2008

WORLD RESOURCES

Roots of Resilience

Growing the Wealth of the Poor

OWNERSHIP ▪ CAPACITY ▪ CONNECTION

United Nations Development Programme

United Nations Environment Programme

World Bank

World Resources Institute

WORLD RESOURCES INSTITUTE   WASHINGTON, DC

The World Resources Institute wishes to acknowledge five organizations whose support has been indispensable in bringing *World Resources 2008* to publication:

Netherlands Ministry of Foreign Affairs

SWEDISH INTERNATIONAL DEVELOPMENT COOPERATION AGENCY

Swedish International Development Cooperation Agency

United States Agency for International Development

UNEP GRID ARENDAL

UNEP/GRID - Arendal

Ministry of Foreign Affairs of Denmark

World Resources 2008:
Roots of Resilience—Growing the Wealth of the Poor

Cite as: World Resources Institute (WRI) in collaboration with United Nations Development Programme, United Nations Environment Programme, and World Bank. 2008. *World Resources 2008: Roots of Resilience—Growing the Wealth of the Poor.* Washington, DC: WRI.

Published by
World Resources Institute
10 G Street, NE
Suite 800
Washington, DC 20002

© 2008 World Resources Institute

The **World Resources Series** is produced collaboratively by four organizations: the United Nations Development Programme, the United Nations Environment Programme, the World Bank, and the World Resources Institute. The views expressed in this volume are those of the contributors and do not necessarily reflect the judgments of the organizations' boards of directors or member governments.

The full report is available online at **www.wri.org**. Materials may be reproduced with the written permission of the World Resources Institute.

ISBN 978-1-56973-600-5

WORLD RESOURCES 2008

CONTENTS

FOREWORD   vii

PART I ROOTS OF RESILIENCE

CHAPTER 1 SCALING UP ECOSYSTEM ENTERPRISE   2
- Our Thesis   5
- The Need to Scale Up   8
  - Box 1.1 Managing Ecosystems to Fight Poverty: The Messages of *World Resources 2005*   9
  - Box 1.2 What is Scaling Up?   10
- Ownership, Capacity, and Connection   13
- Enterprise and Governance   16
  - Box 1.3 The Rural Poverty Imperative   20
- Scaling Up Requires Social Capital   25
- The Changing Development Paradigm   26
- The Resilience Dividend   27
  - Update: Scaling Up Namibia's Community Conservancies   30
  - Update: Scaling Up Local Management of Coastal Fisheries in Fiji   38

CHAPTER 2 BUILDING OWNERSHIP, CAPACITY, AND CONNECTION   46
BUILDING OWNERSHIP   49
- Land and Resource Tenure   50
- Local Demand and Commitment   54
  - Box 2.1 Lessons from the Equator Initiative: Best Practice in Local Ecosystem-Based Entrepreneurship   56
- Participatory Decision-Making   63
  - Box 2.2 Lessons from the Field: Generating and Channeling Local Demand   68

DEVELOPING CAPACITY   71
- A Focus on Local Organizations   71
  - Box 2.3 Women on the Move: Scaling Up Women's Savings Groups in Niger   74
- The Role of Intermediary Support Organizations   77
  - Box 2.4 Watershed Organisation Trust, India   78
  - Box 2.5 Local Empowerment, Upward Influence: The Aga Khan Rural Support Programme   84

CONNECTING RURAL ENTERPRISES: NETWORKS AND ASSOCIATIONS   95
- The Power of Association   95
  - Box 2.6 Curing Poverty? Taking Advantage of the Medicinals Market   98
  - Box 2.7 Ethiopian Coffee Cooperatives: Leverage Through Networks   100
- The Challenges of Association   107

CHAPTER 3 ROUTES TO RESILIENCE: CASE STUDIES   110
■ Fisheries for the Future: Restoring Wetland Livelihoods in Bangladesh   112
■ Green Livelihoods: Community Forestry Enterprises in Guatemala   126
■ Turning Back the Desert: How Farmers Have Transformed Niger's Landscape and Livelihoods   142

CHAPTER 4 DRIVING THE SCALING PROCESS   158
■ Extracting Insights from the Cases   160
  ■ Box 4.1 REDD and Community Forest Management: Reducing Poverty, Reducing Carbon Emissions 164
■ Beyond the Community Level: Addressing Challenges at the Macro Level   168
  ■ Box 4.2 The Difficulty of Devolution: Senegal's Struggle to Shift Forest Management to Local Hands 172

CHAPTER 5 RECOMMENDATIONS: ADVANCING ENTERPRISE AND RESILIENCE   188
■ Cultivating Ownership and Increasing Demand   191
  ■ Box 5.1 Climate Change and the Poor: Resilience and Adaptation   192
■ Developing the Capacity of Local Organizations   195
■ Promoting Enterprise Networks and Associations   197
■ Creating a National Enabling Environment   197
■ Culturing Resilience and Resourcefulness   200

PART II DATA TABLES

1. Population and Human Well-Being   206
2. Food and Water   210
3. Economics and Trade   214
4. Institutions and Governance   218

■ Acknowledgments   222

■ References   224

■ Photo Credits   244

■ Index   245

CREATING ENTERPRISE, FIGHTING POVERTY, FOSTERING RESILIENCE.

THREE-QUARTERS OF THE WORLD'S POOREST CITIZENS—
those living on less than $2 per day—are dependent on the environment for a significant
part of their daily livelihoods. Climate change, therefore, adds a real urgency to the efforts
of the many institutions that work to improve the lives of the poor.

World Resources 2008 argues that properly designed enterprises can create economic,
social, and environmental resilience that cushion the impacts of climate change, and help
provide needed social stability. Increased resilience must be part of the response to the
risks of climate change. The efforts that foster resilience chart the first steps on the path
out of poverty.

What can we say with some certainty about environment and development as we approach
the end of the first decade of the 21st century?

- The world is far wealthier; Brazil, India and China are emerging as new and influential economic powers. At the same time, however, wealth tends to be highly concentrated in a small percentage of the population worldwide.

- The Millennium Ecosystem Assessment of 2005 found that 15 out of the 24 major ecosystem services it assessed are being degraded or used unsustainably.

- We are already experiencing the initial consequences of climate change; the pace of these early changes, such as polar ice melt, is more rapid than any models had predicted.

- We have made commendable progress in reducing the number of people living in poverty, but that achievement has been limited to China and a handful of South Asian countries. The plain fact is that almost half the world's population—2.6 billion people—continues to live on $2 per day or less; one billion of them on $1 per day or less.

- In spite of the news that as of 2007, we have become a predominately urban world, the reality of poverty remains geographical. Three-quarters of the poorest families live in rural areas; they still depend in large measure on natural resources for their existence; they remain vulnerable and their future insecure.

What we know well from successful case studies, and what this volume again argues is that any success in overcoming poverty takes time and persistence; efforts to address rural poverty are linked to natural systems and must abide by natural cycles. Yet time is a growing constraint as the early impacts of climate change emerge and their long-term effects become clearer.

Of equal concern is the fear that progress made over the past decades to overcome poverty may be at risk from the disruptive effects of climate change. This poses a dilemma for the development community: we must not only maintain but scale up our responses to such poverty, to reduce the economic vulnerability of the poorest at a time when many natural resources are being degraded.

World Resources 2005: The Wealth of the Poor examined the relationship between ecosystem management, good governance, and poverty reduction. In it we argued that poverty and the environment are inextricably linked, that the world's rural poor could enhance their livelihoods by capturing greater value from ecosystems.

Our thesis was that income from sustainably managed ecosystems can act as a stepping stone in the economic empowerment of the poor. But this could only happen when poor households are able to reap the benefits of their good ecosystem stewardship. Governance, in the form of tenure reform, can create the self-interest that leads to an improved natural resource base, be it agriculture, forestry, or fishing.

We believe the linkage among poverty, environment, and governance, and the promise it holds for the poor has even more currency today. In this book, we take a closer look at that linkage. We draw on a wealth of experience in community-based natural resource management, much of it supported by the partners in this book.

We identify those elements without which the achievement of any permanent measure of improvement, of any promise of sustained growth, is greatly diminished. We explore three essential factors in some detail: community ownership and self-interest; the role of intermediate organizations (in providing skills and capacity); and the importance of networks—formal and informal—as support and learning structures. When these factors are present, resourceful and resilient communities can emerge.

Resilience is the capacity to adapt and to thrive in the face of challenge. This report contends that when the poor successfully (and sustainably) scale up ecosystem-based enterprises, their resilience can increase in three dimensions: They can become more economically resilient—better able to face economic risks. They—and their communities—can become more socially resilient—better able to work together for mutual benefit. And the ecosystems they live in can become more biologically resilient—more productive and stable.

It is clear that in the coming decades, the rural poor will be tested as the impacts of climate change manifest. There are no cities in the developing world large enough or wealthy enough to absorb the migration of the poor who have no buffer against these dangers, and can find no means to adapt. The political and social instability inherent in such potentially massive movements of people is of increasing concern to the international community.

With the adoption of the Millennium Development Goals in 2000, and the increased attention given poverty with succeeding meetings of the G-8, a renewed and expanded commitment to overcoming poverty is slowly being put in place. There are big strategies being tested, and significant resources being expended, both by donor countries and by NGOs and philanthropic organizations.

We recognize that the concern for poverty extends to the serious problems of urban poverty as well. For this reason, we must continue to support responsible industrial development that generates jobs and opportunity, even as it lessens its burden of pollution. Such urban industrial growth has been a significant factor in East Asia's success over the last two decades in reducing poverty.

But for the rural poor, the challenge is different. Natural resources are still the mainstay of the rural economy. Nature-based enterprises such as community forestry or ecotourism lodges offer the poor a way to use their ecosystem assets and gain business capacities that allow them to participate in an increasingly integrated and globalized economy. They provide the opportunity for diverse livelihood strategies.

And, as we move to reduce carbon emissions, there may well be additional economic opportunity for the rural poor through the mechanism of carbon markets, in which rural communities may receive compensation for carbon reduction or offset programs, such as storing carbon through community forestry projects.

Improved governance is the key. Giving communities the right to manage local natural resources themselves can be a critical catalyst for improving well-being.

Governments committed to end poverty should also begin to remove barriers to rural enterprises, such as lack of competitive markets, lack of transportation infrastructure, and lack of financial services. There is ready help in public and private institutions to assist in these tasks.

Most importantly, the concern over poverty must translate into a real and substantial effort to build the capacity of local organizations to manage natural resources and create viable enterprises. Scaling up such enterprises can provide a potent source of revenue for substantive rural development—the key to a better life for almost 2 billion of the world's poor.

To this imperative is now added the unease that comes from knowing that the time to get ready, the time to help millions prepare, is growing short. The consequences of not acting may well test the depths of our compassion.

Thirty-six years ago—in 1972—the nations of the world came to Stockholm for the first international conference on the human environment. The theme of that historic gathering was "Only One Earth." It marked the onset of our awareness that we all share a common environment, a fact not fully appreciated then or for many years after. Today, the manifest reality of climate change and its certain impact on all of us, no matter how privileged, leaves no doubt as to that fact.

How we embrace that reality does now determine our common future.

Kemal Derviş
ADMINISTRATOR
United National Development Programme

Achim Steiner
EXECUTIVE DIRECTOR
United Nations Environment Programme

Robert B. Zoellick
PRESIDENT
World Bank

Jonathan Lash
PRESIDENT
World Resources Institute

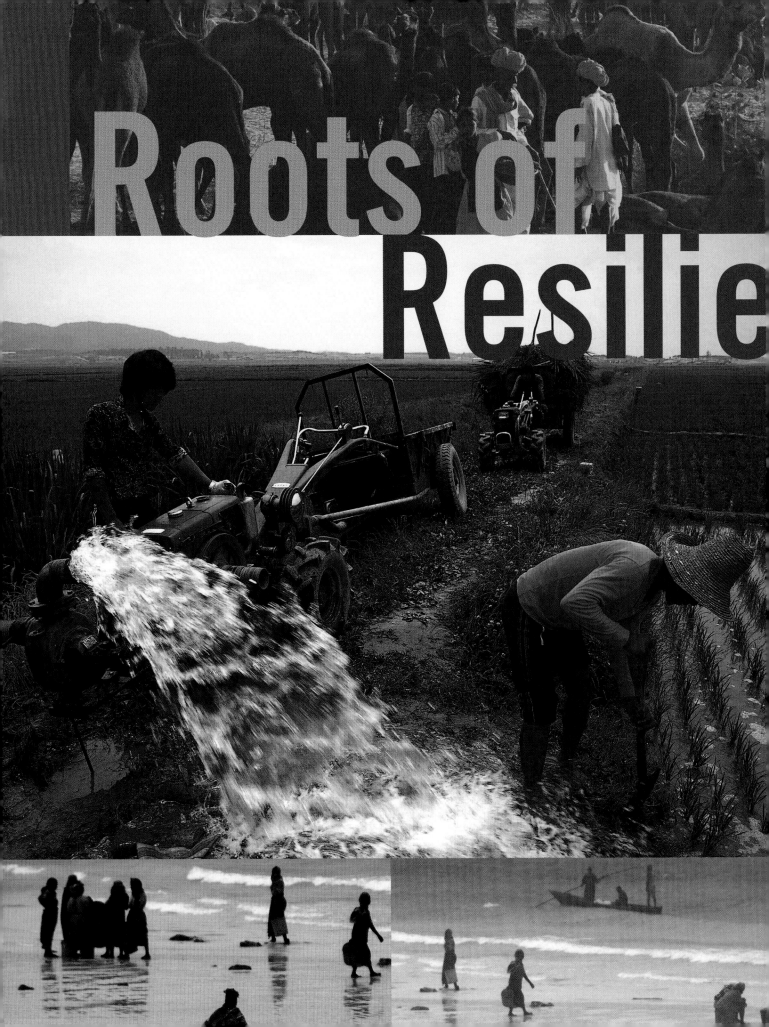

Roots of
Resilie

I PART

nce

1 Scaling Up Ecosystem Enterprise

2 Building Ownership, Capacity, and Connection

■ Building Ownership

■ Developing Capacity

■ Connecting Rural Enterprises: Networks and Associations

3 Routes to Resilience: Case Studies

4 Driving the Scaling Process

5 Recommendations: Advancing Enterprise and Resilience

Scaling up nature-based enterprises offers a clear route to building the resilience of rural communities.

SCALING UP ECOSYSTEM ENTERPRISE

NATURE IS AN ESSENTIAL YET ELUSIVE ASSET FOR THE world's poor. It routinely provides subsistence livelihoods for poor rural households but little prospect for creating opportunity, wealth, and security—the foundations of well-being. This need not be so.

In *World Resources 2005* we showed that ecosystems can become the focus of a powerful model for nature-based enterprise that delivers continuing economic and social benefits to the poor, even as it improves the natural resource base. Evidence shows that poor rural families empowered with secure resource rights can significantly increase their income stream from nature with prudent ecosystem management. To make this possible, a fundamental shift in governance—in the power of the poor to access resources of value and build functional enterprises—is required. *(See Box 1.1 on page 9.)*

The increase in "environmental income" that results from ecosystem-based enterprises can stabilize the household economies of the poor, translating into better nutrition and health, greater access to education, more opportunities for saving and investment, and reduced vulnerability to financial shocks. Social gains accompany these material gains, as the poor assume greater power to manage local ecosystems and become more active players in the local economy. These gains are often associated with an increased voice in resource decisions and greater equity in the distribution of economic benefits from natural resources.

Examples of such economic and social gains from environmental enterprise have grown in recent years. *(See Table 1.2 on page 18.)* It is clear now that helping the poor to increase their environmental income through good resource stewardship, devolution of resource authority, and competent business models can contribute to reducing rural poverty. This must be matched by access to finance and the reform of policies and institutions that keep rural groups and their businesses from competing fairly in rural, national, and international markets.

When these conditions are met, environmental enterprises can become a basis for building more resilient rural communities—resilient in the face of environmental challenges such as climate change. This resilience extends as well to the economic and social challenges associated with rural life in an era of globalization and urban migration. These include the loss of traditional livelihoods, political marginalization, and the breakdown of customary village institutions.

Can this ecosystem-based approach to wealth creation and resilience be scaled up so that it begins to make a difference on a global level? In *World Resources 2008*, we assert that it can.

THIS CHAPTER

In this chapter we present a vision for how the rural poor can use their ecosystem assets to create viable and sustainable enterprises, gain empowerment, increase their income and opportunities, and build their resilience to environmental and social challenges—and do so at a significant scale. The chapter:

- Presents the thesis that scaling up nature-based income and culturing resilience requires the three elements of ownership, capacity, and connection, and defines these terms.

- Defines what we mean by ecosystem-based enterprise and how it relates to community-based natural resource management.

- Presents a rationale for the need to "scale up" and explains the different kinds of scaling.

- Defines the enabling environment of natural resource polices, market regulations, and state support that is needed to foster successful nature-based enterprises of the poor.

- Explains the role of local governments vis-à-vis other local resource institutions such as forest user groups, watershed committees, or fishery committees.

- Relates our thesis to community-driven development as funded and practiced by development organizations today.

- Defines the three dimensions of resilience—ecological resilience, social resilience, and economic resilience—and how scaling up ecosystem-based enterprise helps build the resilience of rural communities and poor families.

Our Thesis

Under the right conditions, programs that give communities the skills and rights to manage their ecosystem assets sustainably have shown they can achieve results on a significant scale, raising environmental income at the village level or district level and, in some instances, even larger scales. In Namibia, for example, community conservancies have grown to cover 14 percent of the land area in less than a decade. Using the authority the state grants them to manage local wildlife, community conservancies have become the foundation of a new rural economy, generating substantial income from tourism and trophy hunting while actually increasing wildlife populations. *(See Update: Scaling Up Namibia's Community Conservancies on page 30.)*

But what are the conditions under which such approaches can go to scale? And how can national governments and international development agencies foster these conditions?

In this volume we explore the essential factors behind scaling up environmental income and resilience for the poor. *(See Box 1.2 on page 10 for a discussion of what we mean by "scaling up.")* Because so many of the forests, fisheries, grasslands, and watersheds that poor families rely on are common pool resources, we concentrate on the governance conditions and local capacities that allow communities to jointly manage these ecosystems in equitable, sustainable, productive, and commercially successful ways. That means we are often speaking of community-based natural resource management (CBNRM). Our consideration of environmental income also includes smallholder agriculture—the most prevalent nature-based livelihood of the poor. This kind of agriculture also benefits from joint approaches to irrigation, soil conservation, pest management, adoption of new technology, and marketing. The capacity for joint action—the result of building "social capital"—is an important feature of successful scaling.

Our thesis is that successfully scaling up environmental income for the poor requires three elements: it begins with ***ownership***—a groundwork of good governance that both transfers to the poor real authority over local resources and elicits local demand for better management of these resources. Making good on this demand requires unlocking and enabling local ***capacity*** for development—in this case, the capacity of local communities to manage ecosystems competently, carry out ecosystem-based enterprises, and distribute the income from these enterprises fairly. The third element is ***connection***: establishing adaptive networks that connect and nurture nature-based enterprises, giving them the ability to adapt, learn, link to markets, and mature into businesses that can sustain themselves and enter the economic mainstream.

When these three elements are present, communities can begin to unlock the wealth potential of ecosystems in ways that actually reach the poor. In so doing they build a base of competencies that extends beyond nature-based enterprises and supports rural economic growth in general, including the gradual transition beyond reliance on natural resource income alone.

They also acquire greater resilience. It is the new capacities that community members gain—how to build functional and inclusive institutions, how to undertake community-based projects, and how to conduct a successful business—that give rise to greater social and economic resilience. It is the insight that ecosystems are valuable assets that can be owned and managed for sustained benefits that builds the foundation of ecological resilience. Together, these three dimensions of resilience support the kind of rural development whose benefits persist in the face of challenge.

Even while stressing these elements, we realize there are numerous other factors that are crucial to creating an environment where poor families have both the authority and the support to engage in ecosystem enterprises. These include state policies on how and to whom natural resource access is granted, as well as how the markets for nature-based products are regulated. Basic democratic rights such as the ability of the poor to have their interests championed within government by representatives that they can sanction and the ability to seek legal recourse when their rights have been violated also form a backdrop of good governance that is essential to real economic empowerment.

On the following pages, Table 1.1 summarizes our view of the key ingredients for successfully scaling up ecosystem-based enterprises to reduce poverty and build resilience, and Figure 1.1 depicts how these ingredients interact to generate ecosystem enterprises and drive them to scale up. At the same time, we realize that enterprise scaling does not proceed by a linear check list or formula. For example, incremental progress can be made without attaining the perfect enabling environment. However, the better the enabling environment, the more effective the scaling-up process and the resulting reduction in poverty.

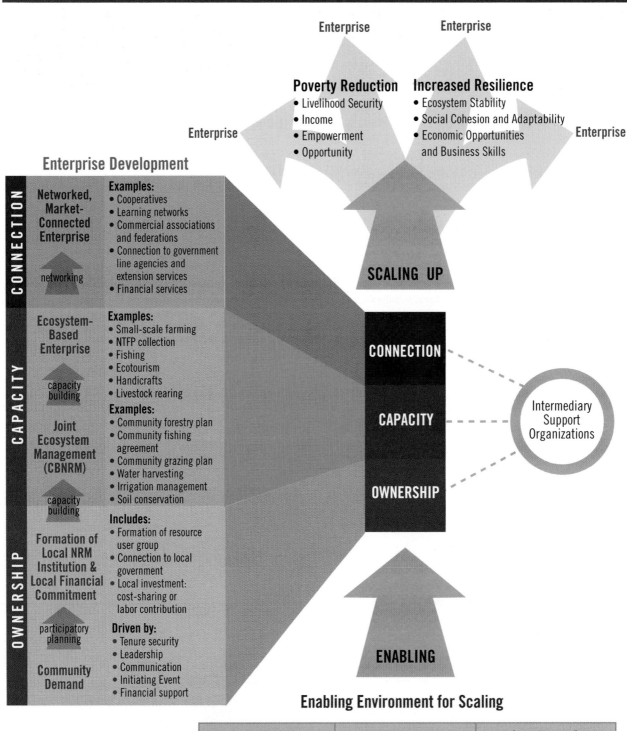

FIGURE 1.1   SCALING UP COMMUNITY-DRIVEN ECOSYSTEM ENTERPRISE

TABLE 1.1 SCALING UP ECOSYSTEM ENTERPRISE: KEY INGREDIENTS

Success Factors for Community-Driven Natural Resource Management

OWNERSHIP: A Local Stake in Development and Enterprise

- Enforceable resource rights
- Community demand for natural resource management
- Community investment of time, money, or other key inputs
- Participation in and influence over decision-making processes

CAPACITY: Social, Technical, and Business Skills to Manage Resources and Establish Enterprises

- Social capacity to embrace a shared goal for resource management and to negotiate an action plan to attain it
- Technical capacity to jointly manage natural resources sustainably, including the ability to monitor resources and enforce rules
- Business capacity to organize an ecosystem-based enterprise and market the resulting products and services
- Local resource management institutions with the capacity to distribute costs and benefits of ecosystem management fairly
- Dynamic community leadership to catalyze demand and mediate disputes
- Intermediary support organizations to help build capacity and influence

CONNECTION: Links to Learning, Support, and Commercial Networks and Associations

- Horizontal links to other rural producers to access information, improve efficiency, and connect to markets
- Vertical links to government and the private sector to build political support, deal with bureaucratic obstacles, and connect to technical and financial support

An Enabling Environment for Scaling

SUPPORTIVE POLICY ENVIRONMENT
- Secure resource rights and fair benefit-sharing arrangements
- Progressive policies on the registration of NGOs, commercial associations, and cooperatives
- Basic democratic rights such as representation and redress

NONDISCRIMINATORY TAX AND REGULATORY ENVIRONMENT
- Reform of subsidies, taxes, licensing requirements, and quotas favoring large enterprises over small enterprises

COMMITMENT OF GOVERNMENT LINE AGENCIES
- Government line agencies reoriented toward service role rather than traditional top-down role
- Interagency coordination

TECHNICAL, RESEARCH, AND MARKETING SUPPORT
- Extension services for resource management and monitoring
- Business planning and enterprise development
- Market research and product development

AVAILABILITY OF FINANCIAL SERVICES AND PUBLIC FUNDING
- Public funds available for ecosystem restoration
- Private and/or public financing available for enterprise development

COMMUNICATION OF SUCCESSES
- Stakeholder engagement via site visits and testimonials
- Momentum among policymakers, funders, line agencies, and local government via media stories, research reports, and site visits

The Need to Scale Up

The scale of global poverty and the scale of peril to rural ecosystems are both great. They require a response at a similar scale. Some 2.6 billion people live on less than $2 per day, with three quarters of them in rural areas. *(See Box 1.3 on pg. 20.)* Their dependence on ecosystems for subsistence and cash is high. Nature-based income often makes up more than half of the total income stream of the rural poor (WRI et al. 2005:39, 52). Unfortunately, rural ecosystems themselves are under unprecedented strain. In 2005 the Millennium Ecosystem Assessment (MA) found that 15 of the 24 ecosystem services it assessed were in global decline—services such as plant pollination or the provision of fresh water, woodfuels, wild foods, and fish. These and similar services provide the basis for many of the livelihoods of the poor. Indeed, the MA concluded that the greatest burden of ecosystem degradation already falls on the poor, and it will do so in increasing measure if current trends persist (MA 2005:1–2).

Scaling Up Community-Based Natural Resource Management for Income and Resilience

These worsening ecosystem trends and the close connection between poverty and the environment drive home the need to scale up income for the poor in a way that helps arrest rather than exacerbate environmental damage. Two decades of experience show that community-based natural resource

management—in the right hands and with appropriate support—has the potential to meet this goal. The question has become how to isolate the key elements of the many local success stories and propel them into wider application. Without an approach to scaling up CBNRM for the poor, these local

Continues on page 12

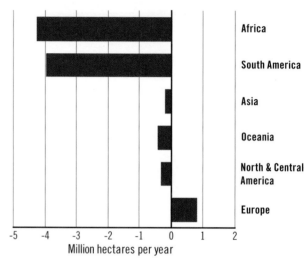

FIGURE 1.2 ECOSYSTEM DECLINE: ANNUAL NET CHANGE IN FOREST AREA BY REGION, 1990-2005

Million hectares per year

Source: FAO 2005a:XV

BOX 1.1 MANAGING ECOSYSTEMS TO FIGHT POVERTY: THE MESSAGES OF *WORLD RESOURCES 2005*

IN *WORLD RESOURCES 2005* WE ARGUED THAT poverty and the environment are inextricably linked and that the world's rural poor could enhance their livelihoods by capturing greater value from ecosystems. The reality is that three quarters of the world's poor people—those living on less than $1 a day—live in rural areas and depend on natural resources to earn a living.

Our thesis was that income from sustainably managed ecosystems can act as a stepping stone in the economic empowerment of the poor. But this can only happen when poor households are able to reap the benefits of their good ecosystem stewardship. Good governance, including secure tenure, can create the self-interest that leads to an improved natural resource base, be it in agriculture, forestry, or fishing.

Unfortunately, an array of governance failures usually stands in the way: lack of secure access to ecosystems, political marginalization, and exclusion from the decisions that affect how ecosystems are managed. Unlocking the economic potential of ecosystems to reduce rural poverty means tackling these obstacles.

Major Findings of *World Resources 2005*

1. **Environmental income is crucial to the livelihoods of the rural poor.** Natural resources anchor the household economies of the rural poor. In the last decade, the connection between environment and the livelihoods of the poor has been well elucidated. Nature-based income, or environmental income, often contributes from one half to two thirds of the total income stream of poor rural families. Small-scale farming and the collection of wild foods, materials, and medicines are the main sources of environmental income. Case studies show that better management of the ecosystems that produce these goods and services can significantly increase household incomes of the poor.

2. **Community-based natural resource management (CBNRM) can be pro-poor.** CBNRM has tremendous potential to increase environmental income of poor households. However, realizing this potential requires a change in governance—a change in the access to and control of natural resources by the poor. Better governance can mean the difference between using nature for simple survival or for wealth accumulation.

3. **A poverty-environment-governance approach is flexible, adaptable, and replicable.** When people have a vested interest in the natural resources they use, this self-interest can

manifest in improved environmental stewardship and improved quality of life. Tenure reform that assures the poor secure resource rights is the first priority in making governance work for the poor. Access and use rights to resources—the basis of resource tenure—are fundamental to tapping the wealth of ecosystems. This includes the right to have access to common pool resources, which are an important source of environmental income but are typically under the control of the state.

4. **Government at all levels plays a critical role.** Everything from resource rights to access to larger markets depends in one way or another on government action and government policy. Getting this policy right so that it facilitates rather than impedes the natural-resource-based livelihoods of the poor is critical.

5. **There are significant obstacles to the success of this approach.** They include the capture of benefits by the elite and powerful, often through corruption; lack of participation by all groups in the community, especially the most disadvantaged; and inequitable distribution of the benefits of natural resource management. Tackling poverty ultimately means political change that enables land reform, finance reform, tax reform, and policy reform in a number of resource sectors. Yet initial steps on the path out of poverty can be taken successfully without the need for every reform to be in place.

Maximizing sustainable environmental income is not, taken alone, a full solution to poverty. But it is a legitimate and important entry route to more stable incomes and greater participation in the market economy of nations. It can support other job creation strategies and economic expansion programs.

Emphasizing good ecosystem management will also directly support attaining the *Millennium Development Goals (MDGs)*. Because of the dependence of the poor on environmental income, the MDGs can never be fully met without utilizing the power of ecosystems to support wealth creation. The converse is also true. Failure to deal with the declining state of ecosystems will increase poverty. Should the ecosystems that the poor rely on most heavily for subsistence and income continue to decline at their present rate or should the poor fail to capture the income derived from these ecosystems, more people will fall into poverty, and the prospect of meeting the MDGs will recede.

Source: *World Resources 2005: The Wealth of the Poor—Managing Ecosystems to Fight Poverty*. Download the full report or the executive summary online: http://www.wri.org/publication/world-resources-2005-wealth-poor-managing-ecosystems-fight-poverty#.

BOX 1.2 WHAT IS SCALING UP?

In general, scaling up refers to increasing the scope or reach of an activity, program, project, or initiative so that it serves more people or delivers more or better benefits.

WHILE THIS SEEMS STRAIGHTFORWARD ENOUGH, the term "scaling up" can be confusing because we use it in several ways. Its meaning depends on *what is being scaled* and the *type of scaling up* that is occurring.

What Are We Scaling Up?

In the broadest sense, we want to scale up:

- *Poverty reduction,* using the assets from ecosystems as a basis for wealth creation, and

- *Resilience of local communities*—especially poor families—to accommodate environmental and social change, particularly arising from climate change.

However, these are ultimate goals. In *World Resources 2008*, we use the term scaling up more specifically to refer to the means to achieve these ultimate goals. Thus we want to scale up:

- *Environmental income*—income from ecosystems and nature-related activities,

- *Access*—the power to use ecosystem resources to support livelihoods and empowerment,

- *Environmental enterprises*—generators of environmental income and livelihood skills, and

- *Community-based natural resource management (CBNRM)*—the basis of much enterprise, social learning, and empowerment.

These four elements are interrelated, as described here:

To reduce income poverty, we focus on increasing the quantity of income from nature—in other words, *scaling up environmental income.* This can result from higher productivity from the natural resource base due to better management, from generating new services like trophy hunting or carbon storage, or from extracting greater value from traditional products like coffee, handicrafts, or medicinal plants due to better business practices or marketing. Environmental income can take the form of subsistence services—food, building materials, or fuel, for instance—but more and more must also translate into the cash economy if the rural poor are eventually to be integrated into mainstream national and global economies.

Environmental income cannot be scaled up unless the poor have *access to ecosystem resources*—or the power to use these resources for benefit within the current economic and political system. With real access comes empowerment and social benefits beyond just income.

Environmental income is realized through some form of *enterprise,* be it farming, fishing, collection of non-timber forest products, or provision of services like tourism. Scaling up environmental income means increasing the scale, viability, and profitability of these enterprises—and doing so sustainably.

For the rural poor, many of these enterprises are best undertaken collectively as community-based schemes, since many of the resources they use are common pool resources. *Scaling up CBNRM,* then, is often the route to scaling up environmental income and environmental enterprise.

Most current development literature uses "scaling up" in this last sense of scaling up a successful CBNRM project, approach, or initiative. While this is certainly desirable, in this volume we do not restrict our definition of scaling up to donor-funded projects or initiatives. We go further to speak of scaling up successful and equitable ecosystem enterprises. Such enterprises are the expression of conducive governance conditions, market and business skills, and good natural resource management, which we believe are the basis of sustainability and resilience.

Five Types of Scaling Up

We can speak in terms of five different modes of scaling up, all of which can help increase the development impact of an enterprise, project, initiative, or organization.

- **Quantitative scaling up.** When an enterprise, program, or organization expands its size, profitability, geographic base, or budget, it is experiencing quantitative scaling. This is the kind of growth and expansion of membership base, constituency, or geographic influence that most people think of when they speak of scaling up. It often involves replicating a successful community-based model or enterprise in new communities or simply spreading the original enterprise or program to cover a larger area—a process sometimes referred to as "scaling out." But quantitative scaling can also simply involve growing an enterprise's size and profitability, and thus increasing its social and financial sustainability (Hooper et al. 2004:132; Uvin and Miller 1994:8-11; Gillespie 2004:8).

- **Functional scaling up.** As enterprises or organizations increase the types of activities they carry out or the scope or integration of these activities with other enterprises or organizations, they are undergoing functional scaling. This allows successful enterprises or CBNRM programs to diversify into complementary activities. For example, a community watershed rehabilitation program may expand to include agricultural marketing activities as the restored watershed becomes more agriculturally productive. Or programs may expand into new areas such as nutrition, health, or even literacy that make use of the trust and community mobilization engendered by the original activities (Hooper et al. 2004:131-132; Uvin and Miller 1994:11-12).

- **Organizational scaling up.** Organizations responsible for community-based projects and enterprises often strengthen their own capacities substantially, allowing them to take on new responsibilities or to carry on their current activities more effectively. They may accomplish this through staff training and personnel development to improve the management and systems of the organization. New sources of funding can also lead to organizational scaling by increasing financial independence and nurturing creativity and critical analysis. Establishing learning links with other public agencies or private organizations is also an important factor in encouraging this type of organizational growth (Hooper et al. 2004:132; Uvin and Miller 1994:16-18).

- **Political scaling up.** This type of scaling involves increasing the political power of an organization or enterprise so that it can influence state actors, negotiate for stronger support or greater latitude in its activities, and advocate for policy changes that facilitate the organization's work or extend the enterprise's commercial or social reach. Through political scaling up, community-based organizations can greatly increase the chances that their work will spread to new jurisdictions or expand into new activities, increasing their impact (Hooper et al. 2004:132; Uvin and Miller 1994:12-13).

- **Institutional scaling up.** This refers to growing and strengthening the public institutions necessary for establishing and distributing the benefits of ecosystem enterprises. Local government is often the focus of this scaling. Replication of the institutional infrastructure of representation—the institutionalized form of participation—and the placement of natural resource functions at the local representative level of government can help spread citizen inclusion in decision-making. Since local government is both replicable across space and sustainable over time, it can be an important partner in scaling up ecosystem enterprises (Ribot 2008).

successes will remain isolated achievements. With such an approach, they may help transform the rural economy and create incentives to manage ecosystems for long-term health as well as profit.

Scaling up CBNRM for the poor needs to be seen as part of a larger strategy to increase the resilience of the rural poor to meet the array of environmental, social, and economic challenges they face. Change is coming to rural communities in many forms—as climate change that threatens agriculture and other nature-based livelihoods; as the general decline in ecosystem health cited by the MA; as a change in traditional rural economies with globalization and the intensification of agriculture; and as increased social instability as village, tribal, and family patterns adjust to new models of ownership and governance and to increasing urban flight. These sources of change are growing exponentially and, with them, the stresses they impose on the poor. So the need for scaling up extends to resilience as well.

CBNRM can become the vehicle for developing the capabilities and connections to accommodate such systemic changes. That, effectively, is the definition of resilience. CBNRM is more than just a means to focus and direct environmental management. It can be a platform for empowerment, a way to develop local institutions, a connection point for local representative government, and a nucleation point for the development of social connections. These aspects encourage knowledge generation and social learning, and these are the basis of greater social resilience. They are also the basis for cooperative enterprise, which can bring greater earning power, so that the poor can expand their financial assets.

At the same time, CBNRM that adopts a stewardship approach supports ecosystem stability, which increases an ecosystem's ability to absorb environmental stresses and remain productive. Reducing pressure on local ecosystems through restoration and sustainable harvest practices can help mitigate longer-term systemic changes like climate change. Thus, scaling up CBNRM through the elements of ownership, capacity, and connection is effectively scaling up resilience in all its dimensions. Such resilience must underlie any attempt at poverty reduction in a rural environment defined by large-scale physical, economic, and social change.

The Potential for Scaling Up

To better understand the need and potential for scaling up environmental income and resilience through good ecosystem stewardship, consider the plight of inland fisheries in Bangladesh. The country's many rivers, wetlands, and shallow lakes make it the world's third largest producer of freshwater fish (not including aquaculture) (FAO 2007a:14). Even so, productivity could be much higher if the nation's freshwater fisheries were not so degraded. As with many of the world's inland fisheries, pollution, development, dams, and unsustainable fishing practices have greatly diminished the annual catch. The consequences for the poor have been grim. Between 1995 and 2000, fish consumption among poor families in Bangladesh's extensive floodplains dropped almost 40 percent (World Bank 2006a:46).

Conscious of the need to try a new approach to managing the nation's inland fisheries, the government of Bangladesh has assented to community control of local fishing waters in 110 villages in three wetland watersheds in the country's northern region. Between 1999 and 2006, fish catches rose 140 percent in these villages as local fishers adopted better fishing practices and restored fish habitat to help fish stocks recover. Fish consumption rose 52 percent, and average daily household income rose more than 30 percent in the affected villages. *(For a more complete account of the fishery restoration, see Chapter 3: Fisheries for the Future: Restoring Wetland Livelihoods in Bangladesh.)*

There is great potential for scaling up the success of the community-based fishery management arrangement in northern Bangladesh. So far, the new approach has directly benefited 184,000 Bangladeshis—most of them poor—in 110 villages

(MACH 2006:2). But the successes there are directly applicable to another 340 neighboring villages in the same watersheds. Beyond these watersheds, many more fish-dependent families could benefit if the government applies the lessons of these communities in the thousands of villages in which freshwater fish make up an important part of the local economy. An estimated 9.5 million Bangladeshis are involved in subsistence fishing on the nation's floodplains, swelling to some 11 million during the monsoon season (Azim et al. 2002:38; FAO 2005b).

Looking farther afield, the number of potential beneficiaries increases even more, since freshwater fisheries are a prime source of income for poor people throughout the developing world. In China, more than 9 million people are involved with inland fisheries and aquaculture. In the Mekong River basin, where fish is a critical part of the diet, as many as 40 million people—from full-time fishers to rice farmers—depend on freshwater fish for at least a portion of their livelihood. Lessons from Bangladesh's success are likely quite relevant in these and other regions where the decline of fisheries still confronts the poor (Kura et al. 2004:36).

Similar estimations could be made for other ecosystems. For example, successful efforts at community-led watershed restoration in arid western India have replenished water tables and boosted crop production and village incomes. These models are now beginning to go to scale, with implications not just for India but for many of the 1.8 billion people in developing countries who live in drylands. About half of all poor families live in drylands; most of them depend on vulnerable rainfed agriculture and livestock rearing in watersheds that are overgrazed and marginally productive (Morton and Anderson 2008:4; UNEP 2007:83). Similarly, community forestry enterprises in Asia, Africa, and Central America have shown that forest loss, poaching, and illegal logging can be arrested as forests become a more reliable source of community income. Since about 1.6 billion of the rural poor rely on forests for at least a portion of their income, the need for scaling up these enterprise models is clear (Forest Trends 2005:1). In all these cases, scaling up successful community-driven approaches is the most promising route to addressing both poverty and ecosystem decline simultaneously.

Ownership, Capacity, and Connection

Ownership, capacity, and connection are essential elements of a strategy to scale up environmental income and ecosystem enterprises and to achieve poverty reduction and increased rural resilience using nature's assets.

Ownership and Demand

Without ownership, poor households and poor communities lack the personal investment necessary to participate in joint resource management efforts, adopt new management techniques, or build enterprises based on long-term stewardship. Ownership here has two aspects. One is ownership of the resource management process, meaning control over decisions on what resources are to be managed and how to manage them. The second is legal ownership or tenure: the recognized right to benefit from resource management. When both of these are aligned, poor families can legitimately be said to have a stake in the benefits that accrue from successful ecosystem management. And that is the first requirement for their engagement at either an individual or community level.

Ownership here should not necessarily be interpreted as the full bundle of property rights associated with private property (the rights to access, to use, to exclude others, to manage a resource, and to sell or transfer these rights). The right to trans-

---

FIGURE 1.3 THE POTENTIAL FOR SCALING UP COMMUNITY-BASED FISHERY MANAGEMENT

3 Watersheds	3 Watersheds	1 Country	15 Countries
110 Villages	340 Adjacent Villages	12,000 Water Bodies	> 50 Million Inland
184,000 Inland fishers		9.5 Million Inland Fishers	Fishers

fer or sell communal or state resources, for example, may not be necessary for establishing a viable enterprise. The crux of ownership—as we use the term—is that local people have *secure rights to use and control ecosystem resources,* including the right to manage the resource and exclude others. Without this power, local groups may find it impossible to protect their resources from exploitation by powerful outsiders (Meinzen-Dick 2008).

Ownership of resources and the resource management process can give rise to local demand for better ecosystem management. Demand can be defined as the expression of desire for something, measured by the contribution that people are willing to make to receive it. In this sense, demand is a spur to action and translates to a willingness to work together for a common goal. Indeed, successful CBNRM often grows directly out of community consensus on the need to act and a commitment on the part of a majority of stakeholders to adhere to an agreed action plan. The impetus for this "local demand" can come from a variety of sources. It may come as a response to resource scarcity or ecosystem decline—the failure of a local fishery, for example. Or it may come in response to successful pilot projects that demonstrate benefits from good resource management in situations similar to those found in a community.

WHAT IS AN ENTERPRISE?

In *World Resources 2008* we focus on building ecosystem-based enterprises as a way to create viable rural livelihoods and reduce poverty. What do we mean by enterprise and how does it relate to human well-being?

We define an enterprise as *any activity undertaken to create a product or service of value.* Ecosystem-based or nature-based enterprises derive their products or services from ecosystem services—from the primary productivity of nature and the functioning of natural systems. Fishing; agriculture; livestock rearing for meat, milk, or wool; timber extraction; collection of non-timber forest products such as rattan, xate palm, thatch, or edible plants and spices; the harvest of medicinal plants; and plant-based handicrafts such as wood carving—are all common nature-based enterprises based on consumptive use. Tourism and recreation are typical nonconsumptive enterprises based on nature.

Enterprises support livelihoods. That is, they are the organized activity that provides the basis for any livelihood, along with the attendant relationships—with markets, social groups, or government—necessary for its success.

It's important to understand that while enterprise is commonly associated with commerce, this is not always so, particularly when speaking of the enterprises of the poor. Realizing the value from the product or service created by an enterprise often occurs when it is marketed within the cash economy, yielding revenue. But value from an enterprise can also be extracted through subsistence use of products or in the form of personal or social benefits such as empowerment, group cohesion, cultural identity, or religious experience. Many of the benefits of community-based natural resource management come in these nonmonetary forms.

Thus our definition of enterprise is a more encompassing one rather than being restricted narrowly to commerce. Enterprise is not only a way to connect to markets, and our emphasis on enterprise is not an attempt to monetize all livelihood benefits. Just as poverty has dimensions beyond lack of income, so enterprises that are poor-friendly have benefits beyond income.

Nonetheless, the commercial aspect of ecosystem-related enterprises for poverty reduction is undeniably important. Developing the business skills, access rights, market connections, finance, and policy support to enable successful business enterprises is an essential part of enabling low-income families to participate in national and global economies and is thus a principal focus of this report.

In sum, enterprise, as we use it here, is both a vehicle for individual and social empowerment, and a means for wealth creation.

How do Ecosystem-Based Enterprises and CBNRM Relate?

Community-based natural resource management (CBNRM) is the foundation of many successful ecosystem-based enterprises. CBNRM plays two important roles in facilitating these enterprises among the poor.

First, CBNRM can improve the natural resource base by encouraging sustainable management and harvest practices. This may mean that there are more fish for fishers to catch and sell, more fodder for pastoralists to feed their livestock, or a higher water table and less erosion, allowing farmers to grow crops more productively.

Second, CBNRM builds social capital among community members and linkages to networks beyond the community that help create successful enterprises. For instance, communities managing forest concessions in Guatemala have used the social capital and linkages to NGOs and government required for this management to create community forest enterprises that export high-grade timber around the world. *(See Chapter 3.)*

The relationship also goes the other way: the promise of improved enterprise encourages greater participation in CBNRM by crystallizing the benefits of working together. A community's demand for joint management of its natural resources is defined by incentives. The prospect of enterprise that produces income or other tangible benefits acts as such an incentive.

Although CBNRM is itself a collective activity, the enterprises associated with CBNRM are not necessarily collective enterprises—they may be individually owned enterprises as well. For example, a community group may collaborate to jointly manage irrigation water, but the benefits the water brings may be realized in an individual small farmer's field—an individual enterprise. However, the collective effort associated with CBNRM may foster networks such as producer cooperatives or Farmer Field Schools that allow individuals to share techniques and technologies, purchase inputs in bulk, and sell their products together to gain market leverage.

So while CBNRM is not a precondition for ecosystem-based enterprises, we argue that the poor's reliance on communal natural resources often makes it a key element in the commercial success of these enterprises, while magnifying their social benefits.

It might also come in reaction to a dynamic leader who presents the community with a compelling vision for good management. The availability of state funds, technical assistance, or reforms to natural resource policy may also factor into the willingness of poor families to change their farming or fishing practices, their grazing habits, or their use of a forest.

Once local demand for a new resource management approach has been expressed, local commitment must follow. This can take a variety of forms, such as a contribution of cash, labor, or other investment that represents both personal ownership of the new management effort and a willingness to participate in a joint undertaking. Sometimes this investment takes the form of adherence to a management plan that restricts harvests for a prescribed period to allow the ecosystem to recover. Without this expression of self-interest and social enterprise, participation in and sustainability of community resource management efforts is likely to be low.

Local Capacity for Development

Ownership and demand are just the first steps in successful environmental enterprise for the poor. When community members take on enforceable rights and the willingness and scope to exercise them, they become empowered "stakeholders." But they must still develop a range of technical, social, and financial skills in order to turn their stake in natural resources into improvements in livelihoods and income. These include the ability to assay their resources, formulate and execute a resource management plan, produce a high-quality product, and market it successfully. This knowledge is the infrastructure of skills and experiences that successful natural resource enterprise requires.

Building these skills is not a haphazard processes for community-based enterprises that succeed. It is an intentional and step-wise process that involves a variety of local organizations—from informal savings or self-help groups to civil society groups like NGOs or unions and to local and municipal governments. In the aggregate, these small-scale, ground-level organizations are the key to drive the scaling process, particularly when it comes to scaling up environmental income for poverty reduction. To be effective for poverty reduction, such local organizations must function along participatory lines and ensure that the interests of the poor are adequately represented.

Other groups beyond local organizations also have important roles to play. Intermediary support organizations or mid-level NGOs that straddle between local groups and state governments are especially powerful actors in building the human, social, and institutional capital required for successful community-driven management of natural resources. These second-order groups—sometimes called "mother NGOs"—play a variety of roles in capacity-building, coordination, service delivery, and as trusted intermediaries between local and state institutions. Fostering the development of such intermediary organizations may be one of the most important steps governments and donors can take to encourage successful scaling.

It is important to note that effective capacity-building is something that enterprises, community groups, and local institutions take on themselves. It is encouraged and facilitated by NGOs and others, but the incentive is born of self-interest. In the largest sense, capacity follows power, and when local people are given enforceable rights over resources of value, their capacities for resource management and entrepreneurship often quickly emerge. In some ways the issue is not so much lack of capacity as it is the inability to exercise capacities due to a lack of political power, contacts, and select skills. As part of this process, local groups can identify those technical and social skill sets they lack and can engage intermediary groups to facilitate these skills and provide opportunities and financial support to apply them.

Networks and Connection

Successful nature-based enterprises depend upon developing dynamic links among local organizations (horizontal linkages) and between local and state institutions (vertical linkages). These linkages, which often take the shape of networks such as cooperatives, federations, unions, or learning networks, are the conduit for information exchange and adaptive learning. They play a critical role in facilitating access to markets, financial services, and other technical and social services that support and sustain community enterprises. Without continued attention to developing and maintaining such networks and connections, the ecosystem enterprises of the poor are not likely to last long. Experience shows that community-based natural resource projects often fail within 5 years without a connection to innovation, encouragement, engagement, and learning (Farrington and Boyd 1997:380–381).

Networks help to create lasting social capital among the poor by increasing cooperation and understanding across a geographic area. In fact, they are the glue of scalability, allowing the efforts of individual organizations in widely separated communities to coalesce into something with broader applicability and impact. In many cases, networks are also the channel through which intermediary organizations reach village clients and deliver their capacity-building services.

The updates on case studies from *World Resources 2005* at the end of this chapter demonstrate the importance and interrelationship of the three elements of ownership, capacity, and connection, using examples of two very different types of ecosystem enterprise that have scaled up significantly in the last few years.

So far this chapter has stressed the potential for nature-based enterprise to enhance the livelihoods of the rural poor and has suggested a strategy to first develop and then scale up such enterprises. The model presented is intentionally schematic, concentrating on a local-level strategy for valuing ecosystem assets and enabling local groups to turn these assets into functional businesses and sources of social empowerment. The remainder of the chapter places this model in the larger context of rural development, acknowledging the governance challenges inherent in fostering the enterprises of the poor and stressing the

importance of an enabling environment of natural resource policy, access to finance, and good communication. The central role of social capital—the web of social networks and relationships that pervade society—in developing successful rural enterprise is also explored, as well as the relationship of nature-based enterprise to "community-driven development" (CDD)—a participatory model of development that devolves decision-making and financial power to local bodies. The chapter ends by considering the potential for a "resilience dividend" when individuals and communities successfully undertake sustainable nature-based enterprises.

Enterprise and Governance

Any model of nature-based enterprise for the poor must wrestle with the fundamental power imbalance that the poor face where natural resources are concerned. For years the poor have been relegated to low-level enterprises and subsistence use of nature, while others have been empowered with access to high-value resources, granted subsidies to develop extractive industries, given favorable tax and regulatory treatment, and permitted to dominate natural resource markets. In other words, wealth is continuously extracted from nature—but not by the poor. They have been excluded from nature's wealth not principally because they lack the business acumen to compete but because the resource rights and market access they need to go beyond subsistence use of ecosystems have been granted to others through state policies (Larson and Ribot 2007:189–191). Successful nature-based enterprises of the poor will not arise—and those that arise will not scale up—without addressing these basic governance challenges.

The Need for Authority and Access

CBNRM can only provide a route for the rural poor to tap nature's wealth if the poor are given sufficient authority over resources and access to markets, technology, and other factors they need to translate their resource management efforts into benefits, monetary or otherwise. We have emphasized the concept of ownership and associated it with secure resource rights and inclusive participation in management and enterprise decision-making. While these are essential, they alone are not sufficient. Poor individuals and groups may be granted resource tenure but lack effective ways to enter the market chains for farm, fish, or forest products. They may lack critical inputs, such as technologies or fertilizers, or lack energy or road infrastructure. They often will lack finance, making productive investment in the resource more difficult. And they will almost certainly be subject to licensing requirements and other regulations that place restrictions on how they can exercise their resource rights.

These common obstacles translate into a lack of true access to nature's wealth. Real access here is more than just physical access to the resource. It encompasses a bundle of powers that includes the ability to tap new technology, gain state support, obtain financing, and negotiate the regulatory and tax systems that the state uses to control resource markets through licenses, quotas, fees, and levies (Ribot and Peluso 2003:161–170).

Honduras provides a good example of the difficulty that the poor often have in acquiring not only the rights to use and manage resources but also the access they need to markets and to a competitive business regulatory environment so that they can conduct successful enterprises. Although in law the Honduran government recognizes the rights of indigenous peoples to their traditional lands, in practice indigenous peoples have found it very difficult to establish legal title to these lands. Indeed, their use rights over forest resources are restricted to non-timber forest products, while the government has the right to grant logging contracts to third parties on indigenous lands without the approval of the indigenous inhabitants (Larson and Ribot 2007:193–196).

Even when rural communities seem to gain an advantage under Honduran law the advantage evaporates under inspection. One provision of Honduran forest law—called the Social Forestry System—grants communities that form an "agroforestry cooperative" the ability to negotiate directly with the state for a contract to tap forest resources, including timber and pine resin. The intent is to foster small-scale forest enterprises. The forest contracts are not only difficult to negotiate, however, but very restricted in their commercial usefulness. For example, agroforestry cooperatives are only permitted to harvest a maximum of 1,000 m³ of timber annually—an amount so small that it is nearly impossible to support a commercial operation. Meanwhile, large-scale timber operators are not subject to similar restrictions. It is no coincidence that the forestry sector is dominated by such large-scale producers, who control both the timber and pine resin markets and who maintain very close relationships with government bureaucrats, often facilitated by sweetheart deals and bribes (Larson and Ribot 2007:193–196).

The situation in Honduras is not unique. Similar obstacles plague the attempts of local groups to undertake community forestry or to organize their use of other ecosystem services—fisheries or wildlife, for instance—into commercial enterprises. A recent study of community forestry enterprises worldwide identified a long list of discriminatory taxes, licensing systems, royalties, and legal limitations that routinely handicap the ability of small forest enterprises to compete against more powerful commercial interests (Molnar et al. 2007:64–68). Thus local nature-based enterprises—even when they are driven by community demand, as we have described—depend for their success on overcoming systemic policy obstacles and power imbalances. Many of these obstacles reflect the fact that the process of decentralizing natural resource authority is still incomplete in most cases.

Creating an Enabling Environment for Enterprise

Wrestling with the problems of authority and access is a necessary precondition for pro-poor enterprise. However, a true "enabling environment" for poor-friendly enterprise will not only remove obstacles but will lend support in many key areas, such as finance, leadership development, communication, and progressive public policy. Much of this will originate at the national level. For example, ensuring that state policies do not unduly restrict the formation or activities of NGOs, producer cooperatives, commercial associations, and other civil society and commercial organizations is essential if these organizations are to provide effective support to rural enterprises. At the same time, the state itself has an important role to play in small enterprise development, whether that be offering technical support for natural resource management, helping small producers to develop business plans, or supporting basic market and product

development that small rural enterprises have difficulty undertaking on their own.

Clearly, an enabling environment for nature-based enterprise also requires access to financial services, since lack of investment capital and start-up funds are frequent barriers to the enterprises of the poor. Both the public and the private sector have parts to play in making financial services available for both small and medium enterprises. Government also has an important regulatory role to encourage the private sector to develop credit and insurance products appropriate for a rural clientele. Governments and international financial institutions can in addition provide funds to undertake basic investments in ecosystem stabilization and restoration, such as watershed restoration to improve water retention and check erosion or aquatic habitat restoration to revitalize fisheries. These funds are often a catalyst for CBNRM and thus a generator of natural assets that can be the basis of enterprise.

Creating an environment in which nature-based enterprises can replicate also requires attention to the role of communication. Media engagement in publicizing successes is almost always necessary to generate interest and local demand for CBNRM and then to build political support among government agencies and donors for funding the scaling process and for building the capacity of intermediary support organizations that will act as midwives for community-driven enterprises. Culturing dynamic community leaders through access to training, mentoring, and secondments is another essential enabling factor. Many of these enabling factors are described in greater detail in Chapter 4.

Continues on page 24

TABLE 1.2 THE RESULTS OF ECOSYSTEM ENTERPRISE: SELECTED EXAMPLES

Enterprise	Background	Results	Scaling
Andavadoaka Fisherman's Cooperative Madagascar Source: UNDP 2006a, Blue Ventures Madagascar 2008	The cooperative formed in 2003 with support from Copefrito, Madagascar's largest exporter of fish. It brings together traditionally competing fishers to coordinate their catches and bargain with buyers.	With technical support from a local NGO and Madagascar's scientific research bureau, the villagers of Andavadoaka created a Marine Protected Area (MPA) plan that includes seasonal bans on octopus fishing. This has increased catches 13-fold, increasing the fishery base on which the co-op depends. Subsistence food supplies and incomes have both grown substantially in the region. The cooperative has enough market power to push for better prices with large businesses. It also fills a lucrative niche in the international sustainable fish market.	A dozen villages nearby are replicating Andavadoaka's MPA and the government is using Andavadoaka's experience as an example for how to manage the rest of the nation's fisheries. The villagers are now building their own ecotourism lodge.
North Western Bee Products, Ltd. (NWBP) Zambia Source: UNDP 2004a	Started as a government-supported community project in 1979, NWBP became a private enterprise owned by the producers in 1988. The company provides training for rural farmers in organic honey production, and then purchases the honey from them. The producers are shareholders in the company and negotiate honey prices to maximize their returns. In 1990, NWBP received the first-ever organic certification for honey production in the world. They maintain this certification today, through the Soil Association in the UK.	NWBP produces 200 metric tons of honey and 50 metric tons of beeswax each year. Along with selling its products throughout Zambia, NWBP exports its honey and beeswax to The Body Shop for use in cosmetic products and to major British grocery stores. Beekeeping provides an incentive for sustainable forest stewardship and an alternative to charcoal production. The average supplementary income to each farmer is roughly enough for a household to purchase a year's supply of soap.	NWBP began with 100 local producers in 1988 and by 2004 had grown to 6,000 producers in an area of 5,000 km². It is looking to increase the number of producers in order to meet product demand. Leaders of NWBP have conducted courses for rural beekeepers in Guyana to share their organic techniques. In addition, NWBP has launched an organic poultry-rearing operation to provide another source of income to the region's communities.
Pred Nai Community Forest Thailand Source: UNDP 2004b	In 1986 community members came together to stop logging and shrimp farming in their mangrove swamp. This decision followed the shrinking of the mangrove from 48,000 ha to about 4,800 ha and the subsequent decline in crab catches. Pred Nai villagers developed a management plan that prohibited large-scale shrimp farming, replanted the mangrove forest, and implemented crab and shellfish harvest regulations and monitoring.	Both the daily crab catches and daily incomes of Pred Nai villagers have doubled. Shrimp, shellfish, and other fish are returning to the mangrove swamp, along with birds and monkeys. The savings and loan group initially established to fund the community's management costs now manages a fund of over US$72,000, raised from its 60 members.	A Mangrove Network has now developed, with other local villages adopting Pred Nai's management program. Pred Nai's leaders spread the lessons they have learned about community management to this new network and to the larger Community Coastal Resource Management Network. They have collaborated with outside fisheries experts, and their efforts have been recognized by Thailand's forestry and fisheries ministries. The community is now using these political connections to push for stricter regulations of trawlers off the coastline.

TABLE 1.2 THE RESULTS OF ECOSYSTEM ENTERPRISE: SELECTED EXAMPLES (CONTINUED)

Enterprise	Background	Results	Scaling
Gokulpura-Goverdhanpura Integrated Watershed Management India Source: ICRISAT 2007	In 1997, in drought-prone eastern Rajasthan, the 1,900 residents of Gokulpura and Goverdhanpura began practicing integrated watershed management to increase agricultural productivity. Their work, supported by a consortium of NGOs, donors, and government agencies, included: creating systems for rainwater harvesting, groundwater recharge, and traditional irrigation; diversifying crops and improving agricultural and livestock-rearing techniques; and implementing an afforestation program.	As of 2005, per capita income among farmers had increased by 28 percent thanks to new agricultural techniques and inputs. Migration from the region—both seasonal and permanent—had fallen noticeably. The communities have become visibly more resilient in the face of drought, both through increased food, fodder, and fuel availability and through higher groundwater levels that recharge local wells. Cut flowers and new high-value crops like fennel and green peas bring in additional income for farmers at local markets. Crop productivity and livestock populations have increased.	The benefits derived from the project have spread beyond agriculture, increasing literacy and spending on health care within the communities. Gokulpura and Goverdhanpura's record is just one of many similar successes within the Indian Government's countrywide effort to promote sustainable agriculture and poverty reduction through integrated watershed management.
Finca Esperanza Verde (FEV) Nicaragua Source: UNDP 2006b; FEV 2008	This 91 ha private forest reserve includes a sustainable coffee farm and eco-lodge. It formed in 1998 through a partnership between a US-based NGO and community members in San Ramón, Nicaragua. The NGO helps to develop the coffee and ecotourism businesses, working with local families to provide guest accommodations; giving grants to local artists, musicians, and farmers; and paying for certification of the coffee farm. The NGO has also linked the coffee business with a US retailer that now buys all of the coffee produced on the farm.	A cooperative of 32 local farmers works on the farm, producing certified shade-grown, organic, Fair-Trade coffee. In 2006, each farmer received US$2,500 from over 10 tons of coffee sold. In the same year, the tourism enterprise generated $100,000 for FEV staff and the local entrepreneurs supporting the venture. The tourism venture has won much international recognition, including being named Best Eco-lodge in Nicaragua in 2004. Smithsonian magazine also awarded it the Sustainable Tourism Award for Conservation in the same year.	Eight small tourism-related businesses have developed as a result of FEV's attraction. Ten percent of revenues from both coffee production and tourism is reinvested in community development each year, and this has funded a school and a drinking water system so far. In addition, FEV has shared its model with others, hosting a delegation from the United Nations as well as groups who want to start similar projects.
Comunidad de Agua Blanca Ecuador Source: Ventura 2006; PIP 2007	This indigenous community of Mataño people is located within the 60,000-ha Machililla National Park on the southern coast of Ecuador. Since the late 1990s, the community has established an ecotourism business based on lodging tourists with local families. Guided tours are offered through the area's unique mix of dry forest and cloud forest. In addition, the area boasts warm sulfur springs, accessible archeological sites, and a museum of Mataño artifacts found nearby.	Migration from the Agua Blanca community has fallen as community members have found new sources of income from tourism, from employment as park rangers, and from selling crafts and supplies to tourists. These economic opportunities have helped the Mataño to maintain their culture and retain their ancestral land. A network of local and international NGOs has extended technical support to the community in agricultural and water harvesting techniques. As a result, the community established a communal garden that all community members work in and take from.	Agua Blanca leaders are now hosting exchanges with surrounding indigenous communities to share their successes and ideas about agricultural techniques, forest management, and tourism in the region.

BOX 1.3 THE RURAL POVERTY IMPERATIVE

REDUCING POVERTY REMAINS A MORAL AND ECONOMIC imperative for most nations. While there has been progress over the last two decades in reducing the number of poor families, poverty persists on a massive scale, with nearly half of the population of the developing world living on less than $2 per day. In addition to the lack of income associated with poverty, the poor experience a range of other deficits in nutrition, health, education, and opportunity, emphasizing poverty's multidimensional nature. Social exclusion and political powerlessness add to the burden.

For these reasons, poverty continues to be one of the most formidable development challenges that nations face. To help meet this challenge, the Millennium Development Goals (MDGs)—adopted by the international community in 2000—establish quantitative and time-bound targets to reach development milestones in income, education, health, and empowerment. At the top of the list of MDGs is the goal to cut in half the number of people living in extreme poverty by 2015 (starting from 1990 levels).

THE DIMENSIONS OF WELL-BEING

Poverty translates into the lack of some or all of the aspects of human well-being. These aspects begin with sufficient income to obtain adequate food and shelter. But other dimensions of well-being are important as well. These include good health, security, social acceptance, access to opportunity, and freedom of choice.

ELEMENTS OF WELL-BEING

Physical and Financial Necessities	▪ Adequate Livelihood
	▪ Sufficient Nutritious Food
	▪ Shelter
	▪ Access to Goods
Health	▪ Strength and Fitness for Activity
	▪ Feeling Well
	▪ Access to Clean Air and Water
Security	▪ Personal Safety
	▪ Secure Resource Access
	▪ Security from Disasters
Good Social Relations	▪ Social Cohesion
	▪ Mutual Respect
	▪ Ability to Help Others
Freedom of Choice and Action	▪ Opportunity to Achieve What an Individual Values

Source: MA 2005:vi

Recent Poverty Trends

Worldwide, the number of people living on less than $1 per day—the international standard for extreme poverty—has dropped from 1.25 billion in 1990 to 986 million in 2004 (the latest year for which data are available). This represents significant progress, given the population growth that occurred during this period. In 1990, 29 percent of the global population lived below the $1 per day level; in 2004, that figure had dropped to 18 percent. The number of people living on less than $2 per day—another recognized poverty marker—has also dropped; nonetheless, some 2.6 billion people still struggle to make do at this marginal income level (World Bank 2007a:63, Table 2.6a).

Although the global drop in poverty has been significant, a more detailed breakdown of poverty trends shows that poverty reduction has been highly uneven across regions. Much of the recent progress on poverty comes from China's extraordinary success in the last several decades in lowering its poverty rate. In 1981, 63 percent of China's population—more than 600 million people—lived on less than $1 per day; by 2004, some 500 million fewer Chinese suffered $1 per day poverty (adjusted for inflation) and the nation's rate of extreme poverty had fallen to just below 10 percent, aided by years of double-digit economic growth (World Bank 2007a:63, Table 2.6a; World Bank 2007b:40–41). *(See Figure on page 21.)*

In contrast, other regions have seen more modest progress. In sub-Saharan Africa, where nearly a third of all poor people live, recent economic growth has helped reduce the share of people in extreme poverty by 4 percent from 1999 to 2004. Nonetheless, population growth has suppressed these gains and kept the number of people suffering $1 per day poverty at nearly 300 million—more than 40 percent of the region's population. Similarly, extreme poverty fell 4 percent in South Asia from 1999 to 2004, but the number of people living on less than $1 per day still exceeds 460 million—32 percent of the region's population (World Bank 2007a:63, Table 2.6a; World Bank 2007b:40–41).

Given these trends, the prognosis is mixed for meeting the Millennium Development Goal of halving the incidence of extreme poverty from 1990 levels by 2015. At the global level, this goal is still within reach: extreme poverty is expected to continue declining to around 12 percent of the global population in 2015. But many countries will not come close to meeting the MDG goal, particularly in Africa. One worrying trend is that severe and persistent poverty is increasingly concentrated in so-called fragile states—countries that suffer from poor governance and weak institutions, are often enmeshed in civil conflict, and have little capacity to address poverty. In these states, poverty levels may actually increase to over 50 percent by 2015, as their

PERCENTAGE OF POPULATION LIVING UNDER $2 PER DAY IN 2004

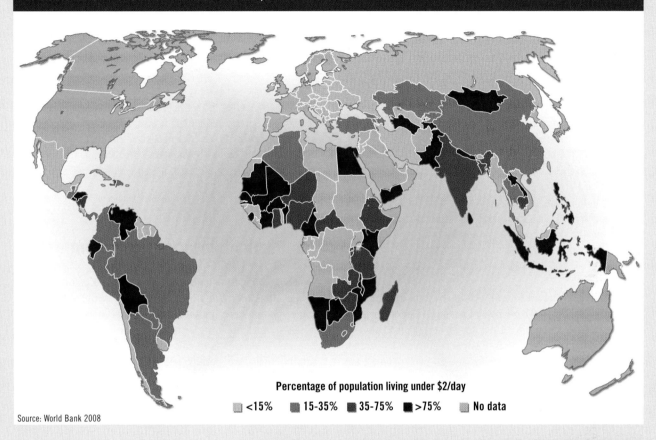

Percentage of population living under $2/day

▨ <15%　▨ 15-35%　▨ 35-75%　■ >75%　▨ No data

Source: World Bank 2008

citizens are shut out of the promising economic trends in other nations (World Bank 2007b:2–4, 40; World Bank 2007a:4).

Even where progress against income poverty has been made, deficits in other aspects of poverty persist. For example, no regions are on track to reach the Millennium Development Goal for reducing child mortality. One third of all children in developing countries remain underweight or stunted from poor nutrition. And half of the residents of developing countries still lack adequate sanitation (World Bank 2007b:1). Even those countries on track to meet their MDG targets will face the challenge of maintaining their current economic growth and progressive poverty policies beyond 2015 so that they continue to lower their national poverty rates.

POPULATION LIVING ON LESS THAN $1 PER DAY, 1981-2004

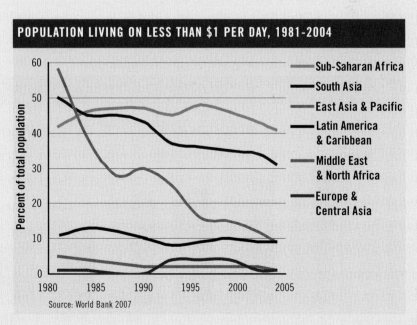

- Sub-Saharan Africa
- South Asia
- East Asia & Pacific
- Latin America & Caribbean
- Middle East & North Africa
- Europe & Central Asia

Source: World Bank 2007

BOX 1.3 THE RURAL POVERTY IMPERATIVE

Poverty Is Predominantly Rural

Although the world's population is steadily urbanizing, the great majority of the world's poor still live in rural areas. New research on the breakdown between rural and urban poverty shows that 75 percent of those who live on less than $1 per day in developing nations live in the countryside—a higher estimate than many observers expected, given the continued growth of urban slums. However, there are considerable regional differences in the urban-rural poverty split. In East Asia, more than 90 percent of the poor live in rural areas. Poverty in China, for example, is overwhelmingly rural and is becoming more so. In Latin America and the Caribbean, on the other hand, poverty is more urban in nature, with only 40 percent of the poor residing in the countryside. The rural poor make up 70 percent of all those surviving on $1 per day in sub-Saharan Africa and 75 percent in South Asia (Ravallion et al. 2007a:38, Table 3; Ravallion et al. 2007b:1–2).

New research also reveals how much of the total rural population lives on less than $1 per day. At a global level, 30 percent of all rural residents live in $1 per day poverty, and 70 percent live on less than $2 per day. By comparison, some 13 percent of urban residents live on $1 per day and 34 percent on $2 per day (Ravallion et al. 2007a:38–39, Tables 3 and 4; Ravallion et al. 2007b:1).

While poverty is still overwhelmingly rural, the balance is slowly shifting as urbanization progresses. In other words, poverty is gradually becoming more urban, in many cases fueled by an influx of poor immigrants from rural areas seeking jobs in the city. Nonetheless, poverty will remain predominantly rural for

decades more. Forecasts for 2030, for example, predict that 60 percent of all poor people will still live in the countryside, even though the majority of people in the developing world will live in cities at that point (Ravallion et al. 2007a:25–26; Ravallion et al. 2007b:2).

The persistence of poverty as a rural phenomenon emphasizes the importance of effective rural development models for scaling up poverty reduction. It also strengthens the case for ecosystem management as a necessary element of such development, since natural ecosystems are one of the principal assets of rural areas—an asset the poor already use extensively.

The Depth of Poverty is Important

Simply knowing the number of people who fall below the $1 or $2 per day poverty line in an area is not sufficient to understand the real depth or severity of poverty there. For that it is necessary to probe how far below the poverty line people fall. One way to do this is to calculate the poverty gap—the mean shortfall from the poverty line of an area's population. The poverty gap captures not only the proportion of people who are poor but also how poor they are, and it is thus an important consideration when designing poverty reduction strategies or measuring their effectiveness. Where the poverty gap is large, escaping poverty is all the more difficult, since families must make substantial income gains just to reach the poverty line. On the other hand, reducing the poverty gap through even small increases in environmental income or wage labor may help

RURAL SHARE OF POVERTY

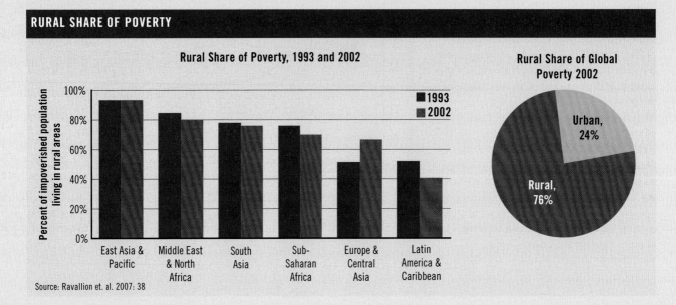

Rural Share of Poverty, 1993 and 2002

Percent of impoverished population living in rural areas

■ 1993
▨ 2002

East Asia & Pacific / Middle East & North Africa / South Asia / Sub-Saharan Africa / Europe & Central Asia / Latin America & Caribbean

Rural Share of Global Poverty 2002

Urban, 24%
Rural, 76%

Source: Ravallion et. al. 2007: 38

relieve some of the symptoms of poverty, even though families remain below the poverty line.

The poverty gap in rural areas can vary markedly from village to village, district to district, or province to province. For example, while the average poverty gap in Kenya (calculated from the national rural poverty line of 59 cents per day) is 19 percent, some districts in Nyanza and Coast Provinces have poverty gaps of 30 percent. These districts have not only more people in poverty but a deeper level of poverty, with family income that is further below the poverty line. In contrast, in many locations in Central and Nairobi Province, the poverty gap is less than 10 percent, and poverty is not as severe (World Resources Institute et al. 2007:13,18–19). Looking across all of sub-Saharan Africa, the large size of the poverty gap—23 percent—gives a good picture of the dimensions of the continent's poverty problem and the challenge of attaining the poverty MDG (Ravallion et al. 2007a:42, Table 8).

Two Imperatives:
More Growth and Greater Equity

Large-scale poverty reduction requires sustained economic growth. A case in point is China, where particularly rapid growth has been paired with steep declines in poverty numbers. Even outside of China, analysis suggests that recent declines in global poverty are largely the product of a resumption of economic growth in many low- and middle-income countries. In a recent analysis of 19 low-income countries, analysts found that a 1-percent rise in gross domestic product per capita—a standard measure of economic growth—was associated with a 1.3-percent fall in the rate of extreme poverty in the countries studied (World Bank 2007b:42).

But growth is not the only factor behind poverty reduction. The distribution of income within a nation—its level of income equality—is also important in determining whether the benefits of economic growth reach the poor or are captured by the well-off. Where income inequality is high, the pace of poverty reduction slows. Inequality results in deficits in many of the factors that determine how economic benefits are shared, such as education, political voice, and access to information, markets, and technology. According to the World Bank, rising inequality over the 1990s offset some of the poverty reduction from economic gains in many countries. In a recent study of trends in growth and inequality, the Bank found that inequality had increased over the last two decades in 46 of the 59 countries studied (World Bank 2007a:4; World Bank 2007c:3).

HOW POOR IS POOR?

Since 1990, poverty analysts have been using the $1 per day standard as the international poverty line for extreme poverty. More precisely, the extreme poverty standard is set at $1.08, figured in 1993 "purchasing power parity" (PPP) dollars, which allows comparison of poverty rates across countries and across years. However, most people in rural areas who live in extreme poverty actually survive on significantly less than $1.08 per day. Recent calculations by the World Bank show that *the mean income of those living below the poverty line in rural areas throughout the world is just 77 cents*. The difference between this mean income and the poverty line—31 cents—indicates that rural poverty is not only extensive but deep.

GLOBAL AVERAGE INCOME OF THE RURAL POOR*

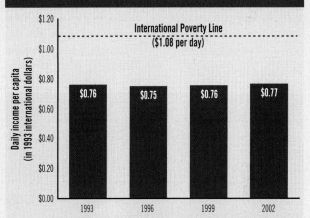

*The rural poor are defined as populations living in rural areas with per capita incomes of less than $1.08 per day

Source: Ravallion et. al. 2007: 38, 42

The need to encourage economic growth with equity is particularly acute in rural areas, where most poverty is centered. Natural resources have been a traditional source of economic activity in these areas, but the kinds of large-scale forestry, mining, fishing, and agricultural development that have been common there have often depleted the resource base. This has not only run counter to the immediate interests of the rural poor, who depend heavily on nature, it has harmed the long-term economic health of nations. In sub-Saharan Africa, for example, net creation of wealth has effectively been zero over the last three decades, as economic gains have been offset by the liquidation of the region's natural resource assets (World Bank 2007b:55). Community-based efforts to manage natural resources offer one route to local enterprises that support sustainable rural growth that both adds to local incomes and builds net wealth at the national level.

The Importance of Local Government

At the heart of our model of nature-based enterprise is the need for local institutions that can competently manage ecosystem assets in a way that enfranchises the poor and distributes the benefits and costs of ecosystem management fairly. Ideally, these institutions would be associated with local levels of government that are based on principles of democratic representation, such as elected village councils. Representation is a critical piece of an enterprise model for the poor; it is the formal mechanism to institutionalize inclusion and citizen participation in local decisions on access and exploitation of natural resources, as well as matters such as business taxes and licenses. Thus when local governments exercise representation effectively, they become critical pieces of the infrastructure of scaling up. By definition, local governments are already "scaled up" geographically and present a vehicle for spreading citizen inclusion laterally over space and time. In other words, local governments can represent an efficient mechanism for institutional scaling (Ribot 2008). *(See Box 1.2 on page 10.)*

However, local governments have struggled both with their ability to represent the poor and their ability to manage local natural resources in a way that enables enterprise. For this reason, other local institutions such as forest user groups, grazing societies, irrigation groups, and watershed committees have

emerged to deal with natural resource issues even when local governments are present. In some cases, these groups evolve from customary institutions such as elders councils or tribal authorities, but in many cases they are deliberately created by local stakeholders or by outside influences such as the central government or international funders. When these groups are empowered with legally recognized resource management powers, they can directly or indirectly compete with the authority of local governments, which is already weak in many cases (Ribot et al. 2008:8).

The question of "institutional choice"—which local institution receives legitimacy and legal empowerment to manage ecosystems—is a challenge for those wishing to foster poor-friendly enterprises, and it has been so for over a decade. On the one hand, transferring substantial powers to resource user committees can undermine the authority of representative government, creating a separate pole of authority outside the traditional governance structure. While such user committees may strive to be inclusive, they are not part of the formal democratic mechanisms of government built on the concept of representation. Under some conditions, they may favor elite capture and actually harm the interests of the poor. On the other hand, they often offer a much greater opportunity for inclusion and participation in actual resource decisions than local government processes, which can be unwieldy and inaccessible to the poor (Ribot et al. 2008:8). In any case, these alternative resource institutions have grown in stature and number and are unlikely to die away soon. They are part of the process of community-driven development as currently practiced.

The challenge, then, is to integrate the functioning of these alternative resource institutions into the processes of local government without handicapping their ability to apply their specialized skills and to motivate citizens to cooperatively manage local resources. There is some precedent to believe that this can be done, although the best routes to accomplish this are by no means well articulated. In the Indian state of Karnataka, for example, communities participating in a World Bank-funded program to revitalize village reservoirs (tanks) formed Tank User Groups to determine how to manage the village tanks for maximum benefit. Villagers were offered a choice as to how their user group would formally relate to the local government. The choices ranged from having members of the local government sit on the Tank User Groups to having the Tank User Group be designated as a legal subcommittee of the local government. The point was to give local government an official role in the decision-making process without disempowering tank users (World Bank 2002:46–49).

Similarly, when the government of Bangladesh transferred authority to manage inland fisheries to communities participating in a special pilot project to rejuvenate depleted fish stocks, it established local Resource Management Organizations composed of all users of the nearby water bodies. But it gave local governments the power to oversee and approve the fishery management plans that the Resource Management Organizations submitted as part of the project. *(See the Chapter 3 case Fisheries for the Future for more details.)* The point here is that addressing questions of institutional choice so that local government and user groups do not work at cross purposes is a critical part of the process of creating governance conditions where the poor can pursue nature-based enterprise.

Scaling Up Requires Social Capital

In considering the challenge of scaling up environmental income, it may be useful to think in terms of natural, human, and social capital.

Nature accounts for much of the wealth of developing nations, particularly the poorest countries. In its 2006 report *Where is the Wealth of Nations?*, the World Bank found that natural capital—a nation's stock of natural resources and biological systems—makes up more than a quarter of the total wealth in low-income countries (World Bank 2006b:20–21). That comes as no surprise when viewing rural economies in the developing world, which are highly dependent on natural resource income, both from small-scale farming, fishing, and forest products and from commercial-scale logging, mining, agribusiness, and fishing fleets.

The implication of this dependence is that careful management of ecosystem resources can be a key contributor to successful development, particularly in the poorest countries (World Bank 2006b:vii). Indeed, the premise of *World Resources 2005* was that ecosystems are reservoirs of natural capital that the poor can tap as a renewable source of income. Giving the poor access to this asset base places this natural capital at the center of rural development and poverty reduction rather than at its fringes, as other development models that ignore the environment-poverty link have done.

But converting the natural capital of ecosystems to sustainable wealth for the poor requires other forms of capital for its success.

One of the most significant findings of the World Bank's analysis of global wealth is that the bulk of the world's wealth exists not as natural capital or physical capital (such as buildings, roads, or goods) but as *human, social, and institutional capital*—the intangible forms of wealth represented by human knowledge and capacity, social networks, and the quality of human institutions such as the rule of law. In developing countries this "intangible capital" accounts for nearly 60 percent of total wealth, but in high-income countries the proportion is far higher—about 80 percent *(See Figure 1.4)*. To a great extent, the key advantages of rich countries are the skills of their labor force, the breadth of their commercial and social networks, and the quality of their institutions—these are essential ingredients behind their high level of economic activity (World Bank 2006b:xiv, 4). For developing countries, making the most of their natural resource wealth will require overcoming their current deficits in these forms of intangible capital.

This insight is relevant to how communities pursue the goal of managing ecosystems for sustainable income. The major challenge in scaling up environmental income for the poor is not identifying opportunities for better ecosystem management or developing better management strategies, although these are very important. The greatest challenge is developing the capacities to take advantage of these opportunities, the local institutions to govern resource management efficiently and fairly, and social networks that are open to the poor. At the village level, a commitment to scaling up is a commitment to deliberately developing human and social capital—to enabling the capacities and willingness for joint resource management.

The capacity for collective action or joint enterprise—cooperative behavior that is mutually beneficial—is one of the defining features of social capital. More broadly, social capital is understood to encompass the social networks and relationships that pervade societies and the shared values and norms that underlie them. Ideas on the importance of social capital have been circulating for some time now, and it is generally accepted that the density of social networks and institutions can greatly affect the efficiency and sustainability of development, including economic growth and poverty reduction (Serageldin and Grootaert 1999:45–47; Grootaert and van Bastelaer 2001:1). Also important is the fact that the formation of social capital can be linked to improvement in natural capital, through the power of collective action (Pretty and Ward 2001:212–214).

Research in the last decade has made it clear that investments in developing social capital may be particularly important to the poor, with major impacts on their income and welfare. The existence of social capital has been found to increase agricultural production and improve the management of natural resources, as well as bringing poor households greater access to water, sanitation, credit, and education (Grootaert and van Bastelaer 2001:xi). Poor people's organizations, such as saving and credit groups, local political advocacy groups, resource user groups, and federations that link such groups into a broader web of support, are a form of structural social capital with proven benefits (Bebbington and Carroll 2000:xiii, 1–2).

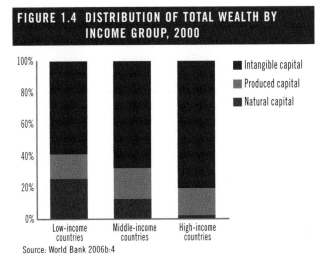

FIGURE 1.4 DISTRIBUTION OF TOTAL WEALTH BY INCOME GROUP, 2000

- Intangible capital
- Produced capital
- Natural capital

Source: World Bank 2006b:4

Investing in the social capital of the poor is particularly important for ecosystem management. Managing the common pool resources that are often at issue requires community approaches—bolstered by the strengths of poor people's groups and social networks. The empowerment, connectedness, and commercial outreach that these groups bring are crucial offsets to the marginalization that plagues the rural poor and isolates their business ventures.

The Changing Development Paradigm

The foundations of a scalable approach to environmental income have been long in the making. Since the late 1980s there has been a growing realization that poor families and rural communities must be the driving force in resource management if this management is to truly benefit them. The move to decentralize natural resource authorities and embrace local participation is just one aspect of a shift in development practice toward "bottom-up" approaches. These community-based approaches—often called community-driven development—see local households and communities as the proper origin and center of development, not simply as beneficiaries of development schemes dictated from above (Shah 2006:1).

The Lessons of Community-Driven Development

Development institutions such as the World Bank and the UN Development Programme have increasingly turned to community-driven development as the shortcomings of top-down development projects have become clear. A 2005 World Bank study showed that projects that include a community-driven component have grown from 2 percent of the World Bank project portfolio in 1989 to 25 percent in 2003 (World Bank 2005:ix).

The Bank's interest stems from years of research and experience indicating that community empowerment has an important role to play in encouraging pro-poor growth, increasing the effectiveness of development projects, and promoting poverty reduction. The lesson is that empowering communities to participate in their own development not only respects their inherent rights, it leads to more successful outcomes (Narayan 2002:1–11).

In addition to empowering communities through participatory processes, CDD—at least as practiced by the World Bank—has four other major components. The first is empowering local governments by granting them significant fiscal powers over development project budgets. A second component is reformulating the role of the central government so that decentralization does not lead to abandoning communities entirely to their own resources but instead joining with them in co-management or joint ventures, drawing on the strengths of each level of government. Improving "downward accountability" is another important dimension of CDD, meaning that service providers and local and central governments must be accountable to local communities for their development decisions. A final vital CDD component is capacity development—enabling local organizations and citizens to improve their skills and problem-solving abilities through training, facilitation, and hands-on experience (Binswanger and Nguyen 2004:9–10).

While there is growing acceptance of the basic tenets of CDD, applying these tenets successfully through normal development channels has achieved mixed results so far, particularly in rural areas. Outcome ratings for World Bank–funded CDD projects undertaken from 1994 to 2003 were, on average, better than those for traditional top-down projects, demonstrating the value of the approach and its ability to be applied at a significant scale. In Benin, for example, community members in 229 villages used a Bank-supported participatory planning approach to identify priority problems, prepare action plans, take part in literacy and technical training courses, and successfully carry out nearly 300 infrastructure projects as part of the Benin Borgou Pilot Project (World Bank 2005:xiii,17). In Senegal, an independent review of the country's National Rural Infrastructures Program—which adopts a community-driven approach to building schools, health clinics, access roads, and water and sanitation infrastructure—found that the program had achieved significant results in extending access to clean water and health services to rural villagers (Arcand and Bassole 2007:1).

But the Bank's CDD projects are not uniformly successful, nor have they met all their project goals. They tend to be more effective in delivering local infrastructure—such as new schools, roads, or other physical improvements—than in building the capacity of communities to use these facilities to reach their development goals. In addition, many CDD projects have not been very effective at reaching the poor, despite efforts to target poor families. Some of this stems from structural factors, such as the fact that many benefits are tied to owning land and thus favor wealthier households with larger land holdings. But some of it derives from a lack of attention to the power dynamics within communities that favor elite capture and make it hard for the poor to participate effectively in community processes (World Bank 2005:xiii–xiv; 19–23).

Attempts to target projects to geographic regions that have high poverty levels, while useful, do nothing to develop a community process that involves the poor and builds their capacity to participate as equal beneficiaries. At the same time, participatory processes are fraught with difficulties for traditionally excluded groups such as women and the poor. In the Benin Borgou Project, traditional village leaders dominated the process of deciding which infrastructure project the village would undertake, and they only later sought the community's approval of their decision—an all-too common form of "participation" (World Bank 2005:126, 20).

Building Capacity Takes Time

According to the Bank's own evaluation, the difficulty that many of its CDD projects have encountered in capacity-building can be traced to the lack of a long-term commitment to systematic and comprehensive capacity-building programs. The typical project cycle for a modest community project—a school, for example—is just 1 year. This may be enough time for a community to assess its needs, generate demand, and actually construct the school, but it is not enough time for residents to develop the social capacity to incorporate the school into the life of the community or the financial and managerial skills to run it effectively. Those capacities require a longer period of gestation. Indeed, the Bank has found that its CDD projects were most successful when they included long-term capacity-building programs or when they took advantage of capacity that had already been built over years of community participation in development projects. For example, one of the factors in the success of Pakistan's Aga Khan Rural Support Programme is that the support of the World Bank and many other funders has stretched over 20 years, allowing the program to capitalize on participatory processes built up over that time (World Bank 2005:19, 21).

The lessons of the World Bank's experience with community-driven development show that while putting communities in the "driver's seat" of local development can bring enormous benefits, it requires a deep commitment to eliciting or channeling community demand, backed by a long-term and comprehensive program of developing skills and the confidence to use them. Most of all, it must catalyze and build on a process of social engagement within the community that gradually cultures social capital sufficient to allow different local stakeholders to work together productively over years rather than months, so that poor families become part of the working model of community action (World Bank 2005:22).

The Resilience Dividend

Resilience is the capacity to thrive in the face of challenge. Communities that are successful in using a community-driven model to manage their ecosystem assets and build them into enterprises can experience a marked increase in their resilience. With increased resilience, these communities are better prepared to survive economic downturns, environmental changes, and social disruptions—challenges whose impacts are often most severe where poverty is highest.

Defining Resilience

Resilience is usually defined as the capacity of a system to tolerate shocks or disturbances and recover. In human systems, this is closely linked to the adaptive capacity of the system—the ability of individuals and the group to adapt to changing conditions through learning, planning, or reorganization. In the context of rural communities, we can speak of three forms or dimensions of resilience: ecological, social, and economic.

- Ecological resilience is the level of disturbance that an ecosystem can absorb without crossing a threshold to a different ecosystem structure or state (Walker et al. 2006:14; Folke et al. 2002:13). The disturbance may be natural, like a storm, or human-caused, like deforestation, pollution, or climate change. The new ecosystem structure that results after crossing a threshold may have lower productivity or may produce differ-

ent things that are not as desirable to those remaining in the ecosystem. Overfishing, forest clearance, and overgrazing are typical disturbances that can challenge ecosystems and ultimately overwhelm their ability to recover, forcing them over the threshold to a new and, from the standpoint of nature-based livelihoods, less desirable state.

- Social resilience is the ability to face internal or external crises and effectively resolve them. In the best cases it may allow groups to not simply resolve crises but also learn from and be strengthened by them (Brenson-Lazan 2003:1). It implies an ability to cohere as a community and to solve problems together in spite of differences within the community. Social capital and a shared sense of identity and common purpose support this aspect of resilience.

- Economic resilience is the ability to recover from adverse economic conditions or economic shocks (Briguglio et al. 2005:6–7). It encompasses having a variety of economic options available if a particular economic activity fails or being able to create more options if necessary. It benefits from being able to call on a wide variety of skill sets and contacts.

Rural environments are subject to increasing challenges as economic globalization, social instability, and large-scale environmental changes disrupt traditional rural social patterns and livelihoods. Turning the natural capital available in ecosystems into the human, social, and institutional capital needed for rural development to succeed generates all three forms of resilience. The concept of resilience started to take hold in development circles in the late 1990s, when it became clear that climate change posed a serious threat to smallholder agriculture in the developing world and that the ability to adapt to it would be crucial to the survival of rural communities (Füssel 2007:155). This adaptability represents resilience writ large, as we use the term here.

But climate change is only one of the high-profile challenges that rural, resource-dependent communities face. Rapid population growth, out-migration from lack of opportunity, the disruption of traditional systems of land tenure, depressed and volatile prices for agricultural commodities, and armed conflict are all serious sources of vulnerability in the modern countryside. Some of these challenges may occur rapidly; others evolve slowly, building in intensity over time. In either case, developing greater resilience can help manage this vulnerability.

Building Resilience

Ecological, social, and economic resilience are all interrelated, creating a strongly coupled system (Glavovic 2005). Depleting or enhancing any of the three dimensions of resilience will affect the other dimensions. For example, exhausting the forest resources in an area through overharvesting—reducing its ecological resilience—may leave the area with fewer economic options, and therefore less economic resilience, particularly if the capital gained from the harvest has not been invested in building

the capacity of the community to move beyond forest-related livelihoods. Reduced economic resilience will, in turn, affect the community's social resilience if it leads to a high proportion of out-migration or causes dissention due to increased competition for the area's remaining resources or jobs (Adger 2000:353–357).

But this strong coupling between ecosystem and society can also create a positive cycle. When communities manage ecosystems for long-term productivity, they increase the resilience of these ecosystems, and this stabilizes the ecosystems' ability to continue to support economic activities. At the same time, the act of cooperatively managing the resource builds the community's social capacity, its set of business skills, and its connection with outside markets and sources of financial and technical support. These sum up to a substantial resilience dividend that consists of different layers of skills, support mechanisms, and biological potential that can allow communities to absorb change and reorganize in new and productive ways rather than disintegrate (Glavovic 2005).

The resilience of the social-ecological system can be increased in a number of ways. For ecosystems, sound management techniques are critical, including harvesting, tillage, and water use practices. For example, contour tilling, agroforestry, organic agriculture, and the use of hedges or vegetative buffer strips can all help stabilize soil structure, reducing erosion and increasing soil organic matter. This increases fertility and raises the moisture holding capacity of the soil. In turn, this decreases vulnerability to high-intensity rainfall, floods, and droughts (FAO 2007b:11). Likewise, water harvesting through the use of contour tilling and check dams can raise water tables, making agriculture on marginal lands less volatile (FAO 2007b:12). In forests, retaining plant diversity can stabilize the ecosystem, making it less vulnerable to extreme weather events and pest damage. These are precisely the kinds of tactics that communities engaged in nature-based enterprises use to increase and sustain production.

Community-driven enterprises also build social resilience because the cooperation and communication skills they demand build the group's functional social capital. For example, new evidence from Nepal, where civil war disrupted village life and affected forest use and agriculture for over a decade, shows that participation in Community Forest User Groups can provide a source of stability during violent conflict (Glenzer 2008). The trust and common purpose developed by managing, harvesting, and marketing forest products together can help bridge potential divides within the community and creates an atmosphere where future cooperation is more likely. Similarly, research in Rwanda shows that the participation of smallholder coffee producers in newly formed cooperatives has provided a shared sense of endeavor and an unexpected opportunity for reconciliation of some Tutsi and Hutu farmers in the aftermath of the nation's genocide (Boudreaux 2007:28–31).

Successful community-based enterprises also depend heavily on their learning skills, and learning is central to resilience and adaptability over time. Indeed, social resilience is not about avoiding change but about gaining the tools to survive

and reorganize when change is inevitable—in other words, learning to adapt (Folke et al. 2002:7). The ability to learn from errors and experiments is a key ingredient of adaptability and thus a key to greater resilience (Walker et al. 2006:15, 20–21).

Resilience experts say that preventing a system under stress from crossing a threshold—in other words, from collapsing to a less desirable state—requires innovation and skills, agreement within the group on what to do, and financial options. These are the kinds of resources that communities build when they undertake community-based enterprises. They gain the ability to work systematically through trial and error, to innovate in order to solve problems, to work together and come to negotiated agreements. At the same time, their business and technical skills give them options to modify their businesses or start new ventures (Walker et al. 2006:19).

When communities in Guatemala's Petén region were first given forest concessions, they confronted widespread illegal forest use that was rapidly degrading the concessions' commercial resources and the ecosystem's biological stability. They had little experience with community action or business development. But the financial and social incentives were strong for joint resource management and were well understood in the communities involved. As a consequence, these communities

have persisted in their efforts for over a decade, working through occasional disagreements and business misjudgments and mastering their business through trial and error—with the support of donors and the government. The result has been the establishment of several viable commercial timber operations that have increased economic options in these communities and yielded valuable—and transferable—business experience. The forest ecosystem itself is no longer in danger of imminent decline because of the actions taken to foster these community forest enterprises. *(See Chapter 3: Green Livelihoods: Community Forest Enterprises in Guatemala.)*

Ultimately, communities that undertake joint resource management, systematically build their social cohesion and business capacities, and expand their learning and commercial networks are greatly increasing their ability to "manage for resilience." This gives them a much better chance of sustaining their success in a world where unforeseen challenges are likely (Folke et al. 2002:10). Moreover, scaling up these kinds of nature-based enterprises offers a clear route to building this resilience on a larger district, regional, or national level. Scaling up resilience in this manner is a recipe for more vital and sustainable rural development.

UPDATE: SCALING UP NAMIBIA'S COMMUNITY CONSERVANCIES

THE LAST EDITION OF *WORLD RESOURCES* highlighted Namibia's Communal Conservancy Program as a successful model of community-based natural resource management with a growing record for poverty reduction. The program empowered rural communities with unprecedented management and use rights over wildlife, creating new incentives for communities to protect this valuable resource and develop economic opportunities in the tourism and trophy hunting industries.

Since its genesis in 1996, the Namibian conservancy program has achieved considerable scale. After a decade of rapid growth, the program has expanded to 50 registered conservancies in 2007, an increase of nearly 20 in the last 3 years alone. Conservancies now cover nearly 11.9 million ha—over 14 percent of the country's area—and benefit more than 230,000 rural Namibians. Many more communities are still in the process of formally establishing conservancies (WWF et al. 2007:ii).

At the same time, there has been a marked increase in the numbers of wildlife in the conservancies after a decades-long trend of decline. In conservancies in the northwest, for example, elephant numbers more than doubled from 1982 to 2000 and populations of oryx, springbok, and mountain zebra increased 10-fold. This recovery is the result of a decrease in illegal hunting and poaching and reflects the economic value that conservancy members now place on healthy wildlife populations—a direct link between wildlife and economic development (NACSO 2006:25; Seitz 2008).

In this update we reexamine Namibian conservancies using the framework for scaling up introduced in this volume, concentrating on the development of local ownership, the building of local capacity for enterprise, and the creation of connections that nurture these enterprises.

Background: The Conservancy Structure

Communal conservancies are legally recognized common property resource management institutions in Namibia's communal lands. They were codified under Namibia's 1996 Nature Conservation Act, which granted rights to any rural community living in the communal lands to form a conservancy, provided they can establish a defined membership, define their geographic boundaries, form a representative management committee, and draft a constitution that guarantees the equitable distribution of economic benefits. The use rights granted to conservancies include the rights to hunt, capture, cull, and sell "huntable game" such as kudu, oryx, springbok,

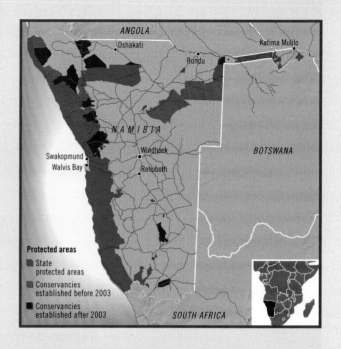

Protected areas
■ State protected areas
■ Conservancies established before 2003
■ Conservancies established after 2003

warthog, and buffalo. These rights are not unlimited, however; for example, the government still determines the overall culling rate and establishes quotas for protected game used for trophy hunting (WRI et al. 2005:115; Seitz 2008; Jones and Mosimane 2007:11).

Conservancies benefit from a variety of income-generating activities, including entering into contracts with large tourism companies, selling hunting concessions, managing small campsite enterprises, selling wildlife to game ranchers, selling crafts, and distributing various in-kind benefits, such as bushmeat. These activities have brought significant profits that, due to safeguards in each conservancy's constitution, have been reinvested into households and communities. Communities add these opportunities to their existing land uses, such as farming and rearing livestock (WRI et al. 2005:117).

The conservancy program has also brought employment to a region where few formal opportunities existed before. Most people were previously engaged in subsistence farming, with a fortunate minority owning and selling livestock. For the poorest, remittances were the only hope for additional income. Conservancies have offered a chance to generate a new source of income and, in some cases, opportunities for social mobility in the country's impoverished communal areas (Boudreaux 2007:13).

Creating Local Ownership

Core to the mission of the conservancy program has been giving communities the local ownership needed to benefit from better natural resource management. By design, communities have considerable control over the relatively nonprescriptive conservancy program. The program's flexibility has enabled it to mold to local conditions across Namibia's diverse communal areas (WRI et al. 2005:115).

Responding to Demand

Conservancies have succeeded as demand-driven institutions because they offer rural communities a vehicle to address unmet needs. People living within the communal areas have long suffered from a paucity of legal rights, particularly when Namibia was under South African apartheid rule, prior to independence in 1990. This has undermined their access to land and economic opportunity. Conservancies allow them a chance to overcome these deficiencies by building political and economic institutions around proven tourism and wildlife industries (Harring and Odendaal 2006: 42–43).

For example, the Nyae Nyae Conservancy in the northeastern part of the country grew out of the Ju/Wa Farmers Union from a demand for a viable economic alternative to farming. The farmers' union was one of the first and most effective formal organizations of the San people—one of the country's poorest and most marginalized minority groups (Harring and Odendaal 2006:37, 38). Due in part to the region's dry and harsh climate, however, the union's agropastoral focus offered little respite to the San. Following the passage of the communal conservancy legislation, the union evolved into the Nyae Nyae Conservancy, taking advantage of considerable potential in the tourism industry. This is now one of the best-performing conservancies, bringing in N\$914,000 (US\$135, 610) in 2006 (WWF et al. 2007:112). A portion of the money was allotted for conservancy reinvestment, while some was used to make cash payouts to members, with each of the conservancy's 657 members receiving N\$300 (US\$44) (Jones and Mosimane 2007:26).

While conservancies do offer substantive rights over wildlife within the conservancy boundaries, they do not confer full land rights over the conservancy area. Conservancy status does not affect other forms of land use such as livestock grazing or agriculture. In practical terms, this sometimes makes wildlife management more difficult if outsiders try to move their livestock onto land the conservancy has reserved for wildlife and tourism. In other words, conservancy status offers only a partial solution to the questions of resource and land tenure, since it does not confer the full right to exclude competing land uses. Nonetheless, it is a large step forward compared with the situation prior to 1996 (Boudreaux 2007:40–43).

Allowing Space for Local Decision-Making

Conservancies themselves are effectively self-selecting units, so they are built around communities' willingness to work collectively. In many instances, they form when neighboring villages and tribal authorities—sometimes with little history of cooperation—agree to trace a boundary around their shared borders and manage the wildlife within this area. Conservancies can also be championed by local groups like farmers' unions, trusts, and veld committees, building on preexisting institutional arrangements—such as the Khoadi Hoas Conservancy, which emerged from a strong association of local farmers known as the Grootberg Farmers' Union (WRI et al. 2005:115; Jones and Mosimane 2007:10; Harring and Odendaal 2006:38).

The flexibility of the conservancy program allows communities to choose diverse strategies to manage wildlife and distribute benefits according to their particular needs, customs, and norms. Conservancies can choose whether wildlife is to be sold, hunted, used for ceremonial purposes, or left alone. Similarly, conservancy revenues are spent according to local discretion—provided that they are equitably distributed. Some conservancies have opted to invest in social services to support schools, local farmers, and other groups in need (NACSO 2006:41–42). Even questions regarding who qualifies as a conservancy member are resolved locally, resulting in arrangements varying from each person within the conservancy boundaries being considered a member to only the heads of households as members. In other cases, membership is open to any individual wishing to participate (NACSO 2006:16).

Participation

Substantive participation of conservancy residents is central to the design of the program, though it has succeeded to varying degrees in practice. The usual challenges to participation exist,

including a limited culture of participation, a distrust concerning the benefits of participation, and gender and ethnic inequalities (NACSO 2006:38–39; Seitz 2008). In the rural context, these challenges are often exaggerated by physical barriers. The Khoadi Hoas Conservancy, for example, in the western semiarid part of Namibia, relies upon a single pickup truck to ferry participants to meetings across the conservancy's many square kilometers (Jones and Mosimane 2007:22).

But as the benefits to participation become clear, even within the sparse rural terrain, communities have spoken up. Particularly when conservancy revenues accumulate, members tend to show more interest in payouts and processes (NACSO 2006:38,40). They begin to demand more accountability from the conservancy management committees and sometimes insist on changes to the constitution that place more power in the hands of members (Jones 2008).

Greater participation is a mechanism for members to apply pressure to conservancy committees, challenging them to deliver benefits fairly. One of the most contentious issues has been the handling of finances, mainly because poor bookkeep-

ing and auditing practices have resulted in missing funds and disgruntled members (NACSO 2006:38). In the Torra Conservancy, for example, members complained that there was no clear process for recording the receipts of payouts. This led to some instances of conflict, but also resulted in recommendations that a third party, like the Ministry of Environment and Tourism, assume an advisory role to oversee the dispersion of payouts (Vaughan et al. 2003:19).

Overall, as the experience of conservancy management committees ripens, the opportunities for participation are growing as well. By 2006, some 80 percent of all conservancies were holding annual general meetings in which conservancy members were able to participate in decision-making, reelect or remove committee members, receive financial reports, and approve conservancy budgets. In three conservancies where the committees did not at first submit audited financial documents for approval, conservancy members insisted that they do so, marking a heightened expectation of accountability (NACSO 2006:38–39).

NAMIBIAN ASSOCIATION OF CBNRM SUPPORT ORGANIZATIONS (NACSO)

Organization	Support Activities
Legal Assistance Centre	Supplies legal advice and advocacy on issues related to community-based natural resource management (CBNRM).
Namibia Community-Based Tourism Association	Serves as an umbrella organization and support provider for community-based tourism initiatives.
Namibia Non-Governmental Organisation Forum	Represents a broad range of NGOs and community-based organizations.
Namibia Nature Foundation Rössing Foundation	Provides assistance through grants, financial administration, technical support, fundraising, and monitoring and evaluation.
Multi-disciplinary Research Centre	Provides training and materials for CBNRM partners.
Namibia Development Trust	Centre of the University of Namibia provides research-related support.
Centre for Research Information	Provides assistance to established and emerging conservancies in southern Namibia.
Action in Africa – Southern Africa Development and Consulting	Provides research, developmental assistance, and market linkages for natural plant products.
!NARA	Conducts capacity training in participatory, democratic management for conservancy communities and institutions supporting communities.
Desert Research Foundation of Namibia	Researches arid land management, conducts participatory learning projects with communities about sustainable management, and engages policymakers to improve regulatory framework for sustainable development.
Rural People's Institute for Social Empowerment	Provides assistance to established and emerging conservancies in southern Kunene and Erongo regions.
Integrated Rural Development and Nature Conservation	A field-based organization working to support conservancy development in Kunene and Caprivi regions.
Nyae Nyae Development Foundation	Supports San communities in the Otjozondjupa region in the Nyae Nyae Conservancy.
Ministry of Environment and Tourism	MET is not a formal member, but attends meetings and participates in NACSO working groups. Provides a broad spectrum of support in terms of policy, wildlife monitoring and management, and publicity.

Source: MET 2005; NEEN 2004a,b,c; Weaver 2007; Jones 2008

Developing Capacity

As institutions, conservancies are in many cases newcomers; they bring together villages, tribal authorities, and other local institutions that often have little experience working together formally. As such, signs of good governance, like participation and a familiarity with accounting and budgeting, develop over time as conservancies learn by doing (NACSO 2006:38). Supporting their evolution are a number of local intermediary support organizations that work with nascent conservancies on capacity-building projects.

At the center of the capacity-building efforts is the Namibian Association of CBNRM Support Organizations (NACSO), which in partnership with the Ministry of Environment and Tourism has helped design and run skills training programs among many diverse communities, institutions, and businesses. These include community-based tourism enterprises, private tourism companies, tribal authorities, villages, and the conservancy committees themselves (NACSO 2005).

The organizations that belong to NACSO—12 local NGOs, the University of Namibia, and several members who participate on a more limited basis *(see Table on previous page)*—undertake the bulk of the capacity-building effort due to their familiarity with issues of development and conservation in rural Namibia (Jones 2007). For example, the Namibian Community-Based Tourism Association (NACOBTA) has been instrumental in helping communities negotiate levies and income-sharing agreements with private tourism companies (Jones 2007). Other capacity-building support has focused on business and natural resources management skills, which has helped the essential day-to-day operations of conservancies. An investigation in 2005 found that most instances of financial mismanagement in the conservancies were due not to graft but to shortfalls in capacity and training—a potent reminder that capacity building is now the conservancies' most critical need (NACSO 2006:38).

Capacity-building efforts have spanned a wide range of activities, from training management teams in financial administration and the writing of annual reports to encouraging local potters to enter the national pottery exhibition and also training workshops on conflict management. In the Caprivi region in northern Namibia, Integrated Rural Development and Nature Conservation—one of the NACSO support organizations—offered tour guide training and even sponsored public speaking workshops specifically intended for women (IRDNC 2006:1,3).

Evolving Governance

Today, with the help of NACSO, some conservancies have become the most functional governing bodies in their regions (Harring and Odendaal 2006:32). Conservancies have revenue, legitimacy from the state, and an ability to work with tribal authorities, giving them political and economic influence (Harring and Odendaal 2006:32–33). For example, when the management committee in Sesfontein Conservancy wanted to distribute bushmeat from regulated hunting, it worked with traditional leaders to allocate and distribute the meat equitably among conservancy members (NACSO 2006:38).

The continued success of conservancies, however, will likely depend on the level of benefits they keep bringing to their members. Addressing this concern, some conservancies have catered their activities more closely around the livelihood needs of local residents, helping to build political support and demonstrate a degree of accountability to the local community. The Khoadi Hoas Conservancy, for instance, has worked with its local farmers' union to support livestock and range management activities, as well as helping to subsidize fuel for water pumps and repair infrastructure damaged by wildlife. It has also reimbursed members for crop losses from elephant and predator damage (Jones and Mosimane 2007:21; NACSO 2006:54)

In some instances, conservancies have taken on larger land use and natural resource management issues in the communal areas. As social and political institutions, they are evolving a capacity to manage land rights issues. Leaders of the Khoadi Hoas Conservancy, for one, have worked with other local figures, such as agricultural extension officers, to offer advice on land and resource disputes (Vaughan and Katjiua 2002:19 as cited in Jones and Mosimane 2007:21). Conservancies have also begun to address social issues such as HIV and AIDS, which affect a large percentage of the population of some areas. In Caprivi, conservancy "peer educators" attended a week-long training workshop in 2006 to improve their AIDS awareness-raising skills (IRDNC 2006:3).

Networks

The success of implementing Namibia's community conservation program has very much been a story of cooperation between institutions. Fifteen years ago the Ministry of Environment and Tourism (MET) began working with a group of nonprofit organizations, along with the University of Namibia, to address the challenges of community-based natural resource management (CBNRM) in Namibia. This cooperative arrangement eventually evolved into NACSO (NACSO 2006:15,19).

GROWTH IN COMMUNAL CONSERVANCIES, 1998-2005

TOTAL LAND AREA UNDER MANAGEMENT

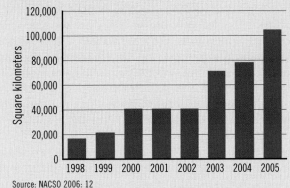

Source: NACSO 2006: 12

POPULATION LIVING IN CONSERVANCY AREAS

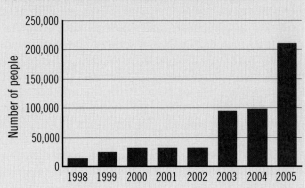

The organic development of NACSO has allowed it to address the evolving challenges faced by communities. Over time, NACSO has worked to build ownership around wildlife management in Namibia's conservancies. This in turn has supported the development of local governance, as well as building the skills and capacities needed to manage wildlife productively for the benefit of the community.

Alongside NACSO's evolution, the Namibia Community-Based Tourism Association has represented and supported the community tourism enterprises sprouting up within conservancies. Currently there are 108 such conservancy-owned enterprises working solely within the conservancy boundaries, with varying levels of success (WWF et al. 2007:92–93). NACOBTA has worked to improve local business skills and, with its membership in NACSO and engagement with the Namibian

government, has also helped bridge the gap between national policy and local needs.

Funding and facilitating the work of NACSO have been a number of international partners, such as the United States Agency for International Development (USAID) and the World Wildlife Fund (WWF). From the beginning, these organizations have been crucial in supporting governance innovations such as the Nature Conservation Act, which provided the legal foundation for the conservancy program, and in providing guidance on establishing community-based wildlife management enterprises (NACSO 2006:15, 19, 55). They have also been very effective at documenting the Namibian conservancy movement and advertising it within the international development community as a model for sustainable environmental management and rural development. This has both strengthened the political position of the conservancy program within the Namibian government and helped it gain the necessary financial resources from other international donors to cover the considerable startup costs of new conservancies.

One downside to the current funding formula is that it has created a certain degree of dependence on external donors, whose funding levels are now declining. This challenges the NACSO organizations to develop alternate funding sources so that they can continue their current level of support to conservancies (Jones 2008).

INCOME FROM CONSERVANCIES AND OTHER COMMUNITY-BASED NATURAL RESOURCE MANAGEMENT IN NAMIBIA, 1994-2005

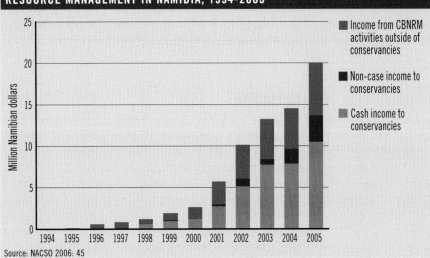

Source: NACSO 2006: 45

CONSERVANCY-RELATED INCOME, 2006

Source of Income	Value in N$	Percentage of Total Conservancy Income
Miscellaneous	34,788	0.1%
Premium hunting	43,600	0.2%
Veld products	39,000	0.1%
Thatching Grass	2,450,481	9.1%
Shoot and sell hunting	504,883	1.9%
Interest earned	161,807	0.6%
Craft sales	474,343	1.8%
Campsites and CBTEs*	3,746,481	14.0%
Trophy meat distribution	870,219	3.2%
Game Donation	860,950	3.2%
Use of own game	739,629	2.8%
Trophy hunting	6,113,923	22.8%
Joint venture tourism	10,794,668	40.2%
TOTAL	**26,834,772**	**100.0%**

community-based tourism enterprises.

Source: WWF et al. 2007:113.

Impacts

Conservancies will not end rural poverty in Namibia on their own, but they are a step in the right direction. In 2006, conservancy income reached nearly N$19 million (US$2.9 million), and this figure has been climbing steadily for the past eight years. Income from small businesses associated with the conservancies but not directly owned by them brings in another N$8 million (US$1.2 million), raising the total economic benefits associated with Namibian conservancies to nearly N$27 million (US$4.1 million) in 2006 *(see table)*, up from N$20 million (US$3 million) just a year earlier. This has established conservancies as a substantial and growing source of employment and revenue generation for rural areas (WWF et al. 2007:ii). Significantly, women have shared in the employment benefit and the empowerment that it brings, capturing many of the new jobs, including being game guards and natural resource monitors, as well as serving tourists in campgrounds and lodges (Seitz 2008; WRI et al. 2005:117).

As conservancy income has risen, so have community benefits. The greatest portion of the money that conservancies take in typically goes toward salaries and benefits for employees in the joint-tourism ventures, campsites, and other tourism and hunting enterprises—some N$7.7 million (US$1.2 million) in 2006. The remainder of the income is used for cash payouts to members, investments in social development and local infrastructure, miscellaneous operating costs, capital development, and purchases of bushmeat for members (WWF et al. 2007:ii; NACSO 2006:52–54). Cash payouts, although relatively small

EXTENDING THE CONSERVANCY CONCEPT: COMMUNITY FORESTS IN NAMIBIA

Based in large part on the success of CBNRM in the conservancies, the Namibian government enacted legislation in 2001 allowing the formation of community forests—areas within the country's communal lands for which a community has obtained management rights over forest resources such as timber, firewood, wild fruits, thatch grass, honey, and even some wildlife (MET 2003). The establishment of the community forest program shows how the scaling-up process can reach across natural resource systems, affecting natural resource policy at the broadest level. Although the community forest program and the conservancy program are now administered separately by different ministries, some groups have expressed interest in merging the programs to allow a more integrated approach to managing natural resources at the community level (Tjaronda 2008).

Establishing a community forest is similar to the process of forming a conservancy. Communities must:

- Submit a formal application to the government;

- Elect a forest management committee from the community;

- Develop a constitution;

- Select, map, and demark a community forest area;

- Submit a forest management plan describing how the community will harvest forest resources sustainably and manage other activities such as grazing and farming within the forest area;

- Specify use rights and bylaws necessary to act on their management plan;

- Craft a plan to ensure the equitable distribution of revenues to all community members; and

- Obtain permission from the area's traditional authority (MET 2003).

As of April 2008, a total of 45 community forests had been formed (although only 13 were officially gazetted), encompassing 2.2 million ha and benefiting some 150,000 Namibians. In the northeastern region alone, 16 registered forests have generated more than N$300,000 (US$38,000) since 2005 (The Namibian 2008; Tjaronda 2008).

in dollar value, play an important role in this cash-scarce society. They are especially helpful when school fees are due or during the dry season, when food can be insufficient (Jones and Mosimane 2007:27).

Expenditures on social development projects are increasing among conservancies, more than doubling from 2003 to 2005. This has made conservancies an increasingly important agent of rural development. Mayuni Conservancy, for instance, donated N$5,000 (US$755) to each of its two schools in 2005, while

UPDATE: NAMIBIA

CONSERVANCIES INCREASE RESILIENCE

The expansion and success of conservancies as sources of rural income, empowerment, social cohesion, and institutional development have increased the resilience of Namibia's ecosystems and rural communities to environmental problems like desertification as well as to the challenges of social and economic change.

Greater Environmental Resilience

- The spread of conservancies means that over 14 percent of Namibia's land mass now benefits from sustainable wildlife management. Reduced poaching and better management have increased wildlife populations over wide areas and helped restore historic game migration patterns (WWF et al. 2007:ii; NACSO 2006:25–29).

- Managing conservancy lands primarily for wildlife has reduced livestock grazing in some areas, lowering the likelihood of overgrazing, which exacerbates desertification (Jones and Mosimane 2007:22).

Greater Economic Resilience

- Greater job opportunities in tourism and related services have diversified local livelihoods, supplementing traditional income from agriculture and livestock rearing. This has reduced vulnerability to drought, which Namibian dryland agriculture is prone to (Jones and Mosimane 2007:3,6).

- Conservancy income has helped bankroll microfinance schemes that have magnified the economic growth associated with the conservancies (NACSO 2006:54).

- The skills necessary to manage wildlife populations, attract and serve a tourist clientele, and distribute conservancy revenues fairly are transferable to other business and social enterprises, opening greater possibilities for small business development within conservancy communities (Boudreaux 2007:15).

Greater Social Resilience

- Conservancies build social capital by offering a platform for collective activities that unite dispersed communities in common cause and for mutual benefit (Boudreaux 2007:3).

- Conservancy management committees provide a forum for participation and empowerment and a laboratory to develop representative and inclusive local institutions whose benefits extend beyond wildlife management into the provision of a variety of social services as well as dispute resolution.

- Conservancy activities build a culture of learning and connection rather than isolation, allowing rural communities to participate in national and global economies and cultures.

paid for the maintenance of school computers. Tsiseb Conservancy has started a microfinance scheme to encourage local enterprises. Soup kitchens and pensioners receive continuing support in Khoadi-Hoas. Many conservancies also make a contribution to the local traditional authority (NACSO 2006:52–54).

Sustainability

A decade after the program began, many conservancies are moving steadily toward economic self-sufficiency. By the end of 2007 there were 16 conservancies covering all their operating costs, up from just 4 in 2003. Another 4 were paying a substantial portion of their costs—as much as 85 percent (Weaver 2007). This sort of financial independence is a crucial long-term goal for conservancies. Strong economic performance increases local buy-in to activities and bankrolls capacity building, which is one of the keys to a conservancy's commercial and social viability. Wealthier conservancies, for example, have started investing in permanent staff to run daily operations. This increases the quality and consistency of conservancy management and ensures that institutional memory is retained longer than when conservancies were managed by a rotating staff of community volunteers (Jones 2007). By 2007, half of the 50 registered conservancies had employed some staff—including conservancy managers, administrators, and field officers—although this was mostly within the conservancies with the highest tourism and game hunting potential (WWF et al. 2007:113).

Torra Conservancy provides an example of what these bodies are capable of. In 2000, it became Namibia's first financially independent conservancy, covering all its operating expenses through conservancy income as well as paying out a surplus dividend to its 450 members (Vaughan et al. 2003:5). This was partly made possible because Torra entered into a joint-venture arrangement with the private company Wilderness Safaris Namibia to run a high-end campground called Damaraland. The conservancy collects 10 percent of the camp's income. Together these joint-venture arrangements are the largest source of revenue for conservancies overall, although only a minority of the conservancies have such an agreement in place. Currently, 16 formal joint-venture agreements exist, with 8 more in development (Weaver 2007).

Challenges to the Conservancies

Despite the economic gains that many conservancies have experienced, there is still considerable work to be done. In 2007, only 34 of 50 conservancies received some kind of income from their activities that was used toward covering operating costs, resource management activities, and payments to members (Weaver 2007). While this is up from 19 in 2004, it indicates that setting up an economically viable conservancy is a difficult and time-consuming process and that the wildlife rights that are devolved to conservancies do not guarantee instant income. Gaining the competence and infrastructure to take advantage of wildlife management rights requires consistent capacity building and institutional support for many years in most cases. Further, a conservancy may gain financial independence before it has a sound governance foundation and may require continuing support in developing good governance practices (Jones 2008).

This need for consistent and continuing support will become a pressing concern in the next few years as international donor support for the conservancies tapers off. Over the past 15 years the Living in a Finite Environment (LIFE) program, which was funded by USAID and implemented by WWF, has supported the Ministry of Environment and Tourism and the NACSO network of NGOs involved in scaling up CBRNM activities in Namibia. The funds have been used to support a variety of existing initiatives, such as strengthening local democratic decision-making in communal areas, helping to develop wildlife management plans, and developing tourism enterprises. But the LIFE program is set to expire in 2008 after receiving US$46 million in support (WWF et al. 2007:1; Jones and Mosimane 2007:5–6).

As the LIFE program phases out, will conservancies have the resources they need to continue their upward trajectory? The answer is unclear. Of course, some conservancies will fare better than others, either because they have more tourist appeal, better functioning institutions, or have benefited from sustained NGO and government capacity-building efforts. But a number of other conservancies—both existing and in the making—will require continued assistance for CBNRM activities to scale up beyond their current level of success.

One likely source of support comes from the Millennium Challenge Corporation (MCC), a 4-year-old United States development agency. With encouragement from the MCC, the Namibian government submitted a US$300-million proposal for assistance in funding economic development objectives over 5 years. Roughly a third of the proposed spending would be used to support tourism ventures, including community conservancies. In its current form, however, the proposal does not primarily focus on conservancies, and it is not clear how much of the money would fund activities that directly or indirectly benefit them. Nor does the proposal specify the kinds of capacity-building and support services that conservancies will clearly continue to need, such as assistance in entering into joint partnerships with private tourism enterprises. This points up the continuing challenge of integrating the growth and maturation of Namibian conservancies into the mainstream of Namibian economic development. That integration will likely determine how successful the scaling up of Namibian conservancies is and how effective this is in achieving long-term rural development and poverty reduction (Morris et al. 2007:5–7, 28).

UPDATE: SCALING UP LOCAL MANAGEMENT OF COASTAL FISHERIES IN FIJI

WORLD RESOURCES 2005 HIGHLIGHTED THE local management of coastal fisheries in Fiji as an example of successful community-based stewardship of natural resources that improved local livelihoods while enhancing marine biodiversity and productivity. A locally managed marine area (LMMA) is an innovative type of marine protected area that blends traditional village management of ocean resources with modern methods of biological monitoring and assessment.

Through the establishment of LMMAs, communities are empowered to improve management of declining marine resources, leading to gradual restoration of productivity and, ultimately, to increased catches of fish and shellfish. Organizing communities into networks actively engaged in the management of their marine resources also helps villagers gain greater access to decision-makers and have more impact on policies that affect their lives.

Since the creation of Fiji's first LMMA in 1997—covering 24 ha near the small village of Ucunivanua on the eastern coast of Fiji's largest island—the use of LMMAs as a tool to address overfishing has spread rapidly throughout Fiji. In 2001, the Fiji Locally-Managed Marine Area (FLMMA) Network was established as a forum for Fiji's LMMA participants to share their methods and monitoring results. As reported in World Resources 2005, the LMMA Network in Fiji encompassed nearly 60 LMMAs, involving 125 communities and covering about 20 percent of Fiji's inshore fishery. By 2007 the Network had scaled up to include some 213 LMMAs, involving 279 villages and covering almost 8,500 sq km (850,000 ha) of coastal fisheries, or about 25 percent of the inshore area (LMMA Network 2005a; LMMA Network 2007a:3; Tawake 2008:2).

At the same time, the LMMA Network has expanded to other countries in the Asia-Pacific region, including Indonesia, Papua New Guinea, the Philippines, the Solomon Islands, and the islands of Palau and Pohnpei. All told, the international LMMA Network encompasses more than 300 LMMA sites, covering in excess of 10,800 sq km (LMMA Network 2007a:3). The LMMA approach has also inspired local management of marine resources in more distant lands, ranging from the Marshall Islands and Vanuatu to Hawaii (LMMA Network 2007b).

In this update, we look at how the LMMA Network has expanded in Fiji and elsewhere in the Asia-Pacific and examine the key factors in that scaling-up and the impact it has had.

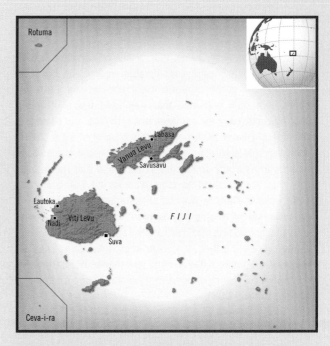

Background: The LMMA Approach in Fiji

The FLMMA Network emerged against a backdrop of long-term depletion of Fiji's inshore fisheries that had accelerated in the 1990s, attributable to increased commercial fishing as well as larger harvests by growing populations of subsistence fishers. The resulting degradation of marine resources impinged sharply on the livelihoods of rural Fijians, most of whom depend on local fish and shellfish catches for some or all of their daily protein intake and income. With fish stocks on the decline, the incidence of national poverty rose from 29 percent in 1991 to about 34 percent in 2003 (Narsey 2007).

The structure of LMMAs in Fiji is based on customary systems of marine tenure, under which communities control traditional fishing grounds, known as *iqoliqolis,* adjacent to their villages. (Leisher et al. 2007b). Communities establishing LMMAs in Fiji today have used these traditional practices, managing their iqoliqolis at the community level and setting aside a portion of this traditional fishing ground (typically 10–20 percent) as a restricted or *tabu* area to allow marine resources to recover (LMMA 2005a).

The location and size of this tabu area is determined within each community, often with suggestions from technical experts. In this aspect, LMMAs are distinct from the more common marine protected areas (MPAs), in which management decisions are made by central authorities with little or no consultation with local people (LMMA 2005b).

As fish and shellfish species recover in tabu areas, their abundance gradually increases in nearby areas of the LMMA where fishing is allowed. This "spillover effect" has boosted local income by as much as 35 percent over 3 years (LMMA Network 2006a:5).

Over the past 7 years of LMMA work in Fiji, communities have collected data on the impacts and benefits of their management efforts and shared these with appropriate government officials. As a result, the LMMA approach has gained increasing acceptance from government, and the Ministry of Fisheries has become a key FLMMA partner. In 2005 the Ministry publicly committed to protecting 30 percent of Fiji's inshore waters by 2020—a commitment that was subsequently joined by Palau and the Federated States of Micronesia (LMMA Network 2006a:5).

GROWTH OF LMMA NETWORK, 2000-2006

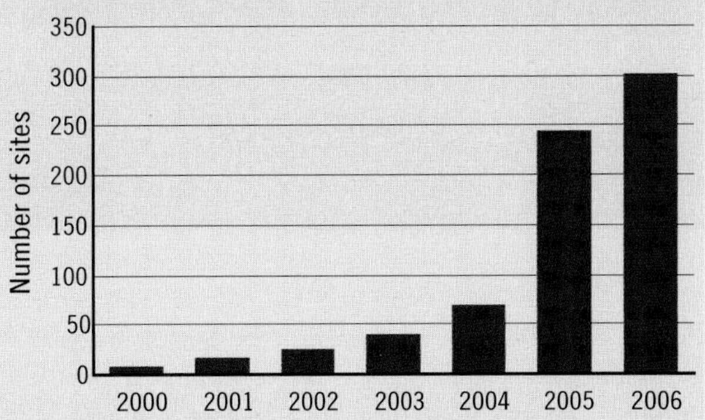

Source: LMMA Network 2007a: 2

LMMA NETWORK PARTICIPATION, 2006

Country	Total Number of LMMAs	Number of Villages	LMMA Area (sq km)
Fiji	213	279	8,497
Indonesia	12	16	700
Palau	1	3	266
Papua New Guinea	16	17	503
Philippines	17	17	270
Pohnpei, FSM	1	4	64
Solomon Islands	42	75	567
Totals	302	411	10,867

Source: LMMA Network 2007a: 3

Creating Local Ownership

Local control of natural resources is the centerpiece of the LMMA Network's approach. The network is a collaborative partnership that aims to demonstrate that marine protected areas can yield impressive conservation results while accommodating a wide range of local needs—economic, cultural, and social—and using modern marine science.

Local Demand

The rapid expansion of the LMMA Network in Fiji and elsewhere in recent years has been driven by demand from communities. When a village creates an LMMA that results in increased fish catches and higher incomes, neighboring communities hear about it and want to learn how these successes occurred and how they can follow a similar path (USP 2007:3–4; Aalbersberg 2008).

Over time, demand for information about the LMMA approach has grown; inquiries now come from as far afield as East Africa (USP 2007:5). As of mid-2007, with more than 200 active LMMA sites in Fiji, 50 to 100 additional villages were at the preliminary consultation stage of the community engagement process (LMMA Network 2007a:3, 23).

Communities engaged in LMMA work tend to retain high levels of commitment to the program, indicative of their sense of ownership and economic stake. For instance, members of the Navakavu community surveyed as part of an extensive international study of the impact of MPAs on poverty reduction indicated that they consider their LMMA to be crucial for themselves and future generations. Ninety-five percent of respondents agreed that dissolving the LMMA now would cause significant problems in the future (Leisher et al. 2007a:9).

Participation and Local Decision-Making

A hallmark of the LMMA Network approach is the use of participatory methods to help communities design simple management plans to address threats to marine resources. Experts from FLMMA partner organizations, such as the University of the South Pacific (USP), the Peace Corps, and the Fijian Fisheries Ministry, provide technical information and advice to support community decision-making but do not dictate it; community members make all final decisions (Tawake et al. 2005:7; Govan et al. 2008:7).

When a community decides to establish an LMMA, participatory planning meetings are held to establish resource rules governing the use of the community's marine resources. Typically an intermediary organization such as USP engages

extensively with the community during this period to provide assistance. Support from a neutral party like USP that is not aligned with any interest group in the community is often very helpful to stakeholders in reaching consensus.

Once rules governing resource use are established, an iqoliqoli committee is formed to coordinate LMMA work as well as to represent the community before relevant institutions on issues involving the LMMA. The iqoliqoli committee has the responsibility, as designated by the *vanua* (traditional community council), for making all management decisions concerning the LMMA, following consultation with residents through village council meetings (van Beukering et al. 2007:11).

In the community of Navakavu, for example, the iqoliqoli committee consists of 21 members, including landowners and the headman from each of the four main villages using the iqloiqoli, as well as the individuals serving in key posts established by the LMMA process: biological monitors, fish wardens (one from each village), and the leader of the youth environmental drama group (van Beukering et al. 2007:11–12).

People in the villages of Navakavu are confident about the committee's competence and its responsiveness to community demands. As one villager noted, "The establishment of the [iqoliqoli] committee has helped each member recognize their assigned duties and has encouraged them to perform well in their area" (Leisher et al. 2007a:8).

The relatively small size of LMMAs (compared with large MPAs administered by central authorities) tends to foster a stronger sense of ownership and engagement by the locals. The limited scale of the resource ensures that the impact of conservation measures can be detected sooner. In the case of Navakavu, the LMMA is even within sight of the managing villages, adding to their sense of control (Leisher et al. 2007a:32).

Compliance and Enforcement

When a community establishes an LMMA, the improvement in the condition of marine resources attracts poachers from both inside and outside the community. Thus monitoring compliance with established resource rules and minimizing poaching is central to a community's LMMA management (Leisher et al. 2007a:10). For instance, in Kadavu alone (Fiji's third largest island), some 52 fish wardens provide enforcement for 26 LMMAs and their protected zones (LMMA 2006a:15).

In many communities, poaching can undermine the levels of cooperation and social cohesion that are needed for successful management. That is especially true when poachers are internal. Rata Aca Vitukawalu, a tribal chief in Daku village in Kadavu province, observes: "The biggest obstacle we are facing right now is people are still fishing illegally in our marine protected area. People have been stealing not only fish but also the buoys which have been left as marks for our MPA boundaries" (LMMA Network 2007b).

In order to ensure tabu compliance, communities select a voluntary fish warden, who patrols local waters, reports illegal entries and collects evidence. Fish wardens are given special training by the fisheries ministry to enable them to arrest violators (LMMA Network 2006a:15).

Developing Capacity

Monitoring and Analysis

When the first LMMAs were established, scientists from USP taught villagers to use simple techniques of sampling and statistical analysis in order to determine a baseline of species abundance in the tabu area and in adjacent, down-current sites. The resulting baseline was then combined with results of annual biological monitoring surveys in order to determine the impact of the LMMA on species numbers (LMMA Network 2006a:6–7).

By 2006, almost 3,000 people—more than 1,000 people each in Fiji and Indonesia, and another 800 or so in other countries, including Papua New Guinea, the Philippines, and Micronesia—had received training in LMMA Network methodologies (LMMA Network 2007a:8). The network has also produced a biological monitoring training DVD for communities.

As community-based management has grown, the methodologies used for monitoring and analysis of results have also evolved. Over the past 2 years, the LMMA Network has devoted particular effort to refining, clarifying, and streamlining data collection and analysis techniques taught to LMMA communities. This has helped to scale up the effort by making it easier to roll out the LMMA approach in new areas (LMMA Network 2006a:7).

One example of this refinement is USP's Learning Framework (LF), which serves as a common language across the LMMA Network. The LF contains methods to measure biological and socioeconomic conditions at LMMA sites, allowing communities to help identify the factors that correlate most strongly with poverty reduction and successful marine resource conservation. Recently, this tool has been translated into local languages, enhancing its accessibility for current and potential LMMA participants (LMMA Network 2006a:7, 35).

The overarching goal of the training provided to LMMA communities is to build their capacity for "adaptive management"—the ability to adjust management practices and rules over time, based on monitoring results (LMMA 2006a:6). Now that communities have been collecting and analyzing monitoring data for several years, many sites are "at the stage where we expect to see more adaptive management happening soon," says Professor Bill Aalbersberg of USP (Aalbersberg 2008).

Enterprise Development

Some LMMA communities are experiencing new economic opportunities, now that villagers spend less time fishing and often have fish surpluses. In communities with good infrastructure and access to urban centers, the men have found jobs in cities or towns and commute daily from the village. In Navakavu, a recently established public bus service has given women access to markets in the capital city of Suva where they can sell their surplus fish and shellfish catch at higher prices, increasing their ability to earn significant amounts of cash (Van Beukering et al. 2007:9–10).

In general, training provided to communities by the LMMA Network and its partners have focused so far on biological monitoring and analysis, with the aim of empowering communities to manage their marine resources better. Yet only a small subsection of the population learns these skills, namely fish wardens, those involved in biological monitoring, and members

of the iqoliqoli committee (Van Beukering et al. 2007:16). Unfortunately, even less emphasis is placed on development of alternative livelihoods for families currently dependent on fisheries or on the acquisition of skills needed to run successful enterprises: accounting, bookkeeping, and management (Van Beukering et al. 2007:16).

Networks

At its core, the LMMA Network is a peer learning system in which members share a strong commitment to supporting each other's activities, including the exchange of information. Community partners who have been trained in LMMA techniques are eager to pass on what they have learned to others. In addition to hosting formal workshops, the LMMA Network also promotes opportunities for informal learning and village-to-village exchanges. Cross-site visits between Network communities enable those involved to learn from each other's experiences, methods, and practices (LMMA Network 2006a:7).

Extending the LMMA Approach

One especially promising development has been FLMMA's creation of subnetworks to extend LMMA work to more remote areas of Fiji. This is being carried out by province-wide teams, which provide systematic support to remote communities. These Iqoliqoli Management Support Teams (QMSTs) are made up of community members, fisheries officers, overseas volunteers, USP students, and provincial government officials. They hold management planning workshops and link LMMA groups province-wide (Tawake et al. 2005:5–6).

This approach has worked well in Kadavu, Fiji's fifth largest island, located to the south of Fiji's main island of Viti Levu. The people of Kadavu rely heavily on fishing and farming for their livelihoods, although a growing tourist industry has begun to provide a few alternative sources of income (Tawake 2008:4). Kadavu faces significant overfishing problems and destructive fishing practices, which have degraded some marine areas.

But due to the Kadavu QMST's efforts to extend the LMMA approach throughout the province, the number of communities that have established tabu areas has increased rapidly in recent years—from 5 in 2002 to 30 in 2005 and 52 in 2008, which represents nearly the entire island (Tawake et al. 2005:5; Aalbersberg 2008). The provincial council has endorsed the team's work and has passed a resolution calling on every community to set up both terrestrial and marine protected areas (Tawake et al. 2005:5).

Similar province-wide approaches are also being pursued in Cakaudrove and Macuata, two of three provinces based on Vanua Levu, Fiji's second largest island, located to the north of Viti Levu (LMMA Network 2006a:5). As of March 2008, some 40 villages (about half of those encompassed by the initiative) had established resource management plans. Of these villages, 24 had established tabu areas of varying sizes (with a maximum of slightly more than 1 sq km) and varying durations (from 3 months to 10 years) (Aalbersberg 2008).

Policy Influence and Political Engagement

Organizing communities into networks enables them to have greater access to decision-makers and greater impact on policy. The efforts of the LMMA Network have helped to secure national governments' recognition of the value of traditional resource management approaches. Indeed, Fiji's government has formally adopted the LMMA approach and has devoted a division of the Fisheries Department to coordinate with FLMMA to promote inshore conservation. The FLMMA Secretariat is now even housed in the Fisheries Department. And as a result of community pressures on the Fisheries Ministry, Fiji has recently set a 12-nautical-mile limit to keep foreign fishing vessels from iqoliqolis (Tamake 2008:2, 8; Aalbersberg 2008).

Impacts

The economic impacts of the LMMA program seem to be significant, although the data so far are not comprehensive. About 20 LMMA Network sites in Fiji have collected detailed survey data on household incomes. However, only 3 of these sites have time-series data to correlate economic benefits from increased fish catch. In Ucunivanua, average household income rose from just over F$430 (US$258) per month in 2002 to about F$990 (US$594) in 2006, an increase of 130 percent. The community of Daku in Kadavu province experienced a gain in average income of just over 30 percent in one year, from about F$235 (US$141) per month in 2005 to F$307 (US$184) in 2006 (Aalbersberg 2007).

The most comprehensive examination of the economic impacts of LMMA work has been a recent study by an international team examining the role of marine protected areas in poverty reduction. The team did extensive interviews with households in the Navakavu community, an LMMA site since 2000. A survey of 300 households found that monthly income in Navakavu averaged F$418 (US$251), while income in control sites with similar demographic and geographic characteristics averaged only F$197 (US$118) per month (van Beukering et al. 2007:20).

The team also investigated whether the tabu had had any significant impacts on fishers. Some 283 fishers were extensively interviewed about their activities, but no significant differences between LMMA and non-LMMA villages could be detected in terms of the types of fish caught, fishing techniques used, fishing frequency, or travel time to fishing grounds (van Beukering et al. 2007:24). Yet LMMA sites generated about three times the income from fishing as non-LMMA sites (van Beukering et al. 2007:28). The ability of fishers from LMMA villages to secure larger fish catches from a smaller harvest zone is testament to the substantial spillover effect from the tabu area into the harvesting zone (van Beukering et al. 2007:28).

The key difference between fishers from LMMA and non-LMMA villages was in their perceptions of changes in fishing conditions over the past 5 years. While some 80 percent of fishers from LMMA villages said that they faced easier conditions, the majority of fishers from non-LMMA villages said that they faced more difficult conditions (van Beukering et al. 2007:26).

Moreover, households in LMMA villages were more likely to rely on income from sources other than fishing, with 28 percent of households in LMMA sites having alternative income sources versus only 17 percent in comparable, non-LMMA villages (van Beukering et al. 2007:28). This increased diversification of income sources boosts resilience in the LMMA villages to threats to future fisheries income from, for instance, the impacts of reef degradation due to coastal pollution, severe storms, or climate change. This resilience comes with other LMMA benefits as well, such as planning skills and closer community cooperation.

Another advantage for LMMA members has been increased consumption of fish. Households in LMMA villages eat more fish because they catch more fish. Some 75 percent of surveyed households in Navakavu reported eating more fish than 5 years ago, while 76 percent of households in the control (that is, non-LMMA) villages reported eating less fish (van Beukering et al. 2007:31).

Despite the challenges of achieving full equity in participation, the ongoing work of the iqoliqoli committees has tended to foster better communication and increased cooperation within LMMA communities, helping to bridge differences between various clans. Typically, local councils in LMMA communities are called on to make many more collective decisions about resource management than was the case before the LMMA's creation. This has revitalized traditional systems of community cooperation and joint decision-making, thus contributing to increased social cohesion (van Beukering et al. 2007:15, 17).

For instance, a survey of villagers in the Navakavu community found that more than 80 percent agreed that since establishment of the LMMA there has been a higher level of participation in community meetings, women have had a stronger voice, and the community has become more united. More than 50 percent agreed that youth have more opportunities to share their opinions and that resource conflicts within the community have declined (van Beukering et al. 2007:30).

In Votua, another LMMA community, social cohesiveness has improved considerably after 3 years of LMMA work. "Through our engagement with LMMA work…our three clan chiefs are now talking to each other after decades of disputes," observed one community member (LMMA Network 2006a:21).

2007a:iv). A separate study in Navakavu showed that the increase in fish caught over this period has provided about US$37,800 in benefits to the community (O'Garra 2007:2). The province-wide approaches established in Kadavu and other provinces of Fiji hold considerable promise as a low-cost and highly effective method for extending LMMA work to remote sites and may provide a model for other LMMA Network countries to emulate (LMMA Network 2006a:35).

It is important to note, however, that successful LMMA work requires a commitment to provide ongoing training for community members who replace people who move away from the village. Likewise, continual training is needed in LMMA Network partner organizations, such as government ministries, since staff move around over the course of their careers and often leave the districts in which they had begun promoting LMMAs.

The role of external funding has also been significant. The cost of the LMMA Network's core operations is about US$500,000 per year, much of which has historically been supplied by U.S.-based charitable organizations, including the MacArthur and Packard Foundations. It has been challenging for the network to secure additional sources of support, especially for core costs (USP 2007:23).

A FLMMA Trust Fund has been established to provide ongoing village assistance costs once donor funding ends. It was originally established with prize money from international awards for FLMMA work. More recently, Conservation International has committed funds in return for FLMMA managing the organization's Fiji Marine Managed Area initiative. A marine bioprospecting venture has also contributed to the fund. Individual communities are being encouraged to establish their own trust funds as well (Aalbersberg 2008).

LMMAs have also enhanced social cohesion by increasing village fundraising for communal purposes, such as to support the local church or schools. Households earning additional income from selling surplus fish and shellfish are better able to meet their traditional social obligation to contribute to village fundraising. For instance, in Waiqanake village in Navakavu, the Community Fundraising Project recently amassed some F$20,000 (about US$12,000), three quarters of which came from the sale of fish and shellfish from the LMMA (van Beukering et al. 2007:9).

Sustainability

The LMMA approach has several distinct characteristics that contribute to its ability to create long-term change. First, it relies on strong commitment and motivation from the communities themselves, which tends to promote enhanced resilience. Experience with the initial LMMAs indicates that communities remain engaged in the collective efforts needed for successful ongoing resource management.

Another favorable aspect is the relatively low cost to establish an LMMA. For instance, the total cost to establish the LMMA in Navakavu is estimated at less than US$12,000 over 5 years—a modest investment that has led to a doubling of average household income for about 600 people (Leisher et al.

Challenges to the LMMAs

In addition to the sustainability challenges described above, the LMMA approach faces other tests as it expands throughout Fiji and the South Pacific.

Representation
Traditional Fijian cultural norms tend to emphasize the involvement of older, male community members in decisions on marine resources. Women and youth are often challenged to make their voices heard.

While the FLMMA protocol recommends equal representation of women, men, and youth in all meetings and committees, this is not always achieved. In some villages, women lead iqoliqoli committees (Aalbersberg 2008). In others, however, women are not represented, despite the fact that many are actively involved in gathering shellfish (van Beukering et al. 2007:15,16–17). In interviews, many women of Navakavu voiced serious criticisms concerning the operation of the iqoliqoli committee in their community, especially the lack of any mechanism for women's grievances to be heard and acted on by the committee (van Beukering et al. 2007:15).

Changing such entrenched traditions will take time, yet the long-term future of any community LMMA depends on both the perception and the reality of equitable treatment and participation. Increases in alternative livelihoods, critical when natural resources are the sole source of income, can provide other avenues of empowerment and representation.

Enforcement

Maintaining the integrity of tabu areas is a continuing problem for LMMA communities, despite the efforts discussed earlier to develop enforcement capacity. Uneven support from regional and national officials and inadequate resources both cause problems. Fish wardens often experience difficulties carrying out their assigned jobs due to this lack of resources. Many LMMA villages consider the availability of a specially desig-nated patrol boat (with an engine) to be a prerequisite for successful enforcement, particularly in areas of conflict with commercial fishers (LMMA Network 2006b:2). While some communities have been able to secure the use of such a boat, they may lack the means to purchase fuel for it.

When violations are detected, only sanctioned fish wardens have the right to take violators to the police. Some transgressors may be brought before community meetings for more traditional forms of enforcement, such as shaming (LMMA Network 2006a:15). But a general lack of consistency and an occasional unwillingness of official law enforcement to get involved often undercut the effectiveness of any compliance program (Rarabici 2007). For instance, in the community of Tavualevu, on the north shore of Fiji's largest island, Viti Levu, the iqoliqoli committee has taken on violators who engage in destructive, illegal fishing using dynamite smuggled out from a nearby gold mine. Despite the confiscation of dynamite and offenders' fishing gear by community fish wardens, many violators have evaded significant penalties due to lack of will within the judicial system to convict them (LMMA Network 2007a:14-15).

A related challenge for communities engaged in LMMA work is addressing the suspicion of favoritism in enforcement. There is a perception that some people, such as extended family members of fish wardens, are more able to "get away with" illegal entry into tabu areas or the use of prohibited gear (van Beukering et al. 2007:12–13). Community support for the LMMA program will be eroded if the appearance of preferential access to marine resources is not addressed.

Other Livelihoods

The long-term success of the LMMA strategy also will depend on LMMA members' capacities for enterprise development and alternative livelihoods. Even with new opportunities for tourism employment, most poor families in Fiji's coastal communities remain heavily dependent on marine resources for their income. Yet as populations grow, if additional livelihood options are not available there is always the danger that poach-ing will become more common and that communities will revert to overharvesting.

Scaling up environmental enterprise for the poor involves creating the conditions for nature-based enterprises to thrive.

BUILDING OWNERSHIP, CAPACITY, AND CONNECTION

SCALING UP ENVIRONMENTAL INCOME FOR THE POOR involves creating the conditions for nature-based enterprises to thrive. The term "enterprise" here spans the range from smallholder farming, fishing, and agroforestry to community-based ecotourism and even commercial logging. The conditions that foster successful ecosystem enterprises are conditions that promote engagement and investment at the individual and community level, skill development to manage resources and yield a desirable product, and the forging of social and commercial links and networks that help isolated rural enterprises to connect to markets and continue growing their business and management capacities over time.

In its three major parts, this chapter probes these three essential conditions for poor-friendly enterprise: ownership, capacity, and connection. Or, to be more precise: creating *a sense of ownership*, developing the *local capacity for resource management and entrepreneurship*, and building the *dynamic networks and connections* necessary to sustain ecosystem-based enterprises. These elements are both sequential and interactive. Ownership provides the initial impulse for enterprise and precedes individual and collective action, but capacity is necessary to allow ownership to bear fruit, and connection is needed to increase and sustain the benefits stream.

This chapter emphasizes the role of local organizations and local branches of government in bringing about these conditions. These local actors, which encompass village councils, savings groups, farmers' organizations, NGOs, producer cooperatives, worker associations, resource user groups, and a range of other formal and informal groups, provide the mechanisms through which joint resource management and enterprise development occur in the rural sphere.

The chapter also examines intermediary support organizations (ISOs) that help connect and enable community-level groups and that act as bridges between local groups and higher levels of government and business. Without these trusted intermediaries, the rural poor would have a much more difficult time gaining the skills, financing, and authority necessary to carry out successful nature-based enterprises. The capacity development that these organizations enable and the political connections that they bring to the table are key elements of successful scaling up.

In examining the elements of scaling up nature-based enterprises, we realize that no list of "best practices," however well-grounded in observation and practice, can be regarded as a blueprint for success. Community-driven enterprises, and particularly nature-based enterprises, are always a product of the unique social, cultural, and resource context in which they arise. Slow and persistent learning by doing, where local participants gradually adapt their collective resource management and business practices to the local situation and capacities of the group, is perhaps the only consistent best practice (Mansuri and Rao 2003:37). Nonetheless, isolating common experiences and challenges within an identifiable theoretical frame, as we do here, offers an undeniable opportunity for learning at a macro level, so that support for scaling up ecosystem enterprise is well conceived.

1. BUILDING OWNERSHIP

Ownership: A Local Stake in Development and Enterprise

OWNERSHIP
- Enforceable resource rights
- Community demand for natural resource management
- Community investment of time, money, or other key inputs
- Participation in and influence over decision-making processes

CAPACITY

CONNECTION

See page 6 for full diagram.

THIS SECTION: OWNERSHIP

In this section, we present the idea that "ownership," broadly conceived, is the bedrock of nature-based enterprise. The incentive for sound resource management grows when individuals and communities possess enforceable resource rights and process rights—that is, when they have secure access to natural resources of value as well as to the decision-making processes around natural resource management. This section:

■ Examines the two components of ownership: secure rights in land or aquatic resources and the ability to participate in decision-making around the management of local ecosystem resources. Both are important to create a real stake in improved resource management.

■ Links the success of community-based natural resources management (CBNRM) to the security of land and resource tenure and looks at recent innovations in tenure reform.

■ Proposes that community demand for better resource management is a crucial element in catalyzing successful ecosystem enterprises and analyzes how this demand arises.

■ Traces how community demand is expressed as collective action—a commitment of resources and time for joint ecosystem management.

■ Explains the importance of participation of community members in the design of local resource management institutions and in the resource management process itself.

■ Probes the weaknesses of current participatory methods with respect to the poor and suggests some strategies for making participation more poor-friendly.

Managing ecosystems productively and sustainably generally requires a significant investment of time and resources. What can catalyze the willingness to make this personal investment, or, even more challenging, the willingness to work and invest collaboratively with others in the community? Ownership is the inducement—having a stake in the benefits that will accrue from ecosystem management. Ownership here involves both *resource rights*—the rights over land and resources known as tenure—as well as *a sense of control* over the larger process of resource development in a community. Local ownership of resource rights and decision-making processes governing resource use provides the motive force for community-driven development of ecosystem enterprises. Without this local stake in ownership, ecosystem management schemes are not likely to be sustainable or effective at poverty reduction.

As mentioned in Chapter 1, our use of the term ownership does not necessarily imply possessing the full bundle of rights attributed to private property. Many different tenure arrangements—from full private ownership to communal tenure to co-management arrangements over state-owned resources like forests or fisheries—can support local nature-based enterprises. The critical factor for ownership is that local people—individually or collectively—have secure rights to use and control the ecosystem resources in question and perceive that their access is secure.

While we do not explicitly take up the topic of decentralization of natural resource governance in this chapter, it provides a necessary backdrop to our discussion of ownership. Decentralization—the shifting of decision-making powers from central to local levels of government—is part of the larger process of devolving resource rights to local-level institutions, which is an important first step on the path to viable ecosystem enterprises. The current reality is that resource rights are often not vested in local governments, communities, or individuals, and the poor are particularly likely to suffer from a lack of control over the ecosystem resources they rely on for their livelihoods. Centralized state control over forest, fishery, mineral, and wildlife resources is still the norm in

STATUS OF LAND TENURE AND PROPERTY RIGHTS, 2005

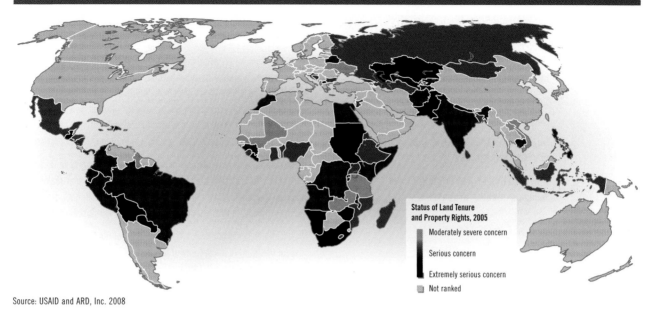

Status of Land Tenure
and Property Rights, 2005

Moderately severe concern

Serious concern

Extremely serious concern

Not ranked

Source: USAID and ARD, Inc. 2008

most developing nations, although this has begun to change as more nations have embraced decentralization reforms. True decentralization shifts power over resources by realigning resource-related decision-making processes to put local institutions—and thus local users—at the center. Devolution of meaningful resource rights can take place within such a decentralization process, with local government playing a critical role. Unfortunately, most current decentralization efforts remain partial, and lack of resource rights is still a serious impediment for most of the rural poor.

Land and Resource Tenure

Access to land and natural resources is the basis for livelihoods, shelter, and social inclusion. Tenure is the right—embodied in law, custom, or convention—to such access. It is the right to use, manage, and profit from resources and to exclude others from access—a bundle often termed property rights. As such, land and resource tenure is the basis for all ecosystem enterprises—from farming to fishing—and lack of secure tenure is one of the most consistent and significant obstacles the poor face in tapping the wealth of nature. In fact, rural poverty is strongly associated with weak property rights or outright landlessness (Cotula et al. 2006:7). Creating the conditions for "ownership" and community buy-in to nature-based enterprises thus requires wrestling early on with the issue of tenure.

The link between successful enterprise and property rights is well established. Those with secure land and resource rights have a reasonable expectation that they will benefit from the use of their "property" and are more willing to invest time and money to

improve or manage it (van den Brink et al. 2006:4). Some studies show that investment doubles on land where tenure is strengthened (Feder 2002:15). It comes as no surprise, then, that strong property rights are associated with increased economic growth (Cotula et al. 2006:7).

The connection between property rights and investment is particularly true of investments that take time to yield benefits, such as using good cultivation and water-management practices, planting long-lived crops such as orchards and plantations, adopting sustainable fishing practices, or installing expensive infrastructure such as irrigation systems or new fishing equipment (Meinzen-Dick and Di Gregorio 2004:1; van den Brink et al. 2006:4). The key here is that the individuals or groups holding the property rights feel these rights are secure, meaning that there is little chance they will be dispossessed of their land or property for a period long enough to ensure that they reap the benefits of their investment.

Secure tenure is also linked to the success of community-based natural resource management. In a 2006 meta-study of 49 community forest management (CFM) cases worldwide, Pagdee et al. found a significant association between a community's security of forest tenure and the project's success (See Figure 1). Conversely, when user rights and benefits were insecure, CFM was more likely to fail. Clearly defined forest boundaries and clear rules for forest use were other factors important to successful community management. All of these are features of robust property rights regimes (Pagdee et al. 2006:43–45, 49).

Challenges to Security

While the benefits of secure tenure are clear, achieving it is often exceedingly difficult for the poor. Tenure regimes are complex and

INEQUITABLE ACCESS TO LAND AND NATURAL RESOURCES, 2005

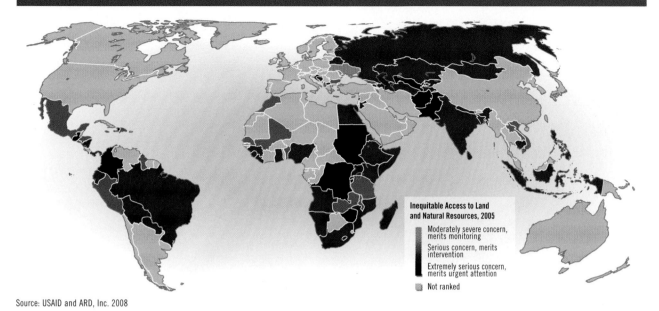

Inequitable Access to Land and Natural Resources, 2005

- Moderately severe concern, merits monitoring
- Serious concern, merits intervention
- Extremely serious concern, merits urgent attention
- Not ranked

Source: USAID and ARD, Inc. 2008

FIGURE 1 SUCCESS RATE OF COMMUNITY FOREST MANAGEMENT (CFM) IN 49 COMMUNITIES STUDIED

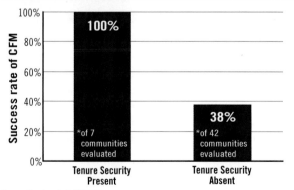

Source: Pagdee et al. 2006:45

the sources of tenure insecurity are many. One particular challenge is the mismatch between modern systems of formalized legal tenure and the systems of informal customary tenure that still prevail in many rural areas. Modern tenure systems are generally based on registered titles that give property owners legally recognized rights sanctioned and enforced by the state.

However, formally codified property rights are uncommon in many rural communities. Access to land in these areas often comes through social networks, kinship, inheritance, and other customary means that bypass the official recognition of the state. Titled property rights in Africa, for example, are still rare, and most land falls under customary tenure. In West Africa, only 2–3 percent of all land is held by formal written title—and most of that is in urban areas or covers higher-value lands such as those near irrigation systems or other infrastructure (Toulmin 2005:34; van den Brink et al. 2006:5).

Responsibility for validating and enforcing customary tenure systems rests with customary authorities such as village elders and tribal chiefs. These systems can be complex, recognizing multiple, sometimes overlapping, rights over the same land or resource. For example, a person may have the right to build a house or grow crops on a piece of land but not to sell it, or the right to graze cattle on a piece of pasture during certain months of the year while another person farms it in other months (Toulmin 2005:33–34). As long as the local institutions that recognize and enforce customary tenure remain strong and unchallenged, research confirms that customary property rights can provide the security landholders need to make long-term investments (Toulmin 2005:29; van den Brink et al. 2006:5).

Unfortunately, customary property rights often overlap state-sanctioned tenure systems, with a single parcel or resource claimed under both systems. The state does not recognize customary title in many of these cases—although this is beginning to change—and the result has been conflict over competing claims and loss of tenure security (van den Brink et al. 2006:14). In many cases, these customary tenure rights take the form of communal rights, meaning they are held in common by a group, tribe, or village, which may allocate different land rights to individuals within the group or to the group as a whole. This provides another point of potential conflict with state tenure systems, where titles are usually granted to individuals (van den Brink et al. 2006:5–6).

State Claims to Land

One of the most frequent sources of tenure conflict is when the state itself claims title to lands and resources long considered by local people to be their own, including forestland, fisheries, and other common pool resources. States routinely grant logging, mining, or fishing concessions to commercial interests without

OWNERSHIP

consultation and with little or no compensation to local inhabitants. Often these are precisely the lands and resources to which the poor require access in order to pursue ecosystem enterprises (Toulmin 2005:31; van den Brink et al. 2006:14).

At the same time, new market forces, demographic trends, and land uses have destabilized many customary tenure regimes. Population growth means that more people are vying for access to land and resource rights in most areas. Modern markets for cash crops, timber, and minerals have also encouraged intensification of land uses. In many areas—particularly near urban centers and lands with high-value resources—land markets have developed that directly compete with traditional methods of land exchange and allocation of resource rights (IIED 2006:2–3; Toulmin 2005:29–31, 34).

For example, in regions of Ghana where land competition is most intense, once-secure inheritance rights over land have begun to break down, with older family members increasingly leasing out family land for income rather than passing it on, resulting in rising landlessness among the young. In other instances, agribusiness firms have worked with local Ghanaian chiefs to expropriate family farming land for conversion to cash crops such as palm oil plantations. The result is increasing distortions of customary tenure practices and a trend toward privatizing land and resource uses to fit the market economy, with the impact falling hardest on those with the weakest property rights: the young, the old, women, and the poor (van den Brink et al. 2006:9; IIED 2006:2–3).

Tenure Innovations

Many governments today are aware of the importance of tenure security to poverty alleviation and economic growth. In a 2005 study of 18 recent national anti-poverty strategies, the International Institute for Environment and Development found that 13 countries made explicit reference to the connection between poverty and the lack of access to land. As a consequence, many countries are experimenting with tenure reform, revising the ways they recognize individual and collective rights to land and resources (Cotula et al. 2006:12; Toulmin 2005:35).

Rural people and governments alike realize that there is an increasing need to formalize their property rights in a way that is legally recognized. To be truly secure, a property right today requires two forms of recognition. It must first be seen as legitimate in the eyes of the community, which must respect the property rights on a daily basis. But it must also be legally recognized by the state and thus capable of weathering a competing claim. While legal recognition may not matter so much if the land is not under pressure and customary tenure arrangements are still strong, it is essential where local land markets are active or there is strong interest in the land or resource rights at issue (Cotula et al. 2006:23). Moreover, where communities seek secure access to natural resources claimed by the state as a basis for environmental enterprise, a formalized agreement between the community and the state that spells out the community's use and management rights is essential.

In the 1970s and 1980s, efforts to make tenure more secure in Africa, Asia, and Latin America focused on large-scale land-titling programs, emphasizing formal land registration and individual title deeds backed by detailed surveys of property boundaries (cadastral surveys). This approach brought some success in Latin America and Asia. In Nicaragua, Ecuador, and Venezuela, research shows that registration of land has brought higher agricultural investment and land values, while Thailand's titling program has increased productivity and investment on titled farm land (Cotula et al. 2006:20; van den Brink et al. 2006:19–20; Feder 2002: 15, 18; Deininger 2003:42–51).

In general, however, traditional titling efforts have not proved to be an effective and cost-efficient approach, particularly in Africa. They tend to be too expensive, time-consuming, and bureaucratically complex and therefore not very accessible to the poor. In 1985, Ghana enacted a registration law intended to help formalize all interests in land, whether under customary tenure or the nation's common law tenure. But the country's registry has not been able to process applications quickly enough and a large backlog remains. In addition, poor quality control in the registration process led to 30,000 disputed titles as of 2000 (Cotula et al. 2006: 20–22; Toulmin 2005:46; van den Brink et al. 2006:12–13).

Titling also brings with it other challenges and unintended consequences. Experience shows that local elites often try to take advantage of the titling process to grab land or to influence the registration process in their favor, such as by registering common lands in their own name. Titling may also work against marginalized groups, such as widows or the poor, who may not have the time, money, or technical understanding to protect their interests against those with more influence or contacts. Titling may even increase land conflicts—at least in the short term—as people with latent disputes realize that registration will be a decisive step in deciding who holds property rights over a given piece of land or resource (Cotula et al. 2006:20).

Using Local Institutions

As a result, the thinking on how best to improve tenure security has now shifted away from wholesale replacement of customary tenure with formal titles. The current consensus is that a broader approach is necessary that builds on local tenure practices and uses local institutions to help execute simpler forms of land and resource registration open to a broader range of rural families. Such registration can be much lower-cost and can offer an intermediate level of formalization that provides a measurable increase in security (Cotula et al. 2006: 21–22; van den Brink et al. 2006:14). In Niger, for example, the government has instituted a community-based system for registering local land rights in the Mirriah region by creating Village Land Commissions. The five-person committees publicize the requests they receive for land registration and, if a request is not contested, they record it in the village land register (Toulmin 2005:48).

Another key to increasing tenure security is rectifying national tenure laws so that they recognize local customary land rights. Countries such as Uganda, Mozambique, Tanzania, Niger, and Namibia have all made efforts to protect such customary tenure in

law and often to recognize it through various forms of registration. On the other hand, under Mozambique's 1997 land law, customary use rights are protected whether they have been registered or not. The law also mandates that communities be consulted when investment projects are proposed within their jurisdiction and be given the right of first refusal (Cotula et al. 2006:21; IIED 2006:7). One potential problem with blanket recognition of customary tenure is that it may formalize existing inequalities in customary tenure arrangements, which often concentrate land rights in authorities such as tribal chiefs (Ribot 2008).

Rights for the Landless

A comprehensive approach to increasing tenure security must also serve those who don't own land. Land leasing arrangements, for example, are an important form of land access for many rural families. Tenure experts point out that full, titled ownership is not always required to give secure access to land and resources. Longer-term lease or tenant arrangements can also provide security and flexibility at much lower cost than land purchases, making them a good entry point for many poor families to increase their land and resource access. Sometimes, NGOs can play a useful intermediary role in helping the poor negotiate land leases. In the Indian state of Andhra Pradesh, an NGO called the Deccan Development Society has helped lower-caste women lease underutilized private land on a tenancy basis (Cotula et al. 2006:25).

Finally, any approach to more secure tenure must include the development of more effective systems to resolve land disputes. Often, several different courts and land dispute tribunals—some part of the national legal system and some operating under customary law—operate in the same jurisdiction without coordination. Those with conflicts often go "forum shopping," looking for the venue where they feel they will get the most favorable ruling. The result is that many land disputes are never fully resolved in a manner that is binding or accepted by all parties. A functional dispute resolution system must include both customary and statutory mechanisms within a single framework, with the connection between the two clearly established (von Benda-Beckmann 1981; Cotula et al. 2006:23).

Forests: Leading Tenure Progress

How quickly such approaches can be applied to bring measurable increases in resource tenure security is uncertain. But it is clear that fundamental changes in the tenure landscape are already under way, particularly with respect to state-owned resources such as forests. Forest tenure has changed substantially in the last few decades, with the area of forest administered by communities doubling in the past 15 years alone to 25 percent of all developing-country forests (White et al. 2007:15) New legislation and reforms now taking place suggest that this increase may continue, with some experts predicting the percentage of community forests may double again by 2020. For instance, in 2006, the Indian parliament passed legislation recognizing the land and use rights of indigenous tribes and other traditional forest dwellers. Meanwhile, the Indonesian government indicated it would allocate 60 percent

OWNERSHIP

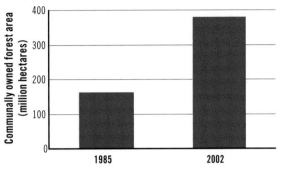

FIGURE 2 GROWTH IN COMMUNITY FOREST OWNERSHIP WORLDWIDE, 1985-2002

Source: White and Martin 2002: 11

of its degraded state forestlands to communities, and the head of China's State Forest Administration said that strengthening local property rights was a top priority (White et al. 2007:15; White and Martin 2002:4-7; Lok Sabha 2006).

How this will play out in terms of actual increases in forest-based enterprises is again unknown. There is often a significant difference between policy and practice on the ground, and the nature of the tenure rights granted to communities varies widely, from substantive to shallow. In addition, there are many requirements for successful enterprise beyond resource access. Nonetheless, current trends show that governments are increasingly aware that ecosystem resources have considerable potential to contribute to rural development if progress on the issue of resource tenure can be made (White et al. 2007:15).

Local Demand and Commitment

Successful ecosystem-based enterprises arise out of an expressed demand from the community. Secure resource rights alone are not sufficient. There must be the desire and willingness to use these rights to jointly manage ecosystems, reflecting the belief that doing so will benefit individuals and the group. *(See Box 2.2.)* Demand manifests itself as community consensus on the need to act and a commitment on the part of the majority of stakeholders to adhere to an agreed action plan. Without this kind of demand from the community, ecosystem enterprises are likely to fail; people will not maintain projects or adhere to management plans over the long term that they do not want or do not consider fair. Similarly, by requiring commitments and investments—of labor, money, or other resources—community-based enterprise encourages a sense of local ownership, in turn engendering sustained involvement on the part of participants.

Insights on the importance of community demand for success in development efforts first arose out of experience with water and sanitation projects in the 1970s and 1980s. Authorities

noted that drinking water or sewer projects that were planned and executed without consultation with local communities often failed to meet community needs and subsequently were underused and poorly maintained. In contrast, projects that responded to focused community demand and involved the community in design, construction, and maintenance had a better performance and cost-recovery record (Deverill et al. 2002:2–3; Breslin 2003:1–10). These lessons provided the groundwork of experience for the community-driven development approach and a point of reference for examining the structure of demand.

The Structure of Demand for Rural Enterprise

In the realm of community development, demand can be defined as "an informed expression of desire for a particular service, measured by the contribution people are willing and able to make to receive this service" (Deverill 2000:1). A "contribution" often includes time and effort, not just goods and money. For nature-based enterprises, the service involved is an ecosystem service, such as increased agricultural production, the provision of timber or non-timber forest products (NTFPs), higher fisheries production, or landscapes and species that attract tourists.

Demand is not static; it develops with changes in the community and the resource base. Among some groups, demand for jointly managing ecosystems has deep historical roots, but it has often broken down as modern tenure patterns and economic forces have disrupted traditional ways. In other instances, degradation of the resource base or new opportunities for resource exploitation offer conditions for the demand for community resource management to arise.

Development of local demand can be envisioned in three stages. First, there is a change, or *initiating event* in the community. Second, participants decide *whether or not to respond* to this change. This usually involves deliberation among the community members, with individuals weighing the costs and benefits to themselves. Third, the participants decide *how to address* the problem. These stages are iterative and not discrete from one another, as people constantly update their information and weigh the consequences of participation or nonparticipation (White and Runge 1995:1685).

The initiating event that leads to demand for a new ecosystem enterprise can come from a number of sources: a change in the information available, a change in the local environment or economy, a change in the financial incentives for investment, or a change in resource rights or access that makes resources more available. A dynamic community leader who can put the change in perspective and advocate for action is often an important part of the mix. In many cases, several of these factors work in concert to create the perception that a new opportunity is at hand. In the end, the decision whether to act on this opportunity is a function of available information, community dynamics, and the perceived costs of action versus inaction (Lobo 2007; White and Runge 1995:1685).

Resource Degradation

A decline in the status or productivity of a local natural resource is frequently a significant factor in generating community demand. A sudden drop in fish catches or the depletion of a certain stock of tree may spur community members to act or to be more receptive to new approaches to managing the resource, particularly if the resource is or was an important part of the household income stream. The decline in the resource must take place over a short enough time span to be noticeable; if changes are too gradual, individuals may not perceive the events as serious enough at any one point in time to justify action (White and Runge 1995:1685). While serious resource degradation may build demand to address the loss of resources, this demand alone may not be sufficient to spur action without a convincing alternative at hand.

Changing Information

Information is always a critical variable in the demand equation. What people know about the changing resource situation in their community, new opportunities for using resources, or the potential return on a new investment is usually the deciding factor in whether they consent to community resource management. New information can come from a variety of sources, with demonstrations and pilot projects being particularly effective in conveying an alternative to the status quo. The "demonstration effect"—when villagers or their leaders see for themselves the benefits that

other communities have gained by managing their watershed, forest, or fishing grounds differently—is often quick and persuasive. In Niger, where NGOs initially helped farmers to regenerate trees and implement basic soil and water conservation practices, the visible and rapid yield increases created by these practices inspired neighboring farmers to follow suit. The spread has been described as "viral," with the techniques now used widely across Niger. *(See Chapter 3: Turning Back the Desert: How Farmers Have Transformed Niger's Landscapes and Livelihoods.)*

However, seeing demonstration projects in person is not the only way that villagers can get new information. Street fairs, theater, radio broadcasts, pamphlets, posters, and video presentations can all broadcast possibilities, shift consciousnesses, and change tastes, making people more aware of options for action (Lobo 2007). Awards and prizes that recognize good practices can also be an effective tool for delivering new information and generating demand. The Equator Prize of the UN Development Programme (UNDP), which profiles and rewards successful ecosystem enterprises, has had a substantial demonstration effect since its establishment in 2002 (UNDP 2008a). *(See Box 2.1.)* This emphasizes the important role that communication plays in building demand at the village level. In most cases, being an effective advocate for community resource management requires some mastery of communication tools and forums.

Engaged Leadership

Effective leaders are able to understand the forces for change in a community, express a guiding vision, offer alternatives for action, and organize their constituents first to make a choice between alternatives and then to carry through on their choice. In this sense, leaders provide both the spark of demand and also a stabilizing force connecting demand to collective action. In the beginning, a leader's personal charisma may be crucial in selling the vision for action and arousing the willingness to make a commitment to a new resource management scheme. Because of their position, education, and experience, leaders can confer legitimacy to a proposed line of action or doom it if they find it unacceptable. Because of their connections to those in power (a form of bridging social capital), they can also communicate this legitimacy to external sources of funding or support. Particularly in those situations where a new management regime or enterprise is stimulated by outside actors (NGOs, governments, etc.), the development of local leaders with the capacity to function within the community according to its norms greatly increases the chances for success (Seymour 1994: 481–486).

New Incentives or Resource Access

Factors originating outside the community, such as changes in state tenure policies or the availability of state or international funds to support a change in resource management, can also be powerful inducements for change. Namibia's conservancies could not take off until the national legislature enacted the Nature Conservation Act in 1996 that devolved wildlife tenure to local groups. Likewise, the widespread adoption of new watershed management practices

Continues on page 61

THE EQUATOR INITIATIVE OF THE UNITED Nations Development Programme (UNDP) champions community efforts to link socioeconomic development and income generation with the conservation and sustainable use of natural resources. The Initiative's name comes from the observation that the most biologically diverse ecosystems and the most acute levels of poverty overlap within the equatorial belt. Bringing together the United Nations, local communities, civil society, businesses, and governments, the Initiative supports community-based organizations and local ecosystem-based enterprises (EBEs) by providing knowledge management services, documenting best practices, and expanding access to policymaking processes that have been recognized as integral to achieving the Millennium Development Goals (Hooper et al. 2005:142).

Since its launch in 2002, the Equator Initiative has accumulated a wealth of knowledge on local best practices through the Equator Prize, an international award that recognizes outstanding local efforts within the equatorial region to reduce poverty through improved environmental stewardship. The selection process is by design a mechanism to identify best practice. Nominations are evaluated by an experienced technical advisory committee whose members have diverse areas of expertise. Winners, which have ranged between five and seven organizations in the past, are selected by a jury of preeminent individuals in the fields of conservation and development.

To distill lessons learned from the process, an ongoing research program reports on Equator Prize finalists and winners. Researchers from the University of Manitoba and the International Development Research Centre have worked firsthand with Equator Prize finalist communities to document and analyze their experiences. They have identified a number of necessary conditions and best practices for successful community-based EBEs (NRI 2007).

Honey Care Africa, Ltd. in Kenya, 2002 Equator Prize Finalist

Preconditions for Success

In order for EBEs to begin to grow and flourish, the stakeholders involved must recognize the economic value of ecosystem-derived resources and also be knowledgeable about how to use these resources to improve local livelihoods. Then EBEs require firm rights to the resource or need to have land (or water) tenure over its use. Without well-established and defensible rights, EBEs cannot make and enforce resource use rules. This is a basic defining principle for success: EBEs must have access to a secure natural resource base and the right to benefit from its use. This is a necessary but not a sufficient condition for EBE success (Berkes and Davidson-Hunt 2007:219).

Another major precondition for success is the availability of sufficient start-up capital and access to financial services, with the amounts needed dependent on the scale and ambition of those involved in the early stages of a project. This "seed money" is often in the form of grants. The Equator Initiative experience has indicated that small grants with few or no conditions (no strings attached) may show better results than large grants during the start-up phase. Large grants create the need for a higher level of financial management capacity to meet many bureaucratic requirements (UNDP 2005:13).

Increasing Access to Markets and Overcoming Barriers to Entry

EBEs are most successful when they engage in innovative strategies to increase access to markets, finding ways to overcome the obstacles they face in the form of local and national regulations, international trade laws, lack of product demand, and channels of distribution (UNDP 2005:24). These obstacles also include physical barriers to getting products to market, such as a lack of roads, bridges, or means of transportation, as well as barriers to knowledge and insight, such as the value of marketing and the need to limit the number of individuals in a value chain in order to capture as much profit as possible for the local community.

Alimentos Nutri-Naturales, an Equator Prize 2006 winner from Guatemala, was founded by 56 women from nine communities in the buffer zone of the Maya Biosphere Reserve. It is completely owned and managed by women. It has successfully overcome barriers to market access through local product sourcing and selling. The women have created a local niche market for the Maya nut, a traditional staple food, whose use had become infrequent and which was becoming threatened by habitat destruction. Sustainable local production and sales, which are cost-effective and locally manageable, have allowed the women of Alimentos Nutri-Naturales to successfully improve local livelihoods and food security. One significant way they have created demand is through a partnership with a school lunch program, whereby biscuits made from Maya nut flour are included in the lunches provided to local schoolchildren (UNDP 2007).

Cross-Scale Linkages
Horizontal Linkages
The Equator Initiative experience has shown that some prize finalists and winners may have 20 or more partners who assume different roles at different phases of program development. Research shows that at least 8–12 partners are needed to provide the levels and kinds of support required to meet all the technical, capacity-building, educational, infrastructural, legal, and marketing needs for program or enterprise growth (Berkes and Adhikari 2006:687; Berkes 2007:15190).

The Village of Andavadoaka in Madagascar, a winner of the 2006 Equator Prize, reacted to declining populations of octopus, the traditional source of local livelihood, by partnering with marine conservationists to stabilize the species and implement a seasonal ban on octopus fishing. The successful partnership encouraged nearby villagers to join Andavadoaka's efforts, resulting in a regional community network that is working to preserve local coral reefs and manage aquatic wildlife populations. To further bolster local livelihoods, the villagers in this remote isolated area have begun to explore ecotourism options in partnership with a UK-based NGO, and a new resort was scheduled to open in late 2007. The overall success of the village's efforts is tied to its work with a number of partners: a national academic institution, two international NGOs, a variety of national government agencies, a private-sector fishing company, and more than a dozen neighboring communities (UNDP 2007; Heid and Streets 2006:4–7).

Vertical Linkages
Research has shown that successful Equator Prize finalists and winners are often connected across four or five levels (community, regional, national, multinational, international) and also demonstrate a system of co-management across the different levels, with vertically integrated responsibilities for program management. If the number of levels a program extends across is truncated, the likelihood of success is diminished (Berkes and Adhikari 2006:687,688).

The Shompole Community Trust, a winner of the 2006 Equator Prize, belongs to the indigenous Maasai people in Kenya. It has been successful in part because it was able to significantly increase community funds by entering into a partnership with a private investor who brought in start-up capital, international hotel standards, and marketing and management skills to establish a luxury eco-lodge. The Shompole Lodge works in close cooperation with the Maasai community, offering local employment and training opportunities. Hotel visitors generate a monthly average income of US$2,000–5,000 that the community invests in social development activities and biodiversity conservation. At the same time, the lodge operations benefit from the Maasai's traditional expertise in managing their ancestral land and wildlife, ensuring a steady flow of ecotourists. Shompole's ability to partner from the community level with a corporate entity that works at the national level, and to use this linkage to attract an international clientele and national and international media attention, has been a significant driver of the Trust's success (UNDP 2002, 2007).

Leadership

Effective leaders and leadership teams are integral to bridging levels and to building and maintaining partnerships. The Equator Initiative has worked closely with representatives of prize finalist and winning communities and has found that these leaders consistently demonstrate an ability to operate in different contexts and across different horizontal and vertical levels. They tend to think systematically about the design of their enterprises, and they catalyze innovative thinking, facilitate communications, and initiate organizational learning (Timmer 2004:4).

Honey Care Africa, an Equator Prize 2002 finalist, illustrates the importance of effective leadership in sustaining successful enterprises. Honey Care was established in 2000 as a social venture to promote local economic development through community-based beekeeping across East Africa. Since then, it has helped more than 9,000 rural beekeepers (over 40 percent of whom are women) earn a supplementary income of US$180–250 per year—often the difference between living above or below the poverty line.

Farouk Jiwa and his co-founders use a holistic strategy for development: in addition to providing beehives to rural farmers and guaranteeing to purchase the honey that is produced, they have also established tree planting and tree nursery programs, using the pollinating habits of the bees to improve local ecosystems. In addition, Honey Care's leaders have created strong networks, partnering with NGOs and donors to support training in sustainable beekeeping and long-term relationships with product retailers abroad. The enterprise's leaders were also willing to take calculated risks, introducing the latest beekeep-

Continues on page 60

BOX 2.1 LESSONS FROM THE EQUATOR INITIATIVE

SUCCESSFUL ECOSYSTEM-BASED ENTERPRISES: SELECTED EQUATOR PRIZE FINALISTS

Ecosystem-Based Enterprise	Product or Service Provided	Description	Benefits
AFRICA			
Pole Pole Foundation Democratic Republic of the Congo Founded: 1992 2006 Equator Prize Finalist	Crafts, carvings, tree nursery, timber, non-timber forest products, construction projects, crop harvesting	Based in Kahuzi-Biega National Park, Pole Pole Foundation provides capacity-building in local communities, including those of displaced pygmies, through wood-carving programs called "poachers to artisans," environmental education, farming and breeding, and reforestation.	Since 1997, Pole Pole has planted more than 426,000 trees, which communities use for timber, firewood, and construction projects. Pygmy women harvest crops and have started at least 140 small businesses. More than 135 children have been supported for three years at a school built by the organization.
Honey Care Africa, Ltd. Kenya Founded: 2000 2002 Equator Prize Finalist	Honey	Honey Care supplies hives and apiculture training to communities, farmers, and organizations and assures them that it will purchase all the honey they produce for a competitive price. Foundations support the initiative by providing start-up funds to the farmers.	Some 2,000 households care for 10,000 hives and earn $200–250 per year in supplemental income.
Shompole Community Trust Kenya Founded: 2001 2006 Equator Prize Winner http://www.shompole.com/	Tourism	This Maasai Community enterprise includes a community-owned and -managed 10,000 ha conservation area that is patrolled by trained local game scouts. The conservation area strategy is designed to decrease poaching and improve environmental conditions, including reforestation and wetland restoration. The community collectively owns 30 percent of an eco-lodge they have helped to establish.	The trust has more than 2,000 registered members. The lodge offers 70 percent of its permanent jobs to community members, with priority given to the poorest. In addition, it provides the community with US$2000–5000 per month in profits, which are used to pay for health care, water, and teacher salaries. Wildlife numbers on the reserve tripled between 2001 and 2004, and small enterprises have spun off from the tourism venture.
ASIA-PACIFIC			
Ngata Toro Community Indonesia Founded: 1993 2004 Equator Prize Finalist	Tourism, artisanal crafts, furniture making	The indigenous Masyarakat Adat of Ngata Toro village live within Lore Lindu National Park. After being granted resource use rights in the park in 2000, the Ngata Toro community established an ecotourism enterprise and complementary agriculture and handicrafts enterprises.	Ngata Toro has revived and implemented customary laws to ensure sustainable extraction of natural resources. They have established duck, pig, and fish farming, implemented organic farming practices, and developed value-added rattan, bamboo, and tree-bark product enterprises. They now host other indigenous communities to share knowledge.
Genetic Resource, Energy, Ecology and Nutrition (GREEN) Foundation India Founded: 1992 2004 Equator Prize Winner	Seeds, garden produce	Developed to increase food security among farmers in the state of Karnataka, GREEN facilitates the creation of seed and gene banks of indigenous varieties of millet, rice, and various vegetables and leads farmer knowledge exchanges and agricultural education programs.	GREEN established 31 community seed banks managed by women farmers, who earn an average of US$52 per year from their work with the seeds. The number of farmers participating in the seed conservation program has grown from 10 in 1992 to more than 1,500 farmers across Karnataka.

SUCCESSFUL ECOSYSTEM-BASED ENTERPRISES: SELECTED EQUATOR PRIZE FINALISTS (CONTINUED)

Ecosystem-Based Enterprise	Product or Service Provided	Description	Benefits
Center for Empowerment and Resource Development (CERD) Philippines Founded: 1996 2006 Equator Prize Finalist	Fish	CERD began a program in Hinatuan Bay in Surigao del Sur called Fishery Integrated Resource Management for Economic Development (FIRMED). The program established a plan among local villages to rehabilitate and conserve fishing resources.	FIRMED established seven fish sanctuaries, restored 117 ha of mangroves, and successfully lobbied for reforms on local fishing laws. Between 2003 and 2005 the number of families engaged in fishing increased by a third while average fish catches have increased by 50 percent. Average household income from fishing has doubled within the community, and income from seaweed farming also more than doubled.
Sepik Wetlands Management Initiative Papua New Guinea Founded: 1998 2006 Equator Prize Finalist	Crocodile eggs and related products	Communities around the wetlands developed a written contract setting guidelines for sustainable harvest of crocodile eggs, as well as protective measures for nesting crocodiles and their habitat. They have implemented a communal monitoring and enforcement program to secure the contract's benefits.	A strong rise in the crocodile population helped Sepik communities earn more than US$90,000 per year from the sale of eggs, skins, and young crocodiles. Revenue goes into a communal fund that is distributed among community members and pays for school fees.

LATIN AMERICA-CARIBBEAN

Ecosystem-Based Enterprise	Product or Service Provided	Description	Benefits
AmazonLife Brazil Founded: 1994 2002 Equator Prize Finalist http://www.amazonlife.com	Treetap® cloth product line, including bags, garments, and footwear	AmazonLife markets Treetap®, a cotton fabric drenched in natural latex that is extracted from wild rubber trees. The cloth producers are co-owners of the patented process. The company contracts third parties in Rio de Janeiro to produce bags, backpacks, briefcases, hats, and footwear with the fabric that are sold nationally and internationally.	As of 2006, some 200 families supplied the rubber for Treetap®, and AmazonLife was selling 40,000 sheets of rubber laminates each year at 10 times the price that local producers had previously received.
Alimentos Nutri-Naturales Guatemala Founded: 2001 2006 Equator Prize Winner http://www.theequilibriumfund.org/	Maya nuts and maya nut products	In this enterprise women harvest the high-protein maya nut from trees in the rainforests and process it at home into whole grain maya nut seeds and flour, drink mix, pancake mix, and cereal. They then jointly market the maya nut products. The group is just one of three women's maya nut enterprises formed in Central America with technical support provided by a regional NGO.	Alimentos Nutri-Naturales brings an annual income of US$24,000 to seven rural communities. The broader maya nut rejuvenation project helps 600 families from 21 communities in Central America to earn more than US$200 per year. The workers have conserved 90,000 ha of maya nut forests and planted 400,000 new trees. Consumption of maya nut products has also improved local nutrition due to its high protein content.
Quibdo Women's Network of Medicinal Plant Producers and Marketeres (Red de Mujeres Productoras y Comercializadoras de Plantas Medicinales de Quibdo) Colombia Founded: 1997 2004 Equator Prize Finalist	Medicinal plants, spices	This community-based enterprise consists of women who grow vegetables, herbs, and medicinal and aromatic plants in their home gardens and in a 2.25-ha community garden. The women's network uses sustainable agricultural practices, makes and markets compost, and coordinates a seed bank. The women and their husbands have built a central storage facility and a processing plant for their produce.	Forty-two families directly benefit from the network. The women's average annual incomes have grown from US$409 per year prior to the enterprise to US$2,863 per year.

Source: UNDP 2007

BOX 2.1 LESSONS FROM THE EQUATOR INITIATIVE

ing technology to ensure high-quality honey. Their solid leadership has created a successful and sustainable enterprise model. Today, Honey Care Africa is the region's largest producer of quality honey and continues to expand its operations, selling its Fair Trade and ecologically certified honey locally and abroad (Timmer 2004:15–18).

Scalability

The vertical and horizontal linkages and leadership conditions for success also apply to scalability. Hooper et al. examined the experiences of Equator Prize finalists and winners and found that their success was defined in large part by their ability to scale up their efforts (Hooper et al. 2005:141–142). Scaling up can be defined as "bringing more quality benefits to more people over a wider geographical area more quickly, more equitably, and more lastingly" (IIRR 2000). Scaling up can take place functionally, in terms of broadening the types of activities undertaken; quantitatively, in terms of increasing participation and scope; organizationally, in terms of increased effectiveness and efficiency of operations; or politically, in terms of a better ability to engage in political processes in order to benefit initiative stakeholders (Hooper et al. 2005: 131-132). The Shompole Community Trust, for example, has shown functional and organizational scalability, while Honey Care Africa has shown strong quantitative scalability.

The experiences of Costa Rica's Talamanca Initiative, an Equator Prize 2002 winner, demonstrate the potential for political scalability. The Initiative is an alliance of more than 20 community-based organizations committed to bringing environmental and socioeconomic benefits to the Talamanca region. It has also provided leadership at many levels beyond the region by establishing and consolidating advocacy groups. The Costa Rican Sea Turtle Conser-

vation Network and the Central American Sea Turtle Conservation Network, for instance, have influenced the development of local and national policies to protect the area's sea turtle population. The Initiative's advocacy efforts have contributed as well to the adoption of rural tourism as the fourth pillar of Costa Rica's tourism marketing plan and the passage of a law to promote organic production methods. Most recently, the Talamanca Initiative has created the National Cacao Chamber (CANACACAO), a multistakeholder group that aims to influence the Costa Rican government to use traditional cacao production techniques nationwide (Asociación ANAI 2006).

Conclusion

Over the past five years, the Equator Initiative has received more than 1,000 nominations for the Equator Prize. Of these, 75 community initiatives stand out as exemplary cases of community-level efforts to conserve biological diversity, alleviate poverty, and ultimately contribute to achieving the Millennium Development Goals. In partnership with academic institutions and research organizations, the Initiative has learned from the experiences of these successful community groups and local EBEs. Analysis shows that local initiatives are most successful when there is a collective understanding of the value of ecosystem-derived resources, secure property rights to these resources, low barriers to market participation, multiple beneficial partnerships, and strong effective leadership. EBEs, when developed with sustainability in mind and operated for the benefit of communities, are a powerful tool in international efforts to protect the environment and promote human development.

This box was written by Elspeth Halverson and Gabriela Tobler, Programme Officers at the UNDP Equator Initiative. More information on the Equator Initiative is available at www.undp.org/equatorinitiative.

Alimentos Nutri-Naturales (ANN) in Guatemala, 2006 Equator Prize Winner

in India did not occur until the government made village-level grants available for undertaking such work. In these situations, demand arose when information about the new opportunity circulated to eligible communities through local NGOs and other intermediaries. *(See Update in Chapter 1: Scaling Up Namibia's Community Conservancies.)* As with resource degradation, policy changes and other incentives from outside rarely create sufficient demand by themselves to lead to action without the advocacy of a leader or other trusted intermediary who can demonstrate how these new policies or funds can translate to local benefits.

From Demand to Commitment

Local commitment is essential to ensure that a community is really invested in the success of an ecosystem-based enterprise. Whereas demand is the expressed desire to engage in an enterprise, based on the projected benefits and costs, commitment is the demonstrated intent of each stakeholder to carry out their respective parts of the project and to make the sacrifices necessary for the

venture to succeed. It is essentially the "down payment" on the community's expression of demand.

Commitment can take many forms in the context of nature-based enterprises. It may be a contract, a public promise, or a demonstration of involvement, with participants all bringing some form of goods, service, or money to offer. It can be a contribution of time or labor, as when members of a forest user group in Nepal volunteer to patrol the forest on a rotating basis to guard against illegal entry or when Indian villagers undertaking watershed restoration activities dig contour trenches together to stop monsoon rains from cascading down the bare slopes. It can also take the form of a monetary contribution used to finance some or all of the costs of the new resource management effort. The important thing is that the commitment must take a tangible form of recognized value. And to have maximum effect, it must be made early in the evolution of the new management effort.

In addition, commitment must be public to be effective. In this way, community members can hold each other accountable for their promise. An important benefit of this accountability is that, over time, as participants make good on their commitments, trust within the group grows, increasing the group's social capital and making communication and coordination among members easier.

Communities as Investors

Without local investment of something of value or a commitment to make a sacrifice, participation in community natural resource management over the longer term is likely to be uncertain. In contrast, by investing in a community undertaking, beneficiaries change its nature. The enterprise moves from something "received" to something "earned." Community members, as active participants, are freer to negotiate for what they want in a project before they contribute their money, time, or goods. In this sense, a show of local commitment opens a path of communication among both community members and outside funders or support organizations, so that the needs and suggestions of participants are taken seriously. Commitment turns community members into active investors (Breslin 2003:1–9).

In concept, the commitment necessary for a nature-based enterprise is similar to the co-financing arrangements that have become common practice in most community-driven infrastructure projects. The World Bank's Ghana Community Water and Sanitation Project, for example, required communities to commit to 5 percent of the project costs to begin with and 100 percent of the operations and maintenance costs. Zambia requires communities to contribute 15 percent of financing costs (with exceptions for particularly indigent communities). In middle-income countries, communities are expected to contribute greater amounts. In Brazil, communities must contribute 10 percent to subproject costs and 15 percent to infrastructure projects (Chebil and Haque 2003:129–130; Breslin 2003:1–9).

Such a substantial monetary commitment may not be possible for community-based resource management efforts that involve many poor families. In these cases, contributions of labor are often more appropriate. Sometimes this "labor" can take the

OWNERSHIP

form of simply adhering to a new ecosystem management regime that calls for reducing harvest levels—a definite sacrifice for poor families whose dependence on the resource may be high. For example, participants in Bangladesh's MACH program (Management of Aquatic Ecosystems through Community Husbandry), which sought to increase fish harvests for lakeside communities, had to forgo fishing in established sanctuaries, stop using certain fishing gear such as mesh nets, and curtail certain types of hunting and gathering. *(See Chapter 3: Fisheries for the Future: Restoring Wetland Livelihoods in Bangladesh.)* The advantage of using nonmonetary forms of commitment is that they tend to increase actual involvement in the endeavor and create a shared sense of effort and mutual sacrifice that furthers the group dynamic and increases the sustainability of the project.

Inspiring Collective Action

At the heart of joint management of natural resources is "collective action" —the willingness to work collaboratively in the pursuit of a common goal. This is what occurs when people decide that it is in their best interest to co-manage a community forest or fishery or work together to insure that an irrigation system operates properly. Most ecosystem-based enterprises depend for their success on collective action because they make use of common pool resources, where many users have access to the resource. Collective action is essential to keep the resource from overexploitation and to make sure benefits are fairly apportioned. This kind of collaboration is nothing new—groups have been engaging in collective resource management for millennia. However, many years of research have confirmed that some conditions are more favorable for inspiring and maintaining collective action than others (Ostrom 1990:88–102; Meinzen-Dick and Di Gregorio 2004:1; Ostrom 2004:1–2; Agrawal 2001:1659).

Demand is the starting point for collective action. Another key condition is that the community or group must have the authority to manage the resource. They must have the autonomy to create and enforce rules—whether formal or informal—for resource use. Without this ability to apply their rules and make them stick, the rationale for joint action quickly diminishes (Bruns and Bruns 2004:1). *(See Figure 3.)*

The will and ability to enforce rules is paramount. Groups need the authority to set boundaries and control access to the resource and the means to monitor the resource for infractions. The rules themselves must have some force behind them, whether it is the threat of punishment, rewards for cooperative behavior, or the threat of alienation from the group. To a certain extent, the details of the rules the group adopts matter less to the success of the collective action than how well these rules are monitored and enforced (Bruns and Bruns 2004:1; Gibson et al. 2005:279–282; Barrett et al. 2005:195).

Not surprisingly, social capital is a fundamental building block of effective collective action. When people in a group are linked by social bonds and share norms and social expectations they are more likely to successfully manage a resource together and succeed

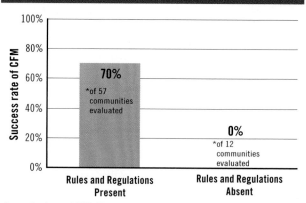

FIGURE 3 INFLUENCE OF COMMUNITY RULES ON THE SUCCESS OF FOREST MANAGEMENT (CFM) IN 69 COMMUNITIES

Source: Pagdee et al 2006:45

at an ecosystem-based enterprise. The social capital of the group greatly influences how effective it is in making and following resource management rules. In the words of one researcher: "Trust lubricates cooperation" (Pretty and Ward 2001:210). It reduces the "transaction costs" of working together, saving time, worry, and money. Where social bonds are strong, the threat of social sanctions alone is an effective means of rule enforcement (Pretty and Ward 2001:210–217; Uphoff 1999:221–231).

Experience working together as a group in the past also contributes to success. Those who already have some experience of the group dynamic are more likely to put their faith in new enterprises that require collective action. It helps, too, if some members of the group have previous experience with the benefits of a particular kind of collective action. This can act as a strong motivator for continued participation in the group endeavor and a source of inspiration for other group members. In a study of Haitian peasant groups who undertook joint watershed management, those groups with at least some members who had experience adopting soil conservation measures in the past were most likely to continue working together (White and Runge 1995:1690–1692). In Mozambique, the fishers of the Inhassoro community rapidly adopted a fisheries co-management arrangement offered by the state in 1995 because years earlier they had informally adopted closed fishing seasons and other management practices on their own, and they knew the advantages and challenges of these practices. They were primed for the opportunity when it came (Chuenpagdee and Jentoft 2007:661).

The proven value of experience, trust, and knowledge of benefits to the success of collective action emphasizes the need to bring these elements into play early when forming nature-based enterprises. Where these elements have not been previously developed in the group, there is a pressing need to employ communication, demonstration, knowledge sharing, and trust-building processes—the motivators behind demand—to fill the void. Building the social capacity of the group to work together also requires embracing the idea and practice of participatory processes, where each member of the group provides input and has a voice in negotiations on the resource management rules and the general conduct of the ecosystem enterprise. Participation anchors the group in a common purpose and provides the means to resolve the disputes that inevitably arise in community resource management.

Participatory Decision-Making

Participation in decisions about how and for what purpose local ecosystems should be managed is an essential part of creating a local stake in development. It is part and parcel of the process of building demand for an ecosystem-based enterprise and a crucial mechanism enabling community-based resource management to succeed.

Participatory decision-making allows local stakeholders to "own" the process of creating and directing environmental enterprises and to specify how and to whom benefits from the enterprise should be distributed. It is the dialogue through which local demand is expressed and thus the basis for "buy-in" to the enterprise and the management activities it requires. Without a mechanism for eliciting what stakeholders want and what they are willing to commit to, community-based resource management efforts can't be "community-driven."

The Benefits of Participation

Since the mid-1970s, the use of participatory approaches to local development has become increasingly common (Pozzoni and Kumar 2005:v). One premise of community-driven development is that broad-based participation is the key mechanism through which communities first define their development and investment priorities and then carry them out. This premise is based on years of experience showing that the more people are involved upstream in the process of planning and carrying out development projects, the more likely they are to contribute to the project and sustain it—to own it (World Bank 1996:8).

The range of participatory methods is broad and, after more than 25 years of application at the community level, fairly well elaborated. At the initial planning stage of an ecosystem-based project, participation techniques often fall under the broad rubric of participatory rural appraisals and can include such activities as joint resource appraisals using mapping and modeling, focus group discussions, structured interviews carried out by an assessment team deputized by the community, and various preference ranking exercises (World Bank 1996:191–192). Ideally, the information, options, and preferences surfaced through these methods provide the basis for a community decision on how to proceed. Once the group decides on an activity, and on an institution—such as a watershed committee or a forest users group—to manage the activity, participation often becomes more structured and formalized. For both these levels of participation, research and practice have confirmed several benefits.

OWNERSHIP

Greater Legitimacy,
Greater Capacity, Better Implementation

Participation by the range of stakeholders in the activity planning process and in the ongoing management of the activity builds the legitimacy of resource and business decisions made. Legitimacy translates to acceptance and "buy-in." Even where there are clear winners and losers, the ownership built in the participatory process can lessen opposition and conflict when the decisions are implemented.

The process of successful participation is itself a learning experience for most stakeholders—a process of social learning. Community members gain awareness of new opportunities and become familiar with their possible costs and benefits. They often acquire new skills: some are technical, such as learning how to monitor resource parameters and trends; others are interpersonal. Community members who otherwise might not have interacted have the chance to build relationships with one another, fostering trust and social cohesion—the currency of social capital. Inclusive participation also deepens the community's democratic culture.

Participation brings well-known empowerment benefits as well, such as confidence, increased social status, self-reliance, and satisfaction at being included in the decision-making process. It may also help connect participants to government services, additional learning opportunities, or other resources of personal benefit (Andersson et al. 2005:70).

Increasing the legitimacy of a community decision-making process and the capacities of the participants leads to better implementation of the project, management plan, or other resource decision. Skills and knowledge developed through a participatory process may give participants greater ability to contribute to the project activity, for example by being a monitor or advisor.

Equally important, the legitimacy granted to a participatory decision usually translates to greater compliance with the terms of the decision, such as fishing or harvest rules. This allows people to make more informed commitments—commitments that they are more likely to keep (Andersson et al. 2005:67–71; Fritsch and Newig 2006:3–5; World Bank 1996:5–6).

Participation is Imperfect

Despite the known advantages of participation, it suffers from documented weaknesses as well. Without conscious management, these weaknesses can advantage certain groups at the expense of others, diminishing the legitimacy of the decisions taken and the prospects for buy-in by the full array of stakeholders.

The Poor Can Be Excluded

Inclusiveness is a particular challenge for many participatory processes, with typically marginalized groups such as the poor and women likely to be left out or their input discounted. Two dimensions of inclusion are essential for true participation. Formal inclusion is the ability for community members to take part in a participatory process—to be present and allowed to speak up. Substantive inclusion relates to the extent that this formal input is actually taken into consideration by others—how well a community member's voice is really heard. Too often, the poor suffer a double exclusion, with fewer poor families taking part in participatory processes overall and, when they do take part, being regarded as minority voices without authority. The participation of poor women is often a worst-case scenario. In a 1994 study of Nepal's Forest User Groups, women only constituted 3.5 percent of all members (Pozzoni and Kumar 2005:4–8; Dahal 1994:78).

There are a number of factors behind the lack of participation of the poor. For one, the costs in terms of time and transportation can be significant, while the immediate benefits of participating are often uncertain, providing little incentive to take time away from their pressing livelihood concerns (Pozzoni and Kumar 2005:29–30; World Bank 1996:147).

In addition, the poor may believe their involvement is of little value, as the processes may be dominated by village elites. While new laws and government practices have begun to increase the level of formal inclusion of marginalized groups in participatory decision-making, research shows that weaker social groups such as the poor still exercise little influence over final decisions compared with more powerful community members (Pozzoni and Kumar 2005:v, 6–7).

Inequality Hinders Cooperation

A related phenomenon is that participatory decision-making is more difficult in communities with high levels of income inequality or strong social or class divisions. One of the strongest criticisms of the generalized application of participatory methods is that it often treats "communities" as if they were more homogeneous than they are, composed of individuals or groups with largely compatible—or at least reconcilable—interests. This ignores the natural heterogeneity of communities and thus ignores the divisions, competing interests, cultural divides, and power imbalances that are typically present in most groups. When these divisions are strong, collective action and participatory processes can suffer.

Some research shows, for example, that cooperating to manage natural resources is more difficult in heterogeneous groups, even when all the members of the group depend equally on the resource (Cardenas 2001:20). In some cases, both the poorest and the richest tend to drop out, as their prospects for getting what they want from the process diminish (Pozzoni and Kumar 2005:9). However, other research shows that group heterogeneity can be tolerated—or managed—and need not hinder successful participation, particularly if the resource at issue is highly valued and the benefits from working together are likely to be substantial (Varughese and Ostrom 2001:762–763).

Benefits and Costs Are Not Equally Shared

If better-off members of the community tend to dominate participatory decision-making, then it is not hard to imagine that they might also share disproportionately in the benefits of participation-based projects. Research on community irrigation developments in Tanzania found that while landowners and tenant farmers both received water, landowners were the main beneficiaries. Both groups had to contribute the same amount of labor to the project, but tenants ended up paying higher land rents since irrigated acreage is more valuable in the land market (Koopman et al. 2001:47–48). In instances where improved community management of ecosystems results in greater productivity—more water, fish, or forest products, for example—those with larger land holdings or more investment capital can often capture a greater share of the increased production. At the same time, landless residents often bear the greatest costs of ecosystem management, particularly if it requires a temporary decrease in their use of common pool resources like fodder, woodfuel, building materials, or bush meat.

Making Participation Poor-Friendly

Addressing the dysfunctions of participation is essential if community-driven ecosystem enterprises are to benefit the poor. Certainly, no standard recipe for successful participation is possible, because each instance of community participation is unique, depending on the natural resource at issue and the social and economic dynamics of the group. Nonetheless, it is possible to identify broad strategies to achieve greater inclusion, facilitate communication, encourage a group vision, build the social capacity to act collectively, and create a viable institution to manage that action. These strategies—which often benefit from the intervention of a trusted outside facilitator such as an NGO—help surmount the initial barriers that local groups face when they contemplate managing natural resources as a community.

Ground Rules: Formal Inclusion and Format

Formal inclusion of all community members is not just a formality, but an essential ground rule. Explicitly recognizing the goal of seeking the input of all stakeholders—men and women—is a significant step in making sure the participatory forum is not unbalanced from the start. Some groups find it useful to specify that management or leadership committees must include members of low-income or marginalized groups. The format for group decision-taking—whether by majority vote, consensus, or other means—is also important. Consensus-based approaches—where the group does not proceed until all parties agree—can help protect the interests of the poor, but they can also be unwieldy. Logistics matter as well. The choice of location and time for the initial and follow-on meetings are simple but important formatting concerns to lower time costs and increase accessibility for the poor.

Fact-Finding and Initial Goal Identification

Initial encounters within a participatory decision-making process need to set a tone of common endeavor and provide the basis for unbiased information. Fact-finding exercises or mapping and modeling efforts can offer a neutral ground for determining the dimensions of the resource base and the range of possible management goals, along with the likely benefits. The discussion and enthusiasm that such exercises often generate can begin to establish a rapport within the group and prepare it for more substantive and controversial topics (World Bank 1996:192; Bruns and Bruns 2004:1–2).

Affinity Groups and Empowerment

Early in the participatory process, the self-selection of affinity groups—composed of individuals with common concerns due to similar economic circumstances, landholdings, or gender—can

65

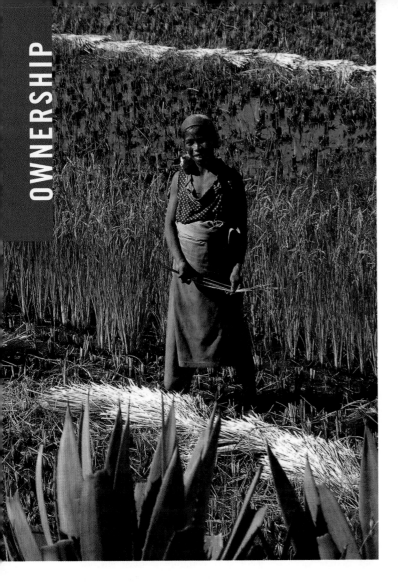

important early task is creating a group vision for what success will look like. Facilitation of the visioning process and subsequent discussions by a trusted outside actor such as a local NGO are often beneficial to provide direction to the process and supply an independent moderator (World Bank 1996:204; Bruns and Bruns 2004:1). On the basis of this vision, the group can proceed to enumerate the challenges to achieving this vision from each stakeholder's standpoint and to negotiate an agreement for collective action. A strong vision of benefits is crucial to maintain the momentum of participation and create space for negotiation.

Building Social Capacities and Technical Skills

To a great extent, the quality of a group's participatory decision-making reflects the social relationships within the group—its stock of social capital. Increasing the inclusion of the poor often requires reconstructing these relationships to build the social capacities of the group. Social capacity-building is thus a big part of successful participation, particularly where marginalized groups are part of the mix. Visioning and other trust-building exercises are one aspect of this, including working side by side to assess, repair, or demark the resource at issue before full community management has begun (Bruns and Bruns 2004:1).

More broadly, social capacity-building is often linked to other forms of capacity-building, such as learning new technical and management skills—the kinds of applied skills necessary to revegetate a watershed, set up a no-fishing zone, or create a harvest plan for a community forest, for example. Linking the two types of learning—social and technical—can often help both proceed more rapidly, so that the capacity for jointly managing the resource is developed as quickly as possible.

Design of Institutions and Formal Rules for Inclusion and Benefits Sharing

A prime focus of participatory decision-making around community resources involves the design of the management rules and the formula for sharing the costs and benefits of the management regime. In both these areas, considerations for how the poor will fare must be in the forefront as negotiations within the group proceed. This requires first a careful accounting of the costs of management that may fall hardest on the poor and the recognition that some form of compensation may be appropriate to allow them to continue to participate in and support the scheme. If poor households will have to reduce their woodfuel harvests to allow a forest to recover or decrease their bushmeat harvest so that tourists can see more wildlife at an ecotourism destination, then provision must be made at the time of rule-making for an adequate substitute. Compensation can come in many forms, such as cash, substitute employment, or increased access to resources at another site. Research confirms that communities are capable of instituting quite complex management rules and compensations if most members believe they are fair and if the community values the resource highly enough (Shyamsundar et al. 2004:10, 95–96; Varughese and Ostrom 2001:759–763).

give marginalized groups the chance to meet and identify common goals and challenges, preparing them to represent their interests within the larger group (Sharma et al. 2005:5; Bruns and Bruns 2004:2). Sometimes these groups find it useful to prepare a formal "action plan" in which they envision their participation in the enterprise and how it can be shaped to meet their needs and respect their constraints. One risk is that members of affinity groups, while they may gain confidence and solidarity by meeting with their peers, may be further stigmatized by more powerful actors in the group as a whole if they function too autonomously. For example, if the landless band together in an affinity group, they may make it easier for the larger community to label them and marginalize their input. To avoid this, when the Indian NGO Watershed Organisation Trust (WOTR) facilitates initial meetings among villagers considering watershed restoration, they divide the entire group into smaller affinity groups that meet simultaneously and in the same location, so that the deliberations of these groups are always considered part of the group process rather than seen as separate and competing with it (Lobo 2007).

Facilitated Group Exchanges to Identify Issues

Once an initial basis of information and group tolerance is established, a broader range of issues can be brought to the table. An

SUMMING UP: OWNERSHIP

Ownership has two aspects in relation to ecosystem enterprises: secure resource rights and meaningful participation rights, or the ability to participate in decisions about the management of local ecosystems. Together they create a real stake—financial and social—in how ecosystems are managed.

FOUR STEPS TO FOSTER OWNERSHIP

STEP 1: Improve the Security of Resource Tenure

- Security of resource tenure supports successful nature-based enterprise. Research confirms that secure tenure is linked to the success of community-based natural resource management. Unfortunately, tenure insecurity is widespread, constituting a major obstacle to ecosystem enterprises among the poor.

- To improve the security of tenure for the majority of poor rural residents, a broader approach is necessary that builds on local tenure practices and uses local institutions to execute simpler, speedier, and lower-cost forms of land and resource registration that are more accessible to rural families. Recognition of local customary land rights must be part of any viable tenure reform. Such reform must also include development of more effective dispute resolution systems that can accommodate both customary and statutory titles within a single legal framework.

STEP 2: Catalyze Demand for Ecosystem Management

- Ecosystem-based enterprises that arise out of community demand are more likely to succeed. Demand is expressed as the willingness for collective action—for joint management of local ecosystem resources. Demand can be catalyzed by factors such as a change in the local environment or economy, a change in the financial incentives for investment, a change in resource rights or access, or a change in information through exposure to pilot projects or demonstrations. Leadership is important in channeling community demand into enterprise.

STEP 3: Inspire a Public Commitment to Collective Action

- To be useful, demand must translate into a public commitment of money, resources, or time—a demonstration of involvement on the part of stakeholders that signals their ownership of the joint effort or enterprise and their commitment to collective action.

STEP 4: Encourage Participatory Decision-Making

- Participatory decision-making allows local stakeholders to own the process of creating and carrying out ecosystem enterprises and is important to building demand for CBNRM and other enterprises.

- Participation by the range of stakeholders builds the legitimacy of business or resource management decisions, which can bring better compliance with management plans. Participation also empowers the poor and builds the social capacities of the group, which can improve cooperation and lessen conflict.

- Making participation more poor-friendly is essential if the poor are to benefit from CBNRM and nature-based enterprise. Some strategies include:

  - *Establishing formal rules for inclusion* of marginalized groups, such as on executive committees;

  - *Undertaking group mapping or modeling exercises* to establish a common ground of endeavor and information sharing;

  - *Establishing affinity groups* to allow the poor to organize and represent their needs effectively;

  - *Engaging in a group visioning process* to establish a model for what successful collective action will look like, understand what its benefits and challenges will be, and establish a basis for negotiation among competing interests; and

  - *Accounting for the costs of resource management* and compensating the poor when these costs fall on them disproportionately

In this piece, Crispino Lobo, one of the founders of the Watershed Organisation Trust, speaks from more than 15 years experience helping villagers in almost 600 watersheds to organize and collectively carry out watershed rehabilitation projects in three arid Indian states.

Crispino Lobo

REGENERATING THE ENVIRONMENT AND REVITALIZING the local economy on a sustainable basis is possible only if the effort is a response to the felt need and demand of the local community. The questions that arise then are: How does one elicit and organize such a response in ecologically and economically stressed communities? How can a commonality of purpose be fostered? How does one gauge the depth of purpose, will, and unity amongst all the major actors in the community? How does one ensure that the interests of disadvantaged groups are not only protected but also become part of the articulated consensus of the community?

Generating Demand, Forging Consensus, Creating Institutions

It is important that people understand the interrelationship between the hardships they are experiencing, the ecological health of their "area of survival," and the way they use their natural resources. Often, the social, economic, and power asymmetries within the community prevent people from seeing these crucial causal relationships.

For a consensus to emerge that galvanizes a community for change and collective action, it is necessary to address the various competing and often hostile interests, agendas, and grievances that permeate the social fabric of a community. For this, it is necessary to surface and discuss exhaustively the conflicts and concerns of the various interest groups. Together, they must arrive at community-endorsed arrangements that protect the legitimate interests of each group, compensate

those who suffer losses resulting from restoration measures, and grant vulnerable groups—women, the landless, small herders and farmers, and indigenous groups—an assured share of benefits both during and after environmental rehabilitation.

If this inclusive process of negotiation, arbitration, reconciliation, compensation, and redistribution results in an agreement that is seen as fair and reasonable by all the major stakeholders, it will become the dynamic that catalyzes a decisive consensus for collective action. Equity is the key to igniting and maintaining community-wide engagement that leads to desired and therefore sustainable results.

Once this dynamic has been created, a local institution must be set up that has effective representation of all the stakeholder groups, is mandated to oversee implementation and enforcement of the actions agreed upon, and is in turn accountable to the community.

This sensitive exercise requires the intervention of a trusted intermediary agency—usually an external one, such as an NGO—that has credibility as well as the ability to leverage the funds necessary for the environmental regeneration to go forward. Unless sufficient financial resources are secured beforehand, the community processes should not proceed. Common purpose and will can only be sustained if people believe that there is a fair chance of the project proceeding and their hopes and aspirations for it being fulfilled.

Assessing Social Capital, Building Capacities, Putting People at the Center

Many projects that begin with great promise quickly lose steam once implementation begins and the agreed upon arrangements and restrictions have to be put into practice. This is because, despite the best intentions, the existing social capital—the bonds of solidarity and goodwill—are not yet strong enough to overcome long-standing internal conflicts, fault lines, and closed mindsets in the community.

To gauge the true extent of positive engagement among community members and decrease the risk of failure, it is helpful to devise a practical "entry test" to help the community determine if it is ready for such a collective undertaking. Such a test must be transparent and resistant to distorting influences like political pressure. More important, it should be "self-selecting" in nature, where success is based on the actions of the community itself rather than the judgment of government or program authorities.

The measures of success must be directly related to the kinds of actions that will be required should the project go forward. For instance, when villages wanting to undertake the regeneration of their watersheds approach the Watershed Organisation Trust (WOTR), they are required to demonstrate their intent and commitment by doing 4 days of voluntary work as a community, such as digging contour trenches or other soil and water conservation work. In dryland areas where the majority of people eke out a subsistence living from the land, this is a substantial contribution, and completing it requires real need, a sufficiently cohesive community, and a functioning and trusted leadership—the minimum amount of social capital needed for complex projects and interventions to succeed.

Once a community has passed the "entry test," it must then enter a capacity-building phase as a prelude to undertaking full-scale project implementation. Capacity-building—as WOTR uses the term—is a time of intense facilitation, support, and skill training, usually by an NGO or other external agent. The community is helped to understand the implications of the agreements they have made as a community and is supported in implementing them and in managing the conflicts that inevitably occur when curbs on customary land and resource uses begin to take effect. Usually this is a time of stress and uncertainty, where internal contradictions and conflicts come to the fore and community institutions undergo changes in membership, functioning, and mandates.

During the capacity-building phase, actual project work should begin at a sufficient scale that it will have some visible short-term impacts. This preliminary work cements trust and builds confidence between the villagers and outside project authorities—a crucial requirement for success and a "goodwill reserve" that can be drawn upon when rough patches are hit. It also provides a cushioning environment for the hardships suffered by some groups by creating incentives—such as increased opportunities for wage labor—to resolve conflicts and adopt new behaviors. These incentives, as well as other short-term results of the project, are a powerful glue that holds together a common consensus and provides a preview of the kind of benefits that will flow to the entire community once the full project is completed. Perhaps most important, this preliminary work during the capacity-building phase provides the experiential basis for imparting skills and competencies to the villagers. In rural communities, the most effective means of knowledge acquisition is through "learning by doing." People learn by directly participating, observing, and experiencing the consequences of their actions and then reflecting upon mistakes made.

Training must be oriented toward empowerment and tailored to the work being undertaken and the needs of the community.

It should therefore include the entire range of skills that a community must acquire in order to be in the "driver's seat" of the effort. Unless people are fully engaged in all aspects of the regeneration effort—planning, implementation, monitoring, evaluation, and maintenance—and are able to implement the project in a technically proficient and managerially sound manner, they will not acquire the necessary "ownership" of the effort nor reap benefits commensurate with their investments and expectations. It is also important to introduce at all levels, especially at the project level, systems that promote transparency, accountability, and free flow of information to all actors and partners so as to secure commitment, foster ownership, and sustain momentum.

A community will maintain and enhance an asset that generates for it a stream of desired benefits on a reliable basis. Hence, it is important to "mate" the village into the local and regional economy and markets as well as with development agencies and resource providers across sectors. This will provide outlets for local products and increase business opportunities and employment.

Box 2.2 LESSONS FROM THE FIELD

It will also provide access to new developmental schemes, financing, technologies, new ideas, and information.

Women are critical in shaping the sustainability of natural resources, whether they be watersheds, forests, or pastures. A major portion of a rural household's daily food consumption comes from the environment and is managed by women. Involving them as decision-makers, with preference given to their needs, ensures that they have a stake in the maintenance of assets created by the project. It also gives them the incentive to encourage their children—the next generation of resources users—to become careful stewards of the resources they inherit.

Making Equity a Community Concern

With projects such as watershed regeneration, it is generally acknowledged that those with access to sizable land resources benefit more that those with less or no land—the impoverished and marginalized. In order to bring about a measure of equity, most of these projects adopt various mechanisms such as increased representation of the marginalized in decision-making bodies, preferential access to resources, and inclusion of a significant livelihood component in the project to augment and diversify the income portfolio of the vulnerable groups.

Unfortunately, equity in natural resources management interventions, as currently practiced, is primarily a concern imposed from outside—usually by donors and some enlightened project authorities. The need for equity and sharing is usually outside the cognitive framework of the village elite. As such, it is often viewed as an irritant to be endured in order to secure project funding. Unless it becomes a part of the "concern set" of the village elite, the underlying inequity will endure. Some of the marginalized will benefit from the interventions or opportunities created for them, but it is unlikely that most of them will experience significant and sustained benefits after the project ends.

To address this, the Watershed Organisation Trust is piloting an approach that promotes inclusiveness and enlists the active cooperation of the village elite in improving the lot of vulnerable groups. Called Wasundhara, which means "the earth" and connotes compassion, caring, co-responsibility, and harmony, it is being implemented in 28 villages in Maharashtra where watershed development projects are under way. It is based on the premise that unless the village elite see reducing poverty and marginalization in their village as a desirable "public good" that also furthers their self-interest, they will not make it their concern, and little will change for the majority of the poor.

Wasundhara engages an entire community in an ongoing dialogue focused on envisaging and realizing a shared and more equitable future, beginning from the smallest unit—the single habitation or neighborhood unit (hamlet)—and building upward to the wider community.

The core components of the approach are:
- Generating awareness by getting groups and the community to understand the nature of their poverty—the events and their causal relationships that led to the present situation;
- Catalyzing community-wide momentum for change by walking them through a process that helps them envision their highest possible realizable good ("visioning") and the steps that are needed to get there;
- Identifying the poor and vulnerable on the basis of a community-led "wealth ranking exercise"; and
- Generating a consensus and affixing responsibilities as to what is to be done, how, and by whom, in order to address identified gaps, particularly the needs of the poor and the underserved areas of the village.

A focused strategy of empowering the marginalized while using the project funds to simultaneously leverage and maintain the political will and commitment of the village leadership to address the needs of the poor and underserved is used.

In addressing these needs, Wasundhara looks beyond the confines of the watershed project that the village is undertaking. This is appropriate since many of the "developmental deficits" of the poor—in infrastructure, education, energy, and so on—are beyond the scope of such a project. The Wasundara approach therefore attempts to link up project villages to government development agencies and other service providers.

Initial results in the 28 villages adopting the Wasundhara approach are very encouraging. Social interactions have improved and relationships between the various community-based organizations and village governance agencies have become more collaborative and less conflict-prone. Fourteen of these villages have already secured funding from various government agencies totaling approximately US$230,000 for development projects such as constructing drinking water systems, classrooms, drip irrigation systems, and connecting roads. They have also contributed more of their own money and labor than they would have otherwise. Such results drive greater sustainability of project gains in the future. If the overwhelming majority of a project village believes that they are appreciably benefiting from watershed restoration and associated developments, it is more than likely that they will continue to maintain these assets in the days ahead.

2. DEVELOPING CAPACITY

Capacity: Social, Technical, and Business Skills to Manage Resources and Establish Enterprises

- **Social capacity** to embrace a shared goal for resource management and to negotiate an action plan to attain it

- **Technical capacity** to jointly manage natural resources sustainably, including the ability to monitor resources and enforce rules

- **Business capacity** to organize an ecosystem-based enterprise and market the resulting products and services

- **Local resource management institutions** with the capacity to distribute costs and benefits of ecosystem management fairly

- **Dynamic community leadership** to catalyze demand and mediate disputes

- **Intermediary support organizations** to help build capacity and influence

See page 6 for full diagram.

THIS SECTION: CAPACITY

In this section, we argue that strong nature-based enterprises are built around functional local organizations with a breadth of social, technical, and business capacities. Developing these latent capacities often requires systematic support from intermediary organizations that can act as honest brokers, facilitators, trainers, organizers, and connection points with government and the private sector. This section:

- Defines local organizations and discusses their function as the keys to implementing and sustaining CBNRM and nature-based enterprise.

- Weighs the strengths and weaknesses of local organizations and describes the need for capacity development to improve inclusiveness and accountability, build critical skills and connections, and find more reliable funding.

- Describes intermediary support organizations, defines their role in catalyzing local nature-based enterprises and delivering critical support services, and profiles several successful ISOs.

- Asserts the ability of ISOs to make nature-based enterprises and CBNRM more pro-poor by building a group's social capacity and setting forth norms for participation and distribution of benefits.

- Examines the role of ISOs in "upward" capacity-building—that is, changing the attitudes of government officials toward local enterprises and increasing government services and political support.

When the "demand cycle" finishes, the "action cycle" begins. Once a community or group of resource users has acquired resource rights and generated the vision and commitment—the demand—for joint enterprise, it enters a new phase of execution. Translating the group's demand into action requires skills. At a minimum, the group must learn to manage the resource, produce and market its product, and organize its own decision-making process to keep group members aligned and involved in the enterprise. Building these skills is at the heart of the process of scaling up rural ecosystem enterprises.

Successful scaling strategies often use a graduated approach that starts with the skills inherent in local organizations and systematically builds these through dedicated capacity-building programs. These programs make a point of building social capital as well as technical skills, emphasizing adaptive and flexible learning. The point is not only to assure the persistence of the resource base but also to build inclusive local organizations with the organizational skills and business experience to succeed in a variety of social enterprises. This is one of the definitions of increasing social and economic resilience.

A Focus on Local Organizations

Local organizations are essential for implementing and sustaining community-based natural resources management. In the developing world, organizations such as forest user groups, watershed committees, and village councils provide the institutional structure for group resource management and the receptacle for resource management authority devolved from the state. Other local groups such as NGOs, unions, savings groups, or producer cooperatives provide technical, financial, and capacity-building services or help marginalized groups organize themselves. These organizations have a distinct advantage in pro-poor development, but they have a number of inherent weaknesses as well. Strengthening such local institutions and their linkages is one of the most effective ways to empower local communities, make their resource management and business efforts technically competent, and ensure that poor families share in the benefits (Alsop and Kurey 2005:5–7).

Defining Local Organizations
The defining feature of "local" organizations is that their dealings are characterized by face-to-face interactions. Their members rely heavily on personal relationships and networks to gain access to

CAPACITY

resources and make decisions within the group. They are human-scale, with trust as an important driver in their activities (Uphoff 1992:3; Uphoff and Buck 2006:5).

Local organizations operate across all sectors and vary widely depending on culture and location. Some are institutions of local government, while others are civil society groups or even businesses. *(See Table 2.1.)* Local organizations also span a spectrum from formal and officially recognized by the government to highly informal, traditional, or organic organizations. In any one rural setting there may be a large number of such organizations with overlapping membership and intersecting functions. In one study of four villages in India, researchers identified 38 different local institutions, including the gram panchayat (official village council), labor and educational organizations, savings groups, youth and religious groups, and marketing groups such as dairy cooperatives (USAID 1984:1–7; Marsh 2003:7).

TABLE 2.1 THE VARIETY OF LOCAL ORGANIZATIONS

Type of Local Organization	Examples
Local Government or Public Institution	Village Councils; Councils of Elders; Public Schools; Local Health Clinics
Resource Management Group	Forest User Groups; Grazing Societies; Watershed Committees; Irrigation Associations; Fishery Management Committees; Farmer Associations
Self-Help Group	Savings Groups; Women's Support Groups, Youth Clubs
Service Delivery, Advocacy, or Networking Group	Non-governmental Organizations; Unions; Church Groups; Cooperatives

Local organizations have a variety of origins: some spring from traditions within a community, while others are created by community members in response to new social, economic, or environmental conditions. Donors and the government also create local groups to take on specific development tasks. In some cases, self-help groups and other local organizations have arisen in response to state failure and lack of government services. Some receive significant support (money, training, resources, or labor) from outside groups, while others are completely self-sufficient (Uphoff 1992:3; Seymour 1994:479; Francis and Amuyunzu-Nyamongo 2005:18–20).

Local groups have been involved with natural resources for as long as these resources have been managed. Many traditional institutions regulating access to natural resources revolved around customary authorities such as tribal leaders. For example, until recently the Borana people of southern Ethiopia used councils of elders and clan leaders to administer carefully delineated rangeland districts on their communities' behalf, specifying where and when to graze based on seasonal weather patterns (Uphoff and Buck 2006:59–60). Today, even as many traditional institutions have declined, the number of local groups involved with fisheries, forests,

pastures, and farms has increased and diversified as rural society has reorganized itself around new ownership patterns, central government structures, and economic realities. Some estimates put the number of new groups related to resource use formed in the last two decades in the hundreds of thousands (Pretty and Ward 2001:214). One principal reason for this expansion has been the trend toward government decentralization and the creation of greater political space for the devolution of resource rights to local groups (Scherr et al. 2001:10). In Nepal alone the government reported the existence of 14,000 community forest user groups by 2005, due to the enactment of the 1993 Forest Act, which set the framework for devolving management authority and harvesting rights to local groups (Pokharel et al. 2006:6).

The Strengths of Local Organizations

Local organizations are central actors in rural development, an insight confirmed by two decades of research and case studies. Their effectiveness stems from being embedded in the community social order. Because of their intimate contact with village life they are good at assessing needs and marshaling local resources to accomplish their work. Their small size and relatively nonbureaucratic nature generally makes them highly adaptable to the changing demands and uncertainty posed by rural life (Satterthwaite 2005:3–7; Uphoff 1992:2–9; Marsh 2003:1–4; Uphoff and Buck 2006:1–10; Scherr et al. 2001:17–18).

The fact that they are populated by people who know each other means that local organizations offer opportunities for collective action and mutual assistance that do not always occur at district, national, or international levels (Uphoff 1992:2–3). For example, in Nepal rotating credit associations called Dhikuri offer the chance for members to tap an informal lending market. Members of the local Dhikuri contribute regularly to a loan fund that each member in turn can draw upon on a revolving basis for

Local NGOs can play a particularly important role in natural resource management and enterprise development. They often provide key services to help strengthen and connect other local organizations, bringing new information and management techniques and offering training in business and management skills to allow resource user groups to do their jobs more effectively. In the Indian states of Maharashtra, Gujarat, Andhra Pradesh, and others, local NGOs have played an essential part in mobilizing communities to take part in watershed restoration schemes and in building the capacity of village watershed committees to manage the restoration work. NGOs also frequently act as advocates for communities, helping to channel local voices to higher levels of government and the private sector and insisting on accountability from these authorities (Marsh 2003:27–28; Scherr et al. 2001:15–16).

Challenges and Limitations

Despite their potential to manage local natural resources, empower community members, and bring political, social, and economic benefits to the community, local organizations suffer from a number of weaknesses.

investment purposes or to meet expenses (Chhetri 1994:449–453). In this instance, trust substitutes for financial or property-based collateral in obtaining the loan (Marsh 2003:26). Local organizations are adept at lowering transaction costs in this way, based on social ties.

Local organizations can be effective at organizing and sustaining collective natural resource management because they naturally tap into the community's understanding of the resource and its connection to local livelihoods. They are likely to be familiar with the different techniques used locally to manage the resource, as well as the problems involved in management. Importantly, they reflect the social norms and work ethic of the community, and for this reason they can often command compliance with management rules through social pressure (Uphoff 1992:2–3; Scherr et al. 2001:17–18). In the village of Mendha-Lekha in the Indian state of Maharashtra, villagers established a *gram sabha* (village assembly) and a forest protection committee in the early 1980s to regulate use of their 1,800-ha village forest. Working in tandem to set rules on forest use, these two local organizations have been highly effective at preventing once-common forest fires, encroachment, and illegal extraction of forest products—so effective, in fact, that the state has ceded all enforcement authority over the local forest to the village (Pathak et al. 2005:59).

Community organizations can offer particular advantages to the poor. Savings groups, self-help groups, resource user groups, and other informal organizations afford members the option to join as the need arises. This opt-in, opt-out structure grants the poor considerable flexibility to participate and provides a safety net in times of need. Local organizations such as political parties, church groups, or farmer cooperatives can also provide an avenue for the poor to achieve some social mobility, at least when these groups are inclusive in their membership. For example, evidence from villages in Mozambique shows that belonging to a church or political group brings opportunities to get ahead in the community (Marsh 2003:25-26).

HOW LOCAL ORGANIZATIONS SUPPORT RURAL DEVELOPMENT

Local organizations provide a range of functions that are essential to rural development, natural resource management, and the development of nature-based enterprises. These include:

- **Financing:** mobilizing and securing funds
- **Staffing:** providing staff to form or support groups
- **Provisioning:** facilitating access to services, natural resources, and local assets
- **Community-Based Action:** physical construction and mobilization of village resources.
- **Capacity-Building:** facilitation or direct provision of training programs
- **Coordination:** coordination with other organizations
- **Monitoring and Evaluation:** tracking organizational inputs, outputs, and performance
- **Conflict Resolution and Accountability:** prevention, mediation, and adjudication of conflict
- **Information-Sharing and Dissemination:** sharing technical, commercial, and political information within and between organizations
- **Advocacy:** pushing for reform of laws or institutions or representing the interests of members to public officials and donors

Source: Adapted from Alsop and Kurey 2005:6–7.

Box 2.3 WOMEN ON THE MOVE: SCALING UP WOMEN'S SAVINGS GROUPS IN NIGER

MATA MASU DUBARA—MMD, FOR SHORT—MEANS "Women on the Move" in Hausa, a language of Niger and the African Sahel (Allen 2002:1). It is also the name of a highly successful savings and loan program based on women's self-help groups. The rapid growth and well-documented success of the program demonstrates that self-initiated local organizations can become effective agents of rural development.

This village-based savings and loan program began in 1991 with six groups of about 30 women in Niger's Maradi region, with funding and technical support from CARE International (Allen 2002:1). Today, MMD's "accumulating savings and credit associations" model provides small short-term loans and strong savings returns to rural women across western and southern Africa. As of August 2005, the MMD program had reached 172,000 women in Niger, resulting in over US$5 million in savings (CARE International 2005:1). By the end of 2006, CARE's Village Savings and Loan program, based on MMD's principles, had reached 500,000 people across Africa—70 percent of them women (CARE International 2007:10).

An MMD group in a rural village typically consists of 30 women who meet on a weekly basis to make a predetermined contribution to a savings pot (FON 2001:1). The group decides each month how it will use the savings. Most often, the funds go toward small loans to petitioning members who make their case to the group. The loans, with interest rates generally between 10 and 20 percent, must then be repaid to the group 4 weeks later. Some groups decide to invest their savings in a group business (Allen 2002:10,19).

At the end of a set time period—usually 9 or 12 months—the savings group dissolves, evenly redistributing its funds among all its members. The fund cycle is timed so that the redistribu-

tion takes place in a season when extra funds are particularly desirable—either before the holidays or during the agricultural planting season. Most groups re-form shortly thereafter to continue the savings and loan process. The program is attractive largely because MMD members receive a median return of 80 percent on their savings (Allen 2002:23).

The rapid growth of MMDs across Niger and in other African states illustrates the scaling capacity of demand-driven local organizations when they are based on a simple model that is supplemented by effective capacity training. The MMD training was initially provided entirely by CARE volunteers. Today, however, the program operates through a "train-the-trainer" model, whereby CARE officials work with select village leaders to bring the model to new areas. The change in strategy greatly facilitated the spread of MMDs. In the four years after the "train-the-trainer" model was adopted in 1998, the number of MMD groups grew from 1,200 to more than 5,600, and membership quadrupled—topping 160,000 (Allen 2002:13).

Women in the region who are interested in forming their own group pay the local trainers a small fee to help establish their MMD. During the first three months of a newly formed group, the trainers attend weekly meetings explaining the procedures and working out the specific rules and the type of loan program the women want to follow. After this "intensive period," the trainer sits in on meetings less frequently but is available to answer questions through the end of the 8-month cycle that new groups typically use as a test period (Allen 2002:18–19).

One key to the simple and flexible MMD model is that no literacy is required of any group members. Instead, the group uses procedures like dropping pebbles into their savings safe-deposit box to mark the number of weeks they have been operating; other records are kept orally, with several women responsible for keeping records, which are then reconciled at each meeting. If women want to contribute more savings each week, they are able to do so in a multiple of the minimum contribution and are considered to represent "multiple persons" in order to simplify the payout process at the end. CARE learned from experience about the unique challenges presented by illiteracy and has formalized these adaptive procedures in its model as a result (Allen 2002:19–20).

CARE's role in MMD's success exemplifies the changing role that external support organizations often play in catalyzing and scaling up the efforts of local organizations. Its transition from a ground-level testing and frontline service to an upper-tier training and advisory organization has allowed CARE to move to the background as local groups have stepped up, promoting local learning and ownership of the program and ensuring that the growth of MMD groups continues to be driven by local demand.

Restricted Focus

The narrow focus of, say, a user group, can foster parochialism and insularity, as members concentrate their energies on increasing the benefits to the group without regard for the effects on other community members or on adjacent communities. For example, a forest protection committee concerned only about enforcing its ban on wood collection by outsiders may show little concern for the broader effects of the ban on nearby communities. Likewise, an irrigation association may succeed at maintaining irrigation structures and apportioning water fairly among its members, but it will likely have little concern for the downstream effects of its water diversions. Without input from other groups, these organizations may miss opportunities for partnerships that meet more than one goal simultaneously and widen the constituency—and base of support—for their actions (Brown and Kalegaonkar 1999:3, 8).

Lack of Capacity

Undoubtedly the greatest weakness of local organizations—particularly newly formed ones—is their lack of social and technical skills and business experience. Many groups form organically through face-to-face interaction, sometimes improvised to solve a particular problem. Others are encouraged to form by outside donors, government agencies, or NGOs in order to enable community-driven development and create an institutional structure for local resource management. The result is that they are largely amateur rather than professionally run organizations. Though their members may be well versed in their livelihood or trade, they are often unfamiliar with business skills such as budgeting, accounting, or negotiation of legal contracts; in the case of resource management groups, they often lack technical knowledge of resource management or monitoring skills. They may also be unfamiliar with organizational processes

and participatory methods that the group may need to plan, make joint decisions, and encourage "ownership" by its members (World Bank 1996:154; Brown and Kalegaonkar 1999:3, 8).

In Namibia's conservancies, lack of capacity is one of the biggest constraints that conservancy management committees face. In the Khoadi Hoas Conservancy, for example, a poorly negotiated contract suppressed income from trophy hunting for several years until professional help was brought in to restructure the deal. Conservancy committees have also had some trouble with auditing and accounting procedures, resulting in cases of misplaced funds. Training in financial management has thus become a high priority for every conservancy committee in the last few years (Jones and Mosimane 2007:11; NACSO 2006:38–40).

Lack of Resources and Connections

Most local organizations are perennially short of funds. This limits their ability to undertake large projects, pay members for their time, or even meet the organization's basic needs for equipment, meeting space, and supplies. Indeed, many rural community groups without a sponsor are low-budget affairs that depend on volunteers for their activities and donations for their expenses. Similarly, they often lack influential contacts within government or the private sector that could advocate for their work, connect them to government support programs, or intervene when they face regulatory obstacles. Recognizing this financial and political isolation, many donors have stepped in to provide support and connection. While this has proved very helpful in many cases, it also tends to weaken the group's autonomy. As local groups become more reliant on a few donors, they run the risk that the donors' goals rather than the needs of their members may begin driving their agendas. In addition, reliance on external support is, in most cases, unsustainable in the long run (Brown and Kalegaonkar 1999:8; USAID 1984:11).

Lack of Accountability

Many local groups are not formed along democratic or participatory lines and lack strong accountability to their members. They are frequently dominated by strong individuals—often those who founded them or prominent members of the community—and don't have good mechanisms to communicate with or elicit feedback from members. They may not have elections, leaving members little ability to sanction leaders or express dissatisfaction. In such situations, members often show little engagement in the governance of the group. Even when local organizations are part of local government, as in the case of official village councils, lack of accountability is still an issue. In Tanzania, some village forest management committees—which are official subcommittees of the elected local government—have withheld crucial information about their forest activities from villagers in order to have a freer hand with their decisions (Alsop et al. 2000:3; Brown and Kalegaonkar 1999:5; Blomley 2006:15).

Lack of Inclusiveness

Achieving greater social inclusion and representation is a major challenge for local organizations around the world. Many local groups—both traditional and modern—still reflect the hierarchical social structure of rural societies and are thus not very inclusive of women, the poor, and other socially marginalized people. Researchers in Guatemala estimated that in 2001 less than 10 percent of the members of community assemblies were women, and women held just 1 percent of leadership positions. In the Indian state of Gujarat, a study of the participation of poor families in rural dairy cooperatives showed that large landowners dominated the cooperatives and captured most of the benefits, while the landless and lower-caste households had not benefited as much. Illiteracy made it difficult for many of the poor to understand the proceedings of the cooperative's general meetings, discouraging their attendance. Moreover, cooperative rules forbade considering illiterate members for spots on the

RESILIENCE AND CAPACITY: MAKING THE CONNECTION

The technical, social, and business capacities that are painstakingly built during the creation and management of nature-based enterprises also foster ecological, social, and economic resilience. The skills and abilities represented by these capacities can be deployed in many other social, resource management, and business settings, increasing the flexibility and adaptability of the members of the enterprise.

CAPACITIES THAT INCREASE ECOLOGICAL RESILIENCE

■ **Technical: mapping and assessing ecosystem resources.** Enables enterprise to demark accurately the resources to be managed and estimate their potential productivity, contributing to better management plans and more enforceable management boundaries.

■ **Technical: monitoring and analyzing resource trends.** Allows enterprise to assess pressures on a resource and determine the effect of the enterprise's management techniques.

■ **Technical: applying resource restoration techniques.** Allows enterprise to increase the ecosystem's baseline productivity.

■ **Technical: applying resource restoration techniques.** Allows enterprise to increase the ecosystem's baseline productivity.

■ **Technical: applying sustainable harvest techniques.** Leaves ecosystem resources to regenerate, providing a continuing stream of environmental benefits.

■ **Technical: processing ecosystem products efficiently.** Allows enterprise to maximize production while minimizing impact.

■ **Social: enforcing management rules.** Enables enterprise to minimize poaching or clearing and to attain its management goals.

CAPACITIES THAT INCREASE SOCIAL RESILIENCE

■ **Social: group visioning and enterprise planning.** Builds the willingness for collective action and guides the formulation of management and business plans.

■ **Social: undertaking collective management activities.** Builds group trust and confidence that enterprise members can work cooperatively toward shared goals.

■ **Social: crafting an equitable benefits distribution plan.** Demonstrates that collective action can result in widespread benefits.

■ **Social: resolving internal management disputes.** Enables enterprise members to overcome obstacles to collective action and joint enterprise.

■ **Social: negotiating with outside funders or government agencies.** Enables enterprise to represent its interests and increases the chance of receiving technical, political, and funding support for the enterprise.

CAPACITIES THAT INCREASE ECONOMIC RESILIENCE

■ **Business: crafting a business plan.** Increases the enterprise's probable returns and improves competitiveness for commercial entities.

■ **Business: applying accounting and fiscal management.** Allows enterprise to handle business transactions and distribute benefits in an efficient and transparent manner that maintains the confidence of enterprise members, funders, and government overseers.

■ **Business: undertaking marketing and communication.** Enables enterprise to expand its customer base and tap support networks.

■ **Business: maintaining quality control.** Allows the enterprise to deliver quality products and services that command a higher market price and inspire customer confidence.

management committee. The persistence of such barriers to inclusion is a central obstacle to realizing the potential of local organizations to drive rural development and foster nature-based enterprises (Pimbert 2006:18–19; Marsh 2003:26, 40–45).

The Need for Capacity Development

Local organizations are in great flux today as traditional groups try to adapt to modern ideas of good governance and as new groups arise to fill the demand for community-driven development. The strengths and weaknesses of these local groups result in a mixed bag of benefits and missed opportunities. They are often in the best position to manage local ecosystems for sustainability and income—and have done so successfully in many cases. But they don't always do so efficiently, in a participatory manner, or with enough consideration for the poor.

The development challenge is to work with local organizations to capitalize on their strengths and facilitate a transformation "from within" that allows them to become more inclusive and competent. This calls for a serious capacity-building effort that supports both social and technical learning. Local organizations are at the ground floor of the creation of ecosystem enterprises, either

participating directly in the enterprise or delivering support services. Unless they raise their level of functioning, scaling up of these enterprises will never occur. Devolving rights to local communities is only one part of the formula. The other necessary element is sufficient capacity within the community to use these rights to good effect, turning them into functional and poor-friendly enterprises (Marsh 2003:32; Satterthwaite 2005:17–19; IIED 2007:1–5).

Experience over the last two decades has demonstrated the perils of ignoring the need for effective capacity-building. More than a decade ago, the World Bank concluded, from its own experience with local organizations, that a common failure was to create an institutional structure—like a watershed committee or irrigation association—without paying sufficient attention to the capabilities, knowledge, and technical skills that these groups would require in order to be successful. In the Bank's experience, many newly formed local groups fail because too much is expected of them, with insufficient capacity-building and time for growth (World Bank 1996:154).

The Role of Intermediary Support Organizations

Intermediary support organizations are characterized by high-level organizing, technical, or political skills. They use these to help local organizations increase their capacity and functioning and to connect to state or regional authorities and funding sources.

Over the last 15 years or so, attention has been directed at a new class of organization—the intermediary support organization—in response to a greater recognition of the constraints of capacity, sustainability, and influence that many local groups face. Intermediary support organizations are typically NGOs or other civil society groups that operate in the space between the state and the local level and often act as intermediaries between the two. Occasionally, private businesses can also act as ISOs.

These groups are sometimes called intermediate, meso-level, grassroots support, or second-order organizations to distinguish them from purely local groups. They are characterized by high-level organizing, technical, or political skills that they use to help local groups increase their capacity and functioning and to connect to state or regional authorities and funding sources. The abilities to manage, coordinate, train, and influence that they possess allow them to catalyze local development projects, extract the elements of success, and spread these as models to other communities. For this reason they are important actors in the scaling up process. Indeed, in nearly every example of successful scaling up of nature-based enterprises, the fingerprints of one or more ISOs are detectable. The Watershed Organisation Trust profiled in Box 2.4 provides a good example of what an effective intermediary organization can achieve.

BOX 2.4 WATERSHED ORGANISATION TRUST, INDIA

IN *WORLD RESOURCES 2005: THE WEALTH OF the Poor,* we profiled the India-based Watershed Organisation Trust (WOTR) in a case study titled "More Water, More Wealth in Darewadi Village" (WRI et al. 2005:124–130). The case examined WOTR's watershed restoration program in Darewadi, a village of 1,000 residents in the western state of Maharashtra.

The Trust, a classic example of an intermediary support organization, helped Darewadi villagers restore their severely degraded terrain through a process of securing land tenure, developing strong institutions and community involvement, and implementing sophisticated regeneration plans. The results were impressive: higher water tables, more land under irrigation, new wells, livestock increases, and crop diversification.

At the start of 2008, WOTR continues to multiply its Darewadi success, leaving a string of similar stories across Maharashtra, Andhra Pradesh, and other Indian states and even other countries (WOTR 2007). WOTR illustrates the pivotal role that intermediary support organizations can play in scaling up successful community development models.

WOTR was officially incorporated in 1993 to serve as the implementing NGO for a German-sponsored development initiative known as the Indo-German Watershed Development Programme. The program was carried out in partnership with the Indian government in an effort to mitigate the rapid degradation of overused, drought-prone lands across India. WOTR began by working directly with individual villages, beginning in Maharashtra state, to help them implement successful management projects.

At the heart of the program is the assumption that these community programs would be organized and facilitated by local NGOs. Government agencies, at both the federal and the state level, would provide administrative and policy support, as well as approving the means and delivery of funding (WOTR 2005:8–9).

Initial success of the first project in Darewadi led to plans for large-scale implementation. The pilot identified certain principles and approaches that WOTR believed were critical to future scaling and implementation success:

■ A development initiative will succeed only if it is "owned" by the community it is trying to help. People need to see themselves not as beneficiaries but as active participants and decision-makers. They should be involved at every stage, and that involvement requires accountability. All others involved, no matter from what sector, have to be facilitators, mentors, teachers—not "doers."

■ Given the many dimensions of poverty, various developmental actors—including those involved in policy development—must be engaged. Creating partnerships and networks across all three sectors—civil society, the private sector, and government—is critical if permanent change is to be achieved.

■ Government has an important but redefined role if successful projects are to scale up. It acts as a validator of the process and as a facilitator to involve new communities.

■ The scope of the project has to be carefully and clearly defined at the outset, so that all involved understand what participation is required and what results can reasonably be expected.

Today WOTR is a true intermediary support organization, going well beyond its original role as village-level implementer and its single focus on watershed management. It takes on multiple responsibilities at various levels: It selects implementing agencies, builds their capacities, brings them together to facilitate shared learning and build relationships, and links them into the local development resource network. It provides financial, technical, organizational, and managerial support to the implementing agencies. Through a variety of communication efforts, WOTR is able to shape pro-poor enabling policies (Lobo 2007).

The WOTR Program

Capacity-Building

WOTR began by developing two training, or "pedagogy," programs: the Participatory Operational Pedagogy (POP) and the Gender Oriented Participatory Operational Pedagogy (GO-POP).

POP is an integrated, sequenced, iterative methodology by which communities (and their facilitating NGOs) are able to develop their organizational capabilities and subsequently learn skills specific to their needs. It contains built-in assessment and monitoring tools. POP is built around the principles of "learning by doing," peer mentoring, and on-site engagement. It is a sequenced program with three components: agency selection (NGOs and villagers), capacity-building within these groups, and implementation of an "operating system" that contains a package of processes that facilitate learning and help realize desired outcomes.

The GO-POP is a stand-alone subcomponent of the overall POP. The GO-POP seeks to weave gender into all aspects of the project. It builds the capacities of women and secures their meaningful representation in the institutional life of the village, while working with men to obtain their support for the women's roles (Lobo 2007).

The capacity-building phase, which WOTR believes is critical to scaling up, must be completed before a project is allowed to go into full implementation mode.

Community

Equally important to the program is the role of the community. WOTR requires active engagement by the community from the outset. Not only does the community have to request the implementation of a watershed restoration program, but that request has to reflect the will of the community arrived at through a process that involved the whole community.

But this will is not enough. WOTR understood the power of self-interest or "ownership." A community must not only want the program that would help them out of poverty, it must "own" a part of it. Community members had to make an investment.

Poor communities have little cash. What they do have is time and labor. So the program also requires community members' commitment to provide the time to attend training sessions that help build the skills and social capital of the community and the labor to construct the catch-basins, ditches, and wells necessary for restoring and improving a small watershed. The self-interest represented by these "investments" is critical to a project's success (Lobo 2007).

Networks and Connections

Successful projects aspire to sustainable (permanent) change that can be scaled up to have greater impact. To avoid operating in a vacuum, a project must make both horizontal and vertical connections.

Expanding the impact of the watershed program has involved sharing its accomplishments and its requirements with other communities. It also required the establishment and training of a network of local NGOs, which were primarily community-grown, and community-based organizations (CBOs) to provide day-to-day support to the projects.

Communicating the opportunity of the watershed restoration program has become a key part of the work of state and local governments. WOTR has managed those delicate relations in a manner that engages government as a partner, ensuring they share credit for project successes.

Those linkages become important as change takes place in communities, as their economic situation improves, as they require additional skills, and as their need for new services increases. WOTR ensures that relevant training and other services are provided, whether by government, the private

sector, or civil society, and it establishes those linkages with each community.

The communities become linked to each other through the process of learning about the program and validating the benefits before joining. WOTR facilitates ongoing communications between the CBOs and local NGOs in each community to share information and best practices. The communities also maintain contacts with government officials.

A crucial element in the WOTR network, one designed to help ensure an enabling institutional framework for the program and support by both the host government and donors, is an effort called the Exposure and Dialogue Program. It brings all parties—donors, government officials, other community leaders—together on a regular basis to spend several days living in poor communities. There they immerse themselves in the daily lives of the villagers, deal with them as equals, and begin to understand the reality of the poor. This experience creates a cadre of motivated, high-level "champions" who understand firsthand what the program does, how it is carried out, and what it requires in policy and funding (Lobo 2007).

Results

Having started in one village, WOTR today supports efforts involving 184 NGOs and agencies that facilitate watershed development in 476 villages in three Indian states. The work has brought improvements to nearly 400,000 ha and more than 650,000 people. Some 150,000 individuals have gone through the WOTR training programs, primarily in India but in 23 other countries as well, thus creating thousands of "ambassadors" spreading the practice of community-driven watershed development (WOTR 2007).

In addition, several other donor and government-funded watershed programs have introduced a capacity-building phase into their programs and adopted some of the approaches and methodologies that WOTR has developed. A major achievement has been the establishment of a National Watershed Development Fund by the government of India that is intended to communicate this program to villages in some of the poorest dryland districts in the country (Lobo 2007).

WHAT DO INTERMEDIARY SUPPORT ORGANIZATIONS DO?

There is no one model that describes intermediary support organizations or what they do. However, their work generally falls into four main categories:

- **Capacity Building.** Building capacity involves imparting a variety of business and social skills, along with the guidance and opportunity to master them. ISOs are involved in at least three different forms of capacity-building:

    - *Building technical, financial, business, and political skills.* This is the more conventional aspect of capacity-building necessary to allow individuals and local organizations to establish and carry out community-based natural resource management and build it into a viable enterprise. ISOs are in a position to identify existing capacity and build upon it to a degree not possible solely at the local level.

    - *Building social and institutional capital.* Putting technical and business skills to good use in nature-based enterprises requires the social capacity for participation and negotiation. ISOs often have particular expertise in catalyzing community processes that develop this social learning.

    - *Upward influence and government capacity-building.* Capacity on the ground will not be enough to sustain community enterprises if government stands in the way. One of the skills of an ISO is that it can engage with government, helping to increase the adaptability and receptivity of the bureaucracy so that it can further rather than hinder community efforts.

- **Facilitating Finance.** As trusted intermediaries, ISOs can be important contacts and conduits for project and business finance. On the one hand, they may solicit and receive funds from government or from local or international donors, which they then disperse at the project level. On the other hand, they may play a crucial role in connecting local nature-based entrepreneurs to sources of investment capital or outside business partners.

- **Increasing Equity and Transparency.** ISOs are often ideally situated to improve the inclusiveness and transparency of community-based resource management efforts by setting forth norms for participation, finance, project management, and the distribution of benefits. This aspect of their work is particularly important to making nature-based enterprises open to the poor.

- **Building Linkages and Networks.** By their nature, ISOs maintain contacts with a variety of organizations, enterprises, and government representatives, as well as a pool of technical experts and other influential actors. They are thus well positioned to help community-based enterprises connect to larger networks for information exchange, market development, and political influence.

Groups like the Watershed Organisation Trust gain their effectiveness from a variety of qualities:

- *They have influence.* Intermediary organizations usually have good relations with or access to government authorities who are a position to clear obstacles at multiple scales.

- *They are good mentors.* They have a "managing" capacity that goes beyond just an "organizing" role, enabling them to mentor other local and mid-level organizations, build capacity within government and donor communities as well as on the ground, and connect different groups to the services, actors, and channels that they need.

- *They communicate well.* They understand the importance of publicizing their successes and sharing their needs and aspirations with those in the position to help.

- *Their endorsement counts.* Their credibility can lend legitimacy to and generate momentum around local initiatives that would otherwise struggle to gain funding and recognition.

Intermediary organizations emerge in a number of ways. They can grow out of grassroots action, be established by external actors, or emerge from a combination of both. They are very often NGOs, but they can be other types of civil society and quasi-governmental organizations. Examples include universities, trade unions, religious organizations, and science and research groups. Local organizations can also grow into or begin to take on some of the functions of intermediary organizations as they mature.

Finally, ISOs are often characterized by adaptability. Success at the community level in natural resource management may lead to demands for new types of information and services. Intermediary organizations that have successfully remained flexible and responsive can adapt to these needs and begin to provide a new array of services, contacts, and strategies.

In this section, we look in greater depth at the core capabilities of intermediary organizations and how they support efforts to sustain and scale up nature-based enterprises that route environmental income to the poor.

ISOs: Capacity-Building

Capacity is the ability of individuals and institutions to perform their functions, solve problems, and set and achieve objectives. It is also the set of attributes, capabilities, and resources of an organization that enables it to undertake its mission.
Source: UNDP 1998:10; Beltran et al. 2004:167; UNDP 2008b.

Building Technical Capacity

Technical capacities that communities need include the ability to use new technologies like improved seeds and more-efficient processing facilities, as well as new techniques such as water harvesting or no-fishing zones. Financial and business skills—from accounting to writing a business plan—also fall under the category of technical capacity, as do monitoring and evaluation skills.

Effective capacity-building is more difficult than many realize. Conventional approaches, which often involve technical experts from government agencies or outside consulting firms, often miss the mark in terms of their relevance to local needs. They may consist of "one-off" efforts that rely on one or two quick training courses, rather than the kind of interactive training that people need to truly absorb useful skills. Perhaps the biggest challenge is to provide capacity-building services that go beyond one-dimensional "how to" training and allow local people to express their creativity and entrepreneurial ability, while providing access to the tools that can help them adapt to changing circumstances.

ISOs help meet these challenges in several ways. First, they typically adopt a long-term and collaborative approach to capacity-building. In many instances they provide training themselves, but just as often they facilitate specialized local NGOs to deliver the training in a way that is locally appropriate. ISOs often coordinate the efforts of these local capacity-builders, providing "training for the trainers" and using their networking ability to provide access to resources that local NGOs typically lack. This ability to nurture and support local service providers has prompted the Watershed Organisation Trust in India to see itself as a "Mother NGO" (Lobo 2008).

The ability to look broadly at capacity-building gives ISOs the power to identify and meet needs on a wider scale, such as across a district or region. For example, the Kalinga Mission for Indigenous Communities and Youth Development, an ISO in the Philippines, recognized a widespread need among Philippine community organizations for better managerial and financial capacity. It worked with some 50 local organizations already engaged in sustainable development projects—including sustainable farming and watershed management—to build their financial accounting, management, and reporting skills. These skill sets increased the financial sustainability of the participating CBOs and increased their confidence when approaching potential donors (Bumacas et al. 2006:299).

When they do participate directly in capacity-building, the most successful ISOs blend an assortment of learning approaches in order to maximize the relevance and effectiveness of their training. For instance, many ISOs emphasize field visits (one village to another), regional workshops and forums for exchange, and a blend of participatory and more traditional methods to build technical skills. The abilities to think holistically about the capacity development process and to draw on their wide reach and system of contacts to facilitate learning are signal characteristics of effective ISOs (Bruneau 2005:43–47; Carter and Currie-Alder 2006:136–138; Berkes et al. 2004:12).

Building Social Capacity

More than technical capacity is required to enable a community-based enterprise to thrive. Many of the capabilities that enable community efforts to succeed over the long term—group organizing and institution building, negotiating and political skills, and the ability to distribute benefits and costs fairly—require significant social capacity within communities.

ISO PROFILE: ASIAN NETWORK FOR SUSTAINABLE AGRICULTURE AND BIORESOURCES, KATMANDU, NEPAL

The Asian Network for Sustainable Agriculture and Bioresources, or ANSAB, is an NGO established in 1992 in Katmandu to raise the living standards of smallholder farmers in South Asia. The organization was founded as a technology-focused initiative, meant to generate knowledge and capacity in agriculture and forestry technology across South Asia. ANSAB evolved through the mid-1990s to emphasize natural resource management and enterprise development, realizing that these two components would be central to its mission of raising living standards (Subedi 2007). The organization's 50 employees are drawn from a variety of fields, including sociology, biology, and economics. Their work is concentrated in five programs: enterprise development, community forestry, policy and networking, marketing information services, and business development services. Within these program areas, ANSAB consults on individual community development projects and also serves as a network coordinator for large-scale initiatives (ANSAB 2007:14–15).

Most of ANSAB's work since this transition has centered on empowering and training Community Forest User Groups (CFUGs) across Nepal, which govern much of the country's forests under the 1993 Forest Law. In addition to assisting with the formation of these CFUGs, in 1995 ANSAB became the coordinator of the Nepal Non-Timber Forest Products Network (NNN). This network brings together communities, businesses, donors, and environmental and government representatives to promote sustainable use of NTFPs in Nepal. NNN coordinators meet biannually to advance their goals of reducing poverty and promoting biodiversity through careful commercialization of NTFPs. Between meetings, ANSAB, among other things, leads trainings for the directors of Community Forest User Groups, publishes and distributes data about NTFP markets, and holds talks with government officials to improve laws for NTFP producers (ANSAB 2005b: 4,7).

Over the last 15 years, ANSAB has facilitated and implemented a wide range of nature-based enterprise initiatives—with visible results. In 2006 alone, their enterprise development work with CFUGs helped 65,351 people to realize US$5.54 million in income (ANSAB 2007:3). In 2005, some 70 percent of the NTFP producers who received ANSAB's market information reported increased bargaining power and therefore higher incomes as a result of the information. In addition, ANSAB's direct work with CFUGs has led to the sustainable management of more than 86,584 ha of forest across Nepal (ANSAB 2007:8).

ANSAB's cross-cutting strategic partnerships are also critical to its success. In 2002, they formed a public-private alliance that brought the Rainforest Alliance together with Nepalese companies, NGOs, and Nepal's federation of CFUGs (known as FECOFUN), to create a program to certify NTFPs produced by the Community Forest User Groups. To date, 24 products, such as handmade paper and cosmetic ingredients, have received Forest Stewardship Council certification under this program. Twenty-one CFUGs are involved in the production of these products (ANSAB 2005b:6). In addition, ANSAB has facilitated the organic certification of dozens of herbs and essential oils within CFUG communities (ANSAB 2005b:12).

CAPACITY

ISO PROFILE: ANAI ASSOCIATION, TALAMANCA, COSTA RICA

The ANAI Association, winner of the 2002 UN Equator Prize, describes itself as a "grassroots support organization," helping other grassroots groups in Costa Rica's Talamanca region to carry out sustainable agriculture projects and conservation initiatives, from agroforestry to sea turtle conservation and ecotourism (ANAI 2005a). ANAI grew out of a loose partnership between North American biologists and Talamancan farmers in the late 1970s, initially formed to provide technical support for conservation-focused community development projects (ANAI 2005b). Since then, ANAI has used training courses, seed grants, networking, and targeted research to support the efforts of 20 grassroots conservation organizations, a 1,500-member farmers' cooperative, and 16 local ecotourism ventures (ANAI 2005c).

When ANAI first began working on agroforestry in the 1970s, there were few local organizations to work with on the ground. As a result, while it was providing seeds and training to community groups willing to participate in agroforestry projects, ANAI also placed an early emphasis on building the organizational and technical capacities of local groups. ANAI's focus on local capacity-building took a major step forward in 1991 when it established its Regional Training Center. Here, ANAI offers agriculture, health, technology, conservation, and leadership workshops to local indigenous communities (ANAI 2005d). Over time, ANAI has evolved into a true intermediary support organization, channeling funds to grassroots organizations and connecting them to sources of technical, financial, and marketing support. It has also become skilled in creating linkages to government agencies, research institutions, and international funders and in promoting the efforts of its clients to these actors (Carroll 1992:217).

The substance and tenor of ANAI's work has changed over the years, largely as a result of the organization's own success. For instance, ANAI began its efforts to conserve Leatherback sea turtles in 1985, concentrating initially on reducing poaching by protecting the beach of the Gandoca-Manzanillo Wildlife Refuge, where the turtles came ashore to breed. Between 1985 and 2004, ANAI developed an entire program to achieve both development and conservation goals through scientific monitoring, community outreach and education, and ecotourism. By 2003, the new ecotourism ventures were generating over US$93,000 for the coastal communities, and poaching was virtually non-existent (ANAI 2005e). The project had become so successful that ANAI's central coordinating role no longer seemed appropriate. The project spun off from ANAI and joined WIDECAST, a global network of turtle conservation groups and researchers (WIDECAST Latin American Program 2007).

ANAI views the spin-off as a mark of its success and its evolution. In fact, its stated purpose is to become part of the local fabric of support, functioning as just one node in a network of self-sufficient local organizations. In ANAI's own words: "The role of locally based Grassroots Support Organizations like ANAI is increasingly recognized as a necessary part of what may be called an 'ecology of organizations,' including specialized technical aid groups, donors, lending institutions, advocacy and watchdog groups, government agencies, and grassroots or 'base' groups....At every stage it has been appropriate for us to ask ourselves what we should be doing for others and what we should be training our neighbors to do [themselves]. Increasingly, though, local groups are taking the initiative to let us know what they think they can do, and what they would like to learn to do, and where they need help" (ANAI 2005a).

HOW DOES ANAI FACILITATE SUSTAINABLE COMMUNITY DEVELOPMENT?

Focus	Activities
Capacity-Building	■ Hold workshops and outreach activities in: ■ Agricultural diversification ■ Organic certification ■ Sea turtle restoration ■ Health ■ Organizational management and leadership
Information	■ Collect, analyze, and distribute information about: ■ Ecotourism markets ■ Agricultural best practices ■ Biodiversity ■ Agricultural markets
Service Provision	■ Work with local enterprises to develop business plans ■ Distribute donor funds to local initiatives
Networking	■ Partner with Costa Rican government to secure good policies for sustainable development projects and conservation of biodiversity ■ Coordinate enterprise and NGO coalitions, such as ecotourism networks and farmers' cooperatives

Source: ANAI 2005a, 2005b, 2005c, 2005d, 2005e.

Evidence indicates that early attention to social processes is worth the effort. In analyses of watershed development projects in India, researchers have found that NGO-led projects have tended to invest more heavily than government-led projects in social organizing. As a result, most NGO projects recorded a higher success rate in terms of creating self-sustaining local institutions—such as village watershed committees—that continued to manage their lands sustainably and profitably (Sharma et al. 2005:2; Kerr et al. 2002:77; Turton et al. 1998:2).

Social capacity-building is a matter of emphasizing process as well as substance. What this often means for ISOs is that guided

social interactions and group learning are deliberately incorporated as part of technical capacity-building courses, in order to induce a new social dynamic in the group. In some cases, these participatory exercises and guided group interactions are broken out separately and become a precursor to the community undertaking group action in the field.

The Watershed Organisation Trust in India has recently begun piloting an approach to social capacity-building when it begins to work with a new community on watershed rehabilitation and water harvesting. It calls its approach *wasundhara*—a term which means "mother earth" and connotes caring and compassion within the community. In it, facilitators from WOTR lead the group through a process of examining the wealth dynamics of the community, including an assessment of needs and aspirations within the village population. This is followed by a visioning process where the community generates a shared goal, agrees upon the steps to get there, and assigns responsibilities for action. In order to cement the agreement and build trust, the group then undertakes several days of cooperative field work together in the watershed. The idea is to engage the entire community in an on-going dialogue focused on creating a more equitable future that offers benefits for every household in the village, rich and poor (Lobo 2007).

While many competent local NGOs can facilitate social capacity-building exercises, WOTR was able to use its extensive experience in nearly 600 villages to design the wasundara approach, which is tailored to the caste and wealth situation in Maharashtra's villages and its relation to water in the arid rural landscape. Villagers tend to respect WOTR as a firm but fair "outsider" with a proven track record in helping villages successfully increase their access to water. This illustrates the point that the established reputation of an ISO can be an important factor in convincing villagers to undertake a social capacity-building process like wasundara in the first place. Indeed, ISO effectiveness depends in some measure on the ISO's own social capacity.

Competent ISOs consciously work on their own visioning process and constantly try to build their connection to their clients, since trust and reputation are sometimes their most valuable assets in their work to guide and empower communities and build networks among stakeholders at many levels (Lobo 2007).

When social capacity-building is successful, it gives rise to capabilities beyond just a shared vision and the ability to work productively together. It can enable groups to internalize learning processes and to problem-solve, and it can give them the confidence and flexibility to collaborate with outside partners and to gain access to outside sources of support. These are the very abilities that help local enterprises sustain themselves in the face of outside shocks, such as economic downturns, unfavorable regulations, or natural hazards such as drought or floods. In this sense, greater social capacity translates to greater social resilience.

"Upward" Capacity-Building

No natural resource can be managed entirely at the local level, even when communities have been granted significant resource rights. All such local efforts ultimately take place within the larger political environment. National policies and the attitudes and competence of elected officials and line-agency staff have a very real impact on the success of management efforts at the local level.

THE AGA KHAN RURAL SUPPORT PROGRAMME (AKRSP) is an internationally funded NGO working to promote development in the remote communities of Pakistan's mountainous northern regions. Its considerable success as an intermediary support organization is a testament to the power of its two-pronged approach: working "downward" to build local institutions and social capacity and "upward" to change government attitudes and development practices.

When AKRSP began to serve the isolated villages of the Chitral and the Northern Areas in 1982, it did so in a governance vacuum at the local level. This vacuum was created in the 1970s when the central government, in a bid to increase its political control of the region, abolished the traditional local governance structures known as mirdoms, which had controlled many aspects of village life and natural resource use. In the fractured governance situation that resulted, local leadership became less effective, and forest and pasture resources degraded quickly (Zehra 2005:22–25). AKRSP decided its initial development efforts must focus on founding and supporting community organizations that could govern and provide for communities on their own, betting that this would be the most effective development strategy for such remote locales in the long term (Zehra 2005:25).

The strategy has paid off. These harsh mountain valleys, historically defined by religious and political divisions, are likely some of the most challenging regions of the world to promote economic opportunities. Yet by focusing on promoting community development, AKRSP has organized nearly 4000 functional village organizations (VOs) that have effectively filled the governance gap that once existed (AKRSP 2003).

The VOs—and parallel women's organizations (WOs), exclusively for women—initially formed around building productive physical infrastructure for the villages. With all village households represented, the VOs convened to make investment decisions based on principles of equity, productivity, and sustainability. Initial investments included transportation and sanitation infrastructure. The communities then began to provide other services through their VOs, such as training in community forestry practices and in veterinary care for livestock. Savings programs were established for each VO, with each member contributing a share. These funds, now totaling over US$8 million, are used as a source of collateral to obtain financing for community projects (Zehra 2005:25–26).

Today the VOs involve about 90 percent of the region's population, and many have federated into clusters to capitalize on economies of scale for larger investments (AKRSP 2003; Zehra 2005:28). AKRSP has facilitated these processes from the start by working closely with the villagers on the ground to establish the VOs, to fund them initially, and to provide technical support and information. All of these efforts have been grounded in AKRSP's goals for social capacity-building among villagers. Participation, self-help, and cooperation are well-established norms among the isolated communities, and AKRSP has used this to its advantage in developing social capital through the village organizations (Zehra 2005:41–42).

The VOs' work has helped to cut poverty rates in the region nearly in half over the last 25 years (Malik and Wood 2003:1). With NGO partners like the World Conservation Union–IUCN and funding from Pakistan's government and bilateral donors, AKRSP has helped communities achieve an impressive range of conservation and development goals (Zehra 2005:32; AKRSP 2003). These include slowing deforestation and providing electricity for 18,000 households through small hydro dam projects. In the process, community decision-making structures have been strengthened. For example, all proposed dams go

through consensus-oriented planning within the village organizations before being approved (Khan 2005:5–7).

Yet even as it has stressed local empowerment and the gradual maturing of local institutions, AKRSP has always understood the inescapable role of government in its work. In its early years of operation, AKRSP focused on earning legitimacy and making gains in natural resource management and renewable energy projects in one region of the country. Its primary concern regarding the provincial and federal government was to convince officials not to actively deter its efforts (Najam 2003:2).

As AKRSP became more established, it began to shift its strategy to explicitly target line agencies and government officials with training sessions and field visits. These efforts began to pay off in the form of new attitudes and approaches to rural development policy in the early 1990s. As a result, the NGO began to have opportunities to collaborate directly with government on education, health, and forestry projects. Leery of the dangers of becoming too closely associated with government, AKRSP's leadership made a conscious effort to avoid over-reliance on government funding. It reserved government collaboration for one portion of its portfolio and treated it as an opportunity for upward capacity-building, particularly in terms of improving social-organizing capacity within government agencies (Najam 2003:2-3).

Finally, after it had been working for more than 20 years, the organization found itself collaborating with officials who had grown up in the villages where AKRSP programs were in place. As it garnered success in the field and earned recognition nationally and internationally, AKRSP found its role with government shifting to that of a respected advisor (Najam 2003:2). The results of this work are visible on the ground. For example, in the late 1990s federal and provincial governments agreed, under guidance from AKRSP, to give 80 percent of all hunting license fees to local conservation funds. These funds are now used by the villages for projects ranging from school construction to compensation for shepherds who sustain losses from snow leopard predation (Zehra 2005:32). AKRSP illustrates that ISOs that are able to attain this level of respectability within government and still retain their flexibility and connections at the grassroots level can become a potent force for change.

AKRSP's successes have inspired a burst of successful imitator NGOs across the region as well as a new government focus on providing support at the local level. This has made what was once a services and governance vacuum a crowded and competitive workspace (Najam 2003:4). By 2000, at least eight rural support programs were modeled on AKRSP's approach, and these programs had catalyzed the formation of 20,000 additional community organizations (Zehra 2005:29).

Intermediary organizations are often in a position to engage with government in a number of different capacities and hence can play an important role in building the capacity of government to further grassroots development. "Upward" capacity-building refers to the efforts of ISOs to improve the skills, adaptability, and receptiveness of government to more participatory approaches and its active engagement with emerging institutions at the local level (Carroll 1992:122–125).

At first, ISO dealings with government often concentrate on mitigating the immediate dysfunctions of government, minimizing harmful interference and neutralizing the often hostile view that official agencies take of local resource management. One of the most effective ways to do this is to act early on to get support from highly placed government officials, based on a compelling vision for the work as well as the solid reputation of the ISO. This can earn the organization some maneuvering room at lower levels of the bureaucracy, and it is one reason that politically savvy leadership can be an important advantage for an ISO.

ISOs may also directly intervene at the policy level on behalf of their local clients. For example, in 2001 ANSAB convinced Nepali forestry authorities to lift their ban on the harvesting of *yarsagumba*, a valuable medicinal fungus. Earlier, unregulated harvesting had badly depleted the fungus; in spite of a total ban on local use, rampant illegal harvesting continued. ANSAB argued that legalizing the harvest and trade of yarsagumba by Community Forest User Groups under careful guidelines would give these groups the incentive to protect the resource. ANSAB's proposal was taken seriously by forest officials since they had worked productively with ANSAB for many years to help local user groups establish sustainable regimes for harvesting other forest products (ANSAB 2005b).

In addition to direct intervention and advocacy, ISOs use a variety of training and engagement strategies, profiled below, to drive positive change in government agencies and build government capacity.

Training and Dialogue. Organizations that are engaged in projects on the ground have a wealth of information and project experience that could inform government activities, but there are few channels to effectively communicate all this to those in government who could use it. One method for reaching policymakers and line-agency officials directly is simply to offer training services that they find worthwhile. These may be technical courses or field demonstrations, or they may involve more dialogue and interactive training in social and policy matters. When carried out skillfully, such training contributes to a wider communication and influence strategy that ISOs use to create the "institutional space" for local programs to succeed. Organizations such as WOTR, Sadguru, and MYRADA—all of which facilitate community-based watershed restoration in India—train government officials at their training centers and organize demonstration visits and workshops for officials (Sharma et al. 2005:10).

ISO-instigated workshops or other public meetings can become a setting in which policymakers and practitioners interact with representatives of poor people in an atmosphere of learning. UNDP's Equator Initiative *(see Box 2.1)* provides an example of this on an international scale. As a respected external actor, UNDP draws attention to successful ecosystem-based enterprises and examples of best practice, and it brings actors from grassroots organizations and governments together on equal footing in international forums (Hooper et al 2004:142).

Staff Exchanges and Partnerships. A very straightforward method for creating dialogue with government is to encourage short- or long-term exchanges of personnel for the purposes of hands-on training and information exchange. A number of the more established ISOs in India and Pakistan have used such secondments to good effect. In its early years of operation, the work of the Aga Khan Rural Support Programme (AKRSP) on rural development in northern Pakistan effectively replaced the weakened government's development role in that area. However, the ISO later played a key role in developing capacity in the public sector through joint activities, training sessions, and deputation of staff from forestry, fisheries, and wildlife departments to work for AKRSP (Zehra 2005:29–30). *(See Box 2.5.)*

ISOs may also influence government attitudes and exchange technical knowledge by working as consultants on government-run projects. When working with reasonably supportive governments, this can be one of the most efficient ways to build capacity within the government bureaucracy itself. AKRSP was able to achieve notable changes in government policy and practice through its direct collaboration with the government of Pakistan on development projects.

Other forms of direct partnership with government can be useful as well. In Namibia, the Ministry of Environment and Tourism (MET) became one of 12 partner organizations that affiliated as the Namibian Association of CBNRM Support Organizations (NACSO), which has acted as an ISO for Namibian conservancies. By joining as a partner of NACSO, the MET has been able to effectively "mainstream" into the government bureaucracy the progressive approach to wildlife governance that NACSO represents.

However, while partnerships between government and ISOs offer many potential benefits, they are always a delicate matter. The origins and terms of the partnership—which party initiated it, who controls funding, and relative levels of competence on both sides—can influence the balance of independence and influence that an ISO is able to maintain. Furthermore, support for collaborative efforts can wane with changes in government leadership, jeopardizing the common ground between the state and an ISO. A larger limitation of collaboration as a model for building capacity is that it rarely influences the underlying incentive structures and organizational attitudes of government agencies. As a result, it may only result in incremental change (Howell and Pearce 2000:75).

The scaling up of CBNRM projects ultimately requires navigating existing policy and enforcement practices—an impos-

sible goal to achieve without engaging government in a constructive manner. Attempting to influence or collaborate with government actors is important in large part because bypassing these institutions is not a viable strategy for the longer term.

ISOs: Building Linkages and Networks

A core strength of intermediary support organizations is their ability to build ties between the diverse actors in development. ISOs are well equipped to facilitate partnerships between community-based organizations and government, between local entrepreneurs and outside sources of support, and among the many NGOs and government actors working—sometimes at cross purposes—in a given area (Edwards and Hulme 1992:84; Brown 1991:812).

This "bridging" or networking function lies at the heart of efforts to sustain and scale up successes in CBNRM and nature-based enterprise. When the ISO bridging function is effective, it supports cumulative learning and builds a web of relationships that persist long after the ISO has exited the scene (Carroll 1992:104). ISOs that are able to build such self-sustaining networks of capable organizations can then gradually withdraw their direct support and focus on replicating their efforts elsewhere. By supporting the growth of other implementing NGOs and improving pathways for communication and learning at the grassroots level, an ISO can also scale out its impact through multiple avenues at once.

Furthermore, a key strength of ISOs is their ability to transcend the limits of localized action, fostering strategic planning across multiple scales and sectors and influencing policy at higher levels. These capacities reflect a combination of horizontal and vertical linkage-building (Bebbington and Carroll 2000:xiii; Bruneau 2005:27).

Horizontal Networking

Horizontal linkages—those between local organizations—enhance the capacity of grassroots organizations for collective action and increase the sustainability and scalability of local development efforts (Brown 1991:810–811). Catalyzing the growth of new relationships and institutional arrangements can be an area of strength for many intermediary support organizations. ISOs often focus on strengthening connections between local groups as part of building social capacity. In other cases, ISOs themselves emerge as the result of groups federating in response to the limitations of local organizations. In both cases ISOs are in a position to be particularly successful networkers. Their efforts can range from creating informal forums for information exchange or more-formal conferences and committees of local representatives to actively supporting the efforts of grassroots organizations to form official networks or federations on their own. Even in places where there is a strong history of grassroots organizing, ISOs can play a networking role by improving

synergies between complementary efforts, allowing for cross-fertilization of ideas and institutional learning and improving groups' access to new services and sources of information.

The People's Rural Education Movement (PREM), an ISO based in the Indian state of Orissa, is a good example of an ISO that is adept at the networking function. PREM, whose development work stresses education, health, and sustainable livelihoods, has been very active in the establishment of formal networks at the regional and national levels. It heads a large supernetwork of 172 independent community-based organizations, from which it has helped several more specialized networks to emerge. These include Utkal Mahila Sanchaya Bikas, a federation of women's self-help groups; the National Advocacy Council for Development of Indigenous People, which represents indigenous communities in 18 states; and the East Coast Fisher People Forum, which organizes and advocates for poor fishing communities. PREM mentors and provides managerial support for these organizations (PREM 2007).

In addition to their obvious importance for scaling up, horizontal linkages can also strengthen existing local initiatives by improving feedback and expanding opportunities. For example, externally funded development projects often suffer from a lack of relevant feedback from the outside. Papa Andina, a regional organization affiliated with the International Potato Center that promotes research and development activities among farmers in the Andes region of South America, noticed

this phenomenon among local development projects within its network. External evaluations rarely produced clear recommendations or significant follow-up and often suffered from the creation of an expert/inexpert dynamic that hindered real capacity-building. In response, Papa Andina began bringing peers from a range of research and development projects in the region together for three-day workshops to evaluate methodologies, conduct site visits, and exchange ideas. These "horizontal evaluations" produced recommendations that were "actionable" and strengthened the confidence and sense of community among participating organizations (Thiele et al. 2006:1).

The concept of horizontal evaluations can also be applied more informally to good effect. WOTR organizes annual "peer review" processes among villages participating in watershed restoration. Representatives from village watershed committees visit and evaluate progress in other villages, creating opportunities to learn from successes and recommend areas for improvement. WOTR has noticed that these reviews spark an element of competitive pride among watershed committees, none of which want to look bad in front of their peers (Das Gupta et al. 2005:27). WOTR also integrates peer reviews into a wider communication strategy by awarding prizes to top performers and involving government officials and neighboring villages in recognizing success stories.

Hence, horizontal evaluations fill several important roles: they help spread the word of successful approaches (evaluators can

CAPACITY

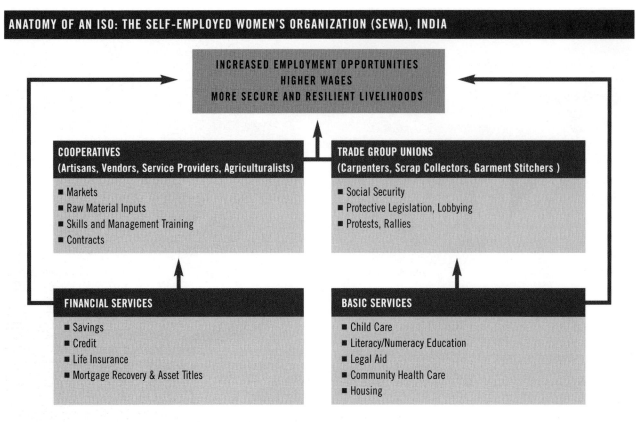

ANATOMY OF AN ISO: THE SELF-EMPLOYED WOMEN'S ORGANIZATION (SEWA), INDIA

**INCREASED EMPLOYMENT OPPORTUNITIES
HIGHER WAGES
MORE SECURE AND RESILIENT LIVELIHOODS**

COOPERATIVES
(Artisans, Vendors, Service Providers, Agriculturalists)

- Markets
- Raw Material Inputs
- Skills and Management Training
- Contracts

TRADE GROUP UNIONS
(Carpenters, Scrap Collectors, Garment Stitchers)

- Social Security
- Protective Legislation, Lobbying
- Protests, Rallies

FINANCIAL SERVICES

- Savings
- Credit
- Life Insurance
- Mortgage Recovery & Asset Titles

BASIC SERVICES

- Child Care
- Literacy/Numeracy Education
- Legal Aid
- Community Health Care
- Housing

More than one million poor women are involved in SEWA, an Indian ISO that combines elements of more traditional trade unions and cooperatives to assist small-scale sellers, producers, and laborers.

Source: Uphoff et al. 1998: ii.

bring lessons learned back to their own communities), build the capacity of local organizations to evaluate and solve technical and management issues on their own, and motivate communities to a higher level of performance. Furthermore, all these interactions strengthen the network of peer groups tackling the same resource and governance issues in a region, opening channels for further learning and collaboration in the future.

Vertical Networking

By virtue of their position of operating between local organizations and higher-level actors, intermediary support organizations are inherently suited to the task of strengthening vertical linkages—connections between local groups and the state or central government, donors, and various international organizations. In some cases, strengthening such linkages can be as straightforward as facilitating access of local groups to funding, or it can be as delicate as improving relationships between state agencies and the poor and paving the way for government to better support local natural resource management. Improving communication and exchanges of learning can also be as important here as in horizontal networking, potentially contributing to greater transparency as well as greater adaptability and responsiveness of actors at different levels.

Capacity-building at the local level plays an important complimentary role in this process, since grassroots organizations interacting with government agencies need confidence, negotiating skills, and credibility. An important part of an ISO's vertical networking ability is its familiarity with the government system and its skill in transferring to grassroots groups the ability to deal with external actors and negotiate unfamiliar procedures (Carroll 1992:122–125; Brown 1991:826; Hooper et al. 2004:136).

In some cases, ISOs are able to use their role as an independent and respected party to create opportunities for equal exchanges between grassroots and government actors. A study of nominees of UNDP's Equator Prize found that one advantage of the program was that it facilitated situations that put community, national, regional, and global leaders all on equal footing, facilitating the rate of political scaling-up for many of the community groups recognized in the process (Hooper et al. 2004:142).

Another example of this process is the Carchi Consortium, an initiative that originated as a roundtable for NGOs and universities to share information on watershed management in northern Ecuador. It soon expanded to involve local stakeholders and government representatives. As it began to gain recognition as a legitimate actor in the region, the consortium evolved into a forum for local and non-local stakeholders to exchange ideas and address conflicts. It has been successful at bringing together municipal governments and local organizations to establish joint watershed planning at the local level and strategic management at a landscape scale. By encouraging ongoing exchanges, the consortium has also created opportunities to raise issues such as women's rights and environmental sustainability across scales. Most important, it provides a neutral space for local stakeholders to interact with the state and influence government processes (Carter and Currie-Alder 2006:132–133).

In practical terms, it is usually impossible to separate the horizontal and vertical networking functions that ISOs perform. They are usually integrated into a unified effort to help local organizations connect to sources of help and support at all levels. The Botswana Community-Based Organization Network (BOCOBONET), for instance, serves as an umbrella organization supporting communities that have been given authority to manage local wildlife. It offers training and communications services, but its most important function is its networking role. BOCOBONET facilitates horizontal linkages by providing a forum for local organizations to exchange experiences and disseminate lessons learned. But it has also strived to use its position to improve dialogue and coordination between community groups, NGOs, the private sector, and the government (IUCN Botswana 2006). Among the policy impacts of its work have been greater support for joint venture activities and a national review of CBNRM in 2003 (IUCN Botswana 2006). Like many active networks, BOCOBONET realizes that building effective capacity on the ground benefits greatly from political connection.

ISOs: Improving Access to Markets

While scaling out nature-based enterprises is an important goal, an equally important objective from a poverty-reduction standpoint is to scale up the income-generating opportunities within these schemes. CBNRM projects in particular are very often hindered by an inadequate focus on the business side of sustainable resource management. One challenge for every nature-based enterprise effort is its dependence upon the viability of local and wider markets and the ability of local people to reach and navigate them. Both of these issues can present daunting challenges to small farmers, foresters, and other natural resource–based entrepreneurs.

Intermediary organizations, by virtue of their connections to the wider world, are potentially well positioned to improve local producers' relationships with local, regional, and—in some cases—international markets. For example, AKRSP's work in northern Pakistan focused primarily on building and supporting community organizations, but it also included an enterprise development arm that was able to use the ISO's size and connections to its advantage *(See Box 2.5)*. Carpet makers and dry fruit merchants are among the industries that gained good access to national and international markets through AKRSP's involvement (Zehra 2005:31).

One source of ISOs' effectiveness in connecting community enterprises to markets is their ability to catalyze "upstream" market research, product development, and process improvements. In the early 1980s, ANAI Association began a series of research and marketing studies to develop higher-value crops and more-efficient cropping systems for local farmers. To bring these to their local clientele, they partnered with a local farmers' cooperative in a three-year crop diversification program. In this instance, ANAI acted like a government research and extension service, but with greater flexibility and accountability to local people (Carroll 1992:214).

ISOs: Facilitating Finance

As trusted intermediaries, ISOs are logical candidates to help community groups and local entrepreneurs connect to sources of finance. In many instances, ISOs act as nodes for the distribution of project funds from governments or international donors. In India, SEWA and WOTR have acted as receptacles for project funds from the government's "watershed development" program, which they then disbursed to village watershed committees for use

TABLE 2.2 INTERMEDIARY SUPPORT ORGANIZATIONS AROUND THE WORLD

PLACE	NAME	YEAR EST.	TYPE	ISO FUNCTIONS	SELECT ACCOMPLISHMENTS
LATIN AMERICA					
Costa Rica Source: ANAI 2005a–f	**Asociación ANAI**	1978	Grassroots Support NGO	Builds capacity of community organizations and local environmental enterprises in forest products, ecotourism, and agriculture. Trains leaders and connects local groups to technical and financial support.	By 2003, ecotourism ventures initiated by ANAI generated $93,000/year for coastal communities, and poaching had been reduced on beaches where ANAI has turtle conservation programs. Farmers co-op that ANAI started provides consistent market and better prices for 1,500 farmers.
Peru Source: AIDER 2007	**Asociación para la Investigación y Desarrollo Integral (AIDER)**	1986	Training NGO	Provides technical support to community organizations to help them generate income and improve living standards while improving the environment.	Helped five communities obtain FSC certification for 25,000 ha of forest. Implemented carbon-capture program through Clean Development Mechanism of Kyoto Protocol. Conducted community forestry management training in 22 communities.
Guatemala Source: Nittler and Tschinkel 2005:10–11; Chemonics 2005:8, 28, 30; Saito 2008	**Asociación de Comunidades Forestales del Petén (ACOFOP)**	1997	Federation of Community Enterprises	Holds technical and managerial training courses for and enables information-sharing among 22 communities that manage forest concessions. In 2003, ACOFOP created FORESCOM—a commercial association of ACOFOP members—to process, market, and certify the communities' forest products.	Has trained 6,839 community forest enterprise members in forestry and processing techniques and business management. FORESCOM halved the cost to receive FSC certification for the 12 enterprises it has certified, which are responsible for 500,000 ha of community concessions. In 2007, coordinated sales of over 2.6 million board feet of timber.
Andes Source: Valcárcel 2007; CIP 2007	**Papa Andina**	1998	Regional Research and Development NGO	Trains smaller Andes NGOs to help potato farmers organize effectively, gain access to new technologies and markets, and innovate market chain solutions.	Taught 1,000 farmers to process native products, generating employment and income and developing new markets. T'ikapapa branding project brings fresh native potatoes from 500 poor farmers to Lima supermarkets.
ASIA-PACIFIC					
Nepal Source: ANSAB 2005a; ANSAB 2007	**Asia Network for Sustainable Agriculture and Bioresources (ANSAB)**	1992	Networking NGO	Works with Community Forest User Groups, offering technical support and linkages to markets, NGOs, and government to promote nature-based enterprise and biodiversity.	In 2006, helped over 65,000 forest dwellers to realize US$5.54 million in additional income. Increased the capacity of over 500 businesses to produce and market natural products. Helped 21 community groups to obtain Forest Stewardship Council certification.
Pakistan Source: Khan 2004:18–19; Zehra 2005:20; AKRSP 2003	**Aga Khan Rural Support Programme (AKRSP)**	1982	Community Support NGO	Builds the capacity of community organizations and government officials, using training sessions, collaboration, and hands-on approaches. Leads natural resource management and poverty reduction efforts in Pakistan's north.	Per capita income in districts where AKRSP works rose from $131 to $241 between 1991 and 2001, while the poverty rate fell from 67 percent to 34 percent. Has helped mobilize US$8 million in savings in 4,000 community organizations it helped established.

TABLE 2.2 INTERMEDIARY SUPPORT ORGANIZATIONS AROUND THE WORLD (CONTINUED)

PLACE	NAME	YEAR EST.	TYPE	ISO FUNCTIONS	SELECT ACCOMPLISHMENTS
ASIA-PACIFIC					
Bangladesh Source: BRAC 2005, BRAC 2007	**Bangladesh Rural Advancement Committee (BRAC)**	1972	Finance, Training, and Research NGO	Facilitates local development, working broadly in health, education, social development, finance, and environmental areas. Offers rural microfinance programs. Partners with World Food Programme and other international NGOs.	As of June, 2007, BRAC microfinance had helped create almost 7 million jobs in agriculture, forestry, trade, and small enterprises. Had loaned over US$4.1 billion, with a repayment rate of 98.3 percent. Operates 17 Training and Resource Centers for literacy, health, and business training.
Philippines Source: FAO 2004; Catacutan and Tejada 2006:1	**Claveria Landcare Association (CLCA)**	1990	Agricultural Extension NGO	Forms and links farmer-led "Landcare" groups. Conducts training sessions and cross-farm visits. Works with local governments to promote sustainable agriculture.	Reaches more than 10,000 farmers through 15 partner institutions. Soil and water conservation are now the norm in villages where it works. Landcare groups have expanded their activities to cut-flower production, post-harvest processing of produce, and furniture-making.
Thailand Source: CODI 2006, Boonyabancha 2005: 34	**Community Organizations Development Institute (CODI)**	2000	Quasi-Governmental Organization	Offers financial and technical assistance to community-based groups in urban slums. Strengthens groups' negotiating and organizational skills, and connects them to political decision-making processes.	As of 2005, helped to secure land tenure for over 12,000 families in the Bangkok slums. Assisted 569 rural towns with community planning for sustainable development and established 40 town "Learning and Pilot Centers" for community members to test agricultural cultivation and processing methods.
Fiji Source: LMMA Network 2007	**Fiji Locally Managed Marine Areas Network (FLMMA)**	2001	Information Forum NGO	Connects and builds the capacity of community groups to manage marine resources. Local NGOs in network share ideas and findings and advocate for changes in government fisheries management policies.	By 2007, over 200 Local Managed Marine Areas (LMMAs) had been established, involving 279 villages and 8,500 sq km of coastal fisheries. Over 1,000 people in Fiji trained in LMMA methods. Incomes are higher in villages involved in the network.
India Source: SEWA 2005, 2007a, 2007b	**Self-Employed Women's Association (SEWA)**	1972	Trade Union	Country-wide federation of trade cooperatives of self-employed women. Provides capacity training, networking, and financing support.	For earthquake recovery project between 2001 and 2005, trained over 4,500 farmers in animal husbandry techniques and established demonstration agricultural farms, salt farms, tool and equipment libraries, and 75 child care centers; 35,000 villagers received capacity training in some form.
India Source: WOTR 2007a and 2007b	**Watershed Organisation Trust (WOTR)**	1993	Capacity-Building NGO	Builds capacity of local NGOs to run watershed development projects across the State of Maharashtra. Has created a network of community watershed groups that helps to maintain and expand these efforts.	As of 2008, collaborates with 184 NGOs and agencies, facilitating watershed development nearly 400,000 ha in three Indian states, benefiting 650,000 people. Has trained nearly 150,000 people in watershed rehabilitation, including participatory methods and planning processes.

CAPACITY

TABLE 2.2 INTERMEDIARY SUPPORT ORGANIZATIONS AROUND THE WORLD (CONTINUED)

PLACE	NAME	YEAR EST.	TYPE	ISO FUNCTIONS	SELECT ACCOMPLISHMENTS
AFRICA					
Namibia Source: USAID and WWF 2007:2–3; NACSO 2003; Buck et al. 2003:16	**Namibian Association of CBNRM Support Organizations (NACSO)**	1996	NGO Umbrella Network	Umbrella group for 11 NGOs and one university. Provides information sharing, technical assistance, capacity-building, regional coordination, and monitoring and evaluation to support the management and enterprises of national conservancies. NACSO secretariat convenes working groups on resource management, business and enterprise, institutional development, etc.	NACSO services such as business training and legal advice have helped move new conservancies from fledgling organizations without enterprise experience to income-generating institutions with high community participation. In 2006, conservancy communities accrued N$26 million in livelihood benefits from tourism and related commerce, creating nearly 6,000 full- and part-time jobs.
Botswana Source: IUCN Botswana 2005a, b, c; Buck at al. 2003:17	**BOCOBONET**	1999		Support network for nine community-based natural resource organizations in Botswana. Promotes information-sharing and connects them to technical support, funding, and government services. Also conducts training, workshops, and lobbying.	Has provided a channel for communication between communities and a platform for rural voices. Its members' work in rural communities has notably shifted attitudes toward natural resources, particularly wildlife.
Zambia Source: COMACO 2006a, b	**Community Markets for Conservation (COMACO)**	2002		A commercial network that has evolved into an ISO. Promotes conservation and farmer access to niche agricultural markets. Builds farmer capacity to gain access to markets and to farm sustainably.	Between 1999 and 2006, trained 30,000 households in conservation farming techniques. Crop yields have consequently risen 6–20 percent. In 2005, earned over US$3,000 profit on soy and honey products, which was reinvested in COMACO's work.

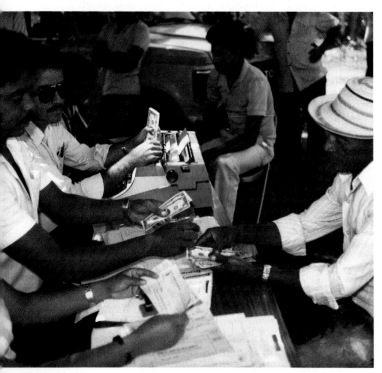

at the project level. In return, ISOs also must act as auditors and information nodes, monitoring progress and passing on to funders data on project accomplishments and lessons learned. They must therefore literally act as honest brokers (Ebrahim 2003:155).

ISOs may also be instrumental in connecting ecosystem-based enterprises to sources of private finance or investment. In fact, in some cases, for-profit, socially responsible businesses can become ISOs, investing their own capital in local enterprises they deem central to their supply chains and providing an array of support services to these enterprises to help them stabilize production, expand their local benefits, and raise their product quality. Dean's Beans—a Fair Trade coffee importer and retailer in the United States—is one such example *(See box on following page).*

ISOs: Increasing Equity and Transparency

As a result of their "mid-level" status in many development efforts, ISOs are well positioned to improve the transparency, accountability, and inclusiveness of the organizations they support, particularly in the beginning phases of a community enterprise. ISOs that offer projects or services that are in high demand can insist that communities meet governance and partic-

PRIVATE SECTOR ISOs: THE EXAMPLE OF DEAN'S BEANS

The private sector can play a crucial part in supporting CBNRM and its associated enterprises in rural communities. In many instances, private sector companies from outside the community can provide market outlets for nature-based products. The markets for Fair Trade items such as coffee, cocoa, and bananas or for Forest Stewardship Council–certified wood work in this way, with retailers specifically advertising the social and environmental benefits of the products as selling points.

In some cases, this marketing link turns into a more direct and substantive partnership between the rural enterprise and the outside retailer. For instance, Alter Eco, a fair trade company headquartered in France, has developed a close relationship with quinoa (a specialty cereal) producers in Bolivia and is helping them to obtain organic certification to further distinguish their crop. Alter Eco pays an NGO with expertise in organic certifications to train the producers' cooperative to adhere to these standards (Alter Eco 2007). Similarly, The Body Shop, a high-end cosmetics company, has developed a Community Trade model in which it buys shea butter and other cosmetic ingredients directly from 36 communities in 23 countries. As part of the Community Trade model, the Body Shop offers communities a long-term market for their products along with a "fair price" guarantee (Body Shop a, b).

Some companies go even farther in their engagement with community enterprises and actually assume the role of an intermediary support organization, providing a range of services such as technical advice, training, finance, and political advocacy on behalf of a community enterprise. Dean's Beans, a coffee and cocoa Fair Trade retailer based in the United States, is one example. In addition to its role as importer, the

company has played a political role, supporting indigenous communities fighting oil pipeline development in Ecuador and Peru. It has helped the communities to negotiate among themselves and with oil companies, and its coffee purchases have broadened the economic opportunities available to the communities.

Dean's Beans also supports development projects within the communities in which it works. In Ethiopia, the company is providing coffee-producing communities with the materials and technical support to build water wells. Elsewhere, it has assisted with health clinics, linking its coffee growers to technical and managerial know-how for these centers and supplying the communities with an extra premium above the Fair Trade minimum price for their coffee to help pay for the clinic. The company even helps to develop other forms of financing for farmers, including a microcredit program for coffee cooperatives in Papua New Guinea (Dean's Beans 2008).

In spite of—or because of—its outlays on social programs and capacity-building, Dean's Beans' business model has proved quite successful, with the company attaining a 14-percent profit margin on US$2.6 million in sales in 2006. The success of Dean's Beans and similar firms shows that social activity and support services—the traditional work of the nonprofit sector—can find their way into commercial business models, benefiting both community enterprises and corporate interests. Dean's Beans argues that its support services and community advocacy are essential elements in controlling its supply chain and delivering consistent quality in its beverages. It acts as an ISO not only to uphold its corporate principles, but also to serve its quality-focused but socially conscious customer base (McFadden 2007).

ipation criteria in order to qualify, such as the equal participation of women in the group activity and in management decisions. Likewise, ISOs can help communities craft schemes for more equitably distributing benefits, such as granting poor families preferential access to water or pastures in restored watersheds. ISOs are also well placed to encourage communities to establish consistent monitoring and reporting regimes, as well as bookkeeping and auditing practices, so that members know the results of their management efforts and can track expenses and the distribution of profits. While these may be outside values at first, they quickly become important to the success of nature-based enterprises, which are predicated on continued support and confidence by community members.

Intermediary organizations can also perform a critical "watchdog" function in places where interactions between government, the private sector, and local communities have little formal oversight. They can help communities monitor and evaluate government actions and compare them to what the government has promised, and they can serve as a repository for information gathered across a larger scale. For government programs they are directly involved in, ISOs can work to build in additional mechanisms for downward accountability. Clearly, this monitoring function needs to be performed deftly so as not to

impair an ISO's ability to partner or intervene with government agencies at other junctures in the enterprise process (Kolavalli and Kerr 2002:232).

Sometimes ISOs can put additional weight behind existing efforts of marginalized groups to gain resource rights or curb abuses of power by government. In one rural district of Orissa, India, local activists in nine villages wanted to initiate a "social audit" of local government—a participatory process for holding *gram panchayat* officials downwardly accountable. The activists collaborated with the national branch of Action-Aid, an international NGO, to implement the process. Although the right to conduct an audit has been a statutory requirement for state-led development projects since 1993, few local groups have sufficient information on how to conduct one or are in a position to confront local elites. The NGO was able to provide information and organizing capacity to local organizers, which brought additional credibility to the process (ActionAid India 2002:14–17).

CAPACITY

SUMMING UP: CAPACITY

Effective approaches to capacity development go beyond one-off technical courses or "how-to" training to allow local people to express their creativity and entrepreneurial ability and to provide opportunities to develop adaptive skills.

Local Organizations

■ Local organizations are essential for implementing and sustaining CBNRM and creating ecosystem-based enterprises. Local organizations include a broad range of bodies including resource management units like forest user groups or watershed committees, as well as local government bodies such as village councils. Community-based organizations like NGOs, unions, cooperatives, church groups, and self-help groups are also local organizations offering important services to local enterprises. As such, they are uniquely equipped to respond to community demand.

■ Because they are populated by people who know each other, local organizations such as resource user groups offer opportunities for collective action and mutual assistance not always present in more geographically dispersed organizations. NGOs and other community-based organizations can provide key services to organize CBNRM and can strengthen user groups through training in business and management skills.

■ Despite their advantages, local organizations often suffer significant weaknesses, including a restricted focus that can foster parochialism and insularity; lack of resources and connections that limits their ability to grow and connect to markets; a lack of accountability to members of the group, particularly if the group is dominated by a powerful leader or local elites; and a lack of inclusiveness of the poor, women, or other socially marginalized groups.

■ The challenge is to work with local organizations to capitalize on their strengths and facilitate a transformation from within that allows them to become more inclusive and competent. Intermediary support organizations can be important contributors to this transformation.

Intermediary Support Organizations

■ In the last 15 years, ISOs have begun to emerge as key actors in the process of scaling-up nature-based enterprises. ISOs are distinguished by high-level organizing, technical, or political skills that they use to help local groups increase their capacity and functioning, and to connect to state or regional authorities and funding sources. They are usually NGOs or other civil society groups such as labor unions, but they can also be private-sector businesses.

■ Effective ISOs are defined by several key qualities: credibility in village circles due to their past successes, influence with government authorities, good communication skills, and an understanding of the power of publicizing.

■ The work ISOs do generally falls into four main categories: social and technical capacity development; facilitating finance for CBNRM and new enterprises; increasing equity and transparency of local organizations; and building linkages and networks for information sharing, political influence, and market connection.

■ ISOs typically adopt a long-term and collaborative approach to capacity-building, often using their mentoring ability to nurture local NGOs and other service providers ("training the trainers") who may be more appropriate to provide direct skills training within a given local context.

■ ISOs pay special attention to the need to develop a group's social capacity. To develop that, ISOs emphasize process, often using guided group interactions, participatory and trust-building exercises, and group visioning processes. In these exchanges, ISOs act as facilitators and honest brokers.

■ ISOs are often in a position to engage in "upward" capacity-building with government agencies—that is, improving the receptivity of government to community-initiated enterprises, improving its ability to deliver training and support services, and securing its policy support to ease regulatory burdens that often handicap rural enterprises.

■ A core strength of ISOs is their ability to build ties between the diverse actors in development. This "bridging" or networking function lies at the heart of efforts to sustain and scale up successes in CBNRM and nature-based enterprise.

■ ISOs are well positioned to communicate the importance of transparency and equity in local enterprises and to lobby communities to put in place auditing, benefits sharing, and participation practices that will maintain the confidence and support of community members.

■ One of the most persistent barriers that rural nature-based enterprises face is the lack of support services that can enable inexperienced communities to grow their business skills and expand their social and institutional capabilities. ISOs, while important, are just one element in a larger web of support that must also include governments, private businesses, civil society groups, donors, international NGOs, and other international organizations and that must persist over the long term.

3. CONNECTION

CONNECTING RURAL ENTERPRISES: NETWORKS AND ASSOCIATIONS

Connection: Links to Learning, Support, and Commercial Networks and Associations

OWNERSHIP

CAPACITY

CONNECTION

— Horizontal links to other rural producers to gain access to information, improve efficiency, and connect to markets

— Vertical links to government and the private sector to build political support, deal with bureaucratic obstacles, and connect to technical and financial support

WHAT ARE NETWORKS AND ASSOCIATIONS?

Networks are dynamic and lasting connections among individuals, groups, and enterprises—a form of structured social capital. They can be informal like learning networks or support groups or can be more formalized, with rules and written charters, such as cooperatives, unions, trade groups, or federations. These more formalized networks we call *associations*.

THIS SECTION: CONNECTION

In this section, we explore the formal and informal networks and associations that ecosystem-based enterprises must rely on to gain information, connect to markets and technology, and organize themselves for political influence. Such networks are part of the essential architecture of scaling up, providing the means for local organizations to share experiences, expand their skills and influence beyond their usual sphere, and sustain themselves in a globalized world. This section:

■ Defines networks and associations and their role in helping rural enterprises to learn and grow, particularly with relation to the poor.

■ Examines the role of formal associations such as cooperatives and consortia in helping small rural enterprises pool resources and achieve economies of scale.

■ Looks at the importance of learning networks that facilitate informal information exchange and foster group learning.

■ Describes the power of federations to magnify the voice of small producers and engage policymakers.

■ Discusses the difficulty of starting and maintaining associations and federations and the problems of keeping them accessible to the poor and free of government manipulation.

If they are to prosper—or even survive—rural enterprises must be connected to learning, support, and commercial networks. Such networks help compensate for the isolation and lack of market power that rural businesses typically suffer, and they help link the diverse array of local organizations to achieve common goals (Best et al. 2005:21–22). As mentioned in the last section, linkages and networks are principal tools in sustaining and scaling up nature-based businesses. Networks link rural producers in information exchanges, in cooperative production and marketing efforts, in product and process research, in financing schemes, and in efforts to achieve political influence.

Networks also help build and extend social capital, creating "institutional spaces" in which the poor can interact and liaise with other groups. They help legitimize and strengthen informal institutions such as savings groups or women's groups, allowing them to institutionalize their processes, solidify their contacts, and thus enter the mainstream of recognized organizations.

There are many kinds of networks. Some, like learning networks, are informal and often amorphous. Others are more structured and take the form of cooperatives, trade groups,

producer organizations, unions, enterprise networks, and federations. Here we will refer to these structured organizations generally as associations. Such associations often have written charters or rules and many—but not all—are legally recognized entities. Associations are essentially networks that have been institutionalized to pursue specific kinds of collective action.

The Power of Association

Associations help small enterprises do collectively what they are unable to accomplish alone. Although the spectrum of their interests is wide, their activities tend to fall into a limited number of categories. These include: creating opportunities to invest in local production; reducing the influence of go-betweens or agents; extending market reach; improving access to credit; facilitating learning networks; and building new opportunities to engage the political process.

CONNECTION

Enabling Local Production and Processing

Perhaps the most basic function of a rural enterprise association is to enable small producers to pool their resources and achieve economies of scale and scope. This can allow them to process locally the raw nature-based products that they once had to send elsewhere—products like timber, rattan, medicinal plants, spices, and other non-timber forest products, as well as traditional agricultural commodities. Bringing processing closer to home is a straightforward way of allowing local enterprises to reach higher on the commodity chain and capture greater value from their efforts.

In Nepal, the formation of community forest user groups has created a platform for villagers who harvest forest products, such as jatamansi and wintergreen, to build local production facilities and improve their profit margins (Subedi et al. 2004; Pokharel et al. 2006:11). Ten years ago, 90 percent of the jatamansi harvested in rural Nepal was exported to India in raw form, with Indian companies profiting from the processing income. Today 75 percent of raw jatamansi is processed into oil by Nepali distillers. Similar progress has been made in the distillation of wintergreen. In 1995, little was processed locally, while today almost 100 percent of the harvest is converted into oil by local distilleries (Pokharel et al. 2006:36).

However, compared with other value-adding business ventures, distilling small batches of wintergreen and jatamansi is relatively inexpensive. When community forest groups have started larger enterprises—like saw and pulp mills—they have relied on larger organizational structures to do so. An example in Nepal's Kavre district is the Chaubas Wood Processing Enterprise, which is essentially a consortium of four community forest user groups, each representing about 75 households. The enterprise functions like a cooperative, where profits are funneled back to the participating community forest groups, after expensing operating costs. The community groups have, in turn, used this money to build roads and schools, among other development projects. In addition to these community benefits, the mill itself employs hundreds of local workers, with a payroll of 500,000 Nepali rupees in 1999 (Subedi et al. 2004:34).

In agricultural communities, associations perform a similar function to promote local crop processing. In the Tecoluca municipality of El Salvador, farmers and workers in the cashew industry have organized under the producer association APRAINORES and are now owners of the Organic Cashew Agroindustrial System (SAMO, by its Spanish acronym), a local cashew production facility. The facility itself employs 68 people and buys cashews from 160 local farmers, most of whom belong to APRAINORES. The sale of cashews has benefited from trade in foreign markets, such as the United Kingdom, the United States, and Belgium (Ford Foundation 2002:42).

While producer associations are frequently key in catalyzing local investment in processing facilities, the reality is that such investment must often be augmented by external support, at least at the start. In the above examples, a number of support groups—most of which are NGOs—supplied financial and logistical support in varying degrees to enable the associations to get off the

ground and build their facilities. For example, the community forest user groups in Nepal that have benefited most from jatamansi and wintergreen distilleries are those assisted by NGOs (Pokharel et al. 2006:1). Likewise, CORDES, an influential Salvadoran NGO, financed and managed SAMO's cashew processing facility initially, as well as assisted in improving the quality and reliability of production—an important prerequisite for access to foreign markets (Cummings 2004:3). This reliance on external start-up support points up the still significant challenges that rural associations face in improving their technical capacity and obtaining commercial finance.

Furthermore, bringing production closer to home does not necessarily guarantee that producers will benefit financially. Despite increases in local employment and marginal increases in the value of the product, traders in the middle can still capture the lion's share of profit by exploiting advantages in market information (Thi Phi et al. 2004:24).

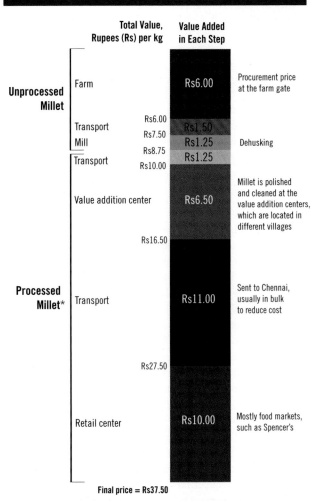

FIGURE 5 MILLET VALUE CHAIN IN INDIA

Final price = Rs37.50

*Prices given per kilogram of processed millet.
About 50% of unprocessed millet is lost during processing.

Source: CAPRi 2007:15

ASSOCIATION PROFILE: SONGTAAB-YALGRÉ ASSOCIATION, OUAGADOUGOU, BURKINA FASO

The Songtaab-Yalgré Association is a women-run organization that facilitates the local production of shea butter, a vegetable fat used in high-end cosmetics that is made by crushing and roasting shea nuts. Collecting shea nuts has long been important to poor women in Burkina Faso, as shea trees grow wild in the West African savannah and the nuts are used in local cuisine. However, the international demand for processed shea nuts has increased in recent years, creating a significant economic opportunity.

In 1997, a study by the UN Development Fund for Women concluded that the economic benefits of selling processed shea butter on the international market were nearly 50 percent higher than selling raw nuts (Harsch 2001:4).

The Songtaab-Yalgré Association has taken advantage of this differential for the benefit of poor women. It has formed relationships with women shea nut collectors in 11 villages near Ouagadougou and works with two women's unions, Siglé and Boussé, to establish a purchase price for the nuts that is considerably higher than what women used to get from private traders. Local women also work in the association's production facilities. In all, the Songtaab-Yalgré Association provides income to some 3,100 women who protect and manage nearly 20,000 shea trees. It sells its product line of traditional and organic shea butter and soaps through a network of distributors in Europe and North America (ASY 2007). Songtaab-Yalgré Association was an Equator Prize winner in 2006.

Gaining Market Influence

By building associations such as cooperatives, rural producers establish a position from which to negotiate with traders or marketing agents or to displace them and deal directly with larger suppliers or retailers. Traders are an integral part of rural market chains, but their incentives are not always aligned with that of rural producers. In Peru, for example, a small number of traders—about 15 percent—dominate the market for straw hats and can often fix the prices paid to rural hat producers (Young and Portocarrero 2007:3). As individuals, rural producers often have poor access to market information and little access to market outlets, putting them at a real disadvantage. Associations can help producers collect and disseminate market information, improve overall bargaining power, and identify new markets. This changes the power balance and helps local enterprises exercise greater control within the market chain (Best et al. 2005:22-23).

Cooperatives are the most common rural enterprise association, offering many examples of successfully organizing nature-based businesses. In 1980, tribal groups in the Mayurbhanj District of Orissa, India, formed a cooperative to harvest and sell sabai, a durable grass used for making rope and string. Prior to that time, local sabai harvesters were at the mercy of traders, who dominated access to markets. The cooperative successfully altered market dynamics in the area by gaining the support of the State Cooperative Department, which helped broker a deal with the State Forest Department in which it promised to purchase sabai only from recognized cooperatives. Since the Forest Department was a large buyer of processed sabai for bundling timber and other forest products, this represented a significant economic opportunity (Harper and Roy 2000:96–97).

Cooperatives have been important organizing forces in countless other commodity areas as well. In Latin America, most small-scale coffee farmers are members of cooperatives that provide technical and marketing assistance to individuals and often give them access to credit or invest in community infrastructure and education. Fair trade certifications for thousands of these cooperatives allow some 420,000 farmers in Latin America to bypass the national coffee purchasing system that historically offered low prices and has boosted these farmers' incomes by between 100 and 200 percent in some cases (Taylor et al. 2003:6-10).

Beyond cooperatives, which are associations of individual producers, rural enterprises also find advantages in banding together in regional networks or clusters to work on mutual technical and marketing concerns. In Nicaragua, 11 small hammock makers—each with about 15 employees—formed a legally constituted business consortium called EcoHamaca with the help of the United Nations Industrial Development Organization (UNIDO). Prior to the formation of the group, the hammock makers had competed in the local market. But once convinced of the need to pool resources, their association allowed them to reconceptualize their product designs and production approaches. For example, they realized that by making their designs more eco-friendly they could enter the lucrative European and United States markets, so they shifted to using natural dyes and substituted more abundant

Continues on page 103

BOX 2.6 CURING POVERTY?
TAKING ADVANTAGE OF THE MEDICINALS MARKET

EVEN IN THE ERA OF MODERN, LAB-DESIGNED pharmaceuticals, medicinal plants are big business. Approximately 47 percent of conventional drugs on the market today are either natural products or directly derived from these products (Newman and Cragg 2007:461). Pharmaceutical companies are putting more resources than ever into bioprospecting in the hopes of finding new cures hidden in the world's forests and deserts (Kursar et al. 2006:1006). In 2007, the global trade in medicinal plants was estimated at US$78 billion and growing, propelled by a burgeoning alternative health care market and increasing demand for natural cosmetics across the United States and Europe. Experts predict that the medicinals trade will continue to grow at about 7 percent annually for the foreseeable future (Lambert et al. 2005:21). Such expansion presents a prime opportunity for rural, nature-based enterprises to capitalize on a market in which they hold a natural advantage. But it also highlights the challenge of advancing what has always been a low-margin business for rural residents into a higher-value enterprise—and doing so without overexploiting the fragile natural resource base.

Rural Advantage

Rural and indigenous communities hold a comparative advantage when it comes to medicinal plant collection and preparation since they already account for much of the global production and use of medicinals. For many rural residents, harvesting medicinals is an important—although limited—contributor to total income. For example, studies show that in India's western Himalaya, nomadic tribes rely on medicinal plant cultivation and sales for 5–10 percent of their income (Shekhar and Badola 2000:275). In rural Kwazulu-Natal in South Africa, the 16,000 medicinal plant gatherers in the region earn an average of between US$67 and US$98 per month for their efforts (Mander 1998:Sec. 5.4). Medicinals also provide direct health benefits to people across the developing world, 80 percent of whom use such treatments as their primary source of health care (WHO 2006). With the knowledge and resources that these communities currently use in their medicinals production, they seem well situated to play a central role in the growing global medicinals market.

Dual Challenges:
Capturing Value, Harvesting Sustainably

Rural communities must address two major challenges if they are to use medicinal plants to their advantage in the long term.

The first is for villagers to capture more value from the medicinals they harvest, requiring a shift away from the current system in which most benefits accrue to pharmaceutical companies and intermediary traders. The second challenge is to make medicinal plant collection more sustainable by reversing the habitat degradation and overharvesting trends common in commercial medicinal production. Fortunately, experience indicates that the solutions to these problems are often complementary.

Ninety percent of the medicinals that are traded on the global market are still harvested from the wild, even though many studies have indicated the importance of increasing medicinal cultivation to meet growing global demand (FAO 2005:5; Schippmann et al. 2002:8–11). The low prices received by harvesting communities and the habitat degradation associated with plant collection stem from the fact that, in most instances, there are no effective government or community controls on the harvest of wild medicinal plants—a de facto open-access situation that undermines ecosystem health and disadvantages poor rural residents, who typically have little market power.

The reality of the supply side is that harvesters rarely own the land on which they harvest (Schippmann et al. 2002:7,10–11). The individuals who collect the specimens tend to work alone, selling their raw products to traders and processors. In areas where employment options are few, these collectors are willing to devote many hours to collection and must accept whatever the traders offer them at the end of the day. Frequently, harvesters are forced to travel farther and farther to find wild medicinal stocks as plants disappear with overharvesting and habitat destruction caused by timber cuts and land conversion (Mander 1998:Sec. 5.1.1.1). One estimate suggests that such destruction and overcollection has led to the endangerment of more than 4,000 medicinal plants worldwide (Schippmann et al 2002:3–4).

The Prunus Africana tree of Cameroon is one of these endangered plants. P. Africana was once harvested primarily by locals who used it for wooden tools and to treat chest pain and malaria (WWF 2002:1). In the 1970s, pharmaceutical companies began to use the plant's bark to treat prostate gland hypertrophy. Cameroon's government eventually allowed all pharmaceutical companies access to its forests as a way to promote competition, and unsustainable harvest practices became the norm. When these practices combined with ongoing deforestation, the P. Africana population plummeted. The rural communities, left without their once-common medicinal resource, reaped few commercial benefits from the deforestation. The trees' harvesters were either outsiders working for foreign pharmaceutical companies or locals who gained little for their efforts because they accepted the low prices offered by intermediary traders (Stewart 2003:566–567).

A New Model:
Community Management of Medicinals

Cameroon's failure to address the open-access issue illustrates the need for national governments and communities to proactively create and enforce guidelines for the medicinals market. Today governments, communities, NGOs, and donors are learning how best to support such efforts. Sri Lanka, Nepal, India, and Ethiopia are a few of the countries serving as test grounds in recent medicinal plant development projects.

Between 1998 and 2004, the World Bank partnered with the Sri Lankan government to establish community management systems for biodiverse areas known to have medicinal species. The Bank contracted with NGOs to help 29 villages form Medicinal Plant Conservation Areas on state-owned lands, meant to act as buffers between village domains and state forest reserves. Village Project Management Committees, partnering with the NGOs and local researchers, oversaw the study of medicinal plants within the area and developed plans for harvesting them sustainably and monitoring their populations over time. The communities involved also started communal gardens in which they cultivated medicinal plants to augment their collection of wild stock. The effort created a greater awareness among local populations of conservation methods and experience with joint forest management practices (Crown 2004:4–5,8–10,46). At the end of the six-year project period, the Bank considered the outcomes and future potential for the project successful enough to pursue a similar effort in Ethiopia (World Bank 2001).

In Nepal, thousands of communities have spent the last 12 years working with NGOs, the U.S. Agency for International Development, and other donors to grow the medicinals market under the state's decentralized forestry law (USAID 2006). NGOs like the Asia Network for Sustainable Agriculture and Bioresources (ANSAB) have helped many of the country's Community Forestry User Groups to craft sustainable harvest plans for medicinal plants and other non-timber forest products and to build processing facilities to add value to them. In 2006 ANSAB's technical and networking efforts, which included securing "organic" and "sustainably harvested" certifications for many forest-derived products, helped more than 65,000 villagers take in US$5.54 million in additional monetary benefits (ANSAB 2007:2). The certified products include 17 different essential oils, such as jatamansi, and 44 single-ingredient herbs, such as juniper, which have various uses in Ayurvedic (a traditional form of Indian health care), Chinese, and modern medicine (ANSAB 2005; Subedi 2001:4–6).

Business's Evolving Role:
The Example of Gram Mooligai Co, Ltd.

Based in Bangalore in southern India, Gram Mooligai Co, Ltd. (GMCL) is a medicinals processing company that uses a different business model from Nepal's community ventures to capitalize on the medicinals market and achieve environmental and social aims. Founded in 2002 with a grant from the Ford Foundation, the company is owned by self-organized groups of medicinal plant gatherers and cultivators from across southern India who hold the company's shares. The company buys all of its raw stock of medicinals from these groups, eliminating intermediaries from its supply chain. As a policy, it pays producers 70 percent of product sale prices to obtain the raw stock—a very high return (GMCL 2006:2). On average, harvesters make a seasonal income of about 3,500 rupees (US$88) per year—a critical contribution for low-income families (Raju 2006: 8).

To protect medicinal plant stocks from overexploitation, GMCL partners with Indian non-profits to train harvesters to carry out their work in a sustainable manner (GMCL 2006:2). The company also encourages organic cultivation of medicinals to augment wild supplies and ease the work of plant collection. The company has established a 12-ha test farm to fine-tune methods for organic plant cultivation. The lessons learned on the farm are then integrated into the training program for producers (GMCL 2006:8).

As part of its larger mission, GCML's business model emphasizes helping women and poor rural consumers. The company fosters rural employment by encouraging women's self-help groups to sell the company's medicinal products in the countryside; the women's groups make 150 rupees for every 500 rupees of medicine they sell (Indian NGOs 2007). At the same time, GMCL hopes that these rural sales will help meet some of the unmet health care needs of the poor. The medicine sold in these areas is certified by Ayurvedic physicians and targets the most common ailments of the rural population (GMCL 2006: 9). The company expects such rural sales to eventually account for 20–30 percent of its total market (GMCL 2006:7).

Overall, Gram Mooligai's business strategy seems to be working. In fiscal year 2005–2006, the company achieved sales of more than US$240,000 (Raju 2006:7,8). Having doubled its sales since 2002, GMCL hopes to expand into northern India and capture 3 percent of the country's medicinals market within the next 5 years (GMCL 2006:6). The company's success is testament to the potential for economic and social impact and environmental sustainability that exists in the medicinals market under the right conditions. With care, medicinals can connect the traditional knowledge and practices of rural communities with the global market economy.

BOX 2.7 ETHIOPIAN COFFEE COOPERATIVES: LEVERAGE THROUGH NETWORKS

THE HUMID MOUNTAINS OF SOUTHWESTERN Ethiopia are the legendary birthplace of Arabica coffee—the most prized coffee variety—and coffee imbues the nation's culture and economy. Ethiopians are some of the world's biggest coffee drinkers per capita, consuming about half of the 280,000 tons of beans the country produces each year (Dempsey and Campbell 2006:5). The remaining coffee is exported, accounting for more than a third of the country's total exports—about US$424 million in fiscal year 2006–2007 (The Economist 2007).

Some 94 percent of Ethiopian coffee is grown by smallholders on 1–2 ha plots, most of it using organic methods (Dempsey 2006:1; Weihe 2005:12). Small coffee producers in Ethiopia, as in many countries, generally earn little from their labors, and poverty among coffee farmers is widespread. But reforms within the nation's coffee sector are bringing change. In the last decade, coffee farmers have revitalized their system of coffee cooperatives and improved their product quality. Greater differentiation of the distinctive flavors produced by different growers and the introduction of organic certification have also added value to the best of the Ethiopian beans, so that they command a higher price. In concert with government reforms of the coffee sales and export system, these changes have allowed many Ethiopian producers to reach more specialized and higher-valued markets, thus increasing income for many farmers.

Reviving Cooperatives, Building Federations

Fundamental to the reform of Ethiopia's coffee sector has been the revival of the nation's coffee cooperatives. Until recently, cooperatives in Ethiopia had fallen into disfavor among farmers because of government interference. The former military regime had used them as a means to control farm production rather than to meet farmers' needs. With the end of military rule in 1991, Ethiopia's new government emphasized liberalizing markets and driving growth through the agricultural sector. This left an opening to reinvent farmer cooperatives and make them more farmer-friendly and market-savvy (Kodama 2007:88–89; McCarthy 2007).

To undertake this task, the Ethiopian Government and the US Agency for International Development (USAID) partnered with a Washington-based NGO called ACDI/VOCA that specializes in agricultural assistance and capacity-building. The first step in rebuilding the legitimacy of cooperatives was to bring a diverse group of Ethiopian officials, farmers, and cooperative directors to visit successful cooperatives in Kenya and the United States

in the early 1990s (Dorsey and Assefa 2005:8). This demonstrated not only the marketing benefits of cooperatives but also their potential as democratic associations acting on behalf of their members.

To help regenerate the cooperative structure, ACDI/VOCA began a farmer-to-farmer training program in 1995. Encouraged by its success, the leaders of the coffee cooperatives involved—along with ACDI/VOCA—petitioned the government to allow them to federate into larger regional associations, called cooperative "unions," to increase their market power and facilitate technical training and coordination. In 1998, the government agreed, and in 1999 the Oromia Coffee Farmers' Cooperative Union was created. Since then, five more coffee unions have formed (Dorsey and Assefa 2005:8–9; Dempsey 2006:4; Kodama 2007:90).

Union leaders have been trained in topics ranging from accounting to bean selection to processing and quality control methods. These leaders are asked, in turn, to train the managers of the different cooperatives within the union. The cooperative managers then train farmers within individual cooperatives, assuring a chain of consistent, high-quality, traceable beans (Dempsey 2006:8).

The government strengthened the role of the cooperatives and unions significantly when it modified its coffee-marketing policies in 2001. Prior to that time, Ethiopian law required coffee cooperatives to sell their products through a national coffee auction rather than directly to roasters and retailers around the world. This requirement meant that coffees, often regardless of quality or region of origin, were lumped together and sold at one price, creating a "lowest common denominator" problem for cooperatives that were working to increase

their bean quality and distinguish their unique regional flavors (Kodama 2007:91; Dempsey and Campbell 2006:5). When the government abandoned this requirement and allowed cooperatives to sell their own products directly, it created a more-efficient and profitable marketing pathway. Producers could now sell their beans to cooperatives, which would then sell to their cooperative union, and unions would directly export their products to wholesalers and retailers worldwide (Kodama 2007:91).

Federating into cooperative unions has brought many advantages, such as greater efficiency and a coordinated, market-chain approach to production and sales. Cooperatives jointly contract for transportation and warehousing, share technical knowledge, and develop solutions to address common logistical problems. They also share market information and business contacts (Dempsey and Campbell 2006:7). ACDI/VOCA has brought union leaders together with experts in Fair Trade and organic certification to help cooperatives get certified. By 2006, more than 70 cooperatives were certified organic and 24 were registered as Fair Trade cooperatives (Dempsey 2006:6; Dempsey and Campbell 2006:6). Fair Trade–certified producers are assured a

minimum price for their beans, which at US$1.26–1.60 a pound can be up to twice the international commodity market price (Geographical 2005:38; Dempsey 2006:6).

Nurturing Direct Trade

Today, roasters and importers around the world buy directly from Ethiopian coffee unions and cooperatives. With improved bean quality and product consistency, coffee unions have been able to concentrate on promoting the impressive array of distinct tastes and aromas from beans originating in different Ethiopian cooperatives. This can translate into a competitive advantage in the world of specialty coffees, in which recognized producers of unique beans can command a considerable price premium. In 2005, for example, Starbucks designated a sun-dried coffee from Ferro Cooperative—a member of the Sidama Union—as a "Black Apron Exclusive" and eventually sold it in its stores for about US$26 per pound (ACDI/VOCA 2006b:16; Olsen 2007).

BOX 2.7 ETHIOPIAN COFFEE COOPERATIVES

Ethiopian coffee marketing has even advanced to the point where there are national contests such as the E-Cafe Gold Cooperative Coffee Competition, in which judges select Ethiopia's best cooperative coffees to market internationally in an Internet auction. In 2005, the average price obtained in this auction was US$3.22 per pound, compared with 65 cents for a pound of regular Ethiopian coffee obtained through the national coffee auction. These direct relationships between cooperatives and roasters have helped raise Ethiopia's profile as a quality coffee producer and will likely spur continued exploration by roasters and retailers for distinct flavors from the region (ACDI/VOCA 2006a:9; ICO 2008).

Cooperative Benefits

Farmers involved in these changes consistently indicate that they are better off, reporting increased household wealth, asset accumulation, higher education levels for their children, improved nutrition levels, and an expansion of farm activities as a result of cooperative membership. They also report more job opportunities across their communities as coffee plots and other crops expanded (Mekasha 2005:19).

New financing mechanisms set up in a partnership between USAID and three Ethiopian banks have also increased the well-being of cooperative members. These banks issue short-term loans to the coffee unions and cooperatives to purchase raw coffee beans each year, providing the initial incentive for farmers to enter the collective process. Many cooperatives use

their earnings and pooled dividends to invest in local infrastructure such as roads, power lines, health care facilities, and schools (Dempsey and Campbell 2006:7; Dorsey and Assefa 2005:49; Mekasha 2005:19). In addition, the federated cooperative structure provides an effective network to achieve other social goals, such as reaching out to rural communities with HIV/AIDS prevention workshops (Wagner:8–9).

Challenges Ahead

Despite the positive repercussions of Ethiopia's specialty coffee boom in some communities, benefits are still limited to a small percentage of producers. Within the Yirgacheffe Union, for example, only 13 percent of coffee is directly exported (Kodoma 2007:96). The rest still flows through the national coffee auction and is subject to international commodity coffee prices that have sometimes reached crisis lows in the last decade due to global overproduction.

One difficulty that the unions must address is that they are, in many ways, victims of their own success. Their achievements in improving the quality and marketing of Ethiopian coffee have led many international roasters and retailers to do business directly with the best cooperatives, leaving fewer specialty buyers to purchase from the unions (McCarthy 2007). This means less funding for the unions to provide training and support for their members. The cooperatives that remain in the unions are in turn unwilling to pay for union membership unless they receive tangible benefits. When cooperatives end up selling through the auction, farmers often leave them to supply directly to traders and thus save themselves the cooperative membership fees.

If the unions can overcome this structural challenge, however, their established network might help address another problem that Ethiopian farmers face: the need to diversify economic opportunities. With such diversification and strong unions, poor farmers will gradually depend less on the volatile coffee industry even as their share of the profit from the coffee they produce grows (Mekasha 2005:17; Dorsey and Assefa 2005:12–13).

102

woods for the rare cedar they had used before. They also adopted the collective brand "Made in Masaya" to promote a local identity. With improved product quality, design, and pricing, the EcoHamaca group was able to successfully penetrate the export market, eventually shipping more than 3,000 hammocks per month (Kanungo 2004:1–2).

Despite the clear advantages, organizing and sustaining cooperatives and other producer associations is not simple. For example, most rural cooperatives start from a base of inexperience, with members who possess low skill levels and little business experience. They attempt to organize in the most difficult economic circumstances, in rural markets that are highly dispersed and very brand- and price-conscious, making their products that much harder to market. For business consortia, setting aside distrust and competitiveness among members is often a major barrier, and frequently requires an outside catalyst, such as an NGO or government department. In addition, co-ops or consortia often require considerable funding from outside sources in order to get off the ground, and finances remain a challenge even for successful associations (Philip 2003:21; Hellin et al. 2007:26; Kanungo 2004:6–7).

Promoting Product Standards and Market Research

Producer associations are an ideal forum in which to develop standards for product quality, harvesting practices, or manufacturing methods to help producers improve their product positioning and reputation. In northeast Brazil, for example, the Valexport producer association helps farmers in the Petrolina-Juazeiro area maintain their melon quality—and export prices—at a high level.

NETWORK PROFILE: COMMUNITY MARKETS FOR CONSERVATION (COMACO), LUANGWA VALLEY, ZAMBIA

Community Markets for Conservation, or COMACO, is a commercial network with a conservation mission, working to expand livelihood opportunities for rural communities in eastern Zambia. Every year, thousands of tourists flock to the Luangwa Valley to visit its game parks. But its people are very poor, with average household incomes under US$200 (Lewis 2005:2). Poverty and food insecurity have encouraged unsustainable agricultural practices and a high incidence of game hunting for subsistence and sale in local markets. Hoping to break this destructive poverty-environment linkage, the Wildlife Conservation Society, an international NGO, formed the COMACO network in 2002 (Middleton 2008).

The centerpiece of COMACO's work is the agricultural extension service it offers to small producer groups of 10–20 households at regional training offices (WCS 2007). At these bases of operation throughout the valley, paid extension officers and volunteers have taught 30,000 villagers—representing over 2,500 producer groups—about livestock care and basic conservation farming techniques, such as natural composting and land preparation without burning. With these techniques, farmers grow higher-quality produce and can provide enough food for their families, even in times of drought. (WCS 2007; Middleton 2008). Upon receiving training from the extension officers, producer group members sign a contract committing themselves to the conservation farming practices in return for the additional benefits that membership in COMACO offers. Included in these benefits are training in other types of farming and access to free and subsidized farm inputs provided by COMACO (WCS 2006a:1).

The biggest incentive that COMACO offers for joining the network and adhering to the contract is that the organization purchases produce with high value-added potential—such as rice, soybeans, honey, peanuts, and fresh vegetables—from network farmers at premium prices. After collecting the produce at its regional centers, COMACO processes and packages the foods at one of its three major plants and sells them under COMACO's "It's Wild" brand through its Web site, in tourist lodges, and in urban markets (Lewis 2005:3; WCS 2007). The producer groups own 20 percent of COMACO shares, and thus receive dividends when the company makes a profit (COMACO 2004:1).

COMACO's extension work and premium payments to farmers are part of a larger strategy to overhaul the incentive structure for Luangwa's farmers, increasing their farm and non-farm income so that they can become less reliant on game hunting and environmentally destructive farming practices (Lewis 2005:3). As part of this strategy, citizens who hand over the firearms they use for game hunting receive an eight-week training course in goat husbandry, beekeeping, dry-season gardening, fish farming, and carpentry in the Poacher Transformation Program (WCS 2007). In addition, COMACO offers those who grow and plant tree seedlings to minimize soil erosion an extra price premium for their produce (COMACO 2007a). COMACO has also helped form an ecotourism enterprise of bush camp accommodations and a line of jewelry made from animal snares that farmers have turned in as part of the Poacher Transformation Program (COMACO 2007b). As it matures and continues to offer an expanded slate of capacity-building and marketing services, COMACO has taken on many of the characteristics of an intermediary support organization, with the goal of geographically scaling its effects throughout eastern Zambia. It has also taken on ISO characteristics in its work with local and national government officials and NGOs at all levels as it expands.

While not yet financially self-sufficient, COMACO has produced positive results for the communities of the Luangwa Valley during its five-plus years of work. One thousand households have begun to grow dry-season gardens and fruit trees using the solar-powered fences COMACO has helped finance. Farmers are now eating more fish, thanks to the 150 fish ponds COMACO has facilitated. On-farm composting combined with other conservation farming techniques (skills taught in COMACO's extension courses) helped increase maize yields of participating farmers by over 19 percent between 2005 and 2006 (WCS 2006b:4). And hunters that formerly used illegal techniques to catch wild game have doubled their legal incomes since joining the program. In fact, former hunters surrendered 40,000 illegal snares and 800 firearms between 2001 and 2006. As a consequence, the local wildlife population has stabilized and slightly increased in some places—a trend that suggests that the network's commercial and conservation missions are compatible (WCS 2006; WCS 2007).

In the 1980s, Petrolina-Juazeiro emerged as a leading melon region, producing year-round fruit for export to European markets. As word of the lucrative business spread, new growers emerged, many of which had little experience. Product quality fell and the region's reputation was tarnished, lowering melon prices (Locke 2002:24).

As a result, four of the area's largest producers formed Valexport. Within a few months 43 additional members had joined, and today Valexport's members include over 200 local producers of different sizes. The association has set region-wide quality standards and routinely collects data on quality control among its members to enforce its standards (Locke 2002:24).

TABLE 2.3 ECOSYSTEM-BASED ENTERPRISE ASSOCIATIONS AROUND THE WORLD

ASSOCIATION	LOCALE	YEAR EST.	MEMBERS	WORK	SELECT ACCOMPLISHMENTS
KLONGNARAI WOMEN'S GROUP Source: Kruijsse and Somsri 2006	Chanthaburi, Thailand	1983	40 women	Women's cooperative cultivates, harvests, processes into various food products, and markets shoots and berries from the local cowa tree.	Women own shares of cooperative, which has attained a profit margin of 18 percent. Members get credit through the cooperative and use cooperative equipment to increase efficiency.
LAGOS STATE FISH FARMERS' ASSOCIATION Source: Basorun and Olakulehin 2007	Lagos, Nigeria	2004	2,100 fish farmers	Association provides marketing strategies and technological information, and also purchases inputs in bulk.	Fish production doubled from 2005 to 2007. Fish production cycle reduced from 8 months to 5 months.
FARMER FIELD SCHOOL (FFS) NETWORKS Source: Braun et al. 2007	Kenya, Uganda, Tanzania	2000	50,000 farmers	Networks coordinate farmer exchanges, help farmers purchase agricultural inputs in bulk, arrange for managerial skills training, and help coordinate product processing and marketing.	Kenya's Kakamega District network, one of 2,000 FFS networks in East Africa, helped farmers process and add value to sweet potatoes, resulting in higher market prices for their produce.
ASSOCIATION OF PALQUI PRODUCERS (APROPALQUI) Source: UNDP Energy and Environment Group 2006:4-6	Potos, Bolivia	2003	31 families	Association manages, processes, and conducts marketing workshops to sustainably use native palqui plants for food and medicinals.	In 2004, each family received US$16 profit from their combined 812 kg of processed palqui.
NAM HA ECOGUIDE SERVICE Source: UNDP 2006a	Luan Namtha, Lao PDR	2001	100 workers	Association trains local villagers as ecoguides, lodge operators, and biodiversity monitors so they can manage ecotourism businesses in and around Lao PDR's protected areas.	From 2001 to 2006, Nam Ha–trained guides earned US$116,603 from 7,700 tourists, and $11,400 more went to village development funds to construct local infrastructure.
WOMEN'S NETWORK OF MEDICINAL AND AROMATIC PLANT PRODUCERS AND RETAILERS (RMPCPMA) Source: UNDP Energy and Environment Group 2006:29-31	Choco, Colombia	1996	85 women	Women's network cultivates, processes, brands, and markets medicinal and herbal plants.	Family incomes have increased 25 percent. Indirectly creates jobs for 385 people in small, mining-dominated community.
SOLOLA ASSOCIATION OF ORGANIC PRODUCERS (APOCS) Source: UNDP Energy and Environment Group 2006:52-54	Rio Abajo, Guatemala	2000	700 farmers	Association links community organizations for watershed planning, coffee processing, and organic certification of farm products.	Members receive 40 percent more for their organic products than traditional farmers. Some products sold in the United States and Europe.

Associations can be important facilitators for achieving product certifications, such as "organic," "sustainably produced," or "Fair Trade"—designations that can add value to products and allow producers to enter select markets. In Nepal, FECOFUN, the national federation of Community Forest User Groups, has helped pioneer new certification standards for many different "sustainably harvested" forest products through the Forest Stewardship Council (FSC) and has encouraged forest user groups to meet these standards as part of their business models. By 2006, 21 communities were harvesting forest products in accordance with the new FSC standards (Pokharel et al 2006:27).

Producer associations are also well positioned to help their members conduct market analyses so that they can tailor their production and marketing efforts better. This involves assessing the current and potential market for a given product, determining the main actors in the commodity chain, and identifying bottlenecks in the supply chain. In Honduras, the Consorcio Local para el Desarrollo de la Cuenca del Rio Tascalapa, a local consortium of farmer organizations in the Yorito region, conducted a market chain analysis for coffee in which it identified critical points and problems in the coffee chain. The analysis, which was jointly undertaken by producers, processors, and traders, brought improved communication to the group and resulted in some farmers deciding to seek organic certification for their coffee (Best et al. 2005:38).

Accessing Credit and Finance

Associations act as important channels for rural finance, providing an access point to microcredit, private finance, or government support programs for small businesses. They provide an organ-

ized and recognized face for producer groups—one that funders can use as a node for communication and contact with dispersed rural enterprises (Macqueen et al. 2006:8). When Indian artisan producers of calico prints created the Calico Printers Cooperative Society in 1999, they gained the attention of the government, which wanted to help small-scale textile producers increase exports of their products by investing in new processes and marketing contacts. As a result, the Small Industries Development Bank of India created the Mutual Credit Guarantee Scheme for calico print makers, which provided microcredit worth Rs 1.5 million to 65 artisans in the co-op. Similarly, small businesses in Nicaragua that joined producer associations or consortia with the help of UNIDO benefited from more than US$300,000 in new investment that they would not have attracted otherwise and gained access to US$100,000 in credit for joint activities (Kanungo 2004:3–4).

Building Learning Networks

By participating in associations, small-scale producers can build learning networks through informal meetings, workshops, site visits, e-mail exchanges, and other types of knowledge sharing. Such exchanges can help spread the latest information on sustainable farming practices, agroforestry, wildlife management, aquaculture, and other knowledge-intensive livelihoods. The learning networks that result allow producers to solve problems collectively, share approaches, and break out of traditional patterns of resource use that may be unsustainable, inefficient, or unprofitable. This important aspect of capacity-building is often self-generated—and self-scaling—when producers are given a forum in which to interact.

In Cuba, the National Association of Small Farmers (ANAP) started a sustainable farming initiative known as the Farmer to Farmer Movement. ANAP worked with farmers, local cooperatives, and government agencies to quickly spread the adoption of sustainable farming practices following the food crisis of the early 1990s, using workshops, farm demonstrations, and other learning exchanges. The Farmer to Farmer Movement was so successful in its information networking that it grew to include 100,000 smallholders in just eight years (Holt-Giménez 2006:37, 173).

In the El Angel watershed of Northern Ecuador, a different kind of learning network evolved, called the Carchi Consortium. The group originally formed as a forum for scientists to share technical information on water issues in the area. It eventually evolved to include not just scientists but also representatives from water associations and farmer groups from around the watershed—many of whom had long been concerned about the use and allocation of water. The consortium's effectiveness rests on its ability to act as a clearinghouse for unbiased information on water flows. As such, the consortium helped end much of the suspicion that plagued earlier debates between farmers. Today, the consortium has expanded in its influence by pulling together additional stakeholders, including representatives from three neighboring

CONNECTION

NETWORKS ENHANCE RESILIENCE

Networks and associations help build the ecological, social, and economic resilience of rural communities and the ecosystems they manage for enterprise:

Ecological Resilience

- *Networks aid adaptive management.* Because they facilitate knowledge sharing among communities and experts with the same ecosystem concerns, networks directly contribute to adaptive management—management that makes changes based on changing conditions or new data, technologies, or capabilities. This kind of learning-based management is a recognized feature of sustainable ecosystem use.

- *Networks enable a synoptic view.* They allow village-level leaders to gain a larger-scale view of ecosystems and their management. Linking with other communities brings a larger geographic scale to bear, so that community management systems can be informed by and connected to management efforts in adjacent ecosystems and can remain aware of synergistic effects.

Social Resilience

- *Networks enhance social capital.* They enlarge the social capital pool by connecting it to other like-minded groups and communities and expanding the universe of useful group processes and experiences, as well as by introducing new ideas and norms of inclusion and public good. In addition, they institutionalize this social capital in official associations, allowing it to take on a legally recognized and commercially relevant form.

Economic Resilience

- *Networks increase commercial access.* They widen and stabilize market penetration, allow businesses to capture greater value from their efforts, provide a route for new technology, act as a conduit for micro or conventional finance, and make available good business practices and opportunities for skills development and training.

municipalities in the watershed. In so doing, it has become both a forum for regional water planning and a de facto dispute resolution mechanism (Carter and Currie-Alder 2006:132–133).

One important aspect of learning networks is their ability to reduce "innovation time"—the time it takes to learn about, understand, adapt, and apply new ideas that will benefit the enterprise. The ANAI Association reports that when it first started working in Costa Rica in the 1970s, it took on average seven years to adopt important new ideas and adapt them to the local situation. Now the ISO says that the communities that it mentors and partners with require only on average two years to take on and implement new ideas of a similar scale and complexity, due to the much larger network of like-minded communities in the region today that support the innovation process by sharing local experiences (Southey 2008).

Engaging Political Processes

Small-scale producers are not known for their influence. At the national level, most small rural enterprises that "go it alone" are politically marginalized compared with their corporate and state-owned counterparts (Macqueen et al. 2005:89; Pimbert 2006: 21). Associations can help producers engage the political process by coordinating and amplifying their voice. They provide a forum for reaching consensus on policy issues and crafting a uniform message that can become the basis for effective lobbying. Associations that are adept at political networking are prime actors in the political scaling of rural nature-based enterprises (Hooper et al. 2004:132; Bebbington and Carroll 2000:9).

The Costa Rican Organic Agricultural Movement (MAOCO) is an example of an umbrella association that has been very effective at influencing local and national farm policy, even as it has catalyzed communication and better product standards within its membership. The network grew out of efforts by smallholders and local NGOs to increase support for organic farming in Costa Rica. Over time, MAOCO attracted champions within government by strategically engaging state officials and universities. It worked on a scale small enough for farmers and their representatives to liaise with local agriculture officials but large enough to engage the national agriculture ministry and development agencies (UNDP 2006b:36–37).

As a result, MAOCO has helped establish a more unified voice on organic farming at a variety of levels. At the local level, MAOCO gave farmers a forum to share lessons and challenges regarding organic farming. At the national and regional levels, MAOCO worked to establish guidelines for the production, preparation, and marketing of organic products. MAOCO eventually helped replace an outdated law on organic farming, paving the way for new organic farming standards and raising awareness among other farmers—organic or not—about the benefits and requirements of organic farming. In addition, MAOCO's work has helped inform a National Strategy for Organic Agriculture (UNDP 2006b:36).

To increase the scale of their political influence, local producer associations often federate into regional or national groups that represent the interests of many similar businesses and present a uniform position on state policies, as well as a convenient contact point for government officials. Federations are associations themselves, but they have a membership base of organizations, not individual enterprises or producers. Many federations exist at the national and state levels, though some operate regionally and internationally.

In 1995, a number of Nepal's Community Forest User Groups established the Federation of Community Forest Users Nepal (FECOFUN) to represent their interests at the national level. By 2005, some 9,000 of the country's 14,000 CFUGs had joined the federation, giving it considerable political clout as well as the ability to offer its members a wide range of technical and marketing services. The federation enables member communities to share information on forest management, biological monitoring, timber and NTFP sales, management plans, and marketing strategies. Politically, FECOFUN's influence has grown over the years as it has forged links with the national ministry that oversees Nepal's land management system. In partnership with the Asian Network for Sustainable Agriculture and Bioresources, FECOFUN played an active role in encouraging the government to develop a national policy on the harvesting of herbs and other non-timber forest products—an area that directly affects the household income of CFUG members. The federation has subsequently become the holder of FSC certification for the sustainable harvest of 23 different forest products. As its confidence and lobbying power has grown, FECOFUN has begun to help local user groups appeal to the government for management rights over larger areas (Pokaharel et al. 2006:17; ANSAB 2005b:5–20)

As FECOFUN's experience shows, federations and umbrella groups can become powerful tools for amplifying local concerns into an effective appeal for expanded rights. In Burkina Faso, an alliance of agricultural producers called the Coordination Framework for Rural Producer Organizations (CCOF in French) has been successful in bringing the concerns of smallholder farmers to government policymakers. The group formed in 1988 when the government began to make changes in national land tenure policies. Government policymakers had not consulted smallholder farmers, and the new tenure policies tended to advantage large farms and agribusinesses and to ignore local customary institutions for land management. CCOF's efforts have helped reorient the tenure policymaking process so that new tenure laws accord equal rights to smallholders (Conway et al. 2002:4).

The Challenges of Association

Formal networking via associations offers indisputable benefits for rural producers, but it also poses challenges, particularly for the poor. By design, many associations are exclusive, open only to the membership of certain individuals or enterprises. Farming cooperatives, for example, tend to only benefit those with land. Furthermore, the formal status of many associations can be restrictive and confounding to rural producers, particularly those who are used to working outside of legal structures. Lack of technical and financial capacity are also common problems that hold rural associations back.

The Closed Doors of Membership Organizations

By their nature, associations are exclusive and not always supportive of the neediest in society. For example, while dairy cooperatives in the Indian state of Gujarat have been highly successful at organizing their members and remaking the Indian dairy market, they have been less successful at opening their doors to low-income producers. Village-level studies suggest that preexisting inequalities—in both land ownership and enforced by caste makeup—are reflected in the makeup of cooperatives (Marsh 2003:40-45).

To address the problem of exclusion, some governments and donors have experimented with quotas that force the inclusion of women and marginalized groups in cooperatives or resource user groups. In Nepal, for example, the government amended its irrigation policy in 1997 to mandate that women account for at least 20 percent of all members of water user associations. Such mandates are often insufficient to spur real acceptance of underrepresented groups, but capacity-building programs have proved effective in some cases. During one canal rehabilitation project funded by the Asian Development Bank, membership of women in the local water user association grew from 25 percent to over 60 percent when a program to train women in canal management and maintenance was included, directed by a newly formed Women's Facilitator Group within the larger water user association (Shrestha 2004:15–17).

Another form of exclusion sometimes encountered in rural associations is related to size. Larger enterprises within an association may seek to exclude smaller ones because they view them as of marginal value to the organization. Sometimes this is a result of institutional failures within a cooperative, where stronger members are able to leverage more decision-making power. In Brazil, the Valexport producer association was initially created for the region's largest and most profitable melon producers. It was not until the government exerted pressure on the cooperative that it opened its doors to smaller producers (Locke 2002:28). Associations also often become less inclusive as they expand beyond their original local areas, with new participants expected to demonstrate a minimum level of experience and wealth (Marsh 2003:26).

The Problem of Informality

Many associations have a formal or legal status that confers a recognizable identity and, in some cases, legal rights. For example, they may be registered under business statutes or recognized under

CONNECTION

FEDERATION PROFILE: THE GUJARAT COOPERATIVE MILK MARKETING FEDERATION

In the Indian state of Gujarat, village dairy cooperatives work within a three-tiered structure of organization that is represented by the national Gujarat Cooperative Milk Marketing Federation. In the Gujarat model, village cooperatives are the lowest level of cooperative society, where membership is typically limited to producers. These cooperatives, however, elect representation in the form of a managing committee and chairperson, which represent the village cooperative at the district level. Cooperative organizations at the district level are called unions, which also elect representation, but for the state-level federation. Generally speaking, the village level handles procurement, the district level handles transportation and processing, and the federation makes decisions on investment, marketing, and planning.

The milk cooperative model in Gujarat was considered so successful that the government of India launched an initiative known as "Operation Flood" to replicate the model in other Indian States (Manikutty 2002:3). The government formed a coordinating agency called the National Dairy Development Board, which has helped scale up the Gujarat model and works with a total of 22 state federations, 170 district level unions, 72,774 village level societies, and 9.31 million milk producers (Manikutty 2002:4).

cooperative law. Thus, one advantage of associations is that they help bring rural enterprises out of the informal sector and increase their visibility and bargaining power with government or private sector actors.

However, making the transition from the informal sector is not always easy. A good deal of business in rural areas still occurs informally, and simple verbal arrangements often govern the rules of business transactions. For example, lending arrangements often rely more on trust and social standing than on financial and asset-based collateral. Partly because of this culture, taking steps toward formalizing rural institutions can be difficult (Marsh 2003:26; UNDP 2004:12).

Many rural workers do not even consider themselves involved in a sector, industry, or enterprise, especially if their work is only seasonal or part-time (Macqueen et al. 2005:84). In addition, much of the rural workforce is self-employed and therefore not necessarily inclined to join an association. In its work to build networks among small producers, UNIDO has found that small businesses are often loath to give up their competitive attitude toward other businesses to work together in a formal organization. Considerable attention to trust-building exercises is sometimes required (Kanungo 2004:3, 6–7). Simplifying regulations surrounding the registration of formal associations can also help reduce barriers to the formation of rural associations.

Even if rural workers and business owners are open to working together, they may be unaware of the possibilities to do so. In South Africa, the Sakhokuhle Association is an umbrella forestry organization for small forestry groups with 1,400 members. The coordinator of the program remarked that when the umbrella

organization was first starting, many forestry groups "had never heard of any umbrella association in forestry" (Bukula 2006:29).

The Involvement of Government

Government policies are critical to the success of rural associations. For one, they determine the rules under which associations can form as well as how they govern and support themselves. When governments favor associations, they can be a principal agent in their scaling up. In West Africa, for example, political liberalization over the past 10 years has directly contributed to the emergence of a number of new producer organizations (Pimbert 2006:13).

But government involvement in associations can be a mixed blessing. At times, governments have sought to use associations for their own political purposes, to the detriment of the associations. The postcolonial period in Africa witnessed a number of examples where governments exerted a paternalistic control over farmer cooperatives, dictating the terms of membership and issuing top-down directives. This bureaucratic approach belied the entrepreneurial nature in which many cooperatives initially formed, resulting in their eventual economic stagnation and disfavor (Chilongo 2005:6–9). Until recently, for example, many small coffee farmers in Ethiopia distrusted cooperatives because of their past affiliation with the government (McCarthy 2007).

In other instances, however, governments may discourage the formation of associations, perceiving them as pressure groups that may campaign against the policies of the state. This reluctance to grant groups the right to free association can be particularly troublesome for those in the informal rural economy, who tend not to be protected under trade unions or other labor laws. In 2002, the International Labour Organization (ILO) issued a recommendation that member states curb their political interference and control of national cooperative movements. The ILO encouraged governments to restrict their involvement to a regulatory and policy-setting role, instead of controlling cooperatives, and to revise their laws to bring them up to the standards put forward by the International Co-operative Alliance. By 2005, 15 countries had acted on the ILO's recommendation and had changed their laws governing cooperatives (Boyd 2005:9–10).

In addition to their political power over associations, governments also wield considerable financial control. In theory, associations have built-in mechanisms for generating revenue, such as membership fees or commissions for wholesaling their members' products. In practice, however, many fail to raise the funds to pay for staff and other support services for their members. This is particularly true of new associations that have not developed established markets. The truth is that many associations are in need of external support and may never get off the ground without start-up finance (Macqueen et al. 2005:84). Governments often fill this role, typically by providing grants, loans, and capacity-building services. While this can provide an essential lifeline, it can also compromise the association's independence and its ability to lobby for change in government policies (Pimbert 2006:13).

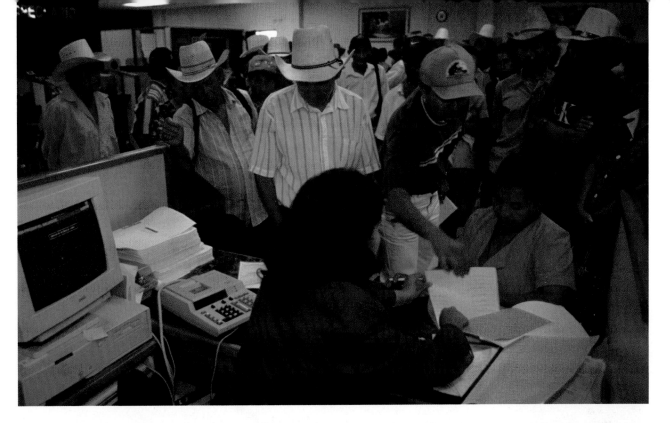

SUMMING UP: CONNECTION

- Networks represent dynamic connections between individuals, groups, and enterprises—a form of structured social capital. They can be informal, like learning networks or support groups, or more formalized, with rules and written charters, such as cooperatives, unions, trade groups, or federations. These more formalized networks we call *associations*.

- Networks and associations are the physical and institutional face of scaling up, giving an organizational form to the growth in information, influence, and market access that allows nature-based enterprises to expand their production, profits, and social benefits.

Networks and the Poor

- Networks create institutional spaces in which the poor can interact with other producers working toward similar goals, building social capital through contact and cooperation.

- They also help to legitimize and strengthen the informal institutions of the poor, such as savings groups or women's groups, by expanding their contacts, helping them to enter the mainstream of recognized organizations.

Association Benefits

- Producer associations enable small rural producers to overcome some of their inherent handicaps, achieving economies of scale in harvesting, processing, and marketing nature-based products and services.

- Cooperatives and marketing associations allow small producers to gain bargaining power with traders in the middle or to bypass them altogether, letting the producers rise higher on the value chain and capture a greater share of the market value of their products.

- Associations provide channels for various forms of microcredit and private finance, acting as a formal node that private banks and public funding agencies can work through to reach a dispersed rural clientele.

- Learning networks are powerful communication links that provide a conduit for sharing information and fostering group learning, reducing innovation time—the time it takes to learn about and adapt new ideas to the local situation. For this reason, they greatly contribute to adaptive management of ecosystem resources, which depends on sharing experiences and lessons learned through a strategic process of trial and error. Cooperatives and producer associations often act as venues for learning new business and technical skills through courses or site visits.

- Federations allow enterprise owners to organize and advocate for their interests within the political process. They provide forums for reaching consensus and crafting a uniform message, amplifying their influence on policy.

Association Challenges

- As with many rural organizations, associations can be exclusive, and they often discriminate against smaller or poorer producers. It is not uncommon for them to be dominated by more wealthy, educated, or politically connected producers.

- Rural associations frequently face funding problems and often depend on grants to cover start-up and running costs. They tend to be financially marginal, with limited budgets, and thus have trouble expanding their activities or offering many services that would benefit their members.

- Government support for rural associations can be crucial for their survival, but it can also interfere with their internal governance. Governments often try to use cooperatives and other associations for political ends, which can destroy their effectiveness as producer-driven organizations.

Enterprises founded on a basis of good environmental governance

can not only improve the livelihoods of the rural poor

but increase their resilience to continuing challenges such as climate change.

ROUTES TO RESILIENCE

IN THIS REPORT WE ARGUE THAT COMMUNITY-BASED NATURAL resource management that springs from genuine community demand can nurture enterprises that both generate considerable income and improve the state of local ecosystems. Under the right conditions, these enterprises can scale up, achieving a significant poverty reduction effect. The case studies in this chapter chronicle three instances where significant scale and income effects have been achieved. The cases detail the governance conditions, principal actors, and enabling conditions that allowed these successes to go forward, as well as the challenges they have faced and must continue to deal with in order to sustain their success.

The cases also demonstrate that enterprises founded on a basis of good environmental governance can not only improve the livelihoods of the rural poor but increase their resilience to continuing challenges. They can become more economically resilient—better able to face economic risks. They and their communities can become more socially resilient—better able to work together for mutual benefit. And the ecosystems they live in can become more biologically resilient—more productive and stable.

The three case studies in this chapter are as diverse in their geography as they are in the ways the communities involved have worked to improve their lives through the management of local natural resources. They illustrate the power of self-interest and community ownership, the enabling value of intermediary organizations, and how communication and networks can provide new ideas and support.

These cases also illustrate simply how hard this all is—that nothing achieves the perfection of plans on paper, that progress takes time and support, but that lives can improve and communities can get stronger.

Fisheries for the Future: Restoring Wetland Livelihoods in Bangladesh
A change in how the government grants access to freshwater fisheries in three major watersheds has restored these fisheries and the lives of the poor in the communities around them. Page 112.

Green Livelihoods: Community Forestry Enterprises in Guatemala
Government-granted forestry concessions in the Maya Biosphere Reserve have reduced illegal deforestation while slowly improving the economies of the communities responsible for them. Page 126.

Turning Back the Desert:
How Farmers Have Transformed Niger's Landscapes and Livelihoods
Long-term engagement by NGOs has transformed traditional and sustainable agricultural practices and in the process has literally changed the landscape of this arid country even as it has improved lives. Page 142.

FISHERIES FOR THE FUTURE
Restoring Wetland Livelihoods
in Bangladesh

EIGHT YEARS AGO, A FULL FISHING NET WAS A RARE SIGHT ON THE EASTERN SHORES of Hail Haor wetland in remote northern Bangladesh. Even the wildfowl for which the area was renowned had been driven away by shrinking habitat and hunters. For the very poor villagers who made up the majority of local residents, and whose food and income depended on fish and aquatic plants, life was increasingly desperate. Households competed fiercely to buy fishing rights from the local elite. These few people, mostly large landowners and businessmen, controlled access to local water bodies (known as *beels*) that contained water year round, purchasing government leases which they then offered to the highest bidder.

Today the residents of Hail Haor area enjoy food and income security. Conflict over fishing rights has been replaced by cooperation, with villagers patrolling a no-fishing sanctuary and voluntarily paying dues to harvest a newly excavated beel. Degraded bird and fish habitat has been restored by local labor. Fish catches have almost doubled, and two locally extinct species have been successfully reintroduced (MACH 2005a; MACH 2005b).

This turnaround in fortunes has been achieved under an innovative pilot program in people-led wetland management that is drawing attention from policymakers across South Asia. Based on the "co-management" of wetlands by new community institutions and local government, the Management of Aquatic Ecosystems through Community Husbandry (MACH) program, funded by the United States Agency for International Development (USAID), has revived fisheries in three degraded wetlands, improving the circumstances of 184,000 of Bangladesh's poorest citizens (MACH 2006:2).

Success is rooted in community self-interest and ownership. In return for adopting conservation measures and sustainable fishing practices, community organizations (each representing several adjacent villages) receive 10-year leases to manage local waterways as well as grants to excavate silted beels and create wetland sanctuaries. To offset the hardships caused by fishing restrictions, poor households also receive skills training and micro-loans to start new enterprises. Between 1999 and 2006, fish catches in project villages rose by 140 percent, consumption went up by 52 percent, and average daily household incomes increased by 33 percent (MACH 2007:10,12,32; Whitford et al. 2006:7).

While the long-term sustainability of these benefits cannot be judged yet, community-led wetlands management and livelihood diversification have improved the ability of some of Bangladesh's poorest inhabitants to survive economic downturns, environmental disruption, and the potential impacts of climate change on the country's low-lying floodplains. By protecting wetlands from further overexploitation and degradation, communities have also improved the environmental resilience of the resources on which their lives and livelihoods depend.

So clear-cut have been the ecosystem and anti-poverty benefits that the government of Bangladesh has replicated key elements of MACH's approach in other fishing areas and in a pilot program for community-led management of protected forest areas. It has also adopted MACH's co-management model in its new Inland Capture Fisheries Strategy, reversing a decades-old policy of centralized control over the floodplains that cover half the country and on which 70 million people depend for food and income (Whitford et al. 2006:5; MACH 2007:47; Thompson 2006:1).

A Road Map for Wetland Revival

Located at the confluence of three major rivers—the Ganges, the Brahmaputra, and the Meghna—Bangladesh is rich in natural resources, especially water and fertile soils. Its freshwater wetlands are among the world's most important, harboring hundreds of species of fish, plants, and wildlife and providing a critical habitat for thousands of migratory birds (MACH 2007:1). But their productivity has come under increasing pressure as the population has increased, exceeding 140 million people in a territory of only 144,000 km²—an area the size of Nepal with nearly five times the population (Whitford et al. 2006:7).

Siltation caused by forest clearance, drainage for agricultural development, and the construction of flood embankments has shrunk inland fishing grounds, especially during the area's six-month dry season. Overexploitation and pollution have decimated fish stocks and other aquatic life, including edible plants harvested by the poor (Thompson 2006:1,3). The consequences have been devastating for millions of fishing households, one of the poorest segments of Bangladeshi society. Between 1995 and 2000, freshwater fish consumption fell by 38 percent among the poorest 22 percent of Bangladeshis (World Bank 2006:46), and in 2000 the World Conservation Union (IUCN) classified 40 percent of Bangladesh's freshwater fish species for which data are available as threatened with extinction (IUCN Bangladesh 2000 as cited in Thompson 2006:1).

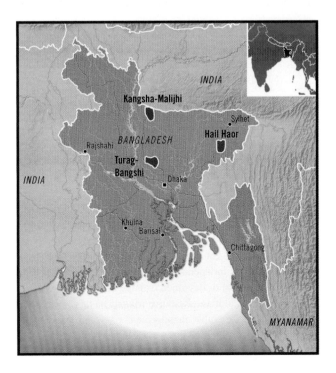

Long-standing government policies intensified this ecological crisis. Bangladesh's ruling classes traditionally viewed wetlands as wastelands to be "recovered" for agricultural production, which fostered indiscriminate development. Between the mid-1960s and the mid-1980s alone, about 0.8 million ha of floodplain were drained (Sultana 2006a:1). Fishing rights were also geared to maximizing government revenue rather than conserving natural resources. Most inland fishing waters in Bangladesh are government property, and the Ministry of Land leased short-term harvesting rights to the highest bidder. This not only encouraged overfishing, it was also fundamentally inequitable. Fishing rights were concentrated in the hands of those wealthy enough to afford the prized leases, while depriving poor fishing households of access (MACH 2006:1).

Recognizing these shortcomings and encouraged by foreign donors, including USAID, Bangladesh's government began restricting wetland drainage in the late 1990s (MACH 2006:2-1, 4-2). It also launched several experimental wetland restoration projects that devolved management rights to communities or local government, with national and international nongovernmental organizations providing capacity-building and technical support (MACH 2006:1).

The nine-year, US$14-million MACH program was perhaps the most successful and high-profile of these projects. Jointly developed and funded by the government of Bangladesh and USAID, MACH's objective was to act as a national testing ground for community-led natural resource management, with field operations in more than 110 rural fishing villages (Whitford et al. 2006:18; Thompson 2006:1).

Four highly experienced NGOs were selected by the Bangladesh government and USAID to implement the program and act as intermediary organizations between communities and local and national government. US-based Winrock International, which specializes in sustainable resource management projects, devised the new institutional arrangements and provided overall program management, while three national NGOs implemented the field work.

The Bangladesh-based Center for Natural Resource Studies (CNRS), which specializes in community-based floodplain restoration, helped communities establish Resource Management Organizations (RMOs), decide environmental priorities, and monitor the impacts of project activities. Caritas Bangladesh, a Catholic human development agency with a long record of working with poor, landless, marginalized communities across the country, oversaw income generation and microcredit lending among poor wetland users. The Bangladesh Center for Advanced Studies, a leading environmental research group, provided short-term specialists in hydrology and fishery biology to inform physical restoration works and fish restocking. Its staff also undertook research and advocacy on water quality, pollution, and cleaner practices in the textile dyeing industry and advised on policy reform (MACH 2007:3-4).

As the program will be completed in 2008, it is too early to assess either the long-term sustainability of the new institutions it established or the durability of benefits to fish stocks and habitats. Still, MACH's success to date has been impressive enough for international donors and government policymakers to view its co-management approach as a potential model for natural resource management beyond Bangladesh's borders (Thompson 2008).

Wealth from Water: The MACH Approach

The three wetlands targeted in the MACH program faced a representative range of development pressures and ecological threats. Hail Haor in the Sreemangal administrative subdistrict in northeast Bangladesh is a wetland region fed by 59 hill streams and renowned for its fish and birdlife but threatened by siltation and soil erosion caused by farming practices in the surrounding hills. Turag-Bangshi, a low-lying floodplain in Kaliakoir just north of Dhaka faces encroachment by agriculture, irrigation works, and industrial pollution. And Kangsha-Malijhi in the Sherpur district of north central Bangladesh is prone to flash floods worsened by the deforestation of surrounding hills (MACH 2003:ix; MACH 2007:5).

Out of 450 villages using these intricate ecosystems of rivers, streams, and beels, the 184,000 people living in 110 communities most dependent on wetland resources were targeted for project activities (MACH 2006:2). Average household income was US$500 a year in 1999 when field operations began (Deppert 2006a). Most families relied either fully or partly on fish and aquatic plants for food and income (MACH 2006:1). Wetlands in Bangladesh are highly seasonal, making year-round livelihoods precarious, a fact of nature exacerbated in the project areas by the overexploitation of dry-season water. In an average year, water coverage shrinks from a wet-season peak of 13,000 ha to a dry-season minimum of 3,000 ha in Hail Haor, from 8,000 to 700 ha in Turag-Bangshi, and from 8,000 to 900 ha in Kangsha-Malijhi (MACH 2007:5).

MACH's approach to reviving these fishing grounds and boosting local incomes was simple but radical: enabling communities to co-manage wetlands and gain access to fishing rights on a secure and equitable basis through new institutions that represented all local stakeholders.

Traditionally, highly-sought-after fishing rights to *jalmohals*—government-owned areas that hold water year-round—were leased to the highest bidder for three years by the Ministry of Land. Fisheries were therefore controlled by well-off lessees, who either hired professional fishers to work for them or charged poor fishers tolls. This system created little incentive to conserve local fish stocks or protect wetland ecosystems, and many poor people were deprived of access (Hughes 2006).

The first step in devolving wetland management was two years of intensive community consultations to identify local

BENEFITING PEOPLE AND NATURE: KEY MACH ACHIEVEMENTS 1999–2006

Building Environmental Capital

- Sixty-three sanctuaries established, covering 178 ha; 57 ha of beel wetland and 31 km of water channels excavated.

- Fishing restrictions have aided habitat and fish stock recovery.

- Fishing pressure in 110 project villages fell by 2,500 person hours per day.

- Some 644,000 trees planted to replace lost swamp forest and reduce erosion.

- Wetlands restocked with 1.2 million fish from 15 native species, including 8 threatened fish species (MACH 2007:11–13; 15; Sultana 2006b:2).

Building Economic Capital

- Members of 5,202 wetland-dependent households received training and credit to start new livelihoods (MACH 2007:32–33).

- Project works provided 2 million days of local employment (MACH 2007:13).

- Average daily household incomes rose by a third, to US$1.31 (MACH 2007:33).

- Fish production rose 140 percent and consumption increased by 52 percent (Whitford et al. 2006:7).

Building Social Capital

- New community institutions provided a forum for cooperation among different interest groups, including poor fishing families, better-off landowners, and local businessmen (MACH 2007:57).

- Co-management arrangements with local government provided support and sustainability for the new community institutions.

- Endowment and revolving credit funds enabled these new institutions to function independently after project finance ended (MACH 2007:45; MACH 2006:4.13–4.17).

wetland threats and develop a consensus on solutions in the form of Participatory Action Plans. In each cluster of villages, field officers from the Center for Natural Resource Studies were careful to bring all stakeholders into the process, including local councilors, small businessmen, landowners, and teachers as well as poor fishing families and the landless (Sultana 2006b:4). While this approach ran the risk of local elites dominating the process, it helped ensure that the new wetland management institutions and their programs for action had full community support. It was applauded by independent evaluators who visited MACH villages in 2006 and described collaboration across interest groups as "essential if the Resource Management Organization is to articulate a credible management plan and stand up to powerful interests, such as former leaseholders or government officials" (Whitford et al. 2006:6–7).

Creating Institutions, Empowering Communities

The next step involved establishing the institutional framework for communities and local government to co-manage the wetlands on their doorsteps. Three new types of institutions were created—at the village, wetland, and local government levels, as well as one village-level federation. *(See Table 1.)*

The first priority was establishing 16 Resource Management Organizations to take over day-to-day control of wetland management. These represented a radical departure from the status quo, as community institutions had rarely played a role in natural resource management in Bangladesh. Each organization had jurisdiction over part of the wetland ecosystem, incorporating several villages. All local wetland users—fishers, farmers, women, aquatic plant harvesters, and other resource collectors—were represented in its membership, along with other local stakeholders such as farmers (MACH 2006:2; Sultana 2006b:1–5).

After each RMO had drawn up a constitution, annual budget, and wetland management plan, with MACH assistance, it was registered with the government's Social Welfare Directorate and awarded 10-year leases to manage and harvest local water bodies by the Ministry of Land. The only condition was prompt payment of annual dues, which were set at lower rates than those charged to individual leaseholders (MACH 2006:2; MACH 2007:19–22).

This granting of medium-term tenure rights was critical to engaging communities' self-interest in the success of the fledgling resource management institutions. Previously fishers and other wetland harvesters could only receive annual permits and had no say over wetland management. Awarding villagers a measure of control over the natural resources on which they depended gave them a compelling reason to invest time and resources in the new governance institutions. By 2006, RMO memberships (ranging from a few dozen to several hundred people) and their elected executive committees had successfully developed, implemented, and enforced wetland restoration plans and equitable harvesting rights across 25,000 ha of permanent and seasonal wetlands (MACH 2007:v, 20).

A second tier of local wetland governance—the co-management institution—was established at the *upazila* (subdistrict) administrative level, in the form of Local Government Committees (renamed and formalized by the Bangladeshi government in 2007 as Upazila Fisheries Committees). These brought together local administrators, elected local councilors, and community representatives from both RMOs and village-based wetland user groups representing poor households. Their role was to coordinate wetland management activities within their boundaries, approving RMO management plans and measures and arbitrating conflicts. They therefore had the final say over wetland development, marking a significant departure from the status quo in which wetland management decision-making was passed down from ministries in Dhaka to local government administrators, bypassing communities (Deppert 2006a).

TABLE 1 WETLANDS MANAGEMENT INSTITUTIONS, MACH PROGRAM		
Management Institution	**Membership**	**Role**
Resource Management Organization (RMO)	All local wetland users and local stakeholders	Exercises day-to-day control of wetland management
Local Government Committee (Upazila Fisheries Committee)	Local administrators, elected local councilors, community representatives from RMOs and RUGs	Coordinates wetland management activities within their boundaries, approves RMO management plans and measures, arbitrates conflicts, has final say in wetland development
Resource User Group (RUG)	Poor fishing families, aquatic plant collectors, and landless people	Creates opportunities for skills training, microcredit loans
Federation of Resource User Groups (FRUGs)	Resource User Groups	Helps RUGs become self-sufficient through training in literacy, record-keeping, and other skills

Sources: Deppert 2006a; MACH 2006:2; MACH 2007:30; Sultana 2006a:2-4; Sultana 2006b: 1-5

Five such committees were established, each chaired by the senior local administrator—the Upazila Nirbahi Officer—with the Upazila Fisheries Officer acting as secretary. Other members included the elected chairmen of local councils (Union Parishads) and local government officials responsible for land management and agriculture as well as the leaders of local RMOs and Resource User Groups (RUGs). Every member had equal voting rights, and the committees provided a new forum for communities to exert influence and voice their needs (MACH 2007:3).

Darrell Deppert of Winrock International, who headed the MACH program until late 2007, describes the innovative Upazila Fisheries Committees as the key to the program's success and long-term sustainability. "They are the backbone required to support community-based institutions in sustainably managing wetlands for the benefit of all users. I am often told by poor community members that to sit at the same table as elected officials and government administrators is very important and empowering" (Deppert 2006a).

While the co-management committees fostered local government investment in sustainable fisheries, the third tier of new institutions created by MACH helped win over the poor. Drawing on existing successful microcredit programs in Bangladesh, Caritas organized village-level Resource User Groups (RUGs), targeting poor fishing families, aquatic plant collectors, and landless people. Each group elected a chairperson, and members applied for skills training and microcredit loans to start new livelihoods. These activities were managed by Caritas Bangladesh, which also provided literacy and nutrition programs (Sultana 2006a:2-4).

The objective was twofold: to prevent the poor being penalized by fishing restrictions imposed by RMOs to regenerate wetlands and to reduce pressure on fisheries by helping the poor gain access to new and more profitable livelihoods. By the end of 2006, project villages boasted 250 RUGs with 5,202 members, bringing income benefits to more than 25,000 people (Sultana

2006a:2; MACH 2007:30; Deppert 2006a). In 2004, the village groups were organized into 13 Federations of Resource User Groups (FRUGs), which employed staff to help member groups become self-sufficient via training in literacy, record-keeping, and other key skills. By 2007, these federations had been registered as independent organizations with the Bangladesh government's Social Welfare Department, had taken control of the revolving microcredit funds built up by the project, and were operating independently of Caritas (MACH 2007:30).

Wetland Management by the People, for the People

Each Resource Management Organization was given jurisdiction over a distinct area of one of the three project wetlands. These were typically made up of a series of beels and streams and a floodplain that were connected during the monsoon months but isolated in the dry season (MACH 2003:25-26).

After it was legally registered, an RMO's first step was to hold community planning meetings to identify the main problems affecting local wetlands. These generally included the following concerns: siltation due to soil erosion, overharvesting and use of harmful fishing gear, destructive fishing methods such as the dewatering of deeper pockets in the floodplain to catch fish sheltering in the dry season, industrial pollution, and blocked fish migratory routes.

To address these problems, the RMOs adopted wetland management plans dictating when and where fishing could take place, banning harmful practices, and outlining physical interventions, such as excavating corridors between dry-season water bodies. These were developed by the membership following community consultations and were implemented by elected executive committees of 10–20 people. Once their plans were approved by Local Government Committees, the

---

TYPICAL COMMUNITY WETLAND MANAGEMENT MEASURES

- Creating small sanctuaries, usually of 10 ha or less, where fishing is banned year-round, enabling fish and other aquatic organisms to repopulate the wider floodplain during the wet season.

- Excavating silted-up channels to create new dry-season habitat and increase water flow and fish movement in the wider wetland.

- Observing two- to three-month fishing bans during the early monsoon fish spawning season.

- Banning damaging practices such as dewatering in the dry season.

- Banning hunting of wetland birds.

- Planting indigenous wetland and riparian swamp trees.

Source: MACH 2006:4.1–4.5

new community organizations were awarded leases for local water bodies, which they paid for by collecting dues from fishers. MACH NGOs provided guidance, technical support, and grants to implement the conservation plans (MACH 2003:xii, 29–31). Field staff from Caritas and the Center for Natural Resource Studies also trained RMO committee members in wetland conservation and tree restoration techniques, accounts and record-keeping, good governance practices, and other key skills (MACH 2003:20).

Promoting Ownership and Equity

Implementing these measures called for significant community investment, cooperation, and sacrifices before the benefits started flowing. Fishing was banned in the sanctuaries that formed the cornerstone of most RMO plans, and fishers had to stop using equipment that encouraged overfishing, such as fine mesh nets that caught immature fish before they had time to reproduce. In some areas, poor families accustomed to supplementing their diet by hunting birds or collecting plants could no longer do so (MACH 2006:4.1–4.2). Those who wanted to join RMOs were expected to volunteer their time free of charge and usually to pay annual dues of about 5 taka (US$1=70 taka) (MACH 2005b).

To win over skeptical citizens, RMOs supported by field-workers from Caritas and the Center for Natural Resource Studies used a variety of measures. In the public arena, these included rallies, public meetings, and street theater to raise awareness of conservation benefits. To foster transparent decision-making and allay suspicions of corruption, RMOs held open meetings from the outset and set two-year term limits for executive committee members. Following early experiences in

which relatively wealthy individuals dominated decision-making, they also mandated that a majority of members must be poor resource users, owning less than 0.2 ha of land (Deppert 2006a; MACH 2007:24–25). Most RMOs also use secret ballots to elect office-holders. Regular meetings are held with fishers and landowners to agree on management plans and rules and to set user fees. In order to broaden participation, most RMOs have also set up subcommittees for financial audits, sanctuary management, and tree plantations (MACH 2007:21).

Perhaps most important for their constituencies, RMOs have provided fair and equitable access to harvesting grounds for all resource users, while adopting a pro-poor approach that has favored a majority of local citizens. Commercial fishers are charged a one-time annual toll during the harvesting season, while those fishing for subsistence receive free access. Dues are lower than those charged by former profit-seeking leaseholders, with executive committees seeking only to cover operational costs and the annual leasing fee (MACH 2007:v–vi, 48).

Independent evaluators commissioned by USAID to visit MACH villages in 2006 reported that the new governance arrangements had significantly empowered the poorest citizens. "The project has been notably successful in improving the social standing of poor fishermen, traditionally near the bottom of the social ladder." One beneficiary eloquently described the improvement of his lot to the evaluation team: "'Before, we were nothing, but now our dignity has increased so that we can shake hands with all kinds of people'" (Deppert 2006a; Whitford et al. 2006:25).

The experience of the Jethua Resource Management Organization in Hail Haor is typical. Its 42 founding members elected a 13-strong executive committee that organized public meetings and won community approval to lease and excavate a 2.4 ha perennial beel, guaranteeing a year-round harvest to local

fishers. Within the beel, a 0.5 ha sanctuary was created where fishing was banned in order to regenerate the wider wetland, and two species of locally extinct fish have been successfully reintroduced. The RMO borrowed 42,000 taka (US$600) from MACH to create the sanctuary, which it repaid through user dues within two years. Within five years, fish catches had almost doubled, to 231 kg/ha. In 2004, having proved its sustainable management credentials and boding well for the future, the RMO obtained leasing rights to a much larger neighboring beel, covering 250 ha (MACH 2005a).

In the few areas where enforcing new rules such as seasonal fishing bans and no-fishing sanctuaries has been a problem, communities have responded by organizing volunteer wetland patrols to deter rule-breakers (MACH 2005c). With community approval, CNRS also pioneered the design and use of concrete fish shelters, using local labor to construct more than 22,000 hexapod-shaped devices and place them in sanctuaries. These both provided additional feeding habitat and made it very difficult to catch fish, which congregate and hide among them (MACH 2006:4-4).

Resource Management Organizations have also exercised newfound influence by successfully overcoming resistance from powerful former leaseholders who did not want to hand over control of wetlands. Such successes have often been achieved with the support of local fisheries officials or council chairmen, underlining the worth of the new co-management arrangements in strengthening communities' hands. Although fisheries law in Bangladesh is generally poorly enforced, in three cases RMOs supported by Upazila Fisheries Committees have succeeded in upholding fines on groups of fishers that broke harvesting rules (MACH 2007:59–61). The evaluation team commissioned by USAID also noted that the co-management structure had "equipped the poor to resist pressure from the powerful" and

that they found "no examples of elite benefit capture" in the project villages (Whitford et al. 2006:8).

Whether this remains the case after project funding ends is an open question. But in 2006–2007 MACH boosted RMOs' survival prospects by awarding the Upazila Fisheries Committees endowment funds whose annual returns could be used to continue making grants to RMOs for habitat restoration and management. By guaranteeing a future revenue stream, these provided a clear incentive for communities to retain their loyalty both to the institutions and to sustainable wetland and fisheries practices (MACH 2007:vi).

Community Dividends: More Fish, New Livelihoods

As a pilot government program, close monitoring of social and environmental impacts was an essential component of MACH's activities. To establish a baseline, NGO field staff set up 23 monitoring locations in 1999, representing all types of wetland habitat. Every 10 days during the project, field staff and village monitors designated by RMOs recorded the number of people fishing, their hours, and the weight of the catches (MACH 2007:35).

The resulting data were dramatic and unequivocal. Fish yields more than doubled with wetlands in community hands, from average catches of 144 kg/ha in 1999 to 327 kg/ha in 2007 (MACH 2007). Fish consumption, recorded every three days by local women in 29 villages, rose by 52 percent overall between 1999 and 2004, from 32 to 48 grams per person a day (MACH 2006:2–3). Wetland diversity also expanded, with threatened fish species successfully reestablished, migrating birds returning, and aquatic plants recovering, including the shingra fruit harvested by poor families (MACH 2007: 12, 112).

For families used to unpredictable fish harvests, the most important benefit has been the revival of fish catches. By 2004, fishing effort had fallen by almost 2,500 hours a day across project

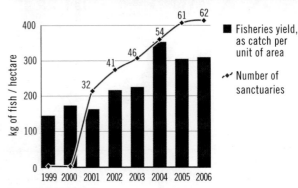

FISH YIELD AND FISH SANCTUARIES, MACH SITES, 1999–2006

■ Fisheries yield, as catch per unit of area

◆ Number of sanctuaries

y-axis: kg of fish / hectare (0, 100, 200, 300, 400)
x-axis: 1999 2000 2001 2002 2003 2004 2005 2006

Sanctuary data points: 32, 41, 46, 54, 61, 62

Source: MACH 2007:11, 53

villages due to harvesting restrictions and a shift among fishing households to alternative livelihoods that offered greater income and stability (Sultana 2006b:2). Yet MACH communities still earned US$4.7 million more from local fish sales in 2004 than they did in 1999 due to the revival of wetland habitats and, consequently, of fish stocks (MACH 2006:4-18). MACH has also speeded this process by funding the reintroduction, under RMO supervision, of almost 1.2 million fish from 15 native species (MACH 2007:12).

New livelihoods have also played a significant role in rising prosperity and ecosystem recovery, underlining the importance of linking conservation activities to income generation. Modeled on established community microcredit schemes in Bangladesh, the first micro-loans were awarded by Caritas a year after MACH began operating. To qualify, households had to own less than 0.2 ha of land, join their local men's or women's Resource User Group, and agree to save a minimum of five taka a week (MACH 2007:34; Costa 2006:2). Members were encouraged to take up new or part-time occupations to compensate for times of year when fishing was banned and to reduce pressure on wetland fisheries against the backdrop of a rising population. They were given access to training and loans covering 35 occupations ranging from poultry, duck, and goat rearing to nursery plantation, mechanics, electricians, and sewing (MACH 2006:4-17). Most beneficiaries sold their goods or services locally, but some reached wider markets. Clothing traders, for example, have begun buying items tailored by RUG members, while wholesalers collect eggs from their poultry farms (Begum 2007).

Between 2000 and 2006, a total of 14,829 loans were handed out to RUG member households, supporting enterprises that collectively brought in more than US$800,000 (MACH 2007:33,53). Four thousand of the borrowing families reported that their incomes rose by at least 70 percent thanks to their new alternative activities (MACH 2007:33). Credit recovery rates are an impressive 96 percent, reflecting the successful outcome of loans and community buy-in (Whitford et al. 2006:8).

MACH infrastructure activities also generated short-term employment for poor households, particularly through the excavation of 31 km of link channels between dry-season water bodies and 57 ha of shallow beels. These excavations provided 2 million days of manual labor while enriching thousands of hectares of wetland by creating new perennial waterways (MACH 2007:13).

Dividends for Women

Women's participation in decision-making of any kind is rare in Bangladesh, particularly in the conservative rural areas where MACH operated. As Bangladeshi women do not fish (although they collect other aquatic resources such as plants), many communities argued that they had no place in wetland management. MACH field staff, however, worked hard to overcome these cultural norms and set a 25 percent target for female membership of resource management organizations. By 2006 all

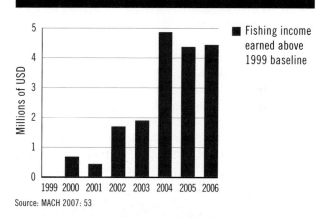

ADDITIONAL INCOME FROM FISHING IN MACH COMMUNITIES

Legend: ■ Fishing income earned above 1999 baseline

(Bar chart, Y-axis: Millions of USD, 0 to 5; X-axis: years 1999–2006)

Source: MACH 2007: 53

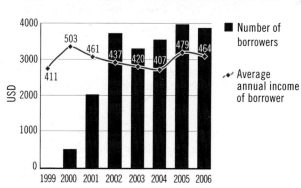

BENEFITS OF ALTERNATIVE INCOME LOAN PROGRAM

Legend: ■ Number of borrowers; ◆ Average annual income of borrower

(Chart, Y-axis: USD, 0 to 4000; X-axis: years 1999–2006; line values: 411, 503, 461, 437, 420, 407, 479, 464)

Source: MACH 2007: 53

Sofia Begum started a home-based poultry business with a loan from her local Resource User Group.

16 RMOs included women on their executive committees and about 20 percent of all members were female (MACH 2006:4-7, 20). Caritas also established 83 women-only resource user groups, to encourage wives to embark on new independent livelihoods (MACH 2007:31).

The evaluation team commissioned by USAID described these efforts to empower poor women as an "outstanding achievement" of the project. "By insisting that a proportion of positions be filled by women...the project has forced the pace of social change," its stated report. "At several sites, the team encountered women members willing to speak forthrightly about their concerns and their role in the project—even interrupting the men" (Whitford et al. 2006:25).

MACH's integrated livelihoods program has also offered a concrete route to female empowerment. A third of village user group members are women, hundreds of whom have benefited from skills training and micro-loans (MACH 2007:31). Toyobul Islam, president of the Kalapur Federation of Resource User Groups in Sreemangal district, has overseen dozens of loans successfully disbursed for new enterprises, including poultry, duck, and goat rearing, tree nursery management, and sewing. "This support has opened up new opportunities for members, especially women," he says. "Traditionally women are confined within the four walls of their houses. Now with money in their hands they have become economically empowered and more confident" (Tanvir 2006:10).

Sofia Begum (see photo above), a former housewife from Chenguria village in the Sherpur district of northern Bangladesh, is a good example. She joined the local women's resource user group in 2002, borrowing 3,000 taka (US$43) to buy wood that her husband made into furniture and sold for a profit. The couple then took out a second loan to open their own small furniture shop. "I knew if we could build more things, better things, we would make more money," she says.

With the shop flourishing, Sofia took out a third loan, for 10,000 taka (US$143), to start a home-based poultry business. She attended a two-day training course and bought 144 chickens. The hens bring in around 11,500 taka (US$164) per month, and Sofia's children now attend school. Once Sofia repays her latest loan, the family will be self-sufficient, now a common pattern in her village. Among the 20 members of the Chenguria women's group, which Sofia chairs, 15 live in households that no longer need to fish for an income (MACH 2005e).

Conservation Dividends

The main job of the 57 sanctuaries established so far by communities was to allow fish to breed and repopulate the wider floodplain, but they also yielded benefits for the ecosystem. A richer diversity of aquatic life as well as bird populations was harbored in the protected waters, with 47 plant species reestablished. In 2003 the government designated eight of the most ecologically sensitive areas as permanent sanctuaries (Thompson 2008; Whitford et al 2006:18; MACH 2006: 4.1–4.2).

The most spectacular example of this trend is the renaissance of Hail Haor's internationally renowned birdlife. The wetland's migratory waterfowl population, once numbering in the tens of thousands, had shrunk to a few dozen by the late 1990s, decimated by overhunting and human disturbance. In 2003 the Ministry of Land agreed to set aside a 100 ha permanent sanctuary in Baikka Beel and to forgo leasing payments, handing over management responsibility to Borogangina RMO,

MACH NGOS AND DONORS: AGENTS FOR CHANGE

The NGOs that implemented the MACH program were not only critical to its success in the 110 project villages. In acting as intermediaries with government agencies, national policymakers, donors, and the wider NGO community, they also had an impact well beyond the program's geographic boundaries. Their work has thus been a practical example of the kind of value added by intermediary NGOs, as discussed in Chapter 2.

Due to MACH's status as a pilot project for potential replication in various natural resource sectors, the government of Bangladesh and the United States Agency for International Development (USAID) decided from the outset to involve prominent and highly experienced organizations in its implementation. Winrock International, a nonprofit NGO with technical experience in natural resource management in 40 countries, was contracted not only to oversee program implementation but also to devise the detailed framework for the makeup, responsibilities, and operation of the new co-management institutions. Likewise, the recruitment of Caritas, the Center for Natural Resource Studies, and the Bangladesh Center for Advanced Studies (BCAS)—three national NGOs with proven track records (in, respectively, livelihood development, fishery and wetland management, and environmental policy) and with highly qualified staff—was based on the desire to lay the groundwork for success in the field.

This approach was costly, both in terms of finances and field staff per hectare (Whitford et al. 2006:18). However, a 2006 evaluation of MACH's effectiveness by independent consultants acknowledged the critical role of intermediaries in its success, stating: "The project correctly recognized that creation and sustaining of beneficiary organizations would require frequent face-to-face contact from project staff with considerable training in rural development and social awareness. Thus the combination of a major consulting firm, with considerable experience in tne technical aspects of the project, with three prominent NGOs, with excellent organizational skills, has proved very effective" (Whitford et al. 2006:18). The evaluation did warn that the "intensity of financial and staff resource use does raise some questions for replicability" (Whitford et al. 2006:18). MACH's final report to USAID estimated, however, that the agency's investment would achieve a "more than healthy" internal rate of return of 56 percent and a benefit-cost ratio of 4.7, based mainly on the documented upsurge in fishing income (Thompson 2008).

The reach, experience, and networking ability of the MACH NGOs also enabled the program's positive lessons to be absorbed by both government officials and other NGOs and to be widely disseminated. Personnel from Caritas and the Center for Natural Resource Studies organized site visits and seminars for policymakers from the Ministry of Fisheries and Livestock and the Ministry of Land and for donors and community development NGOs. They also replicated MACH's physical interventions in nine sites near Dhaka as part of a separate commu-

nity-led wetland management project implemented by the Department of Fisheries (MACH 2007:38–41).

At a macro policy level, the government of Bangladesh has asked MACH staff to advise on a range of natural resource programs, including the high-profile Coastal and Wetland Biodiversity Management Project funded by the United Nations Development Programme and the Global Environment Facility (MACH 2003:xiii). Representatives from Winrock and the Bangladesh Center for Advanced Studies also played a key role in the development of the Ministry of Fisheries and Livestock's 2006 Inland Capture Fisheries Strategy (Whitford et al. 2006:17). BCAS, which helped formulate Bangladesh's environmental policy framework, and Winrock, which shared staff with another project that supported the Department of Fisheries in developing its strategies, were particularly well placed to exert their influence on the strategy, which embraces key MACH approaches (Thompson 2008).

As the program's reputation has spread in development circles, the MACH NGOs' influence and reach has also extended overseas, with delegations of policymakers from Nepal, Cambodia, Viet Nam, Brazil, and other resource-rich developing countries seeking to exchange ideas and learn lessons (Thompson 2008).

Role of USAID

As a major donor to the government of Bangladesh, the US Agency for International Development has developed a broad environmental agenda in the country, with impacts and influence well beyond the funding and scope of individual projects. Its latest Program Objective for Environment seeks to strengthen natural resource management by the Government of Bangladesh and national NGOs via key themes, including implementation of effective community-based resources management mechanisms, habitat restoration, policy promotion, and improved institutional capacity.

The MACH program, mostly funded by USAID, covered all these areas. Its success enabled USAID to influence national policymaking, both through the Inland Capture Fisheries Strategy and the government's latest Poverty Reduction Strategy Paper, its keystone development blueprint. The latter describes floodplain fisheries as having "particular significance for poverty reduction goals." In the future, it stated, the Department of Fisheries would "preserve…and make more productive use of inland capture fishery through community based participation of fishermen and fishery related stakeholders" (MACH 2007:75).

In 2003, USAID's community-led, co-management approach was also formally extended to terrestrial ecosystems, in partnership with the Ministry of Environment and Forests. A pilot program to preserve threatened tropical forests is centered on devolving power to new local institutions in five wildlife-rich protected areas (Whitford et al. 2006:14,19).

which has since banned all fishing, bird hunting, and harvesting of edible water plants (MACH 2007:47). By 2007, a midwinter census recorded more than 7,000 water birds in Baikka Beel, including such rare species as the Pallas' Fish Eagle and Greater Spotted Eagle (MACH 2007:38), and MACH had built a watch tower to accommodate an influx of ecotourists. The Bangladesh government is now applying for Hail Haor to receive international protected wetland status under the Ramsar Convention (MACH 2007:vi).

Land-based habitat management has also brought conservation dividends. Communities planted more than 600,000 trees from 48 native species to restore swamplands and wetland border forests and to counter erosion on the banks of rivers and streams. Over the long term, the tree planting program will also bring economic benefits to communities. While the swamp forests will be preserved, tree branches can be lopped for fuel and for brushwood that is placed in the water to attract fish. MACH also estimates a healthy return from the first felling cycle of non-swamp trees at US$1.04 million in today's prices between 2015 and 2020. Through benefit-sharing agreements a substantial part of this will go to community organizations, with the rest reserved for landowners and local government (MACH 2007:14-15; 53).

Career fisherman Jamir Uddin struggled to survive as once bountiful catches declined across Sherpur wetland in the 1990s. To make extra money he began collecting and selling peanuts, and in 2001 he took out a MACH micro-loan to start his own shop. Three loans later, his expanding general goods store makes 30,000 taka (US$428) a year in profits, a sum he describes as unimaginable in his former occupation: "I saw that if I quit fishing and devoted myself to a shop full time I could make more money," he says as he greets customers. "This shop has changed my life." (MACH 2005d)

Sustaining Success: Lessons and Challenges

Two clear advantages help to explain the MACH program's success as a conservation and anti-poverty initiative: the large sums of donor money invested and government support for decentralizing wetland management. But there were several other key elements that reflect the framework laid out earlier in this book and that have wider resonance.

First and most important, the program was built on communities' self-interests. Villagers were granted rights and powers to use natural resources and responsibilities to manage and protect them. If they failed, their livelihoods and investment (of user dues and time volunteered) were at stake. Second, because of the co-management arrangement with local administrators, these new institutions were not isolated; they worked well within the existing governance framework. Third, the implementing NGOs worked effectively as intermediary organizations—acting as a bridge between villagers and local and national governments to develop democratic, equitable, and effective community-based institutions. Fourth, effective networking, outreach, and organizational scale-up over the nine years of the program prevented the project villages from being mere temporary islands of good practice. Instead, the new institutions were left on a good footing to prosper after donor funds and NGO expertise began to be withdrawn in 2007. Fifth, endowment funds for RMOs and revolving credit funds for resource user groups provided financial security once the project funding dried up.

As a result, the community institutions nurtured by MACH are now self-sufficient enough not only to survive but to prosper. So concluded the team of consultants sent to evaluate the program in 2006, reporting that most resource management organizations and user groups "appear capable of managing the fishery resources and income generation activities respectively [and] should be able to sustain themselves financially for the indefinite future" (Whitford et al. 2006:27).

The slow project phase-out has also helped community

institutions to plan ahead. Several Resource Management Organizations have demonstrated maturity and forward thinking in establishing "post MACH funds," while others have leased additional water bodies to generate more income. Darabashia RMO in Sherpur district, for example, which collects 20 taka a year from its 122 members and rents out access to fish shelters, has saved 33,676 taka ($US481) in a post-MACH fund (MACH 2005b).

Some challenges remain. Literacy rates are very low in some Resource User Groups, which will need to lean heavily on their local federation to survive once project field staff leave (MACH 2006:4.16). Within RMOs there is a risk that female membership will slip or that local elites will seek to re-exert their authority once project oversight is removed. There is also the prospect that, with fish populations recovering, communities will be tempted to overexploit the wetland bounty once again, and RMOs may face challenges to their authority.

The bigger clouds on the horizon, however, are related to national policy and government commitment. While Dhaka has pledged to renew wetland leases to RMOs when they become due, uncertainty remains about how many years the government will commit to. This could undermine community support for sustainable use of wetlands, since interest in the institutions established by MACH is based on long-term tenure.

Competing development priorities are also jeopardizing the impressive fishery gains made by some communities. In Kaliakoir, polluted water from an eightfold increase in textile-related industries over the last three years has caused fish kills in sanctuaries (Chowdhury and Clemett 2006:3). Water quality and treatment regulations exist but are not enforced, despite visits from representatives of the RMOs and the MACH NGOs. To address this, the Bangladesh Center for Advanced Studies, a MACH partner NGO, is working to identify cleaner technologies. It is also adopting a two-pronged lobbying strategy: trying to persuade the polluting industries to install effluent treatment plants while pressing the government to enforce existing water quality standards (MACH 2007: 16–19, 62–63).

Meanwhile, in Hail Haor and Sherpur, continuing deforestation of hills throughout the wetland catchments will result in growing siltation problems unless there are widespread changes in land use practices used in forests, tea estates, and farmland. These problems are common across Bangladesh's floodplains, suggesting that MACH's impressive achievements may not be sustainable over the long term unless its co-management approach is scaled up and applied across larger ecosystems, with full government backing (MACH 2007:76).

Toward a Sustainable Future: Scaling Up Community Fisheries

MACH's success in increasing fish stocks and fishing income was all the more marked in that it occurred against a backdrop of continuing ecological crisis in most of Bangladesh's floodplains. While it remains early, the co-management of wetlands appears to offer a route to preserving their environmental resilience—and hence the fisheries productivity on which millions of poor people depend. Sustainable harvesting, coupled with alternative livelihoods programs, has also boosted communities' economic resilience, while the creation of new community institutions has increased their social capacity. With fishing communities suffering around the country, this lesson has not been lost on the national government, which, with donor support, has begun to replicate MACH approaches both in the field and in national policymaking.

Quantitative Scale-Up

In 2006, for example, MACH field staff began helping Department of Fisheries' officers and communities to copy its physical conservation techniques in 10 degraded wetlands close to Dhaka (MACH 2007:38–39). The villages involved were supported by the Fourth Fisheries Project, a major Department of Fisheries program aimed at reducing poverty through increased fish production, funded by the World Bank and the United Kingdom Department for International Development (Thompson 2007). This project and others overseen by the Bangladeshi Department of Fisheries and Department of Environment have also copied MACH's pioneering efforts to replant native swamp trees along wetland borders. In addition, government agencies directly operating floodplain community projects, such as the Local Government Engineering Department, have adopted MACH best practices such as sanctuaries and habitat restoration (MACH 2007:41–42).

In 2003, MACH approaches were also extended to terrestrial ecosystems, forming the basis for a groundbreaking project to safeguard Bangladesh's threatened forests by devolving power to communities (Whitford et al. 2006:14). Bangladesh has less than 0.02 ha of forestland per person, the lowest ratio in the world, and those fragments that remain are under intense

LEARNING FROM BANGLADESH'S FISHERIES INITIATIVE

Pilot projects can have broader impact. The demonstrable success of the MACH program has spurred its adoption by the national government to cover all inland freshwater fisheries. The government is also instituting a project based on the lessons of the MACH program to safeguard and enhance the country's dwindling forest areas. It remains to be seen how these national commitments will be kept, but national policy recognition establishes a certain measure of accountability that will be hard to abandon.

A long-term commitment is necessary. The kind of political, social, and environmental changes reflected in the MACH program take time to develop and take permanent hold. USAID and Winrock's involvement over 9 years is exemplary for its dedication but also as an object lesson. The World Bank has observed that the single most important factor in the lack of success in community development projects has been the absence of a long-term commitment by donors.

Sustainably-managed resources have limits. Such resources can only provide so much economic benefit; the expanding needs of growing populations have to be accommodated. MACH developed an alternative livelihoods program from the start to help create other options for economic growth for community members, thus avoiding the destructive consequences of overfishing. Villagers were exposed to a variety of potential livelihoods and offered appropriate training.

Accommodate and include women. The alternative livelihoods program was embraced by the women in the communities, traditionally excluded from male-dominated fishing. Engaging women in such enterprises can increase the social capital of a community and hasten its exit from extreme poverty. Microfinance efforts in these communities have also engaged and empowered women, by giving them an important new role in family finances.

Local government is important. The MACH program, while establishing several new organizations—RMOs, RUGs—that aided the restoration and management of the inland fisheries, made sure such groups were not seen as a threat to local governance structures already in place. The legitimacy of local government is critical to continued social stability even as efforts like MACH bring about significant change in livelihoods in a community.

space for new settlements (Whitford et al. 2006:13). Nevertheless, they shelter many threatened and important species, including tigers, elephants, and gibbons, and provide livelihoods and food for around 1 million people. The Co-management of Tropical Forest Resources in Bangladesh project, known as Nishorgo, has set up fledgling stakeholder co-management councils and committees at community and forest ecosystem level in five wildlife-rich areas covering 23,000 ha. If it proves effective, the new governance system, a bilateral initiative of USAID and the Ministry of Environment and Forests, will be replicated across all 19 protected forests in the country (MACH 2006:13, 18–21).

Organizational Scale-Up

MACH's success was also founded on the networks it assiduously built at local and national levels. In particular, setting up Federations of Resource User Groups was vital to the sustainability of the 250 village-based RUGs, most of whose members were poor, illiterate, and lacking in skills and confidence. The 13 federations have offices (built by MACH) and paid employees (including former Caritas field officers) who trained user group office holders such as chairmen and secretaries in such skills as literacy, numeracy, and book and account keeping (MACH 2007:14, 30–32). By mid-2007, revolving credit funds totaling more than US$420,000, set up by Caritas to promote financial stability after project funding ends, had been handed over to the federations to administer (MACH 2007:vi). Without their continued operation and support, the survival of the Resource User Groups—which have helped to lift thousands of people out of severe poverty—would be in jeopardy.

As described earlier, the vertical networking between community institutions and local government at union (local council) and upazila (subdistrict) level has also played an essential role on several fronts: providing a forum for citizens' voices, fostering better local government understanding of wetland problems, and rooting the MACH institutions in existing governance structures.

This has been achieved most obviously through the cross-memberships of poor people in Federations of Resource User Groups, Resource Management Organizations, and Upazila Fisheries Committees. But it has also involved contacts made by RMO leaders and MACH staff with elected local councilors and with upazila officers working in fisheries, agriculture, livestock management, engineering, and social welfare, whose services have been tapped to assist the community institutions (MACH 2003:xi).

Political Scale-Up

The measurable success of MACH's community-led recipe for reviving wetlands (and of other similar projects in Bangladesh and the region) has prompted Dhaka to embrace this approach for all inland waters. In January 2006 the Ministry of Fisheries and Livestock approved a new Inland Capture Fisheries Strategy that adopted key MACH components, namely:

- Co-management of wetlands and fisheries through Upazila Fisheries Committees and community-based organizations; awarding of long-term wetland leases to the latter, for nominal payments, provided they adopted conservation-based plans and practices.

- Promotion of the best practices pioneered by MACH communities, including sanctuaries, restricted fishing seasons, and excavations.

- Alternative income programs for the poorest fishers, although without specified funding sources (Deppert 2006b:3).

If implemented, the strategy would eventually bring some 4 million ha of seasonal floodplains and about 12,000 government-owned year-round water bodies—lakes, marshes, rivers, and estuaries—under community-led control. At a higher policy level, MACH's community-led approach has also been broadly endorsed in the government's latest Poverty Reduction Strategy Paper, which describes floodplain fisheries as having "particular significance for poverty reduction goals" (MACH 2007:47–48).

Putting these paper commitments into practice, however, will require major infusions of political will and public money. Key lessons for successful regional or national scale-up identified by the MACH partners themselves form a daunting to-do list, including:

- Provide all community resource management organizations with endowment funds and wetland leases for at least 10 years.

- Mandate local government to step up support and services for community institutions and to hold themselves accountable to citizens for results.

- Develop criteria and systems for regular reviews of community institution activities, to be jointly conducted by local government and citizens.

- Facilitate the sharing of best practices among community organizations and with government agencies.

- Train community organization representatives in record-keeping, budget preparation, revenue-raising, and preparation of resource management plans.

- At a national policy level, involve all relevant agencies, including those responsible for land management, fisheries, environment, agriculture, and water resources (Sultana 2006b:6).

Azharul Mazumder, Environment Team Leader of USAID/Bangladesh, is confident that sustainable co-management of floodplain fisheries can work for poor communities. But he is under no illusions as to the scale of the task ahead. "Doing business as usual will hardly do the trick," he says. To muster the required political will, "critical wetland habitats should be declared protected areas and brought under an ecosystem-based protected area management system. This will require a mindset change among the policymakers and an institutional change in the way relevant agencies perform management functions" (Mazumder 2006).

The MACH program and similar projects have provided a promising national road map for protecting natural resources while enhancing livelihoods. Policymakers in both developing and donor countries will be watching closely to see whether these efforts will be successfully replicated in the years ahead.

GREEN LIVELIHOODS
Community Forestry Enterprises in Guatemala

GUATEMALA'S NORTHERNMOST REGION, EL PETÉN, HOSTS A UNIQUE BLEND of natural beauty, biological diversity, and archeological heritage dating back to ancient Mayan civilization. The Petén's 33,000 km² of relatively undisturbed lowland tropical forests shelter 95 species of mammals, among them spider monkeys, pumas, and threatened jaguars, and 400 species of birds, including the iconic scarlet macaw (WCS 2006). The region is also home to an expanding melting pot of Guatemalan citizens: indigenous descendants of the Mayans, political refugees who sought refuge during 20 years of civil war, and economic migrants from the country's overpopulated cities and degraded highlands (Pool et al. 2002:92).

A decade ago, deforestation had diminished biodiversity and threatened forest-based livelihoods in the region. But the northern Petén is now the setting for successful community-run forestry enterprises whose sustainably harvested wood and non-timber forest products (NTFPs) are attracting the attention of overseas buyers.

Under the supervision of non-governmental organizations (NGOs), donors, and government agencies, community-owned forestry enterprises steward more than 420,000 ha in the multiple use zone of the renowned Maya Biosphere Reserve (MBR) (Chemonics 2006:16). These enterprises are each in charge of one distinct parcel of land – a concession - that the Guatemalan government has leased to them. Forest product sales from these enterprises have brought new employment, infrastructure, social cohesion, and income.

Between October 2006 and September 2007, the concessions produced some US$4.75 million in certified timber sales and close to US$150,000 in sales of *xate* (palm leaves used for flower arrangements) and other non-timber forest products (Rainforest Alliance 2007a:1; Nittler 2007). Under village management, biodiversity has flourished and forest fires, illegal logging, and hunting have declined dramatically, while continuing unabated in neighbouring national parks (Nittler and Tschinkel 2005:3; Chemonics and IRG 2000: A-IV-8).

By 2000, the forest concessions in the reserve managed by these community enterprises had become the world's largest tract of sustainably certified and community-managed forest (Chemonics and IRG 2000:A-IV-8). Prior to 2004, 10 enterprises had met the international certification standard of the Forest Stewardship Council (FSC) for sustainably harvested wood, and several were selling high-income finished products such as decking and floor panels in addition to timber (Chemonics 2006:17; Rainforest Alliance 2007b:2-3).

This transformation of fragmented communities of farmers and illegal loggers into eco-entrepreneurs did not occur in a policy vacuum. Government decentralization policies, which awarded communities tenure rights and resource management responsibilities, provided an enabling environment and motivation for communities to protect their forests. Substantial assistance from donors and intermediary support organizations provided the funds and the technical expertise to make the concession model work.

Progress toward financial and organizational independence has been slow and sometimes challenging, and the community enterprises are not all assured of a long-term future. The more successful ones now show signs of increased resilience. The overall results have proved promising enough for policymakers to consider scaling up the effort across the region. Already, communities in Honduras are replicating the concession model, while government agencies from Nicaragua, Panama, and Peru have hired members of Petén's community-owned enterprises as consultants in sustainable forest management (Chemonics 2006:41).

From Conflict to Conservation: A New Forestry Approach

Twenty years ago, the region's future looked far less promising. Harvesting of non-timber forest products such as chicle (used to make chewing gum) had been the mainstay of the local economy for decades and had left the bulk of the forest relatively untouched (Chemonics 2006:5). But during the 1980s huge areas were haphazardly cleared as population growth and economic pressures fuelled illegal logging and burning of forests to make way for crops and cattle (Chemonics 2006:5). Illegal land use among new and long-term residents in and around the reserve was also abetted by lack of land tenure, endemic corruption, and the absence of law enforcement (Pool et al. 2002:E-4).

By the end of the 1980s foreign donors, particularly the United States and Germany, were pressuring the Guatemalan government to slow the destruction of this key section of the chain of Mayan forest running through Central America (Nittler and Tschinkel 2005:2).

In response, a new national agency, the National Council of Protected Areas (CONAP) was established in 1989 to

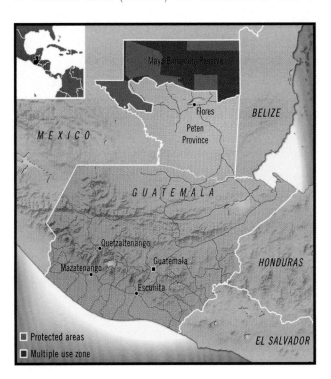

administer and regulate activity within Guatemala's System of Protected Areas (Chemonics 2006:5). A year later, with the approval from the international environmental community, the Congress of Guatemala designated 2.1 million ha in the northern Petén as the Maya Biosphere Reserve (Nittler and Tschinkel 2005:2). Of this, 767,000 ha were designated "core zones" where all extractive activity was banned; 848,440 ha became a "multiple use zone" for sustainable harvesting activities. The remaining 497,500 ha made up a surrounding buffer zone with a mix of state-owned and private lands (Stoian and Rodas 2006a:1). The United States Agency for International Development (USAID) signed an agreement with Guatemala's government to conserve biodiversity and improve management within the Maya Biosphere Reserve, donating about US$10.5 million in the first 10 years. An additional US$11.9 million was contributed by the government of Guatemala and international NGOs (Pool et al. 2002:E-4).

Communities Take Over

CONAP's initial efforts to carry out its mandate to protect the reserve concentrated on battling illegal deforestation in its two designated national parks—Sierra de Lacandón and Laguna del Tigre—and on slowing agricultural clearing in the Buffer Zone (Chemonics 2006:6).

Assisted by local and international NGOs, the new agency emphasized centralized control and enforcement, which alienated local communities. Local loggers unwilling to abide by restrictions attached to CONAP's permits were legally barred from harvesting timber, but the overstretched agency was unable to enforce these bans. Illegal felling and land occupation continued unabated despite the introduction of park guards and checkpoints, measures that angered some members of the local population. CONAP offices were burned, and one official was murdered (Pool et al. 2002:10). Estimates suggested that for every cubic meter of cedar or mahogany cut legally in the region, three meters were illegally felled (Pool et al. 2002: E-2). Intensifying the ecological crisis, the 1992 ceasefire in Guatemala's civil war and subsequent Peace Accords in 1996 prompted returnees from Mexico and other areas of Guatemala to settle in parts of the Petén that had been declared protected parks (Nittler and Tschinkel 2005: 2,5).

By 1994, it was clear that CONAP's punitive approach was not working. As the situation grew increasingly chaotic, a group of concerned foresters proposed awarding communities harvesting rights in the multiple use zone, thus fostering their self-interest in the reserve's success. Backed by national NGOs, their idea soon won support from USAID and the Guatemalan government (Nittler and Tschinkel 2005:3).

Since there was no model for sustainable use of mixed tropical forests in Guatemala, one forestry consultant prepared a management plan for the first concession—a 4,800-ha parcel of forest allocated to a newly constituted legal organization established by the villagers of San Miguel la Palotada. Another consultant proposed how a larger concession scheme might operate, and a local lawyer translated these concepts into draft regulations and a prototype contract between CONAP and the community organization (Nittler and Tschinkel 2005:3–4). "We used the considerable experience on concessions from around the world, especially a study on those in Africa by the World Bank," recalls Henry Tschinkel, part of the founding group and a former Regional Forestry Adviser for USAID (Tschinkel 2008).

In 1994, these legal documents were approved by CONAP's board and the first concession was allocated (Nittler and Tschinkel 2005:4). This mechanism opened the floodgates for other local communities and industries to apply for legal rights to sustainably manage forests under 25-year contracts (Nittler and Tschinkel 2005:3). By September 2006, 11 more concessions were in the hands of communities and 2 more were run by local timber companies, placing the management of most of the multiple use zone in local hands (Pool et al. 2002:E-2). In its effort to slow deforestation in the buffer zone, CONAP has also developed a mechanism to support communities in the buffer that sustainably manage their private land (Chemonics and IRG 2000:A-IV-5). As of 2006, there were four such cooperatives in operation (Stoian and Rodas 2006a:2).

In the early years, most community-harvested timber—primarily high-value mahogany and tropical cedar—was sold as logs to local forest industries, often on unfavorable terms. But as the enterprises matured they began to cooperate across communities, strengthening their negotiating power. In 1999, the early community forestry enterprises, the legally consituted entities that held each forest concession (known as EFCs), formed an umbrella association, the Asociación de Comunidades Forestales del Petén (ACOFOP), which lobbied CONAP and donors on the concessions' behalf, giving member communities the capacity to sell products jointly and generally defend their interests (Chemonics and IRG 2000:A-IV-10).

As their skills and confidence grew, the community forestry enterprises added value to their product by diversifying into wood processing, using the proceeds from selling standing timber to buy chainsaws and later small sawmills (Nittler 2008). Ten enterprises took another step toward diversification and independence in 2003 by setting up FORESCOM, a collective forest products company. Initially funded by USAID, FORESCOM helped its concession members to make the leap from donor subsidy to profitability by providing affordable forest certification services and identifying new markets for timber and other products (Chemonics 2003:21; Nittler and Tshinkel 2005:1; Chemonics 2006:13–14).

By 2007, with some residual training from intermediaries and government agencies, a majority of enterprises were genuine, profit-making businesses, reaching markets in Mexico, the United States, and Europe (Rainforest Alliance 2007a:1).

COMMUNITY FORESTRY ENTERPRISES: KEY ACHIEVEMENTS

Building Environmental Capital

- Community harvesting rights were conditional on sustainable forestry practices; only 0.8–2.4 trees felled per ha (Nittler and Tschinkel 2005:17).

- As of 2008, 9 community concessions, 2 industrial concessions, and 1 cooperative - managing about 480,000 ha in total - maintained certification by the Forest Stewardship Council (Hughell and Butterfield 2008:6).

- Annual forest clearance rates within certified concessions fell sharply to only 0.04 percent of tree cover, one twentieth of the clearance rate in neighboring protected areas; squatting by settlers and illegal logging also declined (Hughell and Butterfield 2008:9).

- Diversity of birds, animals, and insects has been maintained or enhanced (Balas 2004 and Radachowsky 2004 as cited in Nittler and Tschinkel 2005:17).

Building Economic Capital

- More than 10,000 people directly benefit from forest concessions and 60,000 receive indirect benefits. Concession employees receive more than double the regional minimum wage (Saito 2008).

- Trade in timber reached US$4.7 million in 2007, with 2.6 million board feet sold. Sales of non-timber forest products further boosted income from concessions (Rainforest Alliance 2007a:1).

- By 2006, a total of 6,839 members of community enterprises had received intensive training in forestry and business management and in technical skills (Chemonics 2006:8).

- Environmental services payments to communities for avoided deforestation and carbon sequestration are under negotiation (Rainforest Alliance 2007b:3).

Building Social Capital

- Communities received legal rights to manage and harvest forests and security of tenure via 25-year management leases (Nittler and Tschinkel 2005:3).

- New local NGOs were established to assist communities, strengthening civil society (Nittler and Tschinkel 2005:11–12).

- EFCs established an umbrella association and a forest products company, FORESCOM, thereby extending their influence and sales reach (Nittler and Tschinkel 2005:10).

- A share of the revenue from forest products was used for community projects such as installing water supply systems and paying school fees (Rainforest Alliance 2007b:3).

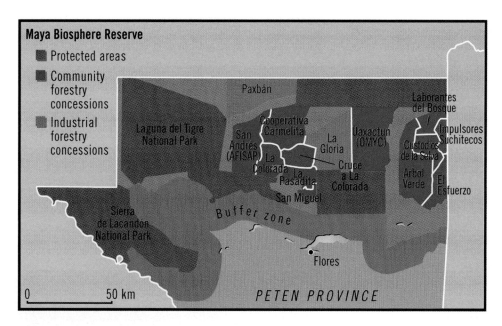

Maya Biosphere Reserve
- ■ Protected areas
- ■ Community forestry concessions
- ■ Industrial forestry concessions

Paxbán
Laborantes del Bosque
Laguna del Tigre National Park
Cooperativa Carmelita
San Andrés (AFISAP)
La Gloria
Uaxactún (OMYC)
Impulsores Suchitecos
Custodios de la Selva
La Colorada
Cruce a La Colorada
La Pasadita
Arbol Verde
El Esfuerzo
San Miguel
Buffer zone
Sierra de Lacandón National Park
Flores
0 50 km
PETEN PROVINCE

parcels of land to be ready for a second harvest, thus creating community self-interest in practicing sustainable forestry management (Tschinkel 2008). It was also long enough for communities to envisage building healthy businesses, especially with significant donor subsidies.

The forest area in the concessions ranges considerably in size from 4,800 to 72,500 ha (Chemonics and IRG 2000:A-iv-7). In a rush to get the concession program established as soon as possible, their borders were drawn on the basis of lobbying by communities and NGOs and of proximity to the park's protected core zones, rather than by the presence and distribution of high-value tree species. As a result, some of the early community enterprises struggled to extract enough valuable trees from the small concessions they had been allocated to support a viable business (Nittler and Tschinkel 2005:4–5). By the late 1990s, due in part to lobbying from the newly formed EFC umbrella organization, ACOFOP, this problem was rectified for later concessions as the national parks agency began awarding larger concessions with greater commercial promise (Chemonics and IRG 2000:A-iv-8).

Each concession was allocated to a legally constituted organization—the community forestry enterprises. Every adult resident of the founding community was free to join, although in many communities, few villagers initially signed up due to concerns about the responsibilities involved (Tschinkel 2007). Early memberships ranged from 29 to 372 and included residents of up to nine villages (Chemonics and IRG 2000:A-IV-11).

Once CONAP approved an EFC's five-year sustainable forest management plan, that plan became part of the legal contract between the enterprise and the national parks agency. EFCs were then legally empowered to harvest and sell timber from their concession, in accordance with each management plan's conditions. They were also required to submit annual operating plans for CONAP's approval, detailing the species and volume to be cut (Chemonics and IRG 2000:II-12; Tschinkel 2008). Enterprises were legally empowered to harvest not only valuable tree species, such as mahogany, but also non-timber forest products, including chicle, allspice, and xate palm leaves (Chemonics 2003:23).

Crucially, the fledgling EFCs were also required by USAID and CONAP to achieve certification under international sustainable forestry standards within three years in order to qualify for continued donor assistance (Chemonics and IRG 2000:A-iv-12). To help them achieve this, the regulations for allocating a concession required that a qualified NGO assume

The Concession Model: An Evolving Blueprint for Sustainable Enterprise

As the concession initiative originated from foresters and as the enabling regulations were rushed through by CONAP against a backdrop of donor pressure, communities living in the multiple use and buffer zones were not widely consulted at the start. As a result, they were initially wary of seeking concessions, with three years passing until a second community sought and received a contract in 1997 (Nittler and Tschinkel 2005:2). After that, as the benefits of forest harvesting rights became apparent, "communities were suddenly standing in line," according to Henry Tschinkel (Tschinkel 2007).

As only six small communities inhabited the densely forested multiple use zone—not enough to manage half a million hectares of land—the remaining concessions were granted to groups of villages in the adjoining buffer zone. The disadvantage of this was that seven of the communities had stronger backgrounds in farming than forestry and faced a steep learning curve for their new trade (Chemonics and IRG 2000:III-6-8). Two additional concessions were awarded to local timber companies, despite opposition from conservation NGOs, on the condition that their operations achieve certification under International Forest Stewardship Council guidelines within three years (Saito 2008). Unable to clear timber and then move on as in the past, these industrial concessions quickly became converts to sustainable forestry practices and formed alliances with community enterprises, buying their wood for processing and sale (Chemonics 2006:16).

Although the multiple use zone remained government property, the concession contracts granted usufruct rights to legally constituted community organizations for 25 years, with an option for renewal (Nittler and Tschinkel 2005:3; Stoian and Rodas 2006a:15). This was estimated as the time needed for the first

considerable technical and financial responsibility over the businesses and that directors and governing boards be elected for each enterprise (Nittler and Tschinkel 2005:11, 8).

Despite early suspicions about CONAP's intentions, these new tenure rights, combined with the desire to tap into growing donor assistance and to develop new livelihoods, created a powerful incentive among communities to bid for concessions and abide by the conditions set.

The concession holders pledged to assume a completely new role, transforming themselves from illegal loggers, farmers, and immigrants into natural resource stewards.

Even with considerable assistance, it took several years for these disparate and often fragmented communities to develop the good governance and resource management practices required to fulfill their contracts (Chemonics 2006:39-40). By December 2000, however, consultants reported to USAID that enterprise members "fully understood" that their economic sustenance depended on a well-managed forest, and they demonstrated this by "their availability for…unpaid jobs and their enthusiasm for learning the technical aspects of the operations" (Chemonics and IRG 2000:A-IV-9-10). It also took time for mistrust of government agencies to abate. But as the early EFCs began to earn income from timber, the perception of CONAP and its NGO partners held by local residents gradually evolved from that of adversary to one of an ally. The result was a marked reduction of tension in the region (Pool et al. 2002:10).

By the end of 1999, CONAP had signed 12 concession contracts covering almost the entire multiple use zone, with 355,000 ha under community management and an additional 132,215 ha managed by the two industrial concessions. Nearly 92,000 ha of the community concessions had been certified to international FSC standards, the largest tract of natural forest under community management in the world at that time (Chemonics and IRG 2000: A-IV-7-8).

ARBOL VERDE: ANATOMY OF A COMMUNITY FORESTRY ENTERPRISE

One of the most successful community forestry enterprises is Arbol Verde, which manages a 64,973-ha concession producing timber and sawn wood for domestic, Caribbean, and Mexican markets and runs a side operation in ecotourism. Certified in 2002, it has the biggest membership of any concession (345) people and its organizational and governance structure typifies how most enterprises have evolved. The administrator and board of directors, elected every two years, operate a sawmill, hotel, and restaurant in addition to managing the forest. In 2006, some 30 people were employed in seasonal timber jobs, 10 people worked in sawmilling, and 19 were in administration, forest management, and patrols and tourism (Chemonics 2006:10; Molnar et al. 2007:44).

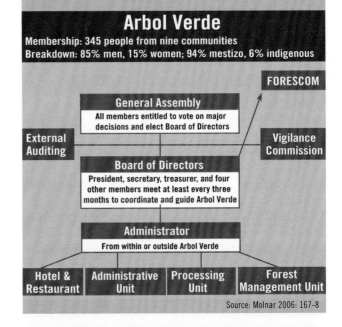

Source: Molnar 2006: 167-8

MAYA BIOSPHERE COMMUNITY CONCESSIONS, 2005			
Legal Status	**Community Forest Enterprise**	**Members**	**Area Under Management (Ha)**
Community Concessions	La Pasadita	121	18, 817
	San Miguel La Palotada	53	7,039
	Cruce a la Colorada	60	20,496
	La Colorada	50	22,067
	San Andrés (AFISAP)	176	51,940
	Cooperativa Carmelita	124	53,797
	Uaxactun (OMYC)	285	83,558
	Arbol Verde	345	64,973
	Impulsores Suchitecos	27	12,218
	Laborantes del Bosque	95	19,390
	Custudios de las Selva	96	21,176
	El Esfuerzo	40	25,386
Industrial Concessions	Paxbán		65,755
	La Gloria		66,460

Intermediaries Help Build Necessary Skills

Given that most EFC members were poorly educated and few had either organizational or business management experience, outside assistance was critical. This role was filled by local and international NGOs funded by donors, primarily USAID but also the UK Department for International Development and others. In the early years, international environmental NGOs including Conservation International, Centro Agrónomico Tropical de Investigación y Enseñanza (CATIE), The Nature Conservancy, CARE, Rodale Institute, and the Wildlife Conservation Society provided technical assistance geared mainly to forest protection (Saito 2008). These organizations had lobbied strongly for the creation of the Maya Biosphere Reserve and were heavily invested in its success.

Working on the basis of Cooperative Agreements and Letters of Implementation with USAID, these NGOs developed monitoring tools, performed environmental impact assessments, fostered conservation awareness, and helped enterprises achieve forest certification. Each international group also worked through local NGOs, whose personnel helped the fledgling enterprises establish basic self-governance procedures and provided basic training for elected officers in organizational management, record-keeping, accounting, and strategic planning (Chemonics and IRG 2000:II-8-9).

Three entirely new local environmental NGOs—ProPetén, Centro Mayo, and Nature for Life—were created to implement USAID-funded activities across the Maya Biosphere Reserve, in itself a major achievement (Chemonics and IRG 2000:II-9). Only one of these, Nature for Life, worked directly with the community enterprises, under the direction of CATIE and with support from The Nature Conservancy (Chemonics and IRG 2000:A-VI-1-2). Yet all three groups have flourished, providing

additional representation for the Petén's isolated forest communities and increasing their social resilience.

The efforts of these early intermediaries, both international and local, were essential in making the concessions a reality. Working with farmers and loggers for whom forestry simply meant felling trees, their expertise in conservation policy and sustainable land management helped to foster conservation awareness and pride among local populations as well as to teach sustainable forestry practices. As a result, the young EFCs exceeded expectations in making the transition to sustainable forestry management. In December 2000, a review of USAID's efforts to preserve the Maya Biosphere Reserve by the development consultancy Chemonics International described the concessions in the multiple use zone as a "stroke of genius" that had "provided the most sustainable aspects of the program" (Chemonics and IRG 2000:III-5).

However, the same review highlighted the urgent need for the EFCs to become viable businesses in addition to successful forestry stewards. Generous subsidies by USAID and others had enabled the enterprises to make profits from timber sales in their first few years without putting sound business practices in place. But this state of affairs was not sustainable over the long term, and the review authors advised USAID that the conservation NGOs assisting the EFCs lacked the business, marketing, and management capabilities that were now required (Chemonics and IRG 2000:A-IV-24).

The consultants also raised two other red flags. They warned that governance failings of enterprises and turf wars among the many NGOs advising them were delaying progress and preventing lessons from being shared (Chemonics and IRG 2000:III-5-6). And they concluded that the free technical assistance to EFCs had "served to develop an unsustainable dependency of the communities on the subsidy and a specific NGO" (Chemonics and IRG 2000:A-IV-24).

A Second Start

These important early lessons caused USAID to streamline its Petén operations and channel all assistance through Chemonics International to local NGOs, thus strengthening local institutions (Chemonics 2006:1; Tschinkel 2007). CONAP also adapted the rules governing concession management to require that a qualified "forestry supervisor" should provide technical supervision, rather than specifically an NGO, enabling EFCs to work with more specialized advisers such as professional foresters (Saito 2008).

From 2002 to March 2006, Chemonics staff worked with local NGOs to improve the community enterprises' internal statutes and financial practices, teach technical forestry skills to improve cost effectiveness, and develop timber processing and marketing outlets (Chemonics 2006:1).

The most difficult problems Chemonics faced was tackling elite capture, corruption, and poor management within some of the community organizations. Institutional corruption remains a serious problem throughout Guatemala, and the new community organizations proved no exception. Making matters worse, the governance conditions required by USAID and the implementing NGOs had often been nominally met by communities in the rush to get enterprises going (Tschinkel 2007).

As a result, decision-making over timber management and sales and financial power were often concentrated among a few individuals, usually the board of directors, with little involvement of the wider membership. Some enterprises also refused membership to residents who had opted out in the early days,

despite contractual requirements that all adults be allowed to join. While concession statutes generally required some investment in community-wide projects, these were often ignored, further alienating the wider community (Chemonics and IRG 2000:A-IV-17; Nittler and Tschinkel 2005:8). Communities' lack of understanding of how to run a good business also resulted in an insistence that new boards of directors and treasurers be elected every year, adding to the organizational disarray (Chemonics and IRG 2000:A-IV-17).

Chemonics took a three-pronged approach to developing the EFCs into viable businesses. First, it helped them to revise regulations along more effective, transparent, and equitable lines (Chemonics 2003:16). Second, it filled the skills void by focusing on intensive training and sales and marketing support. By 2006, some 6,839 enterprise members had participated in training courses and technical assistance events teaching entrepreneurial skills, including business and finance administration, tax and labor laws, banking and credit access, budgeting, sales management, and accounting (Chemonics 2006:8, 19–24). Third, EFCs were helped to develop five-year strategic business plans, weaning them off a year-to-year boom-and-bust approach to doing business (Chemonics 2006:8).

To fulfill its marketing mandate, Chemonics also subcontracted SmartWood, the certification program run by the U.S. nonprofit Rainforest Alliance, to certify the outstanding concessions so they could better tap into the growing global market in sustainable timber (Chemonics 2006:8). In addition, Chemonics'

ENTERPRISING WOMEN: A WORK IN PROGRESS

Among rural Guatemalans, forestry is traditional male territory, a cultural mindset that impeded early efforts to involve women in the community enterprises. In some cases, male leaders argued that forestry management tasks involved physical labor unsuitable for women; in others, wives and daughters were refused membership of EFCs granted to their husbands and fathers (Monterroso 2002:1).

Early NGO training programs also failed to emphasize women's rights. In 2002 only about 15 percent of EFC members were female, with their tasks mostly limited to harvesting non-timber forest products, including berries, xate, and wicker for baskets (Monterroso 2002:1). But addressing this gender gap became a major focus of training programs implemented by Chemonics International, and by 2006 eight EFCs had set up commissions to promote gender equity and appointed at least one woman to their Board of Directors (Chemonics 2006:18).

Chemonics and local NGOs also held workshops to enhance village women's self-esteem and provided day care services to boost their participation in EFC meetings. Practical job training and marketing assistance for non-timber products, such as handicrafts and tourism guiding, were also focused increasingly on women (Chemonics 2006:18–19).

technical support staff supported the establishment of FORESCOM as an umbrella forest products company and drafted its bylaws. FORESCOM began operations in January 2004 and took over certification of its member concessions in 2005. This centralized process for certification cut community costs significantly, enabling EFCs to pay for certification and technical assistance without donor subsidies for the first time (Chemonics 2006:2, 8).

In March 2006, the second phase of USAID-funded intermediary assistance ended and Chemonics withdrew. In a natural progression toward making the EFCs viable businesses, Chemonics was succeeded by a scaled-down USAID program targeted specifically toward diversifying wood and non-timber products from the concessions and expanding their markets. The long-term viability of the concessions depends on the success of this three-year, US$2-million phase, which is managed by the Rainforest Alliance and will end in August 2009 (Rainforest Alliance 2007b:1).

The Paternalism Trap

By August 2009, the US government's aid agency will have spent more than US$11 million on the Petén community forestry enterprises project alone (Nittler and Tschinkel 2005:12; Rainforest Alliance 2007b:1). While the many intermediaries working with the EFCs have helped them become both effective stewards and successful businesses, the scale of support also fostered a culture of donor dependency that has proved difficult to break (Tschinkel 2007). "Self-sufficiency goals were only put in

place after Chemonics arrived," recalled John Nittler, a vice-president of Chemonics International who helped oversee the program. "In the early years...a dependency was created that remains very hard to overcome" (Nittler 2007).

Since 2006, the Rainforest Alliance and government agencies working with the enterprises have sought to foster independence with a "learning through doing" approach (Rainforest Alliance 2007b:2). This provides on-the-job (rather than theoretical) training in the production, processing, packaging, and sale of new processed timber and NTFPs. CONAP's requirement that all concessions hire a forestry specialist as technical supervisor has also helped to professionalize EFCs, as has a recent requirement by the SmartWood certifiers that concession governing boards must retain some members for more than one term of office (Saito 2008; Carrera 2007).

By late 2007, these strategies appeared to be paying off, with 8 of the 12 community enterprises functioning as self-sufficient businesses and facing prosperous futures after USAID subsidies end (Carrera 2007).

Conservation Dividend: Preserving Forests, Protecting Livelihoods

While community forestry enterprises have been slow in gaining organizational independence, they proved to be skillful in forestry stewardship. Aware of the link between sustainable forest management and the income potential of their new venture, virtually every EFC established a low-impact approach to harvesting both timber and non-timber forest products, based on a few common ground rules (Chemonics and IRG 2000:A-IV-9–10).

Ecologically fragile areas and those high in biodiversity were left alone. Elsewhere, harvest management cycles of 25 years were established, with one of 25 blocks of forest to be harvested each year, allowing 24 years for regrowth. Each EFC also prepared annual operational plans, based on a census of individual trees in the block to be harvested, which were approved by CONAP officials (Nittler and Tschinkel 2005:14–15, 11). On average, only 0.8–2.4 trees per ha have been harvested, due in part to a lack of commercial species of sufficient size (Tschinkel 2008).

The 25-year plans included detailed maps, some enhanced with satellite images and aerial photography, showing concession boundaries, vegetation and forest types, and fragile and archeological sites in need of particular protection. Most highlighted 15–20 "commercial" tree species, although until recent years almost all the wood felled was mahogany or tropical cedar (Nittler and Tschinkel 2005:14). This detailed planning also enabled logging roads to be cut efficiently, minimizing ecological impact.

Early fears voiced by some environmental NGOs that any felling activity could harm biodiversity soon proved groundless (Chemonics 2006:37). As one biological monitoring team reported in 2002: "At current extraction levels (0.8–2.4 trees/ha), the ecological impacts of timber extraction are minimal. Modest changes in the community structures of birds, beetles, diurnal butterflies, and game species suggest that current logging practices do not preclude any species from logged areas, but rather increase species richness by augmenting habitat heterogeneity" (Balas 2004 and Radachowsky 2004 as cited in Nittler and Tschinkel 2005:17).

Giving local communities an economic stake in the forest around them has also proved a highly effective driver in curbing illegal activity in the Maya Biosphere Reserve (Saito 2008). To protect their capital investment, the 1,500 members of the 12 community forestry enterprises have invested time, personnel, and money into patrolling and safeguarding their concessions. Every year the EFCs jointly invest around US$150,000 in forest surveillance and fire control measures. Members patrol concession borders; they report fires, illegal logging, and new settlements; and they are compensated for their time from timber sale revenues (Chemonics 2006:37). "Our secret is that we have more than 150 people working in this forest, collecting palm leaves, chicle and allspice, and if one of them sees anything happening that shouldn't be, they report it to us and we send a delegation to that area immediately," says Benedin Garcia, founder member of the community organization that manages the Uaxactun concession (Rainforest Alliance 2007b:3).

The impact of community self-interest and investment in preserving the forests under their control has been dramatic. As early as 2000, deforestation fell sharply in the Maya Biosphere

Reserve's multiple use zone, which contains the concessions; illegal deforestation continues in the core zones where development is banned (Chemonics 2003:10–11). From 2002 to 2007, this trend accelerated, with the average annual deforestation rate in the reserve's national parks (0.79 percent of land area) 20 times higher than that in the FSC-certified concessions (0.04 percent of land area) (Hughell and Butterfield 2008:10). The MBR's protected areas also suffer more wildfires, often set by farmers or illegal settlers, than the neighboring concessions. Since 1998, between 7 percent and 20 percent of forest cover in the Maya Biosphere Reserve has burned annually, while in FSC-certified concessions the figure has fallen steadily from 6.3 percent in 1998, when concessions were first established, to 0.1 percent in 2007 (Hughell and Butterfield 2008:1–2).

CONAP's requirement that EFCs achieve Forest Stewardship Council certification within three years of signing a concession contract also contributed to the speed with which communities adopted effective forest management and surveillance practices (Chemonics 2003: 26). By 2008, all 12 community enterprises and both industrial concessions had achieved FSC status at some point, and 479,500 ha of forest was currently certified (Hughell and Butterfield 2008:6).

While the Petén population's willingness to harvest sustainably depends on a continuing flow of economic benefits, they have laid the groundwork to preserve their forests for the indefinite future. As observers Nittler and Tschinkel reported in 2005: "In general the forest management and operational plans have evolved to a level of sophistication which, if followed, is almost certain to assure the sustained management and long-term conservation of the forest" (Nittler and Tschinkel 2005:15). This is particularly impressive given that tens of millions of dollars have failed to halt deforestation in other parts of the Maya Biosphere Reserve and the wider network of Central American parks to which it belongs.

ANNUAL DEFORESTATION RATE BEFORE AND AFTER 2002

Land class	1986 to 2001	2002 to 2007
Core protected areas	0.26%	0.79%
FSC certified concessions in multiple use zone	0.01%	0.04%
Remainder of multiple use zone	0.31%	0.86%
Buffer zone	1.91%	2.20%
Entire MBR	0.52%	0.88%

Source: Hughell and Butterfield 2008:10

PERCENTAGE OF AREA BURNED IN EACH LAND USE ZONE BY YEAR

Land Use Zone	1998	2003	2005	2007
Core protected areas	23.6%	26.0%	29.6%	10.4%
FSC/RA certified concessions in multiple use zone	6.3%	1.8%	0.1%	0.1%
Remainder of multiple use zone	21.9%	21.3%	12.9%	5.0%
Buffer zone	23.9%	23.5%	19.6%	10.3%
Overall MBR (%)	19.5%	19.1%	18.0%	7.2%
Overall MBR (ha)	404,632	398,280	375,149	149,424

Source: Hughell and Butterfield 2008:1–2

Community Dividends: Jobs, Income, Infrastructure

The success of Guatemala's community forestry enterprises is reflected in growing income and employment among the desperately poor villages scattered through the remote northern forests and lowlands. By 2003, the 12 community enterprises were generating an estimated US$5 million per year in timber sales, while forestry operations generated an estimated 51,309 person-days of work, worth US$359,490 in wages (Nittler and Tschinkel 2005:21). By September 2007, approximately 7,300 people were employed either seasonally or year-round by the enterprises and FORESCOM (Carrera 2008).

Typically, half the wood harvested is highly prized mahogany, sold mostly to local timber companies that export it to the United States. Another valuable species, Santa Maria, is sold for export to Mexico, while other native timber such as Spanish cedar finds ready local markets (Nittler and Tschinkel 2005:17–18).

Enterprise members enjoy distinct advantages over their neighbors. They earn an estimated average of US$1,140 during the two to three months when full time work is available for harvesting and processing within the concessions (Chemonics 2003: 6). The rest of the year they typically take other jobs, such as working on farms or ranches, although some members work year-round on the concessions, processing timber and harvesting and processing non-timber products.

Annual household incomes outside concessions can be as low as US$1,200 a year, the same amount that the average employed concession member earns in two to three months (Chemonics 2003:6). Not only do enterprises typically pay a higher day rate than the regional prevailing wage, but some also pay members an annual dividend (Chemonics and IRG 2000:A-IV-14).

As their income and business acumen has grown, some enterprises have also branched out into ecotourism, independent of donor support, providing additional jobs for local people. Arbol Verde, for example, built a small hotel, while Uaxactun, the gateway to Mayan temple country, has developed tour guide programs and a handicrafts center (Stoian and Rodas 2006b:6; Chemonics 2006:18–19).

Improving Quality of Life

While not all enterprises have fulfilled their own regulations on benefit-sharing with the wider community, most have invested in much-needed local infrastructure and services. In the early years, for example, Unión Maya Itzá purchased two buses and a truck for community use; Carmelita built a bridge, San Miguel installed a potable water system, and La Pasadita built a dispensary (Chemonics and IRG 2000:A-IV-14–15).

More recently, several enterprises have provided social services that are transforming poor families' quality of life and young people's prospects. For example, the Conservation and Management Organization that manages the Uaxactun concession operates an emergency fund that the town's poorest families can draw on for medical care. It also pays several high school teachers salaries and funds computer classes for 22 students in the provincial capital. "We invest in education because we want the next generation to be well-trained and capable of defending our interests," says the organization's board secretary, Floridalma Ax (Rainforest Alliance 2007c:2).

CARMELITA: A CONCESSION SUCCESS STORY

The remote forest town of Carmelita, nestled among Mayan ruins in the central Petén, was among the first to receive a concession contract from CONAP, in 1996. With assistance from U.S. non-profit Conservation International and the Wildlife Conservation Society and later with support from Chemonics and the Rainforest Alliance, it has made productive use of its 53,798 ha of forest (Nittler 2008; Stoian and Rodas 2006a:2). The 127 members of the cooperative enterprise (56 percent male and 44 percent female) that manages the concession have set aside 20,000 ha for timber production and 33,798 ha for harvesting non-timber forest products, primarily xate ornamental palms and chicle gum (Stoian and Rodas 2006a:6). In recent years, the community has offered guided ecotours on foot and horseback into neighboring El Mirador park, which is rich in archeological sites (Stoian and Rodas 2006a:7).

Despite felling timber on less than 1 percent of their land, enterprise members have significantly increased their income by selling certified mahogany and NTFPs and by investing in a community sawmill and carpentry shop. Sawn wood from first-class mahogany fetched US$1,781 per cubic meter in 2006, up from US$742 per cubic meter in 2000 (Molnar et al. 2007:171–172). Since 2003, individual enterprise members have also reaped an impressive average annual income from sales of xate and chicle of around US$2,300 (Chemonics 2003:7).

The community forestry enterprise is the largest local employer, providing seasonal logging and wild plant harvesting work for about 90 people and

30 permanent jobs in sawmills. More than a third of earnings are ploughed back into community development and improved forestry technology and management (Stoian and Rodas 2006a:13).

DAYS OF WAGES PROVIDED BY CARMELITA CONCESSION, 2005

Activity	Non-Members	Members	Total
Timber extraction	250	2,000	2,250
Wood processing	1,000	3,000	4,000
Xate collection	- - -	400	400
Chicle collection	- - -	200	200
Tourism	50	100	150
Total	**1,300**	**5,700**	**7,000**

Source: Stoian and Rodas 2006: 13

The future is not without hazards, as Carmelita's members sometimes have to fend off encroaching settlers, cattle ranchers from the south, and illegal loggers from the north. But the enterprise has strengthened its prospects by expanding markets and pooling resources with other EFCs by joining both FORESCOM and a non-timber forest products marketing alliance (Stoian and Rodas 2006a:5). "Our parents protected this forest for our benefit and it is our responsibility to protect it for future generations," says the enterprise's 23-year-old president Carlos Crasborn (Rainforest Alliance 2007b:2; Pool et al. 2002:94).

Adding Value:
Processing and Wood Products

In the early years, EFC overreliance on donor subsidies and on high-earning but finite supplies of mahogany raised the specter of bankruptcy and subsequent community disillusionment. The NGO intermediaries therefore steered the fledgling enterprises toward capturing greater value from their resource, both by selling more species and by processing timber themselves. By 2003, eight communities owned portable sawmills, two had invested in carpentry equipment, and 55 percent of the 50,000 work days generated across community forests were spent sawmilling, compared with 29 percent spent harvesting (Nittler and Tschinkel 2005:16, 22; Chemonics 2003:7).

Since 2005, the collective forestry services company, FORESCOM, has taken its member enterprises a further step up the economic ladder by expanding markets and developing new products. Building on a marketing strategy developed by Chemonics, FORESCOM has successfully established national and US markets for three lesser-known wood species—pucte, Santa Maria, and danto (Chemonics 2006:24; Nittler and Tschinkel 2005:17–18). It also won government funding to build an industrial processing plant that began

operating in 2007, enabling enterprises to directly manufacture finished products for the lucrative international market in certified wood. With assistance from the Rainforest Alliance, FORESCOM secured orders in 2007 for more than 1.5 million board feet of certified wood, worth US$3 million, including milled lumber, floorboards, and decking (USAID 2005). The plant has already allowed more members of FORESCOM to take advantage of sales contracts for products like decking and flooring with specialty companies in the United States, the Netherlands, and the United Kingdom (Molnar et al. 2007:172–173; Rainforest Alliance 2007a:1).

A Secondary Harvest:
Non-Timber Forest Products

The community enterprises have also garnered extra income and diversified their business by harvesting and selling non-timber forest products (NTFPs). Collecting these products, which include chicle tree sap, xate palms, and allspice, for sale to exporters has been lucrative in the Petén for decades, yielding significant income for thousands of families (Chemonics 2006:5;

Chemonics and IRG 2000:A-V-2). Historically, NTFP collection has been an individual venture, resulting in little awareness of harvest sustainability and limited marketing power for the producers (IRG 2006:1). A few years after the concessions were awarded, however, NGOs began encouraging sustainable and collective harvesting of these products as a supplement to timber cutting (Pool et al. 2002:15). CONAP was subsequently charged with regulating NTFPs' harvesting and transport (IRG 2006:1-2; Chemonics and IRG 2000:A-V-4).

The new focus on NTFPs has paid off for the concession communities. With the assistance of the Rainforest Alliance, more enterprises have improved the management and professional harvesting of wild plants and are exploiting their commercial potential. They are dealing directly with overseas buyers, cutting out the export middlemen, boosting profits, and building relationships with customers (Rainforest Alliance 2007c:2).

In 2007, Carmelita, Uaxactun, and five other concessions created a joint marketing committee for xate palms to coordinate supply and export routes. With the Rainforest Alliance acting as intermediary, these enterprises are selling between 400 and 600 packages of xate a week to a single buyer, Continental Floral Greens in Houston. From January to September 2007 they grossed US$147,948 in US exports (Carrera 2008). Other new markets include the Adventist Churches of Minnesota, which bought 122,000 palms sourced from the Maya Biosphere Reserve over 12 months in 2006–2007 (Rainforest Alliance 2000a:2). For Palm Sunday 2008, these churches purchased 250,000 palms with a 5 cent premium on each palm (Carrera 2008).

To meet the demands of eco-conscious customers, the Rainforest Alliance has helped these communities set sustainable harvesting guidelines for collectors and improve supply and delivery by building two central collection and sorting facilities. With technical assistance, three enterprises—Carmelita, Uaxactun, and San Andres—are on target to achieve FSC certification in 2008 for sustainable xate plantations on 170,000 ha of concession land, the first such management standard in the world (Rainforest Alliance 2007b:2).

Securing the Future:
A Challenging Road Ahead

Both for nature and for people, Guatemala's community forestry enterprises have proved a clear success. As early as 2000, the government's decision to hand over tenure rights and management responsibilities to communities with a direct economic interest in forest protection had paid off. "[They] have exceeded expectations…are dramatically increasing the incomes of concessionaires and have reduced the incidence of forest fires, illegal logging and settlements," reported the authors of a 2000 review of the Maya Biosphere Project for USAID (Chemonics and IRG 2000:III-5).

Xate palms

While the concessions have encountered problems and required millions of dollars in support, they have continued to do far better at protecting forest and biodiversity than CONAP has done in the neighboring national parks. Studies predict that at current rates of deforestation, the Maya Biosphere Reserve will lose 38 percent of its 1986 forest cover by 2050. As a result, the certified concessions are likely to play an increasingly important role in the future in the reserve (Hughell and Butterfield 2008:2).

The commitment of self-interested communities combined with the support of government agencies, NGOs, international donors, and, more recently, overseas buyers has fostered this success story. Yet 14 years after the first concession was granted, four EFCs are in trouble and the long-term future of the remainder, while promising, is not assured (Nittler 2008). The reasons for this uncertainty stem from mistakes made when concessions were first allocated and from failures to address wider policy issues, such as uncontrolled immigration and agricultural encroachment that threaten their future stability.

As described earlier, the borders of some early concessions were hastily drawn without close attention to the makeup of the forests and without input from forestry professionals. Several have since proved too small and devoid of high-value timber species that could provide a viable income from sustainable

timber operations, and they have struggled to make a profit (Nittler and Tschinkel 2005).

Under these circumstances, community commitment to sustainable forestry management has been lacking, with predictable consequences. Corruption has flourished in a number of the smaller concessions, including San Miguel (7,039 ha), La Pasadita (18,817 ha), La Colorada (22,067 ha), and Cruce a La Colorada (20,469 ha). In these concessions, powerful local figures illegally sell parcels of concession land to settlers and encourage farmers to encroach into forest earmarked for sustainable harvest (Nittler 2008; Carrera 2008). In 2004, SmartWood suspended the FSC certification status of San Miguel and La Pasadita, further harming their business outlook and producing a stalemate that has yet to be resolved (Chemonics and IRG 2000:A-IV-24; Carrera 2007).

Poor organization and governance have also continued to hold back some enterprises from thriving as independent small businesses. In 2005, for example, observers noted that the continued insistence by many enterprises on a yearly turnover of board members entrenched "a guaranteed recipe for perpetual incompetence" (Nittler and Tschinkel 2005:8). In the past three years, however, these problems have lessened significantly as EFCs have been required to professionalize their management under conditions specified by the SmartWood sustainable certifi-

cation inspections. At least one manager with proven forestry experience must be hired, for example, and EFC governing boards are required to retain at least one or two members for more than one term of office to ensure continuity of experience (Carrera 2007). Long-term planning has also improved EFCs' business performance. With help from Chemonics, seven enterprises have produced comprehensive five-year plans enabling them to forecast timber supply, improve sales forecasts, and avoid poor investment decisions (Chemonics 2006:26).

In its 2006 completion report, Chemonics International focused on the growing economic and social resilience of the concession communities, describing how villagers had developed into effective entrepreneurs: "Unlike the mindset in 2001, today most [enterprise] members understand the importance of managing their organizations for profit. Board members and managers are more aware of production costs, they have built in administrative and production controls, and are better prepared to negotiate more profitable forest-harvesting contracts" (Chemonics 2006:38). By December 2007, according to José Roman Carrera, regional manager for the Rainforest Alliance's sustainable forestry division, eight enterprises were profitable, operationally self-sufficient, and well placed to prosper once USAID funding to develop new products and markets ceases in August 2009 (Carrera 2007).

LEARNING FROM GUATEMALA'S COMMUNITY FOREST ENTERPRISES

Care must be taken at start-up. In the understandable rush to establish concessions in the early 1990s, little thought was given to the implications of long-term forest stewardship. Territories were carved out with little consideration of what was appropriate and necessary to provide economic opportunities and incentives. The first few concessions were too small, unable to support profitable enterprises under sustainable management. Today, those concessions are rife with corruption, and the forests are degraded by illegal logging and clearing for agriculture.

There is a difference between stewardship and enterprise. Initial skill training for the concession managers focused on forest management. Only after government agencies and NGOs both saw that the expected economic impact was not materializing—and that sustainable practices were suffering as a result—did it become clear that communities also needed skills to manage the business side of the concession: sales, marketing, and certification. This oversight set back the development of profitable community concessions by several years.

Government has an ongoing role that must be exercised. One of the goals of the government's establishment of the Maya Reserve was the preservation of one of the last great swaths of virgin forest in Central America. The track record of the certified concessions shows considerable improvement in the health of the areas under their control. But the National Parks in the reserve itself, ostensibly off-limits to all extractive uses, are losing acreage at an alarming pace because of poaching and illegal farming. The lack of any enforcement undercuts the government's goals and may ultimately jeopardize the achievements of the concessions.

Long-term commitment is needed. This applies in every case. The first concession contract was signed in 1994. Nine years later, NGOs and aid agencies were putting the finishing touches on FORESCOM, the organization formed by nine of the concession communities to provide marketing services and training for concession members and to coordinate sustainable certification of their timber. Twelve years after the first concession, a phaseout plan for USAID is in place, now that nine concessions are well established and profitable.

There is strength in numbers. The forest concessions in Guatemala were thrust from the start into an international market; that is the nature of the high-value timber they were able to harvest. These concessions could never, individually, hope to have all the contacts and skills necessary to successfully navigate that trade. Their willingness to fund the creation of FORESCOM has paid significant dividends. In addition to the services mentioned already, FORESCOM markets the combined harvests of the members to command better prices and encourages the production of additional products. Delegating certain critical management decisions to FORESCOM is one key factor that has made eight of the Petén concessions self-sufficient and profitable today.

Carrera warned, however, that this encouraging prospect depended on the absence of "adverse external developments," particularly the threat of uncontrolled immigration and agricultural encroachment spilling over into community forests (Carrera 2007). Due to rising birth rates and economic migration from the south, illegal settlements and forest clearance by farmers continue to plague the Maya Biosphere Reserve's supposedly protected national parks. By 2006, for example, about 40 percent of Laguna del Tigre National Park along the reserve's western border had been destroyed by illegal logging and wildfires (compared with only 4 percent in the neighboring Uaxactun concession) (Rainforest Alliance 2007c:2).

One problem is that communities in the buffer zone alongside the national parks have not been given the alternative livelihood opportunities enjoyed by the concession communities and therefore lack any incentive to respect park rules. Another is the weakness of CONAP, which remains chronically short of staff and resources and which lacks political support from other government agencies (Chemonics 2006:45). "The government supports the development of the forestry enterprises," says Carrera, "but to protect the concessions it needs to assign enough resources to enforce the protected area laws throughout the Maya Biosphere Reserve" (Carrera 2008).

Scaling Up Community Forest Enterprises

Organizational Scale-Up

The creation of second-tier agencies has been critical in putting Guatemala's community enterprises on a viable business footing. In the early years, ACOFOP lobbied for more and larger concessions to be allocated and it provided fragmented communities with a collective voice (Chemonics 2003:10). Since 2003, the forest products company FORESCOM has enabled nine enterprises to add value to their basic product, timber, and to expand markets (Chemonics 2006:27).

By providing technical assistance in meeting SmartWood's sustainable timber certification conditions, FORESCOM has allowed enterprises to cut compliance costs by up to 80 percent and to end reliance on donor subsidies (Chemonics 2006:13–14; Nittler and Tschinkel 2005:16). With assistance from the internationally networked Rainforest Alliance, the company has also successfully identified national and overseas markets, particularly for lesser-known wood species that FORESCOM sells on its members' behalf. By representing the combined output of nine concessions (with the other three due to join by 2009), FORESCOM is winning big contracts beyond the reach of individual enterprises, such as an annual contract to supply 1 million board feet of timber a year to a Guatemalan building company.

Much of the demand from the US and Europe is for processed wood and finished products. In 2006, FORESCOM received a US$260,000 grant from the Guatemalan government to build a factory that manufactures flooring, decking, and furniture components from lesser-known species. In 2008, the company will also help enterprises set up dry kilning facilities in their communities to refine the processing of high-value mahogany and cedar, further boosting profits (Carrera 2007).

FORESCOM has also built strong working relationships with customers, such as the national timber company Baren Commercial, and strategic alliances with local, national, and international organizations and agencies such as the municipalities of San Benito and Flores in the Petén, the National Forest Institute, the Union Association of Exporters (now a FORESCOM member), and the International Tropical Timber Organization (Chemonics 2006:29; Rainforest Alliance 2007b:1). Individual enterprises have also established strong relationships with specialist US buyers, such as Gibson Guitars and Continental Forest Greens, who are willing to pay premium prices—and often in advance—for, respectively, certified timber and xate (Rainforest Alliance 2007b:3).

Political Scale-Up

Despite the EFCs' well-publicized success, Guatemala's government has rebuffed USAID proposals that the concession approach be extended to core zones of the Maya Biosphere Reserve still being destroyed by illegal development and forest fires (Tschinkel 2007). Its commitment to the existing community concessions, however, is not in doubt. CONAP's 2005–2014 management strategy for the MBR, which includes consolidating the concessions in the multiple use zone, was approved at Cabinet level (Chemonics 2006:33), giving communities at least medium-term security. The national parks agency and the National Forest Institute have also widely adopted and institutionalized the extraction and management practices used in the concessions (Tschinkel 2008).

Since 2006, government agencies have also joined CONAP and the USAID-funded NGOs in helping EFCs achieve profitability and independence. The National Forest Institute is helping refine villagers' technical forestry skills. Two other agencies—PRONACOM (the National Competitiveness Program) and the Technical Training and Productivity Institute—are teaching enterprise members "learning by doing" skills and tools for running a small business, including the supply of finished products to international markets (Rainforest Alliance 2007b:2; Carrera 2008).

These agencies are expected to retain their links with the enterprises after international donors withdraw, deepening the government's investment in the EFCs' future (Carrera 2007). "The importance of the government of Guatemala's political and financial support for the development of the community forestry concession system…and continued enterprise develop-

ment cannot be overstated," says Greg Minnick, Managing Director of the Rainforest Alliance TREES (Training, Extension, Enterprise and Sourcing) Program (Minnick 2008).

Claiming Carbon Credits: A New Policy Tool

The Guatemalan government has also recognized the earning potential represented by preserving the Maya Biosphere Reserve's natural forest cover.

With funding from PRONACOM, USAID, the Inter-American Development Bank, and two private companies, CONAP and the Rainforest Alliance are supporting a pioneering scheme to develop carbon credit markets for the community concessions on the basis of avoided deforestation (Rainforest Alliance 2007b:3). "It is a new concept, the first of its kind in Central America, because we are not working with plantations, but with natural primary tropical forest under certification," says José Roman Carrera (Carrera 2007). The pilot Maya Biosphere Carbon Project has already attracted interest from three buyers, and a quantification and verification process is due to be completed in 2008. The Rainforest Alliance projects that the enterprises will be able to sell 24.9 million tons of avoided carbon dioxide emissions over the next 10 years, creating an impressive new revenue stream in the form of environmental services payments (Rainforest Alliance 2007b:3).

The government's interest reflects the recognition that, as donors withdraw, payments such as these may represent the best guarantee for the reserve's long-term survival, reinforcing local communities' stake in its conservation. According to Carrera, the new income will be partly invested in the four failing community concessions, helping them to develop non-timber forest product industries and sustainable agriculture in areas already stripped of forest. "It's the only way we can preserve biodiversity," he says, "by adding environmental services to other sustainable forms of income and extracting maximum value from the forests" (Carrera 2007).

Replicating the Petén's Success

USAID is funding the first attempt to certify community and family-owned forest plots outside the Petén, by expanding the activities implemented by the Rainforest Alliance to two other regions. Since September 2006, as part of the Forestry Enterprises in Guatemala Program, the NGO has worked in Las Verapaces, to the south of the Petén, and in the Western Highlands area affected by Hurricane Stan, helping communities implement sustainable management practices and expand markets for local mixed forest products. Already, several existing community forestry organizations have reached commercial timber and wooden gift markets for the first time by promoting their timber as "pre-certified" (Rainforest Alliance 2007b:1).

Across Latin America

Neighboring countries with biologically diverse tropical forests are also taking advantage of the skills and lessons learned by the Petén's pioneering enterprises. Following a decade of training, the sophisticated technical capacity of community foresters is so evident that they have been hired as consultants and trainers in sustainable forest management programs in Nicaragua, Panama, and Peru (Chemonics 2006:41). The comprehensive 25-year sustainable management plans developed by the enterprises and intermediaries have also produced "technical models worthy of emulation" by forest managers across tropical regions, according to observers (Nittler and Tschinkel 2005:15). The Rainforest Alliance, for example, is already replicating the concession forest management model in Honduras, helping to build community enterprise skills and access to certified timber markets for 11 villages that manage 100,000 ha within the threatened and wildlife-rich Rio Platano Biosphere Reserve (Rainforest Alliance 2006:1).

Guatemala's community enterprises have taken a long time to become established. In the process, they have become increasingly resilient and better prepared for new external and internal challenges. Their success in keeping deforestation at bay, raising local incomes and quality of life, and developing into established businesses is encouraging and offers prospects and lessons for replication in other tropical regions. Management responsibility for 25 percent of the developing world's forests now lies in the hands of local communities—a figure expected to double by 2015 (Molnar et al. 2007:19; Carrera 2008). This makes identifying and scaling up such local management models, which meet the needs of both people and nature, a compelling and necessary task.

TURNING BACK THE DESERT
How Farmers Have Transformed Niger's Landscapes and Livelihoods

NIGER IS AN UNLIKELY SETTING FOR AN ENVIRONMENTAL SUCCESS STORY OF MAJOR proportions. The West African state ranks 174th out of 177 countries in the 2007–08 Human Development Index prepared by the United Nations Development Programme, based on indicators of health, education, and economic well-being. Sixty percent of Niger's people live on less than US$1 per day (UNDP 2007). Four fifths of its territory falls within the Sahara desert and cannot support food crops. Yet population pressures are intense, with rural women bearing an average of 7.1 children (INS and Macro International Inc. 2007:xxv). Niger's farmland and people—nomadic tribes apart—are concentrated in a southern strip of wind-swept savanna that falls within the Sahelian climatic zone. Rural communities struggle to grow crops in sandy, nutrient poor soils against a backdrop of chronically low and erratic rainfall, an ecological challenge that climate change will only intensify (IPCC 2007:444, 447–48).

Yet Niger is also the scene of an unprecedented, farmer-led "re-greening" movement that has reversed desertification and brought increased crop production, income, food security, and self-reliance to impoverished rural producers. Vast expanses of savanna devoid of vegetation in the early 1980s are now densely studded by trees, shrubs, and crops. The scale of the change is truly astonishing, affecting about 5 million ha of land—about the size of Costa Rica—which amounts to almost half of the cultivated land in Niger (Tappan 2007). By 2007, between a quarter and half of all the country's farmers were involved, and estimates suggest that at least 4.5 million people were reaping the benefits (Reij 2008).

The ecological impacts have been dramatic and include reduced erosion and increased soil fertility (Tougiani et al. 2008:10). Crop harvests have risen in many areas, enabling rural households to enjoy better diets, improved nutrition, higher incomes, and increased capacity to cope with periods of drought (Tougiani et al. 2008:16). In some villages, the *soudure*—the annual "hungry period" when food supplies are nearly exhausted—has been shortened or even eliminated (Larwanou

et al. 2006:1). Large areas of countryside that a few years ago faced constant shortages of fuelwood and fodder now produce surpluses for sale in nearby markets (Tougiani et al. 2008:13).

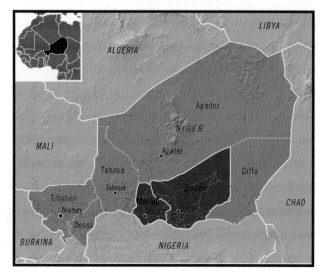

Many rural producers have doubled or tripled their incomes through the sale of wood, seed pods, and edible leaves (Winterbottom 2008).

The re-greening movement has had especially important impacts for some of the poorest members of Nigerien society—women and young men (Larwanou et al. 2006:1–2). The burden on women associated with the gathering of wood for household fuel has been reduced substantially (Boubacar et al. 2005:23). So has the annual exodus of young men seeking urban jobs in Niger and neighboring countries, thanks to new opportunities to earn income in an expanded and diversified rural economy (Larwanou et al. 2006:1–2). With farmers producing more fuelwood to supply urban areas, Niger's shrinking natural forests have also been spared further destruction (Winterbottom 2008).

There have been two key vehicles for this remarkable transformation. First is the adoption of simple, low-cost techniques for managing the natural regeneration of trees and shrubs, known as farmer-managed natural regeneration, or FMNR. In concert with forest management, many communities are also using simple soil and water conservation programs to drive the greening transformation. Both efforts have been encouraged and assisted by intermediaries including NGOs, donor governments, and international aid agencies. While this case study emphasizes the FMNR process, much of Niger's greening success can also be attributed to the simultaneous soil and conservation work. FMNR evolved in the mid-1980s as a response to the problems associated with traditional farming in Niger, in which farmers "cleaned" their land of all vegetation and crop residues before planting crops (Polgreen 2007:2). The past two decades of experimentation and innovation with FMNR in sustainably harvesting native vegetation have resulted in widespread acceptance that tree cover brings both income and subsistence benefits. The government of Niger has played an enabling role, enacting key land tenure and tree growth reforms, having learned from the failures of earlier destructive policies (McGahuey 2008).

In an ecologically vulnerable region expected to experience more frequent drought as a result of climate change, Niger's tree regeneration movement, say natural resource management experts, offers a proven path to greater environmental and economic resilience and increased food security for the inhabitants of Africa's drylands (Harris 2007; IPCC 2007:444, 447–48). Given the explosive rate of population growth in the region, FMNR alone will not enable Niger—or other Sahelian countries—to stay ahead of the food and livelihood needs of their people (McGahuey 2008). Indeed, even though FMNR is used widely today, 50 percent of Niger's children remain undernourished (INS and Macro International Inc. 2007:xxix). But it is one important tool to increase productivity for land-poor farmers and has already proved its capacity to provide them with diverse and sustainable rural livelihoods and economies.

KEY ACHIEVEMENTS OF NIGER'S RE-GREENING MOVEMENT

Building Environmental Capital

- An increase of 10- to 20-fold in tree and shrub cover on about 5 million ha of land, with approximately 200 million trees protected and managed (McGahuey and Winterbottom 2007:7; Tappan 2007; Reij 2008).

- At least 250,000 ha of degraded land reclaimed for crop production (McGahuey and Winterbottom 2007:7).

- Soil fertility improved as higher tree densities act as windbreaks to counter erosion, provide enriching mulch, and fix nitrogen in root systems (Reij 2006:iii).

- In some areas, the return of wild fauna, including hares, wild guinea fowls, squirrels, and jackals (Boubacar et al. 2005:16).

- Return of diverse local tree species that had all but disappeared from many areas and of beneficial insect and bird predators that reduce crop pests (Boubacar et al. 2005:13; Rinaudo 2005a:14).

Building Economic Capital

- Expanded cultivation of cereals and vegetables, with harvests doubling in some areas (Tougiani et al. 2008:16; Boubacar et al. 2005:25).

- Pods and leaves provide critical dry-season fodder supplies for livestock (Tougiani et al. 2008:16).

- New food export markets created, primarily to Nigeria (Reij 2006:ii).

- Rural incomes rose in three regions practicing farmer-managed natural regeneration (FMNR) (McGahuey and Winterbottom 2007:3).

- Creation of specialized local markets in buying, rehabilitating, and reselling degraded lands, with land values rising by 75–140 percent in some areas (Abdoulaye and Ibro 2006:44).

- Empowerment of hundreds of thousands of poor farmers, enabling them to pursue new enterprises and improve livelihoods (McGahuey 2008).

Building Social Capital

- Some 25–50 percent of all rural producers have adopted improved natural resource management techniques (estimate based on Tappan 2007).

- Food, fuelwood, and income provided by trees have increased food security (Reij 2006:iii).

- Nutrition and diets have improved through the availability of edible tree leaves and fruits as well as produce grown on rehabilitated plots (Larwanou et al. 2006:22).

- Improved access to land and income generation for women, widows, and the landless poor (McGahuey and Winterbottom 2007:13).

- Average time spent by women collecting firewood has fallen from 2.5 hours to half an hour (Reij 2006:iii).

- Increased self-reliance among villages; improved social status of women involved in FMNR (Reij 2006:iii; Diarra 2006:27).

- Reduced urban exodus of young men in search of work and creation of new small businesses related to forest products (BBC 2006).

TRENDS IN VEGETATION INDEX, 1982–1999

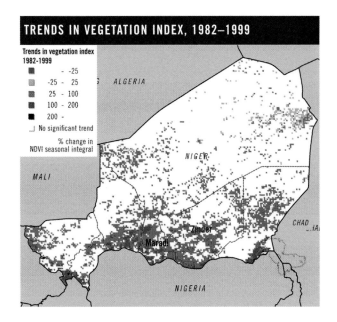

Trends in vegetation index
1982-1999

- ▪   - -25
- ▪   -25 - 25
- ▪   25 - 100
- ▪   100 - 200
- ▪   200 -
- ▫ No significant trend

% change in
NDVI seasonal integral

ALGERIA

MALI

NIGER

Zinder

Maradi

CHAD

NIGERIA

From Famine to Food: The Revegetation of Niger

The farmer-led transformation of Niger's countryside over the past quarter-century stemmed from an ecological and humanitarian crisis that threatened the lives and livelihoods of millions of people and undermined the country's ability to sustain itself.

Through the early 1900s, land use in Niger was characterized by sparse rural populations cultivating small fields amidst surrounding bush. Families were smaller, yields were sufficient, and there were ample supplies of timber from natural woodlands. Fields were left fallow, and trees and shrubs were regenerated to provide extra wood before being cleared for planting (Winterbottom 2008).

Land clearing and tree-felling became more common in the 1930s, as the French colonial government pushed Nigerien farmers to grow export crops and implemented policies that provided disincentives for farmers to care for their land. Such disincentives included a new land law that established the national government as the owner of all trees and required Nigeriens to purchase permits to use them (Brough and Kimenyi 2002).

Perversely, the positive outcomes of the effective French health care system, namely higher life expectancy and lower infant mortality, also increased strain on natural resources (Brough and Kimenyi 2002). So by the time the post-colonial government took power in 1960, Niger's resources were already stretched thin. Throughout the 1960s and 1970s, this pressure multiplied with the policies of the new government, rapid population growth, and a series of devastating droughts.

Niger's postcolonial government extended its predecessor's policy of state ownership over all forest resources. Hoping for better enforcement of the forestry law, it made the Forestry Service into a paramilitary institution (USAID et al. 2002:42). Its

THE GREENING OF NIGER: KEY DATES

- **1935:** French law asserts that all natural resources in Niger, including trees, belong to the state

- **1960:** Independence from France; new government maintains natural resource rules and begins stricter enforcement with paramilitary Forest Service

- **1969 -1973:** 4-year drought cripples country

- **1975:** Multiple donors and NGOs enter Niger to improve food security and combat desertification, including CARE International's Majjia Valley Project

- **1983:** Serving in Mission (SIM) begins implementing Farmer-Managed Natural Regeneration (FMNR) as part of its Maradi Integrated Development Project (MIDP)

- **1984 -1985:** MIDP teams with World Food Program's Food for Work Program in 95 villages in Maradi in response to drought

- **1985:** Government creates Plan to Combat Desertification

- **1987:** Transitional government's Rural Code Secretariat coordinates with international aid groups to revise Rural Code and natural resource governance regulations

- **1993:** New Rural Code signed, transferring tree ownership to property owners

- **1996:** Coup d'état results in suspended donor assistance

- **1998:** Legislation to implement Rural Code at village level enacted

- **2004:** Rural Code enforcement begins at village level

- **2005:** Food shortages due to drought, locust infestation, and population pressures; farmers practicing FMNR and soil and water conservation techniques fare better than those that do not

- **2007:** Satellite images show that over 5 million ha of Niger has new vegetation thanks to regeneration efforts of previous twenty years

officers forbade any felling, harvesting, or selling of trees without government permits (Dan Baria 1999:1, 2). Offenders, including farmers lopping branches from bush trees on their own land, were fined or even imprisoned (Rinaudo 2005a:5). This discouraged people from investing efforts in producing, managing, and selling forest products.

At the same time, government agricultural extension services focused on planting crops in rows, animal plowing, and other measures that also discouraged trees in fields (Rinaudo 2005a:5). The government invested heavily in centrally managed reforestation projects, funded with donor support, which often involved plowing under natural vegetation (McGahuey and Winterbottom 2007:21).

This stripping of Niger's natural tree cover was exacerbated by rapid population growth. By 1975 much of the remaining natural woodland had been converted to farm fields to feed rapidly growing rural communities. But by clearing native trees and shrubs, farmers exposed their fields to the fierce Sahara winds, resulting in plummeting soil fertility and harvests. The loss of tree cover also triggered a rural fuelwood crisis. Poor households were forced to burn animal dung or crop residues instead of using them for compost, reinforcing the downward spiral in soil quality and crop yields (Rinaudo 2007; Winterbottom 2008).

In 1969, Niger's growing stresses developed into a humanitarian disaster with the start of an extreme 4-year drought that triggered famine across the Sahel, afflicting 50 million people (Dan Baria 1999:1). The scale of human suffering attracted global media coverage and drew international aid agencies into Niger. Within a few years these donors, including the United States Agency for International Develop-

ment (USAID), the World Bank, CARE International, the Canadian International Development Agency, Italian Cooperation, the International Fund for Agricultural Development (IFAD), and the German government agency GTZ, had expanded relief efforts to include development projects aimed at restoring rural productivity (Hamissou 2001:34–35).

In the 1970s and early 1980s, these efforts focused on training foresters and establishing exotic tree nurseries and fuelwood plantations. This approach was both intensive and expensive—plantations typically cost US$1,000 per ha to seed and maintain (McGahuey and Winterbottom 2007:4). Local people were rarely consulted before projects began, and the government often appropriated land that farmers and herders had used (Rinaudo 2005a:4). Over 12 years, some 60 million trees were planted in Niger, less than half of which survived (Tougiani et al. 2008:5).

One exception to an otherwise ill-fated program was the Majjia Valley Project, developed by CARE International in 1975, funded by USAID, and implemented by the Nigerien Forest Service and U.S. Peace Corps volunteers (USAID et al. 2002:42; Wentling 2008a). Farms in the tree-denuded river valley had been plagued by high winds that destroyed seeds in Niger's June-to-October growing season. By planting alternating rows of neem *(Azadirachta indica)*—an exotic nursery-grown species—and native *Acacia nilotica* saplings across the valley to act as windbreaks, the project improved soil retention and fertility, lessened the need for repeated sowing, and reduced damage to newly planted crops (Steinberg 1988:1).

Within a few years, overall yields of millet in fields between windbreak rows increased by 15 percent. While this roughly equaled the loss of production due to trees taking up former

crop space, the harvesting of tree branches, leaves, and twigs used for wood fuel, thatching, and livestock fodder rose by 68 percent (Steinberg 1988:1). In a break with previous top-down approaches, the project gave communities responsibility for maintaining the windbreaks, and village committees were established to create and enforce rules governing tree pruning (Steinberg 1988:3; Tougiani et al. 2008:10).

The Search for Sustainable Solutions: Tree Regeneration Takes Root

In its emphasis on improving native soils, harvesting branches, and sharing responsibility with communities, the Majjia Valley Project laid the groundwork for the FMNR revolution. Its capital- and labor-intensive plantation-based approach, however, was not very scaleable, as only a small fraction of Niger's cropland lies within river valleys; the majority is in drier upland areas (Steinberg 1988:2).

By the early 1980s, development agencies operating in Niger began to recognize that simple, low-cost farming techniques held the greatest promise for improving rural livelihoods. At the same time, studies sponsored by USAID's Forest and Land Use Planning project produced compelling evidence that native species were better adapted to local conditions than exotic imports, such as eucalyptus and neem, that were initially used in development projects (Gallegos et al. 1987:86). Not only could the long tap roots of native trees reach low water tables, but they quickly regenerated after lopping (Amoukou 2006:26; Rinaudo 2005a:6). These native trees provided multiple products for resource-poor households, including fuelwood, livestock fodder, and edible leaves and seedpods (Rinaudo 2005a:6).

Armed with this evidence, projects funded by development agencies increasingly shifted from exotic plantations to promoting natural forest management.

The Pioneers: Serving In Mission

One of the key people behind the movement toward natural forest management was Tony Rinaudo, a Christian missionary with a strong background in natural resource issues who spent the 1970s and 1980s working with Serving in Mission (SIM, formerly Society of International Ministries). In 1958, SIM had established a farm school in Maradi, partnering with the Evangelical Church of Niger to assist small-scale farmers in the region (Evans 2005). In response to the drought of the early 1970s, SIM, like other aid organizations at the time, turned its focus in Maradi to tree planting. But by the early 1980s, Rinaudo and some of his colleagues saw that the greening improvements from these efforts were limited, given the amount of time and money invested.

It was then that Rinaudo began to seek out a different solution to desertification (Rinaudo 2005a:6). In 1983 he realized that the fields cleared by project farmers were not barren, as they appeared, but contained "underground forests" of native tree and shrub stumps that could be successfully regenerated at a fraction of the cost of growing nursery tree stock (Rinaudo 2005a:2). As a result, he helped SIM launch the Maradi Integrated Development Project (MIDP), featuring a new approach to reforestation (Rinaudo 2005a:2).

Farmer-managed natural regeneration, as MIDP's approach came to be called, involved supporting the regeneration of trees and their sustainable management to produce continuous supplies of fuelwood as well as non-timber products such as edible seeds and leaves. MIDP's effort entailed very few "rules," instead emphasizing farmer experimentation and choice. Farmers chose how many tree stumps to let resprout in their

---

WHAT IS FARMER-MANAGED NATURAL REGENERATION?

Farmer-managed natural regeneration (FMNR) in the savannas of southern Niger adapts centuries-old methods of woodland management to produce continuous harvests of trees for fuel, building materials, and food and fodder without the need for frequent, costly replanting. Trees are trimmed and pruned to maximize harvests while promoting optimal growing conditions (such as access to water and sunlight). The new feature, pioneered by farmers in Niger and the intermediary organizations that assisted them, was to use these techniques in agricultural cropland and to manage trees as part of a farm enterprise.

For decades, Nigerien farmers had cleared their fields of vegetation, leaving what turned out to be an "underground forest" of living stumps and roots. FMNR is based on the regeneration of native trees and shrubs from these mature root systems, which promote surprisingly fast regrowth. Four key steps are involved:

- Selecting the stumps to regenerate based on the usefulness of the species.

- Selecting stems to prune and protect on each stump—usually the tallest and straightest. Intermediaries promoted five stems per stump as the ideal, but each farmer decides for himself or herself, based on farming objectives and household needs.

- Removing unwanted stems and side branches.

- Removing new stems and regularly pruning surplus side branches (as often as once a day). The longer a stem is left to grow, the higher its value in local wood markets.

The original FMNR model, pioneered by Serving In Mission, promoted harvesting one of the original five stems every year, with a newly resprouting stem chosen as a replacement. However, some farmers regrow many more stems per stump, allowing more than 200 stumps per ha to regenerate. This method quickly creates a young woodland. Typical species regenerated in the region include Ziziphus and Combretum, Guera senegalensis, Bauhinia reticulata, and Piliostigma reticulatum, which provide wood, nutritious fruits, edible leaves, and livestock fodder.

Source: Rinaudo 2005a:6–11

---

fields, how many resprouted stems to grow and harvest, and what to do with the wood (Rinaudo 2005a:8). MIDP workers lived in the project villages and led by example, practicing FMNR on their own farmland. They won recruits by holding village meetings and approaching farmers known to favor planting trees (Rinaudo 2007, 2008).

The FMNR approach asked farmers to abandon lifelong practices. Unsurprisingly, few of them were daring enough to take such a risk (Rinaudo 2005a:9). In the first year, only 12 farmers cultivating a total of 12 ha responded to recruitment efforts, from among thousands of local farmers in the district of Guidan Roumdji (the name of this arrondissement was changed to Groumdjii in 2002). They were mocked by other farmers, and some of their young trees were deliberately damaged or chopped down and stolen for fuelwood (Rinaudo 2007).

According to Rinaudo, the first farmers were motivated by a variety of factors. "In 1983, the thought of leaving trees in crop fields was seen as ludicrous by farmers brought up with the belief that cleared fields were essential for good crop yields. Some of the 12 guys were early adopters and innovators and were used to being different.... Some may have hoped that the project would provide loans for oxen, fertilizer and seed as SIM had done in the past. Some were visionary and were already planting trees, so the idea that FMNR would be simpler and faster appealed to them" (Rinaudo 2007).

Despite the peer pressure, all 12 farmers persevered and benefited from a small fuelwood yield in the first year (Rinaudo 2007). Their crop productivity also increased, as MIDP workers had predicted. The following year, the Sahel was hit with another major drought and subsequent famine, a cycle repeated in 1988. MIDP staff seized the opportunity to expand its tree regeneration efforts by incorporating FMNR in a Food for Work program in 95 villages in three of Maradi's six districts—Guidan-Roumdjii and Madarounfa along the southwest border with Nigeria and Dakoro district in the northwest (Rinaudo 2008). In return for food, farmers were required to regenerate native vegetation on their land. Rinaudo estimates that between 80,000 and 100,000 people were exposed to FMNR in 1984 and 1988, providing "the critical mass of people required for adoption of an innovative approach" (Rinaudo 2007).

Most farmers took part only reluctantly, however, motivated solely by their desire for food aid. Although crops flourished among their field trees, many chopped the trees down after the program ended. About two thirds of the half-million newly regenerated trees were lost, with only a third of farmers continuing with the program (Rinaudo 2005a:9). "Despite regular program messages about the value of trees, most people practiced FMNR only in order to obtain grain," says Rinaudo (Rinaudo 2007).

Nevertheless, MIDP's leaders had seen the benefits of FMNR and were optimistic that it had the potential to help farmers across Niger and beyond. They therefore continued their efforts, working with the thousands of farmers who did

keep their trees to refine regeneration practices. Early progress was slow, obstructed not only by deep-rooted cultural beliefs but also by Niger's forestry laws, which stipulated that trees were state property (Rinaudo 2005a:5, 9). As farmers were liable to be fined for cutting branches in their fields, they lacked incentives to regenerate native bush, and many would slash and burn regrowing stumps (Rinaudo 2005a:1). While government budget cuts in the 1980s began to limit the ability of forestry agents to enforce the laws, the Forestry Service continued to station agents at road blocks to confiscate cut wood, preventing the development of a legitimate commercial market for farm-grown fuel (Rinaudo 2007).

In the late 1980s, however, this problem abated after MIDP intervened with the head of the Maradi Forestry Department, who agreed to suspend enforcement of the tree cutting regulations (Rinaudo 2007). For the first time, this gave farmers the incentive and confidence to protect trees on their land by providing both informal tenure rights and the prospect of new income from timber products. By fostering the perception that farmers "owned" the trees in their fields—although official reform of tree ownership was not implemented until 2004—this cooperation between NGO and local government enabled FMNR to take hold (Rinaudo 2008).

PERCENT OF POPULATION IN THREE NIGER PROJECT VILLAGES ADOPTING COMPLEMENTARY TREE REGENERATION AND SOIL AND WATER CONSERVATION TECHNIQUES				
NRM Technique	Dan Saga, Maradi region (IFAD project)	Control, non-project village (Dourgou in Maradi region)	Kolloma Baba, Tahoua region (GTZ project)	Batodi, Tahoua region (IFAD project)
Protection of natural regeneration of trees	100	6	86	100
Tassa	--	--	91	97
Demi-lunes	--	--	20	46
Stone lines	--	--	97	91

Source: Adapted from Abdoulaye and Ibro 2006:37.

Farmers Spread the Word

Within a few years, farmers throughout the region began to experiment with regeneration. As thousands of households quickly made impressive gains in crop yields and incomes, the practice spread from farmer to farmer and from district to district, driven by self-interest without project intervention. As regenerating trees requires no financial outlays for materials or equipment by poor, risk-averse farmers, FMNR was well adapted to such spontaneous self-scaling (Rinaudo 2005a:17–18).

Farmers became the best spokespersons for woodland regeneration. But the movement was also facilitated by external intermediary support, with donor agencies funding village implementation projects, farmer study tours, and farmer-to-farmer exchanges. By the mid-1990s, FMNR had become standard practice within the MIDP operational area in Maradi. Project staff had also trained farmers and NGO field workers in five of Niger's six other regions, including neighboring Tahoua and Zinder and more distant Tillabéri, Dosso and Diffa (Rinaudo 2008). Other rural development projects adopted and promoted FMNR methods in their programs, including some funded by the German government and the World Bank and implemented by organizations that included IFAD and CARE International (Larwanou et al. 2006; Boubacar 2006:16; USAID et al. 2002:42).

Following a military coup d'état in Niger in 1996, most of this donor assistance was suspended (USAID et al. 2002:42). Yet woodland regeneration continued to spread rapidly, underlining the key role played by farmers themselves in self-scaling (Winterbottom 2008). In 2004—the year in which government reforms formally awarded tree ownership to rural landowners—observers estimated the number of regenerated trees in Maradi's Aguié district alone at about 4 million (Reij 2004:1). By 2006, farmers in the densely populated parts of Zinder had almost universally adopted FMNR on about 1 million ha—without any major donor intervention (Larwanou et al. 2006:12–13, 17).

This remarkable trend, attributed by observers to the high economic value of Zinder's dominant gao and baobab trees, underlines the profound shift that farmer-led regeneration has brought about in national consciousness (Larwanou et al. 2006:12, 14). The gao tree has always been highly valued in Niger—under Hausa tradition, for instance, anyone cutting the sultan's gao trees was subject to physical punishment (Larwanou et al. 2006:14). But with Niger's recent decentralization of natural resource management and the legalization of tree-cutting, the gaos' value can now be translated into economic benefits for the rural farmers that tend them.

While no comprehensive national inventory has been conducted, aerial and ground surveys and anecdotal evidence suggest that by 2006, trees had reappeared on about 5 million ha, nearly half of all cultivated land in Niger (Tappan 2007). In Maradi and Zinder, which account for over half of Niger's cereal production and where 40 percent of its people live, the practice of FMNR is now common (Wentling 2008b: 7; Rinaudo 2005a:5, 9).

Demi-lunes

Tassa

Adding Value: Reclaiming Water and Land

Since the late 1970s, donor efforts to stave off future famines have also included the introduction of simple soil and water conservation techniques to rehabilitate barren land (Reij 2008). As the practice of tree regeneration spread across southern Niger, intermediaries and farmers adopted some of these practices to further boost crop production. Widely adopted methods included rock lining (placing rocks lines along the contour of sloping land to reduce runoff), improved versions of traditional planting pits or tassa, and demi-lunes (crescent-shaped trenches dug along the contour of sloping land to improve water infiltration into soil) (Abdoulaye and Ibro 2006:19).

These techniques enabled cultivation of secondary vegetable crops, which in turn helped rural families improve their diets in a country where half the children suffer from malnutrition (Boubacar et al. 2005:21). For example, improved soils and higher water tables have enabled villages in Tahoua region to grow onions, tomatoes, sweet potatoes, cow peas, watermelon, and asparagus for home use and sale in local markets (Guéro and Dan Lamso 2006:31).

Soil and water conservation methods have proved particularly important in districts with low water tables and severe shortages of cultivable soil. One of the most dramatic success stories is Batodi village in the Illéla district of Tahoua, where the International Fund for Agricultural Development promoted use of improved tassa and demi-lunes (Boubacar et al. 2005:8). According to villagers, the local water table had sunk to 18 meters below ground by the early 1990s (Boubacar et al. 2005:15). Nothing would grow in the barren land around the village, and women typically spent several hours a day fetching water. By 2005, with almost every villager using tassa and demi-

lunes, water tables had risen to three meters below the surface and yields of millet and sorghum, Niger's primary food crops, had increased significantly (Guéro and Dan Lamso 2006:31). Batodi's many women farmers now cultivate dry-season vegetable gardens, irrigated by wells, for household use and sale (Guéro and Dan Lamso 2006:31). Onions are especially high value, with one producer (a male farmer) earning 250,000 CFA francs (US$500) for a crop grown on a quarter of a hectare (Abdoulaye and Ibro 2006:19).

Adoption of these soil and conservation techniques has led to the restoration of land once considered useless. In Tahoua region, for example, entrepreneurial farmers started a new market by buying degraded land to rehabilitate and resell (Reij 2008). Land prices around Batodi doubled between 1990 and 1994 as a result, while in a second village, Roukouzoum, rehabilitated land was resold after two years for triple the original price (Boubacar et al. 2005:10–11, 20). A market in specialized labor has also developed in the region, with self-trained land restorers hired by other farmers to dig tassa and demi-lunes (Boubacar et al. 2005:27). While farmers most able to capitalize on increased land values tend to be the better-off ones, land reclamation has also provided a route for very poor families to relieve hunger and increase income (Boubacar et al. 2005:20–21).

Creating Resilient Landscapes, Livelihoods

The simple and cost-effective practice of farmer-managed natural regeneration has provided an impressively wide range of benefits for Niger's impoverished rural communities. Over the last 20 years or so, about 200 million trees have been protected and managed by farmers and at least 250,000 ha of degraded land has been restored to crop production (Reij 2008; McGahuey and Winterbottom 2007:7). A 2005 survey for USAID recorded tree or shrub stems ranging from 20 to 150 per ha across three regions, a dramatic 10- to 20-fold increase since 1975 (McGahuey and Winterbottom 2007:6–8). This change in the rural landscape has enabled hundreds of thousands of households living on US$2 or less a day to diversify livelihoods and increase income, thus increasing their economic resilience. It has also played a critical role in addressing the chronic hunger of families accustomed to living with unpredictable harvests.

FMNR has also had an enormously empowering effect, demonstrating to hundreds of thousands of people that they were not helpless hostages to poverty and a capricious climate. "[Its success] helped establish a positive mindset about farmers' capacity to take charge of critical farm management decisions," explains USAID natural resources management adviser Mike McGahuey. "It showed that progress against poverty and desertification was strongest when the rural poor worked on their own behalf to achieve their own objectives" (McGahuey 2008).

Money Trees

Fuelwood and Fodder Income

The most immediate benefit for most families practicing FMNR is the availability of fuelwood from pruned tree branches. From the first year, communities are able to harvest light firewood and from the second year to cut branches to sell in local markets for much-needed extra income. According to conservative SIM estimates, farmers regenerating 40 stumps on a 1-ha field could earn an additional 70,000 CFA francs (about US$140) per year—half the average annual income of a poor farming household.

By 2004, researchers had recorded steep increases in fuelwood and fodder production in FMNR communities, with majorities of villagers gaining income from one or other product. Earlier studies indicate that in 100 Maradi villages alone, about US$600,000 worth of wood was sold between 1985 and 1997 (SIM 1999, as cited by Rinuado 2005a:14). And survey results from across villages with land rehabilitation projects demonstrate that residents perceive a marked decrease in poverty around them as a result of the projects (Abdoulaye and Ibro 2006:40).

Crop Income

Revegetation also improves the traditionally poor fertility of Niger's soils, which in turn boosts crop production. Bush trees dotted across fields help hold soil in place, reducing wind and water erosion (Guéro and Dan Lamso 2006:15). Native trees and shrubs draw up nutrients and distribute them in the topsoil at the same time that falling leaves and trimmings are used as mulch

(Rinaudo 2005a:12). Livestock and birds attracted to tree shade and branches leave droppings that fertilize the soil (Rinaudo 2005a:12). Moreover, the growing season on land with trees is longer because farmers only have to sow once, compared with twice or more on fields unprotected from the elements (Rinaudo 2005a:4; Reij 2008). Such benefits are magnified when farmers act collectively, as blanket FMNR villages in Maradi and Zinder regions have discovered. Vegetation in one field affects nearby land by serving as a windbreak and promoting improved water infiltration and soil retention (Winterbottom 2007).

All these FMNR benefits, combined with the soil and water interventions, have resulted in increases in sorghum yields of between 20 and 85 percent and in millet yields of between 15 and 50 percent in intervention villages (Amoukou 2006:25). Other studies suggest that millet yields have even consistently doubled in some FMNR-practicing communities (Tougiani et al. 2008:16). This has enabled households both to store more food against the threat of shortages in the dry season and, occasionally, to sell surplus crops in local markets or for export to neighboring Nigeria (Reij 2006:ii).

SAMPLE WOOD INCOME BENEFITS FOR FARMERS

Area: 1 hectare
No. Trees protected: 40/hectare
No. stems protected per tree: 5 stems/stump

Year 1	40 stems x 0.10 cents	US$ 4
Year 2	40 stems x 0.70 cents	US$ 28
Year 3	40 stems x US$1.50	US$ 60
Year 4	40 stems x US$ 3.50	US$ 140
Year 5	40 stems x US$ 3.50	US$ 140
Year 6	40 stems x US$ 3.50	US$ 140
Total		**US$ 512**

Source: Rinaudo 2005b.

PERCENT OF RURAL HOUSEHOLDS EARNING INCOME FROM WOOD AND HAY IN 2005

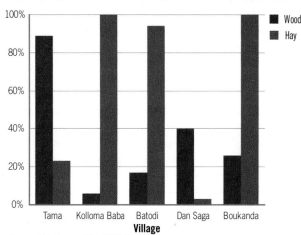

Source: Abdoulaye and Ibro 2006: 43

Storing millet

Nationally, figures from the Niger agriculture ministry show cereal production rising steadily in parallel with the spread of FMNR. In 1980, Niger produced 1,770,700 metric tons of cereals, rising to 2,093,300 mt in 1995 and 2,319,800 mt in 2000. By 2006, when at least a quarter of cultivated land was converted, production reached an impressive 4,055,984 mt (Wentling 2008b:1). These statistics suggest that the farmer-led re-greening movement is having a clear impact on the country's ability to feed itself and improve the rural economy.

Non-Timber Tree Products

Farmers' trees have also yielded direct non-timber benefits in the form of fodder for livestock and edible leaves and seedpods to set aside for times of hunger (Rinaudo 2005a:3). Anecdotal evidence suggests that diet has also improved for many FMNR practitioners as they have a greater diversity of food sources. Some villagers in the Aguié district of Maradi, for example, harvest the leaves of a common scrubland tree, *Maerua crassifolia*, which are rich in vitamin A (Reij 2008). Maradi-based farmers have also used the proceeds of FMNR to embark on new income-generating activities, such as beekeeping (Burns 2008).

While most non-timber tree products are consumed by farming families, some districts have generated significant income from their sale. This is especially true in Zinder province, where FMNR has revived cultivation of the baobab tree. Each baobab can bring in an average of US$20 a year in economic benefits just from the sale of its edible leaves (Larwanou et al. 2006:18). With some farms boasting an average of 50 baobab trees per ha, that can amount to US$1,000 per ha a year—nearly three times the total annual income of much of the population (calculation based on Larwanou et al. 2006:18; Winterbottom 2007).

Providing Food Security, Protecting Against Famine

The return of trees to Niger's densely populated southern plains and dunes has also increased food security for local rural economies at a time when the country is adding 440,000 new mouths to feed every year (Wentling 2008b:2). Since the cereals millet and sorghum make up over 90 percent of the typical villager's diet, it was critical that in 2006 the country was able to produce 283 kg of cereal per capita, almost identical to the 285 kg produced in 1980 despite a near-doubling of the population over 25 years (Wentling 2008b:3, 1).

"In the late 1970s donors thought it would be impossible for Niger to produce enough food to feed a population of 10 million," says Mark Wentling, USAID's country program manager for Niger. "In the past three years, Niger has produced more cereals than ever. Much of this increase can be attributed to higher crop yields achieved through the practice of FMNR... which has been critical to enable Niger...to feed its population of 14 million" (Wentling 2008a).

Over the last 45 years, Niger has been plagued by an average of one bad harvest every eight years, following a growing season of low rainfall (Wentling 2008b:4). Farmers practicing FMNR, who are able to stockpile some grains during good years and to harvest trees for food and income, are better insulated against these deadly cyclical droughts, which are predicted to increase as a result of climate change (Reij 2006:2; IPCC 2007:444, 447–48).

When the most recent drought and accompanying food shortages hit the regions of Maradi, Tahoua, Tillabéri, and Zinder in 2004–05, FMNR villages fared much better than those stripped of vegetation. An estimated 15 children a week died of hunger in Maradi during the summer of 2005 (BBC 2005). Yet villages in Aguié District, where inhabitants could harvest regenerated trees for food, fodder, and firewood to sell in exchange for grain *(see box)* did not rely on famine relief and avoided a single death (Tougiani et al. 2008:13). The contrast between the famine's impacts on FMNR farmers and on their neighbors who did not practice FMNR is a stark reminder of the persistence required to scale up even visibly beneficial and simple changes to entrenched customs. Indeed, despite all its successes, at least half of Niger's farmers still do not use FMNR (Tappan 2007).

Women Reap Dividends

Women are perhaps the biggest winners in Niger's tree regeneration revolution. Traditionally excluded from resource management decisions (despite being skilled in farming and animal husbandry), they have profited from the simple reality that FMNR favors women producers (Tougiani et al. 2008:12). Getting the best results from revegetation requires year-round,

DAN SAGA: PEOPLE POWER TRANSFORMS LOCAL ECONOMY

The Maradi village of Dan Saga and its neighbors are the focus of a concerted effort to build social capacity while promoting natural resource management in Niger. Beset by chronic food shortages due to a lack of land to sustain its rapidly growing population, Dan Saga was chosen as a priority site by the Aguié District Rural Development Project, an initiative launched in 1992 by the International Fund for Agricultural Development (Boubacar 2006:17). The project provided rural credit to several dozen villages and actively promoted farmer-led tree regeneration. Initially it did so using top-down demonstration and instruction to farmers. But these early efforts were undermined by conflicts among villagers, as some people were stealing wood from trees grown by others (Boubacar 2006:17–19).

In 2001, project managers switched focus to empowering communities through capacity-building. Under the renamed Desert Community Initiative, village management committees for natural regeneration were elected by all community members. In a major break with tradition, these included women farmers and herders—two normally marginalized groups—as well as male landowners. The committees laid down strict rules to regulate the exploitation of trees, organized villagers to guard fields against intruders, and imposed fines on those who broke community-approved regulations (Reij 2004; Tougiani et al. 2008:12).

Resource management decisions and action plans were made at monthly village assemblies, held before local elders and the chief, at which committee members fed back information to the community. New bylaws, agreed to by the local administrative authority, embedded these arrangements, while elected committee members were equipped with a uniform and badge, emphasizing their authority. Aguié's departmental government, forestry department, and land tenure commission also approved the new institutional arrangements (Tougiani et al. 2008:10–14).

Their investment thus protected, many more farmers began nurturing bush trees, adopting pruning and trimming techniques that allowed fast vertical growth without hindering the growth of millet in the soil below (Toumieux 2005). By 2007, a total of 53 FMNR community committees had been established, covering 170 villages and encompassing the entire Aguié district (Tougiani et al. 2008:11). Each village made payments toward policing tree regeneration activities. The income raised, together with fines collected, was placed in a village fund and used to support development activities and tree nurseries on common land. This transparent process both enhanced social unity and reinforced public support for tree regeneration (Tougiani et al. 2008:12–13).

By 2007, destructive tree cutting practices had "practically ceased in the whole of Aguié," and 130,000 ha across the district boasted regenerating trees (Tougiani et al. 2008:14). In Dan Saga, this included every household and more than 5,600 ha of land, transforming the local economy (Abdoulaye and Ibro 2006:15). Fields that had previously lain barren contained on average 150 bush trees per ha, compared with only 52 per ha in a nearby non-project village (Abdoulaye and Ibro 2006:36). Villagers reported that FMNR can double their yields (Diarra 2006:18), and some 40 percent of village producers were selling surplus wood, seedpods from gao trees, and fruits and gum Arabic from Acacia seyal trees (Abdoulaye and Ibro 2006:43). Annual per capita income from wood sales alone ranged between US$46 and US$92 (Tougiani et al. 2008: 13).

Food security and resilience to drought—critical issues for a village on the edge of the Sahara—have also improved markedly (Tougiani et al. 2008:2). In 2005, when a deadly combination of locusts and drought struck the region, Dan Saga required no food aid (Toumieux 2005).

even daily, attention to pruning trees. As most men still migrate to urban centers throughout West Africa during the dry season to secure additional cash income, the increasingly valued task of tree husbandry often falls to women (Wentling 2008a).

Women and their families derive a host of material benefits from this role. Using their own wood for cooking eliminates a daily cost of 200 CFA francs (US 40 cents) for purchased firewood (USAID et al. 2005:18). Surplus wood can earn up to 400 CFA francs (US 80 cents) per bundle in local markets

KOLLOMA BABA: WOMEN REVIVE LAND, IMPROVE THEIR STATUS

"These lands are now like our husbands," say the women of Kolloma Baba, describing the thriving plots of millet and sorghum, cow peas, groundnut, and okra around them, the result of years of hard labor (Abdoulaye and Ibro 2006:40, 42). Once barren, boulder-covered, and devoid of vegetation, these patches of reclaimed desert have lifted the women, mostly divorcees and widows, out of grinding poverty and transformed their social status. Today, not only do they harvest enough food for their families; they earn income from selling surplus crops, hay, and tree seedpods, and their land has significantly increased in value (Boubacar et al. 2005:17, 20; Diarra 2006:21).

The women's fortunes were transformed with the help of the Tahoua Rural Development Project, funded by the German government agency GTZ. In the late 1980s, with the agreement of the village chief and local government officials, about 250 widows and divorced women received the rights to abandoned, degraded land in Kolloma Baba, a village where farm productivity had plunged by up to 90 percent (PDRT 1997 as cited by Guéro and Dan Lamso 2006:5; Abdoulaye and Ibro 2006:40). In return the women pledged to restore the land by investing their labor in soil and water conservation techniques (Guéro and Dan Lamso 2006:29; Winterbottom 2008).

After clearing the land of rock, each woman received a plot of about 60 square meters (BBC 2006). In addition to sowing traditional millet and sorghum, many took the initiative to diversify into cow peas, groundnut, and okra (Abdoulaye and Ibro 2006:32). In the early years, female farmers worked through the Kolloma Baba Women's Association, established by the project, with members helping each other to develop their land (BBC 2006). More recently, they have hired male labor, proof of their considerable economic capacity (Boubacar et al. 2005:18, 29). By 2006, they had restored 2,000 ha of degraded land and were selling excess crops, lifting themselves a step out of poverty and increasing their social status. A village committee, principally made up of women, deals with protection of regenerated trees across the community (Saadou and Larwanou 2006:15–16, 18).

Although their land has increased several times in value, and despite persistent pressure from male farmers, the women have vowed not to sell. Says association member Fatima Illiassou: "Thanks to our crops, we can eat. We can buy clothes for our children. We won't go through all that suffering to give men the fruits of our labor" (BBC 2006).

during the dry season; in Zinder, a sack of nutritious, edible baobab leaves can sell for as much as 3,000 CFA francs (US$6), three times the average daily wage for laborers (Larwanou et al. 2006:18). Women farmers use FMNR income to meet household needs, including purchasing food and paying school fees. Many have also diversified their households' livelihoods: some by taking advantage of better soil fertility and water retention to cultivate cash crops such as onions, tomatoes, sesame, and hibiscus; others by using their new earnings to invest in sheep and goats, which live off of tree seedpods (BBC 2006; Reij 2006:iii).

Anecdotal evidence highlights how the status of women has been transformed by their involvement in FMNR. A 2006 field study of FMNR villages across Zinder region found that livestock owners—ranked high on the social ladder—commonly included women (Larwanou et al. 2006:21). In Kolloma Baba village in Tahoua, formerly vulnerable and marginalized widows and divorcees employ male laborers to work their farms (Boubacar et al. 2005:10, 16). During the 2005 food crisis, female FMNR farmers also used their food reserves to assist others, elevating their position in the community (Diarra 2006:12). Women farmers' enhanced status is also clearly demonstrated in FMNR communities that boast village natural resource management committees, where they participate equally with men in decision-making (Tougiani et al. 2008:12).

Re-greening a Country: Key Players and Partners

With millions of trees now carpeting land that was mostly barren only one to two decades ago, Niger's farmers have produced one of the most visibly successful examples of natural resource management in the world today. Although it took several years to take off, Niger's farmers have abandoned a core practice of clearing fields and have embraced the protection and sustainable management of native vegetation.

Why did they do so? One clear reason, say observers, was the impact of the environmental and economic crisis of the late 1970s and early 1980s, combined with Niger's booming population. With more mouths to feed every year, rural communities could see that traditional clearing and farming methods were no longer meeting their needs (Wentling 2008a). The obvious success of early FMNR projects, implemented at little or no cost to farmers, was also a powerful spur to their neighbors. But it is unlikely the movement would have reached such a scale or overcome the barriers to farmer adoption without the input of two key players: Niger's central government and international intermediary organizations.

Role of Government: From Policemen to Allies

One of the biggest hurdles to widespread adoption of FMNR was the state ownership of Niger's trees. Villagers were well aware of the law because the oppressive Forestry Service vigorously enforced it for over 20 years, well into the 1980s, making farmers hesitant to manage trees. However, de facto shifts in the forest and land tenure system began in the late 1980s as part of the government's transition to democracy (USAID et al. 2002:42; Wentling 2008a).

These de facto shifts were driven by a confluence of forces. Macro issues included the fallout from the 1984 drought and Niger's 1987 transition to a democratic government. There were also a range of smaller efforts taking place simultaneously that had an impact on the thinking of the government. One of the most important of these was a USAID project that partnered Niger's Forest Service with rural residents to manage a formerly "off-limits" national park using FMNR and soil and water conservation techniques.

The Forest and Land Use Planning project convinced the Forest Service that such practices were effective and could actually create revenue for the state, as the partnership was based around a sustainable wood harvesting cooperative that divided revenues between the Forest Service and local people (Gallegos et al. 1987:51–52). MIDP and CARE projects were also helping the government realize the goals of its 1985 Plan to Combat Desertification, thereby solidifying the effectiveness of FMNR and these localized conservation techniques in the minds of government officials (Gallegos et al. 1987:24).

In 1987, the transitional government created a Permanent Rural Code Secretariat to begin the process of revising the Rural Code, a body of law that applied to much of Niger and that included the provision establishing government ownership of trees. MIDP, USAID, and others worked with the new Inter-Ministerial Committee on Natural Resources, charged by the government to develop a new Code (Gallegos et al. 1987:25).

The organizations were largely successful in their efforts, though formal legal changes took longer than hoped due to government instability. The Code that was signed in 1993 recognized both customary and formal land use rights and laid the groundwork for transferring tree ownership to property owners (McGahuey 2008). Legislation to implement the new code at the village level was passed in 1998 and came into force in 2004 (Wentling 2008a). For many farmers, having this sense of security about managing trees without fear of legal repercussions tipped the balance of self-interest in favor of embracing FMNR's simple, cheap, and effective practices.

Prompted and assisted by foreign donors, the new government did not limit its reforms to the Rural Code. In pursuit of economic development and improved management of the country's beleaguered natural resources, it also overhauled the country's Forest Code, decentralization laws, Forest Service, and forest fiscal policy (USAID et al. 2002:42). The collective impact was to create an economic and social environment in which sustainable land management practices, such as FMNR and soil

and water conservation, could and did explode across the country. "Under the old system, the spontaneous spread of FMNR would not have likely occurred," says Mike McGahuey. "FMNR demonstrated that the most effective role of government was to reduce barriers and strengthen farmers' incentives to engage in and benefit from environmentally and socially sustainable agricultural practices" (McGahuey 2008).

Role of Intermediaries: Agents of Change

In an effective partnership, international donors and NGOs have had a twofold impact on the spread of Niger's tree regeneration movement: promoting new land management practices among Niger's farmers and facilitating the government reforms that enabled community experiments to reach national scale.

The U.S. and German governments and the World Bank acted as significant catalysts by providing intellectual input, funding, land management expertise, and pressure for policy reform. In the 1980s USAID, GTZ, the French and Dutch governments, IFAD, and the World Bank helped provide the economic rationale for farmer-led tree regeneration by funding research on the superior benefits of native vegetation, including potential markets for forest products (Winterbottom 2008).

While supporting soil conservation and tree management programs, these donors also engaged the government of Niger in a policy dialogue on sustainable natural resource management, stressing the need for community rights, laws providing secure resource tenure, and reform of both the forestry code and the

role of forestry agents (USAID et al. 2002:42). Their advice was adopted in the wholesale reforms of the 1990s described earlier.

USAID's involvement went well beyond advice, however. In the mid-1990s, the agency was deeply involved in helping Niger's new democratic government formulate, implement, and popularize its natural resource management reforms, through a US$28-million agricultural development grant program. This funded, for example, technical support for formulation of the Rural Code and the establishment of the Permanent Secretariat to administer the legislation. The agency also funded all-important efforts to publicize the code to millions of dispersed farmers and herders. This included translating the text into the eight major languages spoken in Niger and communicating the changes via radio and television (USAID et al. 2002:148).

While donors played their part at the macro level, in the field it was the committed and long-term presence of NGOs and specialized agencies such as Serving In Mission, IFAD, and Care International that enabled FMNR to take root. By 2008, SIM had worked with farmers in Maradi for over two decades, while the major IFAD projects in Aguié district had begun 13 years earlier. "After the food-for-work program ended in 1988, the only tools at hand were persuasion and persistence," recalled Rinaudo. "Having staff in the village and giving the same message over and over." In the early years, he added, the catalyzing influence of individual MIDP figures and supportive Maradi forestry staff played a major role in fostering recognition and acceptance of the new farming practices. Without the efforts of such intermediaries, FMNR might not have reached the critical mass that resulted in its scale-up over much of rural Niger (Rinaudo 2008).

A Road Map for Greening Africa's Drylands?

The simple process of regenerating native trees, coupled with progressive policy and institutional reforms, has proved an impressively strong mechanism for leveraging transformational development in Niger. The scope of its impact on one of the world's poorest societies includes poverty reduction, economic growth, agricultural and rural development, and improved governance and health.

Niger's overused farmland and barren savanna are visibly more fertile and resilient thanks to sustainable management practices. And instead of the dire food shortages predicted by aid agencies as Niger's population boomed, farmers adopting FMNR have displayed a new economic resilience that has impressed development experts. "Although challenges remain, the resiliency, innovations and adaptations of rural producers...in the face of environmental and economic stresses... provide encouraging prospects for progress," reported USAID officials in 2007 (McGahuey and Winterbottom 2007:26–27). And progress need not be limited to Niger. For other Sahelian countries facing the triple challenges of population growth, desertification, and climate change, FMNR also offers a cheap and effective model to improve farm productivity and reclaim precious land from the dunes (Rinaudo 2005a:9).

More Food for More People

Yet despite the extraordinary spread of FMNR and the significant benefits generated, population growth will continue to pose a major challenge to food security in Niger, especially against a backdrop of climate change.

In the past 20 years, Niger's population has doubled to 14 million people, and it maintains one of the highest birthrates in the world of about 7.1 children per woman (Wentling 2008b:1; INS and Macro International Inc. 2007:xxv). By 2015, the population will rise to 18.8 million and the area of cultivable land per capita will fall further—from 1.45 ha to 1.12 ha per person (Wentling 2008b:6, 7). Yet already, even in the best harvest years, at least 1 million land-poor Nigeriens need food aid due to localized droughts or pest infestations (Wentling 2008a:5). Similar demographic pressures face Niger's neighbors, including Burkina Faso, Mali, and Chad.

As a result, food production will become an increasing government and donor priority in the region, which makes higher agricultural productivity imperative. In this context, say development experts, FMNR has a major role to play in helping poor rural populations improve food security and ride out the present baby boom. "Niger appears to be a model in buying time," says Mike McGahuey. "FMNR has a track record of allowing people to (a) get more product and more diverse forms of product from the same amount of land and (b) maintain the productive capacity of that land even while more is being taken

155

Sometimes costly technology is less important than patience and persistence. The FMNR approach has succeeded in restoring and improving vast swaths of land in Niger using little more than the time and persistence of the staff of NGOs and aid agencies. No new technology was involved, and no special seeds or other agricultural inputs, simply the willingness of the NGOs to support the first adopters of the practice and to take advantage of every chance to demonstrate the impact of FMNR to other farmers. Even with unexpected setbacks, these organizations stayed close to the farmers and kept encouraging them. The result, over time, has been the significant improvement of more than half the cultivated land in Niger.

Tradition and fear are powerful forces that must be accommodated. The fact that most farmers who had allowed trees to grow on their land in exchange for food support later uprooted the trees, even after the benefits of that practice were apparent, demonstrates the difficulty of securing change in rural and traditional cultures. The NGOs and donors understood the strength of these traditions, and they overcame them with patience and perseverance.

Livelihood improvements can also improve community stability. In rural Sahelian communities, the dry season leaves families seeking alternative sources of income and food. It is something of a ritual for men to leave the village for several months at a time seeking paying work in larger towns and cities. Not only does this exodus increase the pressure on those left behind, it decreases social cohesion within communities and commonly results in the introduction of diseases such as HIV when the men return. One of the important benefits of the increased productivity from FMNR is that it can provide more in-village economic opportunities for men and women, reducing the need to leave to seek work, and so enhancing community resilience. This is a benefit that we have seen in several cases studies in WRR 2008 and 2005.

Simple methods of communication can yield significant benefits. The widespread adoption of FMNR practices in Niger was, to a very large extent, due to simple word-of-mouth…what today is called "viral communication." The program began with a few brave souls willing to break with tradition. It expanded as neighbors witnessed the visible agricultural and economic improvements created by these changes and as farmers conversed about the potential benefits of leaving trees in local and regional markets. Planned visits of farmers to FMNR communities resulted in a continued spread of the practice. Today, about 5 million ha have benefited; more than 250,000 ha of land that was once considered unusable is now producing crops, and a significant portion of the nation's farmers are involved.

Inclusion is important. As communities in Niger began to adopt FMNR and water conservation practices, decisions about the use of common lands and tree protection were necessary. The inclusion of all affected parties, not just land-owning farmers—women, nomadic herders—was critical for broad community acceptance of change and the effectiveness of the new rules.

from it. [Such] approaches… will be more and more important for Niger and for other countries" (McGahuey 2008).

With two thirds of Africa either desert or drylands, this potential has not been lost on donors, neighboring governments, and international NGOs. While the vast, spontaneous spread of re-greening in Niger is unique, tree regeneration and soil and water conservation projects have also been successfully implemented in other Sahelian countries, notably Burkina Faso, Mali, Senegal, the Gambia, and Guinea (Winterbottom 2008). Organisation for Economic Co-operation and Development donor countries, working with the Club du Sahel and the Permanent Interstate Committee for Drought Control in the Sahel, have implemented successful programs supporting decentralized natural resource management, land tenure, and forestry code reforms (Winterbottom 2008).

During the 1990s, USAID duplicated its policy reform assistance to Niger in other West African countries, including Mali, Senegal, and Guinea, where it helped governments reform forest codes. These reforms recognized farmers' rights to manage trees and to redefine the role of forestry officers as extension agents, supporting community-based management (USAID et al. 2002:42, 137). As in Niger, USAID also provided assistance in Mali and Senegal to help implement newly enacted forest codes (USAID et al. 2002: 137).

Barriers remain, however, to achieving the level of scale-up for farmer-led natural resource management witnessed in Niger. "Unfortunately, key enabling conditions are not yet fully established in most countries across West Africa," says International Resource Group natural resources management (NRM) expert Bob Winterbottom, who worked through USAID as Natural Resources Management Advisor to Niger's Ministry of Environment from 1993 to 1996. "An important challenge for donors and governments will [be] to reinforce their efforts to reduce barriers to FMNR, such as high taxes on wood and other 'natural products' harvested and marketed by rural populations, and…onerous permit requirements that discourage investment in producing and marketing forest products" (Winterbottom 2008).

Equally important in creating the incentive to change among farmers is granting secure land and tree tenure—still lacking in some West African countries—and the transfer of rights and authority to local communities to control access to and use of natural resources. As Niger's experience has shown, when farmers are given the rights and tools to control their own economic destiny, both land and people benefit.

Creating Resilience to Climate Change

The Sahel has been identified as one of the areas most vulnerable to increased drought in a warming climate. While rains have been relatively good in recent years (except 2004), the long-term projections are for longer and more frequent droughts across the region as global temperatures rise (IPCC 2007:444, 447–48). In the absence of effective natural resource management approaches such as FMNR in Niger, this raises the threat of future famines approaching the devastating scale of the 1970s; it also promises to further the desertification of fragile lands in the Sahel. Yet development experts and intermediary organizations are hoping that region-wide expansion of FMNR and other proven land management programs will help the region increase its resilience in the face of changing climate (Winterbottom 2008).

Winterbottom notes: "The development community needs better models for poverty reduction and rural development that simultaneously assist these populations in adapting to climate change. The experience in Niger has demonstrated that incorporating FMNR and other NRM practices are key elements of such a model" (Winterbottom 2008). Gray Tappan, a geographer who measures the spread of FMNR across Niger, has seen these tangible effects throughout his travels: "[Adopting communities] have become much more resilient to drought in the last 20 years because of the increase in vegetation cover. Crops can fail, but the farmers, the herders, have something to fall back on. And that is the trees—the wood, the fruit" (Harris 2007).

One opportunity to extend these cost-effective resilience-building techniques to more communities would be to integrate them into the National Adaptation Programmes for Action (NAPAs) of the countries of the Sahel. The NAPAs are adaptation strategy plans written by developing-country governments under the United Nations Framework Convention on Climate Change (CNEDD 2006:3). FMNR can achieve many of the goals of Niger's current NAPA, but unlike the actions recommended in the present version, it would not require extensive external technical and financial assistance (CNEDD 2006:7–8).

Another opportunity to increase the resilience that comes with FMNR across the Sahel is a new international alliance of NGOs and research organizations that is developing a Sahel Re-Greening Initiative. The Initiative will mobilize donor funding to build on the grassroots successes of FMNR across the West African Sahel (Reij 2008).

Niger's current government appears more capable than earlier administrations of instituting the new Rural Code to allow for institutionalization of FMNR and other community conservation practices across Niger. The new government's Rural Code Secretariat, created in 2006, is also getting considerable support from donors (Wentling 2008a). It is hoped that the lessons of the drought in 2004, which left many individuals and communities that did not practice FMNR vulnerable, will help convince farmers who continue to clear their land indiscriminately of the benefits of better management.

But there are new challenges. Where tree regeneration is widely practiced, community and local governments need to act to resolve conflicts over access to natural resources and property rights to formerly abandoned land that has been restored (Winterbottom 2008). In particular, the rights of the more vulnerable—nomadic herders, the landless, and women—to equitably gain access to the benefits of FMNR need to be strengthened (Tougiani et al. 2008:12–15). The gains made by the current generation of women, for example, could be eroded unless Niger's inheritance laws are revised to enable land and livestock to pass from mother to daughter (BBC 2006).

Nevertheless, in its proven impacts and ready scaleability, FMNR and associated soil and water conservation practices provide a potentially transformative model for natural resource management in the drylands of Africa and beyond.

Successfully scaling up ecosystem enterprise

requires a confluence

of community-level and national-level actions.

DRIVING THE SCALING PROCESS

SUCCESSFULLY SCALING UP ECOSYSTEM ENTERPRISES requires a confluence of community-level and national-level actions. As Chapter 2 points out, community stakeholders in ecosystem enterprises must find a compelling rationale for working together and an effective process for learning and applying new skills as a group. For scaling up to occur, this rationale and process must be effectively communicated to other groups in similar circumstances and supported by intermediary organizations. At the same time, national governments, donors, and the private sector must provide an environment that nurtures small rural enterprises and removes some of the political, financial, and physical barriers they face as they struggle to break out of the confines of rural markets.

This chapter looks at both these levels of action—community and national. It first examines the case studies from Chapter 3 to extract cross-cutting lessons on how successful enterprises are founded, sustained, and expanded. It then looks beyond the community level to probe challenges and enabling conditions at the macro level— larger governance, financing, and infrastructure considerations that if left unaddressed will stymie the scaling up process.

In this chapter, we build on the basis of the case studies in Chapter 3, first deriving cross-cutting lessons from the cases, and then looking beyond the community level to examine several national-level actions necessary to create an enabling environment for scaling up nature-based enterprises. The chapter:

■ Derives seven cross-cutting lessons from the case studies in Chapter 3.

■ Looks at the need to make rural markets more amenable to small nature-based enterprises by confronting elite capture, encouraging competition, and rectifying tax and regulatory regimes that discriminate against these enterprises.

■ Examines the rationale for providing technical, research, and marketing assistance to rural enterprises.

■ Argues that representation of rural concerns in national legislatures must improve markedly if the current marginalization of rural producers in national policy is to change.

■ Argues that government line agencies must reorient their missions to emphasize service and to embrace community participation in resource management decisions.

■ Presents the case for a different approach to rural infrastructure development—a community-driven approach specifically attuned to local needs.

■ Examines current trends in rural finance and the government's role in making sure adequate financing and insurance are available for small and medium-size enterprises.

Extracting Insights from the Cases

The cases in Chapter 3 give a tangible expression to the power of giving communities a stake in managing their ecosystem assets, of providing for long-term and comprehensive capacity development of ecosystem enterprises, and of creating political linkages and commercial networks to nurture these enterprises. The cases also contain a number of more nuanced insights into the success of nature-based enterprises and the factors that allow them to scale up.

1. Resource Tenure Need Not Be Perfect to be Useful

One of the biggest catalysts for new and scalable ecosystem enterprises is a change in the resource tenure situation. The prospect of gaining new or more secure resource rights is often more important than the precise form that tenure takes. That said, the details of the tenure situation do affect the ultimate sustainability of an ecosystem enterprise. In addition, the ability to initiate a change in tenure can be a powerful act of community empowerment.

Access to resources is the bedrock of nature-based enterprises, and tenure enshrines this access in law and practice. The case studies make it clear that a variety of different tenure modes can underpin scaling up, though each mode has strengths and weaknesses. In Namibia, for example, conservancies did not offer an unlimited set of resource rights, yet the rights they did offer connected well with opportunities for viable enterprises and with traditional livelihoods. But the more important factor was that conservancies offered a ready vehicle for indigenous communities to use their new tenure rights to their advantage—something they had never had a chance to do before. They offered a new and powerful set of incentives for land use and enterprise.

Likewise, in Bangladesh the chief building block of the Management of Aquatic Ecosystems through Community Husbandry (MACH) program was the opportunity it gave communities to gain new resource rights in the form of 10-year leases—leases they had formerly been shut out of because of cost. In Guatemala, the 25-year forest concessions offered the only real possibility for forest communities to gain enforceable rights to what was until then a de facto open access forest. In Fiji, communities that adopted the locally managed marine area (LMMA) model were essentially voting to adopt a traditional tenure regime that offered a social compact restricting open fishing access.

In all these cases, communities had to understand and act upon the opportunity for a change in tenure made possible by a change in government policy. In Namibia, for instance, communities had to self-organize and formally apply to become a conservancy. The opportunity for tenure change then became an organizing principle and catalyst for action.

One lesson is that if communities themselves can take advantage of a new tenure opportunity, scaling up may be more likely. That is because favorable tenure is the root of local demand, and the opportunity to change tenure is rare. Communities know this. In the case of state-owned resources like common pool forests or fisheries, this implies that governments should establish clear guidelines for how communities may enter into substantive co-management arrangements that devolve real resource authority to them. Then governments must make it clear that communities themselves have the choice to adopt this new regime—a choice that was unavailable before and that rewards community initiative.

At the same time, although many forms of tenure can be acceptable as a basis for ecosystem enterprises, the precise form that tenure takes does have implications for the future. Not all tenure regimes embody the same level of resource rights or the same tenure security. For example, there is no guarantee that the 10-year leases the fishing communities in Bangladesh now hold will be renewed when they expire. In Niger, the government still holds primary ownership of many tree species, and there is no guarantee that government forest policy will not change the incentives once again for forest management. In Fiji, the government has been very supportive of LMMAs but has not granted communities undisputed control of their nearshore waters. In other words, the precise form that local resource tenure takes does matter, insofar as it affects tenure security and benefits sharing arrangements. The details of tenure will therefore be a principal factor in the eventual sustainability of community ecosystem enterprises. Ultimately there is no substitute for strong, formal tenure arrangements with resource rights well defined in duration and geographic extent.

2. High-Profile Demonstrations and Communication Help Scale Up Demand

As a catalyst for local demand and commitment and as a way of generating government and donor support, the power of a high-profile pilot project or demonstration that shows obvious and quantifiable benefits cannot be overestimated. Scaling up will not occur without good communication of success stories.

One of the clearest roles that central governments and donors can play in the scaling up process is creating channels to spread the successes of local enterprises and intermediary support organizations (ISOs). Time and again, demonstration has been shown to be crucial to both quantitative and political scaling up. Exchange visits that allow residents of outside villages to inspect successful community-led ecosystem enterprises are one of the most effective ways to inspire demand. Seeing results on the ground and meeting the people behind these results helps potential adopters to orient themselves and relate their own situations to the social and geographic situation of the demonstration project. This allows them to build a vision of their own, to address pertinent questions, and to argue convincingly to others back in their home villages.

For those who cannot physically visit demonstration sites, such as donors, international NGOs, or government officials, communication of these successful cases in a variety of different formats and depths can be nearly as effective. Today, websites are one of the simplest and most cost-efficient means for communities—often with the help of ISOs—to spread the experiences of their pilot efforts to an international audience. ISOs such as Winrock International, the Watershed Organisation Trust, and the Rainforest Alliance all have articles and pictures on their websites documenting their work with exemplary community enterprises.

International prizes and awards also play a useful role in spreading information and building enthusiasm for new community-based approaches, especially for donors. For example, many of the best examples of enterprises that have successfully scaled up have received recognition—and prize money—from the United Nations Development Programme's Equator Initiative.

(See Box 2.1 in Chapter 2.) This has greatly increased the profile of these programs both internationally and in-country, raising their prestige and opening new channels for interaction and influence.

More-formal research and documentation of benefits, methods, and challenges faced by these enterprises are also a critical part of building their credibility and extending their influence. Indeed, in-depth ecosystem studies and economic analyses have proved to be highly influential among government decision-makers and funders pondering whether their investments have been worthwhile and whether they should continue to fund this model of rural enterprise. In other words, these are often the foundation of high-level "demand"—manifest in political commitment and funding—for scaling up a successful community-led project. For example, in-depth and candid reports on the conservancies in Namibia, the MACH program in Bangladesh, and the forest enterprises in Guatemala have stimulated great interest in the governance and enterprise innovations in these projects and have influenced subsequent funding commitments and natural resource management approaches by the U.S. Agency for International Development and other donors.

3. Capacity Follows Power

Capacity-building for nature-based enterprise is pointless without real devolution of resource authority to local stakeholders. In fact, the devolution itself induces capacity, as those involved in the enterprise find a compelling interest in gaining new competencies and the opportunity to put these into practice in real time.

Even when central governments accept the idea that devolving authority over resources can stimulate the prospects for rural development and poverty reduction, they are often reluctant to relinquish substantive management, regulatory, or budgetary powers to local communities. One reason they put forward is that local organizations lack the technical knowledge and experience to manage forests or fisheries properly without degrading them. Experience from the cases suggests otherwise and drives home the point that success at community-based natural resource management (CBNRM)—at least in the beginning—has more to do with putting proper incentives in place for local action than with technical proficiency. When wildlife management power was granted to Namibian conservancies, they had little trouble reducing poaching because communities had a reason to protect their now-valuable wildlife populations. Similarly, illegal logging and unsustainable fishing practices plunged in Guatemala and Bangladesh, respectively, when communities had the incentive and powers to police their local resources. While there is little doubt that technical training should be a priority early on in the formation of ecosystem enterprises, there is no reason to use it as a reason to slow the devolution process or to put restrictive oversight policies in place.

Earlier and more complete transmission of resource authority to local governments and other local organizations can achieve two ends. First, it can increase commitment to the new ecosystem management regime by eliminating lingering fears about tenure security and management authority. In other words, it can increase local compliance with management rules in the short term as local empowerment is validated. Second, it can provide the conditions necessary to more rapidly gain both technical and social capacities needed to manage over the longer term. Experience is truly the most powerful teacher, and central governments can help maximize this learning environment by mentoring rather than micromanaging.

As mentioned in Chapter 1, institutional choice—which local institution the central government devolves resource authority to—is an important concern, with the need to reconcile the roles of local government and local resource user groups. But there is little dispute that substantial devolution to the local level must occur or the prime incentive for responsible nature-based enterprise will be absent.

By the same token, local institutions to which management powers are devolved must be bound by their new responsibilities as well as their new rights. In Guatemala, the initial rules governing concession management were lax and ill enforced, which created problems of poor governance, exclusion of some community members, and poor business management that took years to set right.

4. Local Resource Management Institutions Require Time to Mature

The local institution responsible for managing a natural resource, whether it is a forest user group, watershed committee, or village council, usually requires a maturation period during which the structure and processes of the institution become more representative and inclusive as well as better able to distribute benefits and costs equitably and resolve disputes fairly.

The development of a capable local resource management institution is essential to the success of ecosystem enterprises. This development includes establishing local legitimacy, setting procedures for decision-making and consultation with community members, and designing processes for enforcing rules and resolving disputes. These are all competencies that build and change over time as the practice of participation deepens and experience with the resource grows. If the institution that is given management power over the resource is a new creation, this maturation process may be lengthy. In Namibia, the general outlines of the conservancy councils were set by the conservancy charter, but there had been no experience with such groups prior to the legal designation of the first conservancy, and little experience with participation. The same was true in Bangladesh with the novel Resource Management Organizations (RMOs). In some Namibian communities, dissatisfactions have surfaced with

how and what benefits are distributed among the group. In Guatemala, the actual resource management scheme was not an issue, even though only a minority of the communities had previously made a living from the forest. Instead, it was a lack of business skills that held them back.

Such growing pains are common, and they point to the importance of an initial institutional structure that is adaptable and responsive enough to accommodate this maturation period. In Bangladesh, the structure of the Resource Management Organizations fostered responsiveness by limiting executive committee members to two-year terms and mandating that a majority of the RMO members come from the ranks of the poorest—those with less than 0.2 hectares of land.

Investing in group visioning and trust-building exercises in the formative stages of community enterprise development can also help by increasing the cohesiveness of the group and its capacity to participate and resolve problems without a rupture. In Bangladesh, communities went through two years of intensive consultation before the RMOs were formed. Experiences of the Watershed Organisation Trust in India emphasize that this initial capacity-building is a singularly effective route to institution-building. In Guatemala, by contrast, the first concessions were hastily demarcated and granted amid political pressure to protect the Maya Biosphere Reserve, with little consultation among local communities or forest management experts.

The effectiveness, legitimacy, and ability of the resource management institution to weather problems also depend on its relationship with other local organizations and levels of government. Care must be taken, for example, that newly empowered resource management organizations do not undermine the role of local representative governments in land use and business development. In Bangladesh, this was avoided by establishing Local Government Committees that brought together government administrators, elected local councilors, RMO members, and local wetland users groups to approve the RMO management plans. The interaction of the RMOs with these other institutions conferred legitimacy on the RMOs, making their role clear without introducing competition among the various groups. This kind of harmony helps give new resource management organizations the space and support they need to mature. In Guatemala, on the other hand, municipal governments were given no role or involvement with the new concessions, and the stumpage taxes they had previously collected were redistributed to the new national park authority, creating resentment.

It is important to note that the necessity for patience as local institutions mature into their role of natural resource managers is frequently at odds with the desire by government or funders for these institutions to move quickly to assume their new duties. One of the challenges in scaling up nature-based enterprises is reconciling this pressure with the reality that institutional growth usually occurs by modest increments. Experience shows that expecting too much from new institutions often undermines progress rather than encouraging it.

THE BENEFITS OF LOCAL NATURAL RESOURCE management and nature-based enterprises reach far beyond the local or even national level: they can also help mitigate climate change.

As we have seen in Guatemala and elsewhere, sustainable management plans that provide local populations with economic alternatives to converting forestlands for agriculture can be highly effective at protecting valuable forest resources, increasing forest cover, and providing a host of other ecosystem services to the surrounding region.

The case study in Chapter 3 describes in detail efforts to establish community enterprises in the Petén region of Guatemala, based on sustainable management of designated forest concessions in the Maya Biosphere Reserve. The program was designed to help alleviate poverty in local communities as well as to combat illegal logging and forest conversion in one of the last unspoiled forest tracts in Latin America.

The environmental benefits were realized within a few years of the program's start, with significant reduction in illegal logging and other forest degradation. Ironically, in the nearby national park, which is a designated "no-harvest" zone, cutting for agriculture and timber poaching have increased. An added dividend is the potential for climate benefits resulting from the improved stewardship of these forest resources.

Climate change now dominates environmental discussions because of the profound effects it is predicted to have on ecosystems around the world. In response, policymakers are seeking fast, effective, and inexpensive ways to mitigate carbon releases. One strategy that has surfaced in international climate change negotiations is referred to as Reducing Emissions from Deforestation in Developing Countries, or REDD.

REDD would function as a global payment for ecosystems services (PES) arrangement, wherein forest owners—either states, communities, companies, or individuals—would be compensated to lower the rate of carbon emissions from their forests below a given reference scenario by reducing forest cover loss. An effective REDD program could become one potentially important option within a menu of global carbon reduction tools, since land use changes account for at least 20 percent of annual carbon emissions worldwide (Myers 2007:19; Huberman 2007: 6-7; IPCC 2007:543). It is unlikely, though, that REDD will ever become a major source of revenue to countries or communities.

There are certain technical issues that REDD must satisfy, however, prior to being accepted by the UN Framework Conven-tion on Climate Change—the broad-based treaty that acts as a forum for international climate negotiations. Carbon emission reference scenarios must be established. Monitoring tools must be created and implemented. Payment mechanisms need to be developed. A robust and accepted carbon trading market has to be in place (Myers 2007:18–19, 26–37).

REDD Flag for the Poor

But even settling these and other technical issues does not guarantee REDD's adoption or success. Experience shows that without careful attention to issues of equity and respect for community rights and rural livelihoods, actions taken under PES programs can backfire, working against the interests of the poor and failing to achieve their environmental objectives. A recent example in Uganda illustrates the potential hurdles for REDD-associated projects that ignore community concerns.

In Mount Elgon National Park, a reforestation program negotiated in the 1990s between a Dutch nonprofit and the national government was designed to offset carbon releases by Dutch power companies. From the government's point of view, the tree planting would improve the landscape of the national park at no cost to the government, attracting more tourists. But the local people who had been evicted from their lands in preparation for reforestation were unwilling to accept the new circumstances imposed upon them by the government. In 2006, after years of fighting to regain their livelihoods, three communities were granted a court injunction that overturned the evictions. After moving back onto their lands, the farmers chopped down the new trees. The Dutch nonprofit that managed the reforestation project was helpless to secure its 12-year, US$4 million investment, and the carbon benefits were lost as well (Faris 2007).

What went wrong? This was a project dictated by the national government, with no involvement by local communities. The traditional tenure rights and livelihoods of local residents were ignored. None of the benefits generated by the project flowed to the local communities.

The outcome could have been different if the program was poor-friendly and created community self-interest by recognizing the rights and needs of the local residents. If the local farmers had been given the opportunity to earn their livelihoods through sustainable management of the new forests or by combining tree planting with their traditional agriculture in an agroforestry scheme, both the economic needs of local residents and the environmental goals of the government and investors would have been served.

The Lessons of PES

There are important lessons from this and other PES experiences, as well as from the community-based natural resource management enterprises described in this report, that could help orient REDD so it can better achieve its goals. By framing REDD initiatives as both pro-poor and pro-environment projects, unintended consequences that could undermine the project in the future have a better chance of being avoided. The Uganda example makes it clear, for instance, that tenure and governance issues cannot be ignored. Creating a community "stake" in a project nurtures the self-interest that inspires community involvement and responsibility.

Another lesson is that payments to communities under a REDD compensation scheme must be substantial enough to make a difference in the household incomes of community members, who otherwise are unlikely to participate in the program or follow through on their commitments. This compensation may come as monetary payments, but it can also be complemented by capacity training or support to develop alternative enterprises.

One way to make REDD's goal of reducing deforestation more amenable to low-income families is to allow them to pursue complementary land uses such as agroforestry, the collection of non-timber forest products, and perhaps even limited timber harvesting. This recognizes the fact that poor families are unlikely to be able to live on PES payments alone and must pursue other activities to round out their livelihoods. The goal should be to make these activities as compatible with carbon storage as possible.

A third lesson is that entry costs to participate in REDD programs—such as licensing and certification costs—must be low if poor people are to participate. Otherwise, only large landowners will be able to join. Prohibitively high entry costs pose a particular problem in cases of contested tenure. Large landowners who can afford the certification costs may stake claims over contested lands, thereby turning REDD into a tool to solidify land claims where tenure has been unclear.

Community-Based Forestry: A REDD Primer

The international development community has a central role to play in assuring that REDD is carried out in an effective and pro-poor manner, first by supporting community-based forestry. Providing this support can bring economic and social benefits to communities while reducing carbon emissions. Community forestry projects can also help build the capacities and resilience of forest communities, making them more capable of handling a REDD project down the line. And such efforts need not wait for REDD's complicated technical questions to be sorted out.

NGOs might also work to establish performance metrics for carbon mitigation that do not rely entirely on precise calculations of emissions created by deforestation. Such metrics could help developing countries to receive international funding outside of the global carbon market—whether through bilateral or multilateral support, or through a global funding mechanism—by reducing their emissions, but without the stringent technical requirements imposed by REDD (Daviet et al. 2007: 5-8). Agroforestry and sustainable harvesting within community forests would likely fit more easily into such performance metrics.

Finally, NGOs and donors can assist in developing social and environmental standards for REDD, using established community-based forestry programs to design social protocols and to test carbon release monitoring techniques. Doing so will mean that if REDD becomes part of global carbon mitigation, communities, donors, governments, and NGOs will already have experience with effectively reducing carbon emissions while improving local economies and increasing social resilience.

Building enterprises through community management of natural resources will certainly not solve all the challenges that REDD faces as a global PES system. Nor will it quickly result in the large-scale projects that climate experts claim are required to make a significant reduction in carbon emissions. Yet these enterprises can be encouraged right now – and they can help meet REDD's major environmental aim while simultaneously serving as a training ground to work out some of the program's technical issues. In this way, community management of natural resources effectively stands at the intersection of climate adaptation, carbon mitigation, and rural development. A well-designed REDD program may serve as one of a number of financial incentives to promote these management efforts in the future.

5. ISOs Provide Focus and Credibility

Intermediary support organizations are often the most efficient way to focus local demand, help communities create an appropriate local institution for resource management, and bring the attention and credibility to the local effort that is needed to engage government and donor interest.

As discussed in Chapter 2, ISOs have capabilities that are especially suited to helping communities organize themselves. ISOs typically have a very strong vision of the advantages of community-led resource management and, based on their deep experience with similar interventions, can articulate the possible benefits of working together to villagers who may lack this vision. They can also be straightforward about costs and potential problems and therefore can act as an honest broker. In addition, they have an understanding of the importance of process and participation to building a firm foundation for group action and can intervene when obstacles arise within the group. In Bangladesh, Caritas and the Center for Natural Resource Studies were instrumental in setting up the initial consultation process within communities to identify local priorities and develop a consensus on how to restore wetland productivity. These consultations were notable for their inclusiveness and political savvy, which paid dividends later on

when actual work began. Meanwhile, another ISO, Winrock International, helped design the innovative institutional arrangement that included Resource Management Organizations and Local Government Committees. The strength of these institutions and their applicability on a broad scale has been a key element in scaling up the MACH program.

ISOs have an ability to intervene with government, funders, and even the private sector to clear obstacles that otherwise might stop a community effort in its tracks. In Niger, for example, it was intervention by Serving in Mission (SIM) that first led the Forest Service to relax its insistence on state ownership of trees, giving farmers the incentive to allow native trees to return to their fields. Without the credibility of SIM, based on its earlier work in Niger, farmer-led regeneration would not have gotten off the ground.

The cases also show that ISOs can usefully work in consortia to increase their effect. In both Namibia and Bangladesh, groups of NGOs and other support organizations coordinated their activities under a single umbrella group, bringing their many different specialties together so that communities could find a range of interlocking services. In Namibia, the 11 members of the Namibian Association of C B N R M Support Organizations even included the Ministry of Environment and Tourism and a trade association, giving conservancies significant access to the government bureaucracy and the business community. Working in tandem in this fashion may be an especially effective model to support scaling up across culturally or geographically diverse communities. In Guatemala, rivalries between the various international and local NGOs working with the communities created the opposite effect, with the fledgling enterprises failing to work together and share best practices in the early years.

6. Accountability Remains Important

Part of the maturation process for local institutions and enterprises is developing appropriate accountability mechanisms so that community interest in maintaining collective action persists.

One of the consistent lessons of successful nature-based enterprises that scale up is that they maintain significant involvement and trust of community stakeholders over time. Stakeholder interest is influenced by many things, such as the value of the resources being managed (the greater the potential benefits, the greater the interest). But trust in community institutions is fostered by transparency of processes and regular accounting for decisions taken. In Bangladesh, all meetings of the Resource Management Organizations are public, and most RMOs have established a separate subcommittee to conduct financial audits and discourage corruption. Biological and socioeconomic data are routinely collected and released so that the community, the government, and funders can measure progress and assess benefits and costs. In addition, the two-year terms for executive committee members mean that elections—the most basic of accountability mechanisms—are held frequently.

Sometimes, accountability mechanisms can be as simple as a public billboard. In some state-funded watershed restoration projects in India, local NGOs have used billboards with great effect to let community members know what kinds of public investments have been promised, how much they have cost so far, and what benefits have accrued.

Such accountability mechanisms may seem like just the rudiments of responsible public action, but they are not trivial, and they are not always easy for inexperienced community institutions to apply consistently. Training in applying such transparent practices as regular audits and public reporting of decisions is one aspect of capacity-building that should not be neglected.

7. High-Level Government and Donor Commitment Is Necessary

No matter how well local demand is marshaled and local capacity expanded, community-driven enterprises still require active acceptance and participation of governments and donors in order to scale up effectively.

It may seem axiomatic, but without a clear, public, and ongoing commitment by government, no strategy to foster nature-based enterprises for poverty reduction can succeed. Government is entwined in nearly every aspect of natural resource management—from granting resource tenure to regulating the transport and sale of ecosystem products. Government's planning, permitting, and oversight roles mean its involvement is nearly always required, even when control over resources has been devolved to the local level. Government's potential to be an obstacle thus looms large as community-based organizations struggle to learn how to manage local ecosystems sustainably and profitably.

But government as potential partner also beckons. Government backing can support pilot projects, ease access to credit, make technical assistance available, and provide capacity development programs that train people in crucial resource management skills. Government also brings a unique synoptic view. It can look broadly at ecosystems regionwide to identify resource trends and assess where there may be conflicts between resource users. It can also look broadly at community-driven enterprises, and when it sees a promising model it can help bring that to scale, bringing the state's planning, budget, and communication powers to bear.

As we see in the cases, the role of a committed government, working in partnership with other key actors, evolves from that of an institution that dictates to communities to one that ensures that conditions are right at every stage for enterprises to grow and prosper. In Bangladesh, the government worked hand in hand with ISOs and communities to analyze the fisheries problems these communities faced, identify alternatives to current practices, design and fund new government and community institutions, and make skill-building programs available for low-income families. In Namibia, the Ministry of Environment and Tourism worked in tandem with conservancies and ISOs to improve wildlife management, create tourist infrastructure, and build tourism demand so that conservancies could capitalize on their wildlife resource. In all these efforts, government involvement extended over years and was at a depth that allowed promising programs to mature naturally.

Donors play a similar and complementary role. One key insight from the cases is the importance of determination, patience, and long-term commitment on the part of both governments and donors. The involvement of the US Agency for International Development in the Namibia, Bangladesh, Guatemala, and Niger cases provides a good example, spanning at least a decade in each instance. Other bilateral donors like the UK Department for International Development and international NGOs such as the World Wildlife Fund have shown similar persistence in these cases. Their mode of extended participation and financial support speaks forcefully to the point that effecting a permanent change in the expectations and livelihoods of the poor requires a long-term approach.

Beyond the Community Level: Addressing Challenges at the Macro Level

Earlier chapters adopt a village-level perspective to nature-based income, concentrating on the capacities that communities must develop and the actions they must take in order to create viable enterprises that reduce poverty. But for such a community-centered model to succeed, a supporting environment of functional national governance, accessible markets, and improved physical and financial infrastructure is required. Scaling up depends critically on actions that governments take to remove obstacles and provide support in matters beyond the local sphere. In the following sections we probe some of the macro-level changes needed to provide the necessary enabling environment to allow community-based enterprises to realize their full potential and scale up their impact. The changes needed to create that environment range from reducing the influence of elites and implementing fair tax and regulatory schemes to improving rural representation in national governments, making ministers more responsive to rural needs, and improving rural infrastructure.

It is an impressive and even daunting list, although it is by no means exhaustive. Behind these recommendations is the understanding, however, that many of the reforms called for have been lacking for decades and that change requires new incentives to alter policy and motivate conduct that is pro-poor. This is not easy. Resistance to the kind of changes that would create such an enabling environment is every bit as persistent as rural poverty itself. This emphasizes the importance of consistent and prolonged commitment by national governments to the goal of pro-poor development and the policy reforms that this requires. With genuine commitment from national leaders to alleviate rural poverty, real change is possible.

Rectifying and Expanding Rural Markets

Rural markets often possess a number of distortions that disadvantage rural smallholders and communities that seek to market nature-based products. Competition is often minimal, and villagers who produce nature-based commodities like charcoal or coffee usually do not capture much of the eventual retail value of their products. Governments have a vital role to play in making markets fairer and thereby able to yield greater income. The right policies can boost employment, helping to ensure viable livelihoods for the poorest.

The willingness of governments to confront the dysfunctions of rural markets must proceed from a genuine belief in the potential for rural small-scale enterprises to contribute to national economic growth. For decades, government policies in every natural resource sector—from agriculture to forestry to fisheries to mining—have favored large-scale producers at the expense of rural small-scale producers. This is in spite of the fact that small-scale rural enterprises are responsible for significant production and most of the employment in these sectors. In India, small forest enterprises account for 87–98 percent of all forest-related businesses and generate more than 80 percent of all revenues. Indeed, small and medium-size forest enterprises frequently account for 80–90 percent of all forest businesses in developing countries (Mayers and Macqueen 2007:1–2; Molnar et al. 2007:1–10). Likewise, smallholders are responsible for 90 percent of all agricultural production in Africa (WRI et al. 2005:35). In the burgeoning palm oil business, smallholders account for up to 90 percent of total production in West African countries and as much as one third of production in Indonesia and Malaysia, the world's two biggest producers (Vermeulen and Goad 2006:4).

The rationale for states to favor large-scale over small-scale operations has been predicated on the belief that the bigger outfits are more efficient and productive. Yet much research points to the fact that small enterprises, when they have the same level of technical help and financing as large ones, can be both efficient and profitable. For example, smallholder palm oil farmers with access to the latest technology have shown they can be as efficient as large-scale plantations and can achieve high net profits (Vermeulen and Goad 2006:6, 26, 28). Similarly, some small forest enterprises in Central America produce high-quality hard woods that are competitive and profitable in a global timber market dominated by larger producers (Molnar et al. 2007:43–46). Extending this productive potential beyond a few successful rural enterprises requires state action to challenge elite capture of resources and reform the regulatory and incentive structures that often determine whether a small business can get off the ground or instead withers quickly. It also requires targeted assistance with technology adoption, product improvement, business planning, and market development.

SMALL FORESTRY ENTERPRISES (SFES) PREDOMINATE						
	Brazil	China	Guyana	India	S. Africa	Uganda
Number of SFEs (% of all forestry enterprises)	>98%	87%	93%	87-98%	33-95%	–
SFE Employees (% of all forestry employees)	49-70%	50%	75%	97%	25%	60%
SFE Revenues (% of all forestry revenues)	75%	43%	50%	82%	3%	60%

Source: Mayers and Macqueen 2007:1–2

Confronting Elite Capture, Encouraging Competition

Elite capture of local resources often proceeds with the government's tacit or explicit help. The more valuable the resource, the more prone it is to being used for political patronage, resulting in distortions in how resource concessions or access are granted. Subsidies may be targeted to a privileged few who qualify. Wealthy landowners or those with political influence have been very adept at using their power to exert control in the countryside and squelch competition. In Indonesia, the businessman Bob Hassan dominated the Indonesian plywood export market from the mid-1980s to the mid-1990s due to his close personal ties to President Suharto. As head of the plywood trade association Apkindo, Hassan—with government compliance —controlled plywood trade quotas and commanded shipping and insurance monopolies that left little room for small forest operators to negotiate (Gellert 2003:55–56, 64–68).

Although Hassan's level of dominance may not be typical, the use of political influence and wealth to gain resource access and discourage competition is still pervasive. Indeed, the rural economy is often beset with anticompetitive practices that end up concentrating profits in the hands of a few who dominate the commodity chain. Collusion among leading businesses in an area often leads to price-fixing in rural commodity markets or the formation of cartels that control trade in natural resources (Molnar et al. 2007:64; Gautam 2005:1–2). These make it hard for smallholders to receive a fair price for their production or labor and for small-scale enterprises to survive. In Senegal's charcoal trade, a handful of high-level traders and brokers capture most of the industry's profit, while woodcutters and low-level transporters and retailers work for subsistence wages. In many instances, the capture of rural commodity chains is enabled by manipulation of government regulations, often with the complicity of officials. Senegal's charcoal barons, for example, have used their dominance of state forest licenses—required of all who harvest, transport, or market forest products—to concentrate their power and control the charcoal market (Ribot 2008:2, 6). *(See Box 4.2.)*

Confronting anticompetitive behaviors such as these is a prerequisite for enabling rural nature-based enterprises to grow. While the necessity of creating a "level playing field" for businesses has long been preached by development banks and donors, many developing nations still lack basic competition laws and have yet to act aggressively to police the marketplace (Gautam 2005:6). Doing so means not only adopting progressive laws and oversight practices; it also requires that governments acknowledge the part their own regulations play in facilitating many anticompetitive behaviors and corrupt practices. Government has an obligation to ensure that regulatory instruments such as production quotas, transport licenses, and user fees are not abused through bribery or patronage and are applied in a manner that widens access rather than restricts it. Greater transparency in the application of such instruments is a necessary first step.

Adjusting Regulatory and Tax Regimes

Unfair capture of natural resource opportunities is not the only hurdle that small businesses face. Over-regulation by government and unfair tax policies also constitute significant burdens

for many nature-based enterprises. The state has a clear role in defining, encouraging, and enforcing sustainable natural resource management. Based on its synoptic view of the nation's ecosystems, the state must make sure that local resource exploitation patterns are compatible with the national vision for resource management and, when summed together, do not degrade the resource base. However, governments have a tendency toward heavy-handed regulation of community groups who manage natural resources. This often manifests as strict prescriptions for "best practices" that communities are required to follow or complex management plans that they must formulate before being granted the necessary permits to harvest or carry out management activities. In many cases these prescriptions are unnecessarily complex, do not respect local institutions or capacities, and impose a severe financial burden (Ribot 2004:54–59; Molnar et al. 2007:64–70). Thus, regulations that may be appropriate for industrial-scale enterprises managing large tracts of forest or significant fishing fleets can be overkill for small community-based enterprises, resulting in a competitive disadvantage.

Under Cameroon's 1994 Forestry Law, for example, the requirements for establishing a community forest include creating a management committee with a constitution, mapping the forest areas at issue and comparing them to the government's overall forest plan, and submitting a forest management plan. These steps have proved too complex and expensive for most communities (Ribot 2004:55). Similar planning and permit obstacles plague forest users in many other countries, including India, Nepal, Tanzania, Bolivia, Guatemala, Senegal, and the Philippines. In Guatemala's community forest concessions in the Petén region, the overlapping inspection requirements of donors, international certifiers (the Forest Stewardship Council), and government agencies burdened fledgling enterprises with high costs and hindered their transition to financial independence. In 2007, a survey of community forestry enterprises worldwide found that artificial and overdemanding rules for management plans and other required permits and procedures—and the high costs associated with them—were major obstacles to the success of community-based businesses (Molnar et al. 2007:66–70).

Overzealous government oversight and micromanagement of community enterprises amounts to resistance to true devolution of resource rights to local communities. It often stems from fear by government bureaucrats that rural communities lack the capacity—and therefore cannot be trusted—to manage resources responsibly and efficiently. This lack of "capacity" is used as an excuse to delay granting the necessary government permission, often without offering any avenue or resources for gaining the required capacities or meeting the required standards. The net result is that the government retains its accustomed role at the center of resource management (Ribot 2004:59–65).

An alternative to the over-regulation of community-based natural resource enterprises would be to adopt a "minimum standards" approach. The national government would establish a minimum set of rules or standards that community members must follow in their management but would grant communities flexibility in how they meet this standard. For instance, environmental standards could be set for how much of a forest can be cut in a single year, what rare or endangered species are not to be harvested, or what seasons are off-limits for fishing in order to encourage spawning and stock replenishment. On the other hand, all activities not specified in the environmental rules or not at odds with the environmental standard would be allowed without the need for a permit or management plan. This would reverse the current regulatory structure in which only activities specified in the management plan are allowed (Ribot 2004:56–59).

Minimum environmental standards or targets could provide the flexibility that local groups need to adapt and innovate in their management without compromising sustainability. Of course, this would only be possible if reasonable sanctions were in place for breaching the standards, such as fines or temporary loss of harvest rights. As in any regulatory scheme, credible monitoring and enforcement would be crucial. Simplicity and clarity of the standards and the consequences of failure to meet them would also be a key factor in the success of this approach (Ribot 2004:56–59).

In addition to their substantial regulatory burden, small nature-based enterprises also commonly suffer from inappro-

FORMAL AND INFORMAL TAXES ON FOREST PRODUCTS, QUANG NINH PROVINCE, VIETNAM, 2004

Tax	Assessed On	Assessed By	Receipt	Amount
Commune road fee	Truck owner	Guard station	No	10,000-50,000 Dong per truck
Village fee	Trader and truck owner	Village	No	20,000 Dong per truck
Commune resource tax	Trader	Commune	Yes	50,000 Dong per truck
Forestry inspection fee	Trader	Forestry inspectors	No	20,000 (for trucks) / 250,000 Dong (for boats at port)
Police fee	Trader	Police	No	20,000 – 250,000 Dong per trader or truck
State forest enterprise	Trader	State	Yes	Variable
Value added tax	Trader	District	Yes	5%
Resource tax	Trader	District	Yes	Up to 13%
Buy-from-afar tax	Trader	District	Yes	10%

Source: Thi Phi et al. 2004:13, 16–17

priate tax policies. In the upland areas of Vietnam, farmers and traders of forest products are subject to as many as nine formal and informal taxes when they market their products, including road fees, village taxes, resource taxes, inspection fees, a value added tax, and a tax on forest enterprises. Road taxes and the expected bribes at inspection stations alone can add as much as 30 percent to the original farmgate price when transporting goods to Hanoi, posing a serious threat to business and suppressing profits. So high was the accumulated tax burden in Vietnam's Ba Che district that cinnamon traders finally abandoned the area (Thi Phi et al. 2004:13, 16–17).

Even established businesses are impeded by such burdens. In the Compostela Valley in the Philippines, one prominent community forestry cooperative in business since 1996 has been consistently hindered by a combination of high regulatory costs and a high tax rate on forest activities (Molnar et al. 2007:69). If small nature-based businesses are to be encouraged, the aggregate burden of taxes, fees, and permit charges must be lowered. In addition, certain kinds of taxes hit small producers particularly hard, such as those applied at the point of resource extraction. Reconfiguring the tax burden so that it falls more heavily at points higher in the value chain could benefit enterprise formation without unduly reducing total tax receipts (Molnar et al. 2007:64, 74).

Other distortions of the rural marketplace also affect small ecosystem enterprises and may likewise need adjustment. For example, governments frequently intervene in agricultural and forest markets by creating state monopolies to control the sale or trade of nature-based products. In Vietnam's Ba Che Province, all producers of bamboo, pine resin, cinnamon, and sandalwood must sell their product to the State Forest Enterprise for processing and trade (Thi Phi 2004:28). Until recently, all coffee producers in Ethiopia had to sell their product through the national coffee auction (Dempsey and Campbell 2006:2). While these entities can offer some stability of prices and an unambiguous outlet for products, they can also stifle local initiative, suppress market prices, and impede the maturation of local enterprises. They constitute another level of state control that is not beneficial to rural entrepreneurs.

Providing Technical, Research, and Marketing Assistance

In addition to correcting market distortions, the government must offer positive encouragement and support to expand rural markets. Governments have a legitimate role in a number of areas, such as helping to set product quality standards and undertaking product research—tasks that small enterprises are ill prepared to perform. In the early 1990s, the government of the Indian state of Andhra Pradesh sponsored research on karaya gum—an exudate collected from gum trees by poor indigenous families in the state and used in the food and pharmaceutical industries. The state knew that karaya gum collection provided an important income source for many rural indigenous families, but poor gum quality suppressed the demand for the product, and poor harvesting techniques injured the trees, decreasing output and shrinking income potential.

Through a state-run corporation, Andhra Pradesh interviewed karaya gum users and conducted lab and field tests on different harvesting, processing, grading, and storing techniques to determine appropriate product standards and pinpoint the optimum methods to harvest and prepare the product. The state corporation then organized training programs to communicate these new methods and distribute better harvesting tools. Due to these initiatives, the quality of the gum has increased considerably, the market has stabilized, and the market price per kilogram has risen two- to threefold, depending on the grade of gum. Gum-related income has risen in step with the higher prices. In essence, a relatively small investment by the state revolutionized the traditional karaya gum trade and made it a more reliable and profitable business (IRG 2005:1–18). Supporting similar research efforts focused on production and quality concerns surrounding medicinals or the many other natural products that form the basis of many rural enterprises could presumably achieve similar increases in market potential and family incomes.

The government also has an important role to play in introducing new technologies, improved seed and plant varieties, and more effective resource management methods that rural producers would have trouble developing on their own. In Indonesia,

EMPOWERING LOCAL COMMUNITIES WITH resource rights seems straightforward, in theory. But transferring meaningful power over local resources to rural communities is often difficult in practice. Forest management in Senegal is a prime example. Senegal's legislature enacted substantive legal reforms in 1996 and 1998 that were intended to shift management and control over local forests from the Forest Department to elected local councils. But a series of obstacles has frustrated the intent of these laws and thwarted real decentralization of forest authority (Ribot 2008a:1).

Since the decentralization reforms, most rural communities have seen little increase in their ability to earn forest income, which was one of the intended benefits of the reforms. Charcoal—made by the partial burning of trees—is the dominant cooking fuel in Senegal's large cities and the principal commercial output of Senegal's forests. Despite supplying lucrative markets with charcoal, the forest villages still cannot profit outside of project areas that are under the protection of donors (Ribot 2008a:3).

Since colonial times, forestry in West Africa has been marked by a top-down approach that has excluded rural communities from forestry decisions and economic gains. In Senegal, authority over forests was exercised by the state Forest Department to serve the commercial sector and meet urban fuel needs. Forests were not managed to develop village economies. Over the past 15 years, Senegalese lawmakers have tried to address this imbalance through successive revisions of the forestry laws. In 1993, they blessed the idea of community forest management by allowing rural councils—the elected bodies that represent the smallest unit of local government—to participate in managing local forests. Under this plan, the country's Forest Department retained total control over the forest resources—allowing villagers to "participate" in the labor of management (Ribot 2008a:4–5).

In 1996 the nation enacted a major decentralization law that required the transfer of direct control over community forests to rural councils. The 1998 Forest Code acted on this directive, granting rural councils the sole right to exploit community forests commercially but also requiring them to develop management plans for their forests so that exploitation would follow good forestry practice (Ribot 2008a:4–6).

In spite of these legal reforms, the old top-down forestry model has by no means died away. For one, professional foresters in Senegal's Forest Department are not convinced that rural communities can manage forests adequately on their own yet—or at least that they will manage them in the best interest of the nation (Ribot 2008a: 1-2). But a more fundamental reason for resistance to the new community forest orientation is its potential to change the dynamics of the nation's charcoal market. The Forest Department has been a key player in a well-established system of forest exploitation that is dominated by urban charcoal merchants. The charcoal market is well oiled with money and political influence, and the current set of vested interests is not anxious to see this situation change (Ribot 2008a:iv).

Under today's system, urban charcoal merchants and distributors have near-monopoly control over the market, allowing them to reap the bulk of the profits. The charcoal process begins when a city-based charcoal merchant hires a team of migrant workers to harvest timber from a forest and convert it to charcoal on-site in an artisanal charcoal kiln (Ribot 2008a:3). The charcoal is then transported by truck or train to cities such as Dakar and sold to distributors, who in turn sell bags of charcoal to individual retail vendors for eventual purchase by city residents (Ribot 2008a:17).

In this system, rural villagers reap virtually no income, because neither the merchants nor the charcoal crews are local. Village chiefs may receive some payoff from charcoal merchants, and the charcoal crews may pay for lodging in village homes, but little else trickles down to the local economy (Ribot 2008a:4). In any case, the charcoal makers—whether local or migrant, work for subsistence wages, while merchants and urban distributors profit handsomely. In 2002, the average merchant reaped

PROFIT DISTRIBUTION ACROSS SENEGAL'S CHARCOAL MARKET CHAIN, 2002

Actor	No. of Actors in Senegal	Average Net Profit Per Actor After Subsistence Subtracted (US$/actor)	Total Market Net Profit (US$)	Distribution of Total Market Net Profit (%)
Woodcutter	9,827	134	642,930	15.9%
Foreman	246	438	52,556	1.3%
Merchant	640	3,815	2,196,053	54.3%
Urban Wholesaler	n.a.	2,922	876,461	21.7%
Urban Retailer	3,306	326	279,256	6.9%
TOTAL	14,018		4,047,255	100.0%

Source: Ribot 2008b.

Hauling charcoal in Senegal

a net profit of $3,815—nearly 30 times the $134 earned by those who cut and produced the charcoal (Ribot 2008b).

Because of the lack of economic benefits for local residents, most are not in favor of letting their forests be cut for charcoal, and their rural councils feel the same way (Ribot 2008a:7). Instead, many communities would like to enter the charcoal market on their own terms and capture more of the benefits. But they are blocked by the Forest Department. In the past several years a few communities have been able to enter the market under the protection of well-financed development projects (Larson and Ribot 2007:197). But outside of the project areas the new laws empowering rural communities are ignored and business-as-usual exploitation continues.

Although the new forest laws technically give rural councils the power to decide whether to allow cutting for charcoal in their forests, the Forest Department has found effective ways to thwart this authority and maintain central control. For example, the Forest Service has set strict rules for the mandatory forest management plans that rural councils must submit before the state will grant them authority over their forests. Local communities find it nearly impossible to develop these detailed plans, which are expensive and, arguably, unnecessarily complex (Ribot 2008a:7). In fact, to date only four rural communities have managed to submit plans acceptable to the government since the 1998 Forest Code was enacted—and those were only completed with support from foreign donors. Without an approved plan, the Forest Department retains management authority over a community's forest (Larson and Ribot 2007:200). In contrast, commercial charcoal harvesters do not need to submit any management plan before harvesting—they

are allowed to cut without plans in areas assigned to them by local forest agents (Larson and Ribot 2007:200).

The Forest Department also has other ways to exact its will. It has authority to require and to allocate permits to produce, store, and transport commercial forest products. It also sets the quota for how much wood will be cut for charcoal—a power it has long used as a source of political patronage and power—and it determines which areas are eligible for cutting (ostensibly, with the permission of the local council) (Larson and Ribot 2007:199, 200). The Department uses these powers to put pressure on local communities. If a rural council questions whether to allow cutting for charcoal, local forest officials, merchants, and powerful political actors will contact the President of the council and usually bully or bribe him to give his permission to cut. Rural councils complain that, with no approved management plan of their own, they have little choice but to comply (Ribot 2008a:16). The result is that real power over harvest and management of forests has not shifted to local communities as intended.

The Senegalese experience demonstrates that without a reasonable set of rights to manage, use, and market natural resources, nature-based income will remain out of reach. In this case, forest villagers are barred from the charcoal market. But Senegal's story equally demonstrates that entrenched economic interests and their Forest Service allies can effectively block the empowerment process, even when progressive laws are in place. Merchants, foresters, and local chiefs with a stake in the Senegalese charcoal industry as currently configured have an incentive to work against the empowerment of elected rural councils and their rural constituents, whose entry into the industry will bring greater competition and will challenge the merchants' dominance of the charcoal market.

Changing this state of affairs will require dismantling the policies that let the Forest Department undermine local authority and allow urban merchants to dominate the charcoal industry. That means abandoning the system of quotas and permits that concentrate market access in the merchants' hands and loosening the requirements for forest management plans. But the political reality is that this will not be easy. Further, when the laws and regulations are changed, the bigger job will be to change practice—especially the culture of domination by forestry agents and urban merchants. The permit and quota systems were, by law, supposed to be phased out in 2001, but the deadline has long passed. In January 2008 the Minister of Environment signed another decree promising to eliminate the quota—even though it was already legally abolished (Ribot 2008b). Will the Forest Department relinquish its sources of power? If not, is the legislature prepared to force the issue?

government-supported nurseries are helping to free small-scale palm oil producers from one of their key competitive constraints by supplying them with the same high-quality seed stock that large plantations use (Vermeulen and Goad 2006:33). Technology interventions need not be highly sophisticated or expensive to be effective. In central and southern Africa, significant increases in honey yields have been realized by introducing new beehive technology, such as replacing traditional bark or clay hives with simple wooden structures with removable slats (Molnar et al. 2007:25; FAO 2005a:19–21).

Government guidance and support should not be confined to technical and production issues. It should also extend to business planning and market analysis—skills that are required early in the enterprise cycle. Local NGOs and intermediary support organizations frequently take on the task of helping local enterprises ascertain their markets and prepare business plans, but governments can sometimes work at a higher level to coordinate these services. In The Gambia, the government adopted a stepwise method of helping communities determine the most suitable forest enterprises for them to invest in for maximum benefit.

The program—called market analysis and development (MA&D)—is directed at communities that have established legally designated Community Forests under the state's community forestry rules, which were put in place in the early 1990s. In each community, the MA&D method proceeds in three phases. First, community members, with the help of a facilitator, assess the community's financial objectives and inventory their forest resources. Second, they identify potential forest products, evaluate their market potential, and select the most promising. In the final phase, the community crafts a business plan, explores financing arrangements, and is guided through a pilot phase of the enterprise (FAO 2005a:9–41).

One of the strengths of the approach in The Gambia is the melding of practical and political concerns. The government saw its adoption of the MA&D program as part of its overall effort to decentralize forest management and enhance forest livelihoods. It integrated the practical step of building local business capacity with the political reform of creating Community Forests, realizing that community forestry would only work well if it resulted in real benefits to the local economy (FAO 2005a:1–3, 59–60, 63).

Another way in which governments can help nature-based businesses expand their markets is in the area of product certification. Many small producers of coffee, spices, tea, timber, vegetables, and a number of other commodities and crafts have added value to their products by certifying them as organic, Fair Trade, or "sustainably harvested." However, certification can constitute a considerable technical and cost barrier for small businesses. Governments can facilitate the process by making sure state regulations support and encourage certification and by providing technical assistance and even financial support in some instances. Certification is not likely to be useful or attainable for all enterprises, however, and governments should be cautious about making certification a requirement for resource manage-

ment—as has happened in some cases—lest it become an inadvertent barrier (Molnar et al. 2007:58).

COST TO PRODUCERS OF INTERNATIONAL CERTIFICATION (US$)		
	Initial Certification	Ongoing Costs
FSC*	$7,500	Yearly Audit: $2000 Documentation: $2,500 Compliance: $10,000
Fair Trade**	$780 application fee + $3,125 certification fee.	Yearly renewal: $1,560 - $2,500 Compliance: Varies

*Average for Oaxaca, Mexico community forests of over 4,000 hectares
**For small farmer organization between 50 and 100 members:

Source: Molnar 2003: 17; FLO-CERT 2008.

Overall, the guiding principle in offering state technology, marketing, research, or other services should be that these programs are rooted in the demand from local enterprises. State extension services are nothing new, but there is abundant evidence that many such efforts fail to achieve their goals. In Indonesia, for example, the government funds nearly 130 separate programs to support small and medium-size enterprises, but evaluations suggest that few meet their goals. A stronger element of local design would undoubtedly improve the effectiveness of these programs (World Bank 2006a:xii).

Improving National Governance

It is not enough to catalyze good governance at the community level if this good practice is undermined at the national level. Rural communities are often marginalized within national policymaking, leading to a lack of policy attention that can work against community enterprises. This is true both within national legislative bodies and within government ministries where the regulatory regime governing natural resource use is forged and enforced. The result is that rural communities face a lack of representation of their interests, often resulting in onerous regulations that handicap their ability to manage local resources. At the same time, government line agencies often perpetuate a top-down mentality that can runs counter to the community-driven approach that is known to foster scaling up of nature-based enterprises. While we concentrate in this section on the challenges of improving rural representation and the importance of reorienting the attitudes of line agencies, we realize that many other steps are necessary to improve national governance for nature-based enterprise, such as more complete decentralization of natural resource governance, less tolerance for natural resource–based patronage and corruption, and greater access to judicial redress for the rural poor whose resource rights have been violated.

Revitalizing Rural Representation in National Legislatures

Most nations have national legislative bodies based on the principle of representation, where legislators ostensibly represent the interests of citizens and are accountable to them—usually through elections. National legislatures are supposed to be the "People's House." They are designed to be the central government's main venue for articulating the popular will in national decisions—a bridge between ordinary citizens and their government. However, they can only fulfill this mission if legislators perform adequately as representatives of their constituents' concerns (Veit 2007:10).

Unfortunately, legislators face a number of disincentives to actually serve the interests of their rural constituents. As a result, they often do not use their lawmaking and oversight powers to protect rural communities from environmental exploitation or to argue their rural constituents' case for greater resource rights (Veit 2007:14). In a recent study of nine African legislatures, the dysfunctions typical of such legislative representation were clear. Across all the countries studied, there were strong incentives to support executive branch and party interests and few to represent local matters. Researchers concluded that "legislators are not downwardly accountable to their electors, do not have sufficient autonomy from political bosses and institutions, and lack the authority and capacity to effectively address their constituents' concerns." The result: many local views are routinely misrepresented in the legislature, and thus rural concerns—particularly concerns related to the environment—are not well represented (Veit 2007:37–38).

Correcting the legislative incentive structure and providing more direct and accountable representation is paramount if legislators are to become forceful advocates for small rural

enterprises based on nature. This will require adjustments of the legislative process itself.

In many legislatures the bond between citizens and their legislators is weak. In part, this is due to the lack of transparency in legislative processes and the difficulty of getting basic information about what legislators are doing and how they are voting. In most African nations, for example, votes by legislators are not recorded and parliamentary sessions are not broadcast on radio or television. Committee meetings are often closed to the public, and special parliamentary reports or investigations are not routinely released to the public or translated into local dialects. This lack of information makes it difficult to hold legislators accountable for their actions (Veit 2007:20). Often the only way local constituents can judge the performance of their representative is by the "constituent services" they deliver—the direct help that legislators sometimes give to constituents to address a particular problem (Veit 2007:20–21).

While legislators may have weak accountability to their rural constituents, they are often quite beholden to more powerful political figures, such as party officials, cabinet ministers, the president, or other members of the executive branch. In fact, the executive branch routinely wields control over legislators through a combination of special favors and intimidation. On the one hand, the executive can offer opportunities for career advancement, such as a cabinet seat, an ambassadorial post, a position in local government, or an appointment to a key parliamentary committee. Many African nations maintain large numbers of presidential appointments for just such patronage purposes. Uganda, for example, has 21 cabinet ministers and 45 ministers of state. On the other hand, failure to support the executive can bring various kinds of harassment and withholding of access and money for constituent services (Veit 2007:24–25).

Political parties are a second pole of influence that demands legislators' attention. Party leaders often play a major role in deciding who will run for office, what committee positions legislators will occupy, and what resources they will have access to. Party officials routinely pressure their members to maintain party discipline and follow the party line. This discourages legislators from taking individual actions such as strongly defending local interests or opposing their party's stand on natural resource issues, including resource concessions, royalties, and subsidies (Veit 2007:25–28).

Even in this environment of weak downward accountability and strong incentives to serve party and executive interests, some legislators do become effective advocates for their rural constituents. But they often pay a political price. In 1997, a Cameroon legislator argued against a forest management agreement that the government had signed with a local forestry company near the Mengame Gorilla Reserve. The legislator objected on the grounds that the volume of timber the company was cutting was greater than it was reporting, while the benefits to his constituents—who lived in that area—were less than their due. Under pressure from the legislator, the agreement was revoked and an advisory board—with some members representing his constituents—was set up to help guide management of the reserve and development in the surrounding communities. For his work against the administration, the legislator was later sanctioned by his party and dropped from its list of candidates in the next election (Veit 2007:29–30).

As this example shows, the current lack of effective and responsive rural representation is not inevitable, but it is deeply entrenched. Addressing the breakdown of legislative representation will require significant reforms of the way power is configured within the legislative and executive branches of government. For example, the accountability of legislators can be raised first by simply increasing transparency and information flow about legislative processes. Adopting Freedom of Information legislation is often vital in this regard. In addition, providing citizens with the authority to recall their legislator in the event of misconduct and shortening the terms of legislators so that they must stand for election with greater frequency will also tend to increase their responsiveness to the electorate (Veit 2007:41–42).

Legislators' autonomy can be increased by limiting the influence of political parties; permitting independent candidates to run for office and allowing lawmakers to switch parties midterm would be a step in this direction. Curbing the executive's influence could be pursued by restricting the number of appointments he or she can make and requiring that all appointees be confirmed by the legislature. Restricting the executive's influence over the selection of legislative leaders such as the parliamentary Speaker or committee chairs would also help. Empowering the legislature to impose sanctions on government officials for poor performance would increase the vital oversight function that legislatures must perform in a healthy democracy (Veit 2007:40–41).

Such political reforms are never simple, but they are certainly not without precedent. Governments in Africa and elsewhere have already initiated wide-ranging political reforms in the last two decades that, if followed through, can empower legislatures, further decentralize power, and make it easier to stand up for rural constituents. In contrast, failure to strengthen rural representation will perpetuate the competitive and political disadvantage that rural enterprises now face with respect to their urban counterparts.

Reorienting Line Agencies toward Participation and Service

In spite of the move to decentralize natural resource rights, government line agencies often persist in their top-down approach to interacting with communities. For at least a decade, proponents of community-driven development and community-based resource management have suggested that government bureaucracies responsible for managing natural resources must reorient their approach. A greater emphasis on delivering support services and a greater embrace of community participation in resource management decisions is necessary if community-driven enterprises are to be developed (Esmail 1997:55–58; Pozzoni and Kumar 2005:22–23; Kolavalli and Kerr 2002:227–233).

Unfortunately, this goes against the culture and training of most natural resource line agencies, which are populated with professional resource managers trained with a mandate to manage the resource for production, not for community development purposes. Line agencies' culture of control derives from their traditional dominance of the planning process as well as the regulatory system of permits, quotas, and licenses that is central to production and marketing of natural resources. Participation and consultation threatens this control and is often seen as outside the agency's core competence, overly complex, and ultimately inefficient. It is not surprising then that, as one researcher noted, "though top-down planning has lost much of its luster in the past decade, it remains a powerful organizational reflex" (Howard et al. 2001:7; Kolavalli and Kerr 2002:228).

Increasing the responsiveness—or downward accountability—of line agencies to rural communities will require a number of interlocking strategies. First is a redefinition of the mission of these agencies, with the focus shifting from control to facilitation and from product to process. Rather than conceiving and measuring success in terms of production targets, the agency must now be seen as encouraging a fruitful decision-making process, balancing community and industry use of ecosystem resources, and delivering capacity-building services that eventually enable community-led production through local enterprises. An important part of this mission shift is the acceptance that the timeframe for a given project or intervention will be lengthened to allow more time for capacity development and strengthening of the local organizations that will become the frontline resource managers (Pozzoni and Kumar 2005:22).

Greater attention to community concerns and capacity development will not happen in a day. It can be hastened by developing a new slate of performance indicators that reflect this change in mission and by tying promotion and compensation to these indicators. NGOs may be able to provide a useful service by acting as community watchdogs, grading agencies on their services and processes (Kolavalli and Kerr 2002:228, 231). There is also a part to be played by the media and other influential parties, such as members of parliament or other government departments. Such actors can often exert indirect pressure to change ineffective attitudes and reward new approaches (Vania and Taneja 2004:117).

Capacity-building within the agencies themselves is obviously a crucial step in making this cultural transition. Few agencies have staff equipped with the professional skills most useful in encouraging participatory processes, and few line staff think of themselves primarily as service providers. Of course, requirements for community participation are not entirely new, and training programs on participatory methods have become more common in recent years. But these have not yet prompted fundamental changes in staff competence or attitudes. Bringing about that kind of shift will require a new incentive structure that rewards staff for attitudes that foster participation, such as openness, tolerance, and adaptability (Pozzoni and Kumar 2005:22; Kolavalli and Kerr 2002:228).

Indeed, many observers suggest that line agencies, to remain effective in their new role, must make greater efforts to become "learning organizations" that give staff more autonomy to make joint decisions with communities and that encourage risk-taking, innovation, and an ability to record and disseminate lessons. Such an organization would be in a good position to help community-based enterprises tackle the management and marketing challenges they face (Bainbridge et al. 2000:12–13).

Improving Physical Infrastructure

One of the most profound obstacles to market penetration and commercial success for rural enterprises is physical isolation. Roads and communication links to the outside world are notoriously inadequate in most villages, restricting the ability of community members to send their products to market, to collect and share market information, or, in the case of tourism, to provide access to the customer base. In the mountainous province of Benguet in the Philippines, rough roads make it a jarring six-hour journey to the lucrative vegetable markets of Manila. Transportation costs and broker fees hit Benguet farmers hard, forcing them to sell their produce for five times as much in Manila as in their home villages, reducing their competitiveness without giving them any extra profit (Beattie 2007:1). Their plight is an example of how important the improvements in rural infrastructure are to bettering the prospects for nature-based enterprises.

Governments have long known that economic growth requires infrastructure investment, and studies in developing countries have particularly identified the economic benefits of roads and telecommunication networks to rural communities (ADB et al. 2005:79–82). Better roads and telecommunications open new markets and attract new business investment, in addition to helping rural people serve their traditional markets better. Inexpensive mobile phone service, for example, has expanded the ability of poor fishers off the southern Indian coast to market their fish, letting them contact wholesalers in a variety of local ports to alert them to the quantity and timing of their catch and allowing the fishers to bargain for a fair price (Sullivan 2006:1). Improved road and communication infrastructure also gives rural people more access to government and financial services and a greater ability to participate in the political process and advocate for their interests (Jahan and McCleery 2005:11, 17).

Infrastructure investments are especially important to the poor (World Bank 2005:74–75). Studies in India, for example, show that investments in roads are nearly twice as effective as other forms of government expenditures in reducing rural poverty (Fan et al. 1999:39–41). In Vietnam, poor households living in communes with paved roads have a 67-percent greater chance of escaping poverty than those without paved roads (Ali and Pernia 2003:6). The poor often define their poverty in terms of access to infrastructure such as roads, schools, and health centers (Fan et al. 2004:26).

In spite of its recognized benefits, infrastructure investment remains difficult and controversial, particularly as it has traditionally been practiced. Large road, dam, energy, irrigation, or telecommunications projects are often expensive, prone to corruption, and subject to poor maintenance, increasing the ratio of costs to benefits. In addition, many infrastructure projects carry high environmental and social costs. While roads increase market access, for example, they also may encourage encroachment and increase competition for natural resources, make enforcing resource management rules more difficult, or raise local land prices, thus increasing land insecurity for the poor. In addition, many rural roads are built not by the government to serve rural communities but by extractive industries for the purpose of tapping rural resources—often the same resources local enterprises would otherwise use. All these factors can work against the success of local nature-based businesses.

The New Paradigm: Community-Driven Infrastructure

To meet the challenges of upgrading rural infrastructure, a new paradigm has emerged that accepts the need to approach such infrastructure with social and environmental sustainability in mind. This requires being more sensitive to local demand and more community-focused, drawing on a process of consultation with affected communities. As much as possible, it also enlists communities in building and maintaining new infrastructure and demands of them a financial commitment—typically 10 or 15 percent of the total cost. This kind of community-driven infrastructure often involves smaller-scale projects that can be planned and undertaken at a local level and then integrated into larger infrastructure networks (Jahan and McCleery 2005:23–45; Torero and Chowdhury 2005:5; Adato et al. 2005:67–69).

Small-scale, community-based infrastructure projects have shown that they can confer a variety of local benefits and can better target these to the poor. In Bangladesh, a project to build portable steel bridges across local rivers has greatly increased mobility in the communities that chose to participate. In the Savar area, travel times to the nearest market, school, and hospital were cut by 75 percent, and travel costs fell by two thirds. Farmers are able to move their perishable products such as milk more quickly and thus realize greater income and less spoilage. Women in particular have benefited from the small, strategically located bridges and can more easily seek wage employment now; girls' school enrollment rates have also climbed with the increased safety of river crossing (Jahan and McCleery 2005:35–36).

PORTABLE BRIDGES SAVE TIME AND REDUCE COST OF MOBILITY IN SAVAR AREA, BANGLADESH

	TIME (minutes)		COST (taka)	
	Before	After	Before	After
Nearest school	60	15	15	5
Nearest hospital	75	22	20	7
Nearest market	60	15	15	5

Source: Jahan and McCleery 2005:35–36

One of the strengths of a community-based approach to infrastructure is that it often directs resources to problems that large-scale infrastructure programs ignore. For example, while many national road projects are focused on building or upgrading primary roads that connect villages and cities, recent research makes it clear that improvements in road infrastructure should not stop there. Feeder roads as well as a variety of informal village paths and tracks are also crucial for the day-to-day transport that supports rural businesses and gives the poor access to natural resources (Hettige 2007:2–3). In Uganda, state investments in rural feeder roads are three times more effective in reducing poverty than expenditures on paved roads, because they directly contribute to greater agricultural productivity (Fan et al. 2004:47). Maximizing the effect of road-building programs on ecosystem-related businesses thus requires reorienting them to include these crucial secondary routes—routes that would be appropriate targets for community-based efforts.

Community-driven infrastructure projects also confer the same kind of empowerment and engagement benefits that other community-based efforts do. Participation of community members in planning and execution of infrastructure projects builds a sense of collective ownership of the roads, water works, or other infrastructure that is built. Cost-sharing and responsibility for long-term maintenance of the facilities reinforce this feeling and make it more likely the infrastructure will continue to deliver benefits in the future. Working together on infrastructure projects builds community solidarity and social capital in the same way that joint resource management does (Jahan and McCleery 2005:36–38; Adato et al. 2005:xi). In fact, the two may reinforce each other, with small-scale infrastructure programs acting as a catalyst for a variety of local enterprises, and these enterprises in turn providing a rationale for continued infrastructure maintenance. Conceived in this way, it is not hard to imagine that infrastructure investments, when appropriately planned and executed in a way that meaningfully involves the user communities, can play a critical role in scaling up nature-based enterprises.

While the community-based approach to infrastructure development has clear advantages, it still depends on strong support from national government to succeed. Infrastructure networks clearly require high-level planning and coordination—traditionally a government responsibility—if they are to provide transportation, communication, power, or water in an integrated and equitable manner. And even if local communi-

ties contribute a portion of the budget through cost-sharing, the bulk of infrastructure financing will appropriately come from state coffers. In addition, government expertise is needed to help communities evaluate the safety of existing infrastructure such as bridges and roads in the face of the increasing risk of natural disasters associated with climate change. Government oversight and facilitation will thus continue to be required even if local communities are given considerable budget authority over local projects. Governments must therefore carefully balance their coordination, oversight, and funding roles without unduly interfering in the conduct of decentralized, small-scale, locally driven projects if they are to discharge their mandate to provide the "built capital" that rural development requires.

Providing Adequate Finance

Like all businesses, small rural enterprises need financing to bankroll their start-up costs and expand their operations as they mature. Yet access to such financing has traditionally been extremely limited. Community-based businesses—particularly when undertaken by the poor—are characterized by high vulnerability and lack of collateral, a financial profile that has left commercial banks reluctant to extend conventional loans to this sector. Loan sharks were often the only available source of funds.

Today the microcredit industry has begun to address this financing void. Over the last three decades, small loans—typically between US$20 and US$500—have become increasingly available to a range of rural and urban enterprises. Inspired by the success of Grameen Bank and other similar initiatives, a host of NGOs, credit unions, community-based organizations, and government funds have entered the microcredit market. The Microcredit Summit Campaign, a nonprofit dedicated to tracking these services for the poorest populations, reported that at the end of 2006 there were 3,316 microcredit institutions worldwide, serving more than 133 million credit recipients (Daley-Harris 2007:2). This growth—and much more—is necessary to finance any substantial scaling up of nature-based enterprises. At the same time, the microcredit field has morphed into the broader "microfinance" industry, expanding into other financial services targeted to the poor, such as "microinsurance." Even remittances—the funds sent home by family members who emigrate to urban areas or to other nations—have become a target of the microfinance industry, as service providers try to reduce the costs and increase the impact of these transferred savings.

The microfinance world is maturing in other ways as well. Urged by governments and encouraged by the success of NGO and government microcredit operations, commercial banks have increasingly entered the microcredit field, servicing over 17 percent of all microcredit customers (Gonzalez and Rosenberg 2006a:6). The private sector role is growing across all forms of microfinance. Many major banks are adding microfinance products, and commercial insurers are seriously considering how to provide life insurance, crop insurance, and even health insurance in a "micro" form to a historically underserved and often unreachable market. In the remittance sector, too, money transfer operations are competing to attract immigrants' business, forcing down the cost of sending remittances. This positive feedback loop between migration and falling remittance costs pushed remittances to developing countries alone to an estimated $239 billion in 2007 (World Bank 2008).

Against this background of change and expansion, government's role is changing too. While financing opportunities for enterprises have definitely expanded, they still fall far short of the need. In India, for example, some 70 percent of small farmers still have no access to credit (World Bank 2007a:1). Overall, some 3 billion people could benefit from microfinance services, but only about 500 million currently have access to them (World Bank 2007b:2). Governments must therefore continue to encourage the expansion of the commercial microcredit industry by providing the basic economic conditions this requires: a stable macroeconomic environment and a legal system that is safe for investment. At the same time, governments must take a more robust role in regulating the microfinance industry and encouraging competition and improved products. In addition, governments will need to remain involved as investors themselves to make sure that the poorest enterprises are served—a market that the private sector may never be able to serve well (Hashemi 2001:1).

Helping Microcredit Mature

Microcredit has proved its effectiveness and profitability since Yunus and his compatriots helped pioneer the concept in the late 1970s. In 2006, microfinance organizations reported an average loan loss rate of just .9 percent: on average, only .9 percent of

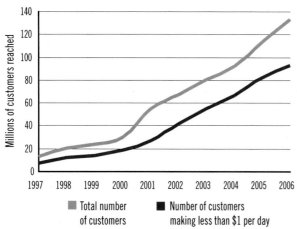

FIGURE 4.1 REACHING THE POOREST WITH MICROCREDIT WORLDWIDE, 1997 – 2006

Millions of customers reached

■ Total number of customers   ■ Number of customers making less than $1 per day

Source: Daley-Harris 2007:22-23

180

the lender's gross loan portfolio is unrecoverable (MIX 2008:44,53). Interest rates on microloans typically range between 18 and 70 percent, depending on the lending institution and the circumstances of the loan (Grameen Foundation 2007).

Attracted by the high repayment rates and interest rate potential, private sector banks have been entering the lucrative and underserved microfinance arena in increasing numbers. Large financial institutions like Citigroup, Deutsche Bank, and American International Group now provide wholesale loans to microfinance institutions around the world, and hedge funds and governments have also begun investing in microfinance (Parks 2007). Such is the interest in microfinance investment that Compartamos, a high-profile microfinance bank in Mexico, held a successful initial public offering (IPO) of stock in 2007 to become a publicly traded company. Since the IPO, Compartamos' net income has risen 38 percent over the previous year (Compartamos 2007; Parks 2007).

The financial resources and management skills that commercial banks can tap have brought new dynamism to microfinance, where 44 percent of all borrowers are now served by profitable institutions (Gonzalez and Rosenberg 2006b:3). Commercial banks also bring advantages that complement the capabilities of the NGOs and community-based groups that pioneered microcredit. For example, regulated banks are not constrained by the same rules for accepting funds and accumulating profits that NGOs typically must follow. NGOs usually have a more difficult time raising money to finance their loans, since they cannot technically accept deposits like a bank and must rely heavily on grants (FAO 2005b:34–35). Likewise, savings cooperatives cannot usually tap commercial credit markets and can only cover their loans by expanding their limited depositor base (FAO 2005b:34–36). Commercial banks thus bring greater firepower and the hope of considerably expanding the credit pool.

The entry of commercial banks into microfinance is not the only transformative change under way in the industry. The Internet has made information on microfinance widely accessible, connecting these institutions around the world to potential donors and investors. For example, the Microfinance Information Exchange Market website contains detailed information on more than 1,000 microfinance institutions and 100 funders, citing statistics on their portfolios, financial standing, and transparency (MIX 2007). Even individuals can now invest in microfinance. Via the Internet, the would-be investor can view the profiles of small entrepreneurs and invest online, receiving repayment at the end of the loan cycle (Kiva 2007). This increased information exchange has been instrumental in microfinance's recent growth, leveraging funds from both small donors and large commercial banks like CitiGroup (Daley-Harris 2006:13–14).

At the same time, new computer and mobile phone technologies are helping to make loan payments and other transactions easier and less costly. For example, mobile phones—already used by 3 billion people worldwide and increasingly penetrating rural areas—

can help rural customers make their loan payments without traveling to the city, by using the services of "rural agents" like shopkeepers. Brazil currently has the most advanced system of banking agents, with 74 different institutions managing about 90,000 "points of sale" across the country (Taylor 2007; Siedek 2007).

Continuing Role for NGOs

Despite the new technology and the entrance of commercial banks, successful finance of rural enterprises still requires many of the institutional skills that gave birth to the microfinance industry decades ago. For this reason, NGOs and self-help cooperatives retain an important role in the industry—as do governments. They are still in many cases the only providers of microfinance services in the poorest and most rural areas or to the most marginal borrowers. Just as important, their missions

generally go beyond only providing finance, and they are more likely to adhere to broad environmental or social objectives that banks may neglect in their search for profits (FAO 2005b:36).

In some ways, scaling up the microfinance industry represents a danger to this larger development mission. Microcredit NGOs have come under pressure to grow their portfolios and recover more of their costs, just like commercial banks. One response to this "mission drift" has been to try to separate "simple" (and profitable) microfinance loans from those that incorporate a wider array of development services—loans that are less likely to be suitable to commercial lenders and may need to be subsidized. For example, the Bangladesh Rural Advancement Committee (BRAC) developed two distinct loan products—one a straightforward microcredit line meant to be self-sustaining through repayments and the other a line subsi-

dized by donors and coordinated with the government to address more complex poverty issues in the poorest segments of the population (BRAC 2005a, 2005b). The second type packages health care and various kinds of skills training with the loan so that recipients gain the capacity for enterprise—and for loan repayment. A high percentage of those receiving these loans "graduate" to conventional microloans later (Matin 2004:7–9).

Major Role for Government

Other innovative programs explicitly target enterprise development among groups. Nepal's Micro-Enterprise Development Programme (MEDEP) is a government initiative that partners with the Agriculture Development Bank of Nepal to provide loans to "microentrepreneur groups" composed of low-income individuals selected primarily for their business potential. Before receiving loan funding, the group receives a staged series of business consulting services and entrepreneurship training that helps them assess their potential market, gain marketing skills, and connect to appropriate technology. In Nepal's rural Parlat district, almost 40 percent of MEDEP's loans have gone to small-scale forest enterprises like beekeeping, bamboo craft making, soap making, or the processing of various medicinals and forest plants. Among these businesses, the loan recovery rate stands at 99.7 percent. The high repayment rate is a testament to the strength of packaging loans and business services together. Although MEDEP's loan administration costs have been high due to the expense of its training and support services, the net profit appears sufficient to sustain the program, even though the loan rate is fixed at 12 percent—a very low rate for microfinance (FAO 2005b:51–58).

A major role for government in spurring the continued maturation of microfinance is to provide a stable investment environment that both attracts new financial institutions into areas where loan availability is still restricted and spurs competition among loan providers in areas where microfinance is already well established.

In addition, government plays a critical role in providing information and training for lending institutions. Lack of staff training is a serious obstacle for many smaller microfinance providers. Subsidizing staff capacity-building could help microfinance institutions cut costs, maximize their investment impact, and diversify their product portfolios. With the high volume of capital flows pushed through microcredit institutions today, it is important that this educational element is not neglected. Government, with its research, technical, and outreach capacities, is the logical entity to assume this task (CGAP 2007:11; FAO 2005b: 84–85).

Meeting Increasing Needs

As microcredit scales up and rural enterprises begin to grow, one emerging issue is how well the industry will serve mid-size businesses. Will an industry geared to loans of less than US$1,000 be able to provide larger loans as enterprises expand? Microfinance institutions tend to hesitate to underwrite such larger loans because, ironically, there is greater risk associated with larger enterprises due to their high capital costs and longer payback periods. It would seem that these mid-size businesses may face a new credit shortage as they succeed (Farrington 2002:6).

Yet competition and the natural evolution of the microfinance industry seems to be filling this void. Where the microfinance market is already saturated, institutions will look to the less-crowded mid-size market to continue their growth, as is already happening in Bolivia. Institutions like BRAC are also beginning to include business loans, ranging from US$20,000 to US$300,000, in their product lines (BRAC 2005a). The presence of successful medium-size businesses may even attract banks to rural areas in order to service this sector. An important role for government in this period of growth will be to develop and manage a credit bureau that assembles and disseminates borrower information, so that businesses with good credit histories at the microfinance level are more visible. Having such a system in place can provide one more incentive for microfinanciers to take on bigger borrowers, propelling these enterprises to the next level (Mylenko 2006:3–9).

Encouraging Microinsurance

Fostering small rural enterprises requires not just greater access to credit but also a reduction in the substantial risks that these enterprises face from accidents, natural disasters, and the ill health of the owners. Without credit, rural entrepreneurs cannot build their businesses; without insurance, however, they may not be able to survive hard times. Insurance is another way that businesses make themselves more resilient in the face of threats. Conventional businesses typically combine insurance into the package of financial services they rely on to stay in business, and small rural businesses deserve no less. In addition, having insurance increases security and therefore promotes investment and growth of the enterprise—a positive cycle that enhances the enterprise's viability and sustainability (Arena 2006:1–3).

Insurance is especially critical for nature-based enterprises that will face increased uncertainty from climate change and other factors beyond their control. Increased droughts and floods, changing geographic distribution of vector-borne diseases, and more severe weather events are just a few of the threats that owners of nature-based enterprises may face. Global economic shifts—now evident in higher food and fuel prices worldwide—are also a source of risk. If fuel prices make flying

substantially more expensive, for example, this could pose a risk to ecotourism destinations like the Namibian conservancies. Microinsurance is one way for nature-based enterprises to increase their resilience in the face of these threats.

Microinsurance is not new. NGOs and community-based organizations have provided microinsurance to some low-income customers for decades, and they currently cover about 10.5 million people, primarily with health, funeral, or life insurance. More recently, the corporate sector has joined in and now commands the largest share of the microinsurance portfolio, with some 38 million policies. Coverage is quite uneven, with policies mostly in a few countries like India, where the govern-

LARGE-SCALE VS. COMMUNITY-LEVEL USE OF NATURAL RESOURCES: ARE THEY COMPATIBLE?

In this volume, we argue the importance of natural capital for rural development. We present a model that relies on community-based development of ecosystem resources to generate income for poverty reduction. But not all natural resources are exploited at the community level. National governments tend to encourage large-scale extraction of natural resources such as minerals, oil, fish, and timber as a source of government revenue through taxes and royalties. In Guinea Bissau, for example, revenue from fishery access agreements for foreign fishing vessels provided 30 percent of all government revenue between 1993 and 1999; in Mauritania, 15 percent; in São Tomé, 13 percent (OECD 2007:55).

Large-scale commercial exploitation thus has the potential to contribute substantially to economic growth in many developing nations. Such extraction is generally organized and regulated at a state or national level—with the revenues accruing there rather than at the community level. In theory, this large-scale, "top-down" use of natural capital can be an important source of development capital—and poverty reduction—if governments use these revenues to fund education, infrastructure, social programs, or—as we suggest—the promotion of rural enterprise (OECD 2007:7-11).

But are these different approaches to the use of natural resources compatible? Both exist side-by-side today, and both are probably necessary to drive economic growth. However, large-scale extraction—through physically extensive forest, fishery, or mining concessions—has the potential to work against the interests of local nature-based enterprises by competing for ecosystem resources or degrading the ecosystems themselves, often aided by corruption. Forest or fishery development that leaves these ecosystems less viable or less available is not a recipe for rural resilience. Even when industrial-scale use of natural resources brings jobs to local people, this may not enhance their resilience if it decreases their opportunities for self-generated enterprises or fails to impart marketable skills that enrich their social and business capacities.

Two principles should guide efforts to make large-scale resource use compatible with community-level uses and a contributor to rural poverty reduction:

1. *Large-scale resource extraction should not undermine the prospects for local enterprises, but co-exist with or support them.* National policies

should not pit these two approaches against one another, but acknowledge the place of both in economic growth. The first practical effect of this acknowledgement should be a commitment to include local interests in the decision-making process when resource concessions or other large natural resource development projects are negotiated. Too often, local communities are effectively left out of the process of determining the size, location, and operating conditions for such projects, and are not compensated if they suffer losses to their traditional livelihoods or lost opportunities for nature-based enterprises. The process of inclusion and respect for local communities is embodied in the practice of "free, prior, and informed consent"—or FPIC. It consists of giving local people a formal role in decisions on large development projects that materially affect the local environment. FPIC is a mechanism, like strong tenure laws, to help communities secure their resource tenure, or to receive reasonable compensation if their tenure rights are involuntarily transferred to others. It is one means to negotiate the interface between large-scale and local extraction modes (Sohn et al. 2007:6-8).

2. *A portion of natural resource revenues should be used to fund local development priorities, particularly local infrastructure.* With foresight and planning, central governments can direct at least some of their resource-derived revenues to activities that foster rural development and reduce poverty. Done properly, this attempt at a fairer distribution of resource benefits can increase the prospects for successful local enterprises if the revenues are used as development capital for local roads, schools, and other basic infrastructure, or to fund microfinance or rural enterprise programs. In some countries, government policies already contain a distributional formula for resource revenues. In Nigeria, for example, 13 percent of oil revenues are returned to the jurisdictions in which the oil was extracted (Veit 2008). Unfortunately, experience shows that the existence of a "fair" distribution formula is no guarantee that revenues will be used wisely or to benefit the poor. Much depends on the capacity of both local and central governments to disperse funds for community-driven infrastructure, education, or other support programs. Developing this capacity for "distributional equity" is a prerequisite for making large-scale resource exploitation both pro-poor and supportive of local enterprise and initiative.

ment requires large insurers to sell a portion of their policies to poor people (Roth et al. 2007:31).

The percentage of poor people around the world with any kind of insurance remains very low—an estimated 0.3 percent in Africa, 2.7 percent in Asia, and 7.8 percent in the Americas (Roth et al. 2007:17, 18). But commercial interest in microinsurance is growing. For instance, AIG Uganda and Delta Life in Bangladesh now both carry insurance products targeted at the poor (Churchill 2006:13). As with microcredit, insurance companies have realized that serving the poor—or at least the moderately poor—can be profitable (Roth et al. 2007:21).

But designing quality microinsurance suited for the rural poor is not easy. Insurers face high costs as they distribute their products in areas where populations are spread out and commercial insurance is unfamiliar. Verifying claims for these distant clients creates high transaction costs. Companies must also deal with higher costs when insuring the rural poor because there is typically low risk diversity among rural clients, meaning that many rural businesses in a given area may face losses from the same risk, such as a cyclone.

One way to cut costs is to make insurance plans for the poor simpler and more flexible. This is necessary for working successfully with small enterprises that must pay their deductibles across a longer time frame because of the episodic nature of small enterprise income (Churchill 2006:22). Group insurance plans are another effective means of cutting down on transaction costs. And all rural insurance plans are most effective when a large insurer partners with a small, community-level channel to distribute the product and verify claims (Loewe 2006:44). These local "agents" might be churches, post offices, employers, or local retailers (Roth et al. 2007:i). The most important qualities of the "on-the-ground" partner are having both the trust of the community members and the competence to educate and provide appropriate insurance packages to the local clientele.

The ideal role for governments with regard to microinsurance may be similar to their role in providing microcredit. They must foster an environment hospitable to investment and competition between insurers in order to ensure that premiums are driven down. Government must simultaneously reach out to the poorest through targeted grants tied to training and partnerships with NGOs.

Governments also play a critical role as providers of information about the industry to potential clients. This is especially important in developing countries where there is no insurance culture and where a mistrust of insurance exists (Trommersauser et al. 2006:513). And while insurance is an important way to promote investment and provide security for small enterprises, the government's primary focus within rural finance should remain on securing more basic finance options like savings and credit first— and then building insurance into these finance channels.

Leveraging Remittances for Rural Investment

Remittances constitute the third growing form of finance for the rural poor and a potential source of investment capital for rural enterprises. As noted earlier, the World Bank estimates that in

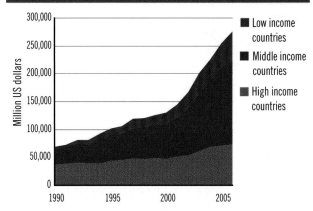

FIGURE 2 GROWTH IN GLOBAL REMITTANCE RECEIPTS, 1990–2006

Source: World Bank 2007e

2007 internal and cross-border migrants from the developing world sent US$239 billion back to their home countries (World Bank 2008). This is more than double the official development assistance (US$103.7 billion) provided to developing countries in 2007 (World Bank 2007c). The International Fund for Agricultural Development estimates that 80–90 percent of such remittances is spent meeting basic needs such as food, shelter, health care, and other necessities. The remaining 10–20 percent is saved or invested—potentially to finance a new business (IFAD 2007:7).

It is hard to assess the impact of remittances on poverty reduction or economic growth, but evidence suggests that even when these monies are not directly invested they have a strong multiplier effect on the local economy (OECD 2006:155). In Mexico, one study suggested that for every remittance dollar spent in the country, the Mexican gross national product increased by about three dollars (Ratha 2003:8). Statistics also indicate that remittances allow more children—especially girls— to go to school and are often designated for this purpose by the sender (World Bank 2006a:126, 2007d).

Governments are beginning to recognize the significant development opportunity that these funds represent. Some are partnering with so-called hometown associations—groups of migrants from a particular region who provide funds and support for their communities from abroad. Local or national governments might provide information to these associations about their communities' needs, establish grant funds to match remittances sent home by the associations, or provide contractors for projects like constructing hospitals or schools. El Salvadorian hometown associations, for example, compete with each other for matching funds from the central government to complete development projects. As of 2004, US$2 million from hometown associations had leveraged almost US$7 million from the government to complete 45 development projects, including infrastructure works and recreational and health facilities (Orozco 2007:234–235).

Yet while individual and collective remittance funds clearly have a significant positive development impact for poor

FIGURE 3 COST OF REMITTANCES TO MEXICO FROM SELECT U.S. CITIES, 1999–2007

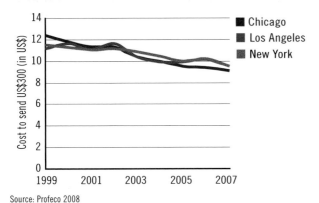

- Chicago
- Los Angeles
- New York

Source: Profeco 2008

communities, the cost of sending remittances is high, and the lack of other financial services such as savings accounts in rural communities makes long-term investment of the funds less likely. Fortunately, competition is lowering these costs, especially in the most heavily used channels, such as between the United States and Mexico (World Bank 2006b:137). The cost of sending US$300 from the United States to Mexico fell nearly 60 percent between 1999 and 2005 (from US$26 to US$11), largely due to the entrance of banks into the remittance transfer business during this time (World Bank 2006a:137–140).

As with microcredit and microinsurance, government has an important part to play in expanding the development benefit from remittances and increasing their ability to finance rural enterprises. Promoting competition within the remittance sector is a definite priority so that transfer costs continue to come down. But governments must also be more active in encouraging group remittances for development purposes by establishing incentives like El Salvador's matching grant programs. With guidance and incentives, remittances could become a more well directed and potent source of local investment finance.

Beyond Microfinance

While access to credit through traditional banking or microfinance channels is a clear necessity for the growth of rural enterprises, it is not the only finance source needed for scaling up. As the case studies in this report attest, project funds from government or multilateral donors remain an important part of the total funding mix for nature-based enterprises.

Particularly during the demonstration phase of new resource management strategies and the growth of nontraditional industries like ecotourism, these external sources of enterprise funding can provide crucial seed money, acting as catalysts for communities. This makes them an invaluable tool in the initial stages of scaling up. Governments therefore have the important task of integrating such public grant funding with the larger pool of traditional loan-based finance so that they reinforce each other, creating a dynamic environment for the growth of rural enterprise.

Encouraging a variety of finance mechanisms for rural enterprise is crucial in the shift toward community-driven development. However, consistent finance for rural populations is only one part of a larger development effort that includes general education, health, and infrastructure investments.

Education provides a higher return on investments because it gives rural citizens a greater capacity to innovate. Where young people in rural areas use their educations to migrate, finances cycle back to rural areas in the form of remittances. Infrastructure promotes microfinance investment by lowering the transaction costs associated with working in rural areas (FAO 2005b:84). Basic health services and sanitation take on added importance because physical labor is at the heart, at least in the early stages, of rural enterprise. Malaria, dysentery, and HIV/AIDS all reduce the productivity and the growth potential of such enterprises.

Thus in addition to their many roles in encouraging microfinance and targeting finance options toward rural enterprises, governments must commit to meeting these other rural needs in order to succeed in their microfinance efforts—and ultimately in their goal of growing the rural economy and reducing poverty.

SUMMING UP: DRIVING THE SCALING PROCESS

SEVEN INSIGHTS FROM THE CASES

- *Resource Tenure Need Not be Perfect to be Useful.* The prospect of gaining new or more secure resource rights is more important to the scaling up of nature-based enterprises than the form this tenure takes, although the precise form does have important implications for the enterprise's sustainability.

- *High-Profile Demonstrations and Communication Help Scale Up Demand.* Scaling up will not occur without good communication of success stories.

- *Capacity Follows Power.* Devolution of resource rights induces capacity development, offering incentive and opportunity to gain entrepreneurial skills.

- *Local Resource Management Institutions Require Time to Mature.* The development of a capable local resource management institution requires patience as the institution gains legitimacy and becomes more representative and responsive.

- *ISOs Provide Focus and Credibility.* Intermediary support organizations focus community demand and help create functional institutions with the necessary technical and social capacities.

- *Accountability Remains Important.* Accountability of the local resource management institution helps maintain the will for collective action and enterprise.

- *High-Level Government and Donor Commitment Is Necessary.* Sustained scaling up cannot occur without clear government and donor commitment over an extended period of enterprise development.

ELEMENTS OF AN ENABLING ENVIRONMENT

1. Fair and Expanded Markets for Rural Enterprise

- *Confront Elite Capture, Encourage Competition.* The more valuable the resource, the more prone it is to being used for political patronage, resulting in distortions in how resource concessions, subsidies, or access are granted. Regulatory instruments such as production quotas or permits are also frequently captured by those with influence. Many developing nations still lack basic competition laws and have yet to act aggressively to police the marketplace or confront resource-related corruption.

- *Adjust Regulatory and Tax Regimes.* Governments have a tendency toward heavy-handed regulation of community groups that manage natural resources, often manifesting as strict prescriptions for "best practices" that communities are required to follow or complex management plans that they must formulate before being granted the necessary permits to harvest or carry out management activities. In many cases these prescriptions are unnecessarily complex, do not respect local institutions or capacities, and impose a severe financial burden. An alternative would be to adopt a "minimum standards"

approach, in which the national government would establish a set of rules or standards that community members must follow in management but would grant communities flexibility in how they meet this standard. In addition, reconfiguring the tax burden away from taxes levied at the point of resource extraction could benefit nature-based enterprise formation.

- *Provide Technical, Research, and Market Assistance.* Governments have a legitimate role to play in helping to set product quality standards and undertaking product research, as well as introducing new technologies, improved seed and plant varieties, and more effective resource management methods that rural producers would have trouble developing on their own.

2. Improved National Governance Related to Rural Enterprise

- *Revitalize Rural Representation in National Legislatures.* Rural communities face a lack of representation of their interests, resulting in onerous regulations that handicap their ability to manage local resources. Rural legislators frequently lack autonomy from political bosses and the executive branch and are not easily held to account by voters for their actions. As a result, they often do not use their lawmaking and oversight powers to protect rural communities from environmental exploitation or to argue their rural constituents' case for greater resource rights or more appropriate regulations.

- *Reorient Line Agencies toward Participation and Service.* Line agencies are typically dominated by professional managers oriented toward resource production rather than community consultation or the development of small enterprises. Changing this situation will require redefining their mission to stress facilitation of community enterprise through capacity development and participatory decision-making.

3. Improved Physical Infrastructure

- *Adopt a More Community-Driven Approach to Infrastructure.* Inadequate roads, communication lines, and energy infrastructure are persistent and profound obstacles to rural enterprise. To meet the challenges of upgrading rural infrastructure, a new paradigm has emerged that accepts the need to approach such infrastructure with social and environmental sustainability in mind. This requires being more sensitive to local demand and more community-focused, drawing on a process of consultation with and participation of affected communities. Small-scale, community-based infrastructure projects have shown they can confer a variety of benefits particularly targeted to rural enterprises and the poor.

4. Adequate Financing

- *Help Microcredit Mature.* The microcredit industry has achieved impressive growth in the last two decades, attracting the interest of the commercial banking industry. Nonetheless, the availability of finance is still a main obstacle in rural enterprise development. A major role for government in spurring the continued maturation of microfinance is to provide a stable investment environment that

SUMMING UP: DRIVING THE SCALING PROCESS (CONTINUED)

both attracts new financial institutions into areas where loan availability is still restricted and spurs competition among loan providers in areas where microfinance is already well established. In addition, government has a critical role in providing information and training for lending institutions.

- *Encourage Microinsurance.* Conventional businesses typically combine insurance into the package of financial services they rely on to stay in business, and small rural enterprises deserve no less. However, the range of microinsurance products available today is still quite limited. Simpler and more flexible plans are required to serve a low-income

rural clientele, coupled with a community-level distribution channel through local institutions like post offices or local retailers.

- *Leverage Remittances for Rural Investment.* Remittances are potentially a significant source of investment capital for rural enterprises. Some emigrants have established informal development funds in which they pool remittances and send them to their home towns to fund development projects. In turn, some governments have established matching grants to encourage this kind of community investment. Bringing down the high cost of sending remittances will be key in making them a more potent source of investment funds.

When ownership, capacity and connection are present,
communities enhance their ability to manage ecosystems collectively
and extract a sustained stream of benefits.

RECOMMENDATIONS:
ADVANCING ENTERPRISE AND RESILIENCE

THIS VOLUME OF THE WORLD RESOURCES REPORT PRESENTS in strategic detail an approach to addressing rural poverty initially examined in our last report, *The Wealth of the Poor.* The "poverty-environment-governance" construct introduced in that volume informs an approach that sets the stage for a community's first steps on a path to a better economic future. We argued there that poverty and the environment are inextricably linked and that the world's rural poor could enhance their livelihoods by capturing greater value from ecosystems. Income from sustainably managed ecosystems can act as a stepping stone in the economic empowerment of the poor. But that can only happen when poor households are able to reap the benefits of their good ecosystem stewardship. Better governance, beginning with improved and predictable resource tenure, is the catalyst.

World Resources 2008 explores the model further. It argues that properly designed nature-based enterprises can not only improve the livelihoods of the rural poor, they can also create resilience—economic, social, and environmental—that can cushion the impacts of climate change, keep communities rooted, and help provide needed social stability.

World Resources 2008 examines what is necessary to allow such nature-based enterprises to scale up so as to have greater impact on rural poverty. It identifies three critical elements: community ownership and self-interest, the role of support organizations in providing skills and capacity, and the importance of networks—formal and informal—as support and learning structures.

When these elements of ownership, capacity, and connection are present, communities enhance their ability to manage ecosystems collectively and extract a sustained stream of benefits, unlocking the wealth potential of nature. In so doing they build competencies that extend beyond nature-based enterprises, allowing them to expand their livelihood options beyond reliance on natural resource income alone.

This approach to rural economic growth and resilience takes on added importance as we look ahead. The World Bank predicts that profound poverty will remain largely rural almost until the end of the century (Ravallion et al. 2007:39). The nature of that poverty, and how the world responds, will be shaped by the larger trends at work right now.

Climate change will, by all accounts, have the greatest impact on the rural poor. Other forces also come into play. An anticipated 50 percent increase in world population by the end of this century will add to the stress on natural resources. Increased consumption by a growing global middle class will continue the erosion of ecosystems, starkly documented by the Millennium Ecosystem Assessment in 2005 (MA 2005).

The emergence of new economic and political power centers with often divergent and competing interests and values will likely make international agreement to solve problems more difficult.

Yet it is precisely the interplay between the persistence of rural poverty and the inexorable trends shaping the twenty-first century that makes addressing this problem so urgent and important.

This chapter outlines specific actions that governments at all levels can take to encourage the creation of nature-based enterprises that build rural resilience as they reduce poverty. It also looks at the important roles that can be played in this process by donors, NGOs, and other institutions working on development issues, particularly with respect to encouraging the development of intermediary support organizations.

In pursuing these actions, a primary goal is to fashion an extensive web of support that can help rural enterprises gain the capacities they require to thrive. One of the most persistent barriers they face is a lack of support services that can enable inexperienced communities to grow their business skills and their institutional capabilities at the same time. Associations and intermediary support organizations (ISOs) are elements of the web of support that rural enterprises require, but governments, donors, international NGOs, and other international organizations must also participate in delivering the capacity that nature-based businesses need over the long term. Such support services are key to turning budding rural enterprises into engines for rural employment and wealth creation—the kind of economic growth that will directly benefit poor families.

Cultivating Ownership and Increasing Demand

1. Complete the Job of Decentralization.

Conferring resource rights on rural communities and individuals means devolving authority over these resources to the local level. An important part of this process is decentralization of natural resource governance to local governments. While devolution of resource rights directly from central government to local user groups can take place without empowering local government, this is not a recipe for long-term success. Local government needs to be part of the mix.

In concept, decentralization was accepted long ago by most governments as an appropriate step to encourage rural development and increase equity. Reforms over the last quarter-century have accomplished the first steps in the decentralization process, delivering new mandates and some new authorities to local governments. But in too many cases decentralization reforms have not been carried through to their logical or necessary conclusion. Political decentralization has not always been matched by fiscal and administrative decentralization that empowers local governments to raise and allocate funds or to regulate local resource management. Central governments still play an outsize role in determining how local ecosystem resources are managed and who will reap the benefits. As a result, local governments continue to suffer from insufficient capacity and authority to catalyze and support nature-based enterprises.

Central governments can help complete the decentralization process by defining more clearly local governments' roles as decision-makers and arbiters of local resource use. This may mean ceding greater budgetary authority and regulatory control—such as permitting authority for resource use—to local authorities, while establishing clear criteria for transparency in spending and permitting to make sure local governments remain accountable to communities.

2. Pursue Tenure Reform That is Flexible and Inclusive.

Many nations have begun to tackle the considerable task of increasing the tenure security of rural residents. On the basis of this experience, several lessons have emerged that should inform government actions.

- **Consider alternatives to formal titles.** Land and resource registration is important, but traditional centralized titling programs have proved costly and contentious. Governments should explore broader approaches that use local institutions to execute simpler and lower-cost forms of registration that provide an intermediate level of formalization in a timely manner.

- **Recognize customary tenure.** National tenure laws need to explicitly recognize—and provide a means to register—local customary land rights, including communal tenure.

- **Provide for long-term land leasing and tenancy.** Governments should not neglect the importance of lease and tenant arrangements to the poor and should encourage long-term leases that can provide adequate tenure security.

- **Clarify co-management responsibilities and rights.** National laws need to explicitly recognize the specific domain of co-management, where the state shares resource tenure with local communities or resource user groups. Co-management arrangements need to specify clearly how resource rights and responsibilities are divided and for what duration in order to provide adequate security for local investment in good management. In addition, the rights devolved must be substantial, with a better balance between local and state authorities than is contained in most current arrangements.

- **Provide a functional dispute resolution mechanism.** Such a mechanism must link the existing customary and statutory mechanisms in a common framework so that conflicting land claims can be settled

3. Support Pilot Projects and Help Communicate Successes.

Governments, NGOs, and donors can all play a positive role in building demand for ecosystem-based enterprises.

- **Fund pilot projects and facilitate exchange visits.** These are among the most effective and cost-efficient means of demonstrating firsthand to community members the benefits of community resource management.

- **Help communities communicate their successes.** This can be done by providing assistance with message development, websites, and the publication of articles, photographs, and other communication tools and with dissemination of these products through state and donor networks.

Continues on page 195

BOX 5.1 CLIMATE CHANGE AND THE POOR: RESILIENCE AND ADAPTATION

OF THE 2.6 BILLION PEOPLE WHO LIVE ON LESS than $2 per day, almost 2 billion live in rural areas, in countries whose economies and people are most dependent on natural resources (World Bank 2007a:63; Ravallion et al. 2007:39). Efforts to meet the Millennium Development Goal of cutting poverty in half in such areas are being stymied by the already-evident impacts of climate change, which has been called "today's crisis, not tomorrow's risk" for developing countries (Alexander 2008).

While climate change impacts will be uneven around the globe, the human impact will be greatest where the poor live—countries at the lower latitudes. Whether the effects relate to food production, human health, desertification, or flooding, location does matter as far as climate change is concerned (World Bank 2007b).

Some examples of the expected effects of climate change:

■ Water will be the defining element of climate change impacts: too much water in the form of more severe storms and resultant flooding, as experienced in 2007 in Bangladesh, or too little, as with desertification—"potentially the most threatening ecosystem change impacting the livelihoods of the poor" (MA 2005:4). According to the Millennium Ecosystem Assessment, desertification is projected to get worse in Africa and Central Asia, and climate change is a key cause (MA 2005:1). More than 300 million Africans, out of a population of some 930 million, live in drought or drought-prone areas (IPCC 2007:437).

■ The Himalayan glaciers are receding at an unprecedented pace. More than 500 million people in southern Asia depend on this previously predictable glacial melt for water, primarily for agriculture. Now that source is at risk (IPCC 2007:493).

■ Agriculture depends on water. In southern Asia, where population growth is expected to add at least 1 billion people by 2050, various climate scenarios project decreases in rice and cereal production of up to 10 percent (UNFPA 2007:91; IPCC 2007:480–481).

■ A 1-meter rise in sea level—the minimum forecast for this century—has the potential to displace nearly 6 million people across South Asia, with Bangladesh's coastal population most threatened. In East Asia, the outlook is even bleaker: a 1-meter rise would displace more than 37 million people, mostly in Vietnam's Mekong and Red River Delta basins (Dasgupta et al. 2007: 2, 28–35).

A recent report on adaptation policy options argued that vulnerability to climate change was a function of two factors: the degree to which an area is exposed—itself a function of climate conditions and the extent and character of the vulnerable area—and the area's capability to respond or adapt (Burton et al. 2006:3)

The countries that are home to the majority of the world's poor *(see Box 1.3: The Rural Poverty Imperative)* are also, by and large, countries with the least developed economies and with a lack of financial and technical resources to support efforts to mitigate climate change effects. They are the least resilient, the most vulnerable.

The poor have limited choices: they can stay where they are and manage the future that faces them with whatever means and mechanism they might have. Or they can move. Though migration may be a necessary recourse for people confronted with conflict or persecution, it must be viewed as the option of last resort.

The World Bank's recent assessment of poverty states that for at least the next 80 years the majority of the poor living on less than $2 per day will live in rural areas (Ravallion et al. 2007:26). That reality defines how the development community must manage the twin and inextricable challenges of abject poverty and climate change.

For the almost 2 billion people already living marginal existences in rural areas, large-scale interventions are not practical or likely. They must be better able to confront the new environmental conditions brought on by climate change so as to maintain and perhaps improve their own circumstances.

Adaptation to the natural variability in climate has been part of rural life for centuries. Anti-poverty strategies that build on the natural resource base and engage the self-interest of the poor have shown the potential to provide a number of important benefits. As the case studies in this book detail, communities that have developed nature-based enterprises have not only improved their livelihoods, they have, over time, become more capable, more adaptable, and more resilient as a result.

That resilience has many dimensions. There is economic resilience, as communities realize income from sustainable management of natural resources, including smallholder agriculture. There is social resilience born of community engagement in the development and operation of such enterprises. And there is environmental or ecosystem resilience from the improved stewardship of natural resources when they come under community control.

The case studies in this book describe programs that were not begun in response to the threat of climate change, yet they had the effect of providing communities with the skills and the tools to help them adapt to that threat. For example, the work of the Watershed Organisation Trust in India has already generated a

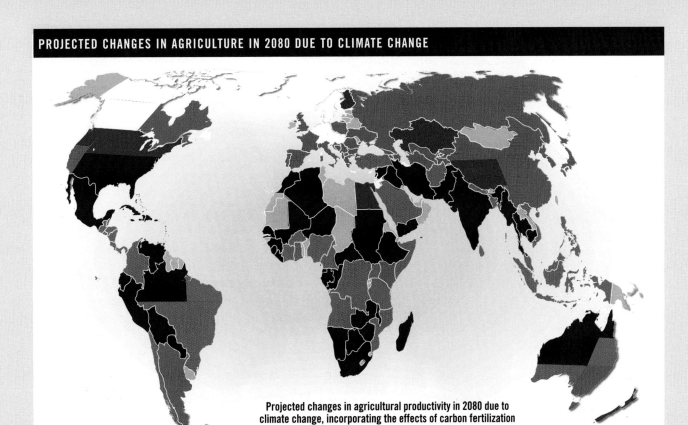

PROJECTED CHANGES IN AGRICULTURE IN 2080 DUE TO CLIMATE CHANGE

Projected changes in agricultural productivity in 2080 due to
climate change, incorporating the effects of carbon fertilization

-50%   -15%   0   +15%   +35%   No data

Source: Cline 2007

range of important benefits—social and economic—for almost 500 watershed communities. Water tables have risen, more land can be irrigated, more livestock can be raised, and there is more paid work for those who do not own land. Other benefits include increased crop variety, including new cash crops; increased income; and increased social cohesion as heads of families leave less frequently to find work elsewhere during what used to be long dry periods. *(See Box 2.4: Watershed Organisation Trust, India.)*

At the same time that the livelihoods of village residents have improved, restoration efforts have made the environment on which they depend—the watershed—more resilient to the expected impacts of climate change.

The same holds true for the farmers in Niger. It has taken more than two decades to restore their agricultural lands to increased fertility and productivity. Now almost half the cultivated land in the country has been "re-greened," densely covered with crops, shrubs, and trees, all of which have contributed to significant increases in food production and improved economic circumstances. Soil and water conservation techniques have resulted in elevated water tables, richer soil, and the reclaiming of over

CHANGE IN AGRICULTURAL OUTPUT POTENTIAL, 2000-2080

Africa
Latin America
Middle East & North Africa
Asia
Developing countries
World
Industrial countries

-20   -15   -10   -5   0   5   10

2080s as % of 2000 potential

Source: Cline 2007

250,000 ha of barren land to productive agricultural use. *(See Chapter 3: Turning Back the Desert: How Farmers Have Transformed Niger's Landscapes and Livelihoods.)*

Niger is one of a number of countries in sub-Saharan Africa whose agricultural productivity has been predicted to be

BOX 5.1 CLIMATE CHANGE AND THE POOR

adversely affected by climate change. While it is impossible to predict what will ultimately happen in Niger, we know that up to half of the country's farmers have adopted land management techniques that make them far more resilient in the future.

The model of enterprise promotion outlined in this book holds promise for addressing the persistence of rural poverty. It appears to deliver other important benefits as well. In the most recent Climate Change Assessment from the Intergovernmental Panel on Climate Change (IPCC), Working Group II identified the critical determinant of "adaptive capacity": the ability make the changes necessary in land use, economic activity, and social organization necessary to respond to climate change. It is worth noting that many of them are the same elements necessary for establishing community nature-based enterprises. The IPCC offered this list of determinants of adaptive capacity from the literature (IPCC WG II 2007:816):

- Access to economic and natural resources

- Entitlements (property rights)

- Social networks

- Institutions and governance

- Human resources

- Technology

There are no guarantees, but experience shows that the poor, rural communities that have nurtured robust nature-based enterprises have, in the process, become more resilient to challenge and more capable of dealing successfully with change in the future.

4. Facilitate Community Participation.

Participatory processes have well-known benefits but require resources and support in order to bring maximum benefits and inclusion. In providing this support, an important goal is to change the power dynamics of participation so that the interests of the poor are adequately represented—an evolution that is both challenging and bound to be gradual.

- **Provide technical support for community resource appraisals.** This can include mapping and work on geographic information systems, as well as government- or donor-led training in monitoring protocols for long-term resource tracking.

- **Encourage representation of marginalized groups on management committees.** Government mandates for formal inclusion of groups such as women or the landless on resource management or executive committees can begin the process of acceptance and true representation of these individuals.

- **Encourage the formation of self-help groups.** Informal associations can be powerful mechanisms for empowerment through capacity development and political organization, helping marginalized groups articulate their concerns within the larger group of resource users.

- **Provide impartial facilitation services for community planning processes.** NGOs are often well placed to help communities engage in productive dialogue, visioning, and planning exercises that must be based on a foundation of trust.

- **Educate agency officials to respect community participation processes.** Government officials themselves often require training in how to elicit community participation, how to incorporate input they receive from communities in government plans, and how to determine what support services the state can offer. Incentives are also required to help officials put into action what they have learned and to catalyze a change in agency culture.

- **Support community enforcement efforts.** Resource management involves rule enforcement. This is best done by the community itself whenever possible. But where the area to be managed is large or contains high-value but widely dispersed resources like wildlife or fish, enforcement may strain the capacity of the community. The state can provide a service by training local community members in enforcement techniques and providing logistical support when needed.

Developing the Capacity of Local Organizations

1. Foster the Development of Intermediary Support Organizations.

Developing the capacity of local organizations involves connecting them with financial and organizational resources, exposing them to new technical and business skills, and helping them improve their inclusiveness and accountability to local people. ISOs are often the most critical actors in this capacity-building process and therefore are key to helping local organizations scale up their ecosystem-focused enterprises.

Supporting the formation of ISOs and helping them meet the many challenges they face should thus be a top priority for governments and donors. The main challenges they face include obtaining a sustainable funding supply, balancing their different roles and relationships, culturing leadership, communicating and disseminating successes and lessons learned, maintaining a learning culture that is flexible and adaptable, and maintaining downward accountability to local citizens. In recognition of the special importance this report places on ISOs, actions that donors and governments can take to promote the growth and maturation of ISOs are broken out below, as well as some steps that ISOs themselves can take to aid in their own development.

Donors can:

- **Provide sustained funding.** This funding should allow ISOs the flexibility to deploy funds as opportunities arise, realizing that the best ISOs are innovative and opportunistic.

- **Support leadership training.** Providing funding and opportunities for off-site training can encourage leadership development. Secondments are one very effective means to accomplish this. This can also include seconding staff from a funder to the ISO.

- **Require accountability for outputs.** This should include regular reporting not just to donors but to citizens to encourage downward accountability to and feedback from local organizations.

- **Recognize achievement with awards.** Awards such as the Equator Initiative prizes can raise the profile and credibility of successful ISOs in national and international circles.

Governments can:

- **Avoid demanding control at the project level.** Governments should recognize that ISOs perform functions that governments themselves cannot readily accomplish. They should therefore endeavor, to the extent practicable, to not interfere with the work of ISOs but to sponsor and share responsibility with them through partnership arrangements that clearly define areas of authority.

- **Be responsive to the lessons that ISOs can teach.** Allow space in the bureaucracy for ISOs to play their role and maintain open channels of communication with them.

- **Facilitate communication of ISO successes and lessons.** This can be done by providing training in message development and media work, as well as by providing government communication networks through which ISO successes can be disseminated.

- **Culture leadership and capacity-building through secondments to line agencies.** As with donors, government agencies are often great sources of technical knowledge, policy analysis, and contacts that can greatly aid ISOs in their work.

- **Create a policy environment that favors the action of civil society organizations like ISOs.** This includes easing restrictions on NGO formation, registration, and funding.

- **Encourage third-party evaluations to improve accountability.** Independent evaluations of publicly funded ISO work can not only provide extremely valuable feedback to ISOs, it can also make it clear to both ISOs and their clients that accountability matters.

ISOs themselves can:

- **Diversify funding sources.** ISOs must negotiate a fine line between dependence and autonomy. They should try not to "put all their eggs in one basket." On the other hand, they should not be desperate in their search for diversified funding; they should be able to turn down money that they realize will compromise their flexibility or reputation.

- **Reserve some unallocated funds.** Keeping some resources unallocated allows ISOs to respond rapidly to developing opportunities.

- **Charge for services.** This may improve the quality of the service and may also raise the perceived value of the service to the community clients. Charges must be commensurate with what users can pay.

- **Establish and avidly pursue a secondment policy.** ISOs must be proactive in seeking learning opportunities. Governments and donors are often eager to share their areas of expertise. And secondments provide an unprecedented level of access and opportunity to change agency culture.

- **Mandate term limits for leaders.** Establish a policy of a limited term for top leadership so that the organization is forced to reckon with leadership development. This is central to remaining a "learning organization" and evolving beyond the vision and capabilities of the founder.

- **Keep a hand in local project work.** This allows the organization to keep in touch with current challenges on the ground and to keep its work as an intermediary in perspective.

- **Create opportunities for clients to evaluate the organization's performance.** Creating accountability mechanisms will help ISOs maintain their status of trusted intermediary, will provide real-time input so that they can maintain the level of the services they provide, and will make it easier to justify themselves to donors. However, it is important to acknowledge that, by their very nature, ISOs will never be accountable in the way that elected officials or government agencies are.

- **Partner with a high-profile organization.** Association with a respected international foundation or organization can be an effective means to improve an ISO's standing and promote its efforts to a wider or more influential circle.

Promoting Enterprise Networks and Associations

1. Create a Policy Environment Conducive to Networking.

Governments can help unleash the power of learning networks and commercial associations by rectifying their legal and regulatory structures.

■ **Establish a right to free association in the national constitution.** This establishes the fundamental legitimacy of all forms of voluntary associations and hinders the government's ability to discourage them.

■ **Simplify registration procedures.** Registration helps formalize rural associations such as cooperatives and business consortia and provides a contact point for government assistance. Onerous registration requirements, on the other hand, can discourage their formation.

■ **Rectify national cooperative laws.** National laws governing cooperatives should be brought in line with the standards put forward by the International Co-operative Alliance and promoted by the International Labour Organization. Doing so will help governments steer clear of attempting to interfere with the activities and governance of cooperatives and other associations.

2. Provide Financial Support for New Associations.

Fledgling associations are notoriously in need of financial support to establish themselves and begin to provide member services. Providing start-up funds can mean the difference between survival and failure. Whether such funds are provided by governments or donors, they should be granted without political interference and with the intent of developing the internal governance abilities of the association. Funds should be gradually phased out to encourage financial sustainability and independence.

3. Extend Capacity Development and Support Services.

As with other aspects of rural enterprise, lack of capacity is a leading obstacle to the growth of functional rural associations.

■ **Advertise the benefits of associations.** Conduct outreach and advertising campaigns to educate rural communities about the benefits of producer associations and to inform them of the capacity-building and support programs available to new organizations from government or NGO sources.

■ **Support training in business and organizational skills.** Associations provide an ideal venue for offering training courses, both to increase the functioning of the association itself and for the benefit of association members.

■ **Encourage the formation of learning networks.** The connectivity of association members can be increased by providing web services and other communication tools, as well as seed funds for regional conferences and other face-to-face encounters between associations.

Creating a National Enabling Environment

1. Foster Competition Through Appropriate Regulation and Transparency.

As overseer of the national economy and regulator of natural resource uses, the central government has a responsibility to make sure small rural enterprises are not held back by uncompetitive practices or regulations and tax structures that puts them at a disadvantage

■ **Enact and enforce basic competition laws.** Many nations have not yet embodied basic market principles in law or do not zealously enforce such laws they already have on the books. While law alone is insufficient to

197

create open markets, basic statutes against price fixing and the formation of monopolies and cartels are an important foundation for oversight and redress.

- **Reverse the bias toward large enterprises.** State subsidies and access policies are often targeted toward industrial-scale resource users rather than small-scale enterprises. One step toward eliminating this bias would be adjusting the procedures that govern the awarding of forest and fishery concessions so that community groups can compete for these concessions on an equal basis or be granted preferred access to a portion of available concessions. Greater transparency in the concession process in general would be a good place to start. In addition, greater attention to including small enterprises in established subsidy programs or creating subsidies targeted to small enterprise development would also help create a better balance between large- and small-scale producers.

- **Increase access to natural resources information.** Too often, rural enterprises lack basic information on the availability, ownership status, and current usage patterns of ecosystem resources. Government has a special responsibility to make available to its rural constituents data on natural resource stocks and flows, on resource tenure, and on market conditions for typical natural resource commodities and services—information that can form the basis of resource management and enterprise planning.

- **Use greater transparency when granting extraction licenses and harvest quotas.** Reducing the use of these regulatory instruments as sources of patronage is a priority. Transparency in how these instruments are obtained and who has obtained them is just a beginning. Creating official avenues for enterprises to pursue administrative redress when these instruments are abused is a second useful step.

- **Apply a "minimum standards" approach to environmental regulations.** Rather than binding communities with a detailed list of resource management requirements, states should consider establishing a set of minimum environmental standards that communities must achieve but should grant latitude in how they meet these standards. Such flexibility can keep small enterprises from becoming bogged down in bureaucratic details that create a significant regulatory burden but do little to increase environmental compliance.

- **Reduce the burden of resource and business taxes.** Taxes and user fees applied at the point of resource extraction are particularly hard on small enterprises. Shifting some of the tax burden to points higher in the value chain may reduce the tax burden on small enterprises without unduly lowering total tax receipts.

- **Increase the ability of small-scale enterprises to market their products directly.** States intervene in the markets of many of the forest and agricultural

products that form the basis of nature-based enterprises; often, rural producers cannot sell their products except through state-controlled auctions or outlets. In the right circumstances, this regulation can help regularize prices and access to commodity markets, but in many cases it squelches competition and restricts the entrepreneurial space that rural enterprises occupy. Creating opportunities for these enterprises to go outside the state-controlled system and market their wares directly can expand their market reach and provide an incentive for product improvement and innovation.

2. Provide Long-Term and Integrated Enterprise Support.

Budding rural enterprises can benefit from a variety of support services sponsored by governments, donors, and NGOs—from business development and marketing support to microfinance programs. Experience shows that these are more effective if administered as an integrated package, where financing follows intensive skills development and business planning and where consistent follow-up is provided as enterprises take their first steps.

- **Provide market analysis, business planning, and mentoring services.** A realistic view of the market and a sound business plan to reach this market are often luxuries that small producers do not have the resources or knowledge to undertake. Filling this gap can greatly enhance an enterprise's chances of success. Business mentoring programs have proved highly effective at reducing the failure rate of new enterprises.

- **Regulate, but don't over-regulate, the microfinance industry.** Microfinance has become a crucial part of the enterprise generation cycle in many rural areas. Although the microfinance industry has grown rapidly, further growth is required to fuel the expansion of nature-based enterprises. Governments have a vital regulatory role, providing oversight as the commercial banking industry enters the microfinance market, encouraging competition to drive down loan costs, and creating product standards that ensure that loan and insurance products are well designed. Governments can also assume an educational role, making training available for smaller microcredit and microinsurance providers.

- **Provide professional business services for continuing support.** Once support services are established, the need for them may persist for many years. One of the most frequent shortcomings of enterprise development programs is their lack of follow-up services, often leaving new enterprises without access to legal, accounting, marketing, technical, and financial services they require to sustain themselves and expand.

3. Reorient the Government Bureaucracy Toward Service.

If the government line agencies that deal with natural resources are to foster community-based enterprise rather than thwart it, they must jettison old attitudes and develop new skills that emphasize service delivery and shared decision-making with local institutions.

- **Redefine the mission of line agencies.** To change their culture, line agencies must begin by redefining themselves. Rather than seeing themselves as sole managers of natural resources, with an emphasis on production alone, they must shift their focus to collaborative management, with a goal of ensuring both a good decision-making process and sustainable resource use based on these decisions. This entails helping communities participate in local resource decisions and use local resources responsibly for their livelihoods.

- **Establish incentives to change agency culture.** Translating this new mission into change within line agencies will require developing performance indicators that embody the agencies' new goals and tying promotions and pay to these performance measures, thus rewarding staff for acquiring participatory skills and delivering technical and advisory services to resource-based enterprises.

- **Develop staff capacity to work collaboratively with local resource users.** Agency staff typically lack training in participatory methods, necessitating a dedicated effort to develop and reward such skills. The goal should be to transform agencies into "learning organizations" that reward innovation and collaboration and that culture cross-cutting skills that combine technical expertise with a mastery of process and social skills.

4. Revitalize Rural Representation.

To compete against larger industries and urban constituencies and to gain access to larger markets, small rural enterprises need their legislative representatives to advocate for their concerns more effectively and to make sure resource policies and regulations treat them fairly. Legislative reforms are needed to realign incentives for rural representatives and increase their downward accountability to their rural constituents.

Not all of these reforms are of the same degree of difficulty. Some, such as increasing legislative transparency through enactment of Freedom of Information legislation, may be accomplished in the short term—and have been in many nations. However, we acknowledge that other more substantive reforms, such as reigning in the power of the executive branch and of political parties, are more challenging and daunting and may require longer-term efforts and significant commitment. But without such major reorientation, rural representation will remain partial, at best, with respect to the interests of the poor and their nature-based enterprises.

- **Increase the transparency of the legislative process.** Rural constituents often face a surprising lack of information about how their representatives have voted, making it difficult to hold them accountable for their actions. Adopting Freedom of Information legislation is a necessary first step to increase information flow. Opening committee meetings that are now held in closed session and requiring that all votes taken and testimony given are officially recorded and made publicly available in local languages would be additional small but significant steps in opening the sometimes arcane world of legislative proceedings. At the very least, these steps would allow the media and NGO watchdog groups to report more accurately on legislators' actions.

- **Restrict the influence of the executive branch.** The considerable influence of the executive branch over legislators often trumps constituent concerns. Curbing this influence—at least somewhat—could be achieved by restricting the number of cabinet appointments (often used as patronage) the executive can make, requiring these appointments be confirmed by the legislature, and restricting the executive's influence over key legislative posts such as the parliamentary Speaker or committee chairpersons.

- **Limit the power of political parties over legislators.** The autonomy of legislators—and thus their willingness to take controversial positions in support of their constituents—can be increased by making sure that independent candidates are permitted to run for office and by ensuring that legislators can switch parties midterm without losing their seats.

Culturing Resilience and Resourcefulness

There is no iron-clad recipe for building the ownership, capacity, and connection that can power successful community management of natural resources, no formula for scaling up ecosystem-based enterprises. Circumstances vary considerably by country and by community, and any set of recommendations is bound to be incomplete. Nonetheless, this chapter has identified a number of fundamental principles that can guide governments, NGOs, and donors, and it offers a discrete set of actions based on these principles—actions that can help create an enabling environment for rural enterprise.

The evidence of success using this approach is scattered and uneven. But the body of evidence continues to grow and the scope of impact—geographically and by sector—widens. And success, even partial, is compelling.

Results are seen in communities with an improved quality of life that can be measured—communities with skills and experiences that can make them more resourceful and more resilient. Improved stewardship of the natural resource base not only creates environmental income, so that the community is stronger financially, it also improves the resilience of the environment itself, rendering it better able to withstand potential future impacts. Nowhere is that more apparent than in Niger and in the improved watersheds in Maharashtra state in India. And finally, the skills wielded by the community as it manages its enterprises builds a confidence—a resilience to the inevitable challenges to come. The foundation for scaling up such community enterprises, whether geographically, as seen in India and Niger, or financially, as seen in Namibia, is set when the project is nurtured at the community level.

To establish, nurture, and grow these natural resource-based enterprises takes time and patience and the right policies. That imperative often runs counter to the natural desire of donors and governments to show progress and claim success. If this approach is to go to scale, it requires a long-term commitment, one that falls on everyone's shoulders: government, funders, and the communities themselves. The conventional criteria that define support of poverty alleviation efforts must change.

Tenure rights, properly framed and put in place, are catalytic; the self-interest they create is critical. But just as important is how the benefits of that tenure—the income and other benefits that result from improved stewardship of natural resources—are allocated. Fairness and equity in the distribution scheme validate the integrity of an enterprise, and that is critical in attracting the support it requires to be sustainable and to grow.

Both donors and ISOs have important responsibilities here as community "buy-in" and active participation take place in the early stages. Donors must ensure that funding is available on an "as needed" basis, when the time is right in the community to move to the next stage. ISOs are critical because of their role both in bringing skills to the community and in determining when it can assume more responsibilities. This stage involves the building of social capital—a process that allows the community to assume responsibility for an enterprise. Skills training and capacity-building to manage an enterprise are, in turn, the processes of building the human capital that will allow the enterprise to grow as other challenges are met. Again, time is required for these skills to take hold and mature.

As the discussion in Chapter 2 details, and as the case studies in Chapter 3 illustrate, the role of government at every level is vital to this approach. At its highest level, there must be an unshakable commitment to help the very poor out of their subsistence conditions, recognizing that it is in a nation's long-term self-interest to do so. That commitment should be reinforced by clear, continuous, and public affirmations.

But that is not enough; it is just the starting point. In addition to the specifics outlined in previous chapters there must be a change in how government sees itself in the process.

We argue that, for success, communities must "own" their enterprise, in that they see its success as their own success and thus make the necessary investments of time and care, supported by informed government policy. Government thus becomes an enabler, providing the legal and other tools that allow these enterprises to take root and flourish. Government, by and large, is no longer the director or the only decision-maker. That doesn't mean government and its officials are relegated to the sidelines. It means that they assume roles of facilitation, service provision, and guidance—roles that become critically important to the ability of enterprises to scale up.

In fact, as Crispino Lobo of the Watershed Organisation Trust has found in India, government officials who accept this new role of enabler realize greater attention, credit, and respect than they did when they were issuing orders and directives. Similarly, Guatemala's National Council of Protected Areas has won the trust of forestry enterprises in the Maya Biosphere Reserve by operating as a facilitator rather than purely regulating their activities.

However, the transition from top-down management to enabling local management and enterprise is not easy. It requires attention to and reinforcement by superiors, and the change challenges the most basic public perceptions of government officials. But the payoff is well worth it. This change of role may be uncomfortable in the early stages of an enterprise, in light of the important place we argue that ISOs must play in the development of the social and business skills required of a successful community enterprise. Seeing these intermediary organizations as allies rather than interlopers is part of that shifting government role.

As outlined in this report, the array of challenges that rural enterprises must meet in order to succeed and scale up can appear overwhelming, even to the most committed of governments and sponsors. However, we hope we have shown the distinctions among the various challenges, both in terms of timing and complexity.

What is important is that the challenges are addressed in a manner appropriate to the enterprise and its move to scale up. Not all challenges can or must be met at once, and the sequencing of activities and funding is essential. For example, improved watershed management programs may ultimately require building new roads in order to market the higher agricultural production that results from greater water availability. But a new road to service urban markets may not be needed immediately, as local markets may be able to absorb the increased production for a time. On the other hand, increased provision of health care and upgraded educational opportunities could be necessary sooner to ensure the continued scaling up of the enterprise. Government as an enabling partner would be in a position to respond appropriately.

Facing the Future

Governments must begin to accept that the success of their broader development initiatives depends on increasing economic, social, and ecosystem resilience. The large-scale trends that are shaping the natural world in this century must be accommodated in development strategies.

Climate change, increased demand for raw materials and foodstuffs, and growing water scarcity are trends unlikely to change in the foreseeable future. They will inevitably have their greatest impact on the rural poor, those whose futures are inextricably tied to the ecosystems in which they live. Rural development strategies must address these challenges head on.

Nurturing and scaling up nature-based enterprises using the approach suggested in this report is an effective route to building the resilience and resourcefulness that rural communities and ecosystems must have to withstand the certain challenges of the future.

Data Tables

1 Population and Human Well-Being

2 Food and Water

3 Economics and Trade

4 Institutions and Governance

WORLD RESOURCES 2008 Data Tables

Each edition of *World Resources* includes a statistical appendix, a compilation of country-level data culled from a variety of sources. This section presents some of the data required to build a basic picture of the state of the Earth in its human, economic, and environmental dimensions. In an increasingly interdependent, globalized world, a picture of the whole is needed to understand the interactions of human development, population growth, economic growth, and the environment.

The four tables in *World Resources 2008* were compiled to reflect the volume's focus on managing ecosystems to reduce poverty. The main text of the book explores how the strategy of using the environmental assets of the poor to raise household income can be scaled up to achieve a major reduction of poverty. These data tables support the volume's analysis by quantifying the poor's assets in terms of food, water, and human capital while measuring background demographic, economic, and governance conditions.

The data tables in this edition of *World Resources* are a subset of a much larger data collection available online through the World Resources Institute's *EarthTrends* website (http://earthtrends.wri.org). *EarthTrends* is a free, online resource that highlights the environmental, social, and economic trends that shape our world. The website offers the public a comprehensive collection of vital statistics, maps, and graphics viewable by watershed, district, country, region, or worldwide.

Table 1: Population and Human Well-Being contains seven core indicators on population, health, education, and poverty. Three of these indicators—poverty rates, infant mortality, and HIV/AIDS prevalence—are measured under the Millennium Development Goals (MDGs), which were established in 2000 to track global progress toward eradicating poverty and improving human well-being. Two other indicators—life expectancy and literacy rates—are elements of the United Nations Development Programme's Human Development Index (HDI), which measures achievement of development goals related to quality of life. In addition, this table displays the Gini Index, a single number that captures the level of income inequality within a country. Recent international attention to the issue of global poverty through the MDGs and the HDI has lead to a substantial improvement in the quality of these indicators in the past decade.

Table 2: Food and Water attempts to show the drivers of global food and water consumption and the consequences for both the environment and human well-being. The intensity of use of agricultural inputs—in terms of land, labor, water, and fertilizer—can be compared across countries with a reasonable level of accuracy. Unfortunately, reliable data do not exist on the actual environmental impacts of agriculture, such as land degradation and nutrient pollution. Similarly, while fish capture can be measured, it is impossible to quantify on a country-by-country basis the extent of fisheries depletion. Water resources indicators are particularly sparse. Nonetheless, we can show the approximate availability of water resources and loosely tie these issues to human well-being with the composite Water Poverty Index.

Table 3: Economics and Trade shows the size and sectoral distribution of national economies, along with some basic financial flows: private investment, exports, foreign aid, and payments to home countries made by laborers working

abroad. In order to capture a country's investment in future growth and development, Adjusted Net Savings is included in this table. Adjusted Net Savings—also known as Genuine Savings or Green GDP—calculates the "true" rate of savings of a country's economy by taking into account human capital, depletion of natural resources, and the damages of pollution in addition to standard economic savings measures.

Table 4: Institutions and Governance measures, at the national level, the governing conditions that need to be in place for sustainable development: personal and political freedom, functioning property markets, responsible government spending, and access to information. Many of these indicators are inherently subjective and can only be captured through an index calculation. Therefore, rigid country comparisons of indices on freedom, corruption, and digital access are discouraged. Unfortunately, many of the enabling governance conditions for scaling up the environmental assets of the poor cannot be measured comprehensively on a national level. Specifically, no data exist to measure security of tenure, access to resources, or the distribution of land and other resources to individuals, communities, and the state.

General Notes

The *World Resources 2008* data tables present information for 155 countries. These countries were selected from the 191 official member states of the United Nations based on their population levels, land area, and the availability of data. Many more countries are included in the *EarthTrends* online database.

Country groupings are based on lists developed by the Food and Agriculture Organization of the United Nations (for developed and developing countries), the World Bank (for low-, medium-, and high-income countries), and the World Resources Institute (for regional classifications). A full listing is available online at http://earthtrends.wri.org/searchable_db/general_notes.

Comprehensive technical notes are available in the pages following each data table. In addition, several general notes apply to all the data tables (except where noted otherwise):

- ".." in a data column signifies that data are not available or are not relevant (for example, country status has changed, as with the former Soviet republics).

- Negative values are shown in parentheses.

- 0 appearing in a table indicates a value of either zero or less than one half the unit of measure used in the table; (0) indicates a value less than zero and greater than negative one half.

- Except where identified by a footnote, regional totals are calculated using regions designated by the World Resources Institute. Totals represent either a summation or a weighted average of available data. Weighted averages of ratios use the denominator of the ratio as the weight. Regional totals are published only if more than 85 percent of the relevant data are available for a particular region. Missing values are not imputed.

- The regional totals published here use data from all 222 countries and territories in the *World Resources / EarthTrends* database (some of these countries are omitted from the current tables). Regional summations and weighted averages calculated with only the 155 countries listed in these data tables will therefore not match the published totals.

- Except where identified with a footnote, world totals are presented as calculated by the original data source (which may include countries not listed in WRI's database); original sources are listed after each data table.

- When available data are judged too weak to allow for any meaningful comparison across countries, the data are not shown. Please review the technical notes for further consideration of data reliability.

Population and Human Well-Being

Sources: United Nations Population Division; United Nations Educational, Scientific, and Cultural Organization; United Nations Children's Fund; Joint United Nations Programme on HIV/AIDS; World Bank

	Total Population Estimates and Projections (thousands of people) {a}		Adult Literacy Rate 2000–2004 (percent)		Human Health			International Poverty and Income Equality			
					Life Expectancy at Birth (years) 2005–2010	Infant Mortality Rate (per 1,000 live births) 2005	Percent Of Adults Ages 15–49 Living With HIV or AIDS 2005	Percent of Population Living on Less Than {b}		Gini Index {c} (0 = perfect equality)	Survey Year
	2007	2030	Women	Men				$1 per day	$2 per day		
World	6,671,226	8,317,707	77	87	67	52	1	..	..	..	..
Asia (excl. Middle East)	3,727,146	4,491,264	71	86	70	..	..	..	..	..	..
Armenia	3,002	2,838	99	100	72	26	0.1	2	31	34	2003 d
Azerbaijan	8,467	9,599	98	100	68	74	0.1	4	33	37	2001 d
Bangladesh	158,665	217,932	..	..	64	54	< 0.1	41	84	33	2000 d
Bhutan	658	851	..	..	66	65	< 0.1	..	..	..	..
Cambodia	14,444	20,761	64	85	60	98	1.6	34	78	42	2004 d, e
China	1,328,630	1,458,421	87	95	73	23	0.1	10	35	47	2004 d
Georgia	4,395	3,807	..	..	71	41	0.2	7	25	40	2003 d
India	1,169,016	1,505,748	48	73	65	56	0.9	34	80	37	2004 d
Indonesia	231,627	279,666	87	94	71	28	0.1	8	52	34	2002 d
Japan	127,967	118,252	..	..	83	3	< 0.1	..	..	25	1993 f
Kazakhstan	15,422	17,142	99	100	67	63	0.1	2	16	34	2003 d
Korea, Dem People's Rep	23,790	25,434	..	..	67	42	..	..	..	..	..
Korea, Rep	48,224	48,411	..	..	79	5	< 0.1	2	2	32	1998 f
Kyrgyzstan	5,317	6,343	98	99	66	58	0.1	2	21	30	2003 d
Lao People's Dem Rep	5,859	8,142	61	77	64	62	0.1	27	74	35	2002 d
Malaysia	26,572	35,270	85	92	74	10	0.5	2	9	49	1997 f
Mongolia	2,629	3,204	98	98	67	39	< 0.1	11	45	33	2002 d
Myanmar	48,798	56,681	86	94	62	75	1.3	..	..	..	..
Nepal	28,196	41,742	35	63	64	56	0.5	24	69	47	2004 d
Pakistan	163,902	240,276	36	63	66	79	0.1	17	74	31	2002 d
Philippines	87,960	122,388	93	93	72	25	< 0.1	15	43	45	2003 d
Singapore	4,436	5,202	89	97	80	3	0.3	..	..	43	1998 f
Sri Lanka	19,299	20,249	89	92	72	12	< 0.1	6	42	40	2002 d
Tajikistan	6,736	9,434	99	100	67	59	0.1	7	43	33	2003 d
Thailand	63,884	69,218	91	95	71	18	1.4	2	25	42	2002 d
Turkmenistan	4,965	6,270	98	99	63	81	< 0.1	21	59	41	1998 d
Uzbekistan	27,372	35,199	..	..	67	57	0.2	2	2	37	2003 d
Viet Nam	87,375	110,429	87	94	74	16	0.5	..	..	34	2004 d
Europe	731,283	706,907	99	99 g	75	..	..	..	..	..	..
Albania	3,190	3,519	98	99	76	16	< 0.1	2	10	31	2004 d
Austria	8,361	8,643	..	..	80	4	0.3	..	..	29	2000 f
Belarus	9,689	8,346	99	100	69	10	0.3	2	2	30	2002 d
Belgium	10,457	10,780	..	..	79	4	0.3	..	..	33	2000 f
Bosnia and Herzegovina	3,935	3,653	94	99	75	13	< 0.1	..	..	26	2001 d
Bulgaria	7,639	6,224	98	99	73	12	< 0.1	2	6	29	2003 d
Croatia	4,555	4,168	97	99	76	6	< 0.1	2	2	29	2001 d
Czech Rep	10,186	9,728	..	..	77	3	0.1	2	2	25	1996 f
Denmark	5,442	5,602	..	..	78	4	0.2	..	..	25	1997 f
Estonia	1,335	1,224	100	100	71	6	1.3	2	8	36	2003 d
Finland	5,277	5,469	..	..	79	3	0.1	..	..	27	2000 f
France	61,647	66,605	..	..	81	4	0.4	..	..	33	1995 f
Germany	82,599	79,348	..	..	79	4	0.1	..	..	28	2000 f
Greece	11,147	11,179	94	98	80	4	0.2	..	..	34	2000 f
Hungary	10,030	9,259	..	..	73	7	0.1	2	2	27	2002 d
Iceland	301	344	..	..	82	2	0.2	..	..	..	..
Ireland	4,301	5,475	..	..	79	5	0.2	..	..	34	2000 f
Italy	58,877	57,519	98	99	81	4	0.5	..	..	36	2000 f
Latvia	2,277	2,012	100	100	73	9	0.8	2	5	38	2003 d
Lithuania	3,390	3,023	100	100	73	7	0.2	2	8	36	2003 d
Macedonia, FYR	2,038	1,966	94	98	74	15	< 0.1	2	2	39	2003 d
Moldova, Rep	3,794	3,388	98	99	69	14	1.1	2	21	33	2003 d
Montegro	598	613	..	..	75	..	..	..	..	..	..
Netherlands	16,419	17,141	..	..	80	4	0.2	..	..	31	1999 f
Norway	4,698	5,366	..	..	80	3	0.1	..	..	26	2000 f
Poland	38,082	35,353	..	..	76	6	0.1	2	2	35	2002 f
Portugal	10,623	10,607	..	..	78	4	0.4	..	..	39	1997 f
Romania	21,438	18,860	96	98	73	16	< 0.1	2	13	31	2003 d
Russian Federation	142,499	123,915	99	100	66	14	1.1	2	12	40	2002 d
Serbia {g}	10,528	10,528	94	99	..	12	0.0	2	..	30	2003 d
Slovakia	5,390	5,217	..	..	75	7	< 0.1	2	3	26	1996 f
Slovenia	2,002	1,901	..	..	78	3	< 0.1	2	2	28	1998 d
Spain	44,279	46,682	..	..	81	4	0.6	..	..	35	2000 f
Sweden	9,119	10,012	..	..	81	3	0.2	..	..	25	2000 f
Switzerland	7,484	8,104	..	..	82	4	0.4	..	..	34	2000 f
Ukraine	46,205	38,053	99	100	68	13	1.4	2	5	28	2003 d
United Kingdom	60,769	66,162	..	..	79	5	0.2	..	..	36	1999 f
Middle East & N. Africa	460,067	649,569	64	82	69	43	0.2 i	2	20	..	2004
Afghanistan	27,145	53,252	13	43	44	165	< 0.1	..	..	..	..
Algeria	33,858	44,726	60	80	72	34	0.1	2	15	35	1995 d
Egypt	75,498	104,070	59	83	71	28	< 0.1	3	44	34	2000 d
Iran, Islamic Rep	71,208	91,155	70	84	71	31	0.2	2	7	43	1998 d
Iraq	28,993	47,376	64	84	60	102	..	..	..	..	..
Israel	6,928	9,160	96	99	81	5	..	..	..	39	2001 f
Jordan	5,924	8,554	85	95	73	22	..	2	7	39	2003 d
Kuwait	2,851	4,273	91	94	78	9	..	..	..	..	..
Lebanon	4,099	4,925	..	..	72	27	0.1	..	..	..	..
Libyan Arab Jamahiriya	6,160	8,447	..	..	74	18	..	..	..	..	..
Morocco	31,224	39,259	40	66	71	36	0.1	2	14	40	1999 d
Oman	2,595	3,865	74	87	76	10	..	..	..	..	..
Saudi Arabia	24,735	37,314	69	87	73	21	..	..	..	..	..
Syrian Arab Rep	19,929	29,294	74	86	74	14	..	..	..	..	..
Tunisia	10,327	12,529	65	83	74	20	0.1	2	7	40	2000 d
Turkey	74,877	92,468	80	95	72	26	..	3	19	44	2003 d
United Arab Emirates	4,380	6,753	..	..	79	8	..	..	..	..	..
Yemen	22,389	40,768	..	..	63	76	..	16	45	33	1998 d

	Total Population Estimates and Projections (thousands of people) {a}		Adult Literacy Rate 2000–2004 (percent)		Human Health — Life Expectancy at Birth (years) 2005–2010	Infant Mortality Rate (per 1,000 live births) 2005	Percent Of Adults Ages 15–49 Living With HIV or AIDS 2005	International Poverty and Income Equality — Percent of Population Living on Less Than {b}		Gini Index {c} (0 = perfect equality)	Survey Year
	2007	2030	Women	Men				$1 per day	$2 per day		
Sub-Saharan Africa	807,425	1,308,461	53	70 g	51	101	6.1 i	41	72	..	2004
Angola	17,024	30,652	54	83	43	154	3.7	..	..	..	..
Benin	9,033	16,076	23	48	57	89	1.8	31	74	37	2003 d
Botswana	1,882	2,358	82	80	51	87	24.1	28	56	61	1993 d
Burkina Faso	14,784	26,505	15	29	52	96	2.0	27	72	40	2003 d
Burundi	8,508	17,232	52	67	50	114	3.3	55	88	42	1998 d
Cameroon	18,549	26,892	60	77	50	87	5.4	17	51	45	2001 d
Central African Rep	4,343	6,214	34	65	45	115	10.7	67	84	61	1993 d
Chad	10,781	19,799	13	41	51	124	3.5	..	..	..	..
Congo	3,768	5,824	..	..	55	81	5.3	..	..	..	..
Congo, Dem Rep	62,636	122,734	54	81	47	129	3.2	..	..	..	..
Côte d'Ivoire	19,262	28,088	39	61	48	118	7.1	15	49	45	2002 d
Equatorial Guinea	507	854	81	93	52	123	3.2	..	..	..	..
Eritrea	4,851	8,433	..	..	58	50	2.4	..	..	..	..
Ethiopia	83,099	137,052	..	..	53	109	..	23	78	30	2000 d
Gabon	1,331	1,791	..	..	57	60	7.9	..	..	..	..
Gambia	1,709	2,770	..	..	60	97	2.4	59	83	50	1998 d
Ghana	23,478	34,234	50	66	60	68	2.3	45	79	41	1998 d
Guinea	9,370	16,170	18	43	56	98	1.5	..	..	39	2003 d
Guinea-Bissau	1,695	3,358	..	..	46	124	3.8	..	..	47	1993 d
Kenya	37,538	62,762	70	78	54	79	6.1	23	58	43	1997 d
Lesotho	2,008	2,252	90	74	43	102	23.2	36	56	63	1995 d
Liberia	3,750	7,797	..	..	46	157	..	..	..	..	..
Madagascar	19,683	32,931	65	77	59	74	0.5	61	85	48	2001 d
Malawi	13,925	23,550	54	75	48	79	14.1	21	63	39	2004 d
Mali	12,337	23,250	12	27	55	120	1.7	36	72	40	2001 d
Mauritania	3,124	4,944	43	60	64	78	0.7	26	63	39	2000 d
Mozambique	21,397	31,117	..	..	42	100	16.1	36	74	47	2002 d
Namibia	2,074	2,678	84	87	53	46	19.6	35	56	74	1993 f
Niger	14,226	30,842	15	43	57	150	1.1	61	86	51	1995 d
Nigeria	148,093	226,855	..	..	47	100	3.9	71	92	44	2003 d
Rwanda	9,725	16,646	60	71	46	118	3.1	60	88	47	2000 d
Senegal	12,379	19,554	29	51	63	77	0.9	17	56	41	2001 d
Sierra Leone	5,866	9,592	24	47	43	165	1.6	57	75	63	1989 d
Somalia	8,699	15,193	..	..	48	133	0.9	..	..	..	..
South Africa	48,577	53,236	81	84	49	55	18.8	11	34	58	2000 d
Sudan	38,560	58,446	52 h	71 h	59	62	1.6	..	..	..	..
Tanzania, United Rep	40,454	65,516	62	78	53	76	6.5	58	90	35	2000 d
Togo	6,585	10,856	39	69	58	78	3.2	..	..	..	..
Uganda	30,884	61,548	58	77	52	79	6.7	..	..	46	2002 d
Zambia	11,922	17,870	60	76	42	102	17.0	64	87	51	2004 d
Zimbabwe	13,349	16,628	..	..	44	81	20.1	56	83	50	1996 d
North America	338,831	405,429	95	96 g	79	..	0.8 i	..	..	..	..
Canada	32,876	39,105	..	..	81	5	0.3	..	..	33	2000 f
United States	305,826	366,187	..	..	78	6	0.6	..	..	41	2000 f
C. America & Caribbean	188,782	235,487	88	90	74	26 j	..	..	..	..	..
Belize	288	413	..	..	76	15	2.5	..	..	..	..
Costa Rica	4,468	5,795	95	95	79	11	0.3	3	10	50	2003 f
Cuba	11,268	11,126	100	100	78	6	0.1	..	..	..	..
Dominican Rep	9,760	12,709	87	87	72	26	1.1	3	16	52	2004 f
El Salvador	6,857	8,935	..	..	72	23	0.9	19	41	52	2002 f
Guatemala	13,354	21,691	63	75	70	32	0.9	14	32	55	2002 f
Haiti	9,598	12,994	..	..	61	84	3.8	54	78	59	2001 f
Honduras	7,106	10,298	80	80	70	31	1.5	15	36	54	2003 f
Jamaica	2,714	2,924	86	74	73	17	1.5	2	14	46	2004 d
Mexico	106,535	128,125	90	92	76	22	0.3	3	12	46	2004 d
Nicaragua	5,603	7,407	77	77	73	30	0.2	45	80	43	2001 d
Panama	3,343	4,488	91	93	76	19	0.9	7	18	56	2003 f
Trinidad and Tobago	1,333	1,400	..	..	70	17	2.6	12	39	39	1992 f
South America	383,406	477,332	90	91	73	26 j	..	..	..	..	..
Argentina	39,531	47,534	97	97	75	15	0.6	7	17	51	2004 f
Bolivia	9,525	13,034	81	93	66	52	0.1	23	42	60	2002 f
Brazil	191,791	236,480	89	88	72	31	0.5	8	21	57	2004 f
Chile	16,635	19,778	96	96	79	8	0.3	2	6	55	2003 f
Colombia	46,156	57,577	93	93	73	17	0.6	7	18	59	2003 f
Ecuador	13,341	16,679	90	92	75	22	0.3	18	41	54	1998 f
Guyana	738	660	..	..	67	47	2.4	2	6	43	1999 f
Paraguay	6,127	8,483	..	..	72	20	0.4	14	30	58	2003 f
Peru	27,903	35,564	82	94	71	23	0.6	11	31	52	2003 f
Suriname	458	481	87	92	70	30	1.9	..	..	..	..
Uruguay	3,340	3,590	..	..	76	14	0.5	2	6	45	2003 f
Venezuela	27,657	37,149	93	93	74	18	0.7	19	40	48	2003 f
Oceania	34,240	43,206	93	94 g	76	..	0.3 i	..	..	..	..
Australia	20,743	25,287	..	..	81	5	0.1	..	..	35	1994 f
Fiji	839	918	..	..	69	16	0.1	..	..	..	..
New Zealand	4,179	4,895	..	..	80	5	0.1	..	..	36	1997 f
Papua New Guinea	6,331	9,183	50.9	63.4	57	55	1.8	..	..	51	1996 d
Solomon Islands	496	762	..	..	64	24	..	..	..	..	..
Developed	1,353,287	1,411,479	99	99 g	76	5	..	..	..	..	..
Developing	5,317,004	6,903,869	70	84	67	57	..	..	..	..	..

a. Medium variant population projections; please consult the technical notes for more information. b. Measures the percent of the population living below $1.08 per day and $2.15 per day at 1993 prices. c. The Gini Index measures the equality of income distribution within the population (0=perfect equality; 100=perfect inequality). d. Based on per capita consumption or expenditure data. e. Poverty Rates for Cambodia were obtained from a 1997 survey. f. Based on per capita income data. g. Data for Serbia include the country of Montenegro (these countries were a single nation from 2003 to 2006). h. Estimates are for North Sudan only. i. Regional totals are calculated by UNAIDS. j. Regional total are calculated by UNICEF and combine South America, Central America and the Caribbean; a list of countries classified in each region is avilable at http://www.unicef.org/files/Table9.pdf.

Population and Human Well-Being: Technical Notes

DEFINITIONS AND METHODOLOGY

Total Population refers to the de facto population of a country, in thousands of people, as of July 1 of the year indicated. For estimates for 2005 and earlier, the United Nations Population Division (UNPD) compiles and evaluates census and survey results from all countries, adjusting data when necessary. Adjustments incorporate data from civil registrations (in developed countries), population surveys (in developing countries), earlier censuses, and, when necessary, population models based on information from similar countries. The future projections reported here assume medium fertility (the UN "medium-fertility assumption"). All future population projections are based on estimates of the 2005 base year population and incorporate the three main components of population growth: fertility, mortality, and migration. For more information on methodology, see *World Population Prospects: The 2006 Revision, Volume III: Analytical Report.*

Adult Literacy Rate measures the proportion of the men or women older than the age of 15 who can both read and write with understanding a short, simple statement on their everyday life. Most literacy data are collected intermittently during national population censuses and supplemented by household surveys, labor force surveys, employment surveys, industry surveys, and agricultural surveys when they are available. The United Nations Educational, Scientific, and Cultural Organization (UNESCO) uses these data to graph a logistic regression model and create the estimates shown here. When census and survey data are not available, literacy rates for a specific country are estimated based on neighboring countries with similar characteristics.

Life Expectancy at Birth is the average number of years that a newborn baby is expected to live if the age-specific mortality rates effective at the year of birth apply throughout his or her lifetime. The United Nations Population Division prepares estimates and projections based on data from national statistical sources. When needed, other sources, mainly population censuses and demographic surveys, are consulted. In countries highly affected by the HIV/AIDS epidemic, estimates of the impact of the disease are made explicitly by projecting the yearly incidence of HIV infection.

Infant Mortality Rate is the probability of a child dying between birth and 1 year of age expressed per 1,000 live births. The indicator is used as a measure of children's well-being and the level of effort being made to maintain child health: more than three quarters of child deaths in the developing world are caused by diseases that can be prevented or cured by low-cost interventions such as immunization, oral rehydration therapy, and antibiotics. The data on mortality of children in infancy are typically obtained from civil registration records on deaths and births, and a ratio can be calculated directly. In many developing countries, however, civil registration records are incomplete. In these instances, several types of surveys may be utilized to collect birth and death histories of sample populations to fill gaps in knowledge.

Percent of Adults Ages 15–49 Living With HIV or AIDS is the estimated percentage of people aged 15–49 living with HIV/AIDS in 2005. These estimates include all people with HIV infection, whether or not they have developed symptoms of AIDS, who are alive at the end of the year specified. Data for this age group capture those in their most sexually active years. Measuring infection within this age range also allows greater comparability for populations with different age structures. Estimates for a single point in time and the starting date of the epidemic were used to plot an epidemic curve charting the spread of HIV in a particular country; these curves are used to create the estimates shown here.

Population Living on Less Than $1 per day is the percentage of the population of a country living on less than $1.08 a day at 1993 international prices, equivalent

to $1 in 1985 prices when adjusted for purchasing power parity (PPP). This amount is used because it is comparable to the poverty lines used in many developing countries, and income below this level is referred to as "extreme poverty."

Population Living on Less Than $2 per day is the percentage of the population of a country living on less than $2.15 a day at 1993 international prices, equivalent to $2 in 1985 prices when adjusted for purchasing power parity. International Poverty Line data are based on nationally representative primary household surveys conducted by national statistical offices or by private agencies under the supervision of government or international agencies and obtained from government statistical offices and World Bank country departments. PPP exchange rates, produced at the World Bank, are used because they take into account local prices and goods and services not traded internationally.

Gini Index is a measure of income inequality that describes the deviation of income or consumption distribution from perfect equality. A score of zero implies perfect equality while a score of 100 implies perfect inequality. If every person in a country earned the same income, the Gini Index would be zero; if all income were earned by one person, the Gini Index would be 100. The Gini index is calculated by compiling income (or expenditure) distribution data. For developing countries, the Gini index is compiled from household survey data; for high-income countries the index is calculated directly from the Luxemburg Income Study database, using an estimation method consistent with that applied for developing countries. Once compiled, income or expenditure distribution data are plotted on a Lorenz curve, which illustrates the cumulative percentages of total income received against the cumulative number of recipients, starting with the poorest individual or household. The Gini index is calculated as the area between the Lorenz curve and a hypothetical (45-degree) line of absolute equality, expressed as a percentage of the maximum area under the line.

Survey Year shows the year that both the poverty rate and income inequality data were collected in each country. Surveys were conducted between 1993 and 2004.

FREQUENCY OF UPDATE BY DATA PROVIDERS

Country-level estimates of population, life expectancy, and HIV/AIDS infection rates are published every two years by UNPD and the Joint United Nations Programme on HIV/AIDS (UNAIDS). Literacy data are updated by UNESCO as new estimates are made available. The United Nations Children's Fund (UNICEF) publishes the most recent infant mortality data in their annual State of the World's Children report. Poverty rates and income equality data are updated irregularly as surveys are conducted in individual countries; new survey results are compiled and released annually in the World Bank's *World Development Indicators.*

DATA RELIABILITY AND CAUTIONARY NOTES

Total Population and Life Expectancy: Since demographic parameters are estimated on a country-by-country basis, reliability varies among countries. For some developing countries, estimates are derived from surveys rather than censuses, especially when countries lack a civil registration system or have one that does not achieve full coverage of all vital events. Also, for developing countries the availability of detailed information on fertility and mortality is limited and the data on international migration flows are generally inadequate. Although estimates are based on incomplete data and projections cannot factor in unforeseen events (such as famine or wars), UN demographic models are widely accepted and use well-understood principles, which make these data as comparable, consistent across countries, and reliable as possible.

Adult Literacy Rate: The availability and quality of national statistics on literacy vary widely. National census and survey data are typically collected only once every decade. In addition, many industrialized countries have stopped collecting literacy data in recent years, based on the sometimes incorrect assumption that universal primary education means universal literacy. When census and survey data are not available for a particular country, estimates are sometimes made based on neighboring countries. Actual definitions of adult literacy are not strictly comparable among countries. Some countries equate persons with no schooling with illiterates or change definitions between censuses. In addition, UNESCO's definition of literacy does not include people who, though familiar with the basics of reading and writing, do not have the skills to function at a reasonable level in their own society.

Infant Mortality: These data tend to be of poorer quality than under-5 mortality data. A concerted effort has been made by UNICEF and its partners to develop a consistent and transparent methodology. However, the data used to derive these estimates come from a wide variety of sources of disparate quality: some countries have several sources of data covering the same period, allowing for data cross-referencing; other countries have many fewer sources and/or have sources of poor quality. In addition, inaccuracies in birth and death totals in civil registries (with death figures typically less complete than those of births) may result in an underestimation of a country's infant mortality rate.

Percent of Adults Living with HIV or AIDS: Data reliability varies on a country-by-country basis. The extent of uncertainty depends primarily on the type of epidemic and the quality, coverage, and consistency of a country's surveillance system. UNAIDS estimates low and high values for the total number of infections in its *2006 Report on the Global AIDS Epidemic;* the values shown here fall between these two estimates. A more detailed analysis of the collection methodology and reliability of HIV/AIDS estimates is available in a series of seven articles published online in the journal *Sexually Transmitted Infections* in August 2004.

International Poverty Rates and Gini Index: Despite recent improvements in survey methodology and consistency, indicators are still not strictly comparable across countries. Surveys can differ in the type of information requested (for example, whether income or consumption is used). Consumption is usually a much better welfare indicator, particularly in developing countries. The households that are surveyed can differ in size and in the extent of income sharing among members, and individuals within a household may differ in age and consumption needs. Differences also exist in the relative importance of consumption of nonmarket goods.

Although the $1/day and $2/day poverty lines are commonly used, there is an ongoing debate as to how well they capture poverty across nations. Values should be treated as rough statistical approximations of the number of people earning or consuming at a given level rather than a certain prognosis of how many people are poor. International poverty rates do not capture other elements of poverty, including lack of access to health care, education, safe water, or sanitation. Estimates are expected to change significantly in the next release of the World Development Indicators, which will incorporate purchasing power estimates benchmarked to 2005 rather than 1993.

SOURCES

Population and Life Expectancy: Population Division of the Department of Economic and Social Affairs of the United Nations Secretariat. 2007. *World Population Prospects: The 2006 Revision.* Dataset on CD-ROM. New York: United Nations. Online at http://www.un.org/esa/population/ordering.htm.

Literacy Rates: United Nations Educational, Scientific, and Cultural Organization (UNESCO) Institute for Statistics. 2006. *World Education Indicators, Literacy Statistics.* Paris: UNESCO. Online at http://www.uis.unesco.org.

Infant Mortality: United Nations Children's Fund (UNICEF). 2006. *The State of the World's Children 2007: The Double Dividend of Gender Equality.* Table 1. New York: UNICEF. Online at http://www.unicef.org/sowc07.

Percent of Adults Living with HIV or AIDS: Joint United Nations Programme on HIV/AIDS (UNAIDS). 2006. *Report on the Global AIDS Epidemic.* Geneva: UNAIDS. Online at http://www.unaids.org/en/HIV_data/2006GlobalReport/default.asp.

Gini Index and International Poverty Rates: Development Data Group, World Bank. 2007. *2007 World Development Indicators.* Washington, DC: World Bank. Online at http://go.worldbank.org/B53SONGPA0.

Food and Water

Sources: Food and Agriculture Organization of the United Nations, Keele University, World Health Organization, United Nations Children's Fund

	Intensity of Agricultural Inputs				Food Security and Nutrition			Fisheries Production		Water Resources			Use of an Improved Water Source (percent of population) 2004	
	Agricultural Land (a) (1,000 ha) 2003	Fertilizer (kg/ha) 2003	Water (m³/ha) 2000	Labor (percent of workforce in agriculture) 2004	Calorie Supply, 2003 (kcal/person/day) Total	Percent from Animal Products	Percent of Population That is Under-nourished 2002-2004	Total Production in 2005 (metric tons)	Percent Change Since 1995	Actual Renewable Water Resources (b) Total (km³)	Per Capita (m³ per person)	Water Poverty Index 2002	Urban	Rural
World	4,423,482	110	..	43	2,809	17	14	157,531,214	26	54,228	8,210	..	95	73
Asia (excl. Middle East)	770,403	221	..	55	2,681	15	15	102,480,487	51	14,514	3,948	..	93	76
Armenia	1,390	19	3,464	11	2,357	19	24	1,033	(47)	11	3,511	54	99	80
Azerbaijan	4,754	8	5,825	25	2,727	14	7	9,016	(18)	30	3,547	61	95	59
Bangladesh	9,019	187	8,999	52	2,193	3	30	2,215,957	100	1,211	8,232	54	82	72
Bhutan	585	..	2,500	94	..	..	..	300	(12)	95	42,035	56	86	60
Cambodia	5,350	4	1,051	69	2,074	9	33	426,000	279	476	32,526	46	64	35
China	554,851	257 c	2,871	64	2,940	22	12	60,630,984	85	2,829	2,125	51	93	67
Georgia	3,006	23	2,006	18	2,646	17	9	3,072	(17)	63	14,406	60	96	67
India	180,000	95	3,289	58	2,473	8	20	6,323,557	26	1,897	1,670	53	95	83
Indonesia	47,600	79	2,250	46	2,891	5	6	6,513,133	48	2,838	12,441	65	87	69
Japan	4,736	366	11,435	3	2,768	21	< 2.5	5,433,436	(28)	430	3,351	65	100	100
Kazakhstan	207,784	6	1,321	16	2,858	25	6	31,589	(37)	110	7,405	58	97	73
Korea, Dem People's Rep	2,950	..	1,771	27	2,178	6	33	712,995	(33)	77	3,403	..	100	100
Korea, Rep	1,902	367	4,651	8	3,035	16	< 2.5	2,711,667	(19)	70	1,448	62	97	71
Kyrgyzstan	10,840	10	6,799	23	3,173	18	4	27	(93)	21	3,821	64	98	66
Lao People's Dem Rep	1,939	..	2,818	76	2,338	7	19	107,800	168	334	53,859	54	79	43
Malaysia	7,870	175	736	16	2,867	18	3	1,424,097	14	580	22,104	67	100	96
Mongolia	130,500	3	196	22	2,250	39	27	366	132	35	12,837	55	87	30
Myanmar	11,293	2	3,109	69	2,912	5	..	2,217,466	169	1,046	20,313	54	80	77
Nepal	4,217	15	4,043	93	2,483	7	17	42,463	101	210	7,447	54	96	89
Pakistan	27,230	150	7,407	45	2,316	20	24	515,472	(5)	223	1,353	58	96	89
Philippines	12,200	88	1,981	37	2,480	15	18	4,145,044	48	479	5,577	61	87	82
Singapore	0	..	950	0	..	..	..	7,837	(43)	1	135	56	100	..
Sri Lanka	2,356	130	6,283	44	2,416	6	22	164,230	(30)	50	2,372	56	98	74
Tajikistan	4,255	..	10,359	31	1,907	10	56	210	(45)	16	2,392	59	92	48
Thailand	18,487	128	4,300	53	2,425	13	22	3,743,398	4	410	6,280	64	98	100
Turkmenistan	32,966	..	12,554	32	2,840	21	7	15,016	32	25	4,979	70	93	54
Uzbekistan	27,259	..	11,268	25	2,312	17	25	5,425	(61)	50	1,842	61	95	75
Viet Nam	9,537	253	5,974	66	2,617	13	16	3,397,200	130	891	10,310	52	99	80
Europe	480,665	80	..	8	3,354	28	<2.5	16,273,014	(15)	7,793	10,686	..	100	..
Albania	1,121	70	1,517	46	2,874	28	6	5,275	207	42	13,184	..	99	94
Austria	3,376	221	14	4	3,732	33	< 2.5	2,790	(16)	78	9,455	75	100	100
Belarus	8,885	153	134	11	2,885	27	4	5,050	(18)	58	6,014	61	100	100
Belgium	1,394	..	..	2	3,634	31	< 2.5	25,767	(29)	18	1,751	61	100	100
Bosnia and Herzegovina	2,148	16	..	4	2,668	13	9	9,070	505	38	9,566	..	99	96
Bulgaria	5,326	126	521	6	2,885	24	8	8,579	(32)	21	2,797	63	100	97
Croatia	3,137	108	..	7	2,795	20	7	48,465	139	106	23,161	68	100	100
Czech Rep	4,270	118	18	7	3,308	25	< 2.5	24,697	9	13	1,290	61	100	100
Denmark	2,658	136	236	3	3,472	36	< 2.5	949,625	(54)	6	1,099	61	100	100
Estonia	829	436	9	10	3,222	26	< 2.5	100,136	(25)	13	9,696	..	100	99
Finland	2,246	118	30	5	3,143	37	< 2.5	146,096	(21)	110	20,857	78	100	100
France	29,690	209	200	3	3,623	37	< 2.5	909,483	(6)	204	3,343	68	100	100
Germany	17,001	226	775	2	3,484	31	< 2.5	330,353	9	154	1,862	65	100	100
Greece	8,431	115	1,622	15	3,666	23	< 2.5	198,951	8	74	6,653	66	..	..
Hungary	5,865	102	510	9	3,552	32	< 2.5	21,270	28	104	10,353	61	100	98
Iceland	2,281	..	29	7	3,275	41	< 2.5	1,690,383	4	170	566,667	77	100	100
Ireland	4,370	452	0	9	3,717	32	< 2.5	352,082	(22)	52	12,187	73	100	..
Italy	15,074	150	1,773	4	3,675	26	< 2.5	480,921	(21)	191	3,289	61	100	..
Latvia	1,582	91	21	11	3,014	28	3	151,160	1	35	15,521	..	100	96
Lithuania	2,541	143	7	10	3,372	27	< 2.5	141,798	140	25	7,317	..	..	..
Macedonia, FYR	1,242	22	..	10	2,852	18	5	1,114	(26)	6	3,137	..	..	..
Moldova, Rep	2,528	7	353	20	2,729	16	11	5,001	137	12	2,783	49	97	88
Netherlands	1,923	580	2,850	3	3,495	30	< 2.5	617,383	18	91	5,539	69	100	100
Norway	1,040	186	261	4	3,511	31	< 2.5	3,203,476	7	382	81,886	77	100	100
Poland	16,169	108	94	20	3,366	26	< 2.5	192,854	(58)	62	1,601	56	100	..
Portugal	3,812	122	3,503	11	3,747	29	< 2.5	218,866	(20)	69	6,485	65	..	..
Romania	14,800	37	1,333	13	3,582	23	< 2.5	13,352	(81)	212	9,837	59	91	16
Russian Federation	216,277	10	108	9	3,118	22	3	3,356,327	(24)	4,507	31,764	63	100	88
Serbia {d}	5,595	434	..	17	2,703	35	9	7,022	82	209	19,870	..	99	86
Slovakia	2,236	92	..	8	2,779	27	7	2,648	(26)	50	9,276	71	100	99
Slovenia	510	334	..	1	2,954	31	3	2,763	(7)	32	16,219	69	..	..
Spain	29,154	119	1,324	6	3,421	28	< 2.5	1,071,178	(25)	112	2,557	64	100	100
Sweden	3,166	118	96	3	3,208	36	< 2.5	262,239	(36)	174	19,131	72	100	100
Switzerland	1,525	178	114	4	3,545	34	< 2.5	2,689	(2)	54	7,354	72	100	100
Ukraine	41,355	13	588	13	3,054	20	< 2.5	274,210	(36)	140	3,066	..	99	91
United Kingdom	16,956	306	47	2	3,450	31	< 2.5	842,271	(17)	147	2,449	72	100	100
Middle East & N. Africa	460,345	77	..	30	3,116	11	6	3,894,801	29	657	1,398	..	94	79
Afghanistan	38,048	..	2,839	66	..	..	..	1,000	(23)	65	2,015	..	63	31
Algeria	39,956	5	481	23	3,055	10	4	126,628	19	14	423	50	88	80
Egypt	3,409	535	17,928	31	3,356	8	4	889,302	118	58	759	58	99	97
Iran, Islamic Rep	63,012	60	4,057	25	3,096	9	..	527,912	43	138	1,931	60	99	84
Iraq	10,019	..	6,791	8	..	..	..	32,970	7	75	2,490	..	97	50
Israel	552	2,329	3,019	2	3,554	21	< 2.5	26,555	26	2	240	54	100	100
Jordan	1,004	619	1,905	10	2,680	10	6	1,071	80	1	148	46	99	91
Kuwait	154	0	19,167	1	3,061	18	5	5,222	(40)	0	7	54	..	..
Lebanon	329	102	2,771	3	3,164	17	3	4,601	5	4	1,206	56	100	100
Libyan Arab Jamahiriya	15,450	28	1,648	5	3,337	11	< 2.5	46,342	34	1	99	..	..	..
Morocco	30,376	53	1,141	33	3,098	7	6	947,777	10	29	895	46	99	56
Oman	1,080	88	15,375	34	..	..	..	150,744	8	1	369	59	..	..
Saudi Arabia	173,798	113	4,074	7	2,840	15	4	74,778	55	2	93	53	97	..
Syrian Arab Rep	13,824	62	3,537	26	3,057	14	4	16,980	46	26	1,314	55	98	87
Tunisia	9,784	21	434	23	3,247	11	< 2.5	111,818	33	5	442	51	99	82
Turkey	40,644	77	1,056	43	3,328	12	3	545,673	(17)	229	3,051	57	98	93
United Arab Emirates	559	237	6,356	4	3,238	23	< 2.5	90,570	(14)	0	31	52	100	100
Yemen	17,734	3	3,787	46	2,020	8	38	263,000	144	4	184	44	71	65

DATA TABLE 2: FOOD AND WATER

	Intensity of Agricultural Inputs				Food Security and Nutrition			Fisheries Production		Water Resources			Use of an Improved Water Source (percent of population) 2004	
	Agricultural Land (a) (1,000 ha) 2003	Fertilizer (kg/ha) 2003	Water (m³/ha) 2000	Labor (percent of workforce in agriculture) 2004	Calorie Supply, 2003 (kcal/person/day) Total	Percent from Animal Products	Percent of Population That is Undernourished 2002–2004	Total Production in 2005 (metric tons)	Percent Change Since 1995	Actual Renewable Water Resources (b) Total (km³)	Per Capita (m³ per person)	Water Poverty Index 2002	Urban	Rural
Sub-Saharan Africa	1,046,854	11	..	61	2,272	7	30	5,925,170	31	5,463	6,957	..	81	43
Angola	57,590	2	64	71	2,089	8	35	240,000	95	184	10,909	41	75	40
Benin	3,467	1	22	50	2,574	4	12	38,407	(13)	25	2,765	39	78	57
Botswana	25,980	..	211	44	2,196	13	32	132	(34)	14	8,215	57	100	90
Burkina Faso	10,900	5	168	92	2,516	5	15	9,007	13	13	890	42	94	54
Burundi	2,345	0	168	90	1,647	2	66	14,200	(33)	4	442	40	92	77
Cameroon	9,160	6	102	55	2,286	6	26	142,682	51	286	16,920	54	86	44
Central African Rep	5,149	..	1	69	1,932	12	44	15,000	7	144	34,787	44	93	61
Chad	48,630	..	54	71	2,147	7	35	70,000	(22)	43	4,174	39	41	43
Congo	10,547	..	7	37	2,183	7	33	58,448	27	832	196,319	57	84	27
Congo, Dem Rep	22,800	..	14	61	1,606	2	74	222,965	40	1,283	20,973	46	82	29
Côte d'Ivoire	19,900	12	88	45	2,644	4	13	55,866	(21)	81	4,315	46	97	74
Equatorial Guinea	334	..	4	68	..	..	..	3,500	52	26	49,336	68	45	42
Eritrea	7,532	2	515	76	1,520	6	75	4,027	13	6	1,338	37	74	57
Ethiopia	31,769	5	487	81	1,858	5	46	9,450	48	110	1,355	35	81	11
Gabon	5,160	2	101	33	2,671	11	5	43,941	9	164	114,766	62	95	47
Gambia	779	..	69	78	2,288	6	29	32,000	35	8	5,019	48	95	77
Ghana	14,735	3	107	56	2,680	5	11	393,428	11	53	2,314	45	88	64
Guinea	12,450	1	850	82	2,447	4	24	96,571	42	226	23,042	52	78	35
Guinea-Bissau	1,630	..	263	82	2,051	7	39	6,200	(2)	31	18,430	48	79	49
Kenya	26,512	79	200	74	2,155	13	31	149,378	(23)	30	839	47	83	46
Lesotho	2,334	..	30	38	2,626	4	13	46	15	3	1,693	43	92	76
Liberia	2,602	..	101	66	1,930	3	50	10,000	13	232	67,207	..	72	52
Madagascar	27,550	2	4,089	73	2,056	8	38	144,900	19	337	17,186	48	77	35
Malawi	4,440	20	362	81	2,125	3	35	59,595	11	17	1,285	38	98	68
Mali	39,479	..	1,262	79	2,237	10	29	101,098	(24)	100	6,981	41	78	36
Mauritania	39,750	..	3,000	52	2,786	18	10	247,577	366	11	3,511	50	59	44
Mozambique	48,580	8	133	80	2,082	2	44	43,751	62	216	10,531	45	72	26
Namibia	38,820	1	260	38	2,290	16	24	552,812	(3)	18	8,658	60	98	81
Niger	38,500	0	143	87	2,170	5	32	50,058	1,271	34	2,257	35	80	36
Nigeria	72,600	7	179	30	2,714	3	9	579,537	58	286	2,085	44	67	31
Rwanda	1,935	..	89	90	2,071	3	33	8,186	142	5	551	39	92	69
Senegal	8,157	13	860	72	2,374	9	20	405,264	11	39	3,225	45	92	60
Sierra Leone	2,845	..	636	60	1,943	4	51	145,993	125	160	27,577	42	75	46
Somalia	44,071	..	3,074	69	..	..	..	30,000	7	14	1,620	..	32	27
South Africa	99,640	51	499	8	2,962	13	< 2.5	830,369	42	50	1,048	52	99	73
Sudan	134,600	4	2,166	57	2,260	20	26	63,608	41	65	1,707	49	78	64
Tanzania, United Rep	48,100	9	926	79	1,959	6	44	354,351	(4)	91	2,291	48	85	49
Togo	3,630	7	29	57	2,358	3	24	29,267	139	15	2,272	46	80	36
Uganda	12,462	1	17	78	2,360	6	19	427,575	105	66	2,133	44	87	56
Zambia	35,289	..	250	67	1,975	5	46	70,125	(6)	105	8,726	50	90	40
Zimbabwe	20,550	33	990	60	2,004	8	47	15,452	(7)	20	1,520	53	98	72
North America	484,646	103	..	2	3,739	28	<2.5	6,872,348	1	5,576	16,558	..	100	100
Canada	67,505	52	104	2	3,605	26	< 2.5	1,255,821	33	2,902	88,336	78	100	99
United States	416,902	118	1,111	2	3,754	28	< 2.5	5,396,735	(6)	2,071	6,816	65	100	100
C. America & Caribbean	141,861	61	..	22	2,902	17	11	2,040,714	5	1,259	6,653	..	96	84
Belize	152	263	303	30	2,876	22	4	14,548	37	19	66,268	66	100	82
Costa Rica	2,865	339	2,724	18	2,813	20	5	46,378	92	112	25,157	67	100	92
Cuba	6,655	13	1,409	13	3,286	11	< 2.5	52,387	(49)	38	3,368	..	95	78
Dominican Rep	3,696	..	1,404	14	2,281	15	29	12,086	(40)	21	2,295	59	97	91
El Salvador	1,704	56	854	27	2,556	13	11	43,317	178	25	3,546	56	94	70
Guatemala	4,652	87	819	44	2,227	9	22	16,756	40	111	8,410	59	99	92
Haiti	1,590	..	846	60	2,109	8	46	8,310	50	14	1,599	35	52	56
Honduras	2,936	41	484	28	2,373	14	23	48,580	61	96	12,755	60	95	81
Jamaica	513	3	704	19	2,690	15	9	18,766	(34)	9	3,520	58	98	88
Mexico	107,300	68	2,210	19	3,171	19	5	1,449,535	3	457	4,172	58	100	87
Nicaragua	6,976	30	502	17	2,291	11	27	40,897	241	197	34,416	58	90	63
Panama	2,230	39	334	18	2,287	24	23	222,756	7	148	44,266	67	99	79
Trinidad and Tobago	133	502	164	8	2,788	17	10	13,414	16	4	2,925	59	92	88
South America	579,599	109	..	16	2,886	21	9	18,316,451	(9)	17,274	44,816	..	96	65
Argentina	128,747	42	747	9	2,959	28	3	933,902	(21)	814	20,591	61	98	80
Bolivia	37,087	4	371	43	2,219	18	23	7,090	12	623	65,358	63	95	68
Brazil	263,600	140	562	15	3,146	21	7	1,008,066	54	8,233	43,028	61	96	57
Chile	15,242	215	3,470	15	2,872	22	4	5,453,882	(31)	922	55,425	69	100	58
Colombia	42,051	196	1,083	18	2,567	16	13	181,074	8	2,132	45,408	66	99	71
Ecuador	7,249	82	4,686	23	2,641	19	6	486,023	(20)	432	31,739	67	97	89
Guyana	1,740	20	3,137	16	2,764	16	8	53,980	12	241	320,479	76	83	83
Paraguay	24,836	69	119	33	2,524	18	15	23,100	9	336	52,133	56	99	68
Peru	21,210	73	3,832	28	2,579	13	12	9,421,130	5	1,913	66,431	64	89	65
Suriname	89	93	9,254	18	2,697	12	8	40,191	209	122	268,132	75	98	73
Uruguay	14,955	99	2,141	12	2,883	27	< 2.5	125,953	(0)	139	39,612	67	100	100
Venezuela	21,640	129	1,166	7	2,272	15	18	492,210	(3)	1,233	44,545	65	85	70
Oceania	459,109	61	..	19	..	..	..	1,582,359	39	1,693	52,674	..	96	83
Australia	439,500	46	356	4	3,135	33	< 2.5	307,392	23	492	23,911	62	100	100
Fiji	460	12	175	38	2,974	17	5	41,597	39	29	33,159	62	43	51
New Zealand	17,235	280	266	9	3,199	32	< 2.5	640,845	2	327	79,893	69	100	..
Papua New Guinea	1,050	101	1	72	..	..	..	250,582	536	801	131,011	55	88	32
Solomon Islands	117	..	..	72	2,260	7	21	28,658	(55)	45	89,044	..	94	65
Developed	1,827,874	86	..	6	3,328	26	<2.5	30,234,605	(13)	14,450	10,637	..	100	93
Developing	2,604,477	131	..	53	2,675	14	17	127,153,044	42	39,837	7,580	..	91	71

a. Includes arable and permanent cropland and permanent pasture. **b.** Although water data were obtained from FAO in 2007, they are long-term averages originating from multiple sources and years.
c. Data from 2002. **d.** Data for Serbia include the country of Montenegro (these countries were a single nation from 2003 to 2006).

Food and Water: Technical Notes

DEFINITIONS AND METHODOLOGY

Agricultural Land, in thousand hectares, is the total area of all arable and permanent cropland and permanent pasture. Arable land includes land under annual crops, temporary meadows, kitchen gardens, and land fallow for less than 5 years. Abandoned land resulting from shifting cultivation is not included. Permanent cropland is cultivated with crops that occupy the land for long periods and need not be replanted after each harvest, including land under trees grown for wood or timber. Permanent pasture is the amount of land used permanently (5 years or more) for herbaceous forage crops, either cultivated or growing wild (wild prairie or grazing land). Data on land use are reported by country governments, in surveys distributed by the Food and Agriculture Organization of the United Nations (FAO).

Fertilizer intensity measures the mass in kilograms of the nutrients nitrogen, potash, and phosphate consumed annually per hectare of arable and permanent cropland. Some countries report data based on the fertilizer year; that is, 2003 data actually encompassed July 1, 2003, to June 30, 2004. Data are collected through the FAO fertilizer questionnaire, with support from the Ad Hoc Working Party on Fertilizer Statistics.

Water intensity measures, in cubic meters, the annual volume of water used in the agricultural sector per hectare of arable and permanent cropland. Water use for agriculture is defined as the water withdrawals that are attributed to the agricultural sector, used primarily for irrigation. WRI calculates water intensity by dividing water use data by the extent of agricultural land, using statistics from FAO's AQUASTAT information system in the FAOSTAT database. To estimate agricultural water use, an assessment has to be made both of irrigation water requirements and of water withdrawals for agriculture. AQUASTAT collects its information from a number of sources, including national water resources and irrigation master plans; national yearbooks, statistics, and reports; reports from FAO; international surveys; and surveys made by national or international research centers.

Labor intensity refers to the percentage of the total labor force economically active in agriculture, hunting, forestry, or fishing. The International Labor Organization (ILO) defines economically active as "all persons of either sex who furnish the supply of labour for the production of economic goods and services." The ILO derives the labor estimates from population censuses and sample surveys. When country data are missing, the ILO estimates figures from similar neighboring countries or by using special models of activity rates. FAO provided the annual figures used for these calculations through interpolating and extrapolating the ILO's decennial series.

Calorie Supply, Total refers to the amount of available food per person per day, expressed in kilocalories. **Percent from Animal Products** refers to the percent of available food that is derived from animal products, including all types of meat and fish; animal fats and fish oils; edible offal; milk, butter, cheese, and cream; and eggs and egg products. FAO compiles statistics on apparent food consumption based on supply/utilization accounts (SUAs) maintained in FAOSTAT, its on-line statistical service. FAO derives caloric values by applying food composition factors to the quantities of the processed commodities.

Percent of Population That is Undernourished refers to the proportion of the population with food intake that is continuously below a minimum dietary energy requirement for maintaining a healthy life and carrying out light physical activity. Data represent country averages over a 3-year period from 2002 to 2004. FAO estimates the number of undernourished individuals using calculations of the amount of food available in each country and a measure of inequality in distribution derived from household income/ expenditure surveys. The total undernourished population is calculated as the number of people who fall below a minimum energy requirement, which is estimated by sex and age group based on a reference body weight. This minimum energy requirement varies by country but typically averages between 1,750 and 2,030 kilocalories per person daily.

Fisheries Production data refer to both the nominal catch (capture) and the harvest (aquaculture) of fish, crustaceans, mollusks, aquatic mammals, and other aquatic animals taken for commercial, industrial, recreational, and subsistence purposes from marine, brackish, and inland waters. Statistics for aquatic plants are excluded from country totals. Data include all quantities caught and harvested for both food and feed purposes but exclude catch discarded at sea. Production of fish, crustaceans, and mollusks is expressed in live weight, the nominal weight of the aquatic organisms at the time of harvest. Most fisheries statistics are collected by FAO from questionnaires sent to national fisheries agencies. When these data are missing or considered unreliable, FAO estimates fishery production based on regional fishery organizations, project documents, industry magazines, or statistical interpolations.

Actual Renewable Water Resources gives the maximum theoretical amount of water annually available for each country in cubic kilometers. **Per Capita Actual Renewable Water Resources** gives the maximum theoretical amount of water annually available, on a per person basis, in cubic meters. Actual renewable water resources are defined as the sum of internal renewable resources (IRWR) and external renewable resources (ERWR), taking into consideration the quantity of flow reserved to upstream and downstream countries through formal or informal agreements or treaties and possible reduction of external flow due to upstream water abstraction. IRWR are composed of the average annual flow of rivers and recharge of groundwater (aquifers) generated from endogenous (internal) precipitation. ERWR are the portion of the country's renewable water resources that is not generated within the country, including inflows from upstream countries and a portion of border lakes or rivers.

Per capita water resources data are calculated by WRI using 2000 population estimates (or other appropriate year as indicated in footnotes) from the UN Population Division. Water resources data were compiled by the FAO from a number of sources: national water resources and irrigation master plans; national yearbooks, statistics, and reports; reports from FAO; international surveys; and surveys made by national or international research centers.

The Water Poverty Index (WPI) measures, for a given country, the impact of water scarcity and water provision on human populations. The WPI is a number between 0 and 100, where a low score indicates water poverty and a high score indicates good water provision. The WPI is the culmination of an interdisciplinary approach that combines both the physical quantities relating to water availability and the socioeconomic factors relating to poverty to produce an indicator that addresses the diverse factors that affect water resource management. The index is composed of five component indices: resources, access, capacity, use, and environment.

Use of an Improved Water Source measures the total proportion of the population with access to an improved drinking water source. An improved water source includes any of the following: household connections, public standpipes, boreholes, protected dug wells, protected springs, and rainwater collection. Improved water sources are more likely to provide safe drinking water than unimproved sources but are not a direct measure of "safe" drinking water. Examples of unimproved water sources include unprotected wells and springs, surface water, vendor-provided water, tanker-provided water, and bottled water if it is not consistently available in sufficient quantities. Both urban and rural access are shown here. Any person not inhabiting an area classified as urban is counted in the rural population. The definition of an urban area varies slightly from country to country; the smallest urban agglomerations typically have a population between 2,000 and 10,000 people. Data are collected by the World Health Organization (WHO) and the United

Nations Children's Fund (UNICEF) using a variety of household survey instruments, including the Demographic Health Surveys, Multiple Indicator Cluster Surveys, Living Standards Measurement Studies, and World Health Surveys.

FREQUENCY OF UPDATE BY DATA PROVIDERS

Land, fertilizer, labor, nutrition, and fisheries data are updated annually by FAO. Water resources data are updated intermittently as new values become available. The Water Poverty Index was created by the Center for Ecology and Hydrology in 2002 and has not been updated. The Use of Improved Water Source data set is a Millennium Development Indicator and is updated every 1–3 years to measure a country's progress toward the Millennium Development Goals.

DATA RELIABILITY AND CAUTIONARY NOTES

Agricultural Land: Data are compiled from various sources, so definitions and coverage do not always conform to FAO recommendations and may not always be completely consistent across countries.

Fertilizer: Data are excluded for some countries with a relatively small area of cropland, such as Iceland and Singapore. In these cases, the calculation of fertilizer consumed per hectare of cropland yields an unreliable number.

Labor: Values vary widely among and within countries according to labor scarcity, production technologies, and costs of energy and machinery. The annual figures for total number of agricultural workers were obtained by interpolating and extrapolating past trends (1950–2000), taken from ILO decennial population series. As a result, fluctuations in the labor force may not be captured in annual figures. Labor intensity may be overestimated in countries with substantial fishing or forestry industries, since the total agricultural labor force includes some workers engaged in these activities.

Calorie Supply: Figures shown here represent only the average calorie supply available for the population as a whole and do not necessarily indicate what is actually consumed by individuals. Even if data are used as approximations of per capita consumption, it is important to note that there is considerable variation in consumption among individuals. Food supply data are only as accurate as the underlying production, trade, and utilization data.

Percent of Population That is Undernourished: Food balance sheets provide data for the available food supply, not specific consumption, so waste and other losses are not accounted for. Also, since production statistics are typically available only for major food crops, non-commercial or subsistence-level production is not always included. Crops that are either continuously or selectively harvested, such as cassava and plantains, may not be accurately accounted for, and subsistence hunting of wild game and insects is typically ignored. Data for 2002–2004 are preliminary. In all likelihood, these numbers will change in future revisions as estimates are refined.

Total Fisheries Production: FISHSTAT provides the most extensive global time series of fishery statistics since 1950. However, country-level data are often submitted with a 1–2 year delay. Statistics from smaller artisanal and subsistence fisheries are sparse. While these figures provide a good overview of regional trends, data should be used with caution and supplemented with estimates from regional organizations, academic literature, expert consultations, and trade data. For more information, consult *Fishery Statistics Reliability and Policy Implications,* published by the FAO Fisheries Department.

Water Resources: While AQUASTAT represents the most complete and careful compilation of water resources statistics to date, freshwater data are generally of poor quality. Sources of information vary but are rarely complete. Access to information on water resources is still sometimes restricted for reasons related to political sensitivity at the regional level. Many instances of water scarcity are highly localized and are not reflected in national statistics. In addition, the accuracy and reliability of information vary greatly among regions, countries, and categories of information, as does the year in which the information was gathered. As a result, no consistency can be ensured among countries on the duration and dates of the period of reference. All data should be considered order-of-magnitude estimates.

Water Poverty Index: The WPI focuses public attention on the important issue of water scarcity and allows individuals to quickly understand the degree of water stress in a country. However, the freshwater data used to build this index are incomplete and frequently incomparable across countries; users of this index should always treat these numbers as order-of-magnitude estimates.

Use of an Improved Water Source: These data have become more reliable as WHO and UNICEF shift from provider-based information (national census estimates) to consumer-based information (survey data). Nonetheless, comparisons among countries should be made with care. Definitions of urban and rural are not consistent across countries. The assessment does not account for intermittent or poor quality of water supplies.

SOURCES

Total Agricultural Land, Fertilizer, Labor, and Calorie Supply: Food and Agriculture Organization of the United Nations (FAO). 2007. *FAOSTAT online statistical service.* Rome: FAO. Online at http://faostat.fao.org.

Percent of Population that is Undernourished: Food and Agriculture Organization of the United Nations (FAO), Statistics Division. 2006. *Food Security Statistics, 2006.* Rome: FAO. Online at http://www.fao.org/es/ess/faostat/foodsecurity/index_en.htm.

Fisheries Production: Food and Agriculture Organization of the United Nations (FAO), Fishery Information, Data and Statistics Unit. 2007. *FISHSTAT Plus: Universal Software for Fishery Statistical Time Series,* Version 2.3. Rome: FAO. Online at http://www.fao.org/fi/statist/FISOFT/FISHPLUS.asp.

Renewable Water Resources: Food and Agriculture Organization of the United Nations (FAO), Water Resources, Development and Management Service. 2007. *AQUASTAT Information System on Water and Agriculture: Review of World Water Resources by Country.* Rome: FAO. Online at http://www.fao.org/waicent/faoinfo/agricult/agl/aglw/aquastat/water_res/index.htm.

Water Poverty Index: Lawrence, P., J. Meigh, and C. Sullivan. 2003. *The Water Poverty Index: an International Comparison.* Staffordshire, UK: Keele University. Online at http://www.keele.ac.uk/depts/ec/wpapers/kerp0219.pdf.

Use of Improved Water Source: World Health Organization (WHO) and United Nations Children's Fund (UNICEF). 2006. *Meeting the MDG Drinking Water and Sanitation Target: The Urban and Rural Challenge of the Decade.* Geneva and New York: WHO and UNICEF. Online at http://www.wssinfo.org/pdf/JMP_06.pdf.

Economics and Trade

Source: World Bank

	Gross Domestic Product (GDP) (constant 2000 $US)			GDP Distribution by Sector (percent) in 2005			Adjusted Net Savings (a) as a Percent of Gross National Income (GNI) 2005	Export of Goods and Services as a Percent of GDP 2005	Financial Flows (million curent $ US)		Workers' Remittances as a Percent of Gross National Income 2005
	Total (million dollars) 2005	Per Capita (dollars) 2005	Average Annual Growth Rate (percent) 1995–2005	Agriculture	Industry	Services			Foreign Direct Investment (net inflows) 2005	Official Development Assistance and Aid (b) 2005	
World	36,352,130	5,647	2.9	4	28	69 c	7	..	974,283	106,372	0.6
Asia (excl. Middle East)	9,370,570	2,665	3.0	6	34	59 c	19	30 c	174,810	16,215	2.6
Armenia	3,405	1,129	8.5	21	44	35	15	27	258	193	21.2
Azerbaijan	9,911	1,182	9.9	10	62	28	(38)	57	1,680	223	6.7
Bangladesh	61,357	433	5.3	20	27	53	17	17	803	1,321	6.4
Bhutan	639	1,003	6.9	25	37	38	..	27	1	90	..
Cambodia	5,660	402	8.2	34	27	39	7	65	379	538	3.3
China	1,889,930	1,449	8.8	13	48	40	32	38	79,127	1,757	1.0
Georgia	4,344	971	5.7	17	27	56	11	42	450	310	5.8
India	644,098	588	6.0	18	27	54	19	21	6,598	1,724	3.0
Indonesia	207,740	942	2.2	13	46	41	(2)	34	5,260	2,524	0.7
Japan	4,992,809	39,075	1.0	2	30	68 c	15	13 c	3,214	..	0.0
Kazakhstan	29,957	1,978	6.8	7	40	54	(38)	54	1,975	229	0.4
Korea, Dem People's Rep	..	..		..	..	..	..	..		81	..
Korea, Rep	637,945	13,210	4.5	3	40	56	22	43	4,339	..	0.1
Kyrgyzstan	1,642	319	4.6	34	21	45	(2)	39	43	269	14.0
Lao People's Dem Rep	2,347	396	6.1	45	30	26	(8)	27	28	296	0.0
Malaysia	112,462	4,437	4.1	9	52	40	9	123	3,966	32	1.0
Mongolia	1,235	483	3.8	22	29	49	17	76	182	212	11.5
Myanmar	..	..		..	..	..	..		300	145	..
Nepal	6,347	234	3.9	38	21	41	23	16	3	428	16.5
Pakistan	92,771	596	3.7	22	25	53	1	15	2,183	1,667	4.0
Philippines	93,727	1,129	3.9	14	32	53	21	47	1,132	562	12.4
Singapore	112,215	25,845	4.6	0	34	66	..	243	20,071	..	..
Sri Lanka	19,663	1,002	4.2	17	26	57	12	34	272	1,189	9.2
Tajikistan	1,544	237	6.3	24	32	44	(2)	54	55	241	21.4
Thailand	156,761	2,441	2.5	10	44	46	18	74	4,527	-171	0.7
Turkmenistan	..	..		20	41	39 c	..	65	62	28	..
Uzbekistan	17,906	684	4.5	28	29	43	(48)	40	45	172	..
Viet Nam	44,718	538	6.9	21	41	38	9	70	1,954	1,905	7.8
Europe	10,072,114	13,785	2.4	2	28	70	10	37	570,253	3,007	5.4
Albania	4,794	1,532	5.8	23	22	56	5	22	263	319	16.0
Austria	208,681	25,346	2.2	2	31	68	15	53	9,057	..	1.0
Belarus	18,261	1,868	6.6	10	41	49	..	61	305	54	1.4
Belgium	249,352	23,796	2.2	1	24	75	11	87	31,959	..	1.9
Bosnia and Herzegovina	6,436	1,647	11.7	10	25	65	..	36	299	546	17.5
Bulgaria	16,033	2,071	2.9	10	32	59	5	61	2,614	..	8.0
Croatia	23,156	5,211	3.8	7	31	62	13	47	1,761	125	3.3
Czech Rep	67,836	6,628	2.3	3	37	60	15	72	..	..	0.9
Denmark	171,208	31,612	1.9	2	25	74	14	49	5,238	..	0.4
Estonia	7,890	5,862	6.3	4	29	67	11	84	2,997	..	2.2
Finland	134,891	25,713	3.4	3	30	68	12	39	3,978	..	0.4
France	1,430,131	23,494	2.3	2	21	77	11	26	70,686	..	0.6
Germany	1,971,486	23,906	1.4	1	30	69	10	40	32,034	..	0.2
Greece	142,125	12,799	4.1	5	21	74	8	21	640	..	0.6
Hungary	57,696	5,720	4.4	4	31	65 c	7	66	6,436	..	0.3
Iceland	10,427	35,136	4.0	7	25	68 c	8	32	2,472	..	0.6
Ireland	124,735	29,991	7.6	3	37	60 c	21	83 c	(29,730)	..	0.4
Italy	1,132,825	19,329	1.4	2	27	71	11	26	19,585	..	0.1
Latvia	11,570	5,029	6.8	4	22	74	9	48	730	..	2.4
Lithuania	16,547	4,846	5.6	6	34	61	11	58	1,032	..	2.2
Macedonia, FYR	3,842	1,889	2.0	13	29	58	12	45	100	230	3.9
Moldova, Rep	1,807	430	2.4	17	25	59	14	53	199	192	29.1
Netherlands	403,042	24,696	2.3	2	24	74	14	71	40,416	..	0.3
Norway	184,787	39,969	2.6	2	43	55	15	45	3,285	..	0.2
Poland	198,578	5,203	3.9	5	31	65	8	37	9,602	..	1.3
Portugal	116,287	11,023	2.4	3	25	73	1	29	3,201	..	1.7
Romania	48,864	2,259	2.1	10	35	55	1	33	6,630	..	5.6
Russian Federation	349,853	2,445	4.4	6	38	56	(10)	35	15,151	..	0.5
Serbia (d)	11,047	1,370	..	16	33	51	..	27	1,481	1,132	17.7
Slovakia	25,651	4,762	3.9	4	29	67	2	79	1,908	..	1.0
Slovenia	22,870	11,432	3.9	3	34	63	16	65	541	..	0.8
Spain	678,021	15,623	3.8	3	30	67	12	25	22,789	..	0.7
Sweden	270,308	29,954	2.8	1	28	71	19	49	10,679	..	0.2
Switzerland	258,647	34,778	1.5	1	28	70 e	..	46 c	15,420	..	0.5
Ukraine	45,188	960	3.8	11	34	55	4	54	7,808	410	0.8
United Kingdom	1,619,534	26,891	2.8	1	26	73	7	26	158,801	..	0.3
Middle East & N. Africa	1,270,018	3,319	4.1	..	..	..	..	47	..	29,783	..
Afghanistan	..	..	..	36	25	39	..	12	..	2,775	..
Algeria	69,698	2,121	3.9	9	62	30	(2)	48	1,081	371	2.2
Egypt	120,216	1,624	4.4	15	36	49	(4)	31	5,376	926	5.4
Iran, Islamic Rep	132,621	1,943	4.7	10	45	45	(16)	39	30	104	0.6
Iraq	19,148	..	(2.3) c	9	70	21 e	..	..	..	21,654	..
Israel	127,167	18,367	2.8	..	..	..	..	46	5,585	..	0.7
Jordan	11,415	2,086	4.6	3	30	68	(1)	52	1,532	622	18.6
Kuwait	52,174	20,578	4.1	1	51	49 e	..	68	250	..	..
Lebanon	20,287	5,672	3.0	7	22	71	(13)	19	2,573	243	21.8
Libyan Arab Jamahiriya	43,998	7,517	4.8	..	..	..	..	..	..	24	0.0
Morocco	40,910	1,356	3.6	14	30	56	24	36	1,552	652	8.7
Oman	22,706	8,961	.. c	2	56	42 c	..	57 c	715	31	..
Saudi Arabia	229,098	9,910	2.9	4	59	37 c	..	61	..	26	..
Syrian Arab Rep	22,369	1,175	2.9	23	35	41	(39)	37	427	78	3.1
Tunisia	24,194	2,412	4.9	12	29	60	9	48	723	377	4.8
Turkey	246,224	3,417	3.2	12	24	65	8	27	9,805	464	0.2
United Arab Emirates	104,151	22,975	6.3	2	56	42	..	94	..	..	..
Yemen	11,121	530	4.4	13	41	45	..	46	(266)	336	10.2

	Gross Domestic Product (GDP) (constant 2000 $US)			GDP Distribution by Sector (percent) in 2005			Adjusted Net Savings (a) as a Percent of Gross National Income (GNI) 2005	Export of Goods and Services as a Percent of GDP 2005	Financial Flows (million current $US)		Workers' Remittances as a Percent of Gross National Income 2005
	Total (million dollars) 2005	Per Capita (dollars) 2005	Average Annual Growth Rate (percent) 1995–2005	Agriculture	Industry	Services			Foreign Direct Investment (net inflows) 2005	Official Development Assistance and Aid (b) 2005	
Sub-Saharan Africa	423,016 f	568	3.6	17	34	49	(6)	34	16,582	30,686	..
Angola	14,935	937	7.1	7	74	19	(39)	74	(1,304)	442	
Benin	2,754	326	4.7	32	13	54	3	14	21	349	1.5
Botswana	8,204	4,649	7.1	2	53	44	..	51	279	71	1.3
Burkina Faso	3,334	252	4.5	31	20	50	..	9	20	660	1.0
Burundi	790	105	0.9	35	20	45	(6)	9	1	365	..
Cameroon	12,057	739	4.3	41	14	45	(3)	23	18	414	0.1
Central African Rep	918	227	0.9	54	21	25	7	..	6	95	..
Chad	2,600	267	7.7	23	51	26	(58)	59	705	380	..
Congo	3,987	997	3.1	6	46	48	(47)	82	724	1,449	0.3
Congo, Dem Rep	5,236	91	(0.7)	46	25	29	1	32	402	1,828	..
Côte d'Ivoire	10,468	577	..	23	26	51	2	50	266	119	1.0
Equatorial Guinea	2,019	4,101	20.3 c	7	89	4 e	..	..	1,860	39	..
Eritrea	757	172	..	23	23	55	3	9	11	355	..
Ethiopia	10,018	141	..	48	13	39	12	16	265	1,937	1.6
Gabon	5,375	3,884	1.2	8	58	35	..	59	300	54	0.1
Gambia	509	335	4.2	33	13	54	8	45	52	58	13.1
Ghana	6,357	287	4.5	38	23	39	13	36	107	1,120	1.0
Guinea	3,621	385	3.6	25	36	39	(6)	26	102	182	1.1
Guinea-Bissau	213	135	(1.2)	60	12	28	1	38	10	79	9.9
Kenya	15,151	442	2.5	27	19	54	8	27	21	768	2.8
Lesotho	988	550	2.3	17	41	41	19	48	92	69	19.2
Liberia	444	135	13.0	64	15	21	..	37	194	236	..
Madagascar	4,340	233	2.8	28	16	56	6	26	29	929	0.1
Malawi	1,986	154	2.7	35	19	46	(11)	27	3	575	0.0
Mali	3,294	244	6.1	37	24	39	5	26	159	692	3.0
Mauritania	1,317	429	3.1	24	29	47	(43)	36	115	190	0.1
Mozambique	5,773	292	8.4	22	30	48	(3)	33	108	1,286	0.9
Namibia	4,231	2,083	3.9	10	32	58	34	46	..	123	0.3
Niger	2,184	156	3.3	40	17	43 e	1	15	12	515	1.8
Nigeria	60,413	459	4.1	23	57	20	(31)	53	2,013	6,437	4.5
Rwanda	2,351	260	7.2	42	21	37	12	11	8	576	1.0
Senegal	5,521	474	4.4	18	19	63	9	27	54	689	7.8
Sierra Leone	1,203	218	5.4	46	24	30	(3)	24	59	343	0.2
Somalia	..	..	..	..	..	..	..	..	24	236	..
South Africa	159,695	3,406	3.1	3	30	67	0	27	6,257	700	0.3
Sudan	16,749	462	6.2	34	30	37	(10)	18	2,305	1,829	4.4
Tanzania, United Rep	12,646	330	..	45	18	38	3	17	473	1,505	0.1
Togo	1,502	244	..	42	23	35	0	34	3	87	6.9
Uganda	7,786	270	5.9	33	25	43	1	13	257	1,198	6.0
Zambia	4,090	350	3.5	19	25	56	(5)	16	259	945	..
Zimbabwe	5,547	426	(3.3)	18	23	59	(9)	43	103	368	..
North America	11,855,976	36,076	3.2	1	22	77 c	3	12 c	143,900	..	0.0
Canada	809,546	25,064	3.5	..	..	..	5	39 c	34,146	..	..
United States	11,046,430	37,267	3.2	1	22	77 c	3	10 c	109,754	..	0.0
C. America & Caribbean	767,298	4,698	2.2	5	26	69	4	31	25,910	**2,923**	5.8
Belize	1,082	3,708	6.3	14	18	68	0	55	126	13	4.4
Costa Rica	19,470	4,499	4.5	9	30	62	16	49	861	30	2.1
Cuba	..	..	..	..	..	..	..	..	..	88	
Dominican Rep	23,396	2,630	5.3	12	26	62	8	34	1,023	77	12.4
El Salvador	14,634	2,127	2.6	10	30	60	2	27	518	199	16.9
Guatemala	21,851	1,734	3.2	23	19	58	3	16	208	254	10.0
Haiti	3,701	434	0.7	28	17	55 e	..	..	10	515	25.4
Honduras	7,098	985	3.1	14	31	55	23	41	464	681	22.3
Jamaica	8,736	3,291	0.9	6	33	61	14	41	683	36	19.8
Mexico	636,268	6,172	3.4	4	26	70	4	30	18,772	189	2.9
Nicaragua	4,577	889	3.8	19	28	53	5	28	241	740	12.3
Panama	14,245	4,408	4.0	8	16	76	2	69	1,027	20	0.8
Trinidad and Tobago	11,856	9,083	6.5	1	60	40	..	..	1,100	-2	0.6
South America	1,434,828	3,829	1.7	9	38	54	3	24	44,660	2,440	3.1
Argentina	313,626	8,094	0.7	9	36	55	4	25	4,730	100	0.2
Bolivia	9,742	1,061	2.9	15	32	53	(20)	36	(277)	583	3.6
Brazil	670,450	3,597	2.1	8	38	54	8	17	15,193	192	0.5
Chile	93,216	5,721	3.7	6	47	48	(6)	42	6,667	152	0.0
Colombia	99,130	2,174	1.8	13	34	53	1	22	10,375	511	3.2
Ecuador	20,496	1,549	2.7	7	46	48	(14)	31	1,646	210	5.9
Guyana	736	980	1.3	31	25	45	(4)	88	77	137	26.1
Paraguay	8,030	1,361	0.8	22	19	59	10	47	64	51	4.4
Peru	65,353	2,337	2.9	7	35	58	5	25	2,519	398	1.9
Suriname	1,147	2,554	3.0	11	24	65	..	41	..	44	0.4
Uruguay	21,632	6,246	0.0	9	31	60	1	30	711	15	0.1
Venezuela	131,270	4,939	0.4	5	52	44 e	(7)	41	2,957	49	0.1
Oceania	538,269	16,566	3.3	4	27	69 c	6	20 c	(32,397)	858	0.6
Australia	468,369	23,039	3.6	3	27	70 c	4	18 c	(34,420)	..	0.4
Fiji	1,863	2,198	2.3	16	25	59	39	..	(4)	64	0.9
New Zealand	62,704	15,298	3.2	..	..	..	15	29 c	1,979	..	0.7
Papua New Guinea	3,783	643	0.9	42	39	19 c	..	..	34	266	..
Solomon Islands	323	677	(1.9)	..	..	..	..	48 c	(1)	198	0.7
High Income	28,546,090 f	28,612	2.5	2	26	72 c	8	..	693,488	..	1.0
Middle Income	6,681,480 f	2,196	5.2	10	39	51	11	37	258,999	43,772	16.0
Low Income	1,132,382 f	494	4.4	21	29	50	10	26	21,796	43,216	10.4

a. Adjusted net savings, formerly called genuine savings, measures the "true" rate of savings by taking into account human capital, depletion of natural resources, and damages from pollution.
b. Represents inflows of development assistance and aid. **c.** 2004 value. **d.** Data for Serbia include the country of Montenegro (these countries were a single nation from 2003 to 2006). **e.** 2003 value.
f. Regional totals calculated by the World Bank.

Economics and Trade: Technical Notes

DEFINITIONS AND METHODOLOGY

Gross Domestic Product (GDP) is the sum of the value added by all producers in an economy. Data are expressed in 2000 constant U.S. dollars. Currencies are converted to dollars using the International Monetary Fund's (IMF) average official exchange rate for 2005. Gross domestic product estimates at purchaser values (market prices) include the value added in the agriculture, industry, and service sectors, plus taxes and minus subsidies not included in the final value of the products. It is calculated without making deductions for depreciation of fabricated assets or for depletion of natural resources. To obtain comparable series of constant price data, the World Bank rescales GDP and value added by industrial origin to a common reference year, currently 2000.

National accounts indicators for most developing countries are collected from national statistical organizations and central banks by visiting and resident World Bank missions. The data for high-income economies are obtained from the Organisation for Economic Co-operation and Development (OECD) data files (see the OECD's monthly Main Economic Indicators). The United Nations Statistics Division publishes detailed national accounts for UN member countries in *National Accounts Statistics: Main Aggregates and Detailed Tables* and updates in the Monthly Bulletin of Statistics.

Gross Domestic Product per Capita is the total annual output of a country's economy divided by the mid-year population. Values are obtained directly from the World Bank.

Average Annual Growth Rate of GDP is the average percentage growth of a country or region's economy for each year between (and including) 1995 and 2005. WRI assumes compound growth and uses the least-squares method to calculate average annual percent growth of GDP in 2000 US dollars. The least squares method works by fitting a trend line to the natural logarithm of annual GDP values. The slope *(m)* of this trend line is used to calculate the annual growth rate *(r)* using the equation $r = e^m - 1$. The growth rate is an average rate that is representative of the available observations over the entire period. It does not necessarily match the actual growth rate between any two periods.

Distribution of GDP by Sector is the percent of total output of goods and services that is a result of value added by a given sector. Value added is the net output of a sector after adding up all outputs and subtracting intermediate inputs. The industrial origin of value added is determined by the International Standard Industrial Classification (ISIC), a classification system for economic activity developed and maintained by the United Nations. **Agriculture** corresponds to ISIC divisions 1–5 and includes forestry and fishing. **Industry** corresponds to ISIC divisions 10–45 and includes manufacturing (ISIC divisions 15–37). It comprises value added in mining, manufacturing, construction, electricity, water, and gas. **Services** corresponds to ISIC divisions 50–99 and includes value added in wholesale and retail trade (including hotels and restaurants); transport; and government, financial, professional, and personal services such as education, health care, and real estate services. Since this value is calculated as total GDP less the portion from agriculture and industry, any discrepancies that may occur in the GDP distribution by sector calculation will appear here.

Adjusted Net Savings (previously "genuine savings") is equal to a nation's private and public net savings (gross domestic product plus net income and transfers from abroad minus consumption of fixed capital) plus education expenditure, minus energy depletion, mineral depletion, net forest depletion, and carbon dioxide and particulate emissions damage. Adjusted Net Savings is an indicator of sustainability; persistently negative rates of savings must lead, eventually, to declining well-being. It measures the true rate of savings in an economy after taking into account investments in human capital, depletion of natural resources, and damage caused by pollution. Data are shown as a percent of gross national income (GNI).

Exports of Goods and Services represents the value of all goods and other market services provided to the rest of the world. Exports include the value of merchandise, freight, insurance, transport, travel, royalties, license fees, and other services, such as communication, construction, financial, information, business, personal, and government services. They exclude labor and property income (formerly called factor services) as well as transfer payments. Data are presented in millions of current US dollars. WRI calculates **Exports of Goods and Services as a Percent of GDP** by dividing total exports by GDP figures provided by the World Bank.

Foreign Direct Investment (FDI) is private investment in a foreign economy to obtain a lasting management interest (10 percent or more of voting stock) in an enterprise. The IMF defines FDI in its manual *Balance of Payments* as the sum of equity investment, reinvestment of earnings, and inter-company loans between parent corporations and foreign affiliates. Data are in million current US dollars. FDI became the dominant means for funds transfer from rich to poor countries after the liberalization of global financial markets in the 1970s and accounts for more than half of financial flows to developing countries. Data are based on balance of payments information reported by the IMF, supplemented by data from the OECD and official national sources. Negative numbers mean that outflows of investment by foreign countries into a particular country (or reinvestment of profits outside the country) exceed inflows.

Official Development Assistance (ODA) and Aid measures the amount of ODA received by a country. It includes concessions by governments and international institutions to developing countries to promote economic development and welfare. The data shown here record the actual receipts of financial resources or of goods or services valued at the cost to the donor, less any repayments of loan principal during the same period. Values are reported in million current US dollars. Grants by official agencies of the members of the Development Assistance Committee (DAC) of the OECD are included, as are loans with a grant element of at least 25 percent as well as technical cooperation and assistance. The data on development assistance are compiled by DAC and published in its annual statistical report, *Geographical Distribution of Financial Flows to Aid Recipients*, and in the DAC annual *Development Co-operation Report*.

WRI calculates **Workers' Remittances as a Percent of GNI** by dividing remittances by gross national income. Both values are originally in current US dollars, and the quotient is expressed as a percentage. Remittances measure the transfer of earned wages by migrant workers to their home country. They include all transfers by migrants who are employed or intend to remain employed for more than a year in another economy in which they are considered residents. Transfers made by self-employed workers are not considered remittances, as this indicator attempts to describe money raised through labor rather than entrepreneurial activity. Since 1980, recorded remittance receipts to low- and middle-income countries have increased sixfold. Data are collected from the IMF's *Balance of Payments Yearbook*. The IMF data are supplemented by World Bank staff estimates for missing data for countries where workers' remittances are important.

FREQUENCY OF UPDATE BY DATA PROVIDERS

The World Bank publishes *World Development Indicators* each year in April. Data for this table were taken from the 2007 online edition, which typically includes values through 2005.

DATA RELIABILITY AND CAUTIONARY NOTES

Gross Domestic Product: The World Bank produces the most reliable global GDP estimates available. However, informal economic activities sometimes pose a measurement problem, especially in developing countries, where much economic activity may go unrecorded. Obtaining a complete picture of the economy requires estimating household outputs produced for local sale and home use, barter exchanges, and illicit or deliberately unreported activity. Technical improvements and growth in the services sector are both particularly difficult to measure. How consistent and complete such estimates will be depends on the skill and methods of the compiling statisticians and the resources available to them. Because values are measured in US dollars, these data do not account for differences in purchasing power among countries.

Adjusted Net Savings: The data that were used to calculate adjusted net savings are mostly from official sources and are generally considered to be reliable. However, due to methodological or data limitations, the calculation omits several important resources including soils, fish, water resources, and water and air pollutants.

Foreign Direct Investment: Because of the multiplicity of sources, definitions, and reporting methods, data may not be comparable across countries. (Data do not include capital raised locally, which has become an important source of financing in some developing countries.) In addition, data only capture cross-border investment flows when equity participation is involved and thus omit non-equity cross-border transactions. For a more detailed discussion, please refer to the World Bank's World Debt Tables 1993–1994, volume 1, chapter 3.

Official Development Assistance: Data are not directly comparable, since the ODA figures do not distinguish among different types of aid, which can affect individual economies in different ways. Because data are based on donor-country reports, they may not match aid receipts recorded in developing and transition economies. According to the World Bank, "the nominal values used here may overstate the real value of aid to the recipient." The purchasing power of foreign aid can decrease when price and exchange rates fluctuate, grants are tied to specific policy restrictions, or technical assistance pays for the work of firms in other countries.

Worker Remittances: Data on worker remittances are reported by the countries receiving the transfers. Variations in reporting standards do exist, particularly in determining the residency status of a worker. This may lead to some differences across countries.

SOURCES

Development Data Group, World Bank. 2007. 2007 *World Development Indicators.* Washington, DC: World Bank. Online at http://go.worldbank.org/B53SONGPA0.

Institutions and Governance

Sources: Freedom House, United Nations Human Settlements Programme, World Bank, Privacy International, International Telecommunications Union, Transparency International

	Freedom Indices (1–7, 1=most free)		Regulatory Barriers to Registering Property, 2007		Government Expenditures (as a percent of gross domestic product)			Press Freedom Index	Access to Information — Status of Freedom of Information Legislation	Digital Access Index	Corruption Perceptions Index
	Civil Liberties Index 2006	Political Rights Index 2006	Average Number of Days to Register	Average Cost to Register (percent of property value)	Public Health 2004	Public Education (a) 2000-2005	Military 2005	(0–100, 0= most free) 2006	2004	(1–100, 100= most access) 2002	(0–10, 10= least corrupt) 2006
World	..	..	..	..	5.9	4.7	2.5	..	..	..	..
Asia (excl. Middle East)	..	..	..	..	4.3	..	1.5	..	..	..	..
Armenia	4	5	4	0.4	1.4	3.2	2.7	64	Law Enacted	30	2.9
Azerbaijan	5	6	61	0.2	0.9	2.5	2.1	73	Pending Effort	24	2.4
Bangladesh	4	4	425	10.3	0.9	2.5	1.1	68	Pending Effort	18	2.0
Bhutan	5	6	64	0	3.0	5.6	..	65	..	13	6.0
Cambodia	5	6	56	4.4	1.7	1.9	1.8	61	..	17	2.1
China	6	7	29	3.6	1.8	..	2.0	83	..	43	3.3
Georgia	3	3	5	0.1	1.5	2.9	3.1	57	Law Enacted	37	2.8
India	3	2	62	7.7	0.9	3.7	2.9	37	Law Enacted	32	3.3
Indonesia	3	2	42	10.5	1.0	0.9	0.9	58	Pending Effort	34	2.4
Japan	2	1	14	5	6.3	3.7	1.0	20	Law Enacted	75	7.6
Kazakhstan	5	6	52	0.9	2.3	2.3	1.1	75	..	41	2.6
Korea, Dem People's Rep	7	7	..	..	3.0	..	..	97	..	..	..
Korea, Rep	2	1	11	6.3	2.9	4.6	2.6	30	Law Enacted	82	5.1
Kyrgyzstan	4	5	4	4.1	2.3	4.4	2.8 b	64	..	32	2.2
Lao People's Dem Rep	6	7	135	4.2	0.8	2.3	..	81	..	15	2.6
Malaysia	4	4	144	2.4	2.2	8.0	1.9	65	..	57	5.0
Mongolia	2	2	11	2.2	4.0	5.3	1.7 b	34	..	35	2.8
Myanmar	7	7	..	..	0.3	1.3	..	96	..	17	1.9
Nepal	4	5	5	6.4	1.5	3.4	2.0	77	Pending Effort	19	2.5
Pakistan	5	6	50	5.3	0.4	2.3	3.4	61	Law Enacted	24	2.2
Philippines	3	3	33	4.2	1.4	3.2	0.8	40	Pending Effort	43	2.5
Singapore	4	5	9	2.8	1.3	3.7	4.7	66	..	75	9.4
Sri Lanka	4	4	83	5.1	2.0	..	2.7	58	Pending Effort	38	3.1
Tajikistan	5	6	37	1.9	1.0	3.5	2.2 b	76	Law Enacted	21	2.2
Thailand	4	7	2	6.3	2.3	4.2	1.1	50	Law Enacted	48	3.6
Turkmenistan	7	7	..	..	3.3	..	..	96	..	37	2.2
Uzbekistan	7	7	78	1.4	2.4	..	..	90	Law Enacted	31	2.1
Viet Nam	5	7	67	1.2	1.5	..	..	79	..	31	2.6
Europe	..	..	..	..	7.0	5.3	1.9	..	..	..	..
Albania	3	3	47	3.5	3.0	2.9	1.4	50	Law Enacted	39	2.6
Austria	1	1	32	4.5	7.8	5.5	0.7	21	Law Enacted	75	8.6
Belarus	6	7	231	0.1	4.6	6.0	1.2	88	..	49	2.1
Belgium	1	1	132	12.7	6.9	6.2	1.2	11	Law Enacted	74	7.3
Bosnia and Herzegovina	3	3	331	5	4.1	..	1.8	45	Law Enacted	46	2.9
Bulgaria	2	1	19	2.3	4.6	4.2	2.4	34	Law Enacted	53	4.0
Croatia	2	2	174	5	6.2	4.7	1.6	39	Law Enacted	59	3.4
Czech Rep	1	1	123	3	6.5	4.5	1.8	20	Law Enacted	66	4.8
Denmark	1	1	42	0.6	7.1	8.4	1.4	10	Law Enacted	83	9.5
Estonia	1	1	51	0.5	4.0	5.7	1.6	16	Law Enacted	67	6.7
Finland	1	1	14	4	5.7	6.5	1.2	9	Law Enacted	79	9.6
France	1	1	123	6.1	8.2	5.9	2.5	21	Law Enacted	72	7.4
Germany	1	1	40	5.2	8.2	4.7	1.4	16	Pending Effort	74	8.0
Greece	2	1	23	4	4.2	4.0	4.5	28	Law Enacted	66	4.4
Hungary	1	1	63	11	5.7	5.9	1.3	21	Law Enacted	63	5.2
Iceland	1	1	4	2.4	8.3	8.1	0.0	9	Law Enacted	82	9.6
Ireland	1	1	38	10.2	5.7	4.5	0.6	15	Law Enacted	69	7.4
Italy	1	1	27	0.6	6.5	4.9	1.8	35	Law Enacted	72	4.9
Latvia	1	1	54	2	4.0	5.3	1.7	19	Law Enacted	54	4.7
Lithuania	1	1	3	0.7	4.9	5.2	1.8	18	Law Enacted	56	4.8
Macedonia, FYR	3	3	98	3.5	5.7	3.4	2.2	49	Pending Effort	48	2.7
Moldova, Rep	4	3	48	0.9	4.2	4.3	0.3	65	Law Enacted	37	3.2
Netherlands	1	1	5	6.2	5.7	5.3	1.6	11	Law Enacted	79	8.7
Norway	1	1	3	2.5	8.1	7.7	1.6	10	Law Enacted	79	8.8
Poland	1	1	197	0.5	4.3	5.6	1.8	21	Law Enacted	59	3.7
Portugal	1	1	42	7.4	7.0	5.9	2.1	14	Law Enacted	65	6.6
Romania	2	2	150	2.8	3.4	3.6	2.1	44	Law Enacted	48	3.1
Russian Federation	5	6	52	0.3	3.7	3.7	3.7	72	Pending Effort	50	2.5
Serbia (c)	2	3	..	..	7.3	3.3	2.7	40	Pending Effort	45	3.0
Slovakia	1	1	17	0.1	5.3	4.4	1.8	20	Law Enacted	59	4.7
Slovenia	1	1	391	2	6.6	6.0	1.7	20	Law Enacted	72	6.4
Spain	1	1	18	7.1	5.7	4.3	1.0	21	Law Enacted	67	6.8
Sweden	1	1	2	3	7.7	7.5	1.6	10	Law Enacted	85	9.2
Switzerland	1	1	16	0.4	6.7	6.1	1.0	11	Pending Effort	76	9.1
Ukraine	2	3	93	3.3	3.7	6.4	2.4	53	Law Enacted	43	2.8
United Kingdom	1	1	21	4.1	7.0	5.5	2.6	19	Law Enacted	77	8.6
Middle East & N. Africa	..	..	..	..	3.5	..	4.8	..	..	..	..
Afghanistan	5	5	250	7	0.7	..	..	69	..	..	..
Algeria	5	6	51	7.5	2.6	..	2.8	61	..	37	3.1
Egypt	5	6	193	1	2.2	..	2.8	61	..	40	3.3
Iran, Islamic Rep	6	6	36	10.6	3.2	4.7	4.5	84	..	43	2.7
Iraq	6	6	8	6.3	4.2	..	..	71	..	..	1.9
Israel	2	1	144	7.5	6.1	7.3	7.9	28	Law Enacted	70	5.9
Jordan	4	5	22	10	4.7	..	7.7	61	..	45	5.3
Kuwait	4	4	55	0.5	2.2	5.1	5.7	56	..	51	4.8
Lebanon	4	5	25	5.9	3.2	2.6	3.8 b	60	..	48	3.6
Libyan Arab Jamahiriya	7	7	..	..	2.8	..	1.9 b	96	..	42	2.7
Morocco	4	5	47	4.9	1.7	6.7	4.3	61	..	33	3.2
Oman	5	6	16	3	2.4	3.6	12.2 b	70	..	43	5.4
Saudi Arabia	6	7	4	0	2.5	6.8	8.2	79	..	44	3.3
Syrian Arab Rep	6	7	34	28.1	2.2	..	6.2 b	84	..	28	2.9
Tunisia	5	6	49	6.1	..	8.1	1.5	83	..	41	4.6
Turkey	3	3	6	3.1	5.6	4.0	3.2	48	Law Enacted	48	3.8
United Arab Emirates	5	6	6	2	2.0	1.3	1.9	65	..	64	6.2
Yemen	5	5	21	3.9	1.9	9.6	5.6	81	..	18	2.6

DATA TABLE 4: INSTITUTIONS AND GOVERNANCE

	Freedom Indices (1–7, 1=most free)		Regulatory Barriers to Registering Property, 2007		Government Expenditures (as a percent of gross domestic product)			Press Freedom Index (0–100, 0= most free) 2006	Status of Freedom of Information Legislation 2004	Digital Access Index (1–100, 100= most access) 2002	Corruption Perceptions Index (0–10, 10= least corrupt) 2006
	Civil Liberties Index 2006	Political Rights Index 2006	Average Number of Days to Register	Average Cost to Register (percent of property value)	Public Health 2004	Public Education {a} 2000-2005	Military 2005				
Sub-Saharan Africa	..	..	..	..	2.6	..	1.6 b	..	..	..	..
Angola	5	6	334	11.1	1.5	2.6	5.0	65	Pending Effort	11	2.2
Benin	2	2	118	11.4	2.5	3.5	..	30		12	2.5
Botswana	2	2	30	5	4.0	10.7	2.5	35	Pending Effort	43	5.6
Burkina Faso	3	5	182	12.2	3.3	4.7	1.5	38	..	8	3.2
Burundi	5	4	94	11.5	0.8	5.1	6.5 b	74		10	2.4
Cameroon	6	6	93	17.8	1.5	1.8	1.3	65	..	16	2.3
Central African Rep	4	5	69	11.7	1.5	..	1.1	61	..	10	2.4
Chad	6	6	44	21.2	1.5	2.1	0.9	73	..	10	2.0
Congo	5	6	137	27.3	1.2	2.2	..	51	..	17	2.2
Congo, Dem Rep	6	5	57	9.4	1.1	..	2.1	81	..	12	2.0
Côte d'Ivoire	6	7	62	16.9	0.9	4.6	..	65	..	13	2.1
Equatorial Guinea	6	7	23	6.3	1.2	0.6	..	88	..	20	2.1
Eritrea	6	7	101	5.3	1.8	5.4	..	91	..	13	2.9
Ethiopia	5	5	43	7.5	2.7	5.0	3.1	75	Pending Effort	10	2.4
Gabon	4	6	60	10.5	3.1	3.9	1.4	67	..	34	3.0
Gambia	4	5	371	7.6	1.8	2.0	0.3	73	..	13	2.5
Ghana	2	1	34	1.3	2.8	5.4	0.7	28	Pending Effort	16	3.3
Guinea	5	6	104	15.3	0.7	2.0	..	67	..	10	1.9
Guinea-Bissau	4	4	211	5.4	1.3	..	..	47	..	10	..
Kenya	3	3	64	4.2	1.8	6.7	1.5	58	Pending Effort	19	2.2
Lesotho	3	2	101	8.2	5.5	13.4	2.4	42	Pending Effort	19	3.2
Liberia	4	3	50	14.9	3.6	..	..	64	..	..	..
Madagascar	3	4	134	11.6	1.8	3.2	..	49	..	15	3.1
Malawi	3	4	88	3.3	9.6	5.8	..	55	Pending Effort	15	2.7
Mali	2	2	29	21.2	3.2	4.3	1.9	24	..	9	2.8
Mauritania	4	5	49	5.2	2.0	2.3	1.0	57	..	14	3.1
Mozambique	4	3	42	8.1	2.7	3.7	1.4	43	Pending Effort	12	2.8
Namibia	2	2	23	9.9	4.7	6.9	3.0	30	Pending Effort	39	4.1
Niger	3	3	32	9	2.2	2.3	1.1 b	56	..	4	2.3
Nigeria	4	4	82	22.2	1.4	..	0.9	54	Pending Effort	15	2.2
Rwanda	5	6	371	9.4	4.3	3.8	2.2	85	..	15	2.5
Senegal	3	2	114	19.5	2.4	5.4	1.5	44	..	14	3.3
Sierra Leone	3	4	235	14.9	1.9	3.8	1.1	59	..	10	2.2
Somalia	7	7	..	..	..	..	..	83		13	..
South Africa	2	2	24	8.8	3.5	5.4	1.4	27	Law Enacted	45	4.6
Sudan	7	7	9	3.2	1.5	..	..	85	..	13	2.0
Tanzania, United Rep	3	4	119	5.3	1.7	..	1.1	50	Pending Effort	15	2.9
Togo	5	6	295	13.9	1.1	2.6	1.5	78	..	18	2.4
Uganda	4	5	227	4.6	2.5	5.2	2.5 b	52	Pending Effort	17	2.7
Zambia	4	3	70	9.6	3.4	2.0	..	64	Pending Effort	17	2.6
Zimbabwe	6	7	30	25	3.5	4.6	3.4 b	90	Law Enacted	29	2.4
North America	..	..	..	..	6.9	5.9	3.9	..		..	..
Canada	1	1	17	1.8	6.8	5.2	1.1	18	Law Enacted	78	8.5
United States	1	1	12	0.5	6.9	5.9	4.1	16	Law Enacted	78	7.3
C. America & Caribbean	..	..	..	..	3.1	5.5	0.4	..		..	..
Belize	2	1	60	4.7	2.7	5.4	..	21	Law Enacted	47	3.5
Costa Rica	1	1	21	3.3	5.1	4.9	..	18	..	52	4.1
Cuba	7	7	..	..	5.5	9.8	..	96	..	38	3.5
Dominican Rep	2	2	60	5.1	1.9	1.8	0.6	37	Pending Effort	42	2.8
El Salvador	3	2	31	3.6	3.5	2.8	0.6	43	Pending Effort	38	4.0
Guatemala	4	3	30	1	2.3	..	0.4	58	Pending Effort	38	2.6
Haiti	5	4	405	6.5	2.9	..	..	68		15	1.8
Honduras	3	3	24	5.8	4.0	..	0.6	52	Pending Effort	29	2.5
Jamaica	3	2	54	13.5	2.8	4.5	0.7	17	Law Enacted	53	3.7
Mexico	3	2	74	4.7	3.0	5.8	0.4	48	Law Enacted	50	3.3
Nicaragua	3	3	124	3.5	3.9	3.1	0.7	44	Pending Effort	19	2.6
Panama	2	1	44	2.4	5.2	3.8	..	43	Law Enacted	47	3.1
Trinidad and Tobago	2	2	162	7	1.4	4.2	..	26	Law Enacted	53	3.2
South America	..	..	..	..	4.2	4.1	1.7	..		..	..
Argentina	2	2	65	7.6	4.3	3.5	1.0	45	Pending Effort	53	2.9
Bolivia	3	3	92	4.9	4.1	6.4	1.9	33	Pending Effort	38	2.7
Brazil	2	2	45	2.8	4.8	4.1	1.6	39	Pending Effort	50	3.3
Chile	1	1	31	1.3	2.9	3.7	3.8	26	Pending Effort	58	7.3
Colombia	3	3	23	2.5	6.7	4.8	3.7	61	Law Enacted	45	3.9
Ecuador	3	3	17	3	2.2	..	2.4	41	Law Enacted	41	2.3
Guyana	3	2	34	4.5	4.4	8.5	..	27	..	43	2.5
Paraguay	3	3	46	3.5	2.6	4.3	0.8	57	Pending Effort	39	2.6
Peru	3	2	33	3.3	1.9	2.4	1.2	39	Pending Effort	44	3.0
Suriname	2	2	193	13.7	3.6	..	..	23	..	46	3.0
Uruguay	1	1	66	7.1	3.6	2.2	1.4	28	Pending Effort	54	6.4
Venezuela	4	4	47	2.2	2.0	..	1.1	72	..	47	2.3
Oceania	..	..	..	..	6.4	5.0	1.7	..		..	..
Australia	1	1	5	4.9	6.5	4.8	1.8	19	Law Enacted	74	8.7
Fiji	4	6	48	12	2.9	6.4	1.2 b	28	Pending Effort	43	..
New Zealand	1	1	2	0.1	6.5	6.8	1.0	13	Law Enacted	72	9.6
Papua New Guinea	3	3	72	5.1	3.0	..	0.5	29	Pending Effort	26	2.4
Solomon Islands	3	4	297	4.9	5.6	..	..	30	..	17	..

a. May include subsidies for private or religious schools. Data are for the most recent year available between 2000 and 2005. b. 2004 value. c. Data for Serbia include the country of Montenegro.

Key to Indices:

Freedom Indices (Freedom House): Scaled from 1 to 7, 1 represents a completely free nation, 7 represents a nation with virtually no freedom.

Press Freedom Index (Freedom House): Scaled from 1 to 100. 1–30 = Free, 31–60 = Partly Free, 61–100 = Not Free.

Status of Freedom of Information Legislation (Privacy International): Legislation is classified as either enacted or pending.

".." indicates that either no data are available for this country, or, more likely, that FOI legislation does not exist.

Digital Access Index (International Telecommunications Union): Scaled from 0 to 100, 100 represents highest access.

Corruption Perceptions Index (Transparency International): Scaled from 0 (most corrupt) to 10 (least corrupt).

DATA TABLE 4: INSTITUTIONS AND GOVERNANCE

Institutions and Governance: Technical Notes

DEFINITIONS AND METHODOLOGY

Freedom Indices, compiled by the nonprofit organization Freedom House, range from 1 to 7, with 1 representing the most free and 7 representing the least free. To determine each rating, researchers answer a series of survey questions, making small adjustments for factors such as extreme violence. Freedom House notes that a poor rating for a country "is not necessarily a comment on the intentions of the government, but may indicate real restrictions on liberty caused by non-governmental terror."

The **Civil Liberties Index** measures freedom of expression, assembly, association, and religion. Countries with a rating of 1 generally have an established and equitable rule of law with free economic activity. A rating of 2 indicates some deficiencies, while a rating of 3, 4, or 5 indicates varying degrees of censorship, political terror, and prevention of free association. Countries with a rating of 6 experience severely restricted freedom of expression and association coupled with political terror (for example, political prisoners). A rating of 7 indicates virtually no freedom.

The **Political Rights Index** measures the degree of freedom in the electoral process, political pluralism and participation, and functioning of government. A rating of 1 indicates free and fair elections, political competition, and autonomy for all citizens, including minority groups. A rating of 2 indicates some corruption, violence, political discrimination, and military influence. These same factors play a progressively larger role in countries with a ranking of 3, 4, or 5. Countries and territories with political rights rated 6 are ruled by military juntas, one-party dictatorships, religious hierarchies, or autocrats. A rating of 7 indicates nonexistent political rights due to extremely oppressive regimes, civil war, extreme violence, or warlord rule.

Regulatory Barriers to Registering Property, published by the World Bank's *Doing Business* database, are compiled via survey in conjunction with academic advisers, using a simple business case to ensure comparability across countries and over time. Surveys are administered through more than 5,000 local experts, including lawyers, business consultants, accountants, government officials, and other professionals routinely administering or advising on legal and regulatory requirements. Broadly speaking, higher values here represent regulatory environments that stifle the formalization of property rights.

Average Number of Days to Register measures the time, in calendar days, necessary for a business to complete the legal and bureaucratic procedures required for registering property. Governments differ significantly in the requirements for this process. Data for registering property are produced assuming a standardized case of an entrepreneur who wants to purchase land and a building in the country's largest business city.

Average Cost to Register measures the cost to a business, expressed as a percent of the property value, needed to complete the legal and bureaucratic procedures required for registering property. Cost includes fees, transfer taxes, stamp duties, and any other payment to the property registry, notaries, public agencies, or lawyers. Other taxes, such as capital gains tax or value added tax, are excluded from the cost measure. Data are produced assuming a standardized case of an entrepreneur who wants to purchase land and a building in the country's largest business city.

Government Expenditures as a percent of gross domestic product roughly indicate the economic importance of public health, public education, and military activities in national economies.

Public Health Expenditure consists of recurrent and capital spending from government (both central and local) budgets, external borrowings and grants (including donations from international agencies and NGOs), and social (or compulsory) health insurance funds. The estimates of health expenditure come mostly from the World Health Organization's (WHO) *World Health Report 2003* and its subsequent updates, and from the Organisation for Economic Co-operation and Development (OECD) for its member countries, supplemented by World Bank poverty assessments and country-sector studies. Data are also drawn from the International Monetary Fund.

Public Education Expenditure consists of public spending on public education plus subsidies to private education at the primary, secondary, and post-secondary levels. Foreign aid for education is excluded. Education expenditure estimates are provided to the World Bank by the Institute for Statistics of the United Nations Educational, Scientific, and Cultural Organization (UNESCO). UNESCO compiles its data from annual financial reports of central or federal governments and state or regional administrations.

Military Expenditure is defined by the Stockholm International Peace Research Institute (SIPRI) as "all current and capital expenditure on: (a) the armed forces, including peacekeeping forces; (b) defense ministries and other government agencies engaged in defense projects; (c) paramilitary forces, when judged to be trained an equipped for military operations; and (d) military space activities." Expenditures include the cost of procurements, personnel, research and development, construction, operations, maintenance, and military aid to other countries. Civil defense, veterans' benefits, demobilization, and destruction of weapons are not included as military expenditures. The World Bank uses data collected by SIPRI for its annual World Development Indicators military expenditure dataset.

Press Freedom is "the degree to which each country permits the free flow of information," according to Freedom House, ranked on a scale of 1 to 100. Countries with a score between 1 and 30 are considered to have a "Free" media; 31 to 60, "Partly Free"; and 61 to 100, "Not Free." This survey does not measure press responsibility; rather, it measures the degree of freedom in the flow of information. Press freedom data are collected from overseas correspondents, staff travel, international visitors, the findings of human rights organizations, specialists in geographic and geopolitical areas, the reports of governments, and a variety of domestic and international news media. The final index is a sum of three separate components that reflect the legal, political, and economic environments that press in each country operate within.

Status of Freedom of Information (FOI) Legislation measures a government's guarantee of public access to information by placing each country in one of three categories: *In Effect: 57* countries legally guarantee public access to government records through comprehensive FOI laws; *Pending:* 39 additional countries are considering adopting freedom of information acts; *None:* countries not listed have no pending FOI legislation (represented by ".." in the data table, which could indicate that no data are available for this country). Access to information about government activities increases transparency and allows citizens to more effectively combat corruption. Data are compiled by Privacy International by author David Banisar on a country-by-country basis. The specifics of each country's legislation and constitutional guarantees are explained in detail in the source publications.

The **Digital Access Index** is a composite score, developed by the International Telecommunications Union (ITU), which reflects the ability of each country's population to take advantage of internet communication technologies. It ranges from 1 to 100, where 100 equals the most access. The Index is calculated as a weighted average of eight variables describing infrastructure, affordability, educational level of the population, quality of information and communication technology services, and Internet usage.

The **Corruption Perceptions Index (CPI)** measures the degree to which corruption is perceived to exist among public officials and politicians. Ratings range in value from 10 (least corrupt) to 0 (most corrupt). The survey measures public sector corruption or the abuse of public office for private gain. It measures local and national governments, not domestic and foreign corporations doing business in these countries. The CPI is compiled from 12 surveys originating from nine different independent institutions. A country is included in the CPI only if there are data available from 3 or more surveys. The surveys measure the perceptions of local residents, expatriates, business people, academics, and risk analysts. Survey results are combined in three-year periods to reduce abrupt variations that could potentially be caused by errors. Thus, figures for 2006 are based on surveys taken not only in 2006, but in 2004 and 2005 as well.

FREQUENCY OF UPDATE BY DATA PROVIDERS

All of the data sets in this table are updated annually by the original providers, with the exception of the Digital Access Index, Public Education Expenditures, and the Status of FOI Legislation, which are updated intermittently.

DATA RELIABILITY AND CAUTIONARY NOTES

Freedom Indices: Data and methodologies are subject to rigorous internal and external reviews, the data are reproducible, the index components are clear, and ratings are assigned by a centralized team of researchers. Thus, the data are considered to be reliable. Nonetheless, this index is measuring ideas and behaviors and not a discrete physical quantity, and, as such, rigid score comparisons and rankings are discouraged. To ensure comparability of the ratings from year to year, any changes to the methodology are introduced incrementally.

Regulatory Barriers to Registering Property: Data are very reliable, but the limited definition of this indicator may restrict its applicability. For example, collected data refer to only businesses in the country's most populous city. In addition, data often focus on a specific business form—a limited liability company of a specified size—and may not be representative of the regulation on other businesses. The methodology also assumes that a business has full information on what is required and does not waste time when completing procedures. In practice, completing a procedure may take longer if the business lacks information or is unable to follow up promptly.

Public Health Expenditure: The values reported here represent the product of an extensive effort by WHO, OECD, and the World Bank to produce a comprehensive data set on national health accounts. Nonetheless, few developing countries have health accounts that are methodologically consistent with national accounting procedures. Data on public spending at the sub-national level are not aggregated in all countries, making total public expenditure on health care difficult to measure. WHO cautions that these data should only be used for an "order of magnitude" estimate and that specific cross-country comparisons should be avoided.

Public Education Expenditure: In some cases data refer only to a ministry of education's expenditures, excluding other ministries and local authorities that spend a part of their budget on educational activities. Spending on religious schools, which constitutes a large portion of educational spending in some developing countries, may be included. The World Bank cautions that these data do not measure the effectiveness or levels of attainment in a particular educational system.

Military Expenditure: The entire data set has been carefully compiled with extensive analysis by a single provider, SIPRI, which makes these data fairly reliable.

When a time series is not available or a country's definition of military expenditure differs from SIPRI's, estimates are made based on analysis of official government budget statistics. Estimates are always based on empirical evidence, not assumptions or extrapolations. SIPRI cautions that military expenditure does not relate directly to military capability or security.

Status of FOI Legislation: While the FOI data have been thoroughly researched, there are unavoidable difficulties in assigning each country to one of three categories. Some countries have laws guaranteeing access, but the laws are not enforced. Still others guarantee access to government documents in specific categories, excluding access in other categories.

Digital Access Index: The variables selected to build this indicator are from a number of reputable sources including ITU's quarterly survey of information and communication technologies around the world. However, as with any complex global dataset, complete accuracy is difficult to ensure.

Corruption Perceptions Index: Overall, the data are considered to be reliable. Survey responses from residents in each country correlate well with responses from experts abroad. The data are reproducible and the index components are clear. Nonetheless, while the CPI can illustrate rough comparisons, rigid international score comparisons are discouraged. While year-to-year variation in scores is affected by changes in survey samples and methodology, findings indicate that in general, trends in the data over time are reasonably accurate. Confidence intervals are published in tabular format by Transparency International.

SOURCES

Freedom Indices: Freedom House. 2007. *Freedom in the World 2007: The Annual Survey of Political Rights and Civil Liberties.* New York: Freedom House. Online at http://www.freedomhouse.org/uploads/press_release/fiw07_charts.pdf.

Urban Population Living in Slums: United Nations Human Settlements Programme (UN-HABITAT). 2003. *Slums of the World: The Face of Urban Poverty in the New Millennium?* Nairobi: UN-HABITAT. Online at http://www.unhabitat.org/publication/slumreport.pdf.

Regulatory Barriers to Registering Property: World Bank Group. 2007. *Doing Business Custom Datasets.* Washington, DC: World Bank. Online at http://www.doingbusiness.org/CustomQuery.

Government Expenditures: Development Data Group, World Bank. 2007. *2007 World Development Indicators.* Washington, DC: World Bank. Online at http://go.worldbank.org/B53SONGPA0.

Status of FOI Legislation: Banisar, D. 2004. *Freedom of Information and Access to Government Records Around the World.* Washington, DC: Privacy International. Online at http://www.privacyinternational.org/issues/foia/foia-survey.html.

Digital Access Index: International Telecommunications Union (ITU), 2003. *World Telecommunication Development Report.* Geneva: ITU. Online at http://www.itu.int/newsarchive/press_releases/2003/30.html.

Corruption Perceptions Index: Transparency International. 2006. *2006 Corruption Perceptions Index.* Berlin: Transparency International. Online at http://www.transparency.org/policy_and_research/surveys_indices/cpi.

Acknowledgments

World Resources 2008 is the 12th volume in a series that dates from 1986. It has evolved from its initial objective as the comprehensive assessment of environment and development trends to a book that provides serious policy analysis of the critical issues arising from human dependence and impact on the environment.

The *World Resources Report* is the work of a unique and continuing partnership between the United Nations Development Programme (UNDP), the United Nations Environment Programme (UNEP), The World Bank, and the World Resources Institute.

For this 12th edition in the *World Resources* series, we would like to express our gratitude to the Netherlands Ministry of Foreign Affairs, the Swedish International Development Cooperation Agency (SIDA), the Office of International Development Assistance of the Ministry of Foreign Affairs of Denmark (Danida), and the United States Agency for International Development (USAID). They have been constant, concerned and engaged supporters of the World Resources Report and of efforts to meet the challenges of profound poverty.

We continue to be thankful for our colleagues in Norway at UNEP/GRID-Arendal for their ongoing involvement in this work, both through their direct contributions of materials, and for their support of outreach efforts to ensure that the findings of the report reach broad and appropriate audiences.

Though we expressed our gratitude in the previous edition of *World Resources*, we wish to acknowledge again the intellectual contribution of Jon Anderson, formerly at USAID, and his colleagues and their publication *Nature, Wealth and Power*, and the members of the Poverty Environment Partnership and their publication *Linking Poverty Reduction and Environmental Management*. Their thinking about poverty remains relevant and important.

In particular, we want to acknowledge the contribution of Crispino Lobo, Executive Director of the Watershed Organisation Trust of India, to our work. His wisdom, practical experience, and documented successes in community-led watershed regeneration have inspired us and informed our theory and writing.

Individual Contributions

The development of *World Resources 2008* had more fits and starts than normal. The patience, goodwill, and understanding of our partners is appreciated well beyond what mere thanks can convey. Peter Gilruth of UNEP, Kirk Hamilton of the World Bank, Charles McNeill of UNDP and Marianne Fernagut of GRID-Arendal have all brought a new dimension to the word partnership, and we do thank them.

We have been equally fortunate with reviewers and advisors who have fielded innumerable requests coupled with demanding schedules without complaint. In particular, we would like to thank Bill Aalbersberg, José Roman Carerra, Darrell Deppert, Elspeth Halverson, David Hughell, Erin Hughes, Brian Jones, Azharul Mazumder, Steve McCarthy, Greg Minnick, Chris Reij, Tony Rinaudo, Rony Rozario, Gretchen Ruethling, Claudio Saito, Sean Southey, Paul Steele, Bhishma Subedi, Alifereti Tawake, Paul Thompson, Gaby Tobler, Henry Tschinkel, Mark Wentling, and Bob Winterbottom.

The staff at World Resources Institute has been equally generous of their time and expertise in helping bring this report to conclusion, under somewhat difficult circumstances. To them we are so grateful: Steve Barker, Hyacinth Billings, Amy Cassara, Emily Cooper, Crystal Davis, Norbert Henninger, Georgia Moyka, Robin Murphy, Jesse Ribot, Jon Talbot, Dan Tunstall, Peter Veit, and Elsie Vélez-Whited. Lauren Withey has worn more than one hat on our staff and Stephanie Hanson, likewise, has taken on a number of duties.

We would be remiss if we did not acknowledge those who started with this volume but had to move on: Alex Acs and Ethan Arpi did early research and writing and Jen Lesar gave us organization and discipline. Dena Leibman laid the early groundwork for this report.

In addition to Greg Mock, our principal writer, we have been fortunate to be able to draw on a small team committed to the project, adaptable to the unpredictability of our schedule, and possessed of good editorial judgment: we owe much to Polly Ghazi and Karen Holmes.

This report began with modest goals and anticipated a length shorter than previous volumes. Thanks to the informed and unstinting engagement of Manish Bapna, with the dedication of Dan Tunstall, Emily Cooper, and Greg Mock, we have produced a much expanded report whose length, we hope, is justified by its value.

That has made the task of our reviewers that much more demanding—more to read under an unconscionably tight timeframe. Their generosity of time and their detailed and thoughtful comments and advice have greatly improved this work. We acknowledge their valuable contributions in the following section, listing each of them by chapter.

Despite all the good advice, careful reviews, and valuable contributions of others, at the end, the WRR staff has to accept final responsibility for the content of this report…and we do.

World Resources 2008 Reviewers

WRI gratefully acknowledges the following individuals for their thoughtful reviews of *World Resources 2008*.

Chapter 1

Bill Aalbersberg, University of the South Pacific
Arun Agarwal, University of Michigan
Jon Anderson, Millennium Challenge Corporation
Anna Balance, DFID
Robert Chase, World Bank
Munyaradzi Chenji, UNEP
Michael Colby, USAID
Emily Cooper, WRI
Marianne Fernagut, UNEP/GRID-Arendal
Norbert Henninger, WRI
Fran Irwin, Independent Consultant
Brian Jones, Independent Consultant
Crispino Lobo, Watershed Organisation Trust
Robin Mearns, World Bank
Ruth Meinzen-Dick, IFPRI
Heather McGray, WRI
Marcos Neto, CARE
Jesse Ribot, WRI
Sara Scherr, Ecoagriculture Partners
Virginia Seitz, Millennium Challenge Corporation
Sean Southey, RARE Conservation
Paul Steele, UNDP
Alifereti Tawake, University of the South Pacific
Frank Turyatunga, UNEP/GRID-Arendal
Chris Weaver, WWF
Robert Winterbottom, International Resources Group

Chapter 2

Arun Agarwal, University of Michigan
Jon Anderson, Millenium Challenge Corporation
Anna Balance, DFID
Ruth Campbell, ACDI/VOCA
Robert Chase, World Bank
Munyaradzi Chenji, UNEP
Michael Colby, USAID
Emily Cooper, WRI
Elisabeth Farmer, ACDI/VOCA-Ethiopia
Marianne Fernagut, UNEP/GRID-Arendal
Norbert Henninger, WRI
Fran Irwin, Independent Consultant
Crispino Lobo, Watershed Organisation Trust
Robin Mearns, World Bank
Ruth Meinzen-Dick, IFPRI
Steve McCarthy, ACDI/VOCA
Heather McGray, WRI
Marcos Neto, CARE

Jesse Ribot, WRI
Sara Scherr, Ecoagriculture Partners
Virginia Seitz, Millennium Challenge Corporation
Sean Southey, RARE Conservation
Paul Steele, UNDP
Frank Turyatunga, UNEP/GRID-Arendal

Chapter 3

Fisheries for the Future

Azhural Mazumder, USAID
Paul Thompson, Winrock International

Green Livelihoods

José Roman Carrera, Rainforest Alliance
David Hughell, Rainforest Alliance
Gregory Minnick, Rainforest Alliance
John Nittler, Chemonics International
Claudio Saito, Chemonics International
Henry Tschinkel, consultant

Turning Back the Desert

Christopher Burns, Peace Corps
Chris Reij, Centre for International Cooperation, Vrije Universiteit
Tony Rinaudo, WorldVision international
Mark Wentling, USAID
Mike McGahuey, USAID
Robert Winterbottom, International Resources Group

Chapter 4

Arun Agarwal, University of Michigan
Virginia Barriero, WRI
Robert Chase, World Bank
Munyaradzi Chenji, UNEP
Florence Daviet, WRI
Christina Deconcini, WRI
Marianne Fernagut, UNEP/GRID-Arendal
Heather McGray, WRI
Bruce McKenney, TNC
Jonathan Pershing, WRI
Jesse Ribot, WRI
Sara Scherr, Ecoagriculture Partners
Paul Steele, UNDP
Fred Stolle, WRI
Peter Veit, WRI

Data Tables

Alan Brewster, Yale University
Norbert Henninger, WRI
Christian Layke, WRI
Daniel Tunstall, WRI
Jaap van Woerden, UNEP/GRID-Geneva

References

Chapter 1

Main Text

- Adger, W.N. 2000. "Social and Ecological Resilience: Are They Related?" *Progress in Human Geography* 24(3):347–364. Online at http://www.uea.ac.uk/env/people/adgerwn/prghumangeog2000.pdf.

- Arcand, J., and L. Bassole. 2007. *Does Community Driven Development Work? Evidence From Senegal.* Paper presented at African Economic Conference 2007, Addis Ababa, United Nations Economic Commission for Africa, Nov. 16. Online at www.uneca.org/aec/documents/Jean-Louis%20Arcand_Leandre%20Bassole.pdf.

- Azim, M.E., M.A. Wahab, and M.C.J. Verdegem. 2002. "Status of Aquaculture and Fisheries in Bangladesh." *World Aquaculture* 34(4):37–40, 67.

- Bebbington, A., and T. Carroll. 2000. "Induced Social Capital and Federations of the Rural Poor." Social Capital Initiative Working Paper No. 19. Washington, DC: World Bank. Online at http://siteresources.worldbank.org/INTSOCIALCAPITAL/Resources/Social-Capital-Initiative-Working-Paper-Series/SCI-WPS-19.pdf.

- Binswanger, H., and T. Nguyen. 2004. *Scaling Up Community-Driven Development for Dummies.* Washington, DC: World Bank. Online at http://info.worldbank.org/etools/library/view_p.asp?lprogram=1&objectid=81570

- Blue Ventures Madagascar. 2008. *Expeditions: Andavadoaka.* London: Blue Ventures. Online at http://www.blueventures.org/expeditions_andavadoaka.htm.

- Boudreaux, K. 2007. "State Power, Entrepreneurship, and Coffee: The Rwandan Experience." Policy Comment No. 15, Mercatus Policy Series. Arlington, VA, USA: George Mason University. Online at http://ssrn.com/abstrats=1026935.

- Brenson-Lazan, G. 2003. *Groups and Social Resilience Building.* West Hartford, CT, USA: Amauta International, LLC. Online at http://www.communityatwork.com/resilience/RESILIENCIAENG.pdf.

- Briguglio, L., G. Cordina, S. Bugeja, and N. Ferrugia. 2005. *Conceptualizing and Measuring Economic Resilience.* Malta: Islands and Small States Institute, University of Malta. Online at http://home.um.edu.mt/islands/resilience_index.pdf.

- FAO (Food and Agriculture Organization of the United Nations). 2005a. *Global Forest Resources Assessment 2005.* Rome: FAO. Online at http://www.fao.org/DOCREP/008/a0400e/a0400e00.htm.

- FAO (Food and Agriculture Organization of the United Nations). 2005b. *National Aquaculture Sector Overview: Bangladesh.* Rome: FAO. Online at http://www.fao.org/fishery/countrysector/naso_bangladesh#tcN110052.

- FAO (Food and Agriculture Organization of the United Nations). 2007a. *State of the World's Fisheries and Aquaculture 2006.* Rome: FAO. Online at ftp://ftp.fao.org/docrep/fao/009/a0699e/a0699e.pdf.

- FAO (Food and Agriculture Organization of the United Nations). 2007b. *Adaptation to Climate Change in Agriculture, Forestry, and Fisheries: Perspective, Framework, and Priorities.* Rome: FAO. Online at ftp://ftp.fao.org/docrep/fao/009/j9271e/j9271e.pdf.

- Farrington, J., and C. Boyd. 1997. "Scaling Up the Participatory Management of Common Pool Resources." *Development Policy Review* 15:371–391.

- FEV (Finca Esperanza Verde). 2008. *About Us.* San Ramón, Nicaragua: FEV. Online at http://www.fincaesperanzaverde.org.

- Folke, C., S. Carpenter, T. Elmqvist, L. Gunderson, C.S. Holling, B. Walker, J. Bengtsson, F. Berkes, J. Colding, K. Danell, M. Falkenmark, L. Gordon, R. Kasperson, N. Kautsky, A. Kinzig, S. Levin, K.-G. Mäler, F. Moberg, L. Ohlsson, P. Olsson, E. Ostrom, W. Reid, J. Rockström, H. Savenije, and U. Svedin. 2002. *Resilience and Sustainable Development: Building Adaptive Capacity in a World of Transformation.* Background Paper for the Environmental Advisory Council to the Swedish Government. Stockholm: Swedish Ministry of the Environment. Online at http://www.sou.gov.se/mvb/pdf/resiliens.pdf.

- Forest Trends. 2005. *Rural Resource Initiative: A New Global Initiative Advancing Forest Tenure, Policy and Market Reforms to Reduce Rural Poverty, Strengthen Forest Governance, Conserve and Restore Forest Ecosystems and Achieve Sustainable Forest-Based Economic Growth: Concept Note.* Washington, DC: Forest Trends. Online at http://www.forest-trends.org/documents/publications/conceptnotes/RRI%20Concept%20Note%20-%20Nov%201[1].doc.pdf.

- Füssel, H-M. 2007. "Vulnerability: A Generally Applicable Conceptual Framework for Climate Change Research." *Global Environmental Change* 17:155–167.

- Glavovic, B. 2005. *Social Resilience: Building Layers of Resilience to Transcend Waves of Adversity.* PowerPoint presentation at Resilient Infrastructure Conference, Rotorua, New Zealand, Aug. 8. Online at http://www.caenz.com/info/2005Conf/pres/Glavovic.pdf.

- Glenzer, K. 2008. "The Power of Local Natural Resource Governance in Conflict Contexts." Powerpoint presentation at Woodrow Wilson International Center for Scholars, Washington, DC. Feb. 28.

- Grootaert, C., and T. van Bastelaer. 2001. *Understanding and Measuring Social Capital: A Synthesis of Findings and Recommendations from the Social Capital Initiative.* Social Capital Initiative Working Paper No. 24. Washington, DC: World Bank. Online at http://go.worldbank.org/W8FMEK6FRO.

- ICRISAT (International Crops Research Institute for the Semi-Arid Tropics). 2007. *Rural Prosperity Through Integrated Watershed Management: A Case Study of Gokulpura-Goverdhanpura in Eastern Rajasthan.* Pantancheru, Andhra Pradesh, India: ICRISAT. Online at http://www.icrisat.org/Journal/volume5/aes/aes6.pdf.

- Kura, Y., C. Revenga, E. Hoshino, and G. Mock. 2004. *Fishing for Answers: Making Sense of the Global Fish Crisis.* Washington, DC: World Resources Institute. Online at http://archive.wri.org/publication_detail.cfm?pubid=3866#1.

- Larson, A., and J. Ribot. 2007. "The Poverty of Forestry Policy: Double Standards on an Uneven Playing Ground." *Sustainability Science* 2(2):189–204.

- MACH (Management of Aquatic Ecosystems through Community Husbandry). 2006. *MACH-II Briefing Packet for USAID Evaluation Team, Part I: Achievement, Influence and Future.* Dhaka: MACH.

- Meinzen-Dick, R. 2008. Senior Research Fellow. International Food Policy Research Institute, Washington, DC. Personal Communication. Feb. 14.

- MA (Millennium Ecosystem Assessment). 2005. *Ecosystems and Human Well-Being: General Synthesis.* Washington, DC: Island Press. Online at http://www.millenniumassessment.org/documents/document.356.aspx.pdf

- Molnar, A., M. Liddle, C. Bracer, A. Khare, A. White, and J. Bull. 2007. *Community Based Forest Enterprises in Tropical Forest Countries: Status and Potential.* Washington, DC: Forest Trends; Rights and Resources Initiative; and International Tropical Timber Organization. Online at http://www.rightsandresources.org/documents/index.php?pubID=109.

- Morton, J., and S. Anderson. 2008. "Climate Change and Agrarian Societies in Drylands." Paper presented at the World Bank workshop The Social

Dimensions of Climate Change, Washington, DC, Mar. 6. Online at http://go.worldbank.org/006G8VNDK0.

- Narayan, D. 2002. *Empowerment and Poverty Reduction: A Sourcebook.* Washington DC: World Bank. Online at http://go.worldbank.org/FD9HH8DH11.
- PIP (Parks in Peril). 2007. *Machililla National Park.* Quito, Ecuador: The Nature Conservancy Ecuador. Online at http://www.parksinperil.org/wherewework/southamerica/ecuador/protectedarea/machalilla.html.
- Pretty, J., and H. Ward. 2001. "Social Capital and the Environment." *World Development* 29(2):209–227.
- Ribot, J. 2008. Senior Associate. World Resources Institute, Washington, DC. Personal Communication. Feb. 12.
- Ribot, J., and N. Peluso. 2003. "A Theory of Access." *Rural Sociology* 68(2):153–181.
- Ribot, J., A. Chhatre, and T. Lankina. 2008. "Institutional Choice and Recognition in the Formation and Consolidation of Local Democracy." Working Paper 35, Representation, Equity, and Environment Series. Washington, DC: World Resources Institute. Online at http://www.wri.org/publication/9397.
- Serageldin, I., and C. Grootaert. 1999. "Defining Social Capital: An Integrating View." *In Social Capital: A Multifaceted Perspective.* P. Dasgupta and I. Serageldin, eds., pp. 40–58. Washington, DC: World Bank.
- Shah, P. 2006. *Supporting the "People Sector." The South Asia Experience in Rural Livelihoods Development and Preliminary Results.* Washington, DC: World Bank. Online at http://siteresources.worldbank.org/EXTSOCIALDEVELOPMENT/Resources/244362-1170428243464/3408356-1170428261889/3408359-1170428299570/People-Sector.pdf.
- UNDP (United Nations Development Programme). 2004a. *Equator Prize 2004 Nomination Form.* New York: UNDP. Online at http://www.equatorinitiative.net/content.lasso.
- UNDP (United Nations Development Programme). 2004b. *Equator Prize 2004 Nomination Form: The Pred Nai Community Forest, Trad Province, Thailand.* New York: UNDP. Online at http://www.equatorinitiative.net/content.lasso.
- UNDP (United Nations Development Programme). 2006a. *Equator Prize 2006 Nomination Form: The Village of Andavadoaka, Madagascar.* New York: UNDP. Online at http://www.equatorinitiative.net/content.lasso.
- UNDP (United Nations Development Programme). 2006b. *Equator Prize 2006 Nomination Form: Finca Esperanza Verde.* New York: UNDP. Online at http://www.equatorinitiative.net/content.lasso.
- UNEP (United Nations Environment Programme). 2007. *Global Environmental Outlook 4: Environment for Development.* Valletta, Malta: Progress Press Ltd.
- Ventura, I. 2006. Leader. Agua Blanca Community, Agua Blanca, Ecuador. Personal Communication. Dec. 10.
- Walker, B., L. Gunderson, A. Kinzig, C. Folke, S. Carpenter, and L. Schultz. 2006. "A Handful of Heuristics and Some Propositions for Understanding Resilience in Social-Ecological Systems." *Ecology and Society* 11(1). Online at http://www.ecologyandsociety.org/vol11/iss1/art13/ES-2005-1530.pdf.
- World Bank. 2002. *Project Appraisal Document on a Proposed Credit in the Amount of SDR 80 Million to India for the Karnataka Community-Based Tank Management Project.* Report No. 23555-IN. Washington, DC: World Bank. Online at http://www-wds.worldbank.org/servlet/WDSContentServer/WDSP/IB/2002/04/19/000094946_02041104044843/Rendered/INDEX/multi0page.txt.
- World Bank. 2005. "The Effectiveness of World Bank Support for Community-Based and -Driven Development: An OED Evaluation." Washington, DC: World Bank. Online at http://lnweb18.worldbank.org/oed/oeddoclib.nsf/

b57456d58aba40e585256ad400736404/cf723fb0d152acd0852570a1005219ea?OpenDocument.

- World Bank. 2006a. "Bangladesh Country Environmental Analysis." Bangladesh Development Series Paper No: 12. Dhaka: World Bank Office. Online at http://go.worldbank.org/SMDBXINT60.
- World Bank. 2006b. *Where is the Wealth of Nations?* Washington, DC: World Bank. Online at http://go.worldbank.org/U055JOCQT0
- World Bank. 2007. *World Development Indicators 2007.* Washington, DC: World Bank. Online at http://go.worldbank.org/3JU2HA60D0.
- World Bank. 2008. *World Development Indicators Online.* Online at http://go.worldbank.org/6HAYAHG8H0.
- WRI (World Resources Institute) in collaboration with United Nations Development Programme, United Nations Environment Programme, and World Bank. 2005. *World Resources 2005: The Wealth of the Poor—Managing Ecosystems to Fight Poverty.* Washington, DC: WRI. Online at http://www.wri.org/project/world-resources.

Box 1.2

- Gillespie, S. 2004. *Scaling Up Community-Driven Development: A Synthesis of Experience.* Washington, DC: International Food Policy Research Institute. Online at http://www.ifpri.org/divs/fcnd/dp/papers/fcndp181.pdf.
- Hooper, M., R. Jafry, M. Marolla, and J. Phan. 2004. "Scaling-Up Community Efforts to Reach MDGs—An Assessment of Experience From the Equator Prize." In *The Millennium Development Goals and Conservation: Managing Nature's Wealth for Society's Health.* D. Roe, ed. London: International Institute for Environment and Development. Online at http://www.iied.org/Gov/mdgs/publications.html.
- Ribot, J. 2008. Senior Associate. World Resources Institute, Washington, DC. Personal Communication. Feb. 12.
- Uvin, P. and D. Miller. 1994. *Scaling Up: Thinking Through the Issues.* Providence, Rhode Island, USA: The World Hunger Program, Brown University. Online at http://www.globalpolicy.org/ngos/intro/growing/2000/1204.htm.

Box 1.3

- MA (Millennium Ecosystem Assessment). 2005. *Ecosystems and Human Well-Being: General Synthesis.* Washington, DC: Island Press. Online at http://www.millenniumassessment.org/en/synthesis.aspx.
- Ravallion, R., S. Chen, and P. Sangraula. 2007a. "New Evidence on the Urbanization of Global Poverty." *Population and Development Review,* 33(4), 667-702.
- Ravallion, R., S. Chen, and P. Sangraula. 2007b. *New Evidence on the Urbanization of Global Poverty.* Summary of World Bank Policy Research Working Paper 4199. Washington, DC: World Bank. Online at http://go.worldbank.org/D92DH5SHP0.
- World Bank. 2006. *Where is the Wealth of Nations?* Washington, DC: World Bank. Online at http://go.worldbank.org/U055JOCQT0.
- World Bank. 2007a. *World Development Indicators 2007.* Washington, DC: World Bank. Online at http://go.worldbank.org/3JU2HA60D0.
- World Bank. 2007b. *Global Monitoring Report 2007.* Washington, DC: World Bank. Online at http://go.worldbank.org/P3JY1Y40Z0.
- World Bank. 2007c. *Poverty At a Glance.* World Bank Issue Brief. Washington, DC: World Bank. Online at http://go.worldbank.org/VL7N3V6F20.

- World Resources Institute, Kenya Ministry of Environment and Natural Resources, Kenya Ministry of Planning and National Development, and International Livestock Research Institute. 2007. *Nature's Benefits in Kenya: An Atlas of Ecosystems and Human Well-Being.* Washington, DC: World Resources Institute. Online at http://www.wri.org/publication/content/9373.

Update: Namibia

- Boudreaux, K. 2007. "Community-Based Natural Resource Management and Poverty Alleviation in Namibia: A Case Study." Policy Comment No. 10, Mercatus Policy Series. Arlington, Virginia, USA: George Mason University. Online at http://www.enterpriseafrica.org/publications/pubID.3745/pub_detail.asp.
- Harring, S., and W. Odendaal. 2006. *Our Land They Took: San Land Rights Under Threat In Namibia.* Windhoek, Namibia: Legal Assistance Centre. Online at http://www.lac.org.na/publications/department.html.
- IRDNC (Integrated Rural Development and Nature Conservation). 2006. *WWF Project Technical Progress Report—Caprivi.* Windhoek, Namibia: IRDNC. Online at http://www.irdnc.org.na/download/Caprivi%20Report%20July%202006%20to%20Dec%2006.doc.
- Jones, B. 2007. Environment and Development Consultant. Windhoek, Namibia. Personal Communication. May 24.
- Jones, B. 2008. Environment and Development Consultant. Windhoek, Namibia. Personal Communication. Jan. 26.
- Jones, B., and A. Mosimane. 2007. *Promoting Integrated Community-Based Natural Resource Management as a Means to Combat Desertification: the Living in a Finite Environment (LIFE) Project and the Khoadi Hoas and Nyae Nyae Conservancies, Namibia.* Washington, DC: International Resources Group. Online at http://www.frameweb.org/ev_en.php?ID=15189_201&ID2=DO_COMMUNITY.
- MET (Ministry of Environment and Tourism). 2003. *Community Based Natural Resource Management (CBNRM) Programme Details: Community Forestry Programme.* Windhoek, Namibia: MET. Online at http://www.met.gov.na/programmes/cbnrm/commfor.htm.
- MET (Ministry of Environment and Tourism). 2005. *Community Based Natural Resource Management (CBNRM): Enhancing Conservation, Development & Democracy in Namibia's Rural Areas.* Windhoek, Namibia: MET. Online at http://www.met.gov.na/programmes/cbnrm/Enhancing%20conse,%20devand%20dem.htm.
- Morris, D., J. Barcomb, M. Bowker, M. Gadd, P. Gaulke, L. Grussing, and O. Pierson. 2007. *Team One Due Diligence Report: Government of Namibia Proposal to the Millennium Challenge Corporation.* Washington, DC: United States Department of the Interior International Technical Assistance Program and United States Department of Agriculture Forest Service International Programs Office. Online at http://www.frameweb.org/ev02.php?ID=86625_201&ID2=DO_TOPIC.
- NACSO (National Association of CBNRM Support Organisations). 2005. *NACSO Services.* Windhoek, Namibia: National Association of CBNRM Support Organisations. Online at http://www.nacso.org.na.
- NACSO (National Association of CBNRM Support Organisations). 2006. *Namibia's Communal Conservancies: A Review of Progress and Challenges in 2005.* Windhoek, Namibia: National Association of CBNRM Support Organisations. Online at http://www.irdnc.org.na/conservancies.htm.
- NEEN (Namibian Environmental Education Network). 2004a. *Namibian Environmental Directory: CRIAA.* Windhoek, Namibia: NEEN. Online at http://www.nnf.org.na/ENVDIR/pages/criaa.htm.
- NEEN (Namibian Environmental Education Network). 2004b. *Namibian Environmental Directory: DRFN.* Windhoek, Namibia: NEEN. Online at http://www.nnf.org.na/ENVDIR/pages/drfn.htm.
- NEEN (Namibian Environmental Education Network). 2004c. *Namibian Environmental Directory: NARA.* Windhoek, Namibia: NEEN. Online at http://www.nnf.org.na/ENVDIR/pages/nara.htm.
- *The Namibian.* 2008. "Community Forestry Project in Omaheke." Windhoek, Namibia: Apr. 8. Online at http://allafrica.com/stories/printable/200804080639.html.
- Tjaronda, W. 2008. "Community Forests a Boon." Windhoek, Namibia: *New Era,* Feb. 15. Online at http://allafrica.com/stories/200802150530.html.
- Seitz, V. 2008. Senior Director of Social and Gender Assessment. Millennium Challenge Corporation, Washington, DC. Personal Communication. Feb. 14.
- Vaughan, K., S. Mulonga, J. B. Katjiua, and N. Branston. 2003. "Cash from Conservation, Torra Community Tastes the Benefits: A Short Survey and Review of the Torra Conservancy Cash Payout to Individual Members." Wildlife Integration for Livelihood Diversification (WILD) Project, Working Paper 15. Windhoek, Namibia: Ministry of Environment and Tourism. Online at http://www.met.gov.na/programmes/wild/WildDownload.htm.
- Vaughan, K., and J. Katjiua. 2002. *An Overview of Community Based Natural Resource Management and Rural Livelihoods in Khoadi Hoas Conservancy—Kunene Region.* Windhoek: Wildlife Integration for Livelihood Diversification (WILD) Project, Ministry of Environment and Tourism. Online at http://www.met.gov.na/programmes/wild/WILDworkingpapers1-5/WP%205%20-%20CBNRM%20Livelihoods%20KHC.pdf.
- Weaver, C. 2007. Chief of Party, Living In a Finite Environment (LIFE) Project. Worldwide Fund For Nature (WWF), Windhoek, Namibia. Personal Communication. Dec. 19.
- WRI (World Resources Institute) in collaboration with United Nations Development Programme, United Nations Environment Programme, and World Bank. 2005. *World Resources 2005: The Wealth of the Poor—Managing Ecosystems to Fight Poverty.* Washington, DC: WRI. Online at http://www.wri.org/project/world-resources.
- WWF (World Wildlife Fund), Namibia Nature Foundation, Cooperative League of United States of America, and International Resources Group. 2007. *Integrated Community Based Natural Resource Management (CBNRM) for Economic Impact, Local Governance and Environmental Sustainability: Living in a Finite Environment Plus (LIFE Plus), Semi-Annual Report for October 1, 2006–April 30, 2007.* Windhoek, Namibia: USAID Namibia.

Update: Fiji

- Aalbersberg, W. 2007. Director of Institute of Applied Science. University of the South Pacific, Suva, Fiji. Personal Communication—Household Income Across FLMMA Sites. Unpublished Data. June.
- Aalbersberg, W. 2008. Director, Institute of Applied Science. University of the South Pacific, Suva, Fiji. Personal Communication. March.
- Govan, H., W. Aalbersberg, A. Tawake, and J. Parks. 2008. *Locally-Managed Marine Areas: A Guide for Practitioners.* Lami, Fiji: The Locally-Managed Marine Area Network.
- Leisher, C., P. van Beukering, and L. M. Scherl. 2007a. *Nature's Investment Bank: How Marine Protected Areas Contribute to Poverty Reduction.* Arlington, Virginia, USA: The Nature Conservancy, Amsterdam: Poverty Reduction

and Environmental Management; Australia: Department of the Environment and Water Resources; Jakarta, Indonesia: Worldwide Fund for Nature. Online at http://www.nature.org/initiatives/protectedareas/files/mpa_report.pdf.

■ Leisher, C., P. van Beukering, and L.M. Scherl. 2007b. *Nature's Investment Bank: How Marine Protected Areas Contribute to Poverty Reduction.* Video. Arlington, Virginia, USA: The Nature Conservancy, Amsterdam: Poverty Reduction and Environmental Management; Australia: Department of the Environment and Water Resources; Jakarta, Indonesia: Worldwide Fund for Nature. Online at http://www.prem-online.org/index.php?p=projects&cid=19.

■ LMMA (Locally Managed Marine Area) Network. 2005a. *History of the LMMA Network.* Lami, Fiji: LMMA Network. Online at http://www.lmmanetwork.org/Site_Page.cfm?PageID=33.

■ LMMA (Locally Managed Marine Area) Network. 2005b. *What is an LMMA?* Lami, Fiji: LMMA Network. Online at http://www.lmmanetwork.org/Site_Page.cfm?PageID=15.

■ LMMA (Locally Managed Marine Area) Network. 2006a. *A Focus on Lessons Learned. Annual Report of the LMMA Network for 2005.* Lami, Fiji: LMMA Network. Online at http://www.lmmanetwork.org/Site_Documents/Grouped/LMMA%202005%20Annual%20Report%20Final%2030%20May%202006.pdf.

■ LMMA (Locally Managed Marine Area) Network. 2006b. Newsletter. Issue 7, October. Lami, Fiji: LMMA Network. Online at http://lmmanetwork.org/Site_Documents/Grouped/LMMA%20Newsletter%207%20Oct%202006.pdf.

■ LMMA (Locally Managed Marine Area) Network. 2007a. *Enhancing LMMA Effectiveness through Continued Learning: Annual Report of the LMMA Network for 2006.* Lami, Fiji: LMMA Network. Online at: http://www.lmmanetwork.org/Site_Documents/Grouped/LMMA%202006%20Annual%20Report%20final%2013%20June%202007.pdf.

■ LMMA (Locally Managed Marine Area) Network. 2007b. *Lessons Learned.* Video. Lami, Fiji: LMMA Network. Online at http://www.lmmanetwork.org/Site_Page.cfm?PageID=67.

■ Narsey, W. 2007. "Truth Behind Our Poverty." *Fiji Times*, June 10.

■ O'Garra, T. 2007. *Estimating the Total Economic Value (TEV) of the Navakavu LMMA (Locally Managed Marine Area) in Vitu Levu Island (Fiji).* Noumea, New Caledonia: Initiative for the Protection and Management of Coral Reefs in the Pacific (CRISP). Online at http://www.icriforum.org/secretariat/gmdc/pdf/CRISP_TEV_REPORT.pdf.

■ Rarabici, V. 2007. "Fish Wardens on Alert for Illegal Fishermen." *Fiji Times Online.* July 23. Online at http://www.lmmanetwork.org/Site_Documents/Grouped/Fiji%20Times%20Online%20July%2007.pdf.

■ Tawake, A. 2008 [Forthcoming]. "Scaling-Up Networks of Locally Managed Marine Areas (LMMAs) to Island Wide Ecosystem Management while Decentralizing the Effort of Fiji LMMA Network and its Implementation from National to Provincial Levels." Suva, Fiji: Institute of Applied Sciences, University of the South Pacific. Pages based on manuscript of June 13, 2007.

■ Tawake, A, L. Nailetica, J. Ravula, M. Crabbe, H. Dugmore, G. Hill, K. Pickering, and R. Tamanivalu. 2005. *Kadavu Yabula Management Support Team: A Report on the Effectiveness and Site Suitability of 5 Tabu Areas (MPAs) in Kadavu.* Institute of Applied Sciences (IAS), Technical Report No. 2005/09. Suva, Fiji: IAS, University of the South Pacific. Online at http://ias.fst.usp.ac.fj/index.php?id=3469&tx_kharticlepages_pi1[page]=4&cHash=044b9cf14b.

■ USP (University of the South Pacific). 2007. *Final Report to the MacArthur Foundation: Improving the Art and Science of Effective Conservation in Fiji and the Western Pacific.* Suva, Fiji: USP.

■ van Beukering, P. J. H., L. M. Scherl, E. Sultanian, C. Leisher, and P. S. Fong. 2007. *Case Study 1: Yavusa Navakavu Locally Managed Marine Area (Fiji).* Arlington, Virginia, USA: The Nature Conservancy; Amsterdam: Poverty Reduction and Environmental Management; Australia: Department of the Environment and Water Resources; Jakarta, Indonesia: Worldwide Fund for Nature. Online at http://www.prem-online.org/archive/19/doc/Country%20Report%20Navakavu%20_Fiji_.pdf.

Chapter 2

Main Text

- ActionAid India. 2002. *Critical Webs of Power*. New Delhi: ActionAid India. Online at http://www.actionaid.org/main.aspx?PageID=278.
- Agrawal, A. 2001. "Common Property Institutions and Sustainable Governance of Resources." *World Development* 29(10):1649–1672.
- AIDER (Asociación para la Investigación y Desarrollo Integral). 2007. Pucallpa, Ucayali, Perú: AIDER. Online at http://aider.com.pe/home.
- AKRSP (Aga Khan Rural Support Programme). 2003. *Introduction*. AKRSP. Online at http://www.akrsplessons.org/akrsp.php.
- Alsop, R., D. Sjoblom, C. Namazie, and P. Patil. 2000. *Community-Level User Groups in Three World Bank Aided Projects: Do They Perform as Expected?* Washington, DC: World Bank. Online at http://povlibrary.worldbank.org/library/view/10285/.
- Alsop, R. and B. Kurey. 2005. *Local Organizations in Decentralized Development: Their Functions and Performance in India*. Washington, DC: World Bank. Online at http://go.worldbank.org/S9B3DNEZ00
- Alter Eco. 2007. *Alter Eco Fair Trade*. San Francisco: Alter Eco, Inc. Online at http://www.altereco-usa.com/main.php?section=home&subsection=main.
- ANAI (Asociación ANAI). 2005a. *About ANAI*. San Jose, Costa Rica: Asociación ANAI. Online at http://www.anaicr.org/gallery/en/index.php?option=com_content&task=view&id=53&Itemid=114. Viewed Jan. 30, 2008.
- ANAI (Asociación ANAI). 2005b. *ANAI History*. San Jose, Costa Rica: Asociación ANAI. Online at http://anaicr.org/index.php?option=com_content&task=view&id=15&Itemid=131. Viewed Jan. 30, 2008.
- ANAI (Asociación ANAI). 2005c. *ANAI Accomplishments*. San Jose, Costa Rica: Asociación ANAI. Online at http://anaicr.org/index.php?option=com_content&task=view&id=16&Itemid=135. Viewed Jan. 30, 2008.
- ANAI (Asociación ANAI). 2005d. *Training and Leadership*. San Jose, Costa Rica: Asociación ANAI. Online at http://anaicr.org/index.php?option=com_content&task=view&id=38&Itemid=82. Viewed Jan. 30, 2008.
- ANAI (Asociación ANAI). 2005e. Gandoca Beach Program. San Jose, Costa Rica: Asociación ANAI. Online at http://anaicr.org/index.php?option=com_content&task=view&id=106&Itemid=182. Viewed Jan. 30, 2008.
- ANAI (Asociación ANAI). 2005f. *Sea Turtle Program Accomplishments*. San Jose, Costa Rica: Asociación ANAI. Online at http://anaicr.org/index.php?option=com_content&task=view&id=114&Itemid=190. Viewed Jan. 30, 2008.
- Andersson, E., R. Wilson, and D. Warburton. 2005. *The True Costs of Public Participation*. London: Involve. Online at http://www.involve.org.uk/index.cfm?fuseaction=main.viewSection&intSectionID=390.
- ANSAB (Asia Network for Sustainable Agriculture and Bioresources). 2005a. *About ANSAB*. Kathmandu, Nepal: ANSAB. Online at http://ansab.org/about.php?linkno=24.
- ANSAB (Asia Network for Sustainable Agriculture and Bioresources). 2005b. *Nepal NTFP Alliance: Final Report*. Kathmandu, Nepal: ANSAB. Online at http://www.frameweb.org/ev02.php?ID=17653_201&ID2=DO_TOPIC. Viewed 1/30/08.
- ANSAB (Asia Network for Sustainable Agriculture and Bioresources). 2007. *Annual Report, 2006*. Kathmandu, Nepal: ANSAB.
- Barrett, C. D. Lee, and J. McPeak. 2005. "Institutional Arrangements for Rural Poverty Reduction and Resource Conservation." *World Development* 33(2):193–197.
- Basorun, Y.O., and J.O. Olakulehin. 2007. "The Lagos State Fish Farmers' Association." *LEISA Magazine, How Farmers Organise* 23(1):10–11. Online at http://www.leisa.info/index.php?url=magazine-details.tpl&p[readOnly]=0&p[_id]=90648.
- Bebbington, A. and T. Carroll. 2000. "Induced Social Capital and Federations of the Rural Poor." Social Capital Working Paper No. 19. Washington, DC: World Bank. Online at http://siteresources.worldbank.org/INTSOCIALCAPITAL/Resources/Social-Capital-Initiative-Working-Paper-Series/SCI-WPS-19.pdf.
- Beltran, J., P. Orozco, V. Zapata, J. Sanz, M. Roa, and A. Schmidt. 2004. "Scaling Out and Scaling Up—The Importance of Watershed Management Organizations." In *Scaling Up and Out: Achieving Widespread Impact Through Agricultural Research*, D. Pachico and S. Fujisaka, eds., pp.152-171. Cali, Colombia: International Center for Tropical Agriculture (CIAT). Online at http://www.ciat.cgiar.org/impact/pdf/scaling_up.pdf.
- Berkes, F., C. Seixas, D. Fernandes, D. Medeiros, S. Maurice, and S. Shukla. 2004. *Lessons from Community Self-Organization and Cross-Scale Linkages in Four Equator Initiative Projects*. Winnipeg, Canada: Natural Resources Institute, University of Manitoba. Online at http://www.umanitoba.ca/institutes/natural_resources/pdf/Lessons%20from%20Community%20Self-Organization%20and%20CrossScale%20Linkages%20in%20Four%20Equator%20Initiative%20Projects.pdf.
- Best, R., S. Ferris, and A. Schiavone. 2005. *Building Linkages and Enhancing Trust Between Small-Scale Rural Producers, Buyers in Growing Markets and Suppliers of Critical Inputs*. Paper presented at the International Seminar Beyond Agriculture: Making Markets Work for the Poor, Church House Conference Centre, Westminster, London, UK. Kent, UK: Crop Post-Harvest Program, Natural Resources International Limited. Online at http://www.cphp.uk.com/uploads/documents/CPHPTheme%20papers.pdf.
- Blomley, T. 2006. *Mainstreaming Participatory Forestry Within the Local Government Reform Process in Tanzania*. London: International Institute for Environment and Development. Online at http://www.iied.org/pubs/display.php?o=14536IIED&n=7&l=71&g=Tanzania.
- Body Shop. a. *Shea Butter*. UK: The Body Shop International. Online at http://www.thebodyshop.com/bodyshop/browse/ingredient_detail.jsp?ingredientId=500208
- Body Shop. b. *Support Community Trade*. UK: The Body Shop International. Online at http://www.thebodyshop.com/bodyshop/values/support_community_trade.jsp?cmre=default-_-Footer-_-ValuesCommunityTrade.
- Boyd, G. 2005. *Organisational Mechanisms that Best Serve the Poor*. Discussion Paper. London: Caledonia Centre for Social Development and International Institute for Environment and Development. Online at http://www.iied.org/pubs/pdfs/13515IIED.pdf.
- BRAC. 2005. *History*. Dhaka, Bangladesh: BRAC. Online at http://www.brac.net/history.htm.
- BRAC. 2007. *BRAC at a Glance*. Dhaka, Bangladesh: BRAC. Online at http://www.brac.net/downloads_files/BRAC%20At%20A%20Glance%20-%20June%202007.pdf.
- Braun, A., J. Okoth, H. Khaamala, and G. Khisa. 2007. "Building FFS Networks in East Africa." *LEISA Magazine, How Farmers Organise* 23(1):18–19. Online at http://www.leisa.info/index.php?url=magazine-details.tpl&p[readOnly]=0&p[_id]=90648.
- Breslin, E. 2003. *Demand Response Approach in Practice: Why Sustainability Remains Elusive*. WaterAid Discussion paper. London: WaterAid. Online at

http://www.wateraid.org/other/startdownload.asp?DocumentID=69&mode=plugin.

■ Brown, L.D. 1991. "Bridging Organizations and Sustainable Development." *Human Relations* 44(8):807–831.

■ Brown, D., and A. Kalegaonkar. 1999. "Addressing Civil Society's Challenges: Support Organizations as Emerging Institutions." *Institute for Development Research Reports* 15(1). Oxford: Institute for Development Research. Online at http://www.worlded.org/docs/Publications/idr/idr_pubs.htm

■ Bruneau, R. 2005. "Watershed Management Research: A Review of IDRC Projects in Asia and Latin America." Rural Poverty and Environment Working Paper No. 18. Ottawa, Canada: International Development Research Centre. Online at http://www.idrc.ca/uploads/user-S/1117113803118Bruneau.pdf.

■ Bruns, B., and P.C. Bruns. 2004. "Strengthening Collective Action." In *Collective Action and Property Rights for Sustainable Development*. R. Meinzen-Dick and M. Di Gregorio, eds., Brief 15. Washington, DC: International Food Policy Research Institute. Online at http://www.ifpri.org/2020/focus/focus11.asp.

■ Buck, L., J. Anderson, and D.C. Behr. 2003. *Strengthening Natural Resource Institutions in Africa – Applying Social Learning to Reconciling Poverty Reduction and Environmental Management Paper*. Presented at International Workshop on Reconciling Rural Poverty Reduction and Resource Conservation: Identifying Relationships and Remedies, Cornell University, Ithaca, New York, May 2–3. Online at http://aem.cornell.edu/special_programs/AFSNRM/Poverty/presentations.htm#Buck,%20Anderson%20&%20Behr.

■ Bukula, S. 2006. *Speaking With One Voice. The Role of Small and Medium Growers' Associations in Driving Change in the South African Forest Sector: Discussion Paper*. London: International Institute for Environment and Development. Online at http://www.iied.org/NR/forestry/projects/associations.html.

■ Bumacas, D., D. Catacutan, G. Chibememe, and C. Rhodes. 2006. "Enabling Local Communities to Develop and Scale Up Ecoagriculture: A Grassroots Perspective." In *Farming with Nature: the Science and Practice of Eco-Agriculture*. J. McNeely and S. Scherr, eds., pp. 286–307. Washington DC: Island Press.

■ CAPRi (CGIAR Systemwide Program on Collective Action and Property Rights). 2007. "Collective Action and Marketing of Underutilized Plant Species: The Case of Minor Millets in Kolli Hills, Tamil Nadu, India." CAPRi

Working Paper No.69. Washington, DC: International Food Policy Resource Institute. Online at http://www.capri.cgiar.org/wp/capriwp69.asp.

■ Cardenas, J-C. 2001. *Wealth Inequality and Overexploitation of the Commons: Field Experiments in Colombia*. Paper presented at the Inequality Cooperation and Sustainability Workshop, Santa Fe Institute, Santa Fe, New Mexico, Sep. 21–23. Online at http://www.santafe.edu/research/publications/workingpapers/02-08-033.pdf.

■ Carroll, T. 1992. *Intermediary NGOs: The Supporting Link in Grassroots Development*. West Hartford, Connecticut, USA: Kumarian Press.

■ Carter, S., and B. Currie-Alder. 2006. "Scaling-up Natural Resource Management: Insights from Research in Latin America." *Development in Practice*, 16(2):128–140.

■ Catacutan, D., and E. Tejada. 2006. *Institutional Issues and Political Challenges in Scaling Up Agroforestry: The Case of Landcare in the Philippines*. Paper presented at ICRAF 2nd National Agroforestry Congress, Camarines Sur, Philippines, Oct. 26–27. Online at www.worldagroforestry.org/downloads/publications/PDFs/pp05125.pdf.

■ Chebil, S., and I. Haque. 2003. "Community Driven Development Programs for Poverty Reduction: Experiences, Issues, and Lessons." *Scientific Journal of Administrative Development*, 1(1):112–141.

■ Chhetri, R. 1994. "Rotating Credit Associations in Nepal: Dhikuri as Capital, Credit, Saving, and Investment." *Human Organization*, 54(4):449–454.

■ Chilongo, T. 2005. *Tanzanian Agricultural Co-operatives: An Overview*. Moshi, Tanzania: Moshi University College of Co-operative and Business Studies. Online at http://internet.fredskorpset.no/upload/24657/TZ%20Co-op%20Overview%20Concept%20Paper.doc

■ Chuenpagdee, R., and S. Jentoft. 2007. "Step Zero for Fisheries Management: What Precedes Implementation." *Marine Policy*, 31(6):657–668.

■ CIP (International Potato Center). 2007. *Press Room/Facts and Figures: Work in the Mountains, Height Programs*. Lima, Peru: CIP. Online at http://www.cipotato.org/pressroom/facts_figures/work_in_the_mountains.asp.

■ CODI (Community Organizations Development Institute). 2006. *Community Master Plan*. Bangkok, Thailand: CODI. Online at http://www.codi.or.th/index.php?option=com_content&task=view&id=1103&Itemid=52.

■ COMACO (Community Markets for Conservation). 2004. *WCS Fact Sheet for Zambia: Community Markets for Conservation and Rural Livelihoods – COMACO: 4*. Lundazi, Zambia: COMACO. Online at http://itswild.org/fact_sheet_for_zambia-4.

■ COMACO (Community Markets for Conservation). 2006a. *About COMACO*. Lundazi, Zambia: COMACO. Online at http://www.itswild.org/about-comaco.

■ COMACO (Community Markets for Conservation). 2006b. *Results*. Lundazi, Zambia: COMACO. Online at http://www.itswild.org/results.

■ COMACO (Community Markets for Conservation). 2007a. *Watershed Protection and Water Management*. Luango Valley, Zambia: COMACO. Online at http://itswild.org/watershed-protection.

■ COMACO (Community Markets for Conservation). 2007b. *Products and Services*. Luango Valley, Zambia: COMACO. Online at http://www.itswild.org/http://itswild.org/products-services.

■ Conway, T., C. Moser, A. Norton, and J. Farrington. 2002. "Rights and Livelihood Approaches: Exploring Policy Dimensions." In *Natural Resource Perspectives*, (78). London: Overseas Development Institute. Online at http://www.odi.org.uk/Publications/nrp/index.html.

■ Cotula, L., C. Toulmin, and J. Quan. 2006. *Better Land Access for the Rural Poor: Lessons from Experience and Challenges Ahead*. London: International

Institute for Environment and Development. Online at http://www.iied.org/pubs/display.php?o=12532IIED&n=11&l=31&k=cotula

■ Cummings, A. 2004. *Against All Odds: Innovative Business Initiatives in Rural El Salvador, Central America.* PhD Thesis, Aalborg University, Denmark. El Salvador: Fundación Nacional para el Desarrollo. Online at http://forskningsbasen.deff.dk/ddf/rec.external?id=auc13211585.

■ Dahal, D.R. 1994. *A Review of Forest User Groups: Case Studies from Eastern Nepal.* Katmandu, Nepal: International Center for Integrated Mountain Development. Online at http://www.odi.org.uk/fecc/resources/greyliterature/joint%20forest%20management/Dill%20Ram%20Dahal/index.html

■ Das Gupta, M., H. Grandvoinnett, and M. Romani. 2003. "Fostering Community-Driven Development: What Role for the State?" World Bank Policy Research Working Paper 2969. Washington, DC: World Bank. Online at http://go.worldbank.org/XXH48NYNF0.

■ Dean's Beans. 2008. *Home.* Orange, Massachusetts, USA: Dean's Beans. Online at http://www.deansbeans.com/coffee/index.html.

■ Deininger, K. 2003. *Land Policies for Growth and Poverty Reduction.* Washington, DC: World Bank; Oxford: Oxford University Press. Online at http://go.worldbank.org/T9WPA67D50.

■ Deverill, P. 2000. *Designing Water and Sanitation Projects to Meet Demands: The Engineer's Role, Background Paper.* Leicestershire, UK: Water Engineering and Development Centre, Loughborough University. Online at http://wedc.lboro.ac.uk/projects/proj_contents0/WEJT1%20-%20Designing%20for%20Demand/www/outputs/Background-paper.doc.

■ Deverill, P., A. Wedgwood, S. Bibby, and I. Smout. 2002. *Designing Water Supply and Sanitation Projects to Meet Demand in Rural and Peri-Urban Communities: Book 1, Concepts, Principles, and Practice.* Leicestershire, UK: Water Engineering and Development Centre, Loughborough University. Online at http://wedc.lboro.ac.uk/staff/staff_details.php?id=37.

■ Ebrahim, A. 2003. *NGOs and Organizational Change: Discourse, Reporting, and Learning.* Cambridge, UK: Cambridge University Press.

■ Edwards, M., and D. Hulme. 1992. "Scaling Up NGO Impact on Development: Learning from Experience." *Development in Practice,* 2(2):77–91.

■ FAO (Food and Agriculture Organization). 2004. *World Overview of Conservation Approaches and Technologies (WOCAT): Impact Analysis, LANDCARE, Claveria Landcare Association (CLCA).* Berne, Switzerland: WOCAT. Online at http://www.fao.org/ag/agl/agll/wocat/wqasum8.asp?questid=PHI04.

■ Feder, G. 2002. *The Intricacies of Land Markets – Why the World Bank Succeeds in Economic Reform through Land Registration and Tenure Security.* PowerPoint presented at Conference of the International Federation of Surveyors, Washington, DC, Apr. 19–26. Online at http://pdf.wri.org/ref/feder_02_the_intricacies.pdf.

■ Ford Foundation. 2002. *Sustainable Solutions: Building Assets for Empowerment and Sustainable Development.* New York: Ford Foundation. Online at http://fordfound.org/pdfs/impact/sustainable_solutions.pdf.

■ Francis, P., and M. Amuyunzu-Nyamongo. 2005. *Bitter Harvest: The Social Costs of State Failure in Rural Kenya.* Paper presented at New Frontiers of Social Policy: Development in a Globalizing World, World Bank, Washington, DC, Dec. 12–15. Online at http://go.worldbank.org/1NX2RIW3B0.

■ Fritsch, O., and J. Newig. 2006. *Improving Environmental Quality Through Participation? A Critical Perspective on the Effectiveness of Public Participation.* Osnabrueck, Germany: Osnabrueck University.

■ Gibson, C., J. Williams, and E. Ostrom. 2005. "Local Enforcement and Better Forests." *World Development* 33(2):273–284.

■ Harper, M., and A. Roy. 2000. *Cooperative Success: What Makes Group Enterprise Succeed.* Warwickshire, UK: Practical Action.

■ Harsch, E. 2001. "Making Trade Work for Poor Women." *Africa Recovery* 15(4):6. Online at http://www.un.org/ecosocdev/geninfo/afrec/vol15no4/154shea.htm.

■ Hellin, J., M. Lundy, and M. Meijer. 2007. "Farmer Organization and Market Access." *LEISA Magazine* 23(1):26–27. Online at http://www.leisa.info/index.php?url=article-details.tpl&p%5B_id%5D=90668.

■ Holt-Giménez, E. 2006. *Campesino a Campesino: Voices from Latin America's Farmer to Farmer Movement for Sustainable Agriculture.* Oakland, California, USA: Food First Books.

■ Hooper, M., R. Jafry, M. Marolla, and J. Phan. 2004. "Scaling-Up Community Efforts to Reach the MDGs: An Assessment of Experience from the Equator Prize." In *The Millennium Development Goals and Conservation: Managing Nature's Wealth for Society's Health,* pp. 129–142. London: International Institute for Environment and Development. Online at http://www.iied.org/Gov/mdgs/publications.html.

■ Howell, J., and J. Pearce. 2000. "Civil Society: Technical Instrument or Social Force for Change?" In *New Roles and Relevance: Development NGOs and the Challenge of Change,* D. Lewis and T. Wallace Bloomfield, eds., Chapter 7. West Hartford, Connecticut, USA: Kumarian Press.

■ IIED (International Institute for Environment and Development). 2006. *Innovation in Securing Land Rights in Africa: Lessons from Experience.* Briefing Paper 2006. London: IIED. Online at http://www.iied.org/pubs/display.php?o=12531IIED&n=1&l=2&k=Innovation%20in%20Securing%20Land%20Rights%20in%20Africa.

■ IIED (International Institute for Environment and Development). 2007. *Learning from Local Organisations about Poverty Reduction and Environmental Management: A Participatory Review.* London: IIED. Online at http://www.povertyenvironment.net/?q=filestore2/download/962/Local%20organisations%20work%20plan%200107%20PEP.doc.

■ IUCN (World Conservation Union) Botswana. 2005a. *Botswana CBNRM Support Program: BOCOBONET.* Gaborone, Botswana: IUCN Botswana. Online at http://www.cbnrm.bw/Partners/BOCOBONET.html.

■ IUCN (World Conservation Union) Botswana. 2005b. *Botswana CBNRM Support Program: Community Based Tourism.* Gaborone, Botswana: IUCN Botswana. Online at http://www.cbnrm.bw/cbnrmbotswana/communitytourism.html.

■ IUCN (World Conservation Union) Botswana. 2005c. *Botswana CBNRM Support Program: Conservation.* Gaborone, Botswana: IUCN Botswana. Online at http://www.cbnrm.bw/cbnrmbotswana/conservation.html.

■ IUCN (World Conservation Union) Botswana. 2006. *Botswana Support Program Achievements.* Gaborone, Botswana: IUCN Botswana. Online at: http://www.cbnrm.bw/supportprogramme/achievements.html. Viewed Sept. 18, 2007.

■ Jones, B., and A. Mosimane. 2007. *Promoting Integrated Community-Based Natural Resource Management as a Means to Combat Desertification: The Living in a Finite Environment (LIFE) Project and the Khoadi Hoas and Nyae Nyae Conservancies, Namibia.* Washington, DC: International Resources Group. Online at http://www.frameweb.org/ev_en.php?ID=42632_201&ID2=DO_TOPIC.

■ Kanungo, P. 2004. *Broadening SME Networking and Cluster Development: UNIDO Initiatives—Glimpses from Nicaragua and India.* Washington, DC: World Bank. Online at http://siteresources.worldbank.org/INTEMPOWERMENT/Resources/15110_Nicaragua_Case_Study.pdf.

- Kerr, J., G. Pangare, and V.L. Pangare. 2002. *Watershed Development Projects in India: An Evaluation.* Research Report 127. Washington, DC: International Food Policy Research Institute. Online at: http://www.ifpri.org/pubs/abstract/127/rr127.pdf.

- Khan, S.S., and J.K. Tareen. 2004. *Scaling Up Poverty Reduction: Case of the Rural Support Programs (RSPs) in Pakistan.* PowerPoint presented at Scaling Up Poverty Reduction Conference, Shanghai, China, May. Washington, DC: World Bank. Online at http://go.worldbank.org/0PVXAD8LO0

- Kolavalli, S., and J. Kerr. 2002. "Scaling up Participatory Watershed Development in India." *Development and Change,* 33(2):213–235.

- Koopman, J., R. Kweka, M. Mboya, and S.M. Wangwe. 2001. *Community Participation in Traditional Irrigation Scheme Rehabilitation Projects in Tanzania: Report of a Collaborative Research Project.* Dar es Salaam, Tanzania: Ministry of Agriculture and Cooperatives, Irrigation Section.

- Kruijssen, F., and S. Somsri. 2006. *Marketing Local Biodiversity in Thailand: Identification of a Possible Good Practice for On-farm Biodiversity Management of Tropical Fruit Trees.* Paper presented at Conference on International Agricultural Research for Develop, University of Bonn, Germany Oct.11–13. Online at http://www.tropentag.de/2006/abstracts/full/221.pdf.

- Lewis, D. 2005. Markets, *Food Security and Conservation: A Model for Rural Development in Zambia.* New York City: Wildlife Conservation Society. Online at http://www.itswild.org/research_and_policy. Viewed 1/30/2008.

- LMMA (Locally Managed Marine Area) Network. 2007. *Enhancing LMMA Effectiveness through Continued Learning: Annual Report of the LMMA Network for 2006.* Suva, Fiji: LMMA Network. Online at http://www.lmmanetwork.org/Site_Page.cfm?PageID=64.

- Lobo, C. 2007. Managing Trustee. Watershed Organisation Trust, Ahmednagar, Maharashtra, India. Personal communication. May and July.

- Lobo, C. 2008. Managing Trustee, Watershed Organisation Trust, Ahmednagar, Maharashtra, India. Personal communication. Feb.

- Locke, R. 2002. *Building Trust and Social Embeddedness and Labor Union Revival.* Paper presented at the Conference on Economic Governance and Political Institutions, São Paulo, Brazil, March. São Paulo, Brazil: Centro Brasileiro De Analise e Planejamento.

- Lok Sabha (Indian House of the People). 2006. *The Scheduled Tribes and Other Traditional Forest Dwellers (Recognition of Forest Rights) Bill, 2006.* Delhi, India: Lok Sabha. Dec. 15. Online at http://forestrightsact.awardspace.com/Act.pdf.

- Macqueen, D., S. Vermeulen, C. Kazoora, F. Merry, S. Ousman, S. Saigal, S. Wen, and H. Weyerhauser. 2005. "Advancement Through Association: Appropriate Support for Associations of Small and Medium Forest Enterprise." In *How to Make Poverty History: The Central Role of Local Organizations in Meeting the MDGs.* T. Biggs and D. Satterthwaite, eds., pp. 79–98. London: International Institute for Environment and Development. Online at http://www.iied.org/pubs/pdfs/11000IIED.pdf.

- Macqueen, D., S. Bose, S. Bukula, C. Kazoora, S. Ousman, N. Porro, and H. Weyerhaeuser. 2006. *Working Together: Forest-Linked Small and Medium Enterprise Associations and Collective Action.* London: International Institute for Environment and Development. Online at http://www.iied.org/pubs/pdfs/14521IIED.pdf.

- Manikutty, S. 2002. "Gujarat Cooperative Milk Marketing Federation Ltd. (GCMMF)." *Asian Case Research Journal,* 6:205–239.

- Mansuri, G., and V. Rao. 2003. *Evaluating Community-Based and Community-Driven Development: A Critical Review of the Evidence.* Washington, DC: World Bank. Online at http://siteresources.worldbank.org/INTECAREGTOPCOMDRIDEV/Resources/DECstudy.pdf

- Marsh, R. 2003. *Working with Local Institutions to Support Sustainable Livelihoods.* Rome: Food and Agriculture Organization of the United Nations, Sustainable Development Department. Online at http://www.fao.org/sd/2002/PE0702a_en.htm.

- McCarthy, S. 2007. Chief of Party, Agricultural Cooperatives in Ethiopia (ACE), 1998–2004. ACDI/VOCA, Washington, DC. Personal Communication. Nov. 27.

- McFadden, S. 2007. "Organic Growth." *Boston Business Journal.* Feb. 2.

- Meinzen-Dick, R., and M. Di Gregorio. 2004. "Overview." In *Collective Action and Property Rights for Sustainable Development.* R. Meinzen-Dick and M. Di Gregorio, eds. Brief 1. 2020 Vision for Food, Agriculture, and the Environment, Focus 11. Washington, DC: International Food Policy Research Institute. Online at http://www.ifpri.org/2020/focus/focus11.asp.

- Middleton, L. 2008. "Community Markets for Conservation: WCS at Work in Zambia." *Wildlife Magazine,* Jan., pp. 22–29. Bronx, New York, USA: The Wildlife Conservation Society.

- NACSO (Namibia Association of CBNRM Support Organisations). 2003. *NACSO Services.* Windhoek, Namibia: NACSO. Online at http://www.nacso.org.na.

- NACSO (Namibian Association of CBNRM Support Organizations). 2006. *Namibia's Communal Conservancies: A Review of Progress and Challenges in 2005.* Windhoek, Namibia: NACSO. Online at http://www.irdnc.org.na/conservancies.htm.

- Ostrom, E. 1990. *Governing the Commons: The Evolution of Institutions for Collective Action.* New York: Cambridge University Press.

- Ostrom, E. 2004. "Understanding Collective Action and Collective Action Problems." In *Collective Action and Property Rights for Sustainable Development.* R. Meinzen-Dick and M. Di Gregorio, eds., Brief 2. 2020 Vision for Food,

Agriculture, and the Environment, Focus 11. Washington DC: International Food Policy Research Institute. Online at http://www.ifpri.org/2020/focus/focus11.asp.

- Pagdee, A., Y. Kim, and P.J. Daugherty. 2006. "What Makes Community Forest Management Successful: A Meta-Study from Community Forests Throughout the World." *Society and Natural Resources,* 19:33–52.

- Pathak, N., A. Kothari, and D. Roe. 2005. "Conservation with Social Justice? The Role of Community Conserved Areas in Achieving the Millennium Development Goals." In *How to Make Poverty History: The Central Role of Local Organizations in Meeting the MDGs.* T. Biggs and D. Satterthwaite, eds., pp. 55–78. London: International Institute for Environment and Development. Online at http://www.iied.org/pubs/pdfs/11000IIED.pdf.

- Philip, K. 2003. *Co-operatives in South Africa: Their Role in Job Creation and Poverty Reduction.* Parktown, South Africa: South African Foundation. Online at http://www.businessleadership.org.za/publications.php.

- Pimbert, M. 2006. *Reclaiming Autonomous Food Systems: The Role of Local Organizations in Farming, Environment and People's Access to Food.* Paper presented at the International Conference on Land, Poverty, Social Justice and Development, The Hague, Netherlands, Jan. 12–14.

- Pokharel, B., S. Madhusudan, I.B. Sapkota, B. Subedi, Asia Network for Sustainable Agriculture and Bioresources, and EnterpriseWorks/VITA for International Resources Group. 2006. *Role of Natural Products in Resource Management, Poverty Alleviation, and Good Governance: A Case Study of Jatamansi and Wintergreen Value Chains in Nepal.* Washington, DC: United States Agency for International Development. Online at http://www.irgltd.com/Resources/Publications/ANE/Nepal%20FRAME%20final%20v5.pdf.

- Pozzoni, B., and N. Kumar. 2005. *A Review of the Literature on Participatory Approaches to Local Development for an Evaluation of the Effectiveness of World Bank Support for Community-Based and -Driven Development Approaches.* Washington, DC: World Bank. Online at http://siteresources.worldbank.org/EXTEFFOFWBSUP/Resources/cbd_cdd_literature_review.pdf.

- PREM (People's Rural Education Movement). 2007. *PREM.* Mandiapalli, Orissa, India: PREM. Online at http://prem.org.in.

- Pretty, J., and H. Ward. 2001. "Social Capital and the Environment." *World Development,* 29(2):209–227.

- Ribot, J. 2008. Senior Associate, Governance and Access, World Resources Institute. Washington, DC. Personal Communication, Feb. 12.

- Satterthwaite, D. 2005. "Introduction: Why Local Organizations are Central to Meeting the MDGs." In *How to Make Poverty History: The Central Role of Local Organizations in Meeting the MDGs.* T. Biggs and D. Satterthwaite, eds., pp. 1–25. London: International Institute for Environment and Development. Online at http://www.iied.org/pubs/pdfs/11000IIED.pdf.

- Scherr, S., J. Amornsanguasin, M.E. Chiong-Javier, D. Garrity, S. Sunito, and Saharuddin. 2001. *Local Organizations in Natural Resource Management in the Uplands of Southeast Asia: Policy Context and Institutional Landscape.* Paper presented at the Sustainable Agriculture and Natural Resources Management Conference Sustaining Upland Development in Southeast Asia, Manila, Philippines, May 28–30.

- SEWA (Self-Employed Women's Association). 2005. *SEWA's Ongoing Struggle.* Bhadra, Ahmedabad, India: SEWA. Online at http://www.sewa.org/index_files/sewastruggle.htm.

- SEWA (Self-Employed Women's Association). 2007a. *Goals.* Bhadra, Ahmedabad, India: SEWA. Online at http://www.sewa.org/aboutus/goals.asp.

- SEWA (Self-Employed Women's Association). 2007b. *Structure.* Bhadra, Ahmedabad, India: SEWA. Online at http://www.sewa.org/aboutus/structure.asp.

- Seymour, F. 1994. "Are Successful Community-based Conservation Projects Designed or Discovered?" In *Natural Connections: Perspectives in Community Based Conservation.* D. Western and R.M. Wright, eds., pp. 472–496. Washington, DC: Island Press.

- Sharma, A., A. Purohit, K.L. Dandsena, and V. Madhu. 2005. *Scaling Up without Losing Quality and Impact: Lessons from Outstanding Watershed Programs in India.* International Water Management Institute–Tata (IMWI-TATA) Water Policy Research Highlight. Mumbai, India: IMWI-TATA. Online at http://www.iwmi.cgiar.org/iwmi-tata/FILES/pdf/PM05/26_Highlight.pdf.

- Shrestha, A. 2004. "Building Gender-Responsive Water User Associations in Nepal." In *Bringing Water to the Poor: Selected ADB Case Studies.* M.A. Asico and L. Lumbao, eds., pp.14–19. Manila, Philippines: Asian Development Bank. Online at http://www.adb.org/Documents/Books/Water_for_All_Series/Water_to_the_Poor/Water_08.pdf#page=11.

- Shyamsundar, P., E. Araral, and S. Weerartne. 2004. *Devolution of Resource Rights, Poverty, and Natural Resource Management – A Review.* Washington, DC: World Bank. Online at http://go.worldbank.org/1Q6TDM92V2.

- Southey, S. 2008. Manager, United Nations Development Programme Equator Initiative. Personal Communication, Feb. 16.

- Subedi, B. 2007. Executive Director, Asia Network for Sustainable Agriculture and Bioresources, Kathmandu, Nepal. Personal Communication. Dec. 11.

- Subedi, B., H.R. Ojha, K. Nicholson, and S.B. Binayee. 2004. *Community-Based Forest Enterprises in Nepal: Case Studies, Lessons and Implications.* Kathmandu, Nepal: Asia Network for Sustainable Agriculture and Bioresources.

- Taylor, P., L. Raynolds, and D. Murray. 2003. *One Cup at a Time: Poverty Alleviation and Fair Trade Coffee in Latin America.* Fort Collins, Colorado, USA: Colorado State University. Online at http://www.colostate.edu/Depts/Sociology/FairTradeResearchGroup/doc/fairtrade.pdf.

- Thiele, G., A. Devaux, C. Velasco, and K. Manrique. 2006. "Horizontal Evaluation: Stimulating Social Learning among Peers." Institutional Learning and Change Initiative Brief 13. Rome: Institutional Learning and Change Initiative. Online at http://www.cgiar-ilac.org/downloads/Briefs/ILAC_Brief13.pdf.

- Thi Phi, L., N. Van Duong, N. Ngoc Quong, and P. Lac Vang. 2004. "Making the Most of Market Chains: Challenges for Small-Scale Farmers and Traders in Upland Vietnam." Small and Medium Forest Enterprise Series No. 2. London: International Institute for Environment and Development. Online at http://www.iied.org/pubs/display.php?o=9313IIED&n=8&l=47&k=Vietnam.

- Toulmin, C. 2005. "Securing Land and Property Rights in Sub-Saharan Africa: The Role of Local Institutions." In *How to Make Poverty History: The Central Role of Local Organizations in Meeting the MDGs.* T. Biggs and D. Satterthwaite, eds., pp. 27–54. London: International Institute for Environment and Development. Online at http://www.iied.org/pubs/pdfs/11000IIED.pdf.

- Turton, C., M. Warner, and B. Groom. 1998. "Scaling Up Participatory Watershed Development in India: A Review of the Literature." Overseas Development Institute (ODI), Agriculture & Extension Network Paper No. 86. London: ODI. Online at http://www.odi.org.uk/networks/agren/papers/agrenpaper_86.PDF.

- UNDP (United Nations Development Programme). 1998. *Capacity Assessment and Development in a Systems and Strategic Management Context. Technical Advisory Paper No. 3.* New York: UNDP. Online at http://www.pogar.org/publications/other/undp/governance/capsystech3-98e.pdf.

- UNDP (United Nations Development Programme). 2004. *Unleashing Entrepreneurship: Making Business Work for the Poor.* New York: UNDP. Online at http://www.undp.org/cpsd/report/index.html.

- UNDP (United Nations Development Program). 2006a. *Equator Prize 2006 Nomination Form: Nam Ha Ecoguide Service.* New York: UNDP. Online at http://www.equatorinitiative.net/files/2006-053_LaoPDR_NamHaEcoguideService.doc.

- UNDP (United Nations Development Programme). 2006b. "The Costa Rican Organic Agricultural Movement (MAOCO)." In *Community Action to Conserve Biodiversity: Linking Biodiversity Conservation with Poverty Reduction.*, pp. 36–37. New York: UNDP. Online at http://sgp.undp.org/index.cfm?module=ActiveWeb&page=WebPage&s=biodiversity_case_st.

- UNDP (United Nations Development Programme). 2008a. *Equator Initiative.* New York: UNDP. Online at http://www.undp.org/equatorinitiative/.

- UNDP (United Nations Development Programme). 2008b. *Capacity Development Homepage.* New York: UNDP. Online at http://www.capacity.undp.org/index.cfm?module=ActiveWeb&page=WebPage&s=capacity_development.

- UNDP (United Nations Development Program) Energy and Environment Group. 2006. *Community Action to Conserve Biodiversity: Linking Biodiversity Conservation with Poverty Reduction.* New York: UNDP. Online at http://www.undp.org/equatorinitiative/documents/pdf/biodiversity_case_studies_english.pdf.

- Uphoff, N. 1992. *Local Institutions and Participation for Sustainable Development.* London: International Institute for Environment and Development. Online at http://www.iied.org/pubs/display.php?o=6045IIED.

- Uphoff, N. 1999. "Understanding Social Capital: Learning from the Analysis and Experience of Participation." In *Social Capital: A Multifaceted Perspective*, P. Dasgupta and I. Serageldin, eds. Washington, DC: World Bank. Online at http://www.worldbank.org.in/external/default/main?pagePK=51187349&piPK=51189435&theSitePK=295584&menuPK=64187510&searchMenuPK=295611&theSitePK=295584&entityID=000094946_99110505361324&searchMenuPK=295611&theSitePK=295584.

- Uphoff, N., and L. Buck. 2006. *Strengthening Rural Local Institutional Capacities for Sustainable Livelihoods and Equitable Development.* Washington, DC: World Bank. Online at http://siteresources.worldbank.org/EXTSOCIALDEVELOPMENT/Resources/244362-1170428243464/3408356-1170428261889/3408359-1170428299570/Strengthening-Rural-Local-Institutional-Capacities.pdf

- Uphoff, N., M. Esman, and A. Krishna, eds. 1998. *Reasons for Success: Learning From Instructive Experiences in Rural Development.* West Hartford: Kumarian Press.

- USAID (United States Agency for International Development). 1984. *Local Organizations in Development. USAID Policy Paper.* Washington, DC: USAID. Online at http://www.usaid.gov/policy/ads/200/localorg/localorg.pdf.

- USAID (United States Agency for International Development) and ARD, Inc. 2008. *Global Land Tenure Master Database. 2007.* Unpublished data. Original graphics published in USAID and ARD, Inc. 2007. "Land Tenure and Property Rights Tools and Regional Reports." Washington, DC: USAID EGAT/Natural Resources Management/Land Resources Management Team and Burlington, Vermont: ARD, Inc. Online at http://prrgp.com/tools.htm.

- USAID (United States Agency for International Development) and WWF (World Wildlife Fund). 2007. *LIFE PLUS Cumulative Progress Towards Achievement of Strategic Objective Results And Intermediate Results for the Period: October 1, 2006 – September 30, 2007.* Washington, DC: USAID and WWF.

- Valcárcel, V. 2007. *T'ikapapa gana el World Challenge 2007.* Lima, Peru: Papa Andina. Dec. 5. Online at http://papandina.cip.cgiar.org/index.php?id=47&tx_ttnews[tt_news]=52&cHash=de3a74ed43.

- van den Brink, R., G. Thomas, H. Binswanger, J. Bruce, and F. Byamugisha. 2006. "Consensus, Confusion, and Controversy: Selected Land Reform Issues in Sub-Saharan Africa." Working Paper No. 71. Washington, DC: World Bank. Online at http://www.icarrd.org/en/icard_doc_down/TD7.pdf.

- Varughese, G., and E. Ostrom. 2001. "The Contested Role of Heterogeneity in Collective Action: Some Evidence from Community Forestry in Nepal." *World Development*, 29(5):747–765.

- von Benda-Beckmann, K. 1981. "Forum Shopping and Shopping Forms: Dispute Processing in a Minanagkabau Village." *Journal of Legal Pluralism* 19:117–159.

- WCS (Wildlife Conservation Society). 2006a. *WCS Fact Sheet for Zambia: COMACO Producer Groups as Entry Points for Food Security and Diversified Livelihoods.* New York: WCS. Online at http://www.wcs.org/international/Africa/zambia.

- WCS (Wildlife Conservation Society). 2006b. *Maize Production in Luangwa Valley in Relation to Farming Practices: Strategies for Sustainable Agriculture and Natural Resource Conservation.* New York: WCS. Online at http://itswild.org/files/maize-production-in-luangwa-valley-in-relation-to-farming-practices.pdf.

- WCS (Wildlife Conservation Society). 2007. *Zambia.* New York: WCS. Online at http://www.wcs.org/international/Africa/zambia.

- White, A., and A. Martin. 2002. *Who Owns the World's Forests? Forest Tenure*

233

and Public Forests in Transition. Washington, DC: Forest Trends and Center for International Environmental Law. Online at http://www.cbnrm.net/pdf/white_a_001_foresttenure.pdf.

- White, T.A., and C.F. Runge. 1995. "The Emergence and Evolution of Collective Action: Lessons from Watershed Management in Haiti." *World Development,* 23(10):1683–1698.

- White, A., A. Khare, and A. Molnar. 2007. *Transitions in Forest Tenure and Governance: Drivers, Projected Patterns, and Implications.* Paper presented at the Conference Illegal Logging and Associated Trade: Exploring Options, Royal Institute of International Affairs, London, Jan. 24. Online at http://www.rightsandresources.org/publication_details.php?publicationID=133.

- WIDECAST Latin American Program. 2007. *Home.* Heredia, Costa Rica: WIDECAST Latin American Program. Online at http://www.latinamericanseaturtles.org/index.php?option=com_frontpage&Itemid=1.

- World Bank. 1996. T*he World Bank Participation Sourcebook.* Washington, DC: World Bank. Online at http://www.worldbank.org/wbi/sourcebook/sbhome.htm.

- WOTR (Watershed Organisation Trust). 2007a. *WOTR: About Us.* Ahmednagar, Maharashtra, India: WOTR. Online at: http://www.wotr.org/aboutus.htm.

- WOTR (Watershed Organisation Trust). 2007b. *WOTR: Activities.* Ahmednagar, Maharashtra, India: WOTR. Online at: http://www.wotr.org/activities.htm.

- Young, T., and J. Portocarrero. 2007. *Hat Making in Peru: A Pathway out of Poverty.* Id21 Research Highlight, Jan. 23. Brighton, UK: Institute of Development Studies. Online at http://www.id21.org/zinter/id21zinter.exe?a=i&w=r5jp1g1.

- Zehra, M. 2005. "Creating Space for Civil Society in an Impoverished Environment in Pakistan." In *Reducing Poverty and Sustaining the Environment: The Politics of Local Engagement.* S. Bass, H. Reid, D. Satterthwaite, and P. Steele, eds., pp. 20–41. Sterling, VA: Earthscan/IIED.

Box 2.1

- Asociación ANAI. 2006. *Talamanca Initiative Case Study.* Sabanilla de Montes de Oca, Costa Rica: Asociación ANAI.

- Berkes, F. 2007. "Community-based Conservation in a Globalized World." Proceedings of the National Academy of Sciences 104:15188–15193. Online at http://www.pnas.org/cgi/content/abstract/0702098104v1.

- Berkes, F., and T. Adhikari. 2006. "Development and Conservation: Indigenous Businesses and the UNDP Equator Initiative." *International Journal of Entrepreneurship and Small Business* 3(6):671–690. Online at http://www.inderscience.com/search/index.php?action=record&rec_id=10920&prevQuery=&ps=10&m=or.

- Berkes, F., and I. J. Davidson-Hunt. 2007. "Communities and Social Enterprises in the Age of Globalization." *Journal of Enterprising Communities* 1:209–221.

- IIRR (International Institute of Rural Reconstruction). 2000. *Going To Scale: Can We Bring More Benefits to More People More Quickly?* Cavite, Philippines: IIRR.

- Heid, E., and J. Streets. 2006. *Partnership for Community-Run Marine Protected Areas in Madagascar.* Berlin: Global Public Policy Institute. Online at http://www.gppi.net/fileadmin/gppi/SEED_CASE_Madagascar_MPA_eh.pdf.

- Hooper, M., R. Jafry, M. Marolla, and J. Phan. 2005. "Scaling-up Community Efforts to Reach the MDGs—An Assessment of Experience from the Equator Prize." In *The Millennium Development Goals and Conservation: Managing Nature's Wealth for Society's Health.* D. Rose, ed., pp. 129–142. London: International Institute for Environment and Development. Online at

http://www.iied.org/Gov/mdgs/documents/MDG2-ch8.pdf.

- NRI (Natural Resources Institute), University of Manitoba. 2007. *Current EI Projects at the NRI.* Winnipeg, Canada: University of Manitoba. Online at http://www.umanitoba.ca/institutes/natural_resources/nri_cbrm_projects _eiprojects.html.

- Timmer, V. 2004. *Characteristics of Leadership and Five Equator Prize 2002 Finalists.* CID Graduate Student Working Paper No. 3. Cambridge, Massachusetts, USA: Science, Environment and Development Group, Center for International Development, Harvard University. Online at http://www.cid.harvard.edu/cidwp/pdf/grad_student/003.pdf.

- UNDP (United Nations Development Programme). 2002. *Equator Initiatives: Shompole Community Ecotourism Development Project (SCEDP) 2002.* New York: UNDP. Online at http://www.equatorinitiative.net/files/2002-0075_ Nom_SCEDP_Kenya.pdf.

- UNDP (United Nations Development Programme). 2005. *Learning From Success: Scaling-up Community-based Enterprises for Biodiversity and the MDGs—A Synthesis of Community Case Studies from Latin America and the Caribbean.* New York: UNDP. Online at http://www.undp.org/equatorinitiative/documents/pdf/completoing.pdf.

- UNDP (United Nations Development Programme). 2007. *Equator Knowledge Zone.* New York: UNDP. Online at http://www.equatorinitiative.net/index.lasso.

Box 2.3

- Allen, H. 2002. *CARE International's Village Savings & Loan Programmes in Africa: Micro Finance for the Rural Poor that Works.* Atlanta, GA: CARE International. Online at http://www.msu.edu/unit/phl/devconference/CAREVillSavLoanAfr.pdf.

- CARE International. 2005. "Women's Groups in Niger Help Stave Off the Worst of the Food Crisis." Atlanta, Georgia, USA: CARE International. Aug. 10. Online at http://www.care.org/newsroom/articles/2005/08/20050810_ niger_mmd.asp?sitewrapper=print.

- CARE International. 2007. *Annual Report 2006—Regions.* Atlanta, Georgia, USA: CARE International. Online at http://www.care.org/newsroom/publications/annualreports/2006/annual2006_regions.pdf.
- FON (Friends of Niger). 2001. "Mata Masu Dubara: Women's Savings and Credit Group Formation." *The Camel Express.* Dec. Online at http://www.friendsofniger.org/newsletters/MMD.htm.

Box 2.4

- Lobo, C. 2007. Co-founder and Executive Director, Watershed Organisation Trust. Ahmednagar, Maharashtra, India: Personal Communication. July.
- WOTR (Watershed Organisation Trust). 2007. WOTR: *Activities.* Ahmednagar, Maharashtra, India: WOTR. Online at http://www.wotr.org/activities.htm.
- WOTR (Watershed Organisation Trust). 2005. *Drop by Drop: The Story of WOTR.* Ahmednagar, Maharashtra, India: WOTR.
- WRI (World Resources Institute) in collaboration with United Nations Development Programme, United Nations Environment Programme, and World Bank. 2005. *World Resources 2005: The Wealth of the Poor—Managing Ecosystems to Fight Poverty.* Washington, DC: WRI. Online at http://www.wri.org/project/world-resources.

Box 2.5

- AKRSP (Aga Khan Rural Support Programme). 2003. *Introduction.* Islamabad, Pakistan: AKRSP. Online at http://www.akrsplessons.org/akrsp.php.
- Khan, M. 2005. *The Microhydel Projects of Aga Khan Rural Support Programme, Chitral, Pakistan.* Aga Khan Development Network. Online at http://www.gdnet.org/pdf2/gdn_library/awards_medals/2005/midp_05_first.pdf.
- Najam, A. 2003. *AKRSP-Government Relations: Looking Back, Looking Forward.* Paper presented at Lessons in Development—The AKRSP Experience Conference, Islamabad, Pakistan, Dec. 2003. Online at http://www.akrsplessons.org/themes.php?goto=government.
- Malik, A., and G. Wood. 2003. *Poverty and Livelihoods.* Paper presented at Lessons in Development—The AKRSP Experience Conference, Islamabad, Pakistan, Dec. 2003. Online at http://www.akrsplessons.org/themes.php?goto=poverty.
- Zehra, M. 2005. "Creating Space for Civil Society in an Impoverished Environment in Pakistan." In *Reducing Poverty and Sustaining the Environment: The Politics of Local Engagement,* S. Bass, H. Reid, D. Satterthwaite, and P. Steele, eds., pp. 20–43. London: Earthscan.

Box 2.6

- ANSAB (Asia Network for Sustainable Agriculture and Bioresources). 2005. *Our Experience of Introducing FSC Certification in Nepal.* Katmandu: ANSAB. Online at http://www.ansab.org/certificates.php?linkno=12.
- ANSAB (Asia Network for Sustainable Agriculture and Bioresources). 2007. *Capability Statement.* Katmandu: ANSAB. Unpublished.
- Crown, R. 2004. "Implementation Completion Report (TF-28370) on a Grant in the Amount of US$ 4.57 Million to the Government of the Democratic Socialist Republic of Sri Lanka for the Conservation and Sustainable Use of Medicinal Plants Project." World Bank Report No. 29629. Washington, DC: World Bank. Online at http://www-wds.worldbank.org/external/default/WDSContentServer/WDSP/IB/2004/12/17/000090341_20041217110244/Rendered/PDF/29629.pdf.
- FAO (Food and Agriculture Organization of the United Nations). 2005. *Trade in Medicinal Plants.* Rome: FAO. Online at http://www.fao.org/docrep/008/af285e/af285e00.htm.
- GMCL (Gram Mooligai Co. Ltd.). 2006. *Business Plan.* Bangalore, India: GMCL. Unpublished.
- Indian NGOs. 2007. *Proposal on Herbal Medicines: Reduction of Health Expenses at Family Level and Livelihood for Women.* Munbai: Indians NCOs Online at http://www.indianngos.com/villageherbals/villageherbs.htm.
- Kursar, T., C. Caballero-George, T. Capson, L. Cubilla-Rios, W. H. Gerwick, M. P. Gupta, A. Ibañez, R. G. Linington, K. L. McPhail, E. Ortegabarría, L. I. Romero, P. N. Solis, and P. D. Coley. 2006. "Securing Economic Benefits and Promoting Conservation Through Bioprospecting." *BioScience* 56(12):1005–1012.
- Lambert, J., P. Ryden, and E. Esikuri. 2005. *Capitalizing on the Bio-Economic Value of Multi-Purpose Medicinal Plants for the Rehabilitation of Drylands in Sub-Saharan Africa.* Washington, DC: World Bank. Online at http://www-wds.worldbank.org/external/default/WDSContentServer/WDSP/IB/2005/11/03/000012009_20051103132923/Rendered/PDF/341170rev.pdf.
- Mander, M. 1998. *Marketing of Indigenous Medicinal Plants in South Africa—A Case Study in Kwazulu-Natal.* Rome: Food and Agriculture Organization of the United Nations. Online at http://www.fao.org/docrep/W9195E/w9195e00.HTM.
- Newman, D., and G. Cragg. 2007. "Natural Products as Sources of New Drugs over the Last 25 Years." *Journal of Natural Products,* 70:461–477.
- Raju, G. 2006. *Gram Mooligai.* Washington, DC: New Ventures. Unpublished.
- Schippmann, U., D. Leaman, and A. B. Cunningham. 2002. *Impact of Cultivation and Gathering of Medicinal Plants on Biodiversity: Global Trends and Issues.* Paper presented at Biodiversity and the Ecosystem Approach in Agriculture, Forestry and Fisheries satellite event at the Ninth Regular Session of the Commission on Genetic Resources for Food and Agriculture, 12–13 Oct. Rome: Food and Agriculture Organization of the United Nations. Online at ftp://ftp.fao.org/docrep/fao/005/aa010e/AA010E00.pdf.
- Shekhar, C., and R. Badola. 2000. "Medicinal Plant Cultivation and Sustainable Development: A Case Study in the Buffer Zone of the Nanda Devi Biosphere Reserve, Western Himalaya, India." *Mountain Research and Development* 20(3):272–279.
- Stewart, K. M. 2003. "The African Cherry (Prunus Africana): From Hoe-Handles to the International Herb Market." *Economic Botany* 57(4):559–569.
- Subedi, B. 2001. *Marketing of Medicinal and Aromatic Plant Products of Nepal in Domestic and International Markets.* Katmandu: Asia Network for Sustainable Agriculture and Bioresources. Online at http://ansab.org/research_papers/marketing%20_MAPs_DOF_training.pdf.
- USAID (United States Agency for International Development). 2006. *Improving Forest Management in Nepal.* Washington, DC: USAID. Online at http://www.usaid.gov/stories/nepal/ss_nepal_forest.html.
- WHO (World Health Organization). 2006. *Plants, Medicinal.* Geneva: WHO. Online at http://www.who.int/topics/plants_medicinal/en/index.html.
- World Bank. 2001. *Ethiopia—Conservation and Sustainable Use of Medicinal Plants Project.* Report No. 21737. Washington, DC: World Bank. Online at http://go.worldbank.org/1LNUAGBMD0.
- WWF (World Wide Fund for Nature). 2002. *Prunus Africana.* Godalming, Surrey, UK: WWF. Online at http://www.wwf.org.uk/filelibrary/pdf/pafricana.pdf.

Box 2.7

- ACDI/VOCA. 2006a. "ACDI/VOCA Beneficiaries Brew Success in Coffee Contest." World Report (ACDI/VOCA). Spring:9. Online at http://www.acdivoca.org/852571DC00681414/ID/resources_worldreportspring06.

- ACDI/VOCA. 2006b. "Another Ethiopian Cooperative Scores Big in the Specialty Coffee Market." World Report (ACDI/VOCA). Spring:16. Online at http://www.acdivoca.org/852571DC00681414/ID/resources_worldreportspring06.

- Dempsey, J. 2006. A Case Study of Institution Building and Value Chain Strengthening to Link Ethiopian Cooperative Coffee Producers to International Markets. Paper presented at Regional Consultation on Linking Farmers to Markets, Cairo, Egypt, Jan. 29-Feb. 2. Online at http://www.globalfoodchainpartnerships.org/cairo/papers/JimDempseyEthiopia.pdf.

- Dempsey, J., and R. Campbell. 2006. "A Value-Chain Approach to Coffee Production: Linking Ethiopian Coffee-Producers to International Markets." World Report (ACDI/VOCA). Spring:5–7. Online at http://www.acdivoca.org/852571DC00681414/ID/resources_worldreportspring06.

- Dorsey, J., and T. Assefa. 2005. USAID Evaluation of Agricultural Cooperatives in Ethiopia (ACE) Program Activities. Washington, DC: The Mitchell Group. Online at http://pdf.usaid.gov/pdf_docs/PDACG205.pdf.

- Geographical. 2005. "Trade Justice: Does it Really Work?" Geographical. October:38–39. Online at http://www.geographical.co.uk.

- ICO (International Coffee Organization). 2008. Historical Coffee Prices Data: Ethiopia. Online at http://www.ico.org.

- Kodama, Y. 2007. "New Role of Cooperatives in Ethiopia: The Case of Ethiopian Coffee Farmers Cooperatives." African Studies Monographs. Suppl. 35, March:87–108.

- McCarthy, S. 2007. Chief of Party, Agricultural Cooperatives in Ethiopia (ACE), 1998 – 2004. ACDI/VOCA, Washington, DC. Personal Communication. Nov. 27.

- Mekasha, W. 2005. "Agribusiness Systems: Improving the Lives of Ethiopian Coffee Farmers." World Report (ACDI/VOCA). Fall/Winter:17–19. Online at http://www.acdivoca.org/852571DC00681414/Lookup/WRFallWinter05-Page17-19-AgribusinessSystemsEthiopia/$file/WRFallWinter05-Page17-19-AgribusinessSystemsEthiopia.pdf.

- Olsen, T. 2007. "Ethiopian Coffee Brings Its Own Aroma." Inter Press Service News Agency. Apr. 3.

- The Economist. 2007. "Ethiopia Industry: More Deals Signed to Secure Coffee Trademarks." The Economist. Oct. 17:10.

- Wagner, H. 2004. Education and the Battle Against HIV/AIDS in Ethiopia. Washington, DC: ACDI/VOCA. Online at http://www.acdivoca.org/852571DC00681414/Lookup/WRSpring04-Page8-9-HIVAIDS/$file/WRSpring04-Page8-9-HIVAIDS.pdf.

- Weihe, T. 2005. Cooperative Fair Trade Coffee: The US Experience. Paper presented at COPAC Conference on Fair Trade Coffee, Berlin, Jan. 21. Online at http://www.coopdevelopmentcenter.coop/Anaylsis/fairtradecoffee.pdf.

Chapter 3

Bangladesh

- Begum, A. 2007. Director of Fisheries Project. Caritas International, Bangladesh. Personal Communication. Aug. 14.
- Chowdhury, N., and A. Clemett. 2006. *Industrial Pollution and Its Threat to Mokosh Beel Wetland in Kaliakoir.* Dhaka: Management of Aquatic Ecosystems through Community Husbandry.
- Costa, T. 2006. "Livelihood Diversification to Reduce Fishing Dependence." Management of Aquatic Ecosystems through Community Husbandry (MACH) Policy Brief 5. Bangladesh: MACH.
- Deppert, D. 2006a. Chief of Party, Management of Aquatic Ecosystems through Community Husbandry, Bangladesh. Winrock International. Personal Communications. June 6, 8.
- Deppert, D. 2006b. L*ocal Government Support to Communities in the Co-management of Wetland Resources in Bangladesh: The MACH Approach.* Management of Aquatic Ecosystems through Community Husbandry (MACH) Policy Brief 2. Bangladesh: MACH.
- Hughes, E. 2006. Senior Program Officer. WINROCK International, Little Rock, Arkansas. Personal Communication. May 25.
- IUCN Bangladesh. 2000. *Red Book of Threatened Fishes of Bangladesh.* Dhaka: IUCN (The World Conservation Union).
- MACH (Management of Aquatic Ecosystems through Community Husbandry). 2003. *MACH Completion Report: Volume 1, Main Document.* Dhaka: MACH. Online at http://www.machban.org/Documents/Documents/Completionpercent20report-Finalpercent20Edited_11percent20Novpercent2003.pdf.
- MACH (Management of Aquatic Ecosystems through Community Husbandry). 2005a. *Community Based Wetland Conservation.* Case Study 1. Dhaka, MACH. Online at http://www.machban.org/casestudies/report_main.htm.
- MACH (Management of Aquatic Ecosystems through Community Husbandry). 2005b. *Managing An Aquatic Natural Resource.* Case Study 6. Dhaka, MACH. Online at http://www.machban.org/casestudies/report_main.htm.
- MACH (Management of Aquatic Ecosystems through Community Husbandry). 2005c. *A Permanent Wetland Sanctuary.* Case Study 3. Dhaka, MACH. Online at http://www.machban.org/casestudies/report_main.htm.
- MACH (Management of Aquatic Ecosystems through Community Husbandry). 2005d. *A Change for the Better.* Case Study 15. Dhaka, MACH. Online at http://www.machban.org/casestudies/report_main.htm.
- MACH (Management of Aquatic Ecosystems through Community Husbandry). 2005e. *From Eggs to Riches.* Case Study 11. Dhaka, MACH. Online at http://www.machban.org/casestudies/report_main.htm.
- MACH (Management of Aquatic Ecosystems through Community Husbandry). 2006. *MACH-II Briefing Packet for USAID Evaluation Team, Part I: Achievement, Influence and Future.* Dhaka: MACH.
- MACH (Management of Aquatic Ecosystems through Community Husbandry). 2007. *MACH-II Completion Report-Volume 1, MACH Achievement.* Dhaka: MACH.
- Mazumder, A. 2006. Environment Team Leader. United States Agency for International Development, Bangladesh. Personal Communication. Aug. 7.
- Sultana, P. 2006a. *Improving Livelihoods of Wetland Users: MACH Lessons.* Management of Aquatic Ecosystems through Community Husbandry (MACH) Policy Brief 4. Bangladesh: MACH.
- Sultana, P. 2006b. *Community-based Co-management: A Solution to Wetland Degradation in Bangladesh.* Management of Aquatic Ecosystems through Community Husbandry (MACH) Policy Brief 1. Bangladesh: MACH.
- Tanvir, O. 2006. *Unsung Heroes of MACH.* Bangladesh: Management of Aquatic Ecosystems through Community Husbandry. Online at http://www.machban.org/mach_folder_web/folders/UH_stan.pdf.
- Thompson, P. 2006. *Restoring Wetland Environments and Biodiversity.* Management of Aquatic Ecosystems through Community Husbandry (MACH) Policy Brief 3. Bangladesh: MACH.
- Thompson, P. 2007. Senior Manager. Winrock International, Bangladesh. Personal Communication. July 14.
- Thompson, P. 2008. Senior Manager. Winrock International, Bangladesh. Personal Communication. Feb. 13.
- Whitford, P., B. Tegler, K. Alam, and A. Islam. 2006. *Evaluation of USAID/Bangladesh Environment Program.* Washington, DC: Weidemann Associates.
- World Bank. 2006. *Bangladesh Country Environmental Analysis: Bangladesh Development Series Paper No: 12.* Dhaka: World Bank Office. Online at http://www.worldbank.org.bd/WBSITE/EXTERNAL/COUNTRIES/SOUTHASIAEXT/BANGLADESHEXTN/0,,contentMDK:21258223~pagePK:141137~piPK:141127~theSitePK:295760,00.html.

Guatemala

- Balas, R. 2004. *The Practical Utility of Biological Monitoring in the Maya Biosphere Reserve.* Guatemala: Biological Monitoring Project (Wildlife Conservation Society; National Council of Protected Areas; United States Agency for International Development; USAID Fortalecemiento Institucional en Políticas Ambientales (FIPA)). Washington, DC: USAID.
- Carrera, J. R. 2007. Regional Manager of Sustainable Forestry Division. Rainforest Alliance Guatemala. Personal Communication. December.
- Carerra, J. R. 2008. Regional Manager of Sustainable Forestry Division. Rainforest Alliance Guatemala. Personal Communication. March 18.
- Chemonics International, Inc. 2003. *Community Forest Management in the Maya Biosphere Reserve: Close to Financial Self-Sufficiency?* Washington, DC: Chemonics International, Inc.
- Chemonics International, Inc. 2006. *Forest Concessions: A Successful Model. BIOFOR Project Final Report.* Washington, DC: Chemonics International, Inc.
- Chemonics International, Inc. and IRG (International Resources Group). 2000. *Guatemala: Assessment of Progress Toward SO5 Goals in the Maya Biosphere Reserve.* Washington, DC: Chemonics International, Inc.
- Hughell, D., and R. Butterfield. 2008. *Impact of FSC Certification on Deforestation and the Incidence of Wildfires in the Maya Biosphere Reserve.* New York: Rainforest Alliance.
- IRG (International Resources Group). 2006. *The Role of Natural Products in Rural Development, Poverty Alleviation, and Governance: The Case of Xate Palm (Chamaedores Spp.) in the Petén Region of Guatemala.* Washington, DC: IRG. Online at http://www.frameweb.org/ev_en.php?ID=14920_201&ID2=DO_TOPIC.
- Minnick, G. 2008. Managing Director, TREES (Training, Extension, Enterprise and Sourcing) Program. Rainforest Alliance, Guatemala. Personal Communication. March 18.
- Molnar, A., M. Liddle, C. Bracer, A. Khare, A. White, and J. Bull. 2007. *Community Based Forest Enterprises in Tropical Forest Countries: Status and Potential.* Washington, DC: Forest Trends, Rights and Resources Initiative, and International Tropical Timber Organization. Online at http://www.rightsandresources.org/documents/index.php?pubID=109

- Monterroso, I. 2002. "Women and Forest Resources: Two Cases from Central America. Latin American Faculty of Social Sciences (FLACSO)." *World Rainforest Movement's Bulletin 63*. Montevideo: World Rainforest Movement. Online at http://www.wrm.org.uy/bulletin/63/women.html.
- Nittler, J., and H. Tschinkel. 2005. *Community Forest Management in the Maya Biosphere Reserve of Guatemala: Protection Through Profits.* Paper submitted to the United States Agency for International Development (USAID) Steering Committee on Nature, Wealth and Power and the Sustainable Agriculture and Natural Resource Management, Collaborative Research Support Program, University of Georgia. Washington, DC.
- Nittler, J. 2007. Senior Vice President. Chemonics International, Inc. Personal Communication. Oct. 23. Washington, DC.
- Nittler, J. 2008. Senior Vice President. Chemonics International, Inc. Personal Communication. Feb. 4. Washington, DC.
- Pool, D. J., T. L. Catterson, V. A. Molinos, and A. C. Randall. 2002. *Review of USAID's Natural Forest Management Programs in Latin America and the Caribbean.* Washington, DC: United States Agency for International Development.
- Radachowsky, J. 2004: *Efectos ecológicos del aprovechamiento de madera certificada en las concesiones forestales en el norte del Petén.* Guatemala: Biological Monitoring Project (Wildlife Conservation Society, National Council of Protected Areas, United States Agency for International Development (USAID), Fortalecimiento Institucional en Políticas Ambientales (FIPA)). Washington, DC.USAID
- Rainforest Alliance. 2006. *Developing Honduras' Sustainable Forestry Concessions to Combat Poverty and Deforestation.* New York: Rainforest Alliance. Online at http://www.rainforest-alliance.org/profiles/documents/honduras_profile.pdf.
- Rainforest Alliance. 2007a. *Results and Achievements of Forestry Enterprises in Guatemala Program, FY 2007.* New York: Rainforest Alliance.
- Rainforest Alliance. 2007b. *Forestry Enterprises in Guatemala.* New York: Rainforest Alliance.
- Rainforest Alliance. 2007c. *Helping Communities Conserve the Maya Biosphere Reserve.* New York: Rainforest Alliance. Online at www.rainforestalliance.org/profiles/documents/maya_biosphere.pdf
- Saito, C. 2005. *Community Forest Concessions in the Maya Biosphere Reserve, Petén, Guatemala.* Presented at United States Agency for International Development, Washington, DC, Jan. 14.
- Saito, C. 2008. Chief of Party, BIOFOR Project. USAID/Guatemala. Santa Catarina Pinula, Guatemala. Personal Communication. Feb. 10.
- Stoian, D., and A. Rodas. 2006a. *Community Forest Enterprise Development in Guatemala: A Case Study of Cooperativa Carmelita, June 2006.* Washington, DC: International Tropical Timber Organization, Forest Trends, and the Rights and Resources Initiative.
- Stoian, D., and A. Rodas. 2006b. *Community Forest Enterprise Development in Guatemala: A Case Study of Cooperativa Arbol Verde, June 2006.* Washington, DC: International Tropical Timber Organization, Forest Trends, and the Rights and Resources Initiative.
- Tschinkel, H. 2007. Forester, Guatemala. Formerly Forestry Consultant. Chemonics, Int'l. Guatemala. Personal Communication. Nov. 9, 19.
- Tschinkel, H. 2008. Forester, Guatemala. Formerly Forestry Consultant. Chemonics, Int'l. Guatemala. Personal Communication. Feb. 11.
- USAID (United States Agency for International Development). 2005. "Mission of the Month: Guatemala." *Frontlines,* Nov. Washington, DC: USAID.
- WCS (Wildlife Conservation Society). 2006. "WCS Guatemala." Online at http://www.wcs.org/international/latinamerica/mesoamerica/Guatemala.

Niger

- Abdoulaye, T., and G. Ibro. 2006. *Analyse des Impacts Socio-economiques des Investissements dans la Gestion des Ressources Naturelles: Etudes de Cas dans les Régions de Maradi, Tahoua, et Tillabery au Niger.* Report part of Etudes Saheliennes, Papers presented at Conference of Study Results of Natural Resource Management Investments from 1980 to 2005 in Niger, Sept. 20–21. Comité Permanent Inter-Etats de Lutte Contre La Sécheresse Dans le Sahel. Online at http://www.frameweb.org/ev_en.php?ID=17812_201&ID2=DO_TOPIC.
- Amoukou, A.I. 2006. *Impacts des Investissements dans la Gestion des Ressources Naturelles sur les Systèmes de Production dans les Régions de Maradi, Tahoua et Tillabery au Niger.* Report part of Etudes Saheliennes, Papers presented at Conference of Study Results of Natural Resource Management Investments from 1980 to 2005 in Niger, Sept. 20–21. Comité Permanent Inter-Etats de Lutte Contre La Sécheresse Dans le Sahel. Online at http://www.frameweb.org/ev_en.php?ID=17815_201&ID2=DO_TOPIC.
- BBC (British Broadcasting Corporation). 2006. *Villages on the Front Line: Niger.* Video. London: BBC.
- BBC (British Broadcasting Corporation). 2005. *Niger Leader "Ignorant" of Hunger.* BBC News, Aug.12. Online at http://news.bbc.co.uk/1/hi/world/africa/4144642.stm.
- Boubacar, Y. 2006. *Rapport d'Etude sur le Foncier, les Institutions Locales et l'Évolution de la Pauvreté.* Report part of Etudes Saheliennes, Papers presented at Conference of Study Results of Natural Resource Management Investments from 1980 to 2005 in Niger, Sept. 20–21. Comité Permanent Inter-Etats de Lutte Contre La Sécheresse Dans le Sahel. Online at http://www.frameweb.org/ev_en.php?ID=18392_201&ID2=DO_TOPIC.
- Boubacar, Y., M. Larwanou, A. Hassane, C. Reij, and International Resources Group. 2005. *Niger Study: Sahel Pilot Study Report.* Washington, DC: United States Agency for International Development. Online at: http://www.frameweb.org/ev_en.php?ID=13117_201&ID2=DO_TOPIC.
- Brough, W., and M. Kimenyi. 2002. *"Desertification" of the Sahel—Exploring the Role of Property Rights.* Bozeman, MT: Property and Environment Resource Center. Online at http://www.perc.org/perc.php?id=142.
- Burns, C. 2008. Program and Development Director. Peace Corps Niger. Personal Communication. Feb. 12.
- CNEDD (National Environmental Council for Sustainable Development, Niger). 2006. *National Adaptation Programme of Action–Niger.* Niamey: CNEDD. Online at http://unfccc.int/resource/docs/napa/ner01e.pdf.
- Dan Baria, S. 1999. *Evolution et Perspectives en Matiere de Gestion des Forets Naturelles au Niger: Quels Progres et Quel Avenir?* Niamey: Conseil National de l'Environnement pour un Développement Durable.
- Diarra, M. 2006. *Restauration de l'Environnement et Changements Sociaux de Genre.* Report part of Etudes Saheliennes, Papers presented at Conference of Study Results of Natural Resource Management Investments from 1980 to 2005 in Niger, Sept. 20–21. Comité Permanent Inter-Etats de Lutte Contre La Sécheresse Dans le Sahel. Online at http://www.frameweb.org/ev_en.php?ID=17818_201&ID2=DO_TOPIC.
- Evans, J. 2005. *Celebrating SIM's 80 Years in Niger.* Charlotte, NC: Serving

In Mission (SIM). Online at http://www.sim.org/index.php/content/celebrating-sim-s-80-years-in-niger.

Gallegos, C., K. Christopherson, M. McGahuey, and H. Schreuder. 1987. *Final Evaluation Niger Forestry and Land-Use Planning Project (No. 683-0230)*. Niamey: United States Agency for International Development Niger.

Guéro, C., and N. Dan Lamso. 2006. *Les Projets de Restauration des Ressources Naturelles et la Fertilité des Sols*. Report part of Etudes Saheliennes, Papers presented at Conference of Study Results of Natural Resource Management Investments from 1980 to 2005 in Niger, Sept. 20–21. Comité Permanent Inter-Etats de Lutte Contre La Sécheresse Dans le Sahel. Online at http://www.frameweb.org/ev_en.php?ID=17817_201&ID2=DO_TOPIC.

Hamissou, G. 2001. *Forest Finance: The Forest Revenue System and Government Expenditure on Forestry in Niger*. Rome: Food and Agriculture Organization of the United Nations.

Harris, R. 2007. *Niger's Trees May Be Insurance Against Drought*. Video report. Washington, DC: National Public Radio. Online at http://www.npr.org/templates/story/story.php?storyId=11608960.

INS (Institut National de la Statistique) and Macro International Inc. 2007. *Enquête Démographique et de Santé et a Indicateurs Multiples du Niger 2006*. Calverton, MD: INS and Macro International Inc.

IPCC (Intergovernmental Panel on Climate Change). 2007. *Fourth Assessment Report: Working Group II Report on Impacts, Adaptation and Vulnerability*. Geneva: IPCC. Online at http://www.ipcc.ch/ipccreports/ar4-wg2.htm.

Larwanou, M., M. Abdoulaye, and C. Reij. 2006. *Etude de la Regeneration Naturelle Assistee dans la Region de Zinder (Niger): Une Premiere Exploration d'un Phenomeme Spectaculaire*. Comité Permanent Inter-Etats de Lutte Contre La Sécheresse Dans le Sahel. Online at http://www.frameweb.org/ev_en.php?ID=17529_201&ID2=DO_TOPIC.

McGahuey, M. 2008. Environment and Natural Resource Management Advisor. USAID, Washington, DC. Personal Communication. Jan. 14 and 16, Feb. 11 and 19.

McGahuey, M., and R. Winterbottom. 2007. *Transformational Development in Niger*. PowerPoint. Jan. Online at http://www.frameweb.org/ev_en.php?ID=23670_201&ID2=DO_TOPIC.

PDRT (Programme de Développement Rural de la Région de Tahoua). 1997. *Gestion Durable des Ressources Naturelles: Leçons Tirées du Savoir des Paysans de l'Adar*. Niamey, Niger: Ministry of Agriculture and Livestock.

Polgreen, L. 2007. "In Niger, Trees and Crops Turn Back the Desert." *New York Times*. Feb. 11.

Reij, C. 2004. *Farmer Managed Natural Regeneration in Niger: Impressions of a Short Field Trip, June 9 to 11, 2004*. Reprinted 2005. North Fort Myers, FL: ECHO. Online at http://echotech.org/technical/IntroductoryArticles.pdf.

Reij, C. 2006. *More Success Stories in Africa's Drylands than Often Assumed*. Notes presented at Forum sur la Souveraineté Alimentaire, Niamey, Nov. 7–10. Niamey, Niger: Réseau des Organisations Paysannes et de Producteurs Agricoles de L'Afrique de L'Ouest. Online at http://www.roppa.info/IMG/pdf/More_success_stories_in_Africa_Reij_Chris.pdf.

Reij, C. 2008. Human Geographer, Center for International Cooperation, VU University Amsterdam. Personal Communication. Feb. 17.

Rinaudo, T. 2005a. *Uncovering the Underground Forest: A Short History and Description of Farmer Managed Natural Regeneration*. Melbourne, Australia: World Vision. Online at http://www.frameweb.org/ev.php?ID=13091_201&ID2=DO_TOPIC.

Rinaudo T. 2005b. "Economic Benefits of Farmer Managed Natural Regeneration." FRAME Web site post. Sep. 27. Washington, DC: FRAME Community, United States Agency for International Development. Online at http://www.frameweb.org/ev.php?ID=12968_201&ID2=DO_TOPIC.

Rinaudo, T. 2007. Natural Resource Management Advisor, World Vision Australia. Melbourne, Australia. Personal Communication. May 27, June 16.

Rinaudo, T. 2008. Natural Resource Management Advisor. World Vision Australia. Melbourne, Australia. Personal Communication. Jan. 5, Feb. 7.

Saadou, M., and M. Larwanou. 2006. *Evaluation de la Flore et de la Vegetation dans Certains Sites Traites et Non Traites des Regions de Tahoua, Maradi et Tillaberi*. Report part of Etudes Saheliennes, Papers presented at Conference of Study Results of Natural Resource Management Investments from 1980 to 2005 in Niger, Sep. 20–21. Comité Permanent Inter-Etats de Lutte Contre La Sécheresse Dans le Sahel. Online at http://www.frameweb.org/ev_en.php?ID=18393_201&ID2=DO_TOPIC.

SIM (Serving In Mission). 1999. *MIDP Summary Report 1994–1997*. Niamey: SIM.

Steinberg, D. (1988) "Tree Planting for Soil Conservation: The Need for a Holistic and Flexible Approach." *Enhancing Dryland Agriculture: LEISA Magazine*, 4(4). Online at http://www.metafro.be/leisa/1988/4-4-20.pdf.

Tappan, G. 2007. "RE: Extent of Natural Regeneration in Niger." FRAME web site post. July 12. Washington, DC: FRAME Community, United States Agency for International Development. Online at http://www.frameweb.org/ev_en.php?ID=52653_201&ID2=DO_DISCUSSIONPOST_LIST.

Tougiani, A., C. Guero, and T. Rinaudo. 2008. "Success in Improving Livelihoods Through Tree Crop Management and Use in Niger." To be published in *GeoJournal*. The Netherlands: Springer Publishing. Page numbers cited from manuscript.

Toumieux, E. 2005. *Trip Report to Niger*. Thies, Senegal: World Vision Senegal.

UNDP (United Nations Development Programme). 2007. *Human Development Report 2007/2008—Niger Statistics*. New York: UNDP. Online at http://hdrstats.undp.org/countries/data_sheets/cty_ds_NER.html.

USAID (United States Agency for International Development), Institutional Resources Group, Winrock International, and Harvard Institute for International Development. 2002. *Environmental Policy Lessons Learned: Report No. 21. Environmental Policy and Institutional Strengthening Indefinite Quantity Contract (EPIQ)*. Washington, DC: USAID.

USAID (United States Agency for International Development), Comité Permanent Inter-Etats de Lutte Contre La Sécheresse Dans le Sahel, and International Resources Group. 2005. *Investing in Tomorrow's Forests : Toward an Action Agenda for Revitalizing Forestry in West Africa*. Washington, DC: USAID.

Wentling, M. 2008a. Country Program Manager for Niger. United States Agency for International Development/West Africa. Accra, Ghana. Personal Communication. Jan. 11.

Wentling, M. 2008b. *Niger—Annual Food Security Report: Current Situation and Future Prospects*. Niamey, Niger: United States Agency for International Development Niger.

Winterbottom, R. 2007. Senior Manager, Environment and Natural Resources Division. International Resources Group, Washington, DC. Personal Communication. December.

Winterbottom, R. 2008. Senior Manager, Environment and Natural Resources Division. International Resources Group, Washington, DC. Personal Communication. March 11.

Chapter 4

Main Text

- Adato, M., J. Hoddinott, and L. Haddad. 2005. "Power, Politics, and Performance: Community Participation in South African Public Works Programs." Research Report No. 143. Washington, DC: International Food Policy Research Institute. Online at http://www.ifpri.org/pubs/ABSTRACT/rr143.asp.

- ADB (Asian Development Bank), World Bank, and Japan Bank for International Cooperation. 2005. *Connecting East Asia: A New Framework for Infrastructure.* Washington, DC: World Bank. Online at http://go.worldbank.org/9RSKZBZQ80.

- Ali, I., and E. Pernia. 2003. "Infrastructure and Poverty Reduction—What is the Connection?" ERD Policy Brief No. 13. Manila: Asian Development Bank. Online at http://www.adb.org/Documents/EDRC/Policy_Briefs/PB013.pdf.

- Arena, M. 2006. "Does Insurance Market Activity Promote Economic Growth? A Cross Country Study for Industrialized and Developing Countries." World Bank Policy Research Working Paper 4098. Washington, DC: World Bank. Online at http://www-wds.worldbank.org/external/default/WDSContentServer/IW3P/IB/2006/12/14/000016406_20061214120343/Rendered/PDF/wps4098.pdf.

- Bainbridge, V., S. Foerster, K. Pasteur, M. Pimbert, G. Pratt, and I. Yaschine Arroyo. 2000. *Transforming Bureaucracies: Institutionalizing Participation and People-Centered Processes in Natural Resource Management: An Annotated Bibliography.* London: International Institute for Environment and Development. Online at http://www.iied.org/pubs/display.php?o=6342IIED.

- Beattie, A. 2007. "Remote Farmers Dig in Over Tariffs." *Financial Times.* May 23.

- BRAC (Bangladesh Rural Advancement Committee). 2005a. *Economic Development, Core Programs: Microfinance.* Dhaka, Bangladesh: BRAC. Online at http://www.brac.net/microfinance.htm.

- BRAC (Bangladesh Rural Advancement Committee). 2005b. *Economic Development, Core Programs: TUP.* Dhaka, Bangladesh: BRAC. Online at http://www.brac.net/cfpr.htm.

- CGAP (Consultative Group to Assist the Poor). 2007. *Building Local Financial Systems That Work for the Poor: Equity and Efficiency.* Washington, DC: CGAP. Online at http://collab2.cgap.org/gm/document1.9.2930/CGAP_IV_Strategy.pdf.

- Cline, W.R. 2007. *Global Warming and Agriculture: Impact Estimates by Country.* Washington, DC: Center for Global Development and the Peterson Institute for International Economics. Online at http://www.cgdev.org/content/publications/detail/14090

- Churchill, C. 2006. "What is Insurance for the Poor?" In *Protecting the Poor: A Microinsurance Compendium.* Churchill, C., ed., pp. 12–64. Munich: Munich Re Foundation and International Labour Organization. Online at http://www.munichrefoundation.org/StiftungsWebsite/Projects/Microinsurance/2006Microinsurance/Microinsurance_Compendium.htm.

- Compartamos. 2007. *Banco Compartamos Reports 3q07 Results.* Mexico City, Mexico: Banco Compartamos, SA. October 25.

- Daley-Harris, S. 2007. *State of the Microcredit Summit Campaign Report 2007.* Washington, DC: Microcredit Summit Campaign. Online at http://www.microcreditsummit.org/pubs/reports/socr/EngSOCR2007.pdf.

- Daley-Harris, S. 2006. *State of the Microcredit Summit Campaign Report 2006.* Washington, DC: Microcredit Summit Campaign. Online at http://www.microcreditsummit.org/pubs/reports/socr/2006/SOCR06.pdf.

- Dempsey, J., and R. Campbell. 2006. "A Value-Chain Approach to Coffee Production: Linking Ethiopian Coffee Producers to International Markets." *The Africa Journal,* Fall. Washington, DC: Corporate Council on Africa. Online at http://acdivoca.org/852571DC00681414/Lookup/AfricaJournalFall06-EthiopiaCoffee/$file/AfricaJournalFall06-EthiopiaCoffee.pdf.

- Esmail, T. 1997. *Designing and Scaling Up Productive Natural Resource Management Programs: Decentralization and Institutions for Collective Action.* Consultation Draft, Dec. 9. Washington, DC: World Bank.

- Fan, S., P. Hazell, and S. Thorat. 1999. "Linkages Between Government Spending, Growth, and Poverty in Rural India." Research Report 110. Washington, DC: International Food Policy Research Institute. Online at http://www.ifpri.org/pubs/ABSTRACT/ABSTR110.HTM.

- Fan, S., X. Zhang, and N. Rao. 2004. "Public Expenditure, Growth, and Poverty Reduction in Rural Uganda." DSGD Discussion Paper No. 4. Washington, DC: International Food Policy Research Institute. Online at http://www.ifpri.org/divs/DSGD/dp/dsgdp04.htm.

- FAO (Food and Agriculture Organization of the United Nations). 2005a. "Empowering Communities Through Forestry: Community-Based Enterprise Development in the Gambia." Forestry Policy and Institutions Working Paper No. 8. Rome: FAO. Online at ftp://ftp.fao.org/docrep/fao/008/j6209e/j6209e00.pdf.

- FAO (Food and Agriculture Organization of the United Nations). 2005b. "Microfinance and Forest-Based Small-Scale Enterprises." Forestry Paper No. 146. Rome: FAO. Online at http://www.fao.org/forestry/publications/en.

- Farrington, T. 2002. "Trends in Microfinance Capital Structure." *MicroRate Latin America*. Online at http://www.microfinancegateway.com/files/14189_Farrington.doc.

- FLO-CERT. 2007. *Cost of Certification*. Bonn, Germany: FLO-CERT. Online at http://www.flo-cert.net/flo-cert/main.php?id=13.

- Gautam, R. 2005. *Competition Policy and Law in Nepal*. Kathmandu, Nepal: Ministry of Local Development. Online at http://siteresources.worldbank.org/INTCOMPLEGALDB/SouthAsia/20965796/Competition_Nepal.pdf.

- Gellert, P. 2003. "Negotiating a Timber Commodity Chain: Lessons from Indonesia on the Political Construction of Global Commodity Chains." *Sociological Forum* 18(1):53–84.

- Gonzales, A., and R. Rosenberg. 2006a. *State of the Microcredit 'Industry': Outreach, Poverty, and Profitability*. PowerPoint presented at the Access to Finance: Building Inclusive Financial Systems Conference, Washington, DC, World Bank, May 30. Online http://info.worldbank.org/etools/library/latestversion.asp?232661.

- Gonzales, A., and R. Rosenberg. 2006b. *The State of Microfinance—Outreach, Profitability, and Poverty*. Notes presented at the Access to Finance: Building Inclusive Financial Systems Conference, Washington, DC, World Bank, May 30. Online at http://info.worldbank.org/etools/library/latestversion.asp?232702.

- Grameen Foundation. 2007. *Frequently Asked Questions About Microfinance*. Online at http://www.grameenfoundation.org/what_we_do/microfinance_in_action/faqs.

- Hashemi, S. 2001. "Linking Microfinance and Safety Net Programs to Include the Poorest: The Case of IGVGD in Bangladesh." CGAP Focus Note 21. May. Washington, DC: Consultative Group to Assist the Poor. Online at http://collab2.cgap.org/gm/document-1.9.2566/FocusNote_21.pdf.

- Hettige, H. 2007. *How and When Infrastructure Investments Encourage Inclusive Growth: Learning from ADB's Experience*. Paper presented at ADB Policy Forum, Agricultural and Rural Development for Reducing Poverty and Hunger in Asia: In Pursuit of Inclusive and Sustainable Growth, Aug. 9–10, Manila, Philippines.

- Howard, J., B. Pozzoni, and P. Clarke. 2001. *Learning Initiative on Citizen Participation and Local Governance: Review and Annotated Bibliography*. Brighton, UK: Institute of Development Studies. Online at http://www.ids.ac.uk/logolink/resources/annotbiblio.htm.

- IFAD (International Fund for Agricultural Development). 2007. *Sending Money Home: Worldwide Remittance Flows to Developing and Transition Countries*. Rome: IFAD. Online at http://www.ifad.org/events/remittances/maps/brochure.pdf.

- IRG (International Resources Group). 2005. *Report on the Gum Karaya Sub-Sector in Andhra Pradesh, India*. Washington, DC: IRG. Online at http://www.frameweb.org/ev.php?ID=13709_201&ID2=DO_TOPIC.

- Jahan, S., and R. McCleery. 2005. *Making Infrastructure Work for the Poor*. New York: United Nations Development Programme. Online at http://content.undp.org/go/cms-service/stream/asset/?asset_id=1420663.

- Kiva. 2007. *What We Do*. San Francisco: Kiva. Online at http://www.kiva.org/about/what.

- Kolavalli, S., and J. Kerr. 2002. "Scaling Up Participatory Watershed Development in India." *Development and Change* 33(2):213–235.

- Loewe, M. 2006. "Downscaling, Upgrading, or Linking? Ways to Realize Micro-Insurance." *International Social Security Review* 59, Feb.:37–59.

- Matin, I. 2004. *Delivering Inclusive Microfinance with a Poverty Focus: Experiences of BRAC*. Dhaka, Bangladesh: BRAC. Online at http://bracresearch.org/reports/delivering_inclusive_microfinance_pdf.pdf.

- Mayers, J., and D. Macqueen. 2007. *Small Forest Enterprises Are Big!* Summary notes presentation at Community Forest Management and Enterprises conference, Rio Branco, Brazil, July 15–20, organized by the Rights and Resources Initiative, International Tropical Timber Organization, World Conservation Union (IUCN), and Global Alliance of Community Forestry. Online at http://www.iied.org/NR/documents/Bigsignificanceofsmallforestenterprises-August2007_000.pdf.

- MIX (Microfinance Information Exchange). 2007. "MIX 2006 MFI Benchmarks Available." *The MIX Market*. Oct. 16. Online at http://www.themix.org.

- MIX (Microfinance Information Exchange). 2007. *MicroBanking Bulletin*. Issue 16, Spring. Online at http://www.mixmbb.org/Templates/PreviousIssues.aspx.

- Molnar, A., M. Liddle, C. Bracer, A. Khare, A. White, and J. Bull. 2007. *Community-Based Forest Enterprises in Tropical Countries: Status and Potential*. Washington, DC: International Tropical Timber Organization, Rights and Resources Initiative, Forest Trends. Online at http://www.rightsandresources.org/documents/index.php?pubID=109.

- Molnar, A. 2003. *Forest Certification and Communities: Looking Forward to the Next Decade*. Washington, DC: Forest Trends. Online at http://www.forest-trends.org/documents/publications/Forest%20Certification%20and%20Communities.pdf

- FLO-CERT. 2007. *Cost of Certification*. Bonn, Germany: FLO-CERT. Online at http://www.flo-cert.net/flo-cert/main.php?id=13.

- Mylenko, N. 2006. *Overview of Credit Reporting and Financial Infrastructure*. PowerPoint presented in Cape Town, Oct.5. Washington, DC: International Finance Corporation. Online at http://info.worldbank.org/etools/library/latestversion.asp?235772.

- New Ventures. 2008a. *About Us*. Washington, DC: New Ventures, World Resources Institute. Online at http://www.new-ventures.org/index.cfm?fuseaction=content&IDsecao=3

- New Ventures. 2008b. *Portfolio Search*. Washington, DC: New Ventures, World Resources Institute. Online at http://www.new-ventures.org/?fuseaction=enterpriseSearchAction&IDsecao=5.

- OECD (Organisation for Economic Co-operation and Development). 2006. "International Migrant Remittances and Their Role in Development." *International Migration Outlook*, pp. 139–161. Paris: OECD. Online http://www.oecd.org/dataoecd/61/46/38840502.pdf.

- OECD (Organisation for Economic Co-operation and Development). 2007. *Natural Resources and Pro-Poor Growth: The Economics and Politics of Natural Resource Use in Developing Countries*. Draft Report, Dec.7. Paris: OECD.

- Orozco, M. 2007. "Central American Diasporas and Hometown Associations." In *Diasporas and Development*. B. Merz, L. Chen, and P. Geithner, eds. Cambridge, MA: Harvard University Press.

- Parks, K. 2007. *Mexico Micro Finance Lender Independencia Plans IPO This Year*. Oct. 17. DowJones Newswire.

- Pozzoni, B., and N. Kumar. 2005. *A Review of the Literature on Participatory Approaches to Local Development for an Evaluation of the Effectiveness of World Bank Support for Community-Based and -Driven Development Approaches*. Washington, DC: World Bank.

- Profeco. 2008. *Quien es Quien en el Envío de Dinero: Comisión Cobrada Promedio, Envios de Dinero por 300 Dólares de Estados Unidos a México*. Mexico City: Profeco. Online at http://www.profeco.gob.mx/envio/

histo_qqed.pdf. Accessed 2/25/2008

- Ratha, D. 2003. "Worker's Remittances: An Important and Stable Source of External Development Finance." In *Global Development Finance 2003*, pp. 157–175. Washington, DC: World Bank. Online at http://siteresources.worldbank.org/INTRGDF/Resources/GDF2003-Chapter7.pdf.

- Ribot, J. 2004. *Waiting for Democracy: The Politics of Choice in Natural Resource Decentralization.* Washington, DC: World Resources Institute.

- Ribot, J. 2008. "Authority over Forests: Negotiating Democratic Decentralization in Senegal: Working Paper 36." *Representation, Equity and Environment: Working Paper Series.* Washington, DC: World Resources Institute.

- Roth, J., M. McCord, and D. Liber. 2007. *The Landscape of Microinsurance in the World's 100 Poorest Countries.* Appleton, Wisconsin, USA: The MicroInsurance Centre. Online at http://www.microinsurancecentre.org/UI/..%5CUploadDocuments%5CLandscape%20study%20paper.pdf.

- Siedek, H. 2007. *Technology Series, Part 1: Banking Agents.* Washington, DC: Consultative Group to Assist the Poor. Online at http://www.microfinancegateway.org/content/article/detail/43155.

- Sohn, J., Herz, S., La Viña, A. 2007. *Development Without Conflict: The Business Case for Community Consent.* Washington, DC: World Resources Institute. Online at http://pdf.wri.org/development_without_conflict_fpic.pdf.

- Sullivan, K. 2006. "For India's Traditional Fishermen, Cellphones Deliver a Sea Change." *Washington Post.* Oct. 15. Online at http://www.washingtonpost.com/wp-dyn/content/article/2006/10/14/AR2006101400342.html.

- Taylor, P. 2007. "Western Union to Transfer Money Cell Phone." *Financial Times.* Oct. 18. Online at http://www.ft.com/cms/s/0/58005146-7da5-11dc-9f47-0000779fd2ac.html.

- Thi Phi, L., N. Van Duong, N. Ngoc Quong, and P. Lac Vang. 2004. "Making the Most of Market Chains: Challenges for Small-Scale Farmers and Traders in Upland Vietnam." Small and Medium Forest Enterprise Series No. 2. London: International Institute for Environment and Development. Online at http://www.iied.org/pubs/display.php?o=9313IIED&n=8&l=47&k=Vietnam.

- Torero, M., and S. Chowdhury. 2005. "Increasing Access to Infrastructure for Africa's Rural Poor." 2020 Africa Conference Brief 16. Washington, DC: International Food Policy Research Institute. Online at http://www.ifpri.org/PUBS/ib/ib32.pdf.

- Trommersauser, S., R. Lindethal, and R. Krech. 2006. "The Promotional Role of Governments." In *Protecting the Poor: A Microinsurance Compendium.* C. Churchill, ed., pp. 508–522. Munich: Munich Re Foundation and International Labour Organization. Online at http://www.munichre-foundation.org/StiftungsWebsite/Projects/Microinsurance/2006Microinsurance/Microinsurance_Compendium.htm

- Vania, F., and B. Taneja. 2004. *People, Policy, and Participation: Making Watershed Management Work in India.* London: International Institute for Environment and Development. Online at http://www.iied.org/pubs/display.php?o=9522IIED&n=8&l=10&s=IP&b=t.

- Veit, P. 2007. *On Whose Behalf?: Legislative Representation and the Environment in Africa.* Feb. 15 draft. Washington, DC: World Resources Institute.

- Veit, P. 2008. Regional Director for Africa, People and Ecosystems Program. World Resources Institute, Washington, DC. Personal communication. Feb. 5.

- Vermeulen, S., and N. Goad. 2006. "Towards Better Practice in Smallholder Palm Oil Production." Natural Resource Issues Series No. 5. London: International Institute for Environment and Development. Online at http://www.iied.org/pubs/display.php?o=13533IIED&n=1&l=1&k=Towards%20Better%20Practice%20in%20Smallholder%20Palm%20Oil%20Production.

- World Bank. 2005. *Pro-Poor Growth in the 1990s: Lessons and Insights from 14 Countries.* Washington, DC: World Bank. Online at http://go.worldbank.org/7WJA36K5G0.

- World Bank. 2006a. *Indonesia: Rural Investment Climate Assessment Report: Revitalizing the Rural Economy: An Assessment of the Investment Climate Faced by Non-farm Enterprises at the District Level.* Washington, DC: World Bank. Online at http://go.worldbank.org/ZCHNNT6SZ0.

- World Bank. 2006b. *Global Economic Prospects: Economic Implications of Remittances and Migration.* Washington, DC: World Bank. Online at http://go.worldbank.org/CGW1GG3AV1

- World Bank. 2007a. "India: World Bank Approves US$600 Million for Government of India to Revitalize Financial Access for Poorest Farmers." Press Release No. 2007/494/SAR, June 26. Washington, DC: World Bank. Online at http://go.worldbank.org/WAD0QC1M00

- World Bank. 2007b. "Microfinance: Breaking the Cycle of Poverty." *North American Affairs Newsletter.* July, Issue 6. Washington, DC: World Bank. Online at http://newsletters.worldbank.org/external/default/main?menuPK=3177873&theSitePK=3177857&pagePK=64133601&contentMDK=21395480&piPK=64129599.

- World Bank. 2007c. *Development Effectiveness.* Washington, DC: World Bank. Online at http://go.worldbank.org/DHT3OTK3U0.

- World Bank. 2007d. "Migration Strongly Benefits Girls in Home Countries, Says New World Bank Book." Press Release No. 2007/496/DEC, June 28. Paris: World Bank. Online at http://go.worldbank.org/7O83TEAUV0.

- World Bank. 2007e. *World Development Indicators 2007.* Washington, DC: World Bank. Online at http://go.worldbank.org/3JU2HA60D0.

- World Bank. 2008. *Migration and Remittances Factbook 2008.* Washington, DC: World Bank. Online at http://go.worldbank.org/59JJA306X0.

- WRI (World Resources Institute) in collaboration with United Nations Development Programme, United Nations Environment Programme, and World Bank. 2005. *World Resources 2005: The Wealth of the Poor—Managing Ecosystems to Fight Poverty.* Washington, DC: WRI. Online at http://www.wri.org/project/world-resources.

Box 4.1

- Daviet, F., H. McMahon, R. Bradley, F. Stolle, S. Nakhooda. 2007. *REDD Flags: What We Need to Know About the Options.* Draft Executive Summary. Washington, DC: World Resources Report.

- Faris, S. 2007. "The Other Side of Carbon Trading." *Fortune.* Aug. 30.

- Huberman, D. 2007. *Making REDD Work for the Poor: The Socio-Economic Implications of Mechanisms for Reducing Emissions from Deforestation and Degradation.* Draft for comment. World Conservation Union (IUCN) on behalf of the Poverty and Environment Partnership. Online at http://cmsdata.iucn.org/downloads/redd_and_poverty_7_dec_07___jtb_dh.pdf.

- IPCC (Intergovernmental Panel on Climate Change). 2007. *IPPC Fourth Assessment Report: Working Group III Report: Mitigation of Climate Change.* Geneva: IPCC. Online at http://www.ipcc.ch/ipccreports/ar4-wg3.htm.

- Myers, E. C. 2007. *Policies to Reduce Emissions from Deforestation and Degradation in Tropical Forests: An Examination of the Issues Facing the Incorporation of REDD into Market-Based Climate Policies.* Washington, DC: Resources for the Future. Online at http://www.rff.org/rff/Publications/Discussion_Papers.cfm.

Box 4.2

- Larson, A., and J. Ribot. 2007. "The Poverty of Forestry Policy: Double Standards in an Uneven Playing Field." *Sustainability Science*, 2(2):189–204.
- Ribot, J. 2008a. "Authority Over Forests: Democratic Decentralization in Senegal." Working Paper 36 in Representation, Equity, and Environment Working Paper Series. Washington, DC: World Resources Institute.
- Ribot, J. 2008b. Senior Associate, Governance and Access, World Resources Institute. Personal Communication, Jan. 22.

Chapter 5

Box 5.1

- Alexander, D. 2008. *Climate Change and Development Tests.* Speech at New York University's Center on International Cooperation, April 14. London: UK Department for International Development. Online at http://www.dfid.gov.uk/news/files/Speeches/alexander-climate-nyc-fulltext.asp.
- Burton, I., E. Diringer, and J. Smith. 2006. *Adaptation to Climate Change: International Policy Options.* Washington, DC: Pew Center on Global Climate Change. Online at http://www.pewclimate.org/global-warming-in-depth/all_reports/adaptation_to_climate_change.
- Cline, W. R. 2007. *Global Warming and Agriculture: New Country Estimates Show Developing Countries Face Declines in Agricultural Productivity.* Washington, DC: Center for Global Development. Online at http://www.cgdev.org/content/publications/detail/14425.
- Dasgupta, S., B. Laplante, C. Meisner, D. Wheeler, and J. Yan. 2007. *The Impact of Sea Level Rise on Developing Countries: A Comparative Analysis.* Washington, DC: World Bank. Online at http://go.worldbank.org/BQMC8FEN30.
- IPCC (Intergovernmental Panel on Climate Change). 2007. *IPCC Fourth Assessment Report, Working Group II Report: Impacts, Adaptation and Vulnerability.* Geneva: IPCC. Online at http://www.ipcc.ch/ipccreports/ar4-wg2.htm.
- MA (Millennium Ecosystem Assessment). 2005. *Ecosystems and Human Well-Being: Desertification Synthesis.* Washington, DC: World Resources Institute. Online at http://www.millenniumassessment.org/documents/document.355.aspx.pdf.
- Ravallion, R., S. Chen, and P. Sangraula. 2007. *New Evidence on the Urbanization of Global Poverty.* World Bank Policy Research Working Paper 4199. Washington, DC: World Bank. Online at http://go.worldbank.org/ZX08OLDGI0.
- UNFPA (United Nations Population Fund). 2007. *State of World Population 2007: Unleashing the Potential of Urban Growth.* New York: United Nations Population Fund. Online at http://www.unfpa.org/swp/2007/english/introduction.html.
- World Bank. 2007a. *World Development Indicators 2007.* Washington, DC: World Bank. Online at http://go.worldbank.org/3JU2HA60D0.
- World Bank. 2007b. *Developing Countries Brace for Climate Change Impact.* Washington, DC: World Bank. Online at http://go.worldbank.org/U2WZTF7MC0.

Photo Credits

244

Index

Italic page numbers refer to figures, tables, and boxes.

A

Aalbersberg, Bill, 41
Access, *10*
    to financial services, *6*, 17, 179–185
    to natural resource information, 198, 200
    need for, 16–17, 190
Accountability. *See also* Transparency
    demand for, 32, 167
    downward accountability, 26
    lack of, 76
    of legislatures, 175–176
    of line agencies, 177, 199
    third-party evaluations for, 196
ACOFOP. *See* Asociación de Comunidades Forestales del Petén
    (Guatemala)
Action plans, preparation of, 66
Adaptability, 28–29. *See also* Resilience
Adjusted Net Savings, 205
AdobeTerra, 181
Advocacy, *72*, 176
Africa. *See also individual countries and regions*
    Equator Prize finalists from, *58–59*
    honey bees in. *See* Beekeeping
    insurance industry in, 184
    legislatures in, 175
    political reform in, 176
    poverty reduction in, *20*
    secure tenure systems in, 53
    small-scale producers in, 168
    technological assistance in, 174
    titled property rights in, 51
Aga Khan Rural Support Programme (AKRSP, Pakistan), 27,
    84–85, 86, 89, *90*
Agriculture. *See also specific crops (e.g., coffee)*
    in Bangladesh, 113, 123
    in Burkina Faso, 107
    CBNRM and. *See* Community-based natural resource
        management
    climate change and, 12, *192*, *193*
    definition of agricultural land, 212
    enterprise and, *14*
    farmers' unions and cooperatives, *31*, *33*, 73, 97, *100–102*,
        107, 108. *See also specific organizations by name*
    food consumption and, 204, 210–213
    forestry management and, *35*, 127, 134, 138, 139, *164*
    horizontal evaluations and, 87
    as income source crucial to the poor, 9
    ISOs and, *81*, *90–92*. *See also* Intermediary support
        organizations
    learning networks and, 105–106

    local crop processing, 96
    marketing activities, *11*, 16, 28, 171, 198–199
    in Namibia, 30–36
    in Niger. *See* Niger's re-greening movement
    organic farming, *104*, 106
    product standards and market research, 103–104
    resilience and, 28, *36*, *192*
    smallholders, 5, 28, 47, 89, 107, 168
    social capital investment and, 25
    sustainable. *See* Sustainable agriculture
    in watersheds, 13, *19*, 201
    in Zambia, *103*
Agroforestry, 17, 28, 47, *82*, 105, *164*, *165*
Aguié District Rural Development project (Niger), 152
AIDER. *See* Asociación para la Investigación y
    Desarrollo Integral (Peru)
AIDS. *See* HIV/AIDS
AIG Uganda, 184
AKRSP. *See* Aga Khan Rural Support Programme (Pakistan)
Alimentos Nutri-Naturales (Guatemala), *56–57*, *59*, *60*
Alter Eco, 93
AmazonLife (Brazil), *59*
American International Group, 180
ANAI Association (Costa Rica), *82*, 89, *90*, 106
ANAP. *See* National Association of Small Farmers (Cuba)
Andavadoaka Fisherman's Cooperative (Madagascar), *18*
ANSAB. *See* Asian Network for Sustainable Agriculture and
Bioresources (Nepal)
Apkindo (Indonesia plywood trade association), 169
APRAINORES (El Salvador), 96
Arbol Verde (Mexico and Caribbean), *129*, *130*, 135
Asia. *See also individual countries and regions*
    Equator Prize finalists from, 58
    insurance industry in, 184
    secure tenure systems in, 53
Asian Development Bank, 107
Asian Network for Sustainable Agriculture and Bioresources
    (ANSAB, Nepal), 81, 85, *90*, 99, 107
Asociación de Comunidades Forestales del Petén (ACOFOP,
    Guatemala), *90*, 129, 139
Asociación para la Investigación y Desarrollo Integral
    (AIDER, Peru), *90*
Association of Palqui Producers (APROPALQUI, Bolivia), *104*
Associations. *See* Networks and associations
Awards and prizes, role of, 55, 162, 195. *See also* Equator Prize
Ax, Floridalma, 135

B

Bangladesh
    climate change and, *192*
    community investment requirement in, 62
    infrastructure investment in, 178, *179*

inland fisheries, 112–125. *See also* Bangladesh inland fisheries
    insurance industry in, 184
Bangladesh Center for Advanced Studies, 113, 121, 123
Bangladesh Coastal and Wetland Biodiversity Management
Project, 121
Bangladesh inland fisheries, 12–13, 24, 112–125
    background, 113–114
    benefits of, *118,* 118–119, *119*
    challenges for, 123
    community involvement in management, *116,* 116–118, 162, 166
    Federations of Resource User Groups (FRUGs), 116
    government role in, 167
    Inland Capture Fisheries Strategy, 112–113, 121, 124–125
    institutional framework for management of, 115–116
    lessons from, 122–123, *124,* 125
    Local Government Committees or Upazila Fisheries
        Committees, 115–116, 118, 163, 166
    Management of Aquatic Ecosystems through Community
        Husbandry (MACH), 112, 113, *114,* 114–116, *115,* 120,
        121, 123–124, *124,* 160
    map of, *113*
    migratory waterfowl and, 120, 122
    new livelihoods and, 118–119, *122*
    ownership and equity, promotion of, 62, 117–118, 163
    Participatory Action Plans, 114
    quantitative scale-up of, 123–124
    reports to promote as scaling up example, 162
    Resource Management Organizations (RMOs) in, 24–25, 113,
        114, 115, 116–118, 123, 163, 166, 167
    resource rights and program success, 160, 161
    Resource User Groups (RUGs), 116, 123
    sustainability of, 123–125
    tree planting and, 122, 123
    women's role and, 119–120
Bangladesh Rural Advancement Committee (BRAC), *91,* 181, 182
Baren Commercial, 140
Beekeeping, *57, 60,* 174
    Honey Care Africa, Ltd. (Kenya), 56, *57, 58, 60*
    North Western Bee Products, Ltd. (Zambia), *18*
Begum, Sofia, 120
Benin Borgou Pilot Project, 26, 27
BOCOBONET. *See* Botswana Community-Based
    Organization Network
The Body Shop, 93
Bolivia
    associations in, *104*
    bureaucratic regulation as obstacle to community forest
        management, 170
    microfinance in, 182
Botswana, vertical networking in, 89
Botswana Community-Based Organization Network
    (BOCOBONET), 89, *92*
Bottom-up approaches, 26.
    See also Community-driven development (CDD)

BRAC. *See* Bangladesh Rural Advancement Committee
Brazil
    banking agents in, 181
    community investment requirement in, 61
    Equator Prize finalist from, *59*
    producer association in, 103–104, 107
Bridges, portable, *179*
Bureaucracy. *See* Government
Burkina Faso
    associations in, 97, 107
    conservation and regeneration projects in, 156

C

Cacao production, *60*
Calico Printers Cooperative Society (India), 105
Cameroon
    Forestry Law, 170
    legislators and rural advocacy in, 176
    medicinals market in, *98–99*
CANACACAO (National Cacao Chamber, Costa Rica), *60*
Canadian International Development Agency, 145
Capacity, *6,* 71–94. *See also* Resilience
    accountability, lack of, 76
    agricultural training, *100*
    CBNRM role. *See* Community-based natural
        resource management
    community-driven development and, 27
    in conservancies, 33
    devolution of resource authority and, 162–163
    ecosystem management and, 190
    element of scaling up, 5, *6, 7,* 15, 27, 195–196
    Fiji LMMA Network, development of, 41–42
    inclusiveness, lack of, 76–77
    intermediary support organizations, role of, 77–93.
        See also Intermediary support organizations
    in line agencies, 177
    local organizations, role of, *72, 74–75. See also* Local institutions
    need for capacity development, 25, 26, 77, 196, 197
    staff exchanges with government, 86
    technical. *See* Technical assistance
    upward capacity building, 83, 86
    Watershed Organisation Trust (WOTR, India), 78–79
    Women on the Move (women's savings groups in Niger), *74*
Carbon credits, 140
Carbon emissions. *See* Climate change
Carchi Consortium (Ecuador), 88–89, 105–106
CARE International, *74,* 131, 145, 148, 154, 155
Caritas (Bangladesh NGO), 113, 116, 117, 121, 166
Carrera, José Roman, 138–139, 140
Cartels, formation of, 169
Case studies illustrating resilience, 111–157
    Bangladesh inland fisheries, 112–125.
        See also Bangladesh inland fisheries

cross-cutting lessons from, 160–167
Guatemala forestry enterprises, 126–141.
  See also Guatemala forestry enterprises
Niger's re-greening movement, 142–157.
  See also Niger's re-greening movement
Cashew industry, 96
CBNRM. *See* Community-based natural resource management
Center for Empowerment and Resource Development
  (CERD, Philippines), *59*
Center for Natural Resource Studies (CNRS, Bangladesh),
  113, 117, 121, 166
Central America. *See* Latin America
Central American Sea Turtle Conservation Network, *60*
Centro Agrónomico Tropical de Investigación y Eseñanza, 131
Centro Mayo, 131
CERD (Center for Empowerment and Resource Development,
  Philippines), 59
Certification of products as Fair Trade. *See* Fair Trade
CFM (Community forestry management), *51*
Changing the development paradigm, 26–27
Charcoal trade in Senegal, 169, *172–173*
Chaubas Wood Processing Enterprise (Nepal), 96
Chemonics International, 132–133, 135, 138
Child mortality, *21*

China
  inland fisheries in, 13
  poverty as rural phenomenon in, 22
  poverty reduction in, *20, 23*
Church membership, *72, 73*
Cinnamon trade in Vietnam, 171
Citigroup, 180
Civil liberties, 221
Claveria Landcare Association (CLCA, Philippines), *91*
Clean water
  local demand and projects for, 54
  Senegal's National Rural Infrastructures Program, 26
  use of improved water source, 212
Climate change
  Niger's re-greening movement and, 157, *193–194*
  Reducing Emissions from Deforestation in Developing
    Countries (REDD), *164–165*
  resilience and, 28, 157
  rural poor and, 190, *192–194*
Club du Sahel, 156
CNRS. *See* Center for Natural Resource Studies (Bangladesh)
Co-financing arrangements, 61
Co-management arrangements, 191
Coffee producers. *See also* Fair Trade

cooperatives, 28, *100–102*
in Ethiopia, *100–102*, 171
Finca Esperanza Verde (FEV, Nicaragua), *19*
in Latin America, 97
in Rwanda, 28
Collective action, 62, 63.
See also Connection; Networks and associations
Colombia
Equator Prize finalist from, *59*
medicinals market in, *59*, *104*
COMACO. *See* Community Markets for Conservation (Zambia)
Commercial banks and microfinance, 180, 199
Common-pool resources, 5, *9*, *10*, 26, 51, 62, 65, 160
Communal property rights, 51
Communication and media, 17, 177–179, 196
Community-based enterprises, *56*
successful ecosystem-based enterprises, list of, *58–59*
Community-based natural resource management (CBNRM),
5, *6*, 8, *9*, *10*, 12
authority and access for the poor in, 16, 17, 162–163
demand as reason to create, 14
effect on poverty levels, *23*, 111
government collaboration and, 86
linkages and networks and, 86
local organizations and, 71
market access and, 89
ownership and, 49
participatory decision-making and, 67, 160
private sector and, 93
relation to ecosystem-based enterprises, *14*
vertical networking and, 89
Community-driven development (CDD), 16, 26–27
building resilience, 28
infrastructure development and, 178–179
Community Forest User Groups (Nepal), 28, 64, 72, 81, 85, 96,
105, 106–107
Community forestry enterprises, 13
Community forestry management (CFM), *51*
Community Markets for Conservation (COMACO, Zambia),
92, *103*
Community Organizations Development Institute
(CODI, Thailand), *91*
Compartamos (Mexico), 180
Competition, fostering of, 169, 197–199
Comunidád de Agua Blanca (Ecuador), *19*
CONAP. *See* National Council of Protected Areas (Guatemala)
Concession model, 127, 128, 129–130, *130*, 135
Congo, Equator Prize finalist from, *58*
Connection, 95–109. *See also* Networks and associations
CBNRM and. *See* Community-based natural resource
management
challenges of association, 107–108
ecosystem management and, 190

element of scaling up, 5, *6*, 7, 15–16
financial support from, 105
government involvement in, 108
informal sectors and, 107–108
learning networks, 105–106, 197
market influence and, 97, 103
membership organizations, 107
power of association, 95–107, 109
product standards and market research, 103–105
resilience and resourcefulness and, 200
Conservancies. *See* Namibia's Communal Conservancy Program
Conservation and Management Organization (Guatemala), 135
Conservation International, 131
Consorcio Local para el Desarrollo de la Cuenca del Rio
Tascalapa (Honduras), 105
Cooperatives, *18*, 28, 97, *100–102*, 107, 108
national laws on, 197
Coordination Framework for Rural Producer Organization
(Burkina Faso), 107
CORDES (El Salvador), 96
Corruption. *See also* Governance; Transparency
Corruption Perceptions Index (CPI), 221
Guatemala forestry enterprises and, 138
of legislatures, 175
Cost-sharing, *6*, 65, 179
Costa Rica
ANAI Association in, 89, *90*, 106
Talamanca Initiative in, *60*
Costa Rican Organic Agricultural Movement (MAOCO), 106
Costa Rican Sea Turtle Conservation Network, *60*
Costs
participatory decision-making and, 67
of REDD programs, *165*
of remittances, 185, *185*
Crasborn, Carlos, 135
Credit associations, 72–73
Cuba, learning networks in, 105
Customary tenure systems. *See* Ownership

D

Damaraland (Namibia), 36
Daugherty, P.J., 50
Deans' Beans, 92, 93
Deccan Development Society (India), 53
Decentralization, 26, 49–50, 162–163, 191
Decision-making. *See* Participatory decision-making
Deforestation
in Bangladesh, 123
Reducing Emissions from Deforestation in Developing
Countries (REDD), *164–165*
Delta Life (Bangladesh), 184

Demand
 conservancies as demand-driven institutions, 31
 defined, 14
 Fiji LMMA Network and, 39
 local demand and commitment, 54–55, 61, 67
 scaling up and, 6
Democratic Republic of the Congo. *See* Congo
Demonstration phase, 55, 161–162, 185, 191
Deppert, Darrell, 116
Desert Community Initiative (Niger), 152
Deutsche Bank, 180
Development paradigm, changing of, 26–27
Dhikuri (Nepal), 72–73
Direct marketing by small-scale enterprises, 198–199
Diseases, effect of, 185. *See also* HIV/AIDS
Dispute resolution. *See* Land disputes, resolution of
Diversification of funding sources, 196
Donor commitment, 167, 195, 200. *See also* Government;
Nongovernmental organizations (NGOs)
Downward accountability, 26
Drinking water. *See* Clean water; Water issues

E

E-Cafe Gold Cooperative Coffee Competition (Ethiopia), 102
East Asia. *See also individual countries*
 climate change and, *192*
 poverty in, *22*
East Coast Fisher People Forum (India), 87
EcoHamaca (Nicaragua), 97, 103
Ecological resilience, 27–28
Economic capital
 in Bangladesh, 114
 in Guatemala, 128
 in Niger, 143
Economic resilience, 28
 Namibia's conservancy program and, 36
Economics and trade, 204–205, 214–217
Ecosystem or ecosystem-based enterprises. *See* Enterprises
Ecosystem resilience, *192*, 201
Ecosystems
 access to resources of, *10*
 decline in, 8, *8*, *9*
 goods and services, 9, *181*, 208, 212, 216
 as renewable source of income for the poor, 25
Ecotourism
 ANAI Association (Costa Rica), *82*, *90*
 Arbol Verde (Mexico and Caribbean), *130*, 135
 Comunidád de Agua Blanca (Ecuador), *19*
 Finca Esperanza Verde (FEV, Nicaragua), *19*
 in Madagascar, *57*
 Ngata Toro Community (Indonesia), *58*
 in Zambia, *103*

Ecuador
 Comunidád de Agua Blanca, *19*
 Dean's Beans in, 93
 land registration in, 53
 learning network in, 105
 vertical networking in, 88–89
Education expenditure, 221
El Salvador
 leveraging remittances for rural investment in, 184, 185
 local production and processing in, 96
Elders councils, 24
Elections and political rights, 221
Elite capture, 24, 27, 53, 169
Empowerment, 6, *10*, 26
Enabling environment, 4, 5, *17*, 126, 168, *197–200*
 for scaling up enterprise, *6*, *7*, 16, 17, 24, 160, 168
EnerSud Ind e Soluções Energéticas (Brazil), 181
Enforcement efforts at community level, *7*, 40–41, 45, 195
Enterprises, 4
 best practices for, *56–60*
 building rural communities and, 4
 commercial aspects of, *14*, 117
 defined, *14*, 47
 ecosystem or ecosystem-based enterprises, 3–45
 environmental income realized from, *10*
 Equator Prize finalists, list of (by region), *58–59*
 examples of successful enterprises, *18–19*
 Fiji LMMA Network, development of, 41–42, 45
 governance and, 16–17, 169–171
 integration of enterprise support initiatives, 199
 nature-based enterprises, 3, 16, 17, 24–25, *49*, 61, *67*, *71*,
  81, 89, *90*, *94*, 162–163, 174, *186*
 preconditions for success of, *56*
 relation to CBNRM, *14*
 scaling up, *6*, *10*
 success stories of, value of, *7*, 161–162
 successful ecosystem-based enterprises, list of, *58–59*
Environmental capital
 in Bangladesh, 114
 in Guatemala, 128
 in Niger, 143
Environmental income
 benefits of, 3–4, *9*
 forms of, *10*
 importance of, *9*
 scaling up, *10*
 smallholder agriculture and, 5
Equator Initiative (case study), *56–60*, 86, 162
Equator Prize, 55, *56–60*, 88, 97, 162, 195
Equity
 in Bangladesh inland fisheries program, 117–118
 favoring large-scale producers over rural small-scale
  producers, 168, 198

in tax regimes and regulation, *6*, *7*, 17, 169–171
in tenure rights. *See* Land and resource tenure
Ethiopia
    coffee producers in, *100–102*, 171
    Dean's Beans in, 93
    government and associations in, 108
    local institutions in, 72
    medicinals market in, *99*
Executive branch influence, 175, 200
Exports of goods and services, 216

F

Fair Trade
    certification, *101*, 105, 174, *174*
    coffee and cocoa, 92, 93, 97
Farmer Field Schools, *14*, *104*
Farmer-Managed Natural Regeneration (FMNR), 143, 146–148,
    150–157. *See also* Niger's re-greening movement
Farmer-to-Farmer Movement (Cuba), 105
Farming. *See* Agriculture
Federation of Community Forest Users Nepal (FECOFUN),
    106–107
Ferro Cooperative (Ethiopia), *101*
Fertilizer, 212
Fiji Locally Managed Marine Area (FLMMA), 38–45
    background, 38–39
    benefits of, 42–44
    capacity, development of, 41–42
    challenges to, 44–45
    compliance and enforcement, 40–41, 45
    enterprise development, 41–42, 45
    as ISO, *91*
    local ownership, creation of, 39–40
    networks and, 42
    participatory decision-making in, 39–40
    representation issues for, 44–45
    resource tenure and program success, 160, 161
    sustainability of, 44
Financial services. *See also* Microfinance; Remittances
    access to, *6*, 17, 179–185
    in India, 105
    rotating credit associations, 72–73
Financial support and commitment, *6*. *See also* Microfinance;
        Nongovernmental organizations (NGOs); Remittances;
        Seed money
    availability of, *6*, *7*
    cost-sharing, *6*, 65, 179
    government as partner and source of funds, *80*, 108, 167,
        174, 183, 185, 200
    ISOs as distribution nodes, 89, 92, 126, 195, 196
    labor contribution, *6*, 15, 61–62, *79*
    local organizations securing, *73*, 75, 77
    official development assistance (ODA), 216

Finca Esperanza Verde (FEV, Nicaragua), *19*
FIRMED (Fishery Integrated Management for Economic
    Development, Philippines), *59*
Fisheries Department (Bangladesh), 121, 123
Fishing
    Andavadoaka Fisherman's Cooperative (Madagascar), *18*
    in Bangladesh's wetlands. *See* Bangladesh inland fisheries
    Center for Empowerment and Resource Development
        (CERD, Philippines), *59*
    in China, 13
    in Fiji. *See* Fiji Locally Managed Marine Area (FLMMA)
    fisheries production, defined, 212
    in Mozambique, 62
FLMMA. *See* Fiji Locally Managed Marine Area
FMNR. *See* Farmer-Managed Natural Regeneration
Food
    Niger's re-greening movement and food security, 142, 143,
        151–152, 155
    security, *57*, *103*, 204, 210–213
    undernourished, definition of, 212
Foreign direct investment (FDI), 216
FORESCOM (Guatemala), *90*, 127, 128, 133, 134, 136,
    139–140. *See also* Guatemala forestry enterprises
Forest Department (Senegal), *172–173*
Forest Stewardship Council, 81, 134
Forests
    in Bangladesh, 112
    in Brazil, *59*
    bureaucratic regulation as obstacle to local communities, 170
    in Cameroon, 170
    community forestry enterprises, 13, *165*
    community forestry management, 50, *51*
    in Congo, *58*
    decline in area of, *8*
    in El Salvador, 96
    in The Gambia, 174
    in Guatemala, 29, *56–57*, *59*, *60*
    in Honduras, 16–17
    in Indonesia, *58*
    in Namibia, *35*
    ownership, 50, *51*, 53–54, *54*
    secure tenure and, 50, *51*
    in Senegal, 170, *172–173*
    small forestry enterprises (SFEs), 168, *168*
    in Thailand, *18*
    in Uganda, *164–165*
Fourth Fisheries Project (Bangladesh), 123
Fragile states, *20*
France, 154
Free, prior, and informed consent (FPIC), 183
Free association, right to, 197
Freedom of Information legislation, 176, 199, 200, 221
Functional scaling up, *11*

G

The Gambia
    community forest enterprises in, 174
    conservation and regeneration projects in, 156
Garcia, Benedin, 134
Genetic Resource, Energy, Ecology and Nutrition (GREEN)
    Foundation (India), *58*
Germany
    Guatemala and, 127
    Niger and, 148, 154
Ghana
    community investment requirement in, 61
    Community Water and Sanitation Project (World Bank), 61
    land ownership in, 52
    land registration in, 53
Global Environment Facility, 121
Gokulpura-Goverdhanpura Integrated Watershed Management
    (India), *19*
Governance. *See also* Government; Local government;
        Representation issues
    in conservancies, 33, 163
    as enabling environment for scaling up, 5, *7, 9,* 17
    enterprise and, 16–17
    measurement of, 205, 218–221
    need to improve on national level, 174
    poor governance of Guatemala forestry enterprises, 138
    poverty-environment-governance approach, *9*
Government. *See also* Decentralization; Governance;
        Local government
    bureaucratic regulation as obstacle to community
        management, 17, 170, *172–173,* 177, 197, 199, 221
    development role of, 168–185, 196. *See also* Marketing;
        Research assistance; Technical assistance
    as enabling environment for scaling up, 24
    expenditures as percent of GDP, 221
    fairness in regulation and, *169–171. See also* Equity
    favoring large-scale producers over rural small-scale
        producers, 168, 198
    involvement in associations, 108
    line agencies' approach to rural communities, 7, 177, 195, 199
    microfinance role of, 182
    "minimum standards" approach to, 170, 198
    national governments and extraction of natural resources,
        183, 198
    as partner and source of funds, 17, 167, 171, 174, 200.
        See also Financial support and commitment
Gram Mooligai Co. Ltd. (India), *99*
Grameen Bank, 179
GREEN (Genetic Resource, Energy, Ecology and Nutrition)
    Foundation (India), *58*
Grootberg Farmers' Union, 31
Gross domestic product (GDP), 216
Group heterogeneity, effect of, 65

GTZ (German Agency for Technical Cooperation), 145, 153, 154
Guatemala. *See also* Guatemala forestry enterprises
    Equator Prize finalist from, *56–57, 59, 60*
    ISO in, *90*
    National Council of Protected Areas, 201
    reports to promote as scaling up example, 162
Guatemala forestry enterprises, 29, 126–141
    authority over resources, 162, 163
    bureaucratic regulation as obstacle to community
        management, 170
    carbon credits, 140
    challenges for, 132–133, 163
    community dividends and, 134–135

concession model and, 129–130, *130,* 135

conservation dividend and, 133–134, *134*

creation of, 127

failure of local NGOs to work with communities, 167

future planning for, 137–139, 140

initial efforts of, 127–128

intermediaries, skill building with, 131–133

key achievements of, 128

lessons from, 139

Maya Biosphere Reserve, 126, 127, *129, 130,* 131, 134, 137, 139, 163, *164,* 201

non-timber forest products and, 126, 133, 136–137

organizational scaling up, 139–140

participatory decision-making and, 163

paternalism trap and, 133

political scaling up, 140

processing and wood products and, 136

quality life, improving, 135

resentment of local government toward, 163

resource tenure and program success, 160

scaling up, 139–141

tax collection and distribution and, 163

women and, 133

Guinea, conservation and regeneration projects in, 156–157

Guinea-Bissau, fishery access agreements in, 183

Gujarat Cooperative Milk Marketing Federation (India), 108

Gum trees, research on, 171

Haiti, watershed management in, 62

Hassan, Bob, 169

Health services

public health expenditure, 221

in Senegal, 26

HIV/AIDS, 33, *102,* 185, 208, 209

Honduras

associations in, 105

concession model in, 127, 141

resources management and the poor in, 16–17

Honey Care Africa, Ltd. (Kenya), *56, 57, 58, 60*

Horizontal networking, *7,* 15, 57, 86–88

Human rights, 221

I

IFAD. *See* International Fund for Agricultural Development

Illiassou, Fatima, 153

ILO. *See* International Labour Organization

Inclusiveness

capacity and lack of, 76–77

large-scale resource extraction and, 183

participatory decision-making and, 65–66

Income. *See* Environmental income

Income equality, 23

India

accountability of local government in, 93

associations in, 105, 107

bureaucratic regulation as obstacle to community forest management, 170

cooperatives in, 97, 108

Equator Prize finalist from, *58*

forest tenure program in, 53

Gokulpura-Goverdhanpura Integrated Watershed Management, *19*

gram sabha (village assembly) and forest association in, 73

infrastructure investment in, 178

insurance industry in, 183

land leasing arrangements in, 53

local institutions in, 72

medicinals market in, *99*

microfinance in, 180

networking in, 87

NGOs, role in, 73

research assistance in, 171

resilience and, 200

Self-Employed Women's Organization (SEWA), 88, 89

small forestry enterprises in, 168

Tank User Groups in, 24

telecommunications in, 177

watershed management practices in, 13, 55, 61, 82, 85, 167

Watershed Organisation Trust. *See* Watershed Organisation Trust (WOTR, India)

Indigenous peoples in Honduras, 16–17

Indo-German Watershed Development Program, *78*

Indonesia

Equator Prize finalist from, *58*

forest tenure program in, 53–54

locally managed marine area (LMMA) in, 38, *39,* 41

palm oil business in, 168, 171, 174

plywood export market in, 169

state assistance programs, effectiveness of, 174

Infant mortality rate, 208, 209

Informal sectors and connection, 107–108

Information, access to, 55, 198, 200

Infrastructure

community-driven infrastructure, 178–179

financing from natural resource revenues, 183

improvement of physical infrastructure, 177–179

Senegal's National Rural Infrastructures Program, 26

Institutional choice, 24, 163

Institutional scaling up, *11*

Insurance industry, 182–184

Intangible capital, 25, *25*

Integrated Rural Development and Nature Conservation (Namibia), 33

Integration of enterprise support initiatives, 199

Interagency coordination, *7, 73,* 166.

See also Intermediary support organizations (ISOs)

InterAmerican Development Bank, 140
Intergovernmental Panel on Climate Change (IPCC), *194*
Intermediary support organizations (ISOs), *6, 7,* 80–93, 94
    ability to facilitate partnerships with government
        and NGOs, 86–89
    access to markets, 89
    equity and transparency, 80, 92–93
    financial sources, 89, 92
    focus and credibility of, 166–167
    horizontal networking, *7,* 15, 57, 86–88
    list of (by region), *90–92*
    private sector, 93
    role of, 15, 77–80, 174, 190, 195–196, 200
    social capacity building, 81–83
    staff exchanges and partnerships and, 86
    success stories of, value of, 161–162
    technical capacity building, 80–81
    training and dialogue and, 85–86
    "upward" capacity building and, 83, *84–85,* 85–86
    vertical networking, 15, 88–89
    Watershed Organisation Trust. *See* Watershed Organisation
        Trust (WOTR, India)
International Co-operative Alliance, 108, 197
International Development Research Centre, *56*
International Fund for Agricultural Development (IFAD), 145,
    148, 149, 152, 154, 155, 184
International Institute for Environment and Development, 52
International Labour Organization (ILO), 108, 197
International Potato Center, 87
Investments. *See also* Infrastructure
    community investment, *7, 49,* 117, *187.*
        See also Cost-sharing; Labor contribution
    microfinance and, 182
    property rights and, 50
IPCC (Intergovernmental Panel on Climate Change), *194*
Iqoliqoli Management Support Teams (QMSTs, Fiji), 42
Iqoliqolis (controlling groups of Fiji fishing grounds), 38, 40, 43, 45
Islam, Toyobul, 120
ISOs. *See* Intermediary support organizations
Italian Cooperation, 145

J

Jethua Resource Management Organization (Bangladesh), 117
Jiwa, Farouk, *57*
Joint action. *See* Networks and associations
Joint ecosystem management. *See* Community-based natural
    resource management (CBNRM)
JuWa Farmers Union, *31*

K

Kalinga Mission for Indigenous Communities and
    Youth development (Philippines), 81
Karaya gum, 171
Kenya
    Honey Care Africa, Ltd., *56, 57, 58, 60*
    networks in, *104*
    poverty gap in, *23*
Khoadi Hoas Conservancy (Namibia), 31, 32, 33, 36
Kim, Y., 50
Klongnarai Women's Group (Thailand), *104*
Kolloma Baba Women's Association (Niger), 153

L

Labor activity, defined, 212
Labor contribution, *6,* 15, 61–62, *79*
Lagos State Fish Farmers' Association (Nigeria), *104*
Land and resource tenure, *6,* 13, 50–54, *51,* 67, 191.
    See also Ownership
    in Bangladesh, 115, 123
    useful even when not perfect, 160–161, 200
Land disputes, resolution of, *7,* 53, 191
Land leasing arrangements, 53, 191
Landless, rights of, 53
Lao People's Democratic Republic, *104*
Latin America. *See also individual countries*
    cooperatives in, 97
    Equator Prize finalists from, *56–57, 59, 60*
    insurance industry in, 184
    networking in, 87
    poverty in, *22*
    secure tenure systems in, 53
    small forest enterprises in, 168
    sustainable forest management and, 141
Leadership
    Equator Initiative and, *57, 60*
    local demand and commitment and, 55
    training for, 195
Learning networks, 105–106, 197
Leasing arrangements for land, 53, 191
Legislatures. *See* Governance
Life expectancy, 208
Line agencies. *See* Government
Literacy
    adult literacy rate, 208, 209
    in Bangladesh, 116, 123, 124
    in Benin, 26
    Women on the Move (women's savings groups in Niger) and, *74*
Livelihood security, *6*
Living in Finite Environment (LIFE) program (Namibia), 37
Lobo, Crispino, *68,* 68–70, 201
Local commitment, *7,* 15, 61–62

Local government, *6, 11, 72*
    accountability and, 93
    in Bangladesh, *124*
    importance of, 24–25
    reconciling with role of resource management organizations, 163
    resource management organizations working with, 163
Local institutions, 24, 53, 71–77, *72*, 94.
      See also Local government
    accountability, lack of, 76
    assessment of, 77
    capacity development, need for, 75, 77, 162–163

challenges and limitations of, 73, 76–77, 163
definition of, 71–72, *72*
example of, *74–75*
inclusiveness, lack of, 76–77
maturation period for, 163
resources and connections, lack of, 75
strengths of, 72–73
Locally managed marine areas (LMMAs)
    in Fiji, 38–45. *See also* Fiji Locally Managed Marine Area (FLMMA)
    in other Asia-Pacific countries, 38, *39*

M

MA. *See* Millennium Ecosystem Assessment
MACH (Management of Aquatic Ecosystems through Community Husbandry). *See* Bangladesh inland fisheries
Macro level challenges, 168
Madagascar
    Andavadoaka Fisherman's Cooperative, *18*
    Equator Prize in, *57*
Majjia Valley Project (Niger), 145, 146
Malaria, 185
Malaysia, palm oil business in, 168
Mali, conservation and regeneration projects in, 156–157
Management of Aquatic Ecosystems through Community Husbandry (MACH). *See* Bangladesh inland fisheries
MAOCO. *See* Costa Rican Organic Agricultural Movement
Maradi Integrated Development project (MIDP, Niger), 146–147, 154, 155
Market analysis and development (MA&D), 174, 199
Marketing
    of agricultural products, *11*, 16, 28, 171, 198–199
    assistance, *7*, 171, 174
    association benefits, *109*
    capacity and, 72, *76*
    cooperatives and, *100–101, 102, 103*
    credit and finance for, 105
    ecosystem-based enterprises and, *104*
    entrepreneurship and, *56–57*
    federation and, *108*
    of forest products, 28, 132, 136, 137, *139*, 157
    intermediaries and, 131
    ISOs and, 81, *82*, 89, 93
    of natural resources and, 177
    political aspects of, 106
    research and, 171
    rural enterprises and, 95, 97, *160*
    scalability and, *60*
    scaling up and, 5, *6, 7, 10–11*
    support and, *181*, 199
    women and, *133, 135*
Mauritania, fishery access agreements in, 183

Maya Biosphere Carbon Project (Guatemala), 140
Mayuni Conservancy (Namibia), 35–36
Mazumder, Azharul, 125
McGahuey, Mike, 150, 154
MDGs. *See* Millennium Development Goals
Media and communication
    in monitoring government accountability, 177
    pilot programs' success stories via, *7*, *162*, *191*, 196
    press freedom, 221
Medicinals market, *59*, 85, *98–99*, *104*, 181
Melons, 103–104
Mengame Gorilla Reserve (Cameroon), 176
MET. *See* Ministry of Environment and Tourism (Namibia)
Mexico
    remittances and, 184, 185
    wood exported to, 135
Micro-Enterprise Development Programme (MEDEP, Nepal), 182
Microcredit Summit Campaign, 179
Microfinance
    in Bangladesh, *124*
    government role in, 182, 199
    maturing of, 179–181
    meeting needs of larger businesses, 182
    NGOs' role in, 181–182
Microfinance Information Exchange (MIX) Market, 180
Microinsurance, 182–184
MIDP. *See* Maradi Integrated Development project (Niger)
Military expenditure, 221
Millennium Challenge Corporation, 37
Millennium Development Goals (MDGs), *9*, 204
    child mortality, *21*
    Equator Initiative and, *56*, *60*
    poverty reduction, *20*, *21*, *23*
Millennium Ecosystem Assessment (MA), 8, 12, 190, *192*
Ministry of Environment and Tourism (MET, Namibia), 33, 37, 86, 166, 167
Ministry of Land (Bangladesh), 113, 114, 115, 120, 121
Minnick, Greg, 140
MIX (Microfinance Information Exchange) Market, 180
MMD (Mata Masu Dubara, Women on the Move), *74*
Monopolies created by state over nature-based products, 171
"Mother NGOs." *See* Intermediary support organizations
Mozambique
    community groups in, 73
    customary land systems in, 53
    fishing co-arrangement in, 62
Mutual Credit Guarantee Scheme (India), 105

N

NACSO. *See* Namibian Association of CBNRM Support Organizations
Nam Ha Ecoguide Service (Lao PDR), *104*
Namibia
    Communal Conservancy Program. *See* Namibia's Communal Conservancy Program
    community forests in, *35*
    customary land systems in, 53
Namibian Association of CBNRM Support Organizations (NACSO), *32*, 33–34, *34*, 37, 86, *91*, 96, 166
Namibian Community-Based Tourism Association (NACOBTA), 33, 34
Namibia's Communal Conservancy Program, 5, 30–37
    background, 30
    benefits of, 35–36
    capacity development in, 33, 75, 162
    challenges to, 37, 163
    demand-driven nature of, 31
    governance of, 33, 163
    growth of conservancies (1998-2005), *34*
    income sources, 35
    local decision-making in, 31, 162
    local ownership, creation of, 31–32
    Ministry of Environment and Tourism role.
        See Ministry of Environment and Tourism (MET, Namibia)
    networks and, 33–34
    participation of residents in, 31–32
    partnerships in, 86
    reports to promote as scaling up example, 162
    resilience of ecosystems and rural communities due to, *36*, 200
    resource rights and program success, 160
National Adaptation Programmes for Action (NAPAs), 157
National Advocacy Council for Development of Indigenous People (India), 87
National Association of Small Farmers (ANAP, Cuba), 105
National Cacao Chamber (CANACACAO, Costa Rica), *60*
National Council of Protected Areas (CONAP, Guatemala), 127–130, 132–134, 137, 139–140. *See also* Guatemala forestry enterprises
National Dairy Development Board (India), 108
National Forest Institute (Guatemala), 140
Natural resources management. *See* Community-based natural resource management (CBNRM)
Nature-based enterprises. *See* Enterprises
Nature Conservancy, 131
Nature Conservation Act (Namibia), 34
Nature Conservation Act (Niger), 55
Nature for Life, 131
Nepal
    Asian Network for Sustainable Agriculture and Bioresources (ANSAB), 81, 85, *90*, *99*, 107
    bureaucratic regulation as obstacle to community forest management, 170

Community Forest User Groups, 28, 64, 72, 81, 85, 96, 105, 106–107
  irrigation policy in, 107
  medicinals market in, *99*
  Micro-Enterprise Development Programme (MEDEP), 182
  rotating credit associations in, 72–73
Nepal Non-Timber Forest Products Network, 81
Netherlands, 136
  Dutch nonprofit and Uganda reforestation project, *164*
Networks and associations, 95–109. *See also* Cooperatives
  benefits of, 197
  challenges of association, 107–108
  in conservancies, 33–34
  credit and finance, 105
  ecosystem-based enterprise associations, list of, *104*
  element of scaling up, 5, *7*, 15–16, 190, 197
  exclusivity of, 107
  Fiji LMMA Network, development of, 42
  financial support for new associations, 197
  financial support from, 105
  government involvement in, 108
  informality, problem of, 107–108
  ISOs and, 80, 86–89.
    See also Intermediary support organizations
  learning networks, 105–106, 197
  local demand and commitment, 61–63
  local organizations as, 71–73, *72*
  local production and processing, 95–101
  market influence, 97, 103
  membership organizations, 107
  political process and, 106–107
  power of association, 95–107, 109
  product standards and market research, 103–105
  social capital and, 25
  Watershed Organisation Trust (WOTR, India) and, *79*
New Ventures (World Resources Institute), 181
Ngata Toro Community (Indonesia), *58*
NGOs. *See* Nongovernmental organizations
Nicaragua
  associations in, 97, 103, 105
  Finca Esperanza Verde (FEV), *19*
  land registration in, 53
  sustainable forest management in, 127, 141
Niger
  conservancies in, 55
  customary land systems in, 53
  land registration in, 53
  re-greening movement, 142–157.
    See also Niger's re-greening movement
  soil and water conservation practices in, 55
  Women on the Move (women's savings groups), *74*
Nigeria, associations in, *104*
Niger's re-greening movement, 142–157

  benefits of, 149–150
  climate change and, 157, *193–194*
  crop income from, 150–151
  famine, protection against, 151–152
  farmers' involvement in, 148, *148*
  food production and, 155–156
  food security and, 142, 143, 151–152, 155
  fuelwood and fodder income from, 150
  government, role of, 154
  income from, *150*, 150–151
  intermediaries, role of, 143, 154–155
  key achievements in, 143
  key people in, 146–147
  lessons from, 155–157
  non-timber tree products and, 151
  partnerships in, 153–155
  resilience and, 200
  resource rights and program success, 161
  revegetation of Niger and, 144–148
  Serving in Mission (SIM) role in, 161
  timeline of, 144
  tree regeneration, 146
  water and land reclamation and, 149
  women and, 152–153
Nondiscriminatory tax and regulatory regimes. *See* Equity
Nongovernmental organizations (NGOs).
    See also Intermediary support organizations (ISOs);
    specific organizations
  associations and, 96
  in Bangladesh wetlands conservation program, 113, 118, 121, 166
  funding for programs from, 167
  intermediary support organizations.
    See Intermediary support organizations (ISOs)
  land leasing arrangements and, 53
  local demand and, *68*
  local organizations and, 75
  in Madagascar, *57*
  medicinals market and, *99*
  microfinance and, 181–182
  microinsurance and, 183, 184
  participatory decision-making, 65, 66
  role of, 73, 174, 177, 181–182, 190, 195
  rural development support by, 73
North Western Bee Products, Ltd. (Zambia), *18*
Nyae Nyae Conservancy (Namibia), 31

O

Official development assistance (ODA), 216
Operation Flood (India), 108
Organic Cashew Agroindustrial System (SAMO), 96
Organic farming, *104*, 106
  product certification, *101*, 105, 174

Organizational scaling up, *11*
    in Bangladesh, 124
Oromia Coffee Farmers' Cooperative Union (Ethiopia), *100*
Ownership, 49–70
    in Bangladesh inland fisheries program, 117–118
    challenges to secure tenure, 50–51, 221
    collective action, *62*, 62–63, 67
    communities as investors, 61–62
    customary tenure systems, 51, 52, 53
    defined for purposes of ecosystem resources, 14
    demand. *See* Demand
    ecosystem management and, 190
    element of scaling up, 5, *6*, *7*, 13–15, 191, 195
    Equator Initiative (case study), *56–60*
    Fiji Locally Managed Marine Area (FLMMA) and, 39–40
    forests, 50, *51*, 53–54, *54*
    informal customary systems, 51
    information, 55
    innovations in tenure, 52–54, 191
    land and resource tenure, 13, 50–54, *51*, 67, 191
    landless, rights of, 53
    leadership, 55
    local commitment, 15, 61–62
    local demand, 54–55, *56–59*, 61–63, 67, *68–70*
    local institutions and, 53
    Namibia's Communal Conservancy Program and, 31–32
    participatory decision-making, 63–67
    resource access, 13, 55, 61
    resource degradation, 55
    resource tenure useful even when not perfect, 160–161
    rural enterprise, 54–55, 61
    state claims to land, 51–52
    tenure security, *6*, 50–51, *51*, 52, 53, 128, 161, 163, 191
    tenure systems, 50–51, 52–53
    watershed organizations, 68, *68*

P

Pagdee, A., 50
Pakistan's Aga Khan Rural Support Programme, 27, *84–85*, 86, 89, *90*
Palau and Pohnpei, locally managed marine area (LMMA) in, 38, *39*
Palm oil business, 168, 174
Panama, sustainable forest management in, 127, 141
Papa Andina, 87, *90*
Papua New Guinea
    Dean's Beans in, 93
    Equator Prize finalist from, 59
    locally managed marine area (LMMA) in, 38, *39*, 41
Participatory decision-making, 7, 63–67
    affinity groups and empowerment, 65–66, 67
    benefits of, 16, 63–64, 160, 195
    in conservancy programs, 31–32
    exclusion of the poor, 27, 64–65
    fact-finding, 65
    Fiji LMMA Network and, 39–40
    free, prior, and informed consent (FPIC), 183
    inclusion of the poor, 65–66
    inequality in, 65
    initial goal identification, 65, 67
    institutional design, 66
    Namibia's Communal Conservancy Program and, 31–32, 162
    social capacities and technical skills, 66
    weaknesses of, 27, 64–65
Patronage, 175, 200
Payment for ecosystems services (PES), *164, 165*
Peace Corps, 145
Peer reviews, 87
People's Rural Education Movement (India), 87
Permanent Interstate Committee for Drought Control in the Sahel, 156
Permanent Rural Code Secretariat (Niger), 154, 155

Peru
associations in, 97
Dean's Beans in, 93
ISO in, *90*
sustainable forest management in, 127, 141
PES. *See* Payment for ecosystems services
Philippines
bureaucratic regulation as obstacle to community forest
management, 170
Equator Prize finalist from, *59*
ISO in, 81, *91*
locally managed marine area (LMMA) in, 38, *39*, 41
tax rates on forest activities in, 171
Pilot projects. *See* Demonstration phase
Plywood export market in Indonesia, 169
Pole Pole Foundation (Congo), *58*
Political parties, 176, 200
Political rights index, 221
Political scaling up, *11*
in Bangladesh, 124–125
Population
definition of total population, 208
growth, 190, *192*
human well-being and, 204, 206–209
Poverty. *See* Rural poverty imperative
Poverty gap, *22–23*
Poverty Reduction Strategy Paper (Bangladesh), 121, 125
Pred Nai Community Forest (Thailand), *18*
PREM. *See* People's Rural Education Movement (India)
Price-fixing, 169
Prizes and awards, role of, 55, 162, 195. *See also* Equator Prize
Producer associations, 103–105
PRONACOM (National Competitiveness Program,
Guatemala), 140
Property rights, benefits of, 50. *See also* Ownership
ProPetén (Guatemala), 131
Public Institution Resource Management Group, *72*

Q

Quantitative scaling up, *10*
in Bangladesh, 123–124
Quibdo Women's Network of Medicinal Plant Producers
and Marketers (Colombia), *59*

R

Rainforest Alliance, 81, 135, 136, 137, 138, 140, 141, 162
Reducing Emissions from Deforestation in Developing Countries
(REDD), *164–165*
Registration of business, 221
Registration of land, 53, 221. *See also* Ownership
Remittances, 179–180, *184*, 184–185, 216

Representation issues, *7*, 24, 195, 199–200
in Bangladesh Resource Management Organizations, 123
in Fiji LMMA Network, 44–45
in national legislatures, 175–176, 199–200
Research assistance, *7*, 171, 174
Resilience
building of, 28–29, 200–201
capacity and, 76
case studies illustrating, 111–157
climate change and, 157, *192–194*
definition of, 27–28
ecological, 27–28, 76, 106
economic, 28, 76, 106
Namibia's Communal Conservancy Program and, *36*
networks and, 106
scaling up and, 5, *6, 10*, 12, 27–29, 200–201
social, 28, 76, 106
Resistance to change, 168
Resource degradation, 55
Resource rights, 49–50
Resource user groups (RUGs), *6*, 73.
See also Bangladesh inland fisheries
Resourcefulness. *See* Resilience
Rinaudo, Tony, 146–147, 155
Rio Platano Biosphere Reserve (Honduras), 141
Road construction, 177–179
Rotating credit associations, 72–73
Rules, natural resource management, 62, 63, 112
Rural Code (Niger), 154, 155, 157
Rural markets, policies to enhance, 168
Rural poverty imperative, *20–23*
climate change and, *192*
depth of poverty, *22–23*
ecosystem decline and, *8, 9*
global average income of rural poor, *23*
growth and increased equity, *23*
population living on less than $1/day, *20, 21, 22, 208*
population living on less than $2/day, *20, 21, 22, 208*
poverty is predominantly rural, *22*
purchasing power parity used for comparison purposes, *23*
recent poverty trends, *20–21*
scaling up and, *6*, 8, *10*
well-being, dimensions and elements of, *20*
Rwanda, coffee cooperatives in, 28

S

Sahel, 157. *See also specific countries*
Sahel Re-Greening Initiative, 157
Sakhokuhle Association (South Africa), 108
Sao Tome, fishery access agreements in, 183
Savings groups, *72, 73*

Scaling up, 3–45, 189–201
    capacity and, 5, *7*, 15, 27. *See also* Capacity
    changing development paradigm and, 26–27
    of community-based natural resource management, 5, 8, *9*, *10*, 12
    of community-driven ecosystem enterprise, 5, *6*, *7*
    connection and, 5, *6*, *7*, 15–16. *See also* Connection
    defined, *10*
    elements of, *6–7*, *10*
    enabling environment for, *6*, *7*, 16, 17, 24
    Equator Prize finalists and, *60*
    Fiji as example of local management of coastal fisheries, *38–45*
    functional, *11*
    future trends and, 201
    governance and. *See* Governance
    institutional, *11*
    Namibia as example of community conservancies, *30–37*
    need for, 8–13
    networks and, 5, *7*, 15–16, 197.
        See also Networks and associations
    organizational, *11*, 124, 139–140
    ownership and, 5, 7, 13–15, 191, 195. *See also* Ownership
    pilot projects' or demonstrations' success as catalyst for, 7, 161–162, 191
    political, *11*, 124–125, 140
    potential for, 12–13
    quantitative, *10*, 123–124
    reconciling local governments with role of resource management organizations, 163
    resilience and, 5, 27–29
    social capital and, 5, 25–26
    successfully driving scaling up process, 159–187
    tenure change and, 160–161
    thesis on, 5–7
    types of, 10–11
Sea turtle protection, *60*, 82
Secondments, 196
Security
    financial, 6. *See also* Financial support and commitment
    food. *See* Food
    insurance and, 183, 184
    as part of well-being, *20*
    social security, *88*
    tenure. *See* Ownership
Seed banks, *56*, *59*, 197
Seed money, *56*, *82*, 185, 197
Self-Employed Women's Organization (SEWA, India), 88, 89
Self-help groups, *72*, 73, 87, 195
Self-interest, 200
    community investment and, *70*, *79*, 115, 127
    impact of, 134
    legal security and, 154
    natural resources and, 9
    necessity of, 15
    REDD and, *164*, *165*
    resilience and, 111, *192*
    spontaneous self-scaling and, 148
    sustainability and, 112, 129
Senegal
    bureaucratic regulation as obstacle to community forest management, 170, *172–173*
    charcoal trade in, 169, *172–173*
    conservation and regeneration projects in, 156–157
    National Rural Infrastructures Program, 26
Sepik Wetlands Management Initiative (Papua New Guinea), *59*
Service delivery groups, 72
Serving in Mission (SIM, Niger), 146, 150, 155, 166
Sesfontein Conservancy (Namibia), 33
SEWA. *See* Self-Employed Women's Organization (India)
Sewers, 54
Shompole Community Trust (Kenya), *57*, *58*, *60*
Shompole Lodge (Kenya), *57*
Sidman Union (Ethiopia), *101*

SIM. *See* Serving in Mission (Niger)

Skill development. *See* Capacity

Small and medium enterprises (SMEs), 181

Small forestry enterprises (SFEs), 168, *168*

Small Industries Development bank of India, 105

SmartWood, 138

Social capital, 5, 16, 25–26, 28, 62

    in Bangladesh, 114

    ISOs and, 80

    in Niger, 143

Social Forestry System (Honduras), 17

Social resilience, 28

    Namibia's conservancy program and, 36

Social security, *88*

Solomon Islands, locally managed marine area (LMMA) in, 38, *39*

Songtaab-Yalgré Association (Burkina Faso), 97

South Africa, associations in, 108

South America. *See* Latin America; *individual countries*

South Asia. *See also individual countries*

    poverty reduction in, *20*

    water needs in, *192*

Sri Lanka, medicinals market in, *99*

Starbucks, Ethiopian cooperative coffee and, *101*

State claims to land, 51–52

State policies. *See* Governance

Stewardship, 12

Sub-Saharan Africa. *See also individual countries*

    poverty gap in, *23*

    poverty reduction in, *20*

Sustainable agriculture, 53, *81, 82, 90–91,* 99, 105, 107, 140

    certification of, 105

Sustainable environment practices, 12

    Bangladesh wetland resources and, *124*

    Fiji LMMA Network and, 44

    income from, *9, 25*

    Namibia conservancy program and, 36

T

Tahoua Rural development Project (Niger), 153

Talamanca Initiative (Costa Rica), *60*

Tank User Groups in India, 24

Tanzania

    accountability in, 76

    bureaucratic regulation as obstacle to community forest management, 170

    customary land systems in, 53

    networks in, *104*

Taxes

    adjustment for equity in, *7,* 170–171, 198

    in Guatemala, 163

    in Vietnam, 171, *171*

Technical assistance, *7,* 15, 171, 174, 195, 197

Technical Training and Productivity Institute (Guatemala), 140

Telecommunications, 177–179

    Digital Access Index, 221

    microfinance and, 180

Tenure rights. *See* Land and resource tenure; Ownership

Thailand

    associations in, *104*

    ISO in, *91*

    land registration in, 53

    Pred Nai Community Forest, *18*

Timber markets. *See* Forests

Titling of land, 53, 191. *See also* Ownership

Torra Conservancy (Namibia), 32, 36

Tourism. *See also* Ecotourism

    in Costa Rica, *60*

    in Namibia, 34, 35, 37

    Shomple Community Trust (Kenya), *57, 58, 60*

Tourism Shompole Community Trust (Kenya), *60*

Trade unions, 108

Traditional organizations, 72

Training. *See* Capacity

Transparency

    in Bangladesh inland fisheries program, 117, 167

    ISOs and, 80, 92–93

    in regulation of markets, 169, 197–200

Tribal authorities, 24

Trust, 163, 167, 195, 201. *See also* Accountability

Tschinkel, Henry, 128, 129

Tseiseb Conservancy (Namibia), 36

U

Uganda

    customary land systems in, 53

    infrastructure investment in, 179

    insurance industry in, 184

    networks in, *104*

    patronage system in, 175

    reforestation program in, *164–165*

UN Development Fund for Women, 97

UN Development Programme (UNDP)

    community-driven development and, 26

    Equator Prize of, 55, *56–60,* 88, 97, 162

    Equator Project of, *56–59,* 86

UN Framework Convention on Climate Change, *164*

Undernourished, definition of, 212

UNIDO. *See* United Nations Industrial Development Organization

Union Association of Exporters (Guatemala), 140

Unión Maya Itzá (Guatemala), 135

Unions. *See* Agriculture; *specific union by name*

United Kingdom Department for International Development

    Bangladesh fisheries project funded by, 123

    funding for programs from, 167

    Guatemala forestry enterprises, 131

United Nations Development Programme (UNDP)
Bangladesh Coastal and Wetland Biodiversity Management Project and, 121
Human Development Index, 204
United Nations Environment Programme (UNEP), 13
United Nations Framework Convention on Climate Change, 157
United Nations Industrial Development Organization (UNIDO), 97, 105, 108
United States Agency for International Development (USAID)
Bangladesh programs supported by, 112, 113, 117, 120, 121, *124*
Ethiopian coffee cooperatives and, *100, 102*
funding for programs from, 162, 167
Guatemala forestry enterprises and, 127–133, 137, 138–139
Living in Finite Environment (LIFE) program, 37
Namibia conservancy program and, 34
Nepal's medicinal market and, *99*
Niger's re-greening movement and, 145, 146, 150, 151, 154–155
West Africa and, 156–157
University of Manitoba, *56*
University of Namibia, 33
University of South Pacific (USP), 39, 41
Upazila Fisheries Committees, 115–116, 118, 163, 166
Utkal Mahila Sanchaya Bikas (women's self-help groups), 87

V

Valexport producer association (Brazil), 103–104, 107
Venezuela, land registration in, 53
Vertical networking, *7*, 15, 57, 88–89
Vietnam
climate change and, *192*
infrastructure investment in, 178
State Forest Enterprise, 171
taxes on forest products in, 171, *171*
Village Land Commissions (Niger), 53
Village organizations (VOs), *84*
Vitukawalu, Rata Aca, 41

W

Wasundhara approach (India), *70*, 82–83
Water issues. *See also* Clean water
availability of resources, 204, 212
in Bangladesh, 123
Water Poverty Indexing (WPI), 212
Watershed management
in Bangladesh, 13, *13*, 68
community involvement, 55, 63
in Haiti, 62
in India, 13, *19*, 61, 82, 85, 167. *See also* Watershed Organisation Trust (WOTR, India)
rehabilitation program, 11, 13, 17

Watershed Organisation Trust (WOTR, India), 66, 68, 77, 78–79, *78–79*, 80, 81, 82–83, 85, 162, 163, *192*
finance, facilitation by, 89
horizontal networking and, 87
as ISO, *91*
Wealth, distribution of, *25*. *See also* Elite capture
poverty gap, *22–23*
Websites to show pilot programs' success stories, 162, 191
Wentling, Mark, 151
West Africa. *See also individual countries*
government and associations in, 108
palm oil business in, 168
titled property rights in, 51
Wetlands
livelihoods in Bangladesh in. *See* Bangladesh inland fisheries
in Papua New Guinea, *59*
Where is the Wealth of Nations? (World Bank), 25
WIDECAST, 82
Wilderness Safaris Namibia, 36
Wildlife conservancies. *See* Namibia's Communal Conservancy Program in Papua New Guinea, 59
Wildlife Conservation Society, 131, 135
Winrock International, 113, 121, *124*, 162, 166
Winterbottom, Bob, 157
Women
in Bangladesh, 119–120, *124*
in Fiji, 41, 45
in Guatemala, 133
in Mexico, 184
in Namibia, 35
in Nepal, 64, 107
in Niger, *74*, 152–153
Self-Employed Women's Organization (India), 88, 89
UN Development Fund for Women, 97
Women on the Move (women's savings groups in Niger), *74*
Women's Network of Medicinal and Aromatic Plant Producers and Retailers (RMPCPMA, Colombia), *104*
Women's organizations (WOs), *84*
World Bank
Bangladesh fisheries project funded by, 123
community-driven development and, 26–27
in Ghana, 61
on income equality, *23*
local institutions and, 77
on long-term commitment by donors, *124*
medicinals market and, *99*
in Niger, 145, 148, 154
on poverty levels, *23*, 190, *192*
on remittances, 184, *184*
Where is the Wealth of Nations?, 25
World Conservation Union on Bangladesh fish species, 113
World Resources Institute's New Ventures, 181

World Resources 2005: The Wealth of the Poor (WRI, World Bank, UNDP, UNEP), *78*
World Wildlife Fund (WWF)
    funding for programs from, 167
    Living in Finite Environment (LIFE) program, 37
    Namibia conservancy program and, 34
WOTR. *See* Watershed Organisation Trust (India)

Z
Zambia
    community investment requirement in, 61
    ISO in, *93*
    network in, *103*
    North Western Bee Products, Ltd., *18*